The Worlds of William Penn

The Worlds of William Penn

Edited by Andrew R. Murphy
and John Smolenski

RUTGERS UNIVERSITY PRESS
NEW BRUNSWICK, CAMDEN, AND NEWARK,
NEW JERSEY, AND LONDON

Library of Congress Cataloging-in-Publication Data

Names: Murphy, Andrew R., 1967- editor of compilation. | Smolenski, John, editor of compilation.
Title: The worlds of William Penn / edited by Andrew R. Murphy, John Smolenski.
Description: New Brunswick, New Jersey : Rutgers University Press, [2018]
Identifiers: LCCN 2018006106 | ISBN 9781978801813 (cloth : alk paper) | ISBN 9781978801776 (pbk. : alk. paper)
Subjects: LCSH: Penn, William, 1644-1718. | Penn, William, 1644-1718—Influence. | Pioneers—Pennsylvania—Biography. | Quakers—Pennsylvania—Biography. | Pennsylvania—History—Colonial period, ca. 1600-1775.
Classification: LCC F152.2 .M88 2018 | DDC 974.802092 [B]—dc23
LC record available at https://lccn.loc.gov/2018006106

A British Cataloging-in-Publication record for this book is available from the British Library.

♾ The paper used in this publication meets the requirements of the American National Standard for Information Sciences—Permanence of Paper for Printed Library Materials, ANSI Z39.48-1992.

www.rutgersuniversitypress.org

Manufactured in the United States of America

Contents

PART III
Restoration Worlds

PART IV
American Worlds

PART V
Quaker Worlds

PART VI
Imperial Worlds

The Worlds of William Penn

Introduction

WILLIAM PENN AND HIS WORLDS

Andrew R. Murphy and John Smolenski

The title of this volume—*The Worlds of William Penn*—indicates its editors' desire to pay homage to, and to build upon, an earlier collection of essays that revolutionized scholarship on the life, career, and thought of William Penn (1644–1718). That volume, *The World of William Penn*, edited by Richard S. and Mary Maples Dunn, appeared in 1986—which, much to our surprise, is now more than thirty years ago—and quickly became an essential reference for everyone working in the field.[1] Twenty authors, many of them leading figures in their fields, approached Penn's complex and multifaceted life from a variety of perspectives, assessed his many accomplishments (and not a few failures and disappointments), and subjected the multiple contexts in which he operated to sustained exploration and analysis. Along with the appearance of five volumes of *The Papers of William Penn* at various intervals during the 1980s (itself a distillation of the fourteen-reel microfilm production of Penn's papers, published in 1975 by the Historical Society of Pennsylvania), *The World of William Penn* served as a kind of icing on the scholarly cake, setting the study of Penn and his roles in England and America on a new and fruitful trajectory.[2]

The year 2018 marks the tricentennial of William Penn's death, and thus provides an ideal opportunity to return to those sources and to reassess Penn's singular importance to English, Irish, American, and Quaker history, to say nothing of the broader emergence of religious toleration and liberty of conscience in early modern political thought and practice. *The Worlds of William Penn* assembles essays from established and emerging scholars—commissioned specially for this volume—to revisit the many contexts and controversies that made Penn's life and times so compelling, reflect on the ongoing legacies of those controversies, and offer new perspectives on the early modern Atlantic world that shaped him and that he in turn did so much to shape. The essays collected here place Penn within a variety of social, political, and religious contexts, approaching him through these different "worlds" to better understand Penn's career, but also to see how examining his life sheds light on the early modern world more generally.

Roughly half of the essays in *The Worlds of William Penn* were originally presented at a November 2015 conference held at Rutgers University in New Brunswick. The conference was sponsored and generously supported by the Rutgers British Studies Center, with additional support from the Rutgers University Department of Political Science and the McNeil Center for Early American Studies at the University of Pennsylvania. We have also been extremely fortunate to have recruited additional essays on Penn and his worlds from a range of accomplished scholars who eagerly agreed to join the project. If the original Dunn and Dunn volume had a limitation, it was disciplinary: of its twenty authors, all but two were historians, and the remaining were scholars of (Quaker) religion. Historians predominate in this volume as well, though *The Worlds of William Penn* brings the work of scholars of literature, art history, material culture, cartography, and political theory into this renewed conversation. The result, we believe, is a volume that provides a fresh and provocative look at William Penn and his worlds, and that does so from an even broader range of perspectives than that earlier, pathbreaking volume.

William Penn was born in 1644, two years after the outbreak of the English Civil Wars. His father, the noted naval commander Sir William Penn, groomed his son to take up the life of an English gentleman and landholder in Ireland. But young William displayed a mystical streak from his early years and was ejected from Christ Church College, Oxford, for religious nonconformity. Following his dramatic 1667 Quaker convincement in Cork, Penn became one of the best-known and most controversial Dissenters in England over the course of the next five decades. He burst onto the public scene as a young agitator for popular liberties and defender of the Society of Friends during the 1670s, convinced Charles II to grant him an enormous amount of land in America early the next decade, and became a confidant of James II and leader of James's attempt to implement toleration during that king's ill-fated reign. In the aftermath of James's expulsion in 1688, Penn fell from grace in dramatic fashion and went into seclusion for a time, losing control of Pennsylvania to the Crown. Reemerging into public life and regaining his proprietorship in the mid-1690s, Penn eventually returned to his colony late in 1699, staying two years before returning again to England, to defend the interests of colonial proprietors against Crown efforts to centralize control. His later years were filled with deep disappointment with his colony and severe financial problems—he spent much of 1708 in debtors' prison—before a stroke disabled him in 1712. During his final six years of life, his wife Hannah essentially managed Pennsylvania and his other business affairs. Penn died in 1718 and was buried at the Jordans Meetinghouse in Buckinghamshire, where he remains alongside his wives and several of his children.[3]

William Penn was a sophisticated political thinker and religious controversialist who made important contributions to the debates of his time. But he was not only a political thinker: he was also an engaged political actor and colonial founder, a role that sets him apart from most of his contemporaries. Reflecting on Penn's legacy—as English theorist and American colonizer, as Public Friend and royal confidant—offers an opportunity to think more broadly about the early modern contexts that gave rise to liberty of conscience, one of the foundational concepts in modern political thought and practice. In other words, it leads us to a renewed consideration of the many worlds of William Penn.

William Penn and His Worlds

As the essays in this volume make abundantly clear, William Penn shaped, and was shaped by, a number of different "worlds" over the course of his long public career. The volume opens with a section that explores Penn as a figure in history and memory, as both a concrete, embodied individual moving through the early modern world and one who quickly became ensconced in myth, legend, and collective memory. Successive chapters explore the multifaceted nature of Penn's body, be it the one buried at Jordans Meetinghouse outside London or Alexander Calder's thirty-seven-foot bronze replica atop Philadelphia City Hall; the homes in which he lived, the countrysides through which he traveled, and the images of Penn that have long shaped public memory of the man; and the important colonizing role played by the extraordinary maps that he and many of those who joined him in Pennsylvania carried with them as they laid claim to their "new" territory. Elizabeth Milroy canvasses the politics of the public spaces Penn envisioned for his capital city and the ways in which subsequent generations of Philadelphians jettisoned the founder's vision as the settlement grew from its seventeenth-century roots. This complex relationship between the city and its founder culminated in an ill-advised and ill-fated attempt to bring Penn's remains back from their resting place at Jordans to Philadelphia in time to mark the 200th anniversary of his first arrival. Catharine Dann Roeber attends to the materiality of Penn's existence—to the fact that his was a peripatetic career characterized by frequent movement and travel across a wide variety of landscapes (rural, urban, Irish, English, American) and that he made his home in numerous abodes, most of which no longer stand, but which were once filled with a range of objects that provide a window into his world. Emily Mann focuses on Penn's use of maps, offering an overview of the important role played by maps in the English colonizing project and engaging in a close reading of the "first map" of Pennsylvania as both a promotional product and a tool of imperial control, cementing Penn's colony to the Crown's purposes. Despite his status as mythical founder and famous Friend, all three authors insist, William Penn lived (and died) in particular places, and moved through the world in complex ways, leaving a legacy as complex and uncertain as the man himself.

Although he was born during the Civil Wars and reached adulthood in Restoration England, the volume begins its consideration of Penn's many worlds with Ireland. The young William Penn spent five years in County Cork, much of it at Macroom Castle, as a member of a colonizing elite living on expropriated land (from native Irish or, in Penn's case, from supporters of the defeated king). It was at Macroom where Penn first met Thomas Loe, the itinerant Quaker who would eventually bring him to the Society of Friends in 1667. Ireland also figured heavily into Penn's lifelong friendship with Sir William Petty, who, as Marcus Gallo makes clear, did so much to solidify English control of Ireland through his oversight of the Down Survey under Cromwell. Petty's influence on Penn was significant. Although he never traveled to America, Petty invested in Pennsylvania and advised Penn on a number of issues related to his colony, emphasizing the crucial importance of accurate land surveys in the successful exercise of English colonizing power. Audrey Horning sketches the broader contours of Penn's involvement in Ireland, which took place against a longer-term backdrop of land confiscation, transportation of native Irish out of their country, and military occupation, each of which intertwined with the Penn family (including not only William but his mother and father as well) in important ways. County Cork also provided the more immediate backdrop, in the form of a severe persecution of Quakers in spring 1670, for Penn's *The Great Case of Liberty of Conscience*. Andrew Murphy lays out both the context and the substance of the work, in which Penn first laid out the theory of toleration that he would refine and develop over the course of his career as activist, theorist, and colonial proprietor.

The importance of Ireland notwithstanding, it was in Restoration England that William Penn became a public figure, noted controversialist, and colonial proprietor. He entered Oxford University, where he would spend two unhappy years, in 1660, joined his father the following spring to observe Charles II's procession to Whitehall for his coronation, and developed a close working relationship with Stuart kings that yielded his colony in 1681. Elizabeth Sauer places Penn in the company of such giants of Restoration literature as John Milton and John Bunyan and emphasizes the Atlantic nature of their influence, tracing the ways in which their ideas traveled to America and enhanced the imagery of New Worlds and, to use Penn's term, "holy experiments." Scott Sowerby uses the relationship between Penn and James II as a window into broader Restoration political and religious dynamics, charting its emergence and development, the ways in which it was tested during the tense months of mid- to late 1688, and the difficulties that subsequent historians have had in making sense of the alliance between the two. Finally, Penn's Restoration career included not only his activism in England and America but also, as Patrick Erben notes, two trips to Germany and the Netherlands during the 1670s. The enduring legacy of those journeys—particularly his 1677 visit in illustrious Quaker company including George Fox, Benjamin Furly, George Keith, and Robert Barclay—would shape Penn's career for years to come. Penn forged deep spiritual and practical connections with German Pietists, connections on which he would later draw in promoting Pennsylvania and that would lead to his close relationship with Francis Daniel Pastorius, the most famous German immigrant to Pennsylvania, and contribute to Penn's posthumous apotheosis among German Pietists. Each of these essays takes up the broader backdrop of Restoration debates over toleration and helps make sense of Penn's role as a bridge between the Society of Friends and a broader universe of Dissenting Protestants (to say nothing of Catholics, like his friend the king).

But regardless of the significance of the Irish and Restoration worlds in which he circulated, for most Americans Penn is first and foremost (and perhaps only!) known as the founder of Pennsylvania. The mythology of Pennsylvania's founding, from euphoric celebrations of its tolerance to Penn's famed gentle treatment of the natives, have long provided the building blocks of a widespread view not only of the man himself but of Friends and their principles. Such a view, as Michael Goode points out, overlooks the fact that the Lenni Lenape themselves had a long history of peaceful engagement with Europeans, a series of agreements and relationships that dated back decades before William Penn arrived on American shores. As a founder, Penn can be profitably viewed against the backdrop of other founders and colonizers, many of whom approached their colonial endeavor with a religious zeal similar to Penn's. Alexander Mazzaferro connects Penn with Winthrop and his fellow New England Puritans, exploring the ways in which the rhetoric of tradition and innovation functioned in their respective undertakings, and the important role played by inductive and empirical methods of inquiry in justifying departures from existing practices in unfamiliar surroundings. Sarah Morgan Smith also emphasizes the connections between Pennsylvania and New England by examining Penn's interactions with Increase Mather when the latter visited London during the 1680s, bringing Penn's political involvement during that decade into an Atlantic frame that enhances approaches highlighting his work on behalf of James's tolerationist agenda.

In all his Restoration and American activities Penn lived, wrote, spoke, and acted not merely on his own behalf—perhaps not at all on his own behalf—but as a leading member of the Society of Friends. Penn remained, from his convincement until his final days, a Quaker controversialist of the first order. That identity was clearly a central one to his own sense of himself as an inveterate defender of George Fox's leadership of the Society and of the Society more generally against its Restoration critics, and his relationship with Fox was one of the most important relationships in his life. Catie Gill takes up Penn's Preface to Fox's *Journal*—also published separately as *A Brief Account of the Rise and Progress of the People Called Quakers*—and traces its role as both an account of Fox and his unrivaled role in the emergence of Quakerism and a response to anti-Quaker polemics of the 1690s, particularly those of Charles Leslie. Penn's aim in *A Brief Account* (which he directed at non-Quakers at least as much as at Friends) was to pay homage to this remarkable man who had made such an impact on his life, and to defend Friends at a critical point in Quaker history. Adrian Weimer, too, approaches the relationship between Quakers and their Restoration counterparts by drawing attention to the ways in which Friends like Edward Burrough sought to emphasize their own peacefulness and loyalty by casting aspersions on other Dissenters (particularly Endicott and the Massachusetts Bay Puritans) and by reviving memories of the 1649 regicide and Cromwellian regime. Rachel Love Monroy draws a broader Atlantic picture of the relationship between Puritans and Quakers, focusing on Mary Dyer's 1660 execution in Boston, Fox's journey to America in the early 1670s, and the transatlantic influence of Henry Barrow's and John Greenwood's separatist congregation. In Monroy's account, the two groups occupy not so much dichotomous categories as communities who shared extensive networks and fluid boundaries.

The volume's final section approaches Penn from perhaps the most expansive "world" to which he addressed himself: the world of the nascent seventeenth-century British empire, which itself sat uneasily alongside French, Dutch, and Spanish colonial systems. As Evan Haefeli explains, Pennsylvania quickly took its place in a robust and growing network of settlements and, its founding mythos notwithstanding, was hardly the only colony to grant religious toleration to its inhabitants. What it did offer to potential settlers was a large territory managed by a politically connected proprietor with deep connections to a wide range of European religious communities. Pennsylvania enabled Penn to put into practice ideas about peaceful coexistence and stability that he had been developing since his early involvement at Carrickfergus in Ireland, when he participated in the suppression of a mutiny of soldiers. Patrick Cecil traces Penn's developing interest in such matters from their Irish roots through his settlement in the Delaware Valley and ultimately to his plan for a European Diet in his 1693 *Essay Towards the Present and Future Peace of Europe* and his "Brief and Plain Scheam" for intercolonial cooperation, which he presented to the Board of Trade in 1697. Such broader dynamics, and the role of Pennsylvania within a broader imperial context, also motivate Shuichi Wanibuchi's exploration of Penn's and Pennsylvania's role in the Restoration imperial system. Here too, Penn's early involvement in Ireland bears fruit in his colonizing endeavor, which both drew upon and contributed to the imperial political economy as well as the scientific impulse animated by the Royal Society, which made Penn a Fellow eight months after he received his colonial charter.

Penn and His Worlds: Four Perspectives

Setting aside for a moment the specific "worlds" outlined above, and into which this book's chapters are organized, we would also point out that the essays in this volume illuminate William Penn's life and times in at least four distinct ways. First, several of the authors enlarge what we know about Penn the man, an individual enmeshed in a range of personal and professional relationships that enabled him to play an outsized role in the affairs of his time. Scott Sowerby's examination of the relationship between Penn and James II helps us reimagine the former's political views. Sowerby demonstrates that the alliance between monarch and Dissenter was more than just a marriage of convenience; instead, it reflected a shared commitment to liberty over democracy, a stance that would carry over into Penn's American endeavor. Patrick Erben and Catie Gill explore new dimensions of Penn's religious life. Erben highlights the importance of Penn's relationship with Pietists in Germany, both as a Quaker missionary in the 1670s and as a proprietor looking for settlers in the 1680s. He gives us a worldlier Penn, tied into a larger Protestant community beyond the Society of Friends. Gill, meanwhile, situates Penn within late seventeenth-century literary debates between Anglicans and Dissenters. She shows how Penn's 1694 *Brief Account* represented, at least in part, a response to anti-Quaker critics. Taken together, they show more continuity in Penn's life than might be apparent at first glance. His religious activism, after all, spanned the founding of Pennsylvania and the Glorious Revolution, even as it took different forms in England and on the Continent. And Shuichi Wanibuchi's essay uses Penn's colonial vision as a point of departure for exploring the intellectual history of improvement and political economy in the seventeenth-century English world. The proprietor's belief that Pennsylvania would be a productive and, more importantly for Penn, profitable settlement stemmed from his active engagement with contemporary mercantilist theory and agricultural science. Wanibuchi's Penn was a scientist as well as an entrepreneur and Dissenter.

Second, the essays in the volume highlight one part of Penn's life that has generally gone underappreciated by scholars: the importance of Ireland in Penn's formation. (In fact, he spent more time in Ireland than in Pennsylvania over the course of his life.) The Penn family legacy on the island loomed large. As a boy during the 1650s, William spent time with his family on their estate at Macroom Castle. He embarked on his first trip to Ireland as an adult in 1666, to defend Sir William's considerable landholdings. That trip saw the most momentous event of Penn's life: his Quaker convincement in 1667, in County Cork. It also gave Penn his first hands-on experience with the realities of being a colonial landlord, something that, as Patrick Cecil shows, would shape his ideas on diplomacy when he later undertook an American colonial project. This journey also marked Penn's first encounter with William Petty, the English cartographer and administrator charged with surveying Ireland so that lands held by rebellious Irishmen could be redistributed to loyal friends of the crown. As Marcus Gallo makes clear, this friendship with Petty deeply influenced Penn's efforts to map and sell land in Pennsylvania in the most efficient way possible. Penn's next trip to Ireland, from 1669 to 1670, saw the publication of *The Great Case of Liberty of Conscience*, written during a wave of anti-Quaker persecution. *The Great Case*, as Andrew Murphy illustrates, represented a breakthrough in Penn's political philosophy, as he made the case for religious toleration as a civic good in and of itself. Murphy elaborates the ways in which its arguments provided a theoretical groundwork for his Restoration career and North American ventures. Gallo, Murphy, and Cecil collectively make the case that Penn came of age as a Quaker and as a colonizer in Ireland.

Third, other chapters provide a deeper understanding of the era in which Penn grew up and lived. Audrey Horning's essay looks at the Penns' time as landholders in Ireland in the context of midcentury struggles over land confiscation in Ireland that took place after the 1652 Act of Settlement, a process in which a major portion of land passed from Catholic to Protestant hands. And if Penn's colonial efforts in America cannot be understood without reference to his experience in Ireland, neither can his experience there be understood without looking at how other major landlords handled these tumultuous times. Rachel Love Monroy shows the reach of Quakerism's transatlantic missionary culture before Penn's convincement. Penn's proprietary endeavors did not represent the beginning of a Quaker Atlantic culture; it merely marked a new phase in the Society's worldwide project of furthering the faith. In her contribution, Adrian Weimer traces the ways in which Friends in the 1660s and 1670s balanced their nascent commitment to pacifism with their efforts to show loyalty to the Stuart monarchy. Suggesting that Puritans and Quakers had more in common with each other than they did with Anglicans, she shows the difficulty that Dissenters faced as they tried to "render unto Caesar" in a post-Restoration world. Penn was one in a long line of Friends who faced this problem as they tried to engage the world politically. Evan Haefeli's chapter compares Pennsylvania's experiment in religious toleration to other colonial efforts that had come before. Looking at colonies that failed—such as the ill-fated New Albion in the Delaware Valley—and those that survived—such as Rhode Island—he highlights those factors that helped Pennsylvania succeed, most significantly its proprietor's strong connections to powerful individuals in England and Europe. Both luck and design helped it succeed where others had foundered. And lastly, Michael Goode's contribution examines how methods of peacemaking that Lenape peoples had developed through their interactions with Dutch and Swedish colonizers from the 1630s through the 1660s shaped their interactions with Pennsylvanian colonizers after 1681. The colony's development as a "peaceable kingdom," Goode argues, stemmed more from Lenape practices of peacemaking than the avowed pacifism of its Quaker proprietor.

Finally, a fourth group of essays takes a somewhat different tack: they use Penn as a case study for broader examinations of seventeenth- and eighteenth-century history and culture. Elizabeth Sauer, for instance, juxtaposes Penn with authors such as John Milton and John Bunyan. Sauer demonstrates that each was part of a transatlantic process, and offers a provocative reinterpretation of major authors in the English literary canon. Comparing William Penn and Massachusetts Bay governor John Winthrop, Alexander Mazzaferro highlights the ambivalent meaning of "innovation" in seventeenth-century colonial political thought. Sharing their English contemporaries' suspicion of innovation in political theory, Winthrop and Penn nonetheless found that American circumstances made it necessary to develop a new intellectual stance that balanced tradition with colonial experimentation. Sarah Morgan Smith compares Penn to other dissenting authors, specifically those individuals who wrote petitions and pamphlets to protect their rights in the aftermath of the Glorious Revolution. Morgan Smith tells of how efforts to restore the original Massachusetts Bay charter (and all of the prerogatives contained therein) morphed into a broader argument defending the rights not just of the colony's Puritan residents but of all of its Protestant subjects. And Emily Mann uses Penn's *Map of Some of the South and Eastbounds of Pennsylvania* (1681), the lesser-known precursor to Thomas Holme's more famous 1685 and 1687 works, to demonstrate the power of cartography in English colonial projects. Maps, she suggests, played a crucial role in colonization not merely as representations of what had been done in imperial settlements but as forms of propaganda offering to investors and potential immigrants a window of what could be done in North America.

All told, these essays represent new explorations into the worlds of William Penn, both topically and thematically. They also chart paths for further study, paths that promise a richer picture of the man, the places he inhabited, and the times in which he lived. To be fair, a number of these chapters downplay Penn's uniqueness. But they do so not simply to debunk the hagiography that has built up around Penn in the three centuries since his death. Instead, they aim to highlight the complexity of both his life and his times. As a politician, scientist, dissident, landlord, and religious controversialist, Penn was part of many worlds throughout his life. He had a wide geographic ambit, with significant ties to Germany and especially Ireland, as well as England and America. And using his career as a case study allows us an opportunity to better understand larger trends in early modern culture and society. Perhaps importantly, these essays show the value of an interdisciplinary approach toward the study of Pennsylvania's founder, one in which fields as diverse as history, political science, literary studies, art history, and archaeology mutually illuminate each other's insights.

The William Penn who emerges from these eighteen chapters is a more complex, multifaceted, and interesting individual than the mythical Founding Father so long presented to scholars and the general public. William Penn was hardly the saint memorialized in denominational histories, children's books, playing cards, department store logos, and even video games. But he remains a seminal figure in the seventeenth- and eighteenth-century worlds and well worth continued study. It is our hope that this collection will contribute to and continue the process of complicating Penn and his project(s) begun thirty years ago by Richard S. and Mary Maples Dunn in their volume, whose name we draw on even as we seek to introduce Penn to a new generation of scholars. There are many worlds yet to discover.

NOTES

1. Richard S. Dunn and Mary Maples Dunn, eds., *The World of William Penn* (Philadelphia: Penn Press, 1986).

2. Richard S. Dunn and Mary Maples Dunn, eds., *The Papers of William Penn*, 5 vols. (Philadelphia: Penn Press, 1981–1987). Volume 5, an exhaustive inventory of Penn's published writings, was edited by Edwin B. Bronner and David Fraser.

3. The most recent biography is Andrew R. Murphy, *William Penn: A Life* (New York: Oxford University Press, 2019).

PART I

Materials, History, Memory

CHAPTER 1

The Elusive Body of William Penn

Elizabeth Milroy

Philadelphians spend their days under William Penn's steady gaze. Since 1894, Alexander Milne Calder's thirty-seven-foot-tall bronze statue of Pennsylvania's founder has stood atop the tower of city hall, which occupies the central public square described in Penn's 1682 plan for his colonial capitol (figure 1.1). Calder rendered the figure in detail (to a degree no pedestrian would ever see), portraying Penn as a young man in his late thirties when he first arrived in his American colony. Handsome, with aquiline features, Penn wears a fashionable beaver hat and lace at his cuffs; his coat and waistcoat are lined generously with buttons—not a costume one would associate with the Quakers' "plain" aesthetic. In his hand, Penn holds the charter signed by Charles II, granting proprietary title to millions of acres constituting the colony of Pennsylvania. Rising more than five hundred feet above street level, the statue is the highest atop any secular building in the world. For decades, a "Gentleman's Agreement" prohibited construction in Philadelphia of any building higher than the Penn statue. That agreement dissolved in the 1980s, and since then skyscrapers have intruded upon Penn's view, but he holds his own.[1]

Calder's Penn is a defining element in Philadelphia's civic iconography. Famed city planner Edmund Bacon called the statue "a sun around which Philadelphia revolves and looks for sustenance."[2] Yet, in spite of this colossal effigy, and the apparent ubiquity of Penn in popular culture, there is a sense that we don't really know the man. John Moretta, for example, states at the start of his 2006 biography of Penn that his aim is to "resurrect from possible historical oblivion an individual who . . . contributed so much to the shaping of the American creed and ideal."[3] As a historical figure, Penn is less approachable than Ben Franklin, whose many impersonators haunt Philadelphia's tourist districts. Franklin was a man

Figure 1.1 Karl F. Lutz (1896–1976). *Cityscape [Philadelphia]*, n.d. Photograph. Karl F. Lutz Collection, Athenaeum of Philadelphia.

of the people, whereas we tend to maintain a respectful distance from Penn. Biographers call him a man of contradictions: the son of privilege, a member of the Stuart court who was also a leading dissenter and principal theologian of the Society of Friends. Penn declared his affection for America, yet he lived in Pennsylvania for less than three years. He was one of seventeenth-century Britain's great religious thinkers and writers. He was also one of seventeenth-century Britain's greatest real estate speculators.[4] Nineteenth-century Philadelphians also worried that Penn was not sufficiently understood or appreciated. "By the majority of careless readers and thinkers, he is regarded merely as a sort of landlord," observed one writer in 1882, "The present generation is almost a stranger to the man."[5] Installing a colossal statue atop the new city hall was one way to redress this situation. But in addition, during the early phases of its construction, a group of citizens sought to add more luster to the municipal building by repatriating Penn's physical remains and reinterring these beneath the main tower. This overlooked chapter in Philadelphia's history reveals a great deal about how our predecessors thought they could deploy the proprietor's body, literally as well as figuratively, to rehabilitate the conflicted spaces of a modern industrial city.

In February, 1881, Dillwyn Parrish, a Philadelphian living in England, wrote to John Welsh, then minister (ambassador) to the Court of Saint James's, with a proposition. Parrish had learned of plans to celebrate the bicentennial of

Figure 1.2 *Jordans' Meeting House and Burial Ground.* From George L. Harrison, *The Remains of William Penn. Pennsylvania's Plea, the Mission to England, Visit to the Grave, Letters, etc.* (Philadelphia, 1882).

William Penn's arrival in North America in 1882, and he suggested that this might be the ideal occasion on which to remove Penn's remains "from their present resting place in an obscure English burying ground to an honored grave in the city of his creation." Parrish volunteered to contact Penn's descendants to gain permission and also to finance the project. More than this, Parrish identified the destination for Penn's remains. "I have also thought that a proper place for the tomb would be under the dome of our new court house, and that a statue in marble over the same would be appropriate."[6] Welsh forwarded the letter to John William Wallace, president of the Historical Society of Pennsylvania (HSP), who arranged to have the letter published (though with the names of the correspondents kept confidential), in order to bring the proposal to the attention of Philadelphia city councils and the state legislature.[7]

The "obscure English burying ground" was Jordans in Buckinghamshire, northwest of London, near Ruscombe, Penn's residence in the last years of his life. The Founder and several members of his immediate family were interred in the burying ground adjacent to the Jordans meetinghouse (figure 1.2). Built in 1688, the meetinghouse had been a principal gathering place for Quakers from the surrounding districts until the late eighteenth century, when declining attendance forced the trustees to suspend meetings and the meetinghouse was closed. By 1806, a Philadelphia writer would complain that Penn, "whose genius

Figure 1.3 Edward Hicks (1780–1849). *The Grave of William Penn*, circa 1847/48. Oil on canvas. National Gallery of Art. Gift of Edgar William and Bernice Garbisch, 1980–62.12.

founded our city, lies nobody knows where. We cannot tell whether he died on this side of the ocean or the other."[8]

Pilgrims and tourists are indefatigable nonetheless. In 1832, Philadelphian Joshua Francis Fisher reported to Roberts Vaux that numerous initials carved into the trunks of trees in the burying ground attested to its growing popularity.[9] Evidently the Penn family encouraged this: earlier in the century the Founder's descendants had commissioned a Dutch artist to imagine the French philosopher Montesquieu visiting Jordans. A lithograph reproduction of the painting was published and copied by the Pennsylvania Quaker artist Edward Hicks (figure 1.3).[10] Fisher mistakenly thought he had found Penn's grave. In fact, at this time, only tumuli indicated the various grave sites because Quakers had rejected the practice of erecting grave markers as prideful acts that were "wrong and of evil tendency."[11]

By 1851, prompted by increasing interest in William Penn and his family, particularly from Americans, the Society of Friends reopened the Jordans meetinghouse for an annual meeting. In the early 1860s, Granville John Penn, William Penn's great-grandson, had stone markers placed at what were generally believed

Figure 1.4 *The Grave of William Penn.* From George L. Harrison, *The Remains of William Penn. Pennsylvania's Plea, the Mission to England, Visit to the Grave, Letters, etc.* (Philadelphia, 1882).

to be the burial locations of the Founder and his family (figure 1.4).[12] Despite these efforts and the fact that articles and pamphlets about Penn's grave were published not infrequently in Britain and the United States, the notion persisted that Jordans was obscure and forgotten, and that William Penn's reputation had suffered as a result.

Dillwyn Parrish was not the first to propose that Penn's remains be returned to Philadelphia. In 1874, John Forney, editor of the *Philadelphia Press*, visited Jordans while touring England and the continent as a commissioner for the upcoming Centennial Exhibition. In a report to readers at home, he expressed surprise at how difficult it was to find the Jordans meetinghouse and cemetery because no one in the district seemed to know of its existence. He had almost given up after wandering along country lanes for several hours when he finally spied a small field "with a few tombstones shining white through the beeches." Nearby was the tiny brick meetinghouse, and as Forney approached the field, he discerned the names of William Penn and his family carved on the headstones, "in a more secluded and desolate spot you could not conceive."[13]

As he pondered Penn's grave, Forney recalled that he had decided to make the pilgrimage while visiting Philadelphia's new public park on the banks of the Schuylkill. "I never supposed . . . that the grave of William Penn would be found in a spot so obscure," Forney remarked, "or that his name would be forgotten in the very neighborhood where he lived and died." Yet Forney saw that opportunity might arise from this neglect. "I am not without hope that the Friends of Philadelphia will make steps to remove the remains of their greatest leader to the State that bears his name, and to the city that he founded," he mused. "There is no place in the world so fitting as Fairmount Park," to receive Penn's remains, Forney proposed, and no time more appropriate as America's 1876 Centennial celebration grew near.[14]

Forney's proposal went no further. But the concept of retrieving Penn's remains resonated among his fellow Philadelphians. John Welsh forwarded Dillwyn Parrish's proposal to the group most likely to give it a sympathetic hearing, because members of HSP were the most enthusiastic proponents of what we might call the "cult of William Penn." Founded in 1824, the society was dedicated to documenting the early history of the state and in particular to commemorating the achievements of Penn, "the father of our happy and prosperous republic."[15] Tourist Joshua Francis Fisher and his correspondent Roberts Vaux were early members. The acquisition and exhibition of archives, artifacts, and relics were central activities. Among the society's cherished artifacts was a wampum belt, said to have been given to William Penn by the Lenni Lenape sachems at the Shackamaxon treaty, which was donated by Granville John Penn when he visited the city in 1859. In 1870, society members had scored an important archival coup by raising money to acquire the Penn Family Papers, numbering more than twenty thousand documents.[16]

HSP's board of councilors had first discussed how to commemorate the bicentennial in the spring of 1880, when they envisioned that celebrations would be comparatively modest: a three-man program committee recommended only that a ceremony be held at the Academy of Music on November 8, 1882 (date of Penn's arrival at the site of Philadelphia), comprising a "historical discourse" by Wayne MacVeagh and a commissioned poem, read by John Greenleaf Whittier.[17] But news of Parrish's proposal raised the stakes considerably. It also resonated beyond HSP, for the response was firmly positive when president Wallace conveyed the proposal to the members of Philadelphia's city councils and to Pennsylvania state legislators. By early May of 1881, the legislature had passed a joint resolution authorizing the governor to correspond with the proper authorities in England and to dispatch an agent posthaste to supervise the exhumation and translation of Penn's remains in time for the 1882 Bicentennial celebrations.[18] By late June, Philadelphia businessman, philanthropist, and HSP member George L. Harrison, carrying credentials from the federal as well as state and local government officials, was on his way to England to pursue negotiations.[19]

The prospect of bringing Penn's physical remains to Philadelphia would have had a considerable symbolic impact within the geography of the city he had designed.

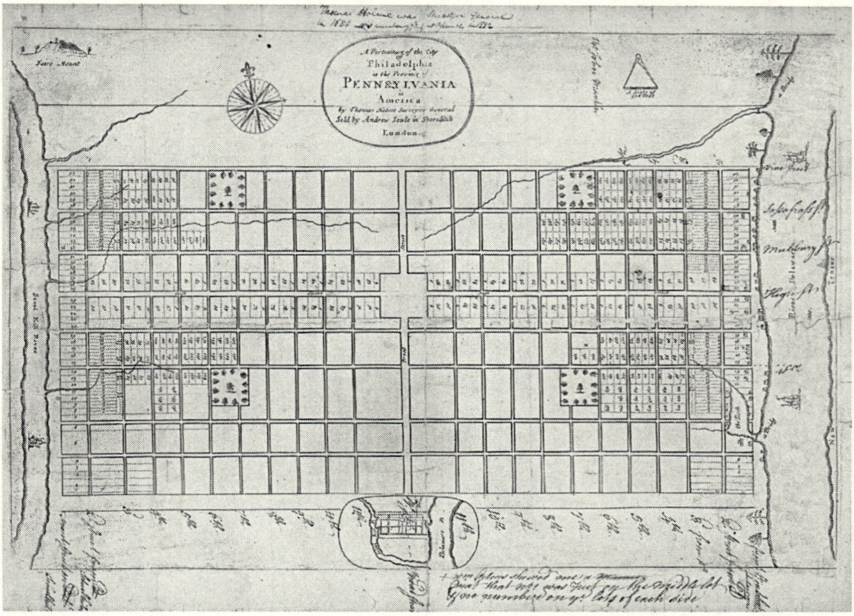

Figure 1.5 Thomas Holme (1624–1695) (with instructions from William Penn). *A Portraiture of the City of Philadelphia in the Province of Pennsylvania in America.* (London: Sold by Andrew Sowle in Shorditch, [1683]). The Athenaeum of Philadelphia.

When Penn published a plan for Philadelphia in 1683 with a letter to the Free Society of Traders, he titled it a "portraiture" of the new city (figure 1.5). This could mean an imagined likeness or the delineation of an existing and tangible thing. On the one hand, Penn's plan promised the future reordering of a specific site, giving concrete form to a still abstract vision. On the other hand, in his letter, Penn described the city as if already "laid out to the great content of those here that are anyways interested therein." The broad and neatly gridded streets embodied his vision of a well-regulated city, safe from fires and disease. The intersection of Broad and High Streets opened out into a ten-acre central square at the corners of which "houses for public affairs" could be erected. Four eight-acre squares drawn in each of the surrounding quadrants would be landscaped as public parks.[20]

By publishing a plan of the new capital, Penn assumed a delicate task. It was his privilege and obligation as proprietor to furnish prospective colonists with viable surveys and settlement plans. Yet Penn certainly recognized that designing a new city might be construed as a supreme act of pride and ambition. Chief among ancient cities laid out on a grid was Babylon itself.[21] But a well-behaved populace could counteract this. In his writings and speeches, Penn repeatedly affirmed the political authority of the people. Well-ordered spaces, in addition

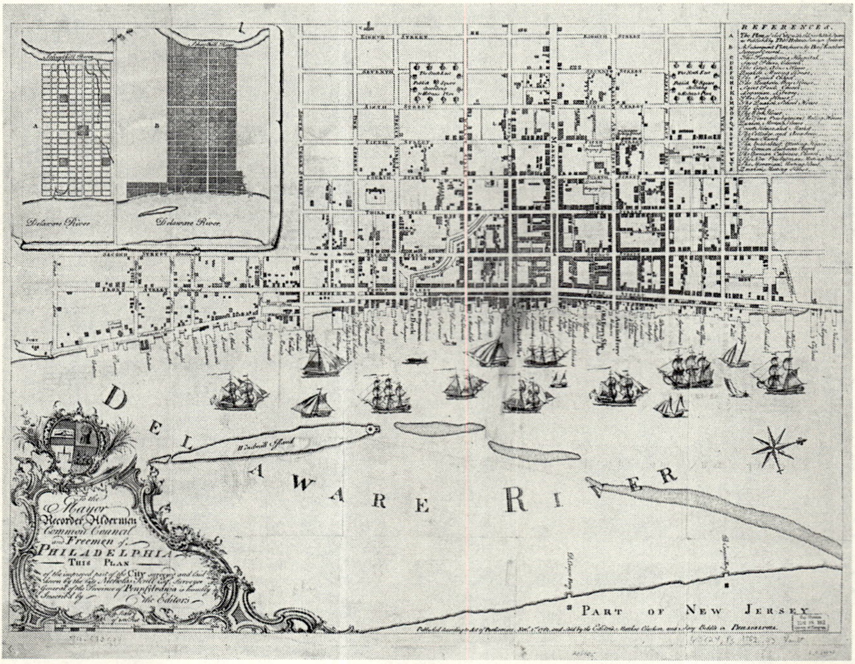

Figure 1.6 Matthew Clarkson (1733–1800) and Mary Biddle (1709–1789). *To the Mayor Recorder Aldermen Common Council and Freemen of Philadelphia This Plan of the improved part of the City surveyed and laid down by the late Nicholas Scull Esq. Surveyor General of the Province of Pennsylvania is humbly inscribed by The Editors,* 1762. Library of Congress, Geography and Map Division.

to firm laws and responsible government, would ensure good behavior. The public squares were crucial to Penn's vision. By comporting themselves in modest and devout fashion, especially in the informal setting of the public square, Quakers would set a valuable example. Just as the order and regularity presented by the new city's street grid would promote social discipline, so too the neatly rectilinear public squares would offer salubrious spaces similar to the private garden.[22]

But when Penn left Pennsylvania for good in 1701 after his second sojourn in the colony, he did not transfer ownership of the squares to the city nor did he leave instructions as to how the Philadelphia plan should be realized or by whom. Philadelphians preserved the street plan but, as a 1762 map documents, they also revised and even abused it by cutting alleyways through city blocks as settlement clustered along the Delaware (figure 1.6). The eastern squares were still on the outskirts of settlement, though the southeast square is somewhat less isolated because of the nearby State House and other institutional buildings along Chestnut Street. There is no sign of the center square or the two western squares because forest still covered much of the western district. Over the course of the eighteenth century, the outlying public squares were used for trash heaps and burying grounds. The center square was, at various times, a fairground, bowling green, race track, and parade ground; for several years executions took place at the gallows just south of the square.[23]

Following independence and divestment of the proprietary, the city of Philadelphia gained title to the public squares, and renovations began in the 1790s, spurred by devastating yellow fever epidemics. In 1797 Philadelphia city councils created the four-man Watering Committee to explore options for bringing fresh water into built-up areas of the city. During these deliberations, committee member Thomas Cope circulated a copy of the *Portraiture* to persuade his associates to build a pumping station for the new municipal waterworks system at the center square.[24] With Penn's plan in hand, the Watering Committee accepted a proposal submitted by Benjamin Henry Latrobe to bring river water from an intake at the Schuylkill near the (projected) end of Chestnut Street to a pumphouse and reservoir at the center square. By 1801, steam engines housed in Latrobe's diminutive rotunda began distributing water throughout the city to provide residents with an adequate supply at low cost. Philadelphia thus became the first American city to develop a publicly funded water distribution system.[25]

By erecting a public works facility at the center square, the Watering Committee neatly finessed the persistent neglect and disorder that had dogged the centerpiece of Penn's plan. Latrobe's pump house revived the square as Philadelphia's symbolic center, bringing progressive utility, municipal benevolence, and respectability to an unruly space. The distribution of Schuylkill water into the city acted much like a transfusion, renewing the physical and psychological health of a city traumatized by disease. Fountains and tree plantings around Latrobe's pumphouse ornamented the modern revision of Penn's plan for "houses for public affairs." And by circulating the *Portraiture*, Cope also had alerted his contemporaries to the pressing need to revive and fulfill the Founder's true intentions.

Improvements at the center square in turn prompted upgrades to the outlying squares, and during the first half of the nineteenth century, private citizens and elected officials worked together to affirm the city's title to Penn's squares and to landscape these spaces as Penn had intended. In 1825, councils formally named the squares: [William] Penn (center), [George] Washington (southeast), [Benjamin] Franklin (northeast), [David] Rittenhouse (southwest), and [James] Logan (northwest). Councils also created standing committees to initiate improvements, and by the 1830s, the two eastern squares had been landscaped and plans were moving ahead to upgrade the two western squares.[26]

Once reacquainted with the original plan, Philadelphians came to regard the city's streets as imbued with the Founder's symbolic presence. "Every part of [Penn's] colonial plan recognized the people as the guardians of the common welfare," declared Job Tyson, another early member of HSP.[27] For Tyson, Penn's spirit of toleration and equality infusing the city's spaces had inspired the nation's founding fathers. "That sacred Charter [the Constitution] was framed by a Convention, who assembled and deliberated in Philadelphia. We may not conjecture how far the influence of the *genius loci*—of a spot consecrated by the universality of its freedom—may have operated upon their deliberations; but we cannot doubt that the ideas of liberty which this colony diffused . . . opened the minds of its framers to the reception of those more catholic principles."[28] But the center square, now called Penn Square, proved more difficult to rehabilitate. Demand soon overwhelmed Latrobe's pumping station, which was taken off-line by 1815 when new waterworks were completed at Fairmount on the Schuylkill, just north of the center city. When proposals to renovate the pumphouse as an observatory or a public library failed, it was demolished, and, in 1829, Market and Broad Streets were cut directly through the square to create four smaller spaces at the city center.[29]

Efforts to reconstitute the center square were under way by the late 1830s, when residents advanced proposals to build a new city hall there. Since the departure of the federal and state governments in 1799 and 1800, the State House, lately renamed Independence Hall, had housed municipal employees and the courts in increasingly cramped quarters. Conditions worsened after 1854, when the city and county of Philadelphia were consolidated to create the modern 130-square-mile metropolis, and the city's bicameral government and the number of employees ballooned. In 1859, members of a state commission appointed to choose between Penn Square and Independence Square voted to build new municipal offices at Penn Square on the grounds that Independence Square was too small and was already slated for a monument to the Revolution. They then announced a building competition and by the summer of 1860 had selected a design by architect John McArthur. Legal challenges, and the looming threat of civil war, brought the project to a halt, and the commission was disbanded.[30]

At war's end, the city hall project was revived. However, to complicate matters, in 1867 a consortium of cultural institutions petitioned to build new facilities on Penn Square "[to] promote learning, knowledge, science and virtue among the people, and elevate the character of the City and the Commonwealth founded by Penn, and increase the happiness of mankind."[31] At that time the Pennsylvania Academy of the Fine Arts, the Academy of Natural Sciences, the Philadelphia Library (now The Library Company of Philadelphia), the American Philosophical Society, and the Franklin Institute operated independently at dispersed sites in the eastern section of center city. Now these institutions proposed to come together at a central site, creating an island of culture within the center city grid. When a referendum was called in 1870, voters were offered two choices: Penn Square or a new site at Washington Square. If the Washington Square site were approved, city councils would give over space at Penn Square to the cultural consortium.[32]

As Charlene Mires notes, "issues of history and urban geography intertwined" in the debates about where to build the new city hall. Employees at the legal and financial firms, federal government departments, publishing houses, and newspaper offices still clustered in the eastern district wanted the municipal government to remain there.[33] And many of Philadelphia's older elite families still lived in the eastern district of center city. But Washington Square was problematic because it carried its own historical associations as a revolutionary-era burial ground. Manufacturers and railroad executives with offices on Broad Street recognized that the city was growing westward. Penn Square was conveniently located between the Pennsylvania Railroad's headquarters and a new station at Thirtieth and Market Streets for trains going out to the western suburbs on the Main Line, where many businessmen now lived.

Class antagonism also surfaced. Doubts were cast on the philanthropic motives of the cultural district supporters when it was revealed that several of them owned property around Washington Square and would benefit if the new municipal buildings were erected at that site.[34] The *Sunday Dispatch* dubbed the cultural district supporters an "aristocracy of corporations . . . a series of mutual admiration societies [whose] members claim to be the elite." Because many of those who belonged to one of the societies also belonged to some or all of the other three, they would be asking for money from the same pool. And several of the organizations had operated in the red for years: the *Dispatch* questioned whether the directors could actually afford the "magnificent buildings" they promised to build. "Because they contribute from five to fifteen dollars a year of their own funds, to be expended for their own gratification," the *Dispatch* contended, "they claim the right to arrogate to themselves peculiar veneration because they represent science, knowledge, respectability and the taste of the city." In the end, simple demographics tipped the balance in favor of Penn Square because more people now lived in Philadelphia's northern and western districts.[35]

Construction of the new municipal complex was entrusted to the Commission for the Erection of Public Buildings, an eleven-man committee appointed by city councils, including the mayor and presidents of the Select and Common Councils. The commission enjoyed considerable autonomy—there were no term limits, and the commissioners controlled the bidding process and approved all contracts. The project would drag on for more than thirty years, in large part because the commissioners could award contracts with a simple majority vote and then request that city councils raise "the amount of money requisite by them" with a special tax.[36] When the building was finally completed in 1901, construction costs had surpassed twenty-four million dollars—more than double the original estimate.[37]

City Hall also presented what one historian has called "the most ambitious sculptural decoration of any public building in the United States," with more than 250 figurative works in stone or bronze on the exterior and interior.[38] This complex program evolved and expanded over time, from relatively sparse ornamentation at the start to the final design, which was likely determined by 1882.[39] In 1887, when the commissioners made final payment to the marble contractors, they noted that "changes in the treatment of the original design of the building have from time to time been made, as artistic developments of the first conception, such for instance as the adoption of human figures as the motif of decoration, instead of conventional foliage."[40] The author of this iconographic program for these decorations is not known, though historian George Gurney credits architect John McArthur, with Alexander Calder serving as his principal assistant.[41]

Work on the Penn statue was similarly protracted. In an early postwar proposal for the Independence Hall site, McArthur drew in a statue of Justice atop the principal tower (figure 1.7). This echoes sculptor Thomas Crawford's figure of *Freedom* surmounting the dome of the Capitol in Washington, which was designed by McArthur's mentor Thomas Ustick Walter (figure 1.8). Sometime later the decision was made to replace the figure of Liberty with a colossal statue of Penn. This decision is usually dated to about 1872 based on a zincograph of a model of city hall published that year, although no document has yet been found that explains the reason for this change (figure 1.9). Again, Walter may have played a role in this change, suggested by a drawing he made in 1873 that shows Penn in much the same pose (figure 1.10). This in turn resembles an eighteenth-century statue of Penn, holding the 1701 Charter of Privileges, that had stood in the grounds of the Pennsylvania Hospital since 1804 (figure 1.11).[42]

In 1875, in response to a request from Samuel Perkins regarding the proper costume for Penn, HSP member George H. Fisher (Joshua Francis Fisher's son) determined that the statue would depict Penn as "about age 38 . . . in full vigor of manhood," dressed in the costume of the last years of Charles II's reign and shown "in speaking attitude holding the original charter of the city of Philadelphia." Word of the request must have inspired some local sculptors to develop prototypes, including Joseph Bailly, Philadelphia's leading sculptor at the time, who exhibited a figure at the Pennsylvania Academy of the Fine Arts in the spring of 1875 that closely resembled Fisher's description. The plaster model officially

Figure 1.7 James Cremer (1821–1893). *Adopted Design for New Public Buildings,* circa 1869. Stereoview. The Library Company of Philadelphia.

endorsed by the Public Buildings Commission, however, was made by two little-known practitioners, Mueller and Quackenbush (also spelled Quakenboss) and unveiled in the fall of 1875, at James Earle's Chestnut Street commercial art gallery (figure 1.12).[43] No documents from this period mention Alexander Milne Calder as designer or sculptor of the figure, though he had been working for McArthur at city hall since 1873 as a "plaster modeler."[44]

Calder was at work on the Penn statue by the mid-1880s, based on surviving models, later signed and dated and cast in bronze. The stance and costume of the figure indicate that he was familiar with the Bacon statue as well as the Bailly, and Mueller and Quackenbush models, though Calder's rendering was more elegantly proportioned. He made three models at one-tenth scale, and a nine-foot quarter-scale maquette, in the process altering the document that Penn holds

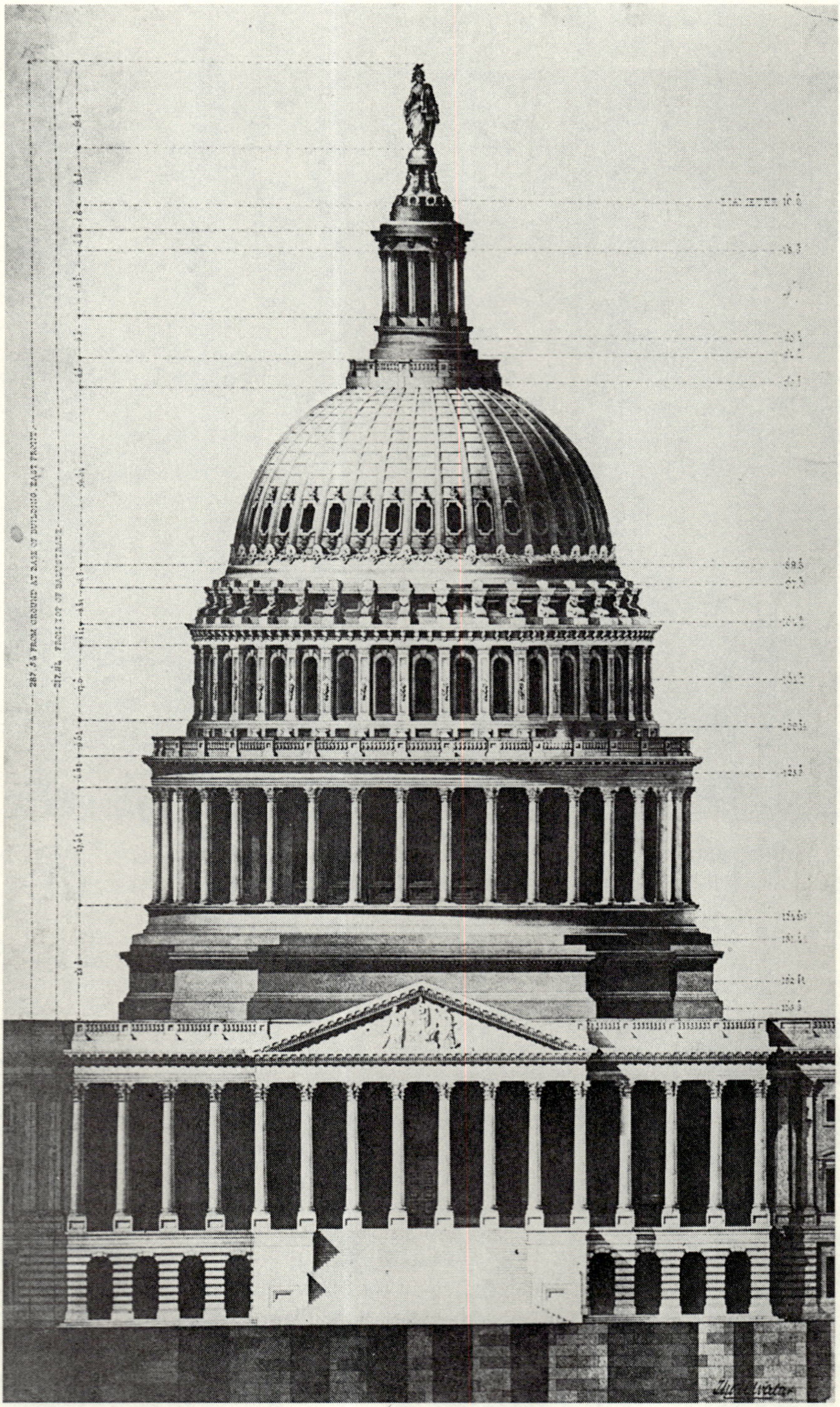

Figure 1.8 Thomas Ustick Walter (1804–1887). *United States Capitol (Washington, D.C.) Dome and Portico. East front. Rendered Elevation*. 1853. Salted paper photograph. Library of Congress. Architect of the Capitol Collection. Retrieved from the Library of Congress, https://www.loc.gov/item/92510798/. (Accessed June 28, 2017)

Figure 1.9 F. A. Wendenroth (1819–1884). *New City Building, Penn Square, Philadelphia. John McArthur, Jr., Architect*, 1872. Photozincograph. The Library Company of Philadelphia.

from the charter of privileges to the 1681 colonial charter (figure 1.13). By the end of 1886, Calder and his assistants were working on enlarging the statue to the full thirty-seven feet, working from a plaster cast of the quarter-scale figure, to fabricate forty-seven plaster sections that would be cast in bronze and bolted together (figure 1.14). The process was interrupted for over a year because there was no foundry in the United States capable of casting the sections. The opening of the Tacony Iron and Metal Works in north Philadelphia in 1889 resolved this problem, and the bronze sections were assembled in the courtyard of city hall in the fall of 1892. The statue was finally installed in November 1894 (figure 1.15).[45]

While the design of the Penn statue was fairly conventional, its siting is curious. Monumental statues depicting religious or secular figures set atop columns date back to antiquity. A notable ancient example was the fourth-century quasi-pagan/quasi-Christian column commissioned by the emperor Constantine for his new capital of Constantinople (Istanbul). Originally, the column was surmounted by a colossal statue of the emperor as Apollo, holding an orb said to have contained pieces of the true cross. A second reliquary at the base of the column held pieces allegedly of the crosses on which the two thieves were crucified and the baskets used for the miracle of the loaves and fishes, as well as a wooden

Figure 1.10 Thomas Ustick Walter. *Figure of Penn for City Hall*, circa 1873. Athenaeum of Philadelphia.

statue of Athena from Troy.[46] By the nineteenth century, this kind of structure was most commonly used to commemorate military heroes. Antoine-Denis Chaudet's bronze figure of Napoleon as Caesar was installed atop the Vendôme Column in Paris in 1810. This figure was replaced in 1833 by Charles Emile Seurre's statue of Napoleon in contemporary uniform, which was in turn replaced by Auguste

Figure 1.11 *South Façade of Pennsylvania Hospital with Statue of William Penn*, n.d. Library of Congress, HABS PA,51-PHILA,39–3.

Dumont's version of Napoleon as Caesar in the 1860s, which we see today. Another example is E. H. Baily's 1843 stone figure of Horatio Nelson atop the column in Trafalgar Square. Closer to home is Enrico Causici's marble statue of Washington atop Robert Mills's Washington Monument in Baltimore, unveiled in 1829 (figure 1.16).

By contrast, typically statues set atop towers are religious figures, such as angels, saints, or the Virgin Mary, that surmount church spires: one example is the statue of the evangelist Mark that crowns the pediment on the principal entrance façade of Saint Mark's Basilica in Venice. An example contemporary with Calder's Penn project is the statue of the angel Moroni, designed by Cyrus Dallin for the Salt Lake City temple of the Church of Jesus Christ of the Latter-Day Saints and installed in 1893; casts of the angel now surmount the spires of most Mormon temples. Statues atop towers could also be allegorical figures, such as the bronze figure designed by Thomas Crawford for the capitol dome. Architect Thomas Ustick Walter originally had intended that this be a figure of Liberty, holding the traditional staff and liberty cap attributes, but Crawford altered the figure by removing the staff and cap. Instead, he portrayed the figure, now called *Freedom*, holding a sword and shield and wearing a star and feather headdress (figure 1.17).[47]

Figure 1.12 Mueller and Quackenbush, *William Penn* (whereabouts unknown), circa 1875. Photograph of plaster model. The Library Company of Philadelphia.

Figure 1.13 Alexander Milne Calder (1846–1923), *William Penn*, 1886. Bronze. Credit: Detroit Institute of Arts, USA Founders Society Purchase, Laura H. Murphy Fund/Bridgeman Images.

Figure 1.14 Photographer unknown. *Man Posing with William Penn's Head*, circa 1892. Credit: Universal History Archive/UIG/Bridgeman Images.

Figure 1.15 Photographer Unknown. *City Hall Tower under construction*, circa 1894. Photograph. Historical Society of Pennsylvania, Society Photograph Collection.

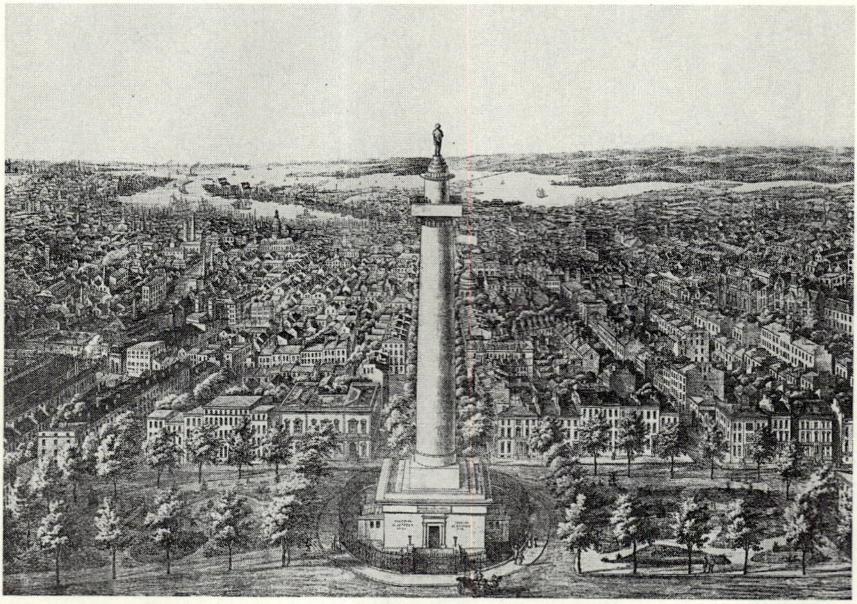

Figure 1.16 A. Sachse & Co., *The City of Baltimore, MD, in 1880. View from Washington Monument Looking South*, 1880. Lithograph. Library of Congress.

Walter had mentored McArthur through Philadelphia's convoluted Public Buildings commission process as this dragged on from 1860 to 1871, and it is not unlikely that McArthur first envisioned a figure of Liberty atop the principal tower as a tribute to Walter—this was also a logical choice for a legislative and judiciary building. The decision to replace this figure with a statue of William Penn may have been prompted by widespread criticism of McArthur's revised plan for a building that entirely covered the center square. Many Philadelphians opposed the design because they feared that the massive complex would destroy the integrity of Penn's plan and subvert the Founder's memory by erasing the principal public square. Adding the statue was daring but effective because this acknowledged the primacy of the center square within Penn's city plan while also affirming this as the proper site for city hall.

The statue could also embody Penn as the kindly overseer, an image that was not unknown. In 1838, for example, H. R. Robinson issued a lithograph slyly titled *A View of the City of Brotherly Love* that chronicles recent civic unrest (figure 1.18). The "view" is William Penn's. The Founder hovers sadly above the fray, holding a calumet and scroll inscribed "Wise Laws and a promt [*sic*] and just administration of them." Below him, volunteer firemen do battle around a fire engine dubbed "Goodwill" while one of their comrades "waters" another riot. Recent financial crises are signaled by the pillared "U.S. Bank," and the failed Penn

Figure 1.17 Thomas Crawford (1814–1857), *Freedom*, 1854–63. Bronze. Credit: Brian Gordon Green/National Geographic Creative/Bridgeman Images.

Figure 1.18 Henry R. Robinson (active 1831–1850). *A View of the City of Brotherly Love,* 1838. Lithograph. Historical Society of Pennsylvania.

Township Bank and J. W. Dyott's Manual Labor Bank. At the right, Pennsylvania Hall is engulfed in flames, memorializing its destruction by an anti-abolitionist mob in 1838. The city's racial divisions are at the center of the tumult, personified by two women, one black, one white, and their offspring wrestling in the foreground. A third boy opens a hydrant on the battling women to add a touch of irony, as if the city's celebrated municipal water system could simultaneously cool and fuel urban unrest.[48]

A statue of Penn could embody the integrity of the Founder's urban vision of an orderly, honest, and benevolent community. But the statue's symbolic power would be considerably amplified if Penn's actual physical remains lay beneath city hall. Harrison sailed for England in late June 1881. But his mission was threatened when the London *Times* published a notice from an American correspondent announcing the Pennsylvania legislature's resolution to acquire the Founder's remains.[49] This news reached the trustees of the Jordans meeting house and burying ground, who quickly conferred and determined to reject the forthcoming request. Harrison was apprised of this opposition after his arrival but was encouraged by Dillwyn Parrish that Penn's descendants were amenable to the proposal and that the Jordans trustees had no legal authority over the Penn family interments. Harrison met with the trustees, but they reiterated their opposition and presented him with a formal rejection letter—which they also sent to the *Times* for publication.[50]

The trustees presented several reasons for their decision. First, it was inappropriate to remove Penn's remains from the site he had selected for his own burial and those of his immediate family. Second, Penn would have considered the removal "to a transatlantic home, amid the pomp and circumstance of a State ceremonial, accompanied in all probability by military honors and parade . . . utterly repugnant." Third, because no marker was used to indicate Penn's burial site at the time of his interment, the true location of his remains actually was not known. And fourth, while it was true that Penn was the founder of Pennsylvania, he had lived in the colony for only a short time: it was in England that his "religious character was mainly formed . . . and [where] he dared to suffer persecution for his religious profession, and took his part manfully in laying the foundation of that system of religious liberty which we now enjoy." The trustees concluded by saying that they had received words of support from Penn's lineal descendants as well as from influential members of the Society of Friends.[51]

Frustrated by the intransigence of the Jordans trustees, Harrison sent a long letter of explanation to the *Times*, no doubt in hopes of gaining general support from its readers. The citizens of Pennsylvania had grounds to request Penn's remains, Harrison averred, because they had the right "to look upon William Penn as a public man, and to use his memory in the most effective way for the public good." And while he could not yet confirm the plan to erect a tomb within city hall, Harrison emphasized the appropriateness of this site, "in the midst of his own square, laid out by himself in the centre of the city of Philadelphia, where now are under construction its great public buildings, through whose avenues thousands must daily pass—as we believe to be elevated for good or restrained from evil by the inevitable consciousness of the high, and pure, and courageous character of the man." Honor was due the man who served the people, and the people were entitled to "have set before them the most effective presentation" in order to imitate that individual's noble character. Surely it was better to celebrate Penn's achievements in his colonial capital than to leave his memory to fade "in an unfrequented neighborhood, whose very existence is comparatively unknown."[52]

The reinterment of William Penn's physical remains in a monumental tomb would have granted Philadelphia's city hall an unusually spiritual dimension. The precise term for this process is *translation*, which refers to the exhumation and relocation of holy bodies, usually to a higher-status location. The repatriation of the remains of heroes and saints dates back to antiquity: Herodotus tells the legend of the return of the bones of Orestes to Sparta. Pausanius relates the true story of the reburial of Alexander the Great's body at Alexandria.[53] The acquisition and veneration of all or parts of the bodies of saints as relics are also long-standing traditions within the Christian faith. Predictably, the translation of the entire saint's body was treated most formally and often accompanied by elaborate vigils and processions. Not infrequently, the remains were housed in

Figure 1.19 Jacopo Robusti, called Tintoretto (1518–1594), *The Finding of the Body of St. Mark*, 1563–1564. Oil on canvas. Credit: Pinacoteca di Brera, Milan, Italy/ Bridgeman Images.

a purpose-built sepulcher or church (figure 1.19). The evangelist Mark was martyred in Alexandria and buried there in about 68 C.E. Eight centuries later, Christians in Alexandria who feared that the saint's remains were threatened by Saracen rulers entrusted the remains to Venetian merchants who carried Mark's remains to Venice, where they were re-interred beneath a newly built chapel dedicated to the saint.[54]

Michael Kammen notes that the widespread desire to ensure the perpetuity of graves in Europe and the United States developed in the early nineteenth century, when the notion of the cemetery as a "resting place" gained popularity. Kammen calls reburial a figurative form of resurrection, specifically the resurrection of reputation, either of the individual or the location to which that individual's remains are relocated. He notes that it was "all about possession and memorialization: matters of reputation, memory, sentiments concerning the most suitable venue, [and] pride of ownership."[55] Commercial development and even tourism came into play. The number of reburial projects increased significantly in the period from 1845 to about 1909. Most of these were secular, instigated principally by politicians and local boosters, rather than by family members.[56] In the United States, reburial projects were often linked to efforts to memorialize the country's founding generation. During the 1830s, Congress considered exhuming George Washington from his crypt at Mount Vernon and reburying the remains under the U.S. Capitol. Washington's descendants prevented this from going forward. Philadelphia-area examples included the removal of the remains of Charles Thomson, General Hugh Mercer, and other colonial heroes to Laurel Hill cemetery in the 1830s and 1840s to enhance that cemetery's prestige and historical value.[57]

The most famous example of a nineteenth-century translation was the removal of Napoleon's remains from the island of Saint Helena to Paris. In 1840, nineteen years after the emperor's death in exile, the British government agreed to release his remains to France to fulfill Napoleon's request that he be buried on the banks of the Seine among the French people "whom I so dearly loved" (figure 1.20). Elaborate parades and ceremonies, including a state funeral, attended the arrival of the remains when these were transported to Paris and laid temporarily in the chapel of Saint Jerome in the dome-church of St. Louis des Invalides. Politics delayed the design and construction of the grand tomb, and the emperor's remains were not moved to the tomb until 1864.[58] Significantly, by that date, Thomas Ustick Walter had modeled the capitol dome in Washington after the dome-church of St. Louis des Invalides.

Parallels between Napoleon, the military genius, and William Penn, the devout pacifist might seem incongruous. Yet Harrison made exactly this parallel in his letter to the Jordans trustees. "No statue of [Napoleon], nor all the exhibitions of him and his exploits, which exist on canvas or in marble, will arouse the adherents of his dynasty to perpetuate it," he declared, "like the tomb in which his relics rest in the Hôtel des Invalides in Paris."[59] Harrison went on to argue that the presence of Penn's remains would inspire Philadelphians to follow his beneficent example, for "neither . . . statue, nor memorial building will serve the purpose so well as a tomb which holds the ashes of the people's benefactor." This mention of Penn's "ashes" was another allusion to Napoleon, whose remains were always described as "les cendres du Napoleon," though neither Napoleon nor Penn were cremated.[60]

The failure of Harrison's mission could have been foreseen. Venerated relics and a public monument certainly were inconsistent with Quaker beliefs. Protests had been voiced as early as April 1881, when a contributor to *Friends' Review* declared

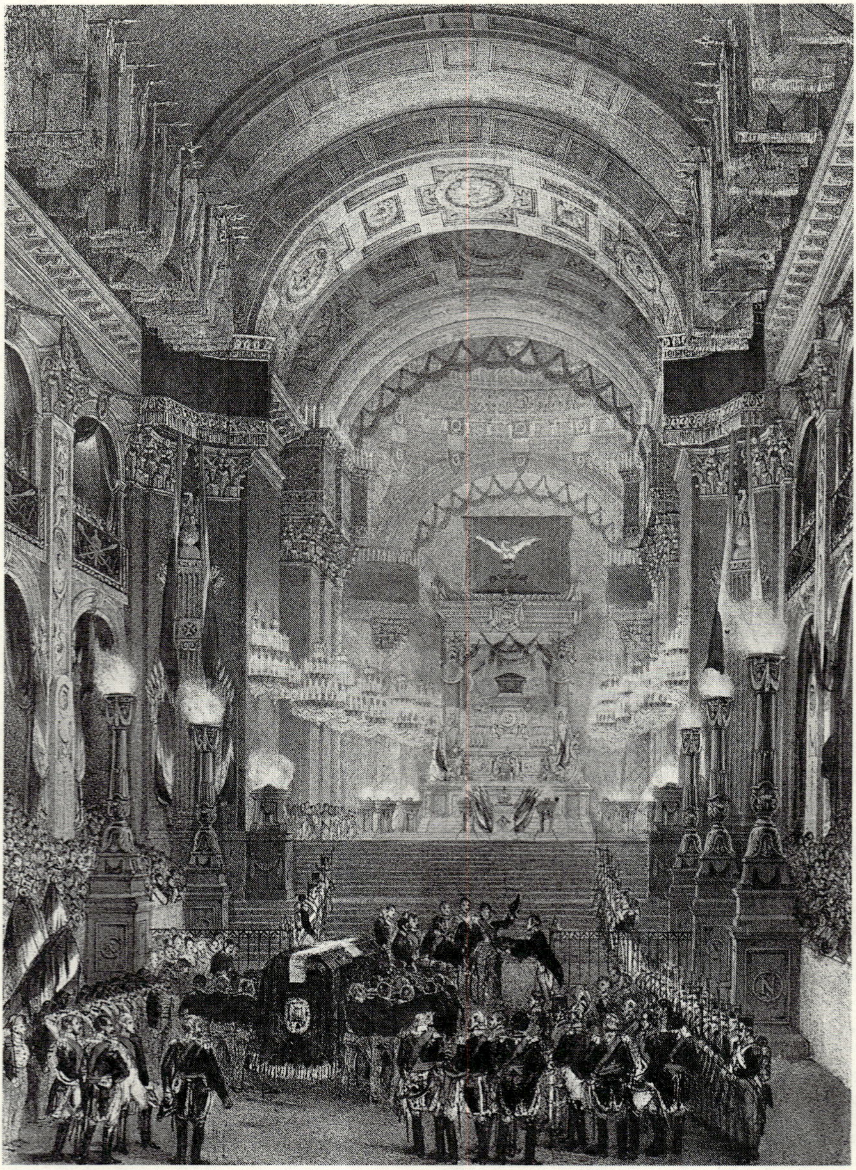

Figure 1.20 French School, (19th century). *The Arrival of Napoleon's Ashes at the Church of the Invalides, 15 December, 1840*. Lithograph. Credit: Musée de la Ville de Paris, Musée Carnavalet, Paris, France/Bridgeman Images.

"this scheme of exaltation . . . a dishonoring act." Instead, the writer directed Philadelphians to honor the Founder with "deeds of righteousness, temperance, virtue and good-will."[61] The *Friends' Intelligencer* concurred: "better to allow [Penn's remains] quietly to moulder away undisturbed, and become a part of that earth from which their elements were drawn. 'Dust thou art and unto dust shalt thou return.'"[62] As did the editors of the *Times*: "It is little better than mockery to think of doing honor to such a man as Penn by the grotesque proposal to disturb his remains. The thing is happily impossible, as the trustees of the burial place state that they are not certain of the exact spot where the remains are interred, but even if it were possible it would surely be instantly forbidden by the instinctive and irresistible sentiments of the two great nations."[63]

Yet it is unlikely that those individuals who supported the project at the federal, state, and local level were aware of its theological contradictions, for their motives were uncontestably political. Harrison's mission and the tone of his report tell us more about how notions of patriotic commemoration were informed by prevailing political conditions in Philadelphia. "Now, more than at any previous time, we seem to need the example which this man affords us," Harrison lamented, "Now, when wealth and office are set up in every public place, as objects to be gained, by the sacrifice . . . of honor and honesty and decency . . . [when] the widow and the orphan . . . [are] ruthlessly cheated and impoverished by the stealthy . . . hypocrite. We should keep before our view this heroic projector of our State; a model of honesty and charity, who surrendered all his chances in life to serve men whom he had never seen."[64]

Sponsoring the return of Penn's body offered an opportunity for citizens who considered themselves the principle stewards of Penn's legacy to exert some influence over a massive and controversial construction project that would define Philadelphia's future for good or ill. Harrison's mission took place at the same time that local reformers redoubled their efforts to combat "extravagance and mismanagement of municipal affairs" and the corrupt practices of Philadelphia's political machine. A decade before, news of the extraordinary powers granted to the Public Buildings Commission, "empowered to tax us without limit, and to spend our money without supervision, to hold office without restriction of time and to fill vacancies in their own body . . . inflicting on us all the evils of taxation without representation," prompted business leaders to form the Citizens' Municipal Reform Association to lobby for a new state constitution that could restrict the powers of similar commissions.[65] The new constitution was passed in 1873, but Philadelphia's ward bosses were undeterred, and corruption continued to infect city government. Just weeks before the HSP councilors learned of Dillwyn Parrish's proposal to translate Penn's remains, reformers among Philadelphia business leaders had come together again to form The Committee of One Hundred in an effort to unseat longtime mayor and machine operative William Stokley.[66] What better way to pay tribute to the Founder and to guide the thousands who would enter city hall to, in Harrison's words, "be elevated for good or restrained from evil by the inevitable consciousness of the high, and pure, and courageous character of the man"?[67] Penn was a tangible example of the honest and decent leader at a time when the city and the country were beset by political corruption. "Now, when the heat and struggle are most fierce and pitiless in the market-place," Harrison declared, "the interests of the unthinking and credulous many . . . sacrificed to those of the keen-witted and unscrupulous few . . . it is needful that we should keep before our view this . . . model of honesty and charity."[68]

Finding that his pleas to the Jordans trustees fell on deaf ears, Harrison hoped that support would come from Penn's descendants, but they vacillated. Peter Penn Gaskell Hall, an American descendant, felt that it would have been more courteous to send a member of the family to Jordans rather than a stranger and volunteered his services.[69] Hall changed his tune when Harrison instead was selected for the diplomatic mission. When contacted by Dillwyn Parrish, British descendants Peter Penn Gaskell and William Stuart initially did not oppose the plan, though Stuart then changed his mind and in a letter to Harrison expressed "great repugnance" at the prospect of disturbing his ancestor's remains.[70] Gaskell still seemed amenable and in early August, Parrish wrote to Harrison that only direct application to the British Home Secretary by Penn's descendants would counter the intransigence of the Jordans trustees. But no such application seems to have been made. Gaskell may have been discouraged by his cousins, and Harrison returned to Philadelphia in mid-August. Deeply embarrassed by his failure, Harrison published an account of his mission that included his report to Henry M. Hoyt, the governor of Pennsylvania, reprints of his credentials and correspondence with the Jordans trustees and Penn descendants, a short biography of William Penn, and a description of a tour of sites in and around Jordans—the publication was distributed by HSP.

I have found no mention of the proposal to build a tomb for Penn's remains under the main tower of city hall in the records of the Public Buildings Commission, though Harrison's mission and the tomb proposal were publicized nationally. No surviving drawings or plans indicate that any kind of tomb or mortuary structure was to be installed in the main tower—though there is an area in the tower basement that might have accommodated a tomb (figure 1.21). But by 1881, construction of the basement and first two stories of city hall was almost complete. Any kind of tomb construction there would have added considerable expense to an already expensive project. Given the numerous controversies and accusations of graft that swirled around their project, Samuel Perkins and fellow members of the Public Buildings Commission likely chose to distance themselves from the translation campaign and controversy.

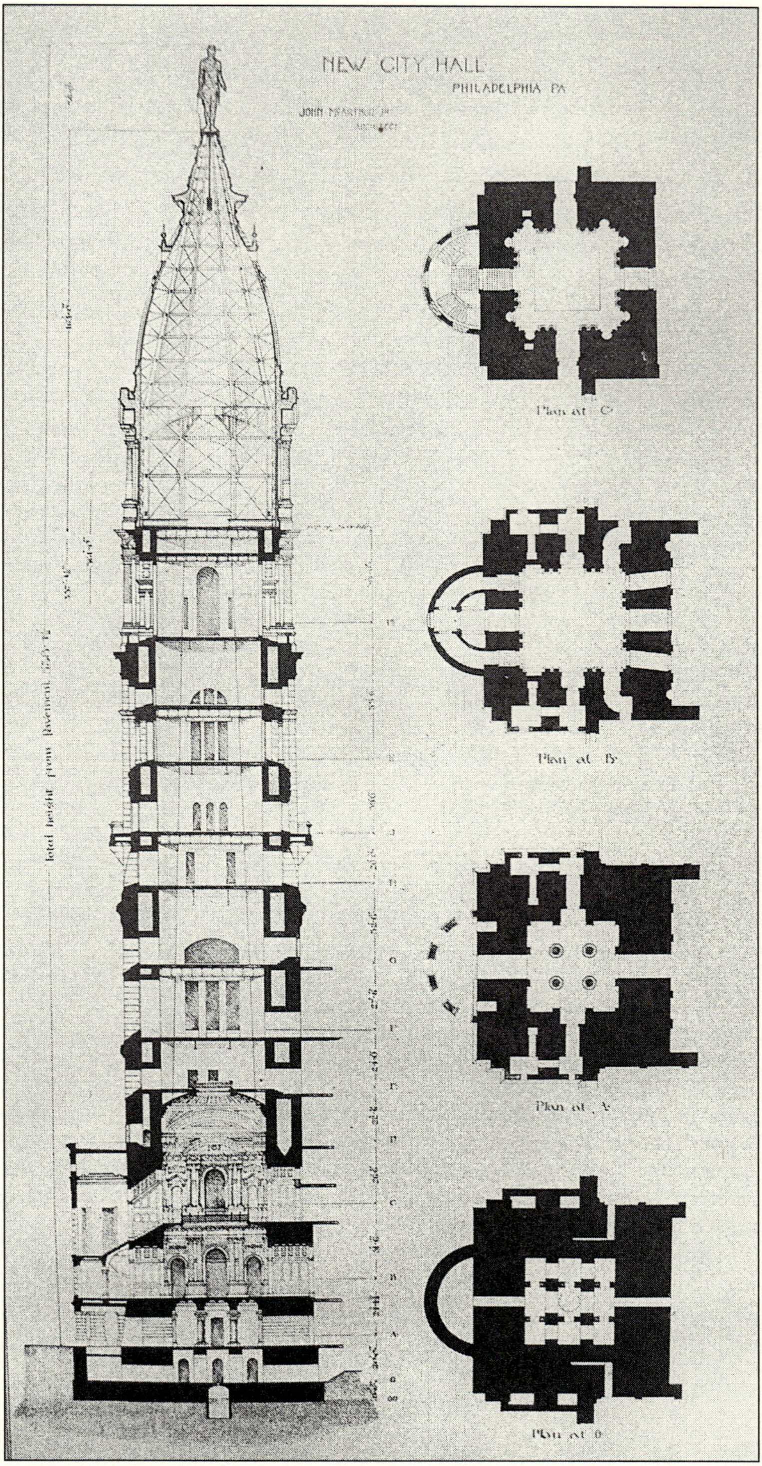

Figure 1.21 *Elevation Drawing of City Hall Tower*, from *The New Public Buildings on Penn Square* (Philadelphia, 1880). City of Philadelphia, Department of Records, City Archives.

Had Harrison and his colleagues succeeded in translating Penn's remains from Jordans to Philadelphia, the new city hall would have become a grand municipal sepulcher—the site of a revered body. As it is, the story of the ill-fated campaign should alert us to the fact that, at least for Harrison and his associates at HSP, the memory of their efforts caused the tower and Calder's statue to combine to form a cenotaph, the "empty" structure that commemorates the bodies of saints or heroes interred elsewhere. At Jordans, William Penn lies, still undisturbed—somewhere—among the graves in a "secluded and desolate spot."

NOTES

1. The height of the tower, including the statue, is 511 feet. The origins of the so-called Gentlemen's Agreement are vague: some sources have dated it to construction of Howe and Lescaze's Philadelphia Savings Fund Society building in 1932, while others credit Edmund Bacon, longtime executive director of the Philadelphia City Planning Commission, with having formulated and enforced the restriction. To distinguish it from the general tradition and practice of gentlemen's agreements, the Philadelphia example is usually capitalized. See Benjamin M. Gerber, "'No Law' Urban Height Restrictions: A Philadelphia Story," *The Urban Lawyer*, 38, no.1 (Winter 2006), 118.

2. Quoted in "Towering over All Comers, Penn Still Defines His City (editorial)," *The Inquirer* (Philadelphia), March 21, 1984, 12A; quoted in Benjamin M. Gerber, "'No Law' Urban Height Restrictions," 114, n. 23.

3. John Moretta, *William Penn and the Quaker Legacy* (New York, NY: Pearson, 2006), xi.

4. A thought-provoking essay that sheds light on the shaky foundations of many Penn legends, including his physical appearance, is J. W. Frost, "'Wear the Sword as Long as Thou Canst': William Penn in Myth and History," *Explorations in Early American Culture*, 4 (2000): 13–45.

5. George L. Harrison, *The Remains of William Penn. Pennsylvania's Plea, the Mission to England, Visit to the Grave, Letters, etc.* (Philadelphia, PA: Privately printed, 1882), 11.

6. The letter is quoted in full in "Bi-Centennial. Proposition for the Removal of Penn's Remains to This City," *The Inquirer* (Philadelphia), March 14, 1881, 3. Welsh's identity is confirmed in the minutes of the Historical Society's board of councilors meeting of April 25, 1881. Historical Society of Pennsylvania, Institutional Records. Parrish was identified by name during a debate on May 10, 1881, in the Pennsylvania General Assembly. See *Laws of the General Assembly of the State of Pennsylvania Passed at the Session of 1881* (Harrisburg, PA: Lane S. Hart, 1881), 182.

Parrish was the son of William D. Parrish (d. 1863) and nephew and namesake of the noted abolitionist and president of the College of Pharmacy. The younger Parrish lived abroad for many years and made his fortune building street railroads and telephone systems in India. Katherine Cox Gottschalk, *The Parrish Family*, compiled and published by Scott Lee Boyd. (Santa Barbara, CA: privately printed, 1935), 200.

7. "Bi-Centennial. Proposition for the Removal of Penn's Remains to This City," *The Inquirer* (Philadelphia), March 14, 1881, 3.

8. "William Penn's Grave," *The Literary Magazine and American Register*, 6, no. 37 (October, 1806), 290. For a history of the meeting-house and burying-ground, see Anna L. Littleboy, *A History of Jordans* (London: Friends' Bookshop, 1925), 7–11, 27–29.

9. "The Grave of William Penn," *The Friend: A Religious and Literary Journal*, 5, no. 40 (July 14, 1832): 314

10. The painting was by H. F. de Cort; Granville Penn donated it to the Historical Society of Pennsylvania in 1834. Hicks made at least five versions of the subject. See Alice Ford,

Edward Hicks, Painter of the Peaceable Kingdom, rev. ed. (1952; repr. Philadelphia, PA: University of Pennsylvania Press, 1998), 105–106.

11. *The Revised Discipline Approved by the Yearly Meeting of Friends Held in Baltimore for the Western Shore of Maryland and the Adjacent Parts of Pennsylvania and Virginia* (Baltimore, MD: John Hayes, 1794), 18. Quoted in Francine W. Bromberg and Steven J. Shephard, "The Quaker Burying Ground in Alexandria, Virginia: A Study of Burial Practices of the Religious Society of Friends," *Historical Archaeology*, 40, no. 1 (2006): 62. Anna Littleboy, however, reports that markers *were* erected when Penn and his family were first buried and were removed late in the eighteenth century in an effort to enforce greater simplicity. Anna L. Littleboy, *A History of Jordans* (London: Friends' Bookshop, 1925), 15.

12. Penn biographer William Dixon credits Granville John Penn with having added the markers, quoted in Arthur Grant, "In England's Pennsylvania," *Atlantic Monthly*, 102, no. 4 (October 1908), 560. Littleboy states that the markers were installed in 1862–1863. Anna L. Littleboy, *A History of Jordans*, 15.

13. Colonel John W. Forney, "Anecdotes of Public Men." *The Press* (Philadelphia), September 28, 1874, 2.

14. Colonel John W. Forney, "Anecdotes of Public Men," 2.

15. Hampton L. Carson, *A History of the Historical Society of Pennsylvania*, 2 vols. (Philadelphia, PA: The Society, 1940), 1:48–60, 1:128–145.

16. Hampton L. Carson, *A History of the Historical Society of Pennsylvania*, 1:243–247, 1:383–398. See also Nicholas B. Wainwright, "The Penn Collection," *Pennsylvania Magazine of History and Biography*, 87, no. 4 (October 1963), 409–412.

17. Meeting of June 12, 1880. Board of Councilors minutes. Historical Society of Pennsylvania, Institutional Records.

18. *Laws of the General Assembly of the State of Pennsylvania Passed at the Session of 1881* (Harrisburg, PA: Lane S. Hart, 1881), 172–182, and Samuel B. Collins, *The Legislative Record, Containing the Debates and Proceedings in the Legislature of Pennsylvania, for the Session of 1881* (Harrisburg, PA: Telegraph Steam Printing House, 1881), pt. 1 and pt. 2.

19. Harrison was president of the Harrison, Havemeyer Sugar Refining Company. No explanation has been found as to why he was selected for the mission. He was a devout Episcopalian, not a Quaker, though he had earned widespread respect as the president of several local charities. See William Welsh Harrison. *The Royal Ancestry of George Leib Harrison of Philadelphia*, edited by William M. Mervine (Philadelphia, PA: printed for private circulation only, 1914), 12–14, and "George L. Harrison," in James Grant Wilson and John Fiske, eds. *Appleton's Cyclopaedia of American Biography*, 8 vols. (New York, NY: D. Appleton and Company, 1887), 3:99.

20. *A Letter from William Penn Proprietary and Governor of Pennsylvania in America to the Committee of the Free Society of Traders of that Province, residing in London* . . . (London: Printed and Sold by Andrew Sowle, 1683), reprinted in Albert Cook Myers, *Narratives of Early Pennsylvania, West New Jersey and Delaware, 1630–1707* (New York, NY: Charles Scribner's Sons, 1912), 239–243. See also Susan Mackiewicz, "Philadelphia Flourishing: The Material World of Philadelphians, 1682–1760," (PhD diss., University of Delaware, 1988), 111 and Elizabeth Milroy, *The Grid and the River: Philadelphia's Green Places, 1682–1876* (University Park, PA: Penn State University Press, 2016), 11–15.

21. Humphrey Prideaux claims that Penn modeled Philadelphia after Babylon in *The Old and New Testament Connected in the History of the Jews and Neighbouring Nations*, 9th ed. (London: R. Knaplock, 1725), 1:135.

22. Elizabeth Milroy, *The Grid and the River*, 17–26.

23. Milroy, *The Grid and the River*, 33–39.

24. Thomas Cope Diary, June 1, 1807. Thomas Cope Papers, Haverford College Quaker Special Collections, Haverford, PA. http://triptych.brynmawr.edu/cdm/ref/collection/HC_Qjournal/id/1915.

25. Histories of the municipal water system include Jane Mork Gibson, "The Fairmount Waterworks," *Philadelphia Museum of Art Bulletin*, 84, no. 360–361 (1988); Andrew Schocket, *Founding Corporate Power in Early National Philadelphia* (DeKalb: Northern Illinois University Press, 2007), 111–116; Carl Smith, *City Water, City Life: Water and the Infrastructure of Ideas in Urbanizing Philadelphia, Boston, and Chicago* (Chicago, IL: The University of Chicago Press, 2013), passim; Elizabeth Milroy, *The Grid and the River*, 181–208; and *Philly H2O: The History of Philadelphia's Watersheds and Sewers*, the website maintained by Adam Levine for the Philadelphia Water Department at http://www.phillyh2o.org.

26. Elizabeth Milroy, *The Grid and the River*, 155–179.

27. Job R. Tyson, *Discourse on the Two Hundredth Anniversary of the Birth of William Penn*. (Philadelphia, PA: John Penington, 1845), 20.

28. Tyson, *Discourse*, 13–14.

29. Elizabeth Milroy, *The Grid and the River*, 165–166.

30. The Select Council grew to twenty-four members, one elected from each of the twenty-four wards into which the city was now subdivided; the Common Council, consisting of one representative elected for every twelve hundred taxpayers, expanded from twenty to seventy-four. Michael P. McCarthy, "Traditions in Conflict: The Philadelphia City Hall Site Controversy." *Pennsylvania History*, 57, no. 4 (October 1990), 302–308; Michael Lewis, "'Silent, Weird, Beautiful': Philadelphia City Hall," *Nineteenth Century*, 11, nos. 3 and 4 (1992): 13–14.

31. "Resolution Requesting an Act of Assembly to Enable the City to Make Grants on Penn Squares for Certain Public Uses," (Appendix No. 295), June 27, 1867. *Journal of the Select Council of the City of Philadelphia* (Philadelphia, PA: E. C. Markley, 1868), 840.

32. Howard Gillette Jr., "Philadelphia's City Hall: Monument to a New Political Machine," *Pennsylvania Magazine of History and Biography*, 97, no. 2 (April 1973), 233–236; Michael P. McCarthy, "Traditions in Conflict: The Philadelphia City Hall Site Controversy," 309; Elizabeth Milroy, *The Grid and the River*, 311–314.

33. Charlene Mires, *Independence Hall in American Memory* (Philadelphia: University of Pennsylvania Press, 2002), 117–121.

34. The *Sunday Dispatch* reported that Henry Charles Lea earned from thirty to fifty thousand dollars per annum in rent from an office building he owned at Fifth and Walnut Streets. Cited in Michael Lewis, "'Silent, Weird, Beautiful,'" 16. See also Charlene Mires, *Independence Hall*, 121.

35. "Penn Square and the Society Beggars," *Sunday Dispatch (Philadelphia)*, September 25, 1870, in George Canby, comp., *The Public Buildings* (1869). Scrapbook, Historical Society of Pennsylvania. Quoted in Elizabeth Milroy, *The Grid and the River*, 313. See also Howard Gillette Jr., "Philadelphia's City Hall, 237; Michael P. McCarthy, "Traditions in Conflict: The Philadelphia City Hall Site Controversy," *Pennsylvania History*, 57, no. 4 (October 1990): 309; and Michael Lewis, "'Silent, Weird, Beautiful,'" 14–16.

36. "The New Public Buildings Act," *Public Ledger (Philadelphia)*, October 3, 1870, 1. See Howard Gillette Jr., "Philadelphia's City Hall, 238–241; Peter McCaffery, *When Bosses Ruled Philadelphia: The Emergence of the Republican Machine*. University Park: The Pennsylvania State University Press, 1993), 22–25; and Andrew David Heath, "'The Manifest Destiny of Philadelphia': Imperialism, Republicanism, and the Remaking of a City and Its People, 1837–1877," (PhD diss., University of Pennsylvania, 2008), 401–406.

37. Roger Butterfield, "The Cats on City Hall," *Pennsylvania Magazine of History and Biography*, 77, no. 4 (October 1953), 442; Peter McCaffery, *When Bosses Ruled Philadelphia*, 24–26.

38. George Gurney, "The Sculpture of City Hall," in Fairmount Park Art Association, *Sculpture of a City: Philadelphia's Treasures in Bronze and Stone* (New York, NY: Walker Publishing Company, 1974), 97.

39. This is based on the date at which William Struthers and Sons, marble contractors for the exterior, reported that the final stone had been put into place on the building's south-

ern façade. George Gurney, "The Sculpture of City Hall," 97; Michael Lewis, "'Silent, Weird, Beautiful,'" 18–20.

40. Gurney, "The Sculpture of City Hall," 97.

41. Gurney, "The Sculpture of City Hall," 98.

42. John Penn, Penn's grandson, donated the lead statue to the hospital in 1804. It has been dated to 1774 based on a description by Benjamin Franklin, who saw the statue when it was installed in the garden of Lord Despencer's country house at Wycombe; John Penn had acquired it after 1788. John Fanning Watson attributed it to John Bacon (the Elder). Henri Marceau, "William Penn's Other Statue," *The Pennsylvania Magazine of History and Biography*, 95, no. 4 (October, 1971), 521–526. See also [Caroline Pitts], "William Penn," in Fairmount Park Art Association, *Sculpture of a City: Philadelphia's Treasures in Bronze and Stone* (New York, NY: Walker Publishing Company, 1974), 20.

43. "Statue of William Penn," *The Inquirer* (Philadelphia), November 13, 1875, 3. See also George Gurney, "William Penn," in Fairmount Park Art Association, *Sculpture of a City: Philadelphia's Treasures in Bronze and Stone* (New York, NY: Walker Publishing Company, 1974), 105–107.

44. Gurney, "The Sculpture of City Hall," 98.

45. Gurney, "William Penn," 107–109.

46. A recent study of the column is Robert Oosterhout, "The Life and Afterlife of Constantine's Column," *Journal of Roman Archaeology*, 27 (January 2014): 304–326.

47. In so doing, Crawford conflated three traditional allegories: Liberty, Minerva, and America. He was responding to the wishes of Jefferson Davis, secretary of war, who disliked the allusion to emancipation conveyed by the liberty cap. Vivien Green Fryd, *Art and Empire: The Politics of Ethnicity in the U.S. Capitol, 1815–1860* (New Haven, CT: Yale University Press, 1992), 189–200.

48. Elizabeth Milroy, *The Grid and the River*, 230–231.

49. "The United States," *The Times* (London), May 14, 1881, 7.

50. Richard Littleboy to the editor of the *Times*, July 18, 1881, enclosing a letter from the Trustees of the Jordans Meeting-house and Burial-ground to George L. Harrison, July 11, 1881, reprinted in George L. Harrison, *The Remains of William Penn*, 40–43.

51. The letter was printed in full in *The Times* (London) on July 20, 1881.

52. George L. Harrison to the editor of *The Times*, July 22, 1881, reprinted in George L. Harrison, *The Remains of William Penn*, 47–52.

53. Michael Kammen, *Digging Up the Dead: A History of Notable American Reburials* (Chicago, IL: University of Chicago Press, 2010), 10–11, 27–29.

54. The story of Saint Mark's translation was well known—Harrison could have read about it in a travel guide, such as Murray's *Handbook for Travellers in Northern Italy*, 4th ed. (London: John Murray, 1852), 303–304.

55. Kammen, *Digging Up the Dead*, 20.

56. Kammen, *Digging Up the Dead*, 17, 24.

57. Kammen, *Digging Up the Dead*, 48–50; Elizabeth Milroy, *The Grid and the River*, 216–218. A later example was the successful effort at the turn of the twentieth century to move the remains of John Paul Jones from a Paris cemetery to a crypt at the United States Naval Academy at Annapolis.

58. "Napoleon's Tomb," *Illustrated Magazine of Art*, 2, no. 10 (1853), 225–249. Modern accounts include Jean Boisson, *Le Retour des Cendres* (Paris: Études et Recherches Historiques, 1973) and Jean-Marcel Humbert, ed. *Napoléon aux Invalides 1840: Le Retour des Cendres*, exhibition catalog (Paris: Église du Dôme des Invalides, 1990); Stanley Mellon, "The July Monarchy and the Napoleonic Myth," *Yale French Studies*, no. 26: *The Myth of Napoleon* (1960), 70–78; Suzanne Glover Lindsay, "Mummies and Tombs: Turenne, Napoleon and Death Ritual," *The Art Bulletin*, 83, no. 3 (September 2000), 491–497 and Michael Kammen, *Digging Up the Dead*, 31.

59. Harrison, *The Remains of William Penn*, 50.

60. Harrison, *The Remains of William Penn*, 49–50. Though "les cendres" literally translates as "ashes," the French use the term to refer to any body remains. See Suzanne Glover Lindsay, "Mummies and Tombs," 501, n. 168.

61. Josiah Leeds, "The 'Entombment' of Penn's Remains," *Friends' Review*, 34 (April 2, 1881), 535.

62. "William Penn's Remains," *Friends' Intelligencer*, 38, no. 23 (July 23, 1881), 358.

63. "[William Penn]," *The Times* (London), July 20, 1881, 11.

64. George L. Harrison, *The Remains of William Penn*, 23–24.

65. Citizens Municipal Reform Association, *Report of the Executive Committee*, October 26, 1871. Henry Charles Lea Papers, Rare Book & Manuscript Library, University of Pennsylvania. See also *Henry Charles Lea [Memoir]* (Philadelphia, PA; Privately printed, 1910), 20; Edward P. Allinson and Boies Penrose, *Philadelphia, 1681–1887: A History of Municipal Development* (Baltimore, MD: The Johns Hopkins University Press, 1887), 259–264; Frank B. Evans, *Pennsylvania Politics, 1872–1877: A Study in Political Leadership* (Harrisburg: The Pennsylvania Historical and Museum Commission, 1966), 74–86; and Peter McCaffery, *When Bosses Ruled Philadelphia*, 22–27.

66. The Committee of One Hundred did remove Stokley from office (though not from a position of influence), and their efforts paved the way the way for passage of the Bullitt Bill in 1885, though this legislation also proved inadequate to destroy machine politics. Peter McCaffery, *When Bosses Ruled Philadelphia*, 71–75.

67. Harrison, *The Remains of William Penn*, 49.

68. Harrison, *The Remains of William Penn*, 24.

69. "William Penn's Remains," *New York Herald*, reprinted in *The Daily Picayune* (New Orleans), June 9, 1881, 2.

70. William Stuart to George L. Harrison, July 9, 1881. Reprinted in George L. Harrison, *The Remains of William Penn*, 87–88.

CHAPTER 2

Where William Penn Slept (and Why It Matters)

Catharine Dann Roeber

In two- and three-dimensional representations of William Penn created as he lay mouldering in his grave, the founder stands, one hand extended, wearing a coat, waistcoat, breeches, stockings, cravat, and hat.[1] Sometimes he faces right, sometimes he faces left. Occasionally he holds a treaty, a charter, or another offering. Sometimes he is surrounded by a group of Quaker Friends or Lenape traders, Pennsylvania Council members or colonial merchants, but he is just as often alone. Penn is fixed in image, fixed in form, and fixed in memory as an unchangeable historical figure representing the lofty political, religious, and social ideals of his Pennsylvania experiment. These renderings of a provincial proprietor frozen in time and space both literally and figuratively rise above any other, dominating popular imagination and governing the skies as the cake topper for the Beaux Arts civic confection, Philadelphia's city hall (built 1871–1901). Yet even a cursory glance at Penn's personal biography reveals a man *of* and *in* the world who was anything but immobile.

Visual depictions and written accounts have relegated Penn to a stereotype, and his legacy has long centered on ideology. His political, spiritual, and intellectual contributions to British colonial society dominate scholarship about a man whom "many know a little, but few know well."[2] Yet what is often lost in scholarship that focuses tightly on his ideas alone is any sense of Penn as a living, breathing person who shaped and was shaped by material and physical circumstances. Tension also exists between the framing of Penn as both mobile in life and immobile in memory.[3] The diversity of his thoughts, words, and actions challenges the noble souls who attempt to reconcile his biography in a neat and tidy package. Penn's peripatetic lifestyle, the relative lack of extant tangible evidence for Penn's material world, and the predominance of mythologized images of the proprietor all obscure the importance he placed on material circumstances for realizing his goals in Pennsylvania and beyond. Admittedly, it is difficult to summarize the life of a man who is often described with words like "paradox" or "complex." It is easier, and was often more politically and socially useful, to cut out the excess details of his life from both written accounts and aesthetic renderings and focus on Penn as the uber-symbol of American colonial liberality, tolerance, and benevolence.

It is important to understand how Penn framed the material world through words and actions in order to move beyond stereotypes that doggedly permeate our understanding of the man. In reference to his material circumstances, scholars and public historians have historically poised Penn as a pious Quaker who shunned all material frivolity, or framed him as a hypocrite, citing his penchant for wig wearing or "French garb." Penn's biographer, Janney, used the opposition to hat doffing as an example of Penn and other early Quakers' persistent faith, suggesting, "The primitive Friends felt it their duty to bear an uncompromising testimony against this custom, as well as all others, which had been adopted for the purpose of flattering human pride." The tension between Penn as hypocrite and Penn as pious leader continues in more recent scholarship. The work on Penn by Richard and Mary Maples Dunn; broader studies of first-period Pennsylvania cultural history, such as Frederick Tolles's historical gem *Meeting House and Counting House*; and exhibits such as the Philadelphia Museum of Art's 1999–2000 exhibit *Worldly Goods* are notable exceptions that embrace a more comprehensive approach to understanding the era of Penn and to studying Penn himself. As these studies suggest, attention to Penn's material world provides a more nuanced picture of a man on a quest to lead Quaker believers and eventually establish a new colony.[4]

Penn's broad exposure to various material surroundings in early life shaped his ability to move fluidly in diverse social settings and provided him with cultural prowess in using and talking about objects, architecture, and landscapes as key components of promoting his colonial projects. More than mere anecdotes or asides, Penn's comments about houses, and fields, and foods were part of an integrated approach to "applied ideology," or a connection between idea and practice, that was better understood by his contemporaries than by twenty-first-century readers.[5]

A Life on the Move

In 1710, William Penn lamented, "I cannot but think it hard measure, that while that has prov'd a Land of freedom & flourishing, it shoul'd become to me by whose means it was principally made a Country the cause of grief Trouble & Poverty."[6] Despite a desire to return to Pennsylvania, William Penn never spent more than a few years in the province he founded. Business and eventually illness and incapacitation hindered his travel to America. Suffering from apoplectic strokes in 1712, Penn was reduced in his abilities to walk or travel, which ended a long life on the move. He lived his last days a resident at his rented house in Ruscombe in Berkshire near Twyford, located approximately an hour from London. This house, like every other main residence of Penn (other than his site of imprisonment at the Tower of London), no longer stands. Due to the lack of extant original buildings, there is no place to study actual architecture that Penn inhabited for any great length of time. Alternately, the one existing reconstruction in America at Pennsbury Manor exemplifies an early twentieth-century colonial revival aesthetic more than seventeenth-century architectural survival. Even if it is difficult to interpret Penn's residences in physical form, it is important to acknowledge his material circumstances and his life on the move. Mary Maples Dunn acknowledged Penn's highly mobile life and summed Penn up as a man who "loved a whirlwind life." Her work on the personality of William Penn emphasizes his mobility to provide psychological insight into a man she understood as restless. She went so far as to ask, "one wonders . . . if he had to keep on the move to avoid meeting even himself."[7] Beyond insight into Penn's personal psychology, the material world and an acknowledgment and understanding of Penn's movements and daily life can be used to glean insights into the ways he used references to the material world to advocate for well-being for himself and others and to promote processes of improvement he envisioned for the Pennsylvania project.

Penn's understanding of the material world's power can be seen in his well-known and much cited expressions of nonconformity. Penn's behavior in refusing to remove his hat is often interpreted in the context of his radical politics and strict adherence to Quaker precepts. But it can also be seen as evidence of his inclination and practice of using the material world for achieving broader goals. Penn was well versed in court behavior, wherein attendees regularly fashioned and refashioned their clothes and comportment to political and social advantage.[8] Only by understanding the importance of hat removal at court and a willingness and commitment to oppositional hat-doffing behavior did Penn achieve any sort of reaction. This is not a man who is oblivious to or misinterpreting social performance. This was evidence of savvy, embodied behavior unleashed at carefully selected moments and in specifically chosen environments.[9]

Penn's awareness of the nuances of actions, combined with his skill with words, supported Penn's ability to react and navigate through the world. In fact, his exposure to, awareness of, and study of city and town plans and improvements of fields and forests; of court dress and reciprocal gifting; and of a rich and diverse material world allowed him fluency in using tangible things and places to navigate his diverse circumstances in America and elsewhere. Details of Penn's material world come from fragments and asides gleaned from his diaries, letters, trip accounts, and the admittedly limited material clues from his life. From these often terse and disperse notes, a sense of the diverse landscapes, places, and objects he encountered come to life. On his trips to Ireland or Germany, or in accounts of his visits to the English countryside and towns, we see a young man led by both faith and duty to pursue betterment in very real and material forms in keeping with his ideological goals.

Penn's peripatetic life began early. Within his first twenty years (1644–1664) he moved from London to Essex to Cork, Ireland, to Oxford, to France, and, briefly, to Italy. We know little about Penn's youth, which is not well represented in historical documents or material remains. Even the *Papers* of William Penn jump from a transcription of Penn's baptismal certificate to the period of young adulthood. Within the fifteen years between 1664 and 1679 he moved extensively throughout England and Ireland and took two trips to Germany and Holland (1671 and 1677).[10] During these travels Penn slept in fields and prison cells, castles, and country houses. Comfortable lodging in private chambers alternated with nights sleeping in wagons with nothing but an "old ragged sheet" or al fresco with "a good bed in the fields." What Penn carried with him besides his clothes and a few linens is difficult to discern, but references to writing letters, reading, and sharing books suggests that he had the equivalent of a traveling bookshop or stationery store to aid in his proselytizing. Soon after, Penn began his administrative connections to the Americas. He traveled widely within England, and during two trips to the colonies (1682–1684 and 1699–1701) he also spent a significant portion of time in transit within the mid-Atlantic.[11] His life was not one of prolonged leisure and repose. This proclivity for movement can be explained by multiple, interrelated factors, including his formal and informal education, family investments and business interests, religious affiliations and leadership, and colonial pursuits.

Accounts of Pennsylvania's founding often begin with some version of the following: "King Charles II owed William Penn £16,000, money which his late father Admiral Sir Penn had lent him. Seeking a haven in the New World for persecuted Friends, Penn asked the King to grant him land in the territory between Lord Baltimore's province of Maryland and the Duke of York's province of New York. With the Duke's support, Penn's petition was granted. The King signed the Charter of Pennsylvania on March 4, 1681, and it was officially proclaimed on April 2. The King named the new colony in honor of William Penn's father."[12] Less often is the origin of William Penn's colonial gaze and mobile lifestyle framed in his family's worldly background and outlook.

His grandparents were Bristol merchants with connections to the Mediterranean, North Africa, and the Levant through grandfather Giles Penn; his mother was of Irish and Prussian/Low Countries stock; and his father, a Bristol merchant and naval officer, was deeply involved in Cromwell's Western Design in the Caribbean and other westward-oriented adventures[13] The Penn family also managed Irish lands acquired after the 1660 Acts of Settlement. The Penns were a multinational and connected family, deeply entwined in the trading of goods and people and the conquest of foreign lands long before William Penn received his Pennsylvania charter from Charles II in 1681.[14] This diverse and outwardly looking experience was true for many colonial Pennsylvania families of all economic backgrounds, and the Penn family outlook and colonial designs must be framed in this broader, worldly context.[15]

Thus, even before William Penn became convinced of the Quaker faith, he was aware of and exposed to English desires to declare sovereignty over people and land in the Americas and the Caribbean. Estate management, enslavement, and other aspects of the colonial experience were within the framework of his youth as was the broader understanding of forming good instincts for being a successful navigator of various social worlds.[16] Penn's experience in Saumur, France, provided a crash course in social graces and was in line with that of other gentlemen of the later seventeenth century who ventured to the Continent for an immersive "finishing school" experience. Although few details of this trip survive, an unknown correspondent with Sir William Penn stated in reference to his son and the eventual proprietor, "indeed the whole Successe of a traveler is in a kind of Crisis, of what Inclinations he carrys with him, and what Conversations he lights in [to at] first."[17] In short, having a firm grasp of social etiquette and an understanding of proper comportment was essential for a gentleman.[18] Rather than only looking to models of sociability closer to home, Penn looked both to England and to the Continent for inspiration to cultivate his behavior, knowledge, and manners. These youthful experiences reinforced his outward gaze. Although there is no evidence that he specifically had designs of his own for creating a colony before the 1670s, his varied experiences and exposure to the world as a young man primed him for later activities. Penn quickly became attuned to life as a traveler, and in 1667, while he was on an excursion managing estates in Ireland, his travels became supercharged when he became convinced of Quakerism and found himself in "a Continual beholding of the Lord's Glory."[19]

With his newfound spiritual awakening and religious identification as a member of the Society of Friends came associations with a community of Quaker itinerant preachers and believers. As Sarah Crabtree suggests, "The Quaker itinerant ministry had built an impressive network of patrons, correspondents, and travelers. But perhaps even more important, they also retained the transnational vision of the Zion tradition and the missionary zeal necessary to sustain and propagate it."[20] Walking and traveling served as meaningful metaphors for Quakers and promoted Quaker beliefs.[21] Participation in a community that accepted and necessitated movement was central to Penn's experiences. He joined a force of women and men who traveled to preach and to find fellowship with others as well as to promote their individual and communal nonconformist views. In this he was generally aligned with other followers and promoters of protestant mysticism active on the late seventeenth- and early eighteenth-century world stage.[22] Indeed, other early Pennsylvania residents, such as Germanic Mennonite-Quaker groups, and followers of separatists, such as Johannes Kelpius, shared a commitment to self-identification as pilgrims.[23] Yet the threat of sin was ever present, and Penn himself admonished fellow Quaker young Sir John Rodes to "Walk wisely" and to stay fixed to the moral path. By doing so he rearticulated Georg Fox's statement that even "The Wayfaring man, Though a Fool, cannot err within."[24] To Penn and others movement was important to further their spiritual mission, so, in turn, regulating and navigating a path through a world deemed uncertain and potentially dangerous was essential.

The spiritual dimensions of itinerancy have been discussed thoughtfully elsewhere, but less attention has been paid to the material ramifications of a wandering life. Literature emphasizes the social connections and resulting economic and religious networks that were formed and strengthened through the Quaker diaspora. As Rebecca Larson noted in her work on female Quaker missionaries, "convinced that they were ushering in the Millennium, early Friends conceived of their mission in worldwide terms," following George Fox's call to "be obedient to the Truth, and spread it abroad, which must go over all the world."[25] These spiritual missions were certainly important to building a strong and wide-reaching Quaker community. Additionally, though, this movement through different countries, landscapes, and architectural settings not only promoted social and spiritual connection in diverse settings, it also both promoted and reinforced a fluid interaction with wide-ranging material circumstances. A picture of Penn's activities in England, gleaned from accounts with Philip Ford in 1672, illustrates how he could easily fill the role of English gentleman on the move. Taking a barge from his house to enjoy the gardens at Vauxhall, procuring fresh provisions purchased from local farmers, dining at London establishments, and acquiring "haberdashery," "silke stockins," or other fine clothes for himself and his family are evidence of his skill with the trappings of civility.[26] But he could just as easily be found "roughing it" on the road for missionary work. Later visual representations of Pennsylvania, such as Thomas Holme's *Map of the Improved Part of Pennsilvania in America*, embodied these varied experiences and knowledge in physical form. This map was a project demonstrating with ink on paper his appreciation of and experience with land management, natural philosophy, and gentlemanly comportment. It reflected his complex role as a colonial leader, rather than as one fixed identity.

Indeed, to posit Penn's interests in Pennsylvania as "Quaker," or even as "English," is reductionist and simplifies the processes of creative reinvention that occur in the provincial setting. In his discussion of Pennsylvania as a creole culture, John Smolenski provides a more sophisticated and satisfactory model for grappling with the various cultural contributions and creations that emerged in Pennsylvania's civic culture. Focus on the built environments and landscapes that Penn knew and inhabited, in addition to the moveable material "toolkit" he employed adds additional insight to Penn as a man, who happened to be a leader, entrenched in the process of creolization.[27] In Penn's world, this ability to negotiate challenging physical and political terrain, to navigate the customs of multiple countries and cultures, and to operate at ease in castles and in prisons promoted his success as a champion of Quaker, American, Pennsylvanian, and Penn family causes.

His early trip to Ireland in 1669–1670 provides a snapshot of how his travels led to varied encounters with people, spaces, objects, and landscapes. As he rode through the landscape on horses described as a "gray gelden," a "stone Coult" a "chestnut nag," "a dun nag," and a "flea bit mare" Penn noted stops at locations both lowly and grand. He "visited the Prisoners" on multiple occasions and "had a meeting in prison at night where we also had dined" and were "kindly entertained." He visited more formal institutions, such as "City Hall" and "County Hall" in Cork, and ate and met in taverns, such as the "Green Dragon" and "the Cow." He also observed the "castle & gardens" of the Gould family. That he "saw the Iron-works" at Montroth and "lay at Thurles, the Ancient manner house of the D. of Ormonde," confirm that he visited sites of both work and leisure. He noted when people "treated me with great civility" and learned what he, as a guest, appreciated and could replicate in his own life. The trip also provided him with opportunities to make observations of the landscape, such as "a road well Improv'd, & much English," or improvements, such as a visit where he "went to see C. [ol. Peter] Wallis trenches In the great Bog where he has made a double ditch 2 miles quicksetted & many great ditches a cross, by which It may be profitable land." On this trip alone he covered "hundreds of miles," met hundreds of people, and visited a wide range of landscapes and built environments. The trip exemplifies the tensions inherent in his circumstances and the multiple roles Penn enacted from day to day and moment to moment. His skillful navigation of geography, culture, and manners set a foundation that became useful for later colonial endeavors.[28]

His later trips in Germany and Holland joined with travels in England to provide the future proprietor both access to and appreciation of physical surroundings he drew on in his provincial projects. This snapshot of his activities only hints at the expansive range of material circumstances Penn experienced, even before arriving on North American shores at New Castle the Lower Counties (Delaware) in 1682. In very specific ways, Penn drew on his accumulated knowledge to craft plans for Pennsylvania. As an example, Elizabeth Milroy, building on previous scholarship, suggests in her recent work that it was Penn and his associates' direct knowledge of Irish expressions of castral plans at Londonderry and Limerick, in addition to awareness of an earlier grid plan of Richard Noble for Burlington, New Jersey, and his exposure to post–London fire urban improvement plans that seemingly inspired the directions he gave for laying out a Pennsylvania city with surveyor Thomas Holme and others.[29] From foundations of knowledge crafted during his pre-provincial life, Penn developed an appreciation for the benefits of managing landscapes and how housing and objects could work to suit his interests. Later biographers similarly harnessed references to the material world in crafting their memories of Penn.

City House(s)/Country House(s)

In 1810, a member of a prominent Philadelphia family, Henry Sandwith Drinker, presented an oak armchair to the Pennsylvania Hospital to commemorate the founder. The chair purportedly came to Drinker from the Crozier family, who had purchased the Pennsbury property in 1783 and who eventually built a frame farmhouse on top of the former Pennsbury house site by 1820.[30] According to lore from eighteenth- and early nineteenth-century tenants of Penn's country plantation the chair was used on an "Area elevated a few steps above the Floor for the convenience of giving Audience to the Indians."[31] Emphasis on the material of oak, known for its density and strength, exemplified the chair's associations with a firm and benevolent founder, who, according to many nineteenth-century Pennsylvanians keen to commemorate the state's past, brought a "civilized" and mannerly approach to negotiations with indigenous peoples.

Objects like these acted as touchstones for community mythmaking, and notable relics like the chair tempted viewers with a visible, tangible record of Penn and the founding era.[32] Because Penn was not in residence at a specific place for an extensive time and instead maintained a relatively mobile lifestyle, it is not as easy to build his biography based on a framework that later historians and interpreters find most comfortable. Penn did not establish a house that he then occupied for years and years nor did he leave an assemblage of well-documented material goods. A plethora of papers exist, but the most personal records were destroyed or lost. Despite these challenges, it should not, by extension, be imagined that Penn lacked awareness of the material world. It simply creates a situation where close attention to detail in the written and material record in combination with reasoned historical analysis must be employed to build a fuller picture of Penn's life. As historian and biographer Annette Gordon-Reed suggests, "We can . . . learn and convey important information about our subjects from the smallest details, if we find ways to work with what we have. . . . The imperfect record can still be of some use." For Penn, this imperfect record includes relics and colonial revival artifacts in addition to a large, but uneven, trove of manuscript material. Identifying the accretions of meaning on objects and events related to the proprietor's past is an important first step in recapturing his material life with greater historical clarity.[33] For items dispersed from the Pennsbury property, like the Pennsylvania Hospital chair or the Library Company bookcase, ownership by Penn is certainly *possi-*

ble, but a firm attribution of ownership and use by the proprietor himself and not simply by other members of the Penn family is elusive. Why is this? Penn resided in the house for less than four years, and within that time he also rented or lodged in other residences in Philadelphia and the surrounding region. Between his two visits and following his departure from Pennsylvania in 1701, Pennsbury was primarily home to multiple enslaved and free workers. In 1704, Penn's son William Jr. made a hasty trip to Pennsylvania and modified the house a bit, and others visited and resided on the site, if not in the house proper, throughout the eighteenth century. So, although Penn certainly funded the furnishing of the house, others could have added to or modified the furnishing plans in the site's multiple buildings. Thus most of the Penn-related objects that remain in institutional collections, such as a razor, the desk and bookcase, a clock, marked linens, and archaeological shards, can certainly serve as fragments available to scholars interested in piecing together Penn's material circumstances during his two visits to America in 1682–1684 and 1699–1701.[34] But lacking hard and fast provenance information, attributions to use by Penn himself should at least be tempered. This does not mean these artifacts and relics should be ignored. In fact, their strong associations with the proprietor serve as important source material for how Penn has been remembered by later generations and act as a testament to a hunger for tangible remains associated with the founder.

The Pennsbury site itself exemplifies creative memory making. It is widely recognized as an important expression of early twentieth-century colonial revival interests and aesthetics in architectural form.[35] To examine the seventeenth- and eighteenth-century history of the site requires delving into the archives. Mark Reinberger and Elizabeth P. McLean produced a detailed study of the site, adding insight as to the original architectural form of the manor house, which they posit was a single-pile T-plan, not the large double-pile structure that Richardson Brognard Okie designed in the 1930s. Their analysis, like many studies of colonial architecture, is site specific. This is often needed for a focused study; however, what is lost is a sense of Pennsbury as only a part of Penn's full residential strategy and experience in the province.[36]

Pennsbury is often held up as Penn's residential and property-holding ideal. He certainly provided the most extensive instructions for this property, and today it is the primary Penn-related historical site available to the public. The site had a great deal of symbolic weight for Penn and for others who saw and visited it. But it would be a mistake to overstate his actual residence in it or to see it as the only space he inhabited. Penn was in residence in Pennsylvania for only about 22 months during his first voyage, and he acquired the Pennsbury property roughly halfway into his stay. His second visit to Pennsylvania was of similar duration. Instead, as he had done in England, Ireland, Germany, and elsewhere, he spent a fair amount of time on the move.

After his arrival on the first visit in 1682, he resided at a number of places, including the home of Friend Robert Wade at "Essex House," a one- and one-half story house in Upland (Chester), Pennsylvania, facing the creek and at Peter Rambo's house on the west bank of the Schuylkill. He traveled throughout the Jerseys, the Lower Counties (Delaware), and elsewhere during both trips. On his second visit, he rented the so-called Slate Roof House (a name applied to the site by the early nineteenth century) and used it as a complementary residence to Pennsbury.

Comparison of Pennsbury and the Slate Roof House provides a view of the complementary relationship between urban and rural setting and city town house and country plantation that shaped Penn's lived experience during his visit in 1699–1701. Not simply a retreat, Pennsbury served multiple functions, including acting as a buffer and symbolic fortress on Pennsylvania's northern border; as a country experimental plantation where he could direct and manage gardening, food cultivation, and fishing; and as a diplomatic center. On the other hand, the Slate Roof House was figured as a governmental administration center deemed by none other than James Logan, then a young provincial secretary, as "the only suitable place to be thought of in town" for the location of meetings of council, Commissioners of Property, and reception of the governor.[37] Accordingly, Penn paid his friend and prominent early settler, Samuel Carpenter, 80 pounds "To 2 years Rent my house Ending the 22th 10month 1701," and he continued to rent the space for governmental use even after his departure from America.[38] Furnishing of the properties reinforced the complementary, and occasionally overlapping, functions. Penn used his plantation house and town house as mutually reinforcing spaces supporting elite culture within an emerging provincial context. From Germany to England to Pennsylvania, this complementary use and role of the built environment flourished among those of enough financial means throughout the colonial world.

Inventories created at the time of Penn's departure from Pennsylvania in 1701 further reveal some of the ways in which the buildings were used by the proprietor. At the Slate Roof House, bed "quiltks" (quilts), close stools (chamber pots), and curtains for privacy in the best chamber and nursery created spaces for sleeping and grooming. Clocks, tables, chairs, maps, knives, forks, and cruet stands in the parlors and hall provided equipage for entertaining and official business. And the pots and pans, candlesticks, and linens in the kitchen acted as tools for a service staff to maintain the activities of the house. This was a multifunctional building to serve personal and professional needs. This is underscored by its continued use as a residence and office by Jacob Taylor and other land surveyors after Penn's departure, and similarly by later owners William Trent and Isaac Norris—all colonial leaders of note.[39]

The property at Pennsbury served different purposes. It was the site of negotiations with Lenape leaders and other colonial officials from Pennsylvania and elsewhere, it was a family home, and it was a working plantation. This residence held a greater number of furnishings appropriate for polite dining and entertaining, such as a variety of damask and diaper linens, "satin" and "green plush" cushions for cane chairs, leather chairs and maps, six salts (vessels or containers holding salt used for communal dining), and a long table with two forms (benches). Ultimately, Pennsbury and the Slate Roof House were satellite locations, accessible via transport on Penn's barge on the Delaware River or by land, serving complementary purposes that were equally essential to the proprietor's business and personal affairs.[40]

Multifaceted residential strategies, allowing access to various property investments and constituents, was a widespread practice among colonial leaders and others of economic means to support the costs of ownership and rental of multiple properties. In Philadelphia alone, James Logan, Isaac Norris, Jonathan Dickinson, and scores of other early residents rented city properties and owned country plantations. This practice of renting a whole house or occasional rooms was also common in other late seventeenth-century and early eighteenth-century colonial American centers.[41] In twentieth- and twenty-first-century America, where home ownership has been crafted as the cultural norm, residential mobility is often conflated with transiency in pejorative terms. In the seventeenth and early eighteenth centuries, many people of all economic levels rented living quarters; home ownership was viewed more as a negotiable commodity than as an end unto itself.[42] Penn was in good company as he moved between houses and followed a circuit of visiting friends and neighbors. How, then, did a man whose mobile lifestyle and flexible, savvy navigation of various material circumstances become trapped in memory as a boilerplate visual image?

Caught in the Curtains: Memory Making and the Road to Myth

In May 1788, Philadelphians had a chance to buy their own William Penn memorabilia. Upon John Penn Jr.'s departure from Pennsylvania, a vendue of his goods featured a set of "hair-colored" (or brown), printed cotton bed hangings and three window curtains with the printed pattern "William Penn's treaty with the Indians." Why did William Penn's grandson own these curtains? While he resided in Pennsylvania, he created an urban gentleman's toolkit complete with a rented town house at the corner of Sixth and Market Streets and a country house, named Solitude, he constructed on the western side of the Schuylkill. For a room in one of these houses, he created this fabric-rich bedchamber, where, swathed by textile portraits of his grandfather, he created a tent of memory celebrating a family origin myth. Perhaps he found comfort in this pleasant image of his grandfather, perhaps he was wistful for this seemingly rosy past, perhaps he hoped to commemorate the artistic interests of his father Thomas, who commissioned the painting, or perhaps he simply liked the design. One thing is clear though, John Penn Jr. was one of many who supported the distillation of the figure of William Penn as benevolent leader through purchase and use of decorative goods.[43]

Following the American Revolution, John Penn Jr. returned to Pennsylvania in hopes of protecting his family's claim to property in the new United States. Since the death of Penn in 1718, the Penn family had faced the challenge of maintaining and managing their interests in Pennsylvania. Even in his lifetime Penn struggled to do so, and his travels were often predicated on the need to conduct business and support his proprietary interests. John Penn Jr., his father Thomas, and other Penn family members needed to promote and create an image of the colony and the founder to suit their familial, political, and monetary interests. And part of this process of familial preservation and pride was managing the founder's image.

Perhaps the most lasting visual legacy of William Penn and early colonial Pennsylvania was the inspiration for the image on the curtains—the painting commissioned by the 73-year-old Thomas Penn in 1770 or 1771. Anyone who has opened an American history book or visited the state of Pennsylvania or the city of Philadelphia has seen some version of the indelible image first painted by the artist Benjamin West, or some derivation of it. Originally titled *William Penn's Treaty with the Indians When He Founded the Province of Pennsylvania in America* when it was first displayed to the public at the Royal Academy in London in 1772, the work was well received.[44] Although Thomas considered sending over a statue of his father to commemorate the preservation of peace in the colony the plan never came to fruition. Thomas eventually determined that a painting would shape and manage the Pennsylvania image within the colony, on the continent, and in the world.[45] Three years after its initial display, engravings were made based on the image, the first of many reproductions.[46] Ann Uhry Abrams recounts how West based the plump Penn image on a likeness of Penn created for an ivory medal carved by the English apothecary Silvanus/Sylvanus Bevan in 1720, two years after Penn's death. This medal was the inspiration for sculptures and important early engravings created by Pierre Eugene Du Simitiere and others, however, the West painting solidified the image, and because it was created in an era with greater printing technology, more reproductions were possible.[47]

To reiterate, more than any house or object, the image of Penn dominates the iconography of Pennsylvania's founder. The Bevan image, and particularly the West image, are evident as models for three-dimensional representations of Penn from the eighteenth-century sculpture presented in 1804 by John Penn (owner of the curtains) to the Pennsylvania Hospital to a carved-wood folk sculpture made in Berks County, Pennsylvania, to the monumental Alexander Calder sculpture of Penn resting atop Philadelphia's city hall.[48] Each of these cultural productions reflects the hand of its individual maker and the style of the era in which it was created. However, the Bevan ivory profile set in motion a tradition of a rather portly, bewigged (but not hat-wearing) man. Benjamin West's image, while it may have looked somewhat to the Bevan model, added a new tradition of depicting Penn with a full-length body, a hat, and one hand extended. From these two traditions the three-dimensional and two-dimensional images exist on everything from ceramics to textiles and other objects of the decorative arts.

These images persist for a few reasons. In the eighteenth century it was widely believed that there was no existing portrait of William Penn created from life. In a widely republished letter from Benjamin Franklin to Lord Kames (Henry Home), in response to an offer of a Penn portrait, Franklin asserts that he knew of no image of Penn and explained his uncertainty of the authenticity. "I have at present some Doubts about it; first, because the primitive Quakers us'd to declare against Pictures as a vain Expence; a Man's suffering his Portrait to be taken was condemn'd as Pride; and I think to this day it is very little practis'd among them. Then it is on a Board, and I imagine the Practice of painting Portraits on Boards did not come down so low as Penn's Time; but of this I am not certain. My other Reason is an Anecdote I have heard, viz. That when old Lord Cobham was adorning his Gardens at Stowe with the Busts of famous Men, he made Enquiry of the Family for a Picture of Wm. Penn, in order to get a Bust form'd from it, but could find none."[49] Since Franklin wrote his letter, two images came to light that are purportedly William Penn, an eighteenth-century copy of a 1666 portrait of him at a young age in armor and a charcoal and chalk portrait by Francis Place. However, as Daniel Richter explains, scholars do not uniformly accept that Penn is the true subject of either image.[50] While their existence was known in the nineteenth century, the Place portrait only came into the possession of the Historical Society of Pennsylvania in 1957, and the earlier portrait in 1833. Until they came into the society's possession and became more accessible for reproduction in histories of Pennsylvania, then, images based on the Bevan and West images were all people had as visual references to Penn's likeness.

The West image survived also because it fit the growing mythology of Penn as a founder and the legacy his family and Pennsylvanians in general perpetuated. After the death of Hannah Penn, the Penn children had to uphold the family business of managing the colony, and they were not ideal leaders.[51] Today, the primary event associated with the Penn children is the grand swindle of the "Walking Purchase," whereby Thomas Penn and others led a masterful land grab that greatly extended the Penns' land claims in western Pennsylvania at the expense of their Lenape/Delaware neighbors. This deception rested on language of a seventeenth-century treaty and on the traditions of William Penn as a friend of colonists and Native inhabitants of the region. Indeed, "their use of the past ratified proprietary power in their present."[52]

These carefully orchestrated acts of remembrance have been noted in scholarship about the legacy of William Penn, and certainly the power of Benjamin

West's painting is widely acknowledged. But little has been said about what is lost in our understanding of Penn's material world as a result of the image-shaping campaign of Thomas Penn, John Penn Jr., and other family members. It was not helpful or desirable for the family to depict William Penn as a young gentleman in armor, as a man on the move, as a skilled and versatile user and promoter of material goods, or as a dispirited and disabled elder. In fact, Penn himself may have shunned these qualities. Instead, the narrative of an impassioned and visionary leader who established foundations of religious and political tolerance was much more appealing. Placing Penn in an outdoor setting, and away from a connection to any particular residence or personal possessions, reinforced the timelessness and versatility of the image. Penn in turn became a character in a founding myth, and Penn the man and his material world were obscured.

The West image and derivations of it, as well as the Bevan-based images of Penn, provide visual reinforcement of a stereotypical role for Penn as removed from the physical world. Partly from a lack of physical fabric, partly because of the success his inheritors had in building a legacy for Penn that supported particular legends above mundane daily existence or a past sullied by complexity, and partly because early Americans from colonial and indigenous backgrounds found use for an idealized historical figure to boost their various interests, the man as represented in the paintings and prints, on John Penn's curtains, and standing atop city hall endured and persists today. As scholars increasingly turn their attention to Penn's material circumstances, to houses and foods and other trappings and trimmings of everyday life, Penn's character, often difficult to define, becomes ever more complex and fascinating. His interactions with people in America and abroad become more apparent, and the character in the images becomes more human once again. We see a man grappling to align his ideals with his existence and set goals for a province he hardly inhabited at all.

NOTES

1. The neck piece Penn is often depicted wearing can be called a cravat, roller, or neck cloth. Thank you to Neal Hurst, Associate Curator of Costume and Textiles at Colonial Williamsburg Foundation, for the proper terminology.

2. Andrew R. Murphy, *Liberty, Conscience, and Toleration: The Political Thought of William Penn* (New York: Oxford University Press, 2016), ix. While Murphy's study examines Penn's political thought and theory, he, like an increasing number of scholars such as those included in this volume, are examining the connections and frequent tensions between Penn's political theory and practice. While William Penn is certainly mentioned in many academic monographs and articles, comprehensive biographies are not overly abundant. Two early works from the nineteenth century on Penn are notable: Samuel M. Janney, *The Life of William Penn: With Selections from his Correspondence and Autobiography* (Philadelphia, PA: Lippincott, Grambo & Co., 1852) and William Hepworth Dixon, *William Penn: An Historical Biography* (London: Chapman and Hall, 1851). In the 1980s, in light of the 300th anniversary of Penn's Charter for Pennsylvania, an uptick in scholarship occurred, including Richard S. Dunn and Mary Maples Dunn, eds. *The Papers of William Penn*. 5 vols.

(Philadelphia: Penn Press, 1982); Richard S. Dunn and Mary Maples Dunn, eds., *The World of William Penn* (Philadelphia: Penn Press, 1986), and Jean R. Soderlund et al., eds, *William Penn and the Founding of Pennsylvania, 1680–1684: A Documentary History* (Philadelphia: Penn Press, 1983). Since then, much of the scholarship on Penn takes a discipline-based or thematic approach to examining aspects of his faith, political activities, relationship with indigenous people, and other aspects of his life and times.

3. For a discussion of objects in motion and the varied meanings of mobility in relation to the material world see Wendy Bellion and Mónica Domínguez Torres, "Editors' Introduction," Objects in Motion Issue, *Winterthur Portfolio*, 45, no. 2/3 (Summer/Autumn 2011): 101–106, "We understand 'motion' in two ways: as a noun indicating the displacement of things from one place to another and as part of the verb 'to set in motion,' that is, to give impetus to particular processes," 103.

4. Pepys Diary 30 August 1664. http://www.pepysdiary.com; Janney, *The Life of William Penn*, 28; Dunn and Dunn, *The Papers of William Penn*; Dunn and Dunn, *The World of William Penn*; Frederick B. Tolles, *Meeting House and Counting House: The Quaker Merchants of Colonial Philadelphia, 1682–1763* (Chapel Hill: University of North Carolina Press, 1948); Jack L. Lindsey, ed. *Worldly Goods: The Arts of Early Pennsylvania, 1680–1758* (Philadelphia: Philadelphia Museum of Art, 1999); Catharine Dann Roeber, "Building and Planting: The Material World, Memory, and the Making of William Penn's Pennsylvania 1681–1726" (PhD diss., The College of William and Mary, 2011). Mary Dunn's work is some of the rare scholarship that mentions anything in the way of specifics about Penn's material interests, noting that "he was always happy to live well" using his purchase of three coaches and orders of "food to set a luxurious table, and clothes and silver fit for a gentleman" as signs of growing distance from his Quaker associates. The scholarship on William Penn she and Richard Dunn published provides the best recording (in printed form) of Penn's commentary or that by his associates. The 2003 edited volume, Emma Jones Lapsansky and Anne A. Verplanck, eds., *Quaker Aesthetics: Reflections on a Quaker Ethic in American Design and Consumption* (Philadelphia: Penn Press, 2003) included rich discussion on the historical meanings of Quaker "plain" aesthetics.

5. As Arjun Appadurai puts it, "We have to follow the things themselves, for their meanings are inscribed in their forms, their uses, their trajectories. It is only through the analysis of these trajectories that we can understand the human transactions and calculations that enliven things. Thus, even though from a theoretical point of view human actors encode things with significance, from a methodological point of view it is the things-in-motion that illuminate their human and social contexts." *The Social Life of Things: Commodities in a Cultural Perspective* (Cambridge: Cambridge University Press, 1988), 5.

6. Dunn and Dunn, *The World of William Penn*, 3:675–676.

7. Mary Maples Dunn, "The Personality of William Penn" in *The World of William Penn*, ed. Richard S. Dunn and Mary Maples Dunn (Philadelphia: University of Pennsylvania Pres, 1986), 3–14.

8. For a good overview of court dress see Susan Vincent, *Dressing the Elite: Clothes in Early Modern England* (Oxford: Berg Publishers, 2003).

9. For an article discussing hat removal and its broader implications during the Penn–Mead trial see Andrew Murphy, "Trial Transcript as Political Theory: Principles and Performance in the Penn-Mead Case," *Political Theory* 41, no. 6 (2013): 775–808. For a good discussion of objects, behavior, and social capital see Rhys Isaac, *Transformation of Virginia, 1740–1790* (Chapel Hill: University of North Carolina Press for the Omohundro Institute of Early American History, 1982). For a good discussion of the symbolic nature of goods and houses, see Bernard L. Herman, *Town House: Architecture and Material Life in the Early American City, 1780–1830* (Chapel Hill: University of North Carolina Press for the Omohundro Institute of Early American History, 2005). Two recent publications with thoughtful discussions of the role of objects and material things in the Atlantic world for further

reading include Zara Anishanslin, *Portrait of a Woman in Silk* (New Haven: Yale University Press, 2016) and Jennifer Van Horn, *The Power of Objects in Eighteenth-Century British America* (Chapel Hill: University of North Carolina Press for the Omohundro Institute of Early American History, 2017).

10. For accounts of Penn's trips to the continent see Dunn and Dunn, *Papers of William Penn*.

11. Penn's letters contain only fragments of information about his material circumstances during his travels. It is clear that he carried multiple copies of books and pamphlets that he distributed on his journeys. Most likely, he also had writing supplies and chests or other furniture for travel containing personal items and a small amount of clothes. Dunn and Dunn, *Papers of William Penn*, 2:463, 488. While in Pennsylvania, Penn moved between a location along the Delaware River and a location in the interior.

12. 1681–1776: The Quaker Province. http://www.phmc.state.pa.us/portal/communities/pa-history/1681-1776.html.

13. Carla Pestana, *The English Conquest of Jamaica: Oliver Cromwell's Bid for Empire* (Cambridge: Harvard University Press, 2017) and Carla Pestana, "English Character and the Fiasco of Western Design" *Early American Studies: An Interdisciplinary Journal* 3, no. 1 (Spring 2005): 1–31.; Nicole L. Greenspan, "News and the Politics of Information in the Mid-Seventeenth Century: The Western Design and the Conquest of Jamaica," *History Workshop Journal*, 69 (2010): 1–26. For information on Giles and earlier Penn family ancestry, see Granville Penn, *Memorials of the Professional Life and Times of Sir William Penn, Knt.* (London: James Duncan, 1833).

14. Kristen Block, "Cultivating Inner and Outer Plantations: Property, Industry, and Slavery in Early Quaker Migration to the New World" in *Early American Studies: An Interdisciplinary Journal* 8, no. 3 (Fall 2010): 515–548.

15. Existing documents do not contain examples of young Penn explicitly articulating a vision of himself as inheritor of his father's worldly outlook. However, we do know that William was well aware of his father's naval activities, management of Irish lands, and other pursuits. Others often reminded him of his lineage as well. In the actions leading to the later infamous trial in 1670, William Mead (according to Penn as recounted in Janney) identified the protesting young man as "Penn's son, who starved the seamen." Penn expressed dismay at the insult to his father and his actions: "I told him I could very well bear his severe expressions to me concerning myself, but was sorry to hear him speak those abuses of my father, that was not present." Janney, 58.

16. Madge Dresser, *Slavery Obscured: The Social History of the Slave Trade in an English Provincial Port* (London: Bloomsbury Press, 2016), 13–14. First published in 2001, Dresser briefly discusses Sir William Penn's ownership of and trade of enslaved people.

17. Dunn and Dunn, "Unknown Author to Sir William Penn, April 24, 1664," in *Papers of William Penn*, 1:31.

18. An issue of *Quaker Studies* (vol. 16, no. 2, 2012) devoted three articles by leading Quaker scholars to William Penn's training and experience at Saumur. They, too, characterize the time in France as in line with an intellectual training fit for a gentleman in training like Penn.

19. Dunn and Dunn, "Two Kingdoms of Darkness and Light," in *Papers of William Penn*, 1:67.

20. Sarah Crabtree, *Holy Nation: The Transatlantic Quaker Ministry in an Age of Revolution* (Chicago: University of Chicago Press, 2015), 152.

21. Meredith Baldwin Weddle, *Walking in the Way of Peace: Quaker Pacifism in the Seventeenth Century* (Oxford: Oxford University Press, 2001).

22. On Penn's spiritualism and mysticism see Dunn and Dunn and others. Scholarship on the religious landscape of early Pennsylvania has grown in recent years with works such as Patrick Erben, *A Harmony of the Spirits: Translation and the Language of Community in*

Early Pennsylvania (Chapel Hill: University of North Carolina Press, 2012); Jeff Bach, *Voices of the Turtledoves: The Sacred World of Ephrata* (University Park: Pennsylvania State University Press, 2003); and A. G. Roeber, ed., *Ethnographies and Exchanges: Native Americans, Moravians, and Catholics in Early North America* (University Park: Pennsylvania State University Press, 2008).

23. Jeff Bach, *Voices of the Turtledoves*. On the definition of mystic/mysticism see pages 5–6; on early Mennonite-Quaker and other separatist/Pietist groups in Pennsylvania see pages 16–17.

24. As quoted in the letter from William Penn to Sir John Rodes York, England, 30th 9mo [November 16] 1680, https://www.raabcollection.com/american-history-autographs/william-penn-rodes; *A Collection of the Works of William Penn* (London: J. Sowle, 1726), 73.

25. Rebecca Larson, *Daughters of Light: Quaker Women Preaching and Prophesying in the Colonies and Abroad 1700–1775*. (New York: Knopf, 1999), 25.

26. "Philip Ford Account No. 1 23 April 1672–24 June 1672," in Dunn and Dunn, *Papers of William Penn*, 1:577–586.

27. John Smolenski, *Friends and Strangers: The Making of a Creole Culture in Colonial Pennsylvania* (Philadelphia: Penn Press, 2010).

28. A transcription of the *Irish Journal* can be found in Dunn and Dunn, *Papers of William Penn*, 1:101–143. For reference to later trips also see Dunn and Dunn, *Papers of William Penn* 1:430.

29. Elizabeth Milroy, *The Grid and the River: Philadelphia's Green Places, 1682–1876* (University Park: Penn State University Press, 2016), 14, 15.

30. Pennsbury chronology, reference to public sale, account of property in 1787. Hoke P. Kimball and Bruce Hensen, *Governor's Houses and State Houses of British Colonial America, 1607–1783* (New York: McFarland, 2017).

31. The History of the Pennsylvania Hospital, https://www.google.com/search?tbo=p&tbm=bks&q=inauthor:%22Thomas+George+Morton%22.

32. Rita Reif, *Antiques: William Penn's Possessions, New York Times, April 7, 1973*; Teresa Barnett, *Sacred Relics: Pieces of the Past in Nineteenth-Century America* (Chicago: University of Chicago Press, 2013).

33. Annette Gordon-Reed, "Writing Early American Lives as Biography" *William and Mary Quarterly*, 3rd ser., 71, no. 4 (October 2014): 491–516. On pages 491–492 Gordon-Reed additionally outlines how "Over time, however, both institutions and landmarks may take on lives of their own as symbols, providing a vehicle for telling the country's history while obscuring the stories of the individuals who helped create and maintain them." I'd suggest that the image of Penn in two- and three-dimensional form is exactly this kind of obscuring figure, and most pertinent here, what these representations obscure is the life of Penn himself.

34. Objects associated with Penn can be found in collections such as the Historical Society of Pennsylvania, the Library Company of Philadelphia, Philadelphia History Museum at the Atwater Kent, the Pennsylvania Hospital, The Pennsylvania State Museum, Pennsbury Manor, and other regional repositories.

35. Carol G. Weener, "Pennsbury Manor: A Study in Colonial Revival Preservation" (master's thesis, University of Pennsylvania, Philadelphia, 1986).

36. Mark Reinberger and Elizabeth P. McLean, "Pennsbury Manor: Reconstruction and Reality" *PMHB*, 131, no. 3 (July 2007): 263–306; Mark Reinberger and Elizabeth P. McLean, *The Philadelphia Country House: Architecture and Landscape in Colonial America* (Baltimore: Johns Hopkins University Press, 2015), 187–188.

37. Dunn and Dunn, *Papers of William Penn*, 4:192.

38. Accounts 1699–1701, Governor William Penn to Samuel Carpenter, Penn-Physick Papers, Buffalo and Erie County Historical Society, Buffalo, New York.

39. Dunn and Dunn, *Papers of William Penn*, 4:135. These items are listed under the section heading "Goods left at Philadelphia/the 20|th of the 9\th Month 1701" in comparison

to those left at Pennsbury; Donna B. Munger, *Pennsylvania Land Records: A History and Guide for Research* (Wilmington, DE: Scholarly Resources, 1991), 32; Roeber, "Building and Planting," 76.

40. For further discussion see Roeber, "Building and Planting."

41. While Penn and other early Quakers may have critiqued the supposed corrupting forces of city living, there was widespread acknowledgment of the need for urban residences and a practice of renting that then followed. For discussions of residential strategies in early Philadelphia see Reinberger and McLean, *The Philadelphia Country House*. For a good discussion of the complementary nature of urban–rural residences and land investments, see Emma Hart, *Building Charleston: Town and Society in the Eighteenth-Century British World* (Charlottesville: University of Virginia Press, 2010).

42. Sharon V. Salinger and Charles Wetherell, "Wealth and Renting in Prerevolutionary Philadelphia," *Journal of American History*, 71, no. 4 (March 1985): 826–840. In fact, the majority of urban American dwellings were not occupied by their owners until 1945.

43. In true colonial fashion, the name "John Penn" was held by multiple people in multiple generations of the Penn family. John Penn Jr. "the poet" and owner of Solitude was the son of Thomas Penn and grandson of William Penn, the founder. William Penn also had a son, John (often called "The American" due to his birth in Pennsylvania). John Penn Jr. also had a cousin John, who was the royal governor of Pennsylvania. See Lorett Treese, *The Storm Gathering: The Penn Family and the American Revolution* (University Park: Penn State University Press, 1992).

44. Joseph Harrison Jr. and his wife Sara acquired the painting in the nineteenth century and donated it to the Pennsylvania Academy of Fine Arts in Philadelphia in the early twentieth century, where it is housed today.

45. Lorett Treese, *The Storm Gathering*, 8. From his first marriage, the surviving children were Letitia and William Penn Jr. Eventually, in 1731, Penn's children by his long-deceased first wife Gulielma and grandchildren accepted a cash payment to release control to their half-siblings. Three of Hannah's children, John, Thomas, and Richard, were left the proprietorship. It was these three and their descendants who managed the proprietary legacy throughout the eighteenth century.

46. Ann Uhry Abrams, "Benjamin West's Documentation of Colonial History: William Penn's Treaty with the Indians," *Art Bulletin*, 64, no. 1 (March 1982): 69, 75; Laura Rigal, "Framing the Fabric: A Luddite Reading of Penn's Treaty with the Indians," *American Literary History* 12, no. 3 (2000): 557–584.

47. Abrams, "Benjamin West's Documentation," 69, 75. Benjamin Franklin also wrote about the Bevan medal in a 1760 letter to Lord Kames, where he recounted an anecdote about the ivory carving: "That when old Lord Cobham was adorning his Gardens at Stowe with the Busts of famous Men, he made Enquiry of the Family for a Picture of Wm. Penn, in order to get a Bust form'd from it, but could find none. That Sylvanus Bevan, an old Quaker Apothecary, remarkable for the Notice he takes of Countenances, and a Knack he has of cutting in Ivory strong Likenesses of Persons he has once seen, hearing of Lord Cobham's Desire, set himself to recollect Penn's Face, with which he had been well acquainted; and cut a little Bust of him in Ivory which he sent to Lord Cobham, without any Letter of Notice that it was Penn's. But my Lord who had personally known Penn, on seeing it, immediately cry'd out, Whence came this? It is William Penn himself! And from this little Bust, they say, the large one in the Gardens was formed." The subject of William Penn's physical appearance came up in the letter because Lord Kames offered a portrait of Penn to Franklin, and Franklin was skeptical of the portrait's authenticity, knowing only of the supposed accuracy of the Bevan medal. See Benjamin Franklin to Lord Kames, January 3, 1760, in *The Papers of Benjamin Franklin*, digital edition, vol. 9, http://www.franklinpapers.org. managed by Packard Humanities Institute.

48. An image of the wood carving by an anonymous artist in Berks County, Pennsylvania (1770–1800) is included in Irwin Richman, *Pennsylvania German Arts: More than Hearts, Parrots, and Tulips* (Atglen, PA: Schiffer Publishing, 2001), 82.

49. Benjamin Franklin to Lord Kames, January 3, 1760, in *The Papers of Benjamin Franklin*, digital edition, vol. 9, http://www.franklinpapers.org.

50. Daniel Richter, "Three Relics of Pennsylvania's Founding," *Pennsylvania Legacies* 4, no. 2 (November 2004): 6–9. See also Roeber, "Building and Planting."

51. John Smolenski sums up the Penn children well: "They swiftly showed that they possessed all their father's defects as a proprietor but nothing of his good intentions." *Friends and Strangers*, 283.

52. Smolenski, *Friends and Strangers*, 285.

CHAPTER 3

Beyond the Bounds

EXPLOITATION AND EMPIRE IN THE FIRST MAP OF PENNSYLVANIA

Emily Mann

Amid the beds, bolsters, blankets, and sundry other material possessions that William Penn left behind at Pennsbury Manor in November 1701, when he departed his American colony for England, were seven maps of different sizes and subjects. Two "large Mapps" were displayed in the "Best Parlour," likely hung on the wall but perhaps sometimes spread out for close scrutiny on the two tables in the same room, surrounded by assorted chairs with cushions of satin and green plush.[1] Five further maps adorned the "little Hall," which was otherwise furnished only with six leather chairs and two wooden ones—forming a waiting room of sorts.[2] Even more maps featured among the smaller assortment of goods left at the Penn family's rented house in Philadelphia (known as the Slate Roof House), four in the main parlor and six in the "other Parlour," where they could be studied after dark by the light of the sconces on the walls.[3]

The prevalence of maps in the surviving inventories of Penn's colonial properties at the turn of the eighteenth century is remarkable but rarely commented on.[4] Apart from cushions and curtains, these printed or manuscript images appear to have provided the only decoration in the proprietor's domestic world. "Beyond a few maps," wrote Mark Reinberger and Elizabeth McLean in their critical appraisal of Pennsbury's reconstruction in the twentieth century, "apparently nothing hung on the walls."[5] Thus the interiors reflect, it has been suggested, "a distinct lack of pretension, grandeur, or extravagance" on Penn's part; a vision that was neither "grandiose nor particularly ornamental."[6] Yet such a conclusion risks underestimating not just the monetary value but also the rich, multifaceted purpose and significance of maps—their potency as manifestations of both art and science, at once "ornamental" and "necessary" in elite self-fashioning and expression.[7] And a focus on Penn and his household risks losing sight of the variety of viewers whose interactions with and interpretations of the maps contributed to their meaning. As recent historians of cartography have amply documented and demonstrated, maps made visual and textual appeals to hearts and minds; they were tools of government, expansion, and diplomacy, conveying information and ideas with the aim of asserting or contesting cultural, economic, and political claims.[8] While they are still sometimes reproduced as incidental illustrations, they are immensely valuable historical documents, often rare and very vulnerable, dog-eared through years of display and repeated use.[9] Dominating the walls of Penn's all-important parlors—the most public rooms in both his city and his country homes, which themselves doubled as administrative centers—his maps were so much more than modest wallpaper, or mere pieces of paper showing the way from one place to another. These geographic representations defined and described Penn's proprietary identity and interests, asserting his authority even in his prolonged absences. Moreover, through both their composition and consumption, they inscribed relations of power between himself, the land, and the people who inhabited and worked it, including indigenous peoples and those enslaved.

As objects whose meanings were "entangled with the world beyond [their] edges," Penn's maps provide routes to exploring his American colonial project in its wider context.[10] We cannot be certain about which specific maps he chose to display in either of his colonial dwellings (the inventories merely give the number found in each room), but the collection of seventeen likely included the *Map of Some of the South and Eastbounds of Pennsylvania in America* (figure 3.1). Produced in England in the months following Charles II's grant of land to Penn in March 1681 and presented to the Royal Society on Penn's election as a fellow in November that year, this first map of Pennsylvania hangs in the shadows of subsequent, seemingly more impressive and now iconic images.[11] The surveyor Thomas Holme's *Portraiture of the City of Philadelphia* (figure 3.2), printed in 1683, and *Map of the Improved Part of the Province of Pennsilvania in America* (figure 3.3), printed in 1687 and successive versions, have attracted far greater attention and admiration. It is these two images, as Catharine Dann Roeber put it, "that were successful enough to remain the dominant visual representations of the region until the mid-eighteenth century," and they retain their appeal in histories of the place to this day.[12] The apparent sparse and simplistic detail of the *Map of Some of the South and Eastbounds of Pennsylvania*, as well as the still-vague and fluid territory hinted by the title, were surpassed by Holme's prospects of a sophisticated gridded city and comprehensively settled, cultivated, and carved-up country beyond. The subsequent dominance of Holme's images does not render the first map a less relevant object of study now, however, any more than it immediately became a redundant instrument, or blunt tool, then. The "William Penn map" of Pennsylvania (as the *Map of Some of the South and*

Eastbounds is sometimes called) laid vital groundwork. By constructing a memory of what had been, it played a part in both the conceptualization and creation of what came to be, and endured as a reference point against which the "improved" parts could be measured and assessed. The *Map of the Improved Part of the Province of Pennsilvania in America* (likely one of the "large Mapps" in Penn's best parlor) invokes the first map with its subtitle "Begun by Wil. Penn Proprietary Governour thereof Anno 1681."

This chapter puts the first map of Pennsylvania back in the spotlight. Renewed study of the print's visual and textual strategies, and consideration of the map as a material object, offer insights into Penn's vision for his colony and, to borrow the words of Richard and Mary Dunn, "the multifaceted seventeenth-century environment in which he lived and worked."[13] More specifically, exploration both within and beyond the edges of the map illuminates the inextricable relationship between Penn's colonial new world and the wider imperial world of which it was a crucial part from the very start. The best-known surviving copy of the *Map of Some of the South and Eastbounds of Pennsylvania*—the one reproduced here (figure 3.1), beautifully colored and complete with printed description pasted below—is part of a seventeenth-century collection known today as the Blathwayt Atlas, named after the "imperial fixer" William Blathwayt, the secretary to the Lords of Trade and Plantations in London who both accumulated the maps and was involved in redrafting Penn's charter for the province.[14] The forty-eight print and manuscript maps that remain together in the atlas, believed to be just a sampling of what was once a very extensive working archive, represent the enormous expansion of England's territorial and trading interests through the seventeenth century.[15] Their subjects range from Hudson's Bay in northern America to Suriname in the south; from the Atlantic archipelago of Bermuda to the Caribbean island of Barbados; and from the shores of Carolina to the coast of West Africa, and further still to the harbor of Bombay in India. Together, these diverse images set the "scene of a vast interaction," as the American geographer Donald Meinig described the Atlantic world, and it is within this expansive scene that Penn's map and its subject, indeed Penn himself, should be seen.[16]

Just as Penn has remained "a man apart . . . a figure whom many know a little, but few know well"—a political thinker in the shadow of the likes of Locke, Milton, and Boyle—his colony is often set apart, treated as singular and relatively isolated from narratives and investigations of England's emerging empire.[17] Placing the first map of Pennsylvania in a connected history of mapping supports and sheds light on his colony's place (and so his thinking as he founded it) in a connected history of the empire. This opens up not just a "transatlantic view of William Penn," as the Dunns sought to delineate, but an even more encompassing, interoceanic framework for analyzing his activities and aims.[18] It was a rapidly globalizing world, after all, that transported a "payre of ben gall [Bengal] Curtains" and "one spice box" to Penn's parlor in Pennsylvania in the early years of the 1680s.[19]

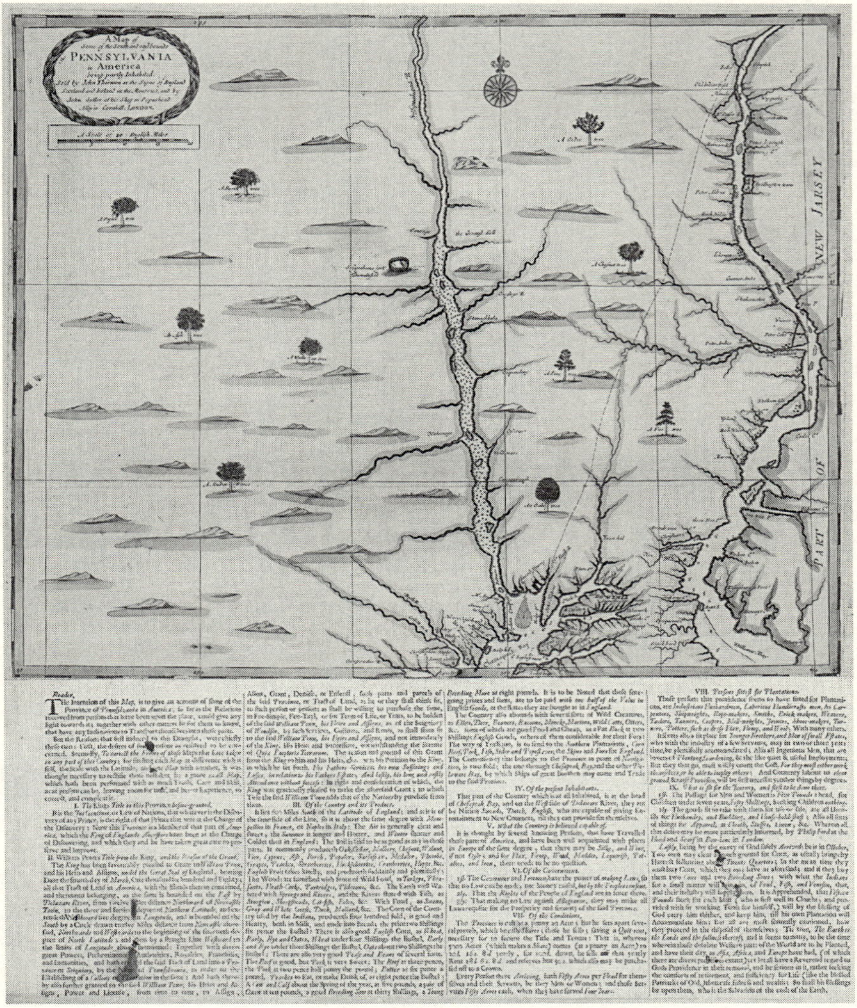

Figure 3.1 *A Map of Some of the South and Eastbounds of Pennsylvania in America* (London: John Thornton and John Seller, 1681). Courtesy of the John Carter Brown Library at Brown University.

A World of Maps

When Penn, wielding his royal charter, launched his publicity campaign for Pennsylvania in the spring of 1681, he would have been acutely aware that a map was essential to secure official approval as well as to attract wider interest and support. That much he had learned from his experience colonizing conquered and confiscated land in both America and Ireland (the latter surveyed by his friend and fellow Irish landowner William Petty), and from the close ties he nurtured with England's ruling class. Both King Charles II and his brother James,

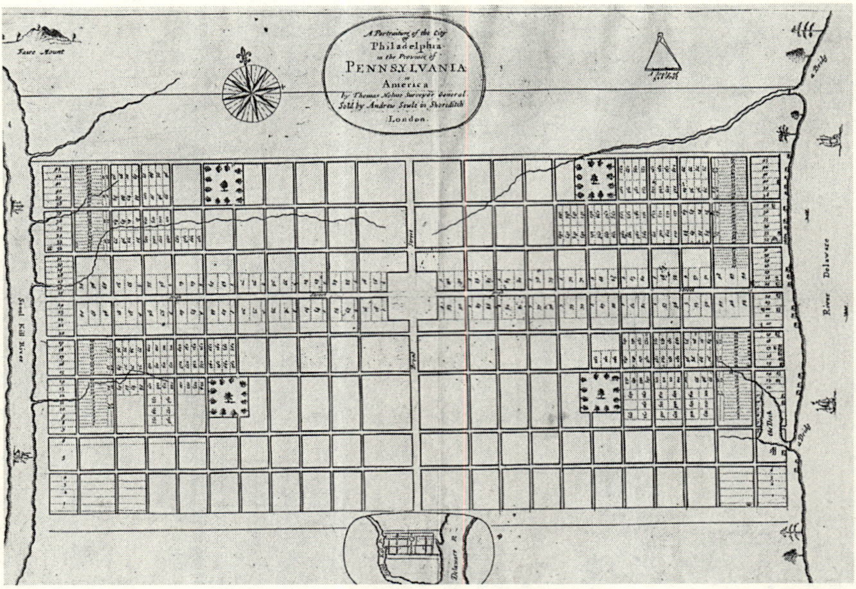

Figure 3.2 Thomas Holme, *A Portraiture of the City of Philadelphia in the Province of Pennsylvania in America* (London: Andrew Sowle, 1683).

Figure 3.3 Thomas Holme, *A Map of the Improved Part of the Province of Pennsilvania in America. Begun by Wil. Penn Proprietary Governour thereof Anno 1681* (London: John Thornton and Robert Greene, first printed 1687). Library of Congress, Geography and Map Division.

Duke of York, were map enthusiasts and frequently received cartographic objects as gifts.[20] Visiting Whitehall shortly after the king's restoration in 1660, the diarist John Evelyn (another of Petty's admirers) marveled at the "vast book of Mapps in a Volume of near 4 yards large" presented by the Dutch merchant Johannes Klencke in hope of royal favor.[21] A decade later, in May 1671, Evelyn recorded a board meeting of the Council for Foreign Plantations (of which he had been appointed a member a few months earlier) in "a very large room furnished with atlases, maps, charts, globes, etc."[22] Shortly before, Penn had been forced to search among the "many" maps in the collection of his recently deceased father, the admiral, for a "Draught of the River Medway" that had gone missing from the Navy Office, probably in his possession in relation to the Dutch raid on the river in the county of Kent in 1667 but still deemed necessary "to answer that frequent use, the Kings Service."[23] The storage and display of maps in the halls and offices of Westminster, as in Penn's parlors and closets, confirms their perceived value and use in the daily business of government and international affairs. Kept on hand near the king and his councilors and commissioners, they were drawn upon—often literally—alongside other official documents of state and, as Helen Wallis pointed out, retained that purpose even "when old enough to be considered mainly archival."[24] Writing to the navy commissioners about the lost Medway map, which seems never to have been retrieved, Penn recognized the "publique benefit" of such a document at the same time as pointing out its self-aggrandizing potential as a "Relique" of his father, "that may be deem'd a badge of his Trade, which rendred him what he was, and Us, his Relations, what we are."[25]

The "Aboundance of Mapps & Sea-Chards . . . & Pieces relating to the Navy" admired by Evelyn in Charles II's private library in September 1680, as officials consulted on Penn's petition for a colony in America, were closely bound up with the restored monarch's expansionist spirit and activity.[26] The process of surveying and the production of maps had long been highly strategic and symbolic in European colonizing projects. Interdependent with writing, building, and other performative acts, such as the feudalistic turf and twig ceremony that Penn would enact on American soil in 1682, surveying and mapping established territorial claims, invested them with an aura of legitimacy, and communicated them to others.[27] Penn's father, once he had redeemed himself as the admiral who led the English seizure of Jamaica from Spanish control under Oliver Cromwell in 1655, likely presented or pored over charts in the king's collection. In Whitehall in March 1661, the naval administrator Samuel Pepys recorded coming across Penn senior, now a Navy Board commissioner, with William Coventry, private secretary to the Duke of York (Lord High Admiral, the titular head of the navy), "teaching of him upon the mapp to understand Jamaica."[28] The map studied by Penn and Coventry in 1661 probably provided the basis for the earliest printed map of Jamaica under the English (figure 3.4), published the same year in

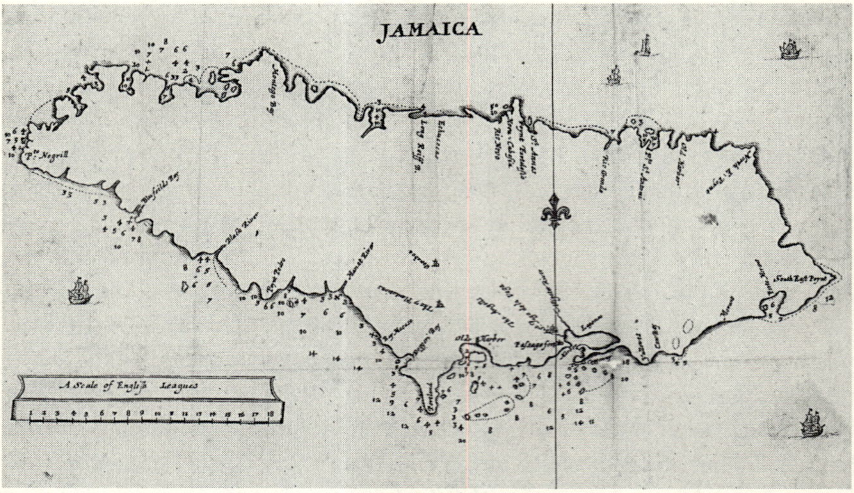

Figure 3.4 Jamaica from Edmund Hickeringill's *Jamaica Viewed* (London: John Williams, 1661). Courtesy of the John Carter Brown Library at Brown University.

Edmund Hickeringill's *Jamaica Viewed*.[29] The purpose of this volume was made explicit in the opening dedication to Charles II: "*All your* Dominions, *being the happy* Subjects *of your care, are therefore, the proper* objects *of your* view."[30] There is a hint that, without such a text and its map, the king might not have "care" over places he could not see. England's seventeenth-century colonies were built out of view of the government, and written and visual representations aimed to bring them into view and under a level of centralized control—not necessarily favorable to colonists, as Penn would fully realize in the late 1690s when Crown officials and courts cracked down on Pennsylvania's freedoms and independence.[31]

The restored monarch confirmed his commitment to imperial expansion and coherence through the reformulation of government committees to report and advise on colonial matters in the 1660s and 1670s, and he specifically charged them with collecting maps to perform that role. In 1670, he ordered the Council for Foreign Plantations to "by all Wayes and meanes . . . procure exact Mapps, Platts or Charts of all and Every [of] our said Plantations abroad, togeather with the Mapps and Descriptions of their respective Ports, Harbours, Forts, Bayes, Rivers with the Depth of their respective Channells comming in or going up, and the Soundings all along upon the said respective Coasts from place to place, and the same so had, you are carefully to Register and Keepe."[32] The instruction was reiterated (in not quite so many words) to the new Council of Trade and Foreign Plantations in 1672 but evidently to little avail, because when the Lords of Trade took charge of colonial administration in 1675 they complained of "a want of maps" and ordered that all overseas governors "send home

Figure 3.5 Richard Ford, *A New Map of the Island of Barbadoes* ([London]: Sold by Mr. Overton and others, [c. 1675]). Courtesy of the John Carter Brown Library at Brown University.

maps of their plantations."[33] The Blathwayt Atlas includes maps sent to London after repeated demands—the *New Map of the Island of Barbadoes* (figure 3.5) took almost five years to arrive, a delay that was suspected to signal willful resistance against its being brought into view—while others are purchases made by the plantations office in an attempt to fill the gaps.

With the *Map of Some of the South and Eastbounds of Pennsylvania*, presented and publicized when his colony had barely begun, Penn proved himself ahead of the game. He very likely conceived of his map as the finishing piece in a bigger picture. Inserted into the colonial collection between charts showing existing English claims on American territory to the north, south, and east (as seen in the arrangement of the Blathwayt Atlas), it filled a substantial and strategic gap. His province was the missing link in the slightly earlier *Mapp of Virginia, Mary-Land, New-Jarsey, New York, & New England* (figure 3.6), however much the blank spot north of Maryland was disguised by the title in its decorative cartouche, and his map was to some extent an elaborated, expanded detail of this similarly sized and colored work. The leading chartmaker John Thornton was

Figure 3.6 *A Mapp of Virginia, Mary-Land, New-Jarsey, New-York, & New England* (London: John Thornton and Robert Greene, [1678–1679]). Courtesy of the John Carter Brown Library at Brown University.

involved in making and selling both these prints (and, moreover, Holme's later maps shown in figures 3.2 and 3.3), while his collaborator on the Pennsylvania map, John Seller, had worked with Penn on another Blathwayt Atlas map that served as a model: the striking depiction and description of the Quaker colony newly carved out of New Jersey (figure 3.7). The incorporation of this impressive piece of propaganda into the official archive can only have encouraged publisher and proprietor to follow the format.

Figure 3.7 *A Mapp of New Jersey in America* (London: John Seller and William Fisher, 1678). Courtesy of the John Carter Brown Library at Brown University.

The map of Pennsylvania was a keystone in an extensive and highly successful advertising campaign, an integral part of the promotional literature that we must consider alongside the drafts of constitutions and frames of government, as Andrew Murphy has stressed, to "plumb the meaning(s) at the heart of Penn's colonizing endeavour."[34] For Richard Dunn, the map was "one of the most effective promotional devices" in what turned out to be "the most effective English colonial recruitment drive since the Puritans had founded Massachusetts half a century before."[35] Yet exactly how and why the map was so effective is not well established. The image is less studied and cited than the contemporary parallel texts—notably Penn's first promotional pamphlet, the ten-page *Some Account of the Province of Pennsilvania in America*, and the eight-page *Brief Account of the Province of Pennsylvania*, in which the map was advertised as a postscript—an imbalance that reflects the common relegation of maps as lesser evidence than the written word.[36] Indeed, the map is little discussed or reproduced in tandem with the text included here in figure 3.1, even though it was pointedly advertised as being printed "together with a Description at the End of it."[37] The written description was specially composed and designed to be pasted and perused beneath the map, evidently with the aim of enhancing and emphasizing the visual description above, thus we should consider word and image as an integral whole, a single text.[38] If Penn were trying to sell land today, Jean Soderlund has speculated, he would produce a "flashy brochure filled with many pictures" instead of what she characterizes as a series of "sober and restrained" tracts.[39]

But the prospect provided by the map and its description may be viewed very much as the seventeenth-century equivalent of the flashy brochure or eyecatching full-page poster ad.

The ad, measuring a manageable half-meter or so wide and long, was hot off the press around midsummer and circulated through the City of London and far beyond. It was presumably on view at the establishments where the *Brief Account* suggested those "desirous to be concern'd in the Province . . . may be treated with, and further Satisfied," that is, Philip Ford's shop off Cheapside, and Thomas Rudyard's or Benjamin Clark's off Lombard Street; and on sale (as indicated in the cartouche) at Thornton's shop in the Minories near Tower Hill, Seller's near the Royal Exchange, and perhaps also his occasional stall in Westminster Hall; and it was probably studied or discussed in the coffeehouses and other cultural and commercial spaces dotted in between, as well as the Royal Society's meeting room at Gresham College near Bishopsgate, where on November 9 the fellows admitted Penn into their circle "with much respect" and "returned their thanks" for his map.[40] Petty and Pepys, well-established and esteemed fellows, each acquired a copy.[41] Penn presumably took the map with him when he traveled through the country signing up settlers and investors in his scheme—it was produced first and foremost, as the text explains, to meet "the desires of such persons as resolved to be concerned"—and he apparently dispatched copies through his religious and secular networks: in late August he wrote to his go-between in Dublin, the Quaker merchant Robert Turner (who signed up himself and others), that he had sent "maps & accounts too by Fr[iend] Tho[mas] Lurting."[42] Publication almost certainly came too late for William Markham to carry the printed map with him to America as Penn's deputy governor in early summer, but it would be strange if the land commissioners who departed England in the autumn did not have one or more copies in their bundle of assorted papers.[43] By the time Penn and hundreds of others arrived in Pennsylvania the following winter, many different eyes had scanned and scrutinized the *Map of Some of the South and Eastbounds*.

Pennsylvania Viewed

What the eyes of imperial overseers and prospective investors and emigrants were meant to see in the map was an ideal balance of minimal existing settlement and maximum space for improvement: a land of possibility. Title and text stress that this represents but "some" of the province, promising an expansiveness that is seemingly confirmed in visual form by the two great rivers flowing up to and over the map's borders to the north and by the unnamed—and so, in European minds, unclaimed—hills and plains rolling inland to the west. The sparse detail presents the province as an uncluttered stage, easy to comprehend and claim.[44] Would-be subscribers and settlers were encouraged to project their

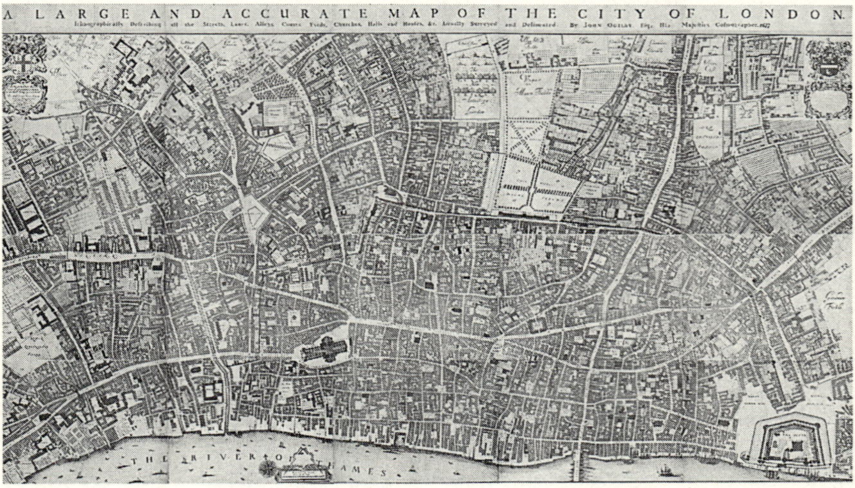

Figure 3.8 John Ogilby, *A Large and Accurate Map of the City of London* (London: John Ogilby and William Morgan, 1677). British Library.

future hopes and aspirations on to this wide-open territory, to map and begin cultivating in their minds the shares of acres as set out in the "Conditions" below. The seductiveness of the space for contemporary viewers is understandable by comparison with the recent map of Barbados (figure 3.5), which shows the island fully inhabited and barely a patch uncultivated—"too small a Hive for such a swarm of people," as Hickeringill described it in the process of promoting Jamaica as a relative blank canvas (figure 3.4); or indeed the latest map of London (figure 3.8), published a decade after its destruction by the Great Fire of 1666, in which the crowded, crazy-maze city is shown rebuilding along old lines but beyond all its old bounds.[45] Nonetheless, the subtitle's clarification that the province was "partly Inhabited" offered the perfect inducement to settlement. The text elaborates that the "part of the Country which is at all Inhabited [the addition of "at all" helping to minimize the reader's sense of the scale of habitation] is at the head of *Chesapeak Bay*, and on the *West* side of *Delaware* River, they are by Nation *Sweads*, *Dutch*, *English*, who are capable of giving Entertainment to New Commers, till they can provide for themselves." All very reassuring. The riverbank settlements would provide stepping stones for settlers and traders, enabling access to the spaces in between and beyond. With these words, reflected on the map through a smattering of selected planter and place names, this document served to contain existing European claims on the territory, turning them to the service of Penn and his new colonists.

Still more significantly subdued by the map, if not altogether silenced, are indigenous people's connections to and rights over the land—as well as water. The Delaware River, which served as Pennsylvania's eastern and West Jersey's western border, had already been extensively colonized by the English, and by Swedes, Finns, and Dutch before them, causing severe disruption to Lenape life in the area (the shifting dominion and process of separation marked by the renaming of the river and the region).[46] The placement of the Susquehanna River straight down the center of Penn's map confirms that he had this, too, squarely in his sights, along with the land on both sides and the trade that extended its entire length; that from the beginning he envisaged a greater Pennsylvania absorbing vast tracts of land used by various Native groups.[47] And he armed himself with European legal concepts associated with Roman imperial practice, backed up with English narratives of North America's "discovery" in the early decades of the seventeenth century.[48] The first item in the map's accompanying text, on "*The* Kings *Title to this* Province *before-granted*," invokes "*Jus Gentium*, or Law of Nations" to claim English rights over the territory pictured above: "whatever is the Discovery of any Prince, is the right of that Prince that was at the Charge of the Discovery: Now this *Province* is a Member of that part of *America*, which the *King of Englands Ancestors* have been at the Charge of Discovering, and which they and he have taken great care to preserve and Improve." Penn's emphasis on improvement in justifying the colonization of inhabited land in America was carried over from his Irish experience.[49] As for the emphasis on "the Charge of the Discovery," it is no coincidence that the plantations office, at the same time as bringing together the Blathwayt Atlas maps, purchased "histories" of English colonization of America by Captain John Smith, Samuel Purchas, and John Ogilby, among others.[50] The foundational myths constructed through word and image thus became part of the official record, employed to assert English possession and dispossess others. The only mentions of indigenous peoples in the paragraphs that follow beneath the map sweep them aside in a simple, nonnegotiated transaction—principally in the line explaining that, to the king's grant, "Penn adds that of the Natives by purchase from them"—and present them as the source of useful resources (land, corn, meat), not the benefactors. Potential resistance to English colonization is written out, and mapped out, of this reconstructed place.

Here, then, is the "room" that Penn imagined to be available to him "there, though not here [in England, that is]" for a "holy experiment" that would be "free from any Indian incumbrance."[51] The map's juxtaposition of names concentrated along the shorelines and unmarked land beyond may be compared to the first English map of Jamaica (figure 3.4), in which the comprehensively charted coastline contrasts starkly with the blank interior. Both maps, with the involvement of Penn senior and Penn junior, respectively, were tools in a process of erasure and reinvention; of peopling and depeopling.[52] The former was involved in the work of de-establishing Spanish and Taíno Jamaica and establishing English Jamaica amid ongoing struggle against the new occupiers following Admiral Penn's initial but incomplete seizure of the island. Penn junior's map—of the province named by the king for his father—was involved in the work of smoothing over earlier claims and clearing space for what he viewed as "my country." The simple border of the title cartouche may suggest a certain speed and restraint on the artist's part, but laurel wreaths potently denoted victory and conquest to contemporary eyes, and for that reason may be found on roughly contemporary maps of Jamaica.[53] Conquest is inscribed on to the territory in the depiction of "Sesquahana fort Demolished" on the west bank of the river, albeit believed to be the result of earlier conflict between the Susquehanna and Iroquois, and irrespective of the likelihood that some Susquehanna still lived there. These three blunt words—like "Old Indian feild" located north-west of the Delaware—seem calculated to remove from viewers' minds "any Indian incumbrance" and plant in its place the concept of *vacuum domicilium*, vacant land free for the taking. We have to allow for the fact that, in time, the "Indian incumbrance" would have figured among the map's viewers, as their representatives visited Pennsbury to sign over parcels of land.

The demolished fort is perhaps the map's most forceful, fraudulent sign in another, lastingly significant respect. On the map produced by Augustine Herrman for Maryland's proprietor Lord Baltimore and published in 1673 (figure 3.9)—which Thornton and Robert Greene used in the creation of their chart including Virginia and Maryland (figure 3.6), which in turn provided the model for large areas of Penn's map of Pennsylvania—the "present Sasquahana Indian fort" straddles a dotted line marking the 40th degree of north latitude, the disputed border between the two colonies. As the Duke of York's secretary Sir John Werden wrote to Blathwayt in June 1680, the location of the lines of both latitude and longitude were "so very little known, or so ill observed" that it was impossible to say where the proper boundaries should be.[54] For Baltimore, the fort's position in relation to latitude was key to what he called "this business of the ascertaining [of] the bounds betwixt Mr Penn and me."[55] As one historian noted, "It is no exaggeration to state that there was no point within the present bounds of Pennsylvania before Penn's arrival of equal importance to that of Susquehannock fort."[56] Before Penn was granted his charter, he had accepted that the fort marked his colony's southern boundary with Maryland. But just as the location of the 40th degree was uncertain, there was also haziness over which Susquehanna fort was meant in the negotiations, and the exact site of the principal fort was a matter of bitter dispute into the eighteenth century. Penn's map seems deliberately to muddy the waters further, not only by declaring the fort "demolished" but by placing the 40th degree of north latitude almost fifty miles further south, at the bottom of the map, and removing all reference to Maryland and Baltimore.

The wild inaccuracy, which ensured serious and sustained acrimony between the proprietors and their heirs, has not helped the map's historical reputation. But that is the problem with judging maps for their accuracy alone rather than

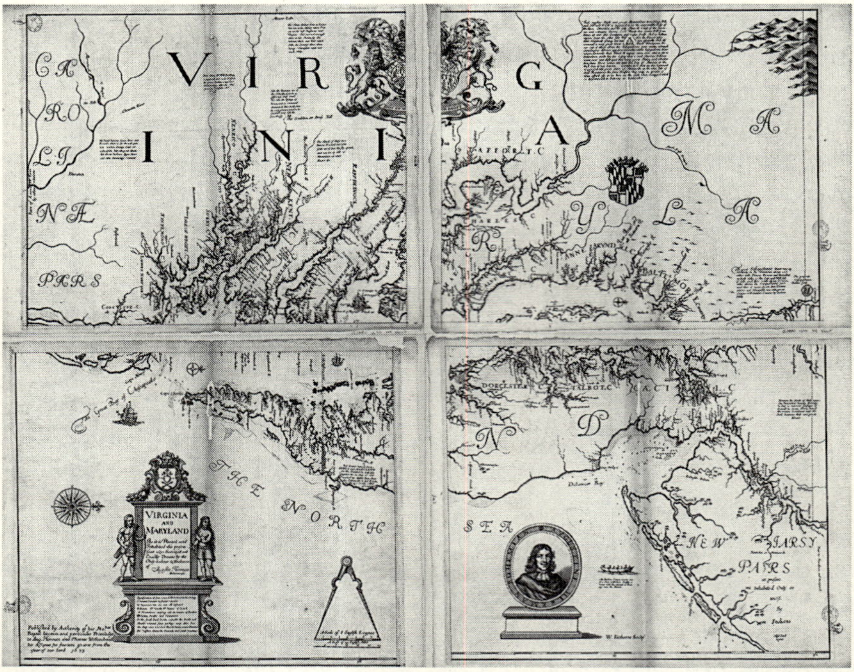

Figure 3.9 Augustine Herrman, *Virginia and Maryland as it is Planted and Inhabited this present Year 1670* (London: Augustine Herrman and Thomas Withinbrook, 1673). Library of Congress.

seeking to understand the ideas they contained and communicated. It certainly suited Penn to exploit the prevailing uncertainty over the 40th degree, as Antoinette Sutto has shown.[57] The continuation of the border dispute, in which Penn asserted his deference to the king's dictates on the issue and represented Baltimore's opposition as a challenge to royal authority, dramatizes the inseparability of material interests and ideas that defined the map.[58] Quite simply, as Sutto put it, Penn wanted ocean access.[59] His map positioned the 40th degree so as to give his province access to two great rivers and control over their all-important mouths, and emphasized the importance of these waterways by making them the strongest visual elements. The text explained that "the Conveniency that belongs to the *Province* in point of *Navigation*, is two fold; the one through the *Chesapeak Bay*, and the other *Delaware Bay*, by which Ships of great Burthen may come and Trade to the said *Province*." The map of New Jersey (figure 3.7) had similarly emphasized the value of a tract of land (the newly formed colony of West New Jersey) "bounded with two Navigable Rivers," in this case the Hudson and the Delaware; the access thus provided "to many good *Harbours* for Shipping" made the country "compleat." The Delaware was, as Roeber put it, the "geographic hinge that connected the surrounding areas and opened the region to the world."[60] Without a "back door" to the Susquehanna via the Chesapeake, Penn feared the valley that held so much promise for his new province would "prove but a dead lump of earth."[61] In putting his case to the Lords of Trade, he explained that he was motivated not by "the love or need of the land, but the water," and it was perhaps on receiving and digesting Penn's letter that Blathwayt or his assistant John Povey added "Cheseapeak Bay" by hand on the map.[62] The annotation underlines how the missing piece in the English jigsaw of colonial America didn't quite fit.

The mistake made on Penn's map may have been encouraged by the confusion of the grid on Thornton and Greene's chart (figure 3.6), which did not represent latitude or longitude as might be supposed at a glimpse (the degrees of latitude are marked in the margins), but were apparently "squaring up" lines for the purpose of copying the map.[63] One of the grid lines was taken as the base point for Penn's map, and in a muddle may have been misidentified as the 40th degree. However, enough maps in circulation countered such a position by some distance (including a few in the Blathwayt collection, and not least the New Jersey map sponsored by Penn) for this to remain a case of someone seeing and sticking with what they wanted themselves and others to believe. As if anticipating that the map's geographical claims might cause controversy, the text is quick to concede that "time, and better Experience" might "correct, and compleat it"—but not before insisting that it may be relied on as drawn from "Relations received from persons that have been upon the place," and that it aimed to "*correct the Errors of those* Maps *that have taken in any part of this Country*; for finding each *Map* at difference with it self, the Scale with the Latitude, and one *Map* with another, it was thought necessary to rectifie those mistakes, by a more *exact Map*, which hath been performed with as much Truth, Care and Skill, as at present can be." Seller may have been prone to take shortcuts with his maps, but he nevertheless had a reputation to keep as hydrographer to the king.[64] That the map of Pennsylvania was proudly presented to the Royal Society months after it was produced indicates that it was deemed suitably authoritative and valuable for the eyes of this revered scientific body, rather than dubious and discredited. To understand the anomaly, it helps to recognize that maps were weapons in the border war. Markham, in England in 1683 pleading Penn's case against Baltimore, reported back that "a draft" of Maryland had arrived in England and, having heard it was at Blathwayt's office, he went to see it, but Richard Burke, Baltimore's agent, had taken it away again.[65] By subterfuge, Markham got inside Burke's house to see the map, and to find that it "makes the line of 40 to run as near as I can guess over Philadelphia."[66] In retaliation for Penn's low blow, Baltimore sought to carve up his beloved city, as well as his river access.

A feature of Penn's map that appears to have been neither noted nor explained is the dotted line that cuts across the heart of the province to connect Chesapeake Bay with the Delaware Falls, where the river might be crossed for access far to the north and near where Pennsbury Manor would soon be built. This, too, is a claim being staked. Confirming the importance for Penn not only of the two great rivers but also of the relationship and movement between them (exaggerated by their twisted orientation toward each other on the map), the trail suggests a crucial backbone through the colony with the proprietor's country estate at its head. It is perhaps the first indication of how the Pennsbury site formed, as Roeber has defined it, "a strategic crossroads facilitating establishment of a buffer against former territorial claims as well as a gateway to future expansion."[67] The dotted line may represent a route established by indigenous peoples and traced by Europeans—perhaps by James Wasse, who made a number of now lost surveys for Penn and whose plantation of five thousand acres, as marked in the Thornton and Greene map (figure 3.6), lay near the line's northerly destination, on the other side of the Delaware Falls. The plantation belonging to Herrman, whom Wasse was instructed to look up in Maryland as an "able surveyer," is not too distant from the line's southerly end.[68] The value of the tract of land traversed by the line is signaled in a note on the map Herrman made for Lord Baltimore (figure 3.9). A few lines of text, engraved across the 40th degree of north latitude between the Susquehanna and Delaware like the fort above, explain that "between the Heads of these opposite Branches being Swampy is but a narrow passage of Land to come down out of the maine Continent into the Neck between these two great Rivers." The dotted line on Penn's map seems to chart just such a narrow passage, thereby claiming his province's hold over the all-important trade route connecting colonies to north and south. It also represents a path through the wilderness—or rather, the dense and potentially dangerous forest, which the map similarly tames through the scattering of stylized trees. Easily dismissed as decoration or simple illustration of the meaning of "Pennsylvania" (Penn's woods), these arboreal motifs are laden with as many potential meanings as they might have leaves, and indeed bear the weight of Penn's economic as well as religious ambition and claims.

The Wood for the Trees

It was common for colonial maps to mask the unknown and appeal to the viewer through artfully placed trees. Those on Penn's map were also artfully drawn. The attention to detail (see, for example, figure 3.10) may have been inspired by the diversity of leafy forms found on Captain John Smith's renowned map of the Chesapeake, *Virginia Discovered and Discribed*, published decades earlier in 1612 yet copied and reworked as the prototype for the area at least until Herrman's *Virginia and Maryland* of 1673. The Farrer (or Ferrar) map of Virginia, a version of which dating from around 1652 was acquired by the Office of Trade and Plantations and survives as part of the Blathwayt Atlas, features a similar variety of trees and even names one, the sassafras, which could command high prices in

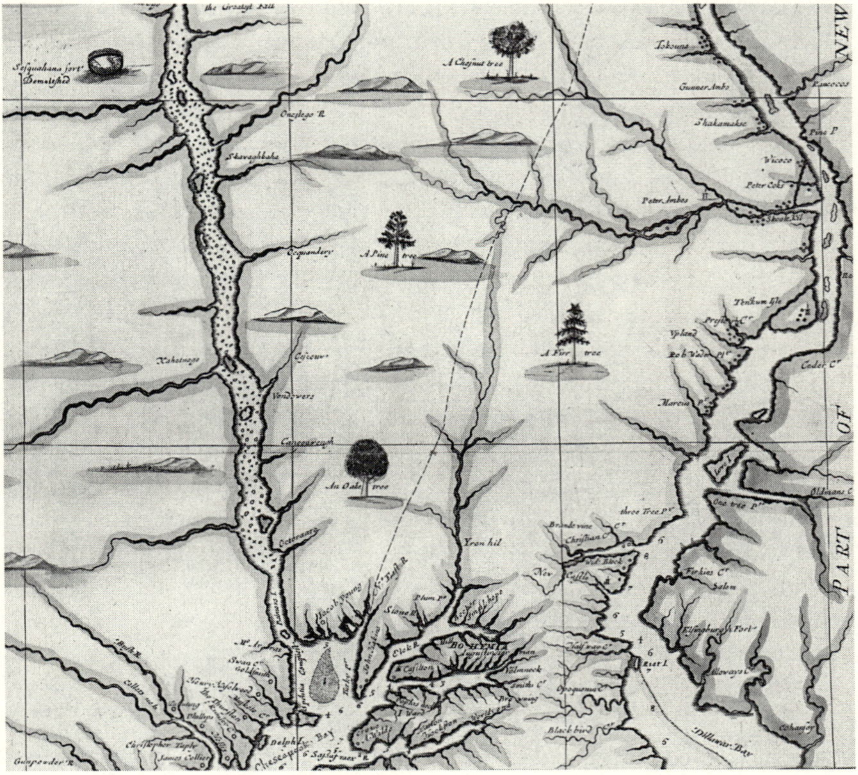

Figure 3.10 Detail of *A Map of Some of the South and Eastbounds of Pennsylvania in America* (London: John Thornton and John Seller, 1681). Courtesy of the John Carter Brown Library at Brown University.

Europe for its purported herbal healing powers.[69] Penn's map is striking for its ten individually named species—an arboreal alphabet from ash to walnut—and the specificity indicates they were intended as more than added ornament. Considered as a visualization of the tree catalogue of classical poetry and colonial tracts (which came together in the courtier-planter Edmund Spenser's *Faerie Queene*, a work on late sixteenth-century English forfeiture and transformation of the Irish landscape that surely resonated with Penn), the map's trees partly served to smooth and soothe the journey of the viewer's mind, and ultimately body, from familiar to strange territory.[70] Like the sassafras, their names spoke to their audience, and their branches reached out to them with the hope of health and wealth. Their roots were firmly embedded and entwined in Penn's personal and proprietorial plan of sustainable development for his colony: the "two plantations—the inward and the outward," as Frederick Tolles (drawing on the Society of Friends founder George Fox) characterized the duality of spiritual and worldly impulses.[71]

Trees were a matter close to Penn's heart. Before he put forward his vision of a "greene country towne," its streets lined with and named after trees, his map laid out the green country itself. The spiritual appeal was clear. Just as Penn celebrated his chartered territory as a gift from God, Quakers and other religious audiences would have been prone to see the hand of Providence in the vision of a divinely wooded landscape; an Eden restored in which they could lead the innocent, wholesome, harmonious life that eluded them elsewhere.[72] The text beneath the map appeals explicitly to those with "a Reverend regard to Gods Providence" who were "seeking the comforts of retirement, and sufficiency for Life." The "mystically minded near-Quaker" Thomas Tryon, in his *Planter's Speech to His Neighbours and Country-Men of Pennsylvania, East and West-Jersey* (1684), compared the colonists themselves to replanted, regenerated trees: "That as Trees are transplanted from one Soyl to another, to render them more Thriving and better Bearers, so we here in Peace and secure Retirement under the bountiful Protection of God, and in the Lap of the least adulterated Nature, might every one the better improve his Talent, and bring forth more plentious Fruits to the Glory of God, and publick Wellfare of the whole Creation."[73] In that vein, each tree stands on the map as a "seed of a nation," to use Penn's emblematic expression—a new nation growing "as on a *Virgin Elysian Shore*" (Tryon's analogy), in place of and thus shrouding native ones.[74]

Both Tryon's metaphor and Penn's map, reflecting the project of Pennsylvania as a whole, contain a tension between a desired state of nature (or "the least adulterated") and the impulse to "improve" it. Sprouting up through little green patches on the print, the trees at once lend a sense of natural inevitability to the colonizing process and, through their typological presentation, underline the implantation and intervention inherently at work. Commonly used as boundary markers on the ground, on the map the trees immediately signaled orderly and productive stewardship of the land, from which prospective colonists might be reassured of their future safety and protection. The weighty literature of improvement that Penn carried in his baggage or had shipped to America, packed alongside seeds (walnuts and other "rare good" ones) and even young trees, testifies to his vision of himself as the Quaker ideal of the godly husbandman.[75] Yet the motivation and popularity of such books as John Worlidge's *Systema Agriculturae: The Mystery of Husbandry Discovered* (in its third edition in 1681) and Moses Cook's *The Manner of Raising, Ordering, and Improving Forrest-Trees*—two of almost a dozen agricultural manuals kept in the "Governers Closet" at Pennsbury before the gardener there took custody of them—was less spiritual sustenance than material profit: the social and economic gains hinted at in Tryon's "public Wellfare."[76]

Since the earliest English colonizing ventures across the Atlantic, arguments for expansion centered around trees. Richard Hakluyt, the Anglican minister, geographer, and advocate of English exploration and colonization under Elizabeth

I and James I, promoted expeditions to North America because it had been discovered to be "infinitely full fraughte with sweet wooddes . . . and divers other kinds of goodly trees."[77] The diversity he celebrated may explain the effort to indicate distinct species on Smith's map of Virginia. Such was the value of the trees in Hakluyt's view, both as raw material and manufactured into countless goods, that "were there no other peculier commodities, this onely [wood] I say were ynoughe to defraye all the chardges of all the begynnynge of the enterprise, and that oute of hande."[78] For Hakluyt, as for subsequent promoters of English colonization, trees provided a guarantee of financial success. Money really did grow on trees.

Penn's marketing strategy followed suit, and he backed it up on his first visit to the province by sending presents of lumber to some of his English patrons.[79] The third section of the text beneath the map ("Of the Country and its Produce") provides a comprehensive list of trees that the soil "commonly produceth," adding to the species depicted—that is, oak, poplar, ash, walnut, beech, mulberry, cedar, chestnut, pine, fir—the cyprus, sassafras, and assorted fruit trees. English fruit "takes kindly, and produceth suddainly and plentifully," the text stresses, and the woods are not only valuable in their own right, but "are furnished with Store of Wild Fowl, as *Turkeys*, *Pheasants*, *Heath-Cocks*, *Partridges*, *Pidgeons*, &c." Trees are presented as both lifeblood and livelihood; the essential natural resource (coupled with the navigable, fish-filled rivers) out of which life might be carved.[80] The benefits would have been clear to contemporary English audiences, those experiencing depression and dispossession in the countryside as much as urban dwellers. As Joan Thirsk pointed out, the "inhabitants of forests generally in the seventeenth century had advantages over those living in more arable regions. They had many different resources at their disposal, many alternative ways of earning a living."[81] *Some Account*, in which Penn appealed to those who were "much clogg'd and oppress'd about a Livelyhood," stressed that "for Timber and other Wood there is variety for the use of man," but particularly "sufficient for Shipping," and it follows that first among the "Persons fittest for Plantations" (section eight in the map's accompanying text) are "Industrious Husbandmen" and "Laborious Handicrafts men" such as carpenters and shipwrights.[82]

The reference to shipbuilding, an echo of Hakluyt's promise that America would give England access to "plenty of excellent trees for mastes, of goodly timber to builde shippes and to make great navies," points to how the map's trees formed a message not just to potential settlers and investors but also, perhaps even more calculatingly, to imperial officials and interested elites.[83] The necessity of reliable timber supplies for the construction of commercial and naval ships made trees potent symbols of English national and international strength, and a century or more of growing concern over declining supplies put trees at the forefront of Restoration minds, especially within the circles in which Penn and his father mixed. In 1662 the principal officers and commissioners of the navy, including Penn senior and led by the Duke of York, approached the Royal Society with "certain Queries" aimed at encouraging the "Preserving of Tymber now growing And planting more," which were answered by John Evelyn in a lecture subsequently published as *Sylva, or A Discourse of Forest-Trees and the Propagation of Timber in his Majesties Dominions* (1664).[84] The successive editions of this volume, which was the newly established society's first publication and received royal approval, indicate the great importance of the issue and the influence of the ideas set out by Evelyn and his collaborators. The work's commercial success and depth of penetration among the English upper classes has been deemed "remarkable," and the third edition appeared in 1679, just as Penn was developing his scheme for an American colony.[85]

In both his dedication to the king and his address to the reader, Evelyn focused attention on wood as the basis of the monarch's "Lustre *and* Glory" and the nation's wealth and safety. Forests were the "Treasure and Ornament of this Nation," he wrote; they furnished it with "Trojan Horses" and facilitated unimpeached navigation around the world.[86] The "so great a scarcity of Tymber" that deeply troubled the English navy in 1662 was a symptom of a wider European energy crisis, or at least a far-reaching and long-running discourse of wood scarcity based on increasing competition between Europe's seafaring powers over territory, its resources, and trade.[87] French officials likewise launched a commission in 1662 to investigate the depletion of timber supplies for their navy.[88] More and more wood, converted to charcoal and white coal, was being used to fuel iron and glass production, and a range of other growing industries, such as brick, lime, and lead. Forests seemed to shrink at an alarming rate, and rising demand pushed up the prices of both wood and charcoal.[89]

Laws aimed at conservation and increasing future supplies of timber through planting were enacted from the mid-sixteenth century in England, but the problem was exacerbated for the restored king and his government in the mid-seventeenth century following further destruction of woods and forests (including the royal preserves) during the civil wars and commonwealth years—the latter, under Cromwell, simultaneously ushering in aggressive commercial and military policies that increased demand for timber and wood products vital to shipping. In 1668, after the second Anglo-Dutch war (1664–1667) had shown domestic supplies of timber to be invaluable, Parliament passed "An Act for the Increase and Preservation of Timber within the Forest of Dean." The following year, Louis XIV's chief minister and secretary of state for the navy, Jean-Baptiste Colbert, introduced the *Ordonnance des eaux et forêts* in the fear that France, too, would perish for the want of wood: "*La France périra faute de bois.*" The English navy's proposal (put forward in the "Queries") to "forbid the building of Houses, in or about the Citty of London, the Liberties of the same or within 10 Miles of the said Cittie, with Oken Tymber, unless for Ground Plates" proved even more persuasive in the aftermath of the Great Fire that destroyed the City in 1666. In the interests of timber preservation as well as fire protection, the 1667 Act for the Rebuilding of the City of London stipulated that new houses should be built of brick or stone, and the external use of wood was severely restricted. The majority of any wood used in rebuilding was imported, notably firs from Scandinavia, and the relaxation of the Navigation Acts which opened up this trade, and encouraged a more general dependence on foreign supplies of timber and fuel, deepened concerns over English vulnerability on an international stage. Such concerns perhaps contributed to the scheme hatched by Penn senior, Pepys, and the master shipwright Phineas Pett to transport timber and deals from Scotland, "which while London is building, will yield good money."[90] While Dutch merchants were only too eager to engage in the trade, war with the Netherlands threatened to interrupt supplies of Baltic and Nordic resources on which naval construction and now London's reconstruction relied.[91]

Despite the early promises of Hakluyt and others, England's colonies at this point provided little comfort. Caribbean islands prized for their dense and diverse woods were looking increasingly barren. Barbados, once covered to the shoreline with forests "so thick and most of the Trees so large and massie . . . they were not to be falne," had been almost entirely deforested by the late 1660s to make way for and fuel the booming sugar industry (as the crowded map shown in figure 3.5 testifies).[92] The island was itself dependent on imports for construction and energy, including coal from Newcastle and Wales, and when its own capital of Bridgetown was destroyed by fire, two years after London in 1668, timber for rebuilding arrived in Dutch ships from Europe and Suriname.[93] Meanwhile, the English colony on Saint Kitts was devastated in 1666 by the French with whom the island had been partitioned and occupied. In an act that confirms the contemporary physical and symbolic value of trees, and which shook the English to the core, the French cut down the trees in the woods and on the mountains of the English territory, dispossessing the colonists and making them "incapable of rebuilding."[94] A decade later, in 1676, Colonel Philip Warner declared starkly: "There is no wood."[95]

New England was a critical source of lumber for the Caribbean islands and the metropole. It had the finest natural supply of naval stores outside the Baltic, as Bernard Bailyn pointed out, and the arrival of four ships with a cargo of masts on the south coast of wartime England in 1666 was greeted by Pepys as "a blessing, mighty unexpected, and without which (if for nothing else) we must have failed the next year."[96] However, New England's reliability was questioned by officials in London through the 1670s. Not only were some Massachusetts towns experiencing timber shortages but the colony was, in Evelyn's account of the plantations council meeting in May 1671, "appearing to be very independent as to their regard to old England, or his Majestie, rich and strong as now they were."[97] The colony's condition was such, Evelyn wrote, "that they were able to contest with all our Plantations about them, and feare there was, of their altogether breaking from all dependence on this nation."[98] The brutal war between colonists and Native peoples beginning in 1675 left New England's environment and economy in ruin, and its future relations with England an even greater concern. Similarly, in the Chesapeake, the conflict commonly known as "Bacon's Rebellion" (1676–1677) caused imperial officials to judge colonists in Virginia "ill Qualified as to their Obedience and incouraged at soe remote a Distance from England to cast off the Yoke."[99]

Penn's map presents an oasis between these conflict-ridden and contested landscapes, with the trees creating a picture of solid, upright responsibility and reliability, a colony firmly yoked to the Crown. Here is new life and endless energy, viewers were encouraged to believe: a richly sustainable new world for settlers and a dependable supply of raw materials to repower the old world and its wood-stripped plantations at home and overseas. Presented to the Royal Society (its president, Lord Brouncker, a navy commissioner and comptroller) by John Houghton (an advocate of improvement and a more commercialized fuel market), Penn's map may be seen as a direct response to the economic and expansionist argument made in Evelyn's *Sylva*—continued in his 1674 treatise on navigation and commerce—specifically, the appeal to landowners to do their patriotic duty by improving their estates (and by extension their dominions) through the planting of timber trees.[100] The "*Planting* and *Improving* of *Wood*, is a right *noble* and *royal undertaking*," Evelyn had concluded, "more worthy of a *Prince* who truly consults his glory in the highest *Interest* of his *Subjects* than that of gaining *Battels*, or subduing a *Province*."[101] Penn's plan for his province may not have been directly militaristic, but he nonetheless implied its contribution to strengthening the nation's "Wooden-walls," as Evelyn described England's ships, a subject in which Penn had a personal interest as his father's career-long concern: "his Trade," as Penn had put it, which defined the family as much as the father and hints at a heraldic quality to the trees on the map.[102] Tree types considered indispensable for ship construction are prominent in both map and text: the "precious" oak ("The *Land* and the *Sea* do sufficiently speak for the improvement of this excellent material; *Houses*, and *Ships*, *Cities* and *Navies* are built with it"); the "martial" ash ("in Peace and War it is a wood in highest request"); the "speedy growing . . . useful and profitable" fir ("They make our best *Mast*, *Sheathing*, &c" and "an incredible mass of ready *Money* is yearly exported into the *Northern Countrys* for this sole commodity, which might all be saved were we *industrious* at *home*").[103] Across his promotional material, Penn claimed his trustworthiness in recognizing the crucial importance of timber and understanding how to cultivate and manage supplies. In the "conditions" of settlement he formulated while work proceeded on the map in 1681, he stressed that, in clearing the ground, "care be taken to leave one acre of trees for every five acres cleared, especially to preserve oak and mulberries, for silk and shipping."[104]

Trees also represented a healthy iron industry. Map and text signal Pennsylvania's potential as a rich seam of iron: Yron Hill, named for its deposits, is marked east of Newcastle, and iron is included in the section on "What the Countrey is believed capable of." Demand had increased massively in England between the 1630s and 1680s—such that Evelyn described the period as an "*Iron-age*"—but output had failed to respond.[105] Like timber, iron had many uses, but an important one on official minds in Restoration England was guns and other armaments. The industry's potential had attracted the attention of numerous owners of Irish estates, including Petty, who in the 1670s attempted to revive iron manufacture on his recently acquired lands in County Kerry. As Toby Barnard remarked of his motives for the project, Petty saw the woodland there as an asset to be converted as speedily as possible into cash, and iron production offered better profits than exporting the timber for ship and house building and as staves.[106] Perhaps the same motive encouraged Petty's purchase of ten thousand acres in Pennsylvania, though it came to nothing.[107] It was the interrelation of commercial timber production and iron smelting, according to the author of "Directions for Establishing a Plantation in Ireland," that would contribute to the improvement not just of land but also of the landowner's "fortune by his industry."[108] Penn himself owned ironworks at Hawkhurst in Kent and was anxious to see them built in his American colony.[109] Again, Evelyn provided inspiration and justification. Addressing the "exorbitance, and increase of devouring *Iron-mills*" in England, he pondered: "what if some of them were even remov'd into another *World*? 'twere better to purchase all our *Iron* out of *America*, than thus to exhaust our *Woods* at *home*."[110] Returning to the question in his conclusion, he suggested that New England colonists should use "their surfeit of the *Woods* which we want" to supply "their *Mother* old *England*" with iron and so help preserve the nation's forests.[111] "This were the only way to render both our Countries habitable indeed, and the fittest sacrifice for the Royal-Oaks," Evelyn argued, and he snippily suggested that the colonists owed "more than a slight submission" to the restored king whom the royal oak symbolized.[112]

Submission was more critical than ever by 1681, at the height of the political crisis over the succession to the throne. Where New England had disappointed, Penn positioned his province to succeed and supplant. Through the variegated trees, the wide open space on the map was transformed into prime real estate and loyal colony in front of viewers' eyes—as King Charles indeed seemed to design by insisting on the name of "Penn's woods." Far from weakening the "motherland" by draining it of people and resources, as critics of colonization complained (notably Roger Coke in his 1670 *Discourse of Trade* and William Petyt in his 1680 *Britannia Languens*, both of whom lamented migration to Ireland as well as across the Atlantic), the province as promoted by the map would strengthen both England and its hold on America.[113] Like *Some Account*, which countered objections with its opening salvo on the "credit and benefit of *plantations*," the map presented an economic and political argument in favor of colonization. This was always a hard-headed "holy experiment."

Infused with the spirit of *Sylva*, the first map of Pennsylvania is a visualization of Evelyn's "seminary" designed to provide "*Timber, Shelter, Fuel*, and *Ornament*, to an incredible Advantage."[114] It was no coincidence that, discussing the matter of improvement, Royal Society fellow John Beale (who contributed to *Sylva*) cited Penn for his proposals for American plantations and John Seller for his maps: the two were brought together in the *Map of Some of the South and Eastbounds of Pennsylvania in America*.[115] The map expressed far and wide Penn's commitment, made an obligation through its articulation in the first lines of the royal charter, to "enlarge our *English* Empire, and promote such usefull comodities as may bee of Benefit to us and Our Dominions," and indeed to "reduce the savage Natives."[116] Quite what the Native peoples with whom Penn held court in his parlors might have made of their reduction in the maps, the fort demolished and their lands replanted with alien ideas of improving nature, we cannot presume. It seems pertinent, however, that the tree with which Penn became most associated and which still stands for Pennsylvania's benevolent origins—the elm, under which legend says he treatied with the Lenape leaders in 1682—is entirely missing from the map and the text.[117] The iconic elm's absence helps us to see beneath the great canopy of myth that grew up around Penn's aims and attitudes, and to take a closer, harder look at his colony's deep imperial roots.

NOTES

1. "A Catalogue of Goods left at Pen[n]sbury the 3d of the Tenth Month [December] 1701," in William Penn's Cash Book, 1699–1703, American Philosophical Society [APS], MSS B. P38, printed in Richard S. Dunn and Mary Maples Dunn, eds., *The Papers of William Penn, Volume 4: 1701–1718* (Philadelphia: Penn Press, 1987), 132–135 (132).

2. "A Catalogue of Goods left at Pen[n]sbury," 134.

3. "Goods left at Philadelphia the 20th of the 9th Month [November] 1701," in William Penn's Cash Book, 1699–1703, APS, MSS B.P38, printed in Dunn and Dunn, *Papers of William Penn, Volume 4*, 135.

4. One recent exception, which has informed my discussion of the maps here, is Catharine Dann Roeber's "Building and Planting: The Material World, Memory, and the Making of William Penn's Pennsylvania, 1681–1726" (PhD diss., College of William and Mary, 2011).

5. Mark Reinberger and Elizabeth McLean, "Pennsbury Manor: Reconstruction and Reality," *Pennsylvania Magazine of History and Biography* [*PMHB*] 131, no. 3 (2007): 263–306 (300).

6. Reinberger and McLean, "Pennsbury Manor," 301.

7. On the nature and functions of maps in early modern Europe, see, for example, Peter Barber, "Maps and Monarchs in Europe 1500–1800," in *Royal and Republican Sovereignty in Early Modern Europe*, ed. Robert Oresko, G. C. Gibbs, and H. M. Scott (Cambridge: Cambridge University Press, 1997), 75–124 (75); and "Necessary and Ornamental: Map Use in England under the Later Stuarts 1660–1714," *Eighteenth Century Life* 14, no. 3 (1990): 1–28. On understandings of maps as decorative as well as useful objects in early America, see Martin Brückner, "The Spectacle of Maps in British America, 1750–1800," in *Early Ameri-*

can Cartographies, ed. Brückner (Chapel Hill: University of North Carolina Press, 2011), 389–441.

8. Barber, "Maps and Monarchs," 75.

9. It is striking that the documentary history *William Penn and the Founding of Pennsylvania*, ed. Jean R. Soderlund (Philadelphia: Penn Press, 1983), classifies the maps as illustrations rather than documents (80, 320–21, 337). An important new study focusing on a single map as a rich and complex historical document (one closely related to the subject of my own essay) is Christian J. Koot's *A Biography of a Map in Motion: Augustine Herrman's Chesapeake* (New York: New York University Press, 2018).

10. The quotation, from Robert Blair St. George's *Conversing by Signs: Poetics of Implication in Colonial New England Culture* (Chapel Hill: University of North Carolina Press, 1998), 5, is used in relation to maps as material "things" by Brückner in "The Spectacle of Maps," 396.

11. Penn's nomination and election are recorded in the Royal Society Journal Book for 1681–85, JBO/7, 32.

12. Roeber, "Building and Planting," 139. Roeber discusses Holme's 1687 map at length. See also Walter Klinefelter, "Surveyor General Thomas Holme's 'Map of the Improved Part of the Province of Pennsilvania,'" *Winterthur Portfolio* 6 (1970): 41–74. On Holme's *Portraiture*, see especially Elizabeth Milroy, "'For the like Uses, as the Moore-Fields': The Politics of Penn's Squares," *PMHB* 130, no. 3 (2006): 257–281.

13. Richard S. Dunn and Mary Maples Dunn, eds., *The World of William Penn* (Philadelphia: Penn Press, 1986), xx.

14. On Blathwayt's roles in government, see Stephen Saunders Webb, "William Blathwayt, Imperial Fixer: From Popish Plot to Glorious Revolution," *William and Mary Quarterly*, 3rd Ser., 25, no. 1 (1968): 3–21, and "William Blathwayt, Imperial Fixer: Muddling Through to Empire, 1689–1717," *William and Mary Quarterly*, 3rd Ser., 26, no. 3 (1969): 373–415; and on the Pennsylvania charter, "'The Peaceable Kingdom': Quaker Pennsylvania in the Stuart Empire," in *World of William Penn*, ed. Dunn and Dunn, 173–194 (esp. 185–189).

15. The maps in the atlas became part of Blathwayt's personal library at his country estate of Dyrham Park in Gloucestershire, England, where they stayed until offered for auction by his descendants in the early twentieth century and were purchased by the John Carter Brown Library in Providence, Rhode Island. Other copies with the description are held by the Historical Society of Pennsylvania (uncolored), the British Library and the Pepys Library, Magdalene College, Cambridge. As curator at the John Carter Brown Library, Jeannette D. Black provided commentary on the maps in volume 2 of *The Blathwayt Atlas*, 2 vols. (Providence: Brown University Press, 1970–75); for the Pennsylvania map see 2:102–108. For a recent, brief analysis of the atlas, see S. Max Edelson, *The New Map of Empire: How Britain Imagined America before Independence* (Cambridge, MA: Harvard University Press, 2017), 24–27.

16. D. W. Meinig, *The Shaping of America: A Geographical Perspective on 500 Years of History*, vol. 1 (New Haven, CT: Yale University Press, 1986), 65.

17. Andrew R. Murphy, *Liberty, Conscience, and Toleration: The Political Thought of William Penn* (New York: Oxford University Press, 2016), 255.

18. Dunn and Dunn, *World of William Penn*, xx.

19. Hubertis M. Cummings, "An Account of Goods at Pennsbury Manor, 1687," *PMHB* 86 (1962): 397–416 (408).

20. Barber, "Maps and Monarchs," 105; and "Necessary and Ornamental," 16.

21. Evelyn cited by Helen Wallis in "The Royal Map Collections of England," *Revista da Universidade de Coimbra* 28 (1980): 461–468 (466).

22. Evelyn cited by Charles M. Andrews, "British Committees, Commissions, and Councils of Trade and Plantations 1622–1675," *Administrative and Political History* 26 (1908): 1–152 (136).

23. Letters from Penn to the Commissioners of the Navy, 2 December 1670 and 31 December 1670, National Archives Kew [NAK], SP 29/286. The first letter is printed in Mary Maples Dunn and Richard S. Dunn, eds., *The Papers of William Penn, Volume 1: 1644–1679* (Philadelphia: Penn Press, 1981), 183–184; my thanks to Andrew Murphy for pointing me to the later, unpublished letter.

24. Helen Wallis, "Material on Nautical Cartography in the British Library, 1550–1650," *Revista da Universidade de Coimbra* 32 (1985): 187–197 (188).

25. Letter from Penn to the Commissioners of the Navy, 2 December 1670, in Dunn and Dunn, *Papers of William Penn, Volume 1*, 183.

26. Wallis, "Royal Map Collections," 466.

27. Patricia Seed proposed nationally specific "symbolically significant gestures" (for example, Spanish speeches, French processions, Dutch mapping, English building) in *Ceremonies of Possession in Europe's Conquest of the New World 1492–1640* (Cambridge: Cambridge University Press, 1995). Her argument has since been nuanced by examinations of how Europeans drew on shared concepts of property and imitated each other, such as Lauren Benton and Benjamin Straumann, "Acquiring Empire by Law: From Roman Doctrine to Early Modern European Practice," *Law and History Review* 28, no. 1 (2010): 1–38. Roeber discusses Penn's turf and twig ceremony at Newcastle in "Building and Planting," 36–42.

28. Pepys, March 20, 1661, in *The Diary of Samuel Pepys*, ed. Robert Latham and William Matthews, 11 vols. (London: Bell & Hyman, 1971; repr. HarperCollins, 1995), 2:56.

29. Edmund Hickeringill, *Jamaica Viewed* (London: John Williams, 1661). On the map, see Black, *Blathwayt Atlas*, 2:187–188.

30. Edmund Hickeringill, *Jamaica Viewed*, 2nd ed. (London: John Williams, 1661), A2^{r-v}. The first edition was printed the same year by John Redmayne, without the dedication to Charles.

31. On Penn's trouble with royal officials, especially over the Navigation Acts, see Murphy, *Liberty, Conscience, and Toleration*, 222–230.

32. Item 16 of "Instructions for the Council for Foreign Plantations, 1670–1672," in Andrews, "British Committees," 122.

33. "Draft of Instructions for the Council of Trade and Foreign Plantations, 1672–1674," in Andrews, "British Committees," 131 (item 43). Minutes of the Committee of Trade and Plantations, September 16, 1675, *Calendar of State Papers Colonial* [*CSPC*], accessed August 20, 2017, http://www.british-history.ac.uk/cal-state-papers/colonial/america-west-indies/vol9/pp271-293. Journal of the Lords of Trade and Plantations, January 21, 1676, *CSPC*, accessed August 20, 2017, http://www.british-history.ac.uk/cal-state-papers/colonial/america-west-indies/vol9/pp330-345.

34. Murphy, *Liberty, Conscience, and Toleration*, 130.

35. Richard S. Dunn, "Penny Wise and Pound Foolish: Penn as a Businessman," in *World of William Penn*, 37–54 (43, 37). Worthington C. Ford connected the map to the promotion literature in "The First Map of Pennsylvania," *Proceedings of the Massachusetts Historical Society* 57 (1923): 172–183, and Hope Frances Kane took the discussion further in "Notes on Early Pennsylvania Promotion Literature," *PMHB* 63 (1939): 144–168.

36. *Some Account of the Province of Pennsilvania in America* (London: Printed by Benjamin Clark, 1681). *A Brief Account of the Province of Pennsilvania* (London: Printed for Benjamin Clark, 1682).

37. *Brief Account*, 8. In addition to missing the text, key scholarly works have reproduced only part of the map (for example, Soderlund, *Founding*, 80; and Dunn, "Businessman," 44).

38. G. N. G. Clarke argues that the different elements of a map are a "single text" in "Taking Possession: The Cartouche as Cultural Text in Eighteenth-Century American Maps," *Word and Image* 4, no. 2 (1988): 455–474. Black makes the point in relation to the map of West Jersey (*Blathwayt Atlas*, 2:97).

39. Soderlund, *Founding*, 58.

40. *Brief Account*, 8. John Aubrey, *Brief Lives*, ed. Richard Barber (Woodbridge, Suffolk: Boydell Press, 1982; repr. 1998), 240. Raymond Phineas Stearns, "Colonial Fellows of the Royal Society of London, 1661–1788," *Notes and Records of the Royal Society of London* 8, no. 2 (1951): 178–246 (196–197).

41. Black, *Blathwayt Atlas*, 2:108.

42. Richard S. Dunn and Mary Maples Dunn et al., eds, *The Papers of William Penn, Volume 2: 1680–1684* (Philadelphia: Penn Press, 1982), 110. "Go-between" is how Gary Nash described Turner in "The Free Society of Traders and the Early Politics of Pennsylvania," *PMHB* 89, no. 2 (1965): 147–173 (149).

43. For the commissioners and Penn's instructions to them, see Dunn and Dunn, *Papers of William Penn, Volume* 2, 118–123.

44. Meinig describes Pennsylvania as a "new expansive and uncluttered stage": *Shaping of America*, 1:134.

45. Hickeringill, *Jamaica Viewed*, 17. On what the Barbados map does not show, see Emily Mann, "A Promotional Map of Barbados, c. 1675," *Common-place.org* 17, no. 3 (2017), accessed August 20, 2017, http://common-place.org/book/vol-17-no-3-mann/. In the 1690s, the governor of Barbados remarked that significant numbers of colonists had left the island for Pennsylvania.

46. On the Swedish, Dutch, and English struggle for control of the Delaware, see Koot, *Map in Motion*, 106–114. Also Thomas J. Sugrue, "The Peopling and Depeopling of Early Pennsylvania: Indians and Colonists, 1680–1720," *PMHB* 116, no. 1 (1992): 3–31.

47. Gary Nash discusses the prominence of the river on the map and in Penn's thoughts in "The Quest for the Susquehanna Valley: New York, Pennsylvania, and the Seventeenth-Century Fur Trade," *New York History* 48, no. 1 (1967): 3–27 (5).

48. On early modern European use of Roman theory and practice, see Benedict Kingsbury and Benjamin Straumann, eds, *The Roman Foundations of the Law of Nations: Alberico Gentili and the Justice of Empire* (Oxford: Oxford University Press, 2010).

49. Penn noted the "improved" character of the Earl of Cork's "great seat" in his "Irish Journal": see Nicholas Canny, "The Irish Background to Penn's Experiment," in *World of William Penn*, ed. Dunn and Dunn, 139–156 (quotation 139); also, on the process of ideological transfer more generally, Canny's "The Ideology of English Colonization: From Ireland to America," *William and Mary Quarterly* 30, no. 4 (1973): 575–598.

50. Black, *Blathwayt Atlas*, 2:11.

51. Letter from William Penn to James Harrison, August 25, 1681, in Soderlund, *Founding*, 77. *Some Account*, 5.

52. Sugrue, "Peopling and Depeopling of Early Pennsylvania."

53. Roeber wrote that the "simple braided-wreath border around the title and lack of an elaborate cartouche suggest a map made quickly and without additional artistic flair" ("Building and Planting," 151–152). For laurel wreaths, see the maps of Jamaica in *The Laws of Jamaica* (London: Charles Harper, 1683) and the second edition of 1684.

54. Letter from Sir John Werden to William Blathwayt, June 23, 1680, in Soderlund, *Founding*, 26.

55. Letter from Lord Baltimore to William Markham, June 5, 1682, in Soderlund, *Founding*, 154.

56. D. H. Landis, "The Location of Susquehannock Fort," in *Papers Read Before the Lancaster Country Historical Society* 14, no. 3 (1910): 81.

57. Antoinette Sutto, "The Borders of Absolutism: William Penn, Charles Calvert, and the Limits of Royal Authority, 1680–1685," *Pennsylvania History* 76, no. 3 (2009): 276–300.

58. Sutto, "Borders of Absolutism," esp. 285–292, 296.

59. Sutto, "Borders of Absolutism," 295.

60. Roeber, "Building and Planting," 22.

61. Soderlund, *Founding*, 153.

62. Letter from Penn to the Committee of Trade, August 14, 1683, in Soderlund, *Founding*, 301.

63. As suggested by Harold Cramer in "Placing Pennsylvania on the Map: The First Steps," accessed August 20, 2017, http://www.mapsofpa.com/article1.htm.

64. For a critical assessment of Seller's contribution to map-making, see Coolie Verner, "John Seller and the Chart Trade in Seventeenth-Century England," in *The Compleat Plattmaker: Essays on Chart, Map, and Globe Making in England in the Seventeenth and Eighteenth Centuries*, ed. Norman J. W. Thrower (Berkeley: University of California Press, 1978), 127–157.

65. Letter from William Markham to Penn, March 27, 1684, in Soderlund, *Founding*, 364.

66. Letter from William Markham to Penn, March 27, 1684, 364.

67. Roeber, "Building and Planting," 55.

68. The instructions given to James Wasse are printed in Dunn and Dunn, *Papers of William Penn, Volume 1*, 410–418 (quotation 412).

69. On the Farrer map, see Black, *Blathwayt Atlas*, 2:141–144.

70. Thomas Herron argues for the omnipresence of the colonial in Spenser's literary project and compares his tree catalogue with Thomas Hariot's in his report on Virginia, in *Spenser's Irish Work: Poetry, Plantation and Colonial Reformation* (Aldershot, Hampshire: Ashgate, 2007). The tree catalogue's function in "tricking [the mind] out of recognition of what's going on" was discussed by Ellen Martin in "The Shady Trope in Spenser's Trees: Inside the Catalogues of the *Parliament of Fowls* and *Faerie Queene* I.i," paper presented at the Twenty-Eighth International Medieval Congress, May 1995.

71. Frederick B. Tolles, *Meeting House and Counting House: The Quaker Merchants of Colonial Philadelphia, 1682–1763* (Chapel Hill: University of North Carolina Press, 1948), 4.

72. On providence and Pennsylvania, see J. William Frost, "William Penn's Experiment in the Wilderness: Promise and Legend," *PMHB* 107, no. 4 (1983): 577–605.

73. [Thomas Tryon], *The Planter's Speech to His Neighbours and Country-Men of Pennsylvania, East and West-Jersey* (London: Andrew Sowle, 1684), 6. The description of Tryon is Peter Brock's in *Pioneers of a Peaceable Kingdom: The Quaker Peace Testimony from the Colonial Era to the First World War* (Princeton: Princeton University Press, 1968), 64n3.

74. Letter from Penn to Robert Turner, March 5, 1681, in Soderlund, *Founding*, 54–55 (55). [Tryon], *Planter's Speech*, 5.

75. On books and seeds carried to Pennsylvania, see Cummings, "Goods at Pennsbury Manor, 1687." On the Quaker ideal, Erin A. Bell, "From Ploughing the Wilderness to Hedging the Vineyard: Meanings and Uses of Husbandry among Quakers, c.1650–c.1860," *Quaker Studies* 10, no. 2 (2006): 135–159.

76. John Worlidge, *Systema Agriculturae: The Mystery of Husbandry Discovered* (London: Printed by T. Johnson for Samuel Speed, 1669). Moses Cook, *The Manner of Raising, Ordering, and Improving Forrest-Trees* (London: Printed for Peter Parker, 1676). Cummings, "Goods at Pennsbury Manor, 1687," 407.

77. Hakluyt cited by Eric Rutkow in *American Canopy: Trees, Forests, and the Making of a Nation* (New York: Scribner, 2012), 13.

78. Hakluyt cited by Eric Rutkow in *American Canopy*, 13.

79. Ford noted the attention given to trees in the successive written accounts ("First Map," 177n1). On the presents, see Markham's letter to Penn in Soderlund, *Founding*, 362–367 (365, 367n15).

80. Rutkow, *Canopy*, 22. Roeber discusses the importance of fish (especially sturgeon) as a resource in "Building and Planting."

81. Joan Thirsk, "Agricultural Conditions in England, circa 1680," in *World of William Penn*, ed. Dunn and Dunn, 87–97 (87, 95).

82. *Some Account*, 5–6.

83. Hakluyt cited by Rutkow, *Canopy*, 15.

84. John Evelyn, *Sylva, or A Discourse of Forest-Trees and the Propagation of Timber in his Majesties Dominions* (London: Printed by John Martin and James Allestry, 1664). The queries are transcribed as Appendix I in Beryl Hartley, "Exploring and Communicating Knowledge of Trees in the Early Royal Society," *Notes and Records of the Royal Society* 64 (2010), 229–250 (245).

85. Lindsay Sharp, "Timber, Science and Economic Reform in the Seventeenth Century," *Forestry* 48 (1975): 51–86 (65). On the enduring influence of Evelyn's *Sylva*, and the earlier influences on his work, see Felicity Stout, "Before Evelyn: Trees, Tree Planting and Tree Management in Sixteenth- and Early Seventeenth-Century England," *Arboricultural Journal* 37, no. 3 (2015): 150–165.

86. Evelyn, *Sylva*, A3^{v}. B1^{r}.

87. Debates over the extent and depth of the energy crisis are summarized by Stout in "Before Evelyn," 154–155. See also Brinley Thomas, "Was There an Energy Crisis in Britain in the Seventeenth Century?" *Explorations in Economic History* 23 (1986): 124–152.

88. Gregory Allen Barton, *Empire Forestry and the Origins of Environmentalism* (Cambridge: Cambridge University Press, 2002), 12.

89. On English timber and charcoal prices in the first half of the seventeenth century, see Thomas, "Energy Crisis," 127.

90. Pepys, September 28, 1666, cited by Gillian Darley in *John Evelyn: Living for Ingenuity* (New Haven and London: Yale University Press, 2006), 224.

91. Thomas, "Energy Crisis," 135.

92. Richard Ligon, *A True and Exact History of the Island of Barbados* (London: Printed for Humphrey Moseley, 1657), 24. I am grateful to Ryan McGuinness for sharing with me his thesis, "'They can now digest strong meats': Two Decades of Expansion, Adaptation, Innovation, and Maturation on Barbados, 1680–1700" (PhD diss., University of Edinburgh, 2017) and his draft essay on fuelwood in Barbados in the period.

93. Barbados planter Nicholas Blake noted the use of coal for boiling sugar in a letter to the king, February 28, 1669, NAK, CO 1/67.

94. "Matter of Fact of Injuries Received Since ye Peace with Attested Probacions of Them," British Library, Egerton MS 2395, 509^{r}.

95. Philip Warner, "Account of the Caribbee Islands, America and West Indies: April 1676," *CSPC*, accessed August 20, 2017, http://www.british-history.ac.uk/cal-state-papers/colonial/america-westindies/vol9/pp365-388.

96. Bernard Bailyn, *The New England Merchants in the Seventeenth Century* (Cambridge, MA: Harvard University Press, 1955; repr. 1979), 139.

97. Susan Q. Stranahan, *Susquehanna, River of Dreams* (Baltimore, MD: Johns Hopkins University Press, 1993), 78n4. *The Diary of John Evelyn, Volume 3: Kalendarium,1650–1672*, ed. E. S. de Beer (Oxford: Oxford University Press, 1955; Oxford Scholarly Editions Online, 2012), accessed August 20, 2017, 10.1093/actrade/9780198187509.book.1.

98. *Diary of John Evelyn, Volume 3*.

99. Royal commissioners cited by Stephen Saunders Webb, *1676: The End of American Independence* (New York: Knopf, 1984; Syracuse University Press, 1995), 10.

100. On Houghton's agenda, see William M. Cavert, *The Smoke of London: Energy and Environment in the Early Modern City* (Cambridge: Cambridge University Press, 2016), 20n10, and chapter 8.

101. Evelyn, *Sylva*, 111–120.

102. Evelyn, *Sylva*, 1. See n25. Penn's broad and long-running concern about the supply of timber for shipbuilding is reflected in his offer to the navy, in the mid-1690s, of 500 trees from his Warminghurst estate, "which he offers for the Service": letter from Penn to the Navy Board, March 10, 1695, NAK, ADM 106/474/239.

103. Evelyn, *Sylva*, 15, 23, 53, 54.

104. Item 18 in "Certain Conditions or Concessions," printed in Soderlund, *Founding*, 72–76 (74).

105. Thomas, "Energy Crisis," 124–125.

106. T. C. Barnard, "Sir William Petty as Kerry Ironmaster," *Proceedings of the Royal Irish Academy* 82C (1982): 1–32.

107. Marion Balderston, "The Mystery of William Penn, the Royal Society, and the First Map of Pennsylvania," *Quaker History* 55, no. 2 (1966): 79–87 (80).

108. Petty and Penn may have been aware of this document (among the Strafford Papers in Sheffield Archives), which compares the relative costs of timber and iron production on Thomas Wentworth's estates in England and Ireland: see Nicholas Canny, *Making Ireland British, 1580–1650* (Oxford: Oxford University Press, 2001), 282, 399–401.

109. Arthur Cecil Bining, *Pennsylvania Iron Manufacture in the Eighteenth Century*, 2nd ed. (Harrisburg, PA: Pennsylvania Historical Museum Commission, 1973), 14.

110. Evelyn, *Sylva*, 109.

111. Evelyn, *Sylva*, 114.

112. Evelyn, *Sylva*, 114.

113. Roger Coke, *A Discourse on Trade* (London, 1670). William Petyt, *Britainnia Languens, or a Discourse on Trade* (London, 1680).

114. Evelyn, *Sylva*, 6.

115. Beale cited by Paul Slack, *The Invention of Improvement: Information and Material Progress in Seventeenth-Century England* (Oxford: Oxford University Press, 2015), 161.

116. Jon L. Wakelyn, ed., *America's Founding Charters: Primary Documents of Colonial and Revolutionary Era Governance*, 3 vols. (Santa Barbara, CA: Greenwood, 2006), 1:249–250.

117. James O'Neil Spady reconsiders the story of Pennsylvania's benevolent origins in "Colonialism and the Discursive Antecedents of Penn's Treaty with the Indians," in *Friends and Enemies in Penn's Woods: Indians, Colonists, and the Racial Construction of Pennsylvania*, ed. William A. Pencak and Daniel K. Richter (University Park: Penn State University Press, 2004), 18–40.

PART II

Irish Worlds

CHAPTER 4

William Penn, William Petty, and Surveying

THE IRISH CONNECTION

Marcus Gallo

During the seventeenth century, English imperialists embraced the technology of geometric surveying that intellectuals had begun to popularize during the sixteenth century. This new style of surveying, with its emphasis on quantitative measurement, differed from medieval surveys that focused on enumerating tenants' traditional rights and assessing land with qualitative descriptions. While geometric surveys could help lords modernize their estate management, overseas conquests provided the fullest demonstration of how surveyors could empower both private speculators and the state. As the land market developed throughout the spreading English empire, surveyors embraced a new mathematical and geographical literacy.[1]

Although he was only a child during the conquest of Ireland, William Penn numbered among the prominent men whose Irish experience convinced him of the usefulness of geometric surveys. During the 1650s, technocratic surveying experienced a turning point with the Down Survey in Ireland, which measured Irish lands and apportioned them into English hands. Successful surveying on that island convinced English elites to export surveying to North America, along with the conceptions of private property that surveying enabled. Penn's familiarity with the effects of surveying on his family's estates deeply influenced his plans for the settlement of Pennsylvania.[2]

English and Irish history had intertwined for centuries prior to Cromwell's decisive colonization in the seventeenth century. Normans first invaded Ireland in 1169, and "Old English" Norman lords soon controlled the Pale around Dublin with virtual autonomy. The Old English mixed with Gaelic elites and formed a hybrid society that became almost totally isolated from England. In the early sixteenth century, the English returned to conquer Ireland once again. Faced with staunch resistance, English elites established lordship over Irish subjects through military campaigns and institutionalized terror, such as the atrocities in Munster in 1569, when Sir Humphrey Gilbert decapitated each day's Irish casualties and decorated his camp with the heads. This reconquest took a century, culminating in 1659 with the Down Survey and the attendant redistribution of Irish lands among English landlords. English efforts took place on a huge scale, with large invasion forces followed by hundreds of thousands of immigrating settlers in the mid-seventeenth century.[3]

The crown employed the lure of Irish lands to finance its military campaigns. Beginning in 1565, Elizabeth authorized entrepreneurial younger sons of the gentry to form joint-stock companies to pacify specific groups of Irish "rebels" and take their lands. Many of the English conquerors came from the West Country around Devon, and some, like Gilbert and Richard Grenville, later became influential in American colonization projects. In another example, Ralph Lane left Ireland after a short stint to oversee the colony at Roanoke in 1585 and 1586. After Roanoke failed, Lane returned to Ireland for more than a decade, overseeing combat forces and establishing a plantation. The earliest attempts at English colonization often ended in military disaster on both sides of the Atlantic, but this did not stop continued invasions, and Ireland became an early model for franchising empire across the sea.[4]

The English justified their invasions in two ways: by claiming ancient Norman titles to Irish lands and by asserting that the culturally inferior Irish needed English civilization. Norman titles provided a legal right, but the cultural argument satisfied those Englishmen more deeply troubled about the ethics of conquering the Irish. Although in theory the English had reigned over parts of Ireland for four centuries, the "New" English had practically no contact with the Irish prior to their invasions. The foreignness of Gaelic Irish culture allayed English qualms. Had the Irish simply been Catholic, this alone might have justified would-be cultural imperialists. Worse than encountering Catholics, the English discovered a nation of ignorant priests and ruined churches, where unfamiliar pagan practices tinged Christian rites. English theorists like Sir John Davies claimed that the English would civilize Ireland, just as the Romans had civilized ancient Britain and the Spaniards had brought civilization to the Americas.[5]

Among Irish incivilities, perhaps the most heinous was improper land use. While the invading English had begun enclosing their commons, many Irish clung to an antiquated form of pastoral agriculture, allowing their herds to meander between open meadows. This especially held true in the upland regions dominated by the Gaelic Irish, where a lack of arable land prevented intensive agriculture, and low population densities allowed high geographic mobility. Combined with the fact that families and clans, rather than individuals, held property, the Irish tended not to invest in improvements to their buildings and lands to the extent that the English did.[6]

In the late sixteenth century, the English colonist Thomas Smith compared the Irish to roving herdsmen like Tartars or Arabs. Edmund Spenser felt that the nomadic Irish must have been the barbaric descendants of nomadic Scythians. As late as 1655, Richard Lawrence, an English planter living in Ireland, wrote that the Irish had created a "waste Wilderness" with their lands. During the 1590s another English philosopher of colonization, William Herbert, wrote that, "Colonies degenerate assuredly when the colonists imitate and embrace the habits, customs, and practices of the natives. . . . Once you have removed those things which can alienate hearts and minds, they will both become united, first in habits, then in mind." Breaking Irish control over Ireland entailed breaking Irish culture, and that meant disrupting Irish land-use practices. Otherwise, in Herbert's view, the conquerors themselves would degenerate into barbarians, just as the Old English had assimilated into barbarous Irishness.[7]

In 1641, a revolt in Ulster by Catholic landholders prompted the final military stage of Ireland's conquest. Taken by surprise and horrified by the flight of several thousand Protestant settlers, the English hung suspected rebels without trials, specifically targeting women and other civilians. English ferocity cowed the initial rebellion but also caused many of the formerly placid Catholic inhabitants to join the revolt, including many of the Old English.[8]

Although few Protestants died in the early days of the revolt, the death toll from the unrest eventually rose to ten thousand people, evenly split between both sides. Despite the relative bloodlessness of the initial uprising, the memory of Catholic Irish atrocities motivated English actions for the next decade. In 1650, Oliver Cromwell referred to the Irish actions in the "Massacre of 1641" as "unprovoked . . . the most unheard of and most barbarous massacre (without respect of sex and age) that ever the sun beheld." Irish rejection of the obvious material benefits of English rule particularly galled Cromwell. He pointed out that the Irish rebelled even though, "through the example of English industry, through commerce and traffic, that which was in the natives' hands was better to them than if all Ireland had been in their possession, and not an Englishman in it."[9]

Meanwhile, in 1642, tensions heightened between the Crown and Parliament, giving rise to the first English Civil War. In response to the ongoing troubles in Ireland, a distracted Parliament returned to earlier models of colonization by passing the Adventurer's Act, which would grant land to participating "adventurers" in return for their financial investment in the reconquest, at the rate of one shilling per acre. This amounted to a huge discount on Irish land, which typically sold for six to twelve times that amount. In 1643, adventurers could double the amount of land they received by giving an additional quarter of the money they had originally advanced. Nonetheless, by the end of the war, adventurers had only covered the costs of about a tenth of the subjugation effort.[10]

Following the Doubling Ordinance, the opposing forces conducted a truce. Charles I installed a royalist governor who transferred many of his soldiers from Ireland to England to fight the parliamentarian forces. Hostilities flared seriously in 1647, following the king's initial defeat. With Parliament now in control in Dublin, English commanders conducted pitiless attacks against the rebels, including the massacre of between three and five thousand fleeing soldiers and prisoners at Dungan's Hill in August 1647.[11]

Due to the onset of the second English Civil War, parliamentary forces in Ireland became temporarily isolated, causing them to sue for a truce with the Irish in 1649. Despite the execution of the king in January 1649, the royalists remained well organized in Ireland, causing Oliver Cromwell to bring his twelve-thousand-man New Model Army across the Irish Sea that August. Fearing that Irish Catholic soldiers could be used to advance the royalist cause, Cromwell struck quickly, massacring three thousand Irish soldiers and inhabitants at the Siege of Drogheda in September 1649, and another two thousand at Wexford in October.[12]

The bloody displays at Drogheda and Wexford encouraged a variety of other Irish forces to surrender without a fight. By May 1650, when Cromwell left Ireland to turn his attention to Scotland, almost all the principal towns of Ulster, Leinster, and Munster lay in English hands. Over the next few years, fighting in Ireland entered a new phase as royalist and Irish armies lost control of their last urban strongholds. Ireland became the site of an extended counterinsurgency operation against guerrilla units led by Catholic aristocrats. The English divided the countryside into "protected" and "outlawed" zones: in outlawed regions, the army could kill people and cattle, destroy buildings, and set fire to crops without cause.[13]

Exacerbating an already dire situation, in 1649 Atlantic shipping brought the bubonic plague to Galway in the western, heavily Catholic region of Connacht. While English scorched-earth tactics helped produce famine, military movements and forced migrations helped spread this devastating epidemic around the island. Taken as a whole, disease and starvation combined with military and civilian casualties to kill perhaps as much as 25 percent of Ireland's population of almost two million. By the 1650s, following massacres, reprisals, total warfare, and mass death, the English felt little empathy for their Irish subjects. To bring security and English civilization to the island and to pay for the subjugation effort, the conquerors now looked to engage in an unprecedented bureaucratic effort to redistribute Irish property to Protestants. In total, more than thirty thousand soldiers and 1,500 adventurers would gain access to approximately eleven million acres of land.[14]

The effort to survey Ireland began long before the 1641 rebellion. In 1537, Henry VIII asked for descriptive surveys of royal lands around Dublin, with an eye toward increasing rents. By the 1540s, English officials pressed for a variety of surveys and military maps. Edward VI installed Ireland's first surveyor general to oversee crown lands in 1548. Beginning in the 1560s, English cartographers leveraged increasingly accurate surveys to produce detailed maps of contested portions of Ireland. Immediately before the rebellion, between 1633 and 1636, the English conducted the Strafford Survey in Connacht in anticipation of further colonization. This survey took the form of an index of place names and landowners, with descriptions of the soil, its inhabitants and buildings. At the time, Ireland had not been comprehensively surveyed, and the Strafford surveyors made no attempt to measure the land or assess the value of its acreage.[15]

By the mid-1650s, the English government had an annual deficit of £450,000 due to its operations in Ireland. Because the English intended to pay their soldiers and adventurers with Irish land, delay in distributing those lands created additional debts. Facing these budgetary constraints, parliament passed an act to conduct a comprehensive survey of the island's forfeited lands in 1653. As a result, Ireland's surveyor general, Benjamin Worsley, began to conduct what became known as the Gross Survey. Prospective English landholders paid one pound for every five hundred acres of land to be measured and mapped. The Gross Surveyors conducted their work quickly, estimating lands rather than carefully measuring and evaluating them. Soldiers objected to this shoddy work, which halted in the fall of 1654.[16]

As a result, in 1654 civil administrators began to conduct the Civil Survey in counties that had not already been examined by the earlier Strafford Survey. In contrast to the Strafford Survey, the Civil Survey noted landowners along with their acreage, distinguishing between profitable and unprofitable acres. The Civil Survey used interviews with Irish locals to develop a comprehensive account of the lands in most of the island, but it created no maps. This approach harkened back to medieval methods, failing to provide the English authorities with workable documents for the military control and redistribution of the land.[17]

In December 1654, Dr. William Petty took charge of a renewed surveying effort that became known as the Down Survey. Dismissing prior surveys as expensive and poorly organized, he pointed out that surveyors who had actually measured land with care received less money than those who worked quickly and inaccurately. As a consequence, surveyors had relied too much on estimation and local Irish accounts. Petty's more systematic Irish surveys became a catalyst for legitimizing land seizures and reallocations.[18]

To remedy the failures of the initial surveys, he broke the process of surveying into its constituent parts, farming out specialties to English soldiers in assembly-line fashion: fieldwork, protracting, calculating, converting measurements, drawing maps, describing surveys in writing, and oversight. Working together, the soldiers calculated acreage from scale measurements made on paper. Petty standardized field books and issued a standard set of tools and instructions for conducting surveys. His men made qualitative judgments, defining profitable lands as "meadow, arable, [or] pasture" and dividing pasture lands into a variety of categories: "common pasture, healthy pasture, rocky pastures, mountaine pasture, or boggy pasture." In all, he organized around a thousand soldiers to not only measure the land but also evaluate its quality and assign it a monetary value. These men endured imperfect working conditions, including unclear boundaries between lordships, tiny fields that necessitated careful individual surveys, inadequate descriptions of the lands to be surveyed, and fellow surveyors who pawned their instruments. Cutting across the boundaries of existing domains, the Down Survey created many new landholdings and erased old property rights in the process. As a result, the outright hostility of the native Irish necessitated that a constant military guard accompanied the surveyors. Despite this, in County Wicklow, eight of Petty's surveyors died at the hands of Irish rebels. This violence foreshadowed the later struggles of North American surveyors who often found themselves in the cross fire between legal proprietors, squatters, and Indians.[19]

Because the crown intended to redistribute land for the benefit of the empire, the Down surveyors paid greater attention to some lands than others. The English did not reallocate lands controlled by Protestants, so those estates did not receive surveys. Similarly, surveyors lacked interest in surveying marginal lands; Petty received £7.3.4 for every thousand acres of profitable land, and only £3.0.0 for every thousand acres of unprofitable or undistributable land. This discrepancy in pay led the disgruntled to charge that surveyors had corruptly claimed marginal lands as profitable, causing soldiers to receive land bounties of lesser value.[20]

Although the Down Survey intended to demystify the question of landholding in Ireland, drawing precise boundaries often had the opposite effect. Squabbles over the survey occupied much of Petty's time, and the process of land settlement dragged on slowly, despite the speed with which Petty executed the survey. Because surveying remapped economic value onto real estate, many owners felt that the surveying process had improperly evaluated their land. In addition to recipients of "profitable" lands maintaining that they had in fact received marginal lands, those who had financed their own military campaigns, the "adventurers," relied on earlier surveys that underestimated the size of Irish lands. They used these false estimates to claim that they should receive a proportionally larger section of land, now that Ireland proved bigger than previously imagined. Ireland's surveyor general, Benjamin Worsley, accused Petty of using his influence to assist his friends. Although governmental commissions later exonerated Petty of wrongdoing, these legal entanglements prevented the swift and regular settlement that the English meant for surveying to effect. Whether in Ireland or later in North America, the process of land settlement became messy, especially when powerful interests contested the same plots of land. As legal documents, surveys became another tool that allowed contesting parties to prolong court cases about land disputes.[21]

Between 1654 and 1659, the Down Survey had assessed and mapped virtually the whole of Ireland—an unprecedented feat in European history. English elites acquired huge amounts of Irish land, both because the Down Survey turned up more profitable land than expected and because many adventurers and common soldiers sold their shares in Irish land cheaply to officers. Nonetheless, agents for the adventurers and officers demanded more land for payment than the government could supply, resulting in the displacement of many "innocent" Catholic Irish lords (who had not resisted English invasion) farther and farther west. Most eventually settled in the counties of Connacht.[22]

With the return of the English monarchy in 1660, shortly after the Down Survey concluded, thousands of adventurers and soldiers who had allied with the republican government found it difficult to apply to the crown to confirm their claims of Irish land. Nevertheless, the survey resulted in the transfer of most of the lands in Ireland into Protestant hands. Protestants held less than one-fifth of Irish land in 1600, but more than half of that land in 1641, and more than 85 percent in 1700. As these numbers indicate, the English never confiscated the entirety of Ireland. Instead, they intended for soldiers to take up land in contiguous townships and dominate neighboring Catholics. Ultimately, this plan did not come to fruition, as some Catholic lords returned to their home provinces after years of western exile. Regardless of who ruled the great estates, Catholic tenants remained the backbone of the economy and a heavy majority of the population.[23]

Despite English misgivings about Irish barbarity, the island's people had long engaged in market agriculture. In the centuries leading up to the Cromwellian conquest, Gaelic elites operated market towns, and the Old English oversaw the regular trade of raw materials from Irish farms to other western European countries. However, the transfer of Catholic land to the English accelerated the rise of export-based agriculture in Ireland. English lords desired pasturelands that would turn the island into a center for the production of leather goods. To create these pastures, and also to ensure lines of sight for defense, the English cleared the island of trees, financing a lumber industry that deforested much of Ireland in the forty years from 1590 to 1630. From 1530 to 1730, the acreage used for agriculture increased by almost 20 percent. The "Big House," the landlord's home, walled and hedged off from his tenants, became the central building from which planters and overseers directed their Irish tenants' farming activity. In addition, the English promoted the use of planned, rectilinear market towns not just as hubs for plantation agriculture but also as centers of military and judicial activity. The turn toward market agriculture accelerated throughout Ireland after the Cromwellian settlement during the 1650s, even affecting the western province of Connacht, where the English had the least penetration.[24]

William Penn's family benefited directly from the Cromwellian settlement of Ireland. In 1654 his father, Admiral William Penn, received estates worth £300 in rent per year "in consideration of the great losses sustained by General Pen and his wife by the rebellion in Ireland." The family took up land in Macroom in County Cork and bought nearby lands in Kilcrea. In 1655, Admiral Penn commanded the naval invasion of the Spanish West Indies. The expedition failed, resulting in Cromwell imprisoning the admiral in the Tower of London. After his release later that year, he moved his family to Macroom. It was there that a young William Penn first encountered Quakers.[25]

Following the Restoration and Charles II's ascent to the throne, Ireland's titles fell into disorder as the king sought to restore land to royalist favorites. These realignments affected the Penn family, despite the admiral's support for the royalists. His lands in Macroom and Kilcrea had originally belonged to the aristocratic MacCarthy dynasty of Muskerry. In 1658, Charles II had already granted the lord of Muskerry the title of the earl of Clancarty. After regaining the throne, he took the Penn family's lands to restore them to their original Irish owners. Between 1665 and 1667, the admiral sent his son William, then in his early twenties, to advocate on the family's behalf for compensation. As a result, the crown's Court of Claims awarded the Penns a series of estates near County Cork's coastline. By 1670, Admiral Penn held sixty-eight separate holdings in three baronies, approximately 12,000 acres in all.[26]

During the trip to Ireland in the mid-1660s, William Penn became committed to Quakerism, which resulted in his own imprisonment in the Tower of London. Upon his release in 1669, his father dispatched him to Ireland again, to manage the family estates there until the admiral's health began to fail in 1670. While Penn spent most of his time in Ireland visiting with the members of high society and his fellow Quakers, his principal business on the island was to put his family's finances on a firm footing. This meant bargaining with the locals who would rent out the family estates and overseeing disputes about the particulars of the tracts of land. Penn recorded making six separate new surveys, and he checked his findings against the Civil Survey records and official maps. To aid his understanding, Penn commissioned maps for his estates. This process became complicated by the patchwork nature of official surveys: at Geiragh and Knocknacaple, he held lands for which no surveys had been made, because Protestants had previously held them. His mapmaker assumed the official outline and acreage of those holdings by comparing them to records he had already made of neighboring lands. As a whole, the Penn family estate brought in approximately £1,100 in yearly revenue at this time, about one-tenth of which went to the crown as quitrents.[27]

Penn's attitude toward his family's lands and their inhabitants was typically English. When visiting Captain Boles, one of his father's tenants in Shanagarry, Penn commented only that the land was "well Improv'd." On the way, he traveled by "a road well Improv'd & much English." When assessing the rent for other sets of lands, he debated the worth of a windmill or included the "Considerable Improvements" on the land in the price. However, Penn "showed very little interest in the oppressed native population" of Ireland during his visits, as the editors of *The Papers of William Penn* point out. As noted by Hiram Morgan, Penn's mentions of Irish locals were perfunctory and unkind: "They are rarely surnamed, let alone first-named and they are the subject of passing derogatory remarks about their barbarous, superstitious customs." For example, Penn dismissed a local burial as "Barberous like the heathen."[28]

While in Ireland, Penn became friends with William Petty. Penn was a guest in Petty's home in 1667 and visited with him more than once during his later trip to Ireland. It is reasonable to assume that Penn examined Down Survey maps, and possibly other records related to his estates, while at Petty's home. In 1675, Petty appealed to Penn to ask for a reduction in the quitrents that he needed to pay for his extensive Irish lands. Pressed with his own difficulties in paying quitrents, Penn lobbied successfully on Petty's behalf. Penn felt warmth toward Petty: in his letter describing these lobbying activities, he wrote, "I will run, goe, or doe ten times more for thee at any time."[29]

Penn's experience in Ireland helped cement his conception of how a state could properly direct landownership for the benefit of the landholding class. Surveys in Ireland had made land fungible: lands need not hold their traditional values and confusing medieval land tenures if they could instead be measured for acreage and evaluated for quality. New lords like the Penns could substitute holdings in Macroom with holdings elsewhere in Cork, without much material loss. In addition, surveys effectively eliminated the rights of traditional occupants while bolstering the rights of titleholders. All the while, surveys and maps made bewildering tangles of landholdings comprehensible and tangible for nonresident landowners and potential purchasers. If anything, Ireland's surveys were not comprehensive enough: Penn found it inconvenient that the hodgepodge of Irish surveys had failed to measure and map Protestant lands, which made it necessary for him to conduct resurveys.[30]

Over time, in the reign of Charles II, and especially in the reign of James II (from 1685 to 1688), Protestant landholders in Ireland felt less secure. Charles II had many supporters among Catholics, and James II openly supported Catholics. The government's support for old Irish titleholders soon became apparent, causing Protestants' land values to drop. As early as 1671, Petty began to write about the possibility of transplanting Irish Catholics into England and more Protestants into Ireland. His argument was social and economic: socially, Catholics would be less of a threat as minorities in England (or would strengthen Catholic interests there, a spin he put on his position once James II took power). Economically, with the Irish mostly gone, Ireland's countryside could be put to the best possible use. In Petty's view, the island could be turned into a cattle ranch.[31]

As Ireland became increasingly problematic, America began to hold increasing allure as a region where scientific management could yield profits for English landholders and the empire as a whole. By 1680, William Penn already had experience with Quaker settlements in West Jersey. He petitioned Charles II for a province, hoping that he could both create a zone of religious freedom and permanently improve his financial situation: over the course of the 1670s, he had already amassed approximately £10,000 of debt from lavish spending. Because of Penn's personal relations with members of the court, the crown likely granted the province as a personal favor and also as a cheap way to repay a debt to his father, Admiral Penn, who had spent £11,000 supplying the government with provisions in Ireland. By 1680, the interest on this debt amounted to £16,000.[32]

Pennsylvania provided an opportunity for surveying to place new values on previously untapped lands on a grand scale, and both Penn and Petty found the prospect exciting. The two friends corresponded regularly, and Petty acquired one of the first maps of Pennsylvania made after Penn acquired his proprietorship of the colony. Petty was one of the first investors to buy a five-thousand-acre plot, but did not settle his land before his death in 1687. Penn also arranged for Petty's wife Elizabeth to receive twenty thousand acres in combination with one of her relatives, but they eventually backed out of the deal and Penn found other purchasers.[33]

Although Petty never settled his land, he ruminated on various schemes for how a large landholder could make money in Pennsylvania. He speculated that five thousand acres of land would need two hundred families (one thousand people) to make it productive. If they cleared all of the land quickly over the winter, one thousand acres could be left for planting, and four thousand acres for cattle. Paying for the passage of the people, cattle, food, and materials needed would amount to a cost of £30,100. Petty estimated that the returns on the rent would amount to £5,300 per year, so that a developer could expect to break even after seven years. Later, in 1686, Petty wrote up a proposal for Penn to grant him a region of bottomland laying along 12 miles of riverfront, and stretching back into the countryside for 6.5 miles. In return for this tract of fifty thousand acres, Petty would pay a yearly rent of one one-hundredth of all of the crops and animals produced on the land. Nothing ever came of this proposal.[34]

Petty also wrote up a series of questions about Pennsylvania's native inhabitants, trying to imagine how they might be put to profitable use in the English empire. He wanted to learn demographic information, including age distributions, rates of stillbirth, and the length of time it took mothers to wean. He also inquired about the Indians' physiques, facial features, language, religion, laws, economy, and capacity to wage war, among other subjects. His final sentences addressed questions truly critical to Penn's colony: "What is their manner and rate of selling Lands to the English?" and "Is there much Lying and Fraude amongst them?"[35]

In addition to the questions about Native Americans, Petty wrote a document entitled "General Cautions Concerning Pennsylvania," which he likely intended for Penn's benefit. Some of Petty's advice was not particularly practical; for example, he suggested that the general population should pay to raise all the children collectively, that a single sermon should be preached in all congregations, and that "matters of fact which cannot bee decided, bee left to Lott." On the other hand, Petty also wanted registries set up for all contracts, and exact accounts made of arrivals, births, and deaths. Men should not study the classics, but "arithmetic & measuring & drawing." Unemployment should be avoided in a colony with such a low population density, so criminals should be punished with whippings, not imprisonment. Similarly, debtors should forfeit their land and improvements, without facing prison time. He also believed that Pennsylvania should "admit the Native Women into freedome," presumably to add to the colony's population. Petty generously estimated the colony to contain nearly fifty million acres—by charging rent of one half-penny per year, Penn could eventually make the princely sum of £100,000 annually.[36]

Perhaps most importantly, Petty cautioned his friend to "Avoyd Stragling plantations." In America's southern colonies, no townships were surveyed prior to settlement, so the first colonists in a region chose where to purchase their own lands. This practice, known as indiscriminate location, often resulted in irregularly shaped tracts of land, where individual farms might monopolize desirable bottomlands while leaving less desirable uplands unpurchased. If Penn followed the southern model and allowed his purchasers to have plantations that straggled into the backcountry, his revenue would suffer in the unwanted gaps between settlements. Following a clear township system would also allow him to plan for urban centers, which could increase the desirability of his lands and lead to more income. Because English theorists typically justified their presence as colonizers by their proper use and improvement of the natural landscape, Petty's opinions in this regard were both practical and ideological.[37]

While Penn did not embrace all of the particulars of Petty's plans, he did see the obvious benefits of maintaining control over land distribution in his colony. From its founding, Pennsylvania continuously maintained the office of surveyor general, whose responsibilities included managing deputy surveyors and reviewing the legality of their returns of survey for the Land Office. This highly centralized surveying structure contrasted with the decentralized surveying regime in other American colonies founded before the Down Survey, such as Virginia. Surveys would help Penn market his territory to potential buyers, keep track of purchases, and later guarantee future income in the form of quitrents. Maintaining a centralized depository for surveys connected to land sales would obviate the problems that Penn encountered trying to piece together a picture of his landholdings in Ireland.[38]

In a variety of ways, Penn based his initial vision for Pennsylvania on Irish precedents. In April 1681, he published *Some Account of the Province of Pennsylvania*, in which he described his plan to people his colony with buyers, renters, and servants. He intended to sell lands in five-thousand-acre blocks for £100, with a permanent quitrent of 5 shillings per year (renters and servants would receive higher yearly burdens). One-tenth of the land would be reserved permanently for his family's use. To encourage settlement, he would allow occupants the rights to the underground mineral wealth. Penn imagined that adventurers would form companies in his new endeavor, and that they could divvy up lands among themselves. He wrote, "if the persons concerned please, a tract of land shall be surveyed, say *fifty thousand acres to a hundred adventurers*, in which some of the best shall be set out for towns or cities . . . the remainder of the fifty thousand acres shall be shared among the said *adventurers* . . . The manner of the dividend I shall not be strict in." This vision harkened back to the conquest of Ireland, where "adventurers" risked their money and sought their repayment in widely separated plots of land.[39]

Even in his early descriptions of Philadelphia, Penn painted a vision of a town that resembled the rural countryside of Ireland more than an early modern city. Penn wanted a city of ten thousand acres, with hundred-acre lots for each five-thousand-acre share in his colony. Each lot would front the river for a distance of 825 feet. Penn wanted houses "in the middle of its plot as to the breadth of the way of it, that so there may be ground on each side for gardens or orchards or fields, that it may be a green country town, which will never be burnt and always be wholesome." The result of such a distribution would have dotted a sprawling, fifteen-square-mile tract with one hundred big houses on huge farm plots, creating a miniature version of Ireland's estates. Such a city truly could never catch on fire.[40]

Penn soon had to adapt his early plans to realities on the ground and the whims of his customers: in July 1681 he noted, "I cannot make money without special concessions." Unable to find enough purchasers of 5,000-acre tracts, Penn reduced the preferred size of his plots to 500 acres and began selling tracts as small as 125 acres. For a purchaser of large amounts of acreage, like the merchant Ralph Fretwell who bought 40,000 acres, Penn could discount his prices. Early purchasers would receive bonus lots in Philadelphia, which took on a new, less ambitious character. Since the site for his new colony rested on top of the earlier colony of New Sweden, whose inhabitants still farmed there, the original plan for a green country town could not be sustained. By the spring of 1682, Penn's agents could only acquire 300 acres of riverfront land for Philadelphia, and the scale of the city needed to be massively reduced.[41]

Because Pennsylvania was not empty, Penn had to negotiate with both Native American and European inhabitants in order to sell and settle his lands. His interest in and attitude toward Pennsylvania's native inhabitants bore little resemblance to his earlier lack of concern about the Irish. By August 1683, Penn had spent enough time with local Lenapes to answer many of Petty's questions about Native Americans in detail. He punctuated a discussion of their language, attitudes, religion, and customs with personal anecdotes—albeit without the statistical precision that Petty may have preferred. Although we have no direct evidence, it is possible that Petty's interest in Indian culture may have helped spark Penn's fascination. It is also possible that once Penn decided that it would be moral and expedient to purchase land from the Indians, he realized that he would need to understand them better. No such need arose in Ireland. With regard to land sales, Penn endeavored to treat the local Indians honestly, but he also warned his agents in 1681 that they must be vigilant when making purchases, because the Indians would "sell one another's [land] if you be not careful."[42]

From 1682 to 1684, Penn conferred regularly with the local Lenapes, paying £1,200 in goods for the lands surrounding the site of Philadelphia. The Lenapes balked at Penn's terms as they began to understand the massive scale of Penn's undertaking and the population density that would come with his new colony, but both sides avoided bloodshed. In 1686 in central Bucks County, the Lenapes threatened to kill surveyors making further measurements without payment in full from Penn. To defuse the situation, Pennsylvania officials wrote up a deed (but never paid for the land), leaving an opening for his descendants to conduct the infamous, fraudulent Walking Purchase of 1737. With regard to the European settlers, Penn's government initially incorporated the former Swedish settlers into the court system, but his agents also systematically pressured them to sell their lands. As time passed, their numbers paled in comparison to incoming settlers, and they lost what little political clout they had. By 1700, almost half had left the colony to settle in West Jersey. This exodus mirrored a similar development in the Indian community, where disease and outmigration left the population about a quarter of the size it had been when Penn began his negotiations.[43]

Another complication precluded the easy settlement of Pennsylvania. Penn wanted access to the whole of the Delaware River in order to control Philadelphia's route to the ocean. The title to this territory was disputed: Maryland had claimed and already settled some of the lower Delaware. The king's brother James, Duke of York, who had control over the land east of the Delaware, granted Penn what is now the state of Delaware, but his authority to do so was dubious. Furthermore, Penn believed that his charter for Pennsylvania took precedent over Maryland's northern border, which had been fixed at 40 degrees north latitude. Officials from the two colonies could not agree on a survey line, and when James became king in 1685, he ruled in Penn's favor. Much as had been the case with the allegations of corruption against Petty in Ireland, surveys alone could not solve political problems without consensus.[44]

The job of regulating and mapping Pensylvania's early settlements fell primarily to the surveyor general. Penn initially appointed his cousin, William Crispin, to fill this role. When Crispin died en route to Pennsylvania, Penn turned to the fifty-eight-year-old Thomas Holme as his first acting surveyor general. Like Penn, Holme was an English Quaker with deep ties to Ireland. As a young man, Holme had served as a captain in Cromwell's army, then transitioned to serving as a surveyor for the Civil and Down Surveys. Through payments for his national service and by speculating on the lands of other soldiers, he amassed an estate of more than four thousand acres in Wexford, Ireland. In the aftermath of Cromwell's military campaign, Holme joined the Society of Friends and soon became one of the most prominent organizers and writers on their behalf. His religious activities and proselytization caused him to be arrested numerous times and would have made him well known to Penn. They certainly would have met during the course of Penn's time in Ireland in 1669, when Thomas Loe converted Penn (and Penn spent extended time with William Petty). It is possible that they may have met as early as Penn's initial introduction to the Quaker religion during the mid-1650s, when Admiral Penn invited Loe along with other Quaker speakers to give a discourse on their religion in the Penns' home in Macroom. By 1677, Holme had moved to live in William Crispin's house in Waterford, Ireland, where he was operating as a merchant, shipping goods to America. Given his background, Holme became an obvious choice to replace Crispin. As a mark of Penn's faith in Holme's ability, he also made him an assistant to the deputy governor William Markham, another of Penn's cousins.[45]

Upon arrival, Holme had to evaluate the countryside and navigate the problem of land warrants being issued to different purchasers on a single plot of land. Because of the small size of Philadelphia, purchasers would only receive less than an acre each inside the rectilinear city, with the remainder being given to them in the "liberty lands" outside Philadelphia. In time, Holme had established a series of townships that stretched into the countryside around the city. In Penn's view, townships should "lie square," with at least ten families living in five-thousand-acre blocks, keeping their homes in the middle of the township. While Penn was still in the colony, in August 1684, he counted at least fifty settled townships. Holme's 1687 map shows a series of more or less gridlike purchases that wend their way around the tributaries of the Delaware and the Schuylkill. The grid stopped abruptly in Bucks County, where the surveyors faced Indian opposition. As time went on, this scheme for orderly development slowly eroded. Pressure to expand into the backcountry caused this neat township system to languish, and Pennsylvania's interior increasingly resembled the "Stragling plantations" that Petty had warned against.[46]

Unlike many of his predecessors in English colonization, Penn harbored no illusions that his new colony would provide vast wealth from untapped mineral reserves or exotic farm products. Instead, Pennsylvania would be a site where Quakers and other Protestants could practice their religions in peace, while Penn profited from the land: a better version of Ireland. He summed up this sentiment neatly in July 1681: "Though I desire to extend religious freedom, yet I want some recompense for my trouble." Unfortunately, the colony never proved to be the financial boon that he imagined, and his finances remained precarious throughout his life, despite his collecting more than £9,000 from over 700,000 acres of land sales by 1685.[47]

Although his reach exceeded his grasp, Ireland's land distribution practices served as a model for William Penn. Given his life story, this should not be particularly surprising: Irish experiences were foundational to his identity. His path to religious conversion took place in Ireland, and Ireland was also where he began to make serious decisions about managing large estates. Penn adopted typically English attitudes about land use in his time as a lord, along with typically English attitudes about the Irish. Over time, his attitudes about people evolved, but his attitudes about land changed very little.

In 1662, when writing his treatise on taxes, William Petty had waxed rhapsodic about the prospects of the English taking control over Ireland when the country was "as a white paper." After conquering the island, surveying it, mapping it, and redistributing its lands, Ireland could reasonably appear like a white paper on which the English could write the future. One can imagine how Petty's vision could captivate an idealistic and ambitious William Penn. We cannot know for sure if Penn first glimpsed maps of the Down Survey in Petty's Irish home, but we can see the Down Survey's influence on the orderly grids stretching away from the Delaware Valley that Thomas Holme depicted on his 1687 map of Pennsylvania. Much as the Down Survey had helped turn Ireland into a "white paper," centrally organized geometric surveys allowed Penn to erase the traces of his province's previous inhabitants and make "wilderness" lands legible to educated nonlocals. Armed with maps and round numbers of acres, he could market his lands to prospective buyers in Europe and maintain control over how the colony would spread into the interior.[48]

NOTES

1. On medieval surveys and the development of geometric surveys, see E.G.R. Taylor, "The Surveyor," *Economic History Review*, 17, no. 2 (1947): 121–124; D. Chilton, "Land Measurement in the Sixteenth Century," *Excerpt Transactions of the Newcomen Society*, 31 (1957–58 and 1958–59): 112; Peter Barber, "Mapmaking in England, ca. 1470–1650," ed. David Woodward, *The History of Cartography: Cartography in the European Renaissance*, vol. 3, part 2 (Chicago, IL: University of Chicago Press, 2007), 1593–1594.

2. For an introduction to the impact of Irish colonization on Penn, see Nicholas Canny, "The Irish Background to Penn's Experiment," ed. Richard S. Dunn and Mary Maples Dunn, *The World of William Penn* (Philadelphia: University of Pennsylvania Press, 1986), 139–156. For the origins of the Down Survey and its effect on English rule in Ireland, see Patrick Carroll, *Science, Culture, and Modern State Formation* (Berkeley: University of California Press, 2006), especially 81–89, 100–106. On surveying in Pennsylvania, see J. Barry Love, *The Colonial Surveyor in Pennsylvania* (1970; repr., Harrisburg: Pennsylvania Society of Land Surveyors, 2000). For a discussion of how land surveying in Penn's colony compared to contemporary settler societies, see Marcus Gallo, "Land Surveying in Early Pennsylvania: A Case Study in a Global Context," *Journal of Early American History*, 6, no. 1 (May 2016): 9–39.

3. On English imperialism in Ireland, see J. C. Beckett, *The Anglo-Irish Tradition* (Ithaca, NY: Cornell University Press, 1976), 13–27; Nicholas P. Canny, "The Ideology of English Colonization: From Ireland to America," *William and Mary Quarterly* 3rd Ser., 30, no. 4 (October 1973): 575–598; Nicholas Canny, *From Reformation to Restoration: Ireland, 1534–1660* (Dublin, Ireland: Criterion Press Limited, 1987), 220. For estimates of British settlers in Ireland, see Wayland F. Dunaway, *The Scotch-Irish of Colonial Pennsylvania* (1944; repr., Baltimore: Genealogical Publishing, 1985), 20–25 and William J. Smyth, *Map-making, Landscapes and Memory: A Geography of Colonial and Early Modern Ireland, c. 1530–1750* (Notre Dame, IN: University of Notre Dame Press, 2006), 430–431 and 455–456 (for standing armies). Tensions between the Irish and the Old and New English around the Pale blurred into the Elizabethan invasions of Ireland: see R. H. Buchanan, "Towns and Plantations, 1500–1700," in William Nolan, ed., *The Shaping of Ireland: The Geographical Perspective* (Cork, Ireland: Mercier Press, 1986), 87, and Smyth, *Map-making, Landscapes and Memory* for differing periodizations for the beginning of the conflict.

4. Canny, "Ideology of English Colonization": 576–578. Audrey Horning, *Ireland in the Virginian Sea: Colonialism in the British Atlantic* (Chapel Hill: Omohundro Institute of Early American History and Culture by the University of North Carolina Press, 2013), 60–91. Lane also deployed symbolic decapitation as a terror tactic, first in the New World, then in Ireland.

5. John Patrick Montaño, *The Roots of English Colonialism in Ireland* (Cambridge: Cambridge University Press, 2011), 1–21. Canny, "Ideology of English Colonization": 576–595.

6. Montaño, *The Roots of English Colonialism in Ireland*, 13–18. The English overstated the importance of herding in the Irish economy as a whole. See Horning, *Ireland in the Virginian Sea*, 31–37. With regard to the reality of Irish land use, the majority of Ireland prior to English invasion contained small, divided plots of land, such as ballliboes and ploughlands. See J. H. Andrews, "Geography and Government in Elizabethan Ireland," in *Irish Geographical Studies in Honour of E. Estyn Evans*, ed. N. Stephens and R. E. Glasscock (Exeter, England: Department of Geography, Queen's University of Belfast, 1970), 179.

7. Canny, "Ideology of English Colonization," 587. On the importance of land usage for English colonists in Ireland, see Montaño, *The Roots of English Colonialism in Ireland*, especially 22–153. Lawrence quoted in Sarah Barber, "Settlement, Transplantation and Expulsion: a Comparative Study of the Placement of Peoples," in *British Interventions in Early Modern Ireland*, ed. Ciaran Brady and Jane Ohlmeyer (New York: Cambridge University Press, 2005), 293; Herbert quoted in Hinderaker and Mancall, *At the Edge of Empire: The Backcountry in British North America* (Baltimore: The Johns Hopkins University Press, 2003), 3. Old English: Horning, *Ireland in the Virginian Sea*, 27–28. Early Anglo-Americans decoupled the two English justifications for Irish land ownership (legal claims and material improvements to the land). In many regions, this caused proprietors who made no improvements and squatters without titles to engage in prolonged struggles over legitimate landownership. For a brief introduction to the two types of land claims, see Alan Taylor, *Liberty Men and Great Proprietors: The Revolutionary Settlement on the Maine Frontier, 1760–1820* (Chapel Hill: Omohundro Institute of Early American History and Culture, University of North Carolina Press, 1990), 24–29.

8. Micheál Ó Siochrú, "Atrocity, Codes of Conduct and the Irish in the British Civil Wars, 1641–1653," *Past & Present*, 195 (May 2007): 55–86 at 58–62.

9. Ó Siochrú, "Atrocity, Codes of Conduct," 59–60. Cromwell quoted in S. C. Lomas, ed., *The Letters and Speeches of Oliver Cromwell*, 3 vols. (London: Methuen & Co., 1904), 2:4,8.

10. Danielle McCormack, *The Stuart Restoration and the English in Ireland* (Woodbridge, UK: Boydell and Brewer, 2016), 5–6.

11. Ó Siochrú, "Atrocity, Codes of Conduct," 63–73.

12. Ó Siochrú, "Atrocity, Codes of Conduct," 73–78.

13. On the Cromwellian conquest, see Smyth, *Map-making, Landscapes and Memory*, 153–165; for an alternative view, see Carroll, *Science, Culture*, 81–83.

14. Smyth, *Map-making, Landscapes and Memory*, 158–165, 178–181.

15. On sixteenth-century surveying and mapping, see Montaño, *The Roots of English Colonialism in Ireland*, 154–212. For Ireland's surveyors general before 1641, see W. H. Hardinge and Ths. Ridgeway, "On Mapped Surveys of Ireland," *Proceedings of the Royal Irish Academy (1836–1869)* 8 (1861–1864): 39–55. "Strafford's Survey of Connaught," *The Journal of the Royal Historical and Archaeological Association of Ireland*, 4th ser., 6, no. 55 (July 1883): 176–177. For a map that was likely based on the Strafford Survey, see Smyth, *Map-making, Landscapes and Memory*, 108.

16. W. H. Hardinge, "On Manuscript Mapped and other Townland Surveys in Ireland of a Public Character, embracing the Gross, Civil, and Down Surveys, from 1640 to 1688," *The Transactions of the Royal Irish Academy* 24, Antiquities (1873): 3–118, at 6–13. The English had similarly rushed the 1584 survey of Munster: Montaño, *The Roots of English Colonialism in Ireland*, 202–204.

17. Hardinge, "On Manuscript Mapped and other Townland Surveys," 13–20; J. G. Simms, "The Civil Survey, 1654–6," *Irish Historical Studies*, 9, no. 35 (March 1955): 253–263. For an example of the returns of the survey, see Conleth Manning, "Transcripts from the Civil Survey of Counties Carlow and Kilkenny," *Journal of the Royal Society of Antiquaries of Ireland* 132 (2002): 57–76.

18. Englishmen created approximately one hundred maps of Ireland during the sixteenth and early seventeenth centuries but produced nothing that approached the comprehensiveness of the Down Survey's map. See J. H. Andrews, "Colonial Cartography in a European Setting: The Case of Tudor Ireland," ed. David Woodward, *The History of Cartography: Cartography in the European Renaissance*, vol. 3, part 2 (Chicago, IL: University of Chicago Press, 2007), 1672–1675. For the Civil and Down Surveys at the local level, see William Nolan, *Fassadinin: Land, Settlement & Society in South-East Ireland, 1600–1850* (Dublin, Ireland: Geography Publications, 1979), 57–83, 248–250. The Down Survey took its name from the process of scaling down the surveys from large field notes onto small maps. Petty wholeheartedly believed that applied science benefited the state. He advocated a host of measures for the government to adopt but found little support for most of his projects. See Carroll, *Science, Culture, and Modern State Formation*, especially 47, 53–106. Petty later became the principal contemporary historian of the Down Survey, and he chronicled both the execution of the surveys and the infighting surrounding their results. On Petty's criticisms of Worsley, see William Petty, *The History of the Survey of Ireland, Commonly Called the Down Survey* (1851; repr., New York: Augustus M. Kelley, 1967), 2. On Petty's attempts to subject politics and economics to mathematical rigor, see Patricia Cline Cohen, *A Calculating People: The Spread of Numeracy in Early America* (New York: Routledge, 1999), 30–34.

19. Petty, *The Down Survey*, 17–18, 36–38, 46–50, 53, 123,173–175, 322–324; quotation, 36. For dangers, see Smyth, *Map-making, Landscapes and Memory*, 54–55. Petty also received a 270,000-acre estate as payment for the Down Survey. See Carroll, *Science, Culture, and Modern State Formation*, 54. For an example of Lenape Indians who killed colonists with chains and tomahawks, the tools used to mark out land in Pennsylvania, see Jane T. Merritt, *At the Crossroads: Indians and Empires on a Mid-Atlantic Frontier, 1700–1763* (Chapel Hill: Omohundro Institute of Early American History and Culture, University of North Carolina Press, 2003), 183–184. On English surveys and maps erasing Irish land use patterns, see Montaño, *The Roots of English Colonialism in Ireland*, 163–169, 180–181, 196, 204–206, 210–212.

20. On Protestant land, see Smyth, *Map-making, Landscapes and Memory*, 170; for pay rates, see Petty, *The Down Survey*, 27.

21. See Petty, *The Down Survey*, for his acerbic take on his opponents. He alleges further corruption charges in Marquis of Lansdowne, ed., *The Petty Papers: Some Unpublished Writings of Sir William Petty*, 2 vols. (1927; repr., New York: Augustus M. Kelley Publishers, 1967), 1:49–55.

22. Smyth, *Map-making, Landscapes, and Memory* 167, 177–197; on speculative practices among officers and pushing the Irish to the west, see also Nicholas Canny, *From Reformation to Restoration*, 220–221. For western Indian dislocations around the Great Lakes, see Richard White, *The Middle Ground: Indians, Empires, and Republics in the Great Lakes Region, 1650–1815* (New York: Cambridge University Press, 1991), 1–10.

23. Smyth, *Map-making, Landscapes and Memory*, 190, 196, 248, 270–273, 377, 441. For post-Cromwellian land redistributions, see also Nolan, *Fassadinnin*, 57–58, 74–75.

24. Early Irish economy: Horning, *Ireland in the Virginian Sea*, 19–25, 33–35, 87. On deforestation and farming, see Smyth, *Map-making, Landscapes and Memory*, 91–101. On the "Big House," see Smyth, *Map-making, Landscapes and Memory*, 12, 142–146, 382–383, and Plate 1j, fig. 2.15. On towns, see, R. H. Buchanan, "Towns and Plantations, 1500–1700," in William Nolan, ed., *The Shaping of Ireland: The Geographical Perspective* (Cork, Ireland: Mercier Press, 1986), 93–98. On Connacht, see, Jean M. Graham, "Rural Society in Connacht, 1600–1640," in N. Stephens and R. E. Glasscock, eds., *Irish Geographical Studies in Honour of E. Estyn Evans*, 206.

25. Howard M. Jenkins, "The Family of William Penn," *Pennsylvania Magazine of History and Biography*, 20, no. 1 (1896), 1–29, at 25–26; quotation, 25. On the invasion of the Spanish West Indies, see Carla Gardina Pestana, "English Character and the Fiasco of the Western Design," *Early American Studies* 3, no. 1 (Spring 2005): 1–31. Mary Maples Dunn and Richard S. Dunn, eds., *The Papers of William Penn*, 5 vols. (Philadelphia: Penn Press, 1981) 1:49.

26. On the Penn family's lands in Ireland, see Jenkins, "The Family of William Penn," 26–27; Howard M. Jenkins, "The Family of William Penn, Continued," *Pennsylvania Magazine of History and Biography* 20, no. 2 (1896), 158–175, at 167; Dunn and Dunn, *Papers of William Penn*, 1:39, 44–45, 570–573. The results of the Down Survey have been digitized online. To search for Ireland's landowners in 1641 and 1670 (including Admiral Penn), go to http://downsurvey.tcd.ie/landowners.php [accessed June 15, 2016]. In 1670, William Petty held 310 separate properties spread across southern and eastern Ireland.

27. Jenkins, "The Family of William Penn, Continued," 168–171; Dunn and Dunn, *Papers of William Penn*, 1:101–167, 571; quotation on 102. For a dispute between tenants, see 111. Another version of Penn's "Irish Journal," is available online at the Corpus of Electronic Texts of Ireland: http://www.ucc.ie/celt/published/E660001-002.html [accessed June 16, 2016]. For maps, see note 59.

28. Dunn and Dunn, *Papers of William Penn*, 102, 110–111, 115, 124; quotations on 102, 110–111. For Morgan's introduction, see http://www.ucc.ie/celt/published/E660001-002.html [accessed June 16, 2016].

29. Dunn and Dunn, *Papers of William Penn*, 1:47, 101–107, 333–334.

30. For Petty's proposals for a comprehensive land registry in Ireland, see Lansdowne, *The Petty Papers*, 1:75–111.

31. Lansdowne, *The Petty Papers*, 1:45–72.

32. Jean R. Soderlund, ed., *William Penn and the Founding of Pennsylvania: A Documentary History* (Philadelphia: University of Pennsylvania Press, 1983), 3–5, 19–20, 23.

33. Lansdowne, *The Petty Papers*, 2:95–98. For Petty's purchase in Pennsylvania, see Samuel Hazard ed., *Annals of Pennsylvania, from the Discovery of the Delaware, 1609–1682* (Philadelphia: Hazard and Mitchell, 1850), 643. The Thornton and Seller map is available online: http://www.mapsofpa.com/17thcentury/1681morden.jpg [accesssed June 19, 2016].

34. Lansdowne, *The Petty Papers*, 2:110–111, 121. Petty's math was off—his own numbers suggested that he would break even in less than six years. Petty's estimate of twenty-five acres per family was reasonable, but on the small side for a sustainable family farm. See

Bettye Hobbs Pruitt, "Self-sufficiency and the Agricultural Economy," *William and Mary Quarterly* 41, no. 3 (July 1984): 334–364.

35. Lansdowne, *The Petty Papers*, 2:115–119.

36. Lansdowne, *The Petty Papers*, 2:109–120, quotations on 114–115.

37. Lansdowne, *The Petty Papers*, 2:114. On the concept of indiscriminate location, see Edward T. Price, *Dividing the Land: Early American Beginnings of Our Private Property Mosaic* (Chicago, IL: University of Chicago Press, 1995), 13–14, 21, 89, 334–335. On the legal basis of Penn's proprietorship and the theoretical underpinnings that justified English settlement, see Christopher Tomlins, *Freedom Bound: Law, Labor, and Civic Identity in Colonizing English America, 1580–1865* (New York: Cambridge University Press, 2010), 133–190.

38. J. Barry Love, *The Colonial Surveyor in Pennsylvania*, 108–110, 123. On Penn's landholdings and his cultivation of Quaker merchants, see Gary B. Nash, "The Framing of Government in Pennsylvania: Ideas in Contact with Reality," *William & Mary Quarterly*, 23, no. 2 (1966): 183–209. On Virginia's decentralized surveying regime, see Sarah S. Hughes, *Surveyors and Statesmen: Land Measuring in Colonial Virginia* (Richmond: The Virginia Surveyors Foundation and the Virginia Association of Surveyors, 1979).

39. Soderlund, *William Penn and the Founding of Pennsylvania*, 58–66, 71–72; quotation on 63. Hannah Benner Roach, "The Planting of Philadelphia: A Seventeenth-Century Real Estate Development, I," *Pennsylvania Magazine of History and Biography*, 92, no. 1 (January 1968), 3–47, at 10.

40. Roach, "The Planting of Philadelphia, I," 10–11, 17–22. Quotation: Soderlund, *William Penn and the Founding of Pennsylvania*, 85.

41. Quotation: Roach, "The Planting of Philadelphia, I," 9. Soderlund, *William Penn and the Founding of Pennsylvania*, 71–72, 82. On Fretwell, see Gary B. Nash, *Quakers and Politics: Pennsylvania, 1681–1726*, new ed. (Boston: Northeastern University Press, 1993), 90–94.

42. Soderlund, *William Penn and the Founding of Pennsylvania*, 84, 312–317. On the context for Indian purchases, see Daniel K. Richter, *Trade, Land, Power: The Struggle for Eastern North America* (Philadelphia: University of Pennsylvania Press, 2013), 135–154.

43. Jean R. Soderlund, *Lenape Country: Delaware Valley Society before William Penn* (Philadelphia: University of Pennsylvania Press, 2015), 149–176.

44. Antoinette Sutto, "The Borders of Absolutism: William Penn, Charles Calvert, and the Limits of Royal Authority, 1680–1685," *Pennsylvania History: A Journal of Mid-Atlantic Studies* 76, no. 3 (Summer, 2009): 276–300; Nicholas B. Wainwright, "Tale of a Runaway Cape: The Penn-Baltimore Agreement of 1732," *Pennsylvania Magazine of History and Biography* 87, no. 3 (July 1963), 251–293, especially 253–254. The border was not fully fixed until the Mason-Dixon line was run between 1763 and 1767.

45. Munger, *Pennsylvania Land Records: A History and Guide for Research* (Wilmington, DE: Scholarly Resources, Inc., 1991), 32; Irma Corcoran, *Thomas Holme, 1624–1695: Surveyor General of Pennsylvania* (Philadelphia, PA: Memoirs of the American Philosophical Society, 1992), 42–83.

46. Corcoran, *Thomas Holme, 1624–1695*, especially 98–100; Holme's map is in the frontispiece. On Philadelphia, see Dunn and Dunn, *Papers of William Penn*, 2:334, 358–360. For Penn's 1685 description of townships, see Albert Cook Myers, ed. *Narratives of Early Pennsylvania, West New Jersey, and Delaware: 1630–1707* (New York: Barnes & Noble, 1912), 263. On surveying halting in Bucks, see Soderlund, *Lenape Country*, 174. On Pennsylvania's subsequent land development, see Gallo, "Land Surveying in Early Pennsylvania: A Case Study in a Global Context."

47. Quotation: Roach, "The Planting of Philadelphia, I," 9. For sales numbers, see Soderlund, *William Penn and the Founding of Pennsylvania*, 5.

48. Charles Henry Hull, ed. *The Economic Writings of Sir William Petty*, 2 vols. (Cambridge: Cambridge University Press, 1899), 1:9.

CHAPTER 5

The Irish Worlds of William Penn

CULTURE, CONFLICT, AND CONNECTIONS

Audrey Horning

The role of Ireland in Penn's extraordinary career is oft cited if surprisingly underanalyzed. Routinely noted for serving as the locale of his 1666 convincement to Quakerism; as the place where he learned skills as a landlord; and for his involvement in an intellectual milieu including thinkers such as Sir William Petty, the deeper role played by his exposure, at a young age, to a land marred by warfare and characterized by the fundamental gap between colonial rhetoric and practical realities is more often assumed than assessed. In general terms, parallels are commonly drawn between the colonial character of English engagements in Ireland and their subsequent influence in settling the Pennsylvania frontier. However, to truly understand the ways in which Penn's Irish experience influenced his activities as a proprietor and particularly the manner in which he engaged with the Native peoples of the Delaware and Susquehanna Valleys, requires much greater appreciation of the complexities of Ireland in the period. In the earlier *World of William Penn*, Galway historian Nicholas Canny addressed some of this background, principally focusing on the broader context of post-Cromwellian settlement in County Cork where the Penn family held their lands.[1] Clearly the social circle within which Penn moved while in Cork was critical to the evolution of his ideologies and the ways in which he approached colonization in Pennsylvania, and this is explored further in this chapter. But Cork was not the only part of Ireland with which William Penn was familiar, nor can it stand as an exemplar for the whole of the island.

Penn of course spent time in Dublin, and numerous early Philadelphia merchants left businesses in Dublin.[2] But Ulster would loom large in the migration to Pennsylvania. Myers enumerates over two hundred Quakers who emigrated from Ulster to Pennsylvania, principally drawn from meetings in County Armagh.[3] There is also reason to suspect that the peculiarities of Ulster society contributed to Penn's perspective on toleration. Unmentioned in Canny's earlier consideration was Penn's role in suppressing a mutiny in the Ulster port and garrison town of Carrickfergus in May 1666. Significantly, this event occurred prior to Penn's Quaker convincement, and while fleeting in the documentary record, is worthy of further scrutiny. A closer look at the wider circumstances of the mutiny, the cultural character and composition of Carrickfergus, and Penn's own actions suggests that this event may have been more of a formative experience than previously acknowledged. The cultural context of Ulster as witnessed by Penn in the 1660s contrasted with that of Munster and Dublin, both more familiar to Penn. Importantly, it was the experiences of Protestant planters in Ulster, the circumstances of the 1641 Rising/Rebellion in the north, and the at times hysterical memories of violence that together informed and shaped the post-Cromwellian land redistribution from which the Penn family clearly benefited.[4] The intricacies and complexities of plantation and of transplantation, and how best the Crown might gain stable, long-term control over the island of Ireland, were topics that obsessed thinkers of the day, perhaps none more so than Penn's intellectual companion and fellow Royal Society member Sir William Petty. Petty (see chapter 4), advocated a transformationist approach to subduing Ireland that relied upon intermarriage between Irish men and English women—in effect, appealing to the baser instincts of Irish men and a belief in the power of women to impose English values.[5] But Petty was far from the only Irish influence on Penn as he developed his own ideas of toleration.

Penn's experiences with Ireland stretch back to childhood, and he came of age during a period of momentous and lasting change on the island. This period, in the wake of Cromwellian warfare to the Ascendancy ushered in by William III, was crucial to the entrenchment of patterns of inequality, religious discrimination, and economic control. Protestant hegemony was ultimately assured in the aftermath of the Williamite Wars, which saw the accession of Prince William of Orange to the English throne. However, the impact of Cromwellian land confiscations and resettlement, and further reordering during the Restoration, has tended to be far overshadowed by assumptions about the impact of earlier British plantation efforts in cementing the unequal power relations between Irish and British, Catholic and Protestant, colony and kingdom. Themes around displacement, migration, and language are key to understanding Ireland in the latter half of the seventeenth century and are also key to the American dimension of Penn's career. This chapter therefore explores the ways in which Penn's Irish experiences during this transformative period contributed to his approach and attitude toward indigenous people in Pennsylvania.

Background: Ireland at Midcentury

Ireland at midcentury was a war-torn land with an uncertain future. Vested interests sought to reimagine, recast, and recalibrate the political and demographic composition of the island's populace. The project of plantation, which had taken hold in the early part of the century as a means of ensuring British control over the island through the importation of loyal, mainly Protestant settlers, had abruptly come to an end. Thirty-odd years of relative peace based upon an uneasy accommodation between the numerically dominant Irish and the incoming planters was shattered by the outbreak of violence in Ulster in 1641. While initially a localized movement primarily intended to ensure the rights of property-holding Ulster Gaelic elites, the 1641 Rising/Rebellion soon spread throughout the island. What began as an armed constitutional protest, intended to restore and guarantee the role of Catholic elites in the governance of Ireland as a kingdom, devolved into a more overtly religious conflict as one front in the broader War of Three Kingdoms. English and Scottish Catholics joined Irish compatriots in the Confederacy, initially fighting against the Protestant forces of the Crown. Cromwell's intervention in 1649 accelerated the violence, with Protestants in Ireland dividing their allegiances between the Parliamentarian and Royalist forces, and Confederate Catholics compelled to forge an alliance with the exiled Charles II. The redistribution of landholdings that took place in the aftermath of the warfare, made manifest in the 1652 Act of Settlement, ultimately brought far more radical changes to Irish settlement and society than had the plantations of the first half of the century, notwithstanding historical memories to the contrary. To illustrate the scale of the transformation, in 1641, 59 percent of land still remained in the hands of Catholic landowners (both Gaelic and Old English); that figure diminished to a mere 22 percent by 1688.[6]

Following the cessation of hostilities, opinions were clearly divided over how to knit the country back together and ensure Protestant English rule. Government plans were punitive and focused on eliminating Catholic power. Lands were to be confiscated and redistributed to Protestant New English, and scores of Irish were to be transplanted to the West Indies as part of Cromwell's wider Western Design.[7] William Penn's father, Admiral William Penn, was a key participant in Cromwell's Atlantic project, leading the forces that in May 1655 wrested the Jamaica colony from the Spanish (albeit failing to capture Hispaniola).

Confiscation and transplantation were not universally accepted as the best way forward. The most articulate critic of the government's approach was Vincent Gookin Jr., the son of a Cork planter who had made his own fortune by adopting Gaelic Irish economic activities: cattle pastoralism and pilchard fishing. While the elder Gookin professed his hatred of the Irish (while happy to profit from Irish commodities), his son strongly favored a more integrationist approach.[8] In his estimation, harsh treatment of the Irish would only breed opposition, whereas returning to the patterns of cohabitation and accommodation that had characterized the relatively peaceful years of 1610 to 1641 would eventually see the Irish accept English mores and Protestant religion.[9] Language was critical to debates over how best to achieve this end. Vincent Sr. was strongly opposed to the use of Irish. In an ill-tempered letter to Lord Deputy Thomas Wentworth in 1633 that earned him censure, he asserted that he "ever will stand at a distance from the Irish, and will not so much as suffer my children to learn the language."[10] Sir Vincent Gookin may have believed he was preventing his children from going native by forbidding them to learn the language, but in reality, English planters who did not learn the tongue were at a considerable disadvantage, reliant solely upon translators—liminal figures who de facto could not be trusted.[11]

Unlike his father, Vincent Jr. understood the value of linguistics, noting that "The frequent use of the Irish language in all commerce, and the Englishes habituating themselves to that language, was one great means of Irishifying the English colonies." Now, he believed, it was time for the English language to predominate: "But now the Language will be generally English; and if the Irish be mingled with the English, they will probably learn and be habituated to the English tongue."[12] Throughout 1655 and 1656, a prolonged war of words ensued between Gookin and the principal advocate for transplantation, Colonel Richard Lawrence.[13] Meanwhile, efforts to implement Cromwell's Western Design focused on peopling the newly captured Jamaica with unwanted Irish. On September 27, 1655, Vincent Gookin Jr.'s cousin Captain Daniel Gookin Jr. accepted orders to organize a venture in which "one thousand Irish girls, and the like number of youths, be sent into Jamaica."[14] Daniel's Jamaican adventure was unsuccessful and remains principally a footnote to his more well-known career as first a Virginia planter, then close associate of John Eliot, and finally the surveyor general of Massachusetts. Not coincidentally, Daniel was in London in 1655 at the same time that Vincent was vociferously opposing transplantation.[15]

Daniel's later actions in relation to the integration of English and Native in Massachusetts strongly indicates that the cousins discussed shared concerns and broadly agreed on principles. Echoing Vincent's approach to language, Daniel Gookin advocated proximity and discourse between English and Indian, conducted in the English language. As part of that strategy, he set out plans to build a school for both English and Indians at Okommakamesit (Marlborough, Massachusetts) so that "the Indians will be able to converse with the English familiarly; and thereby learn civility and religion from them."[16] At the same time, Gookin pragmatically encouraged colonists to learn Native languages, evidenced in the use of "Massachusett" in the early Natick town records.[17] As was the case in Ireland, knowledge of language was a double-edged sword—knowledge of English held by Native people was empowering, while English ignorance of Native languages fostered fears, often accurate, of subversion. Daniel Jr. directly compared his emphasis on teaching English to the Praying Indians to promote assimilation with the situation in Ireland: "And the changing of the language of a barbarous people, into the speech of a more civil and potent nation that have conquered them hath been an approved experiment, to reduce such a people unto the civility and religion of the of the prevailing nation. And I incline to believe, that if that course had been effectually taken with the Irish, their enmity and rebellion against the English had been long since cured or prevented."[18] The violence and devastation of King Philip's (Massassoit's) War in New England frustrated Daniel Gookin's approach. In Ireland, as noted by Toby Barnard, Vincent Gookin Jr.'s integrationist approach "prevailed, but for practical rather than humanitarian reasons."[19] Transplantation, and the attendant loss of the laboring classes, was simply not economically feasible on any large scale.

The Young Penn and Ireland

What did the young Penn know of this long-standing conflict, the debates over its resolution, and their transatlantic resonances? Certainly the discussions taking place in the 1650s over the best way to bring English notions of "civility" to Ireland would echo in the discourses over treatment of the indigenous populations of the lands that would become the Pennsylvania colony. When he was a child, it is certain that the topic of warfare in Ireland would have arisen at home in London, given that the family lost lands in Ireland during the conflict. His mother Margaret was raised in County Clare and had inherited substantial estates from her father and then from her first husband, a Dutch merchant trading in Ireland. Those estates were damaged and lost during the violence of 1641 to 1652, and it is inconceivable that the young Penn was not privy to at least some of the reports from Ireland. The elder Penn was partially compensated for his Irish losses by a grant from Cromwell of lands in Cork to the value of £300 per year in December of 1654, although the Protector's generosity has been viewed as principally an inducement to Penn to participate in the effort to capture and plant Jamaica.[20]

The lands that the elder Penn received, and to which the family relocated in 1656, were those of the MacCarthys at Macroom, County Cork. The site of at least one skirmish in the 1640s, it is unclear what condition the property was in when the Penns took possession. The surrounding countryside certainly would have borne the scars of the conflict, visible to the young Penn on his arrival with the family. The main dwelling at Macroom, a castle of likely fifteenth-century date, must have been sufficiently habitable for the family and their retainers. Macroom was the former seat of the Gaelic Irish Viscount Muskerry, himself an active participant in the plantation society of early seventeenth-century Cork. Despite his Catholicism, Muskerry, like other powerful Irish lords, managed to hold onto power and to simultaneously uphold and subvert plantation rhetoric.[21] In Muskerry's case, he planted the adjacent town with English recusant families[22] but upgraded his property to reflect English fashion; his gardens at Macroom have been interpreted as a "sign of confident emulation of English ways."[23] How many additional modifications and improvements were made to the castle by the Penns is unknown without archaeological investigation, as only portions of the structure now survive. However war-damaged it may have been, the Macroom estate materially reflected the processes of accommodation and hybridization inherent to colonial entanglements and the lived experience of plantation. By all accounts, Admiral Penn was "rapidly assimilated into Munster society, sharing the conservative inclinations of the established settlers, serving as a justice of the peace for Cork in 1658, and on the presidential council of Munster in 1660."[24] His new estate symbolized his new identity, simultaneously manifesting familiar English notions of polite architecture and landscape design, while at the same time representing the vanquished "other" in the traces of its fifteenth-century Gaelic fabric.

Regardless of the extent to which the Penns made themselves at home in Macroom Castle, their tenure was not to last. The Restoration brought back a successful counterclaim by the previous occupant, and the Penns were ultimately compelled to accept a substitute in the form of another County Cork property, Shanagarry. While extolled by Penn biographer William Hepworth Dixon as "a still nobler property,"[25] Shanagarry Castle itself was in actuality an austere sixteenth-century masonry tower house that unlike Macroom, had not been updated to reflect seventeenth-century architectural fashions.[26] Shanagarry was also not blessed with extensive gardens like those created by Muskerry at Macroom, and alluded to in Admiral Penn's 1660 testimony, which noted that his property at Macroom "possessed gardens and nurseries brought to great perfection."[27] Nothing is recorded of the personal impact of the Penn family having to surrender Macroom Castle back to the MacCarthys, but it takes only a small amount of imagination to envision the disruption and disappointment caused by having to move from the well-appointed Macroom Castle, to the smaller, darker, and certainly less impressive Shanagarry Castle. Admiral Penn, now busily engaged in the politics of Restoration, elected to remain in London rather than reside in his consolation prize. The younger Penn appears to have been the only member of the family to spend any time at Shanagarry, which he referred to as "my father's house"[28] in December 1669 (he would inherit it following his father's death in September 1670). Penn resigned himself to simply using the rather old-fashioned tower as a base while managing the estate and collecting rents (or seeking to) on behalf of his father, not being in any position to invest money in the rather more fashionable manor houses built by other Cork elites. His time would come decades later when he was able to design his own fashionable Pennsbury Manor in Pennsylvania. Penn inherited his father's estates, but noted with regret in 1695 that "I have not seen my estate since I had it, 24 years

& an 1/3," referencing his last visit in 1669–1670.[29] But before further exploring the time Penn did spend at Shanagarry, it is worth examining in greater detail his brief military service in 1666, prior to shouldering the mantle of a County Cork landlord.

Andrew Murphy (chapter 6) has rightly commented on Penn's dual identities as a Friend and as a landlord. To that we might add servitor, given Penn's brief but not unimportant involvement in the military service that had long been the arm of English authority in Ireland. That the principal action seen by Penn was in quelling a rebellion of English troops, rather than fighting against the Irish he and his family had dispossessed, only highlights the convoluted realities of the Restoration period. What was the cause of this internal rebellion? Not politics, but pay. The soldiers billeted at Carrickfergus, by their own account, had loyally served nine months without pay. While their grievance may have been just, any unrest in Carrickfergus rang multiple alarm bells in Dublin and in London. As expressed by the Irish Lord Lieutenant (James Butler, first Earl of Ormonde) in a May 24 letter to Secretary Arlington: "Carrickfergus is inhabited by many Scotch and Presbyterians who perhaps have and will further foment this disorder." His concern led him to assert a day later that "I am resolved myself to go to Carrickfergus tomorrow to prevent the mutiny from spreading. I shall hasten there to prevent Lord Donegall giving them those assurances of pardon which he seems inclined to give. . . . The mutiny of four companies may seem a small thing to draw me thither, but considering how near Carrickfergus is to the disaffected part of Scotland, and the ill inclinations of so many in Ulster, I think it best to make the journey."[30] Clearly Ormonde was deeply troubled by the potential of the revolt to precipitate further unrest.

The Lord Lieutenant was not only concerned about the recent history of conflict. Carrickfergus, first established as an Anglo-Norman garrison in the late twelfth century, had a long history of cultural and political entanglement with Scotland, and not just with the Lowland Scotland of the Presbyterian planters. Carrickfergus was situated in a strategic position on Belfast Lough, and in the late sixteenth century lay at the interface of the territories of the powerful Gaelic Clann Aodha Buidhe Uí Néill (Clandeboye O'Neill) and the Highland Scottish Clann Domhnaill (MacDonnell). English commanders of the garrison at Carrickfergus castle (figure 5.1) more often than not acted strategically and pragmatically in balancing conflicting allegiances and the practical need for Carrickfergus merchants to engage with any and all comers.[31] Even during the fraught and violent years of the latter half of the sixteenth century, when England extended control through warfare leading to colonial control via plantation in the early seventeenth century, Carrickfergus was noted as a node of interaction between the Gaelic Irish, the English (both military and planter), and the Catholic Highland Scots who strategically aligned themselves with either the Irish or the English depending on circumstances and exigencies.

Figure 5.1 Carrickfergus Castle. Photo by A. Horning.

Carrickfergus was also one of the two seats of Lord Donegall, the title given to the preeminent military man and early seventeenth-century lord deputy of Ireland Sir Arthur Chichester, and held by his nephew and namesake Arthur when Penn found himself in Carrickfergus in 1666. The first Lord Donegall had fought in Elizabeth's Irish wars, sailed to the New World on Francis Drake's final voyage, and ultimately settled down to direct the implementation of the Ulster Plantation in 1609.[32] Chichester built two mansions for himself; one in Belfast (then a subsidiary port to Carrickfergus) and the other, styled Joymount, in Carrickfergus.[33] Chichester very clearly set himself up as the epitome of English civility and a firm supporter of the Ulster Plantation project. But Chichester was not doctrinaire when it came to peopling either settlement. The seventeenth century would see the Lowland Presbyterian Scots, who would come to dominate aspects of Ulster society and later form a significant pool of migrants for the Pennsylvania colony, added to the mix. Material evidence for this convoluted melange of identities and associations in Carrickfergus comes from a series of archaeological excavations, which have uncovered objects referencing the multiple identities of inhabitants, such as hand built Irish earthenware, North Devon sgraffiti, and Scottish grayware, as well as continental and Mediterranean ceramics indicative of the burgeoning mercantile world of the seventeenth century, of which Carrickfergus was an integral part.[34]

Regardless of any stabilizing influence that may have been brought by the Chichesters, Carrickfergus remained fundamentally a multicultural meeting place and, as such, a locale predisposed to the potential for violence and disarray.

The upheavals of the 1640s had only exacerbated this volatility, bringing as they did a fundamental split between the Scottish and English Protestant communities, with the Ulster Scots of the time "fighting for a new form of Presbyterian royalism under Charles II," while the Ulster English Protestant community principally embraced the parliamentary cause.[35] Furthermore, while Carrickfergus had not suffered any attacks during the 1640s, the replacement of the primarily Scottish troops in the castle with an English regiment, and the use of the castle for imprisoning Presbyterian clergy, inflamed tensions.[36] Small wonder that word of unrest in the garrison town in 1666 sparked fear and a swift reaction. War-weary residents struggled with trade disruption and the loss of income from the soldiery, as expressed in a declaration made by the rebelling soldiers: "The town is so much impoverished for want of pay from us, that they are no longer nor will to trust us further."[37] It is unsurprising, then, that the Lord Donegall at the time, Sir Arthur Chichester's nephew Arthur, sought to calm the situation. Having a far more intimate understanding of the peculiarities of Carrickfergus and its pluralist makeup, his aim was to appease the soldiers through promise of pardons in an effort to return the town to some semblance of stability.

Donegall tried fruitlessly to convince the lord lieutenant that the mutineers "will 'moulder away' if your Grace promises pardon to those who submit, and orders payment for present subsistence for them."[38] Instead, Ormonde ordered troops under the command of his son, the Earl of Arran (Richard Butler), to suppress the revolt. Arran's forces, including the young William Penn, swiftly subdued the mutineers, executing nine by hanging and imprisoning the rest as a prelude to threatened transplantation to Barbados. In the end, these prisoners were soon reconscripted to wage battle against so-called tories, or Catholic bandits. The Carrickfergus mutineers notably subdued the Catholic outlaw Edward Nangle on July 17, 1666, in an armed confrontation at Longford, an opportunity reportedly welcomed by the soldiers who "earnestly desired this in order that they might repair the reputation which they had lost at Carrickfergus."[39]

As the mutineers were pondering their own postmutiny futures, so too was William Penn. By all accounts he had acquitted himself well in the successful effort to take the castle and capture the soldiers. The brevity and ease with which the rebellion was subdued may have contributed to Penn's brief enthusiasm for a military career, given the thrill of success without significant losses or the psychological and physical challenges of a long, drawn-out campaign. After the action, Penn evidently was hosted by Donegall in Joymount, an opulent mansion that was unfortunately demolished in 1768.[40] Joymount was described in the same year as Penn's visit as possessing "as many windows as there are days in the year; the top is turreted and defended with wall balustrades, the entry is handsome . . . Its staircase is admirable; and its gate or door much more so, on account of the many pieces of sculpture with which it is ornamented."[41] Those windows would have afforded views not only of the town, castle, and Belfast Lough but also of the mountainous hinterland. In gazing out through those windows, did conversation turn to the cultural complexity of the town and its history? Did Chichester seek to educate his visitors in the nuances of Ulster life and the delicate accommodations that had long characterized discourse within the port and garrison?

The only conversation we know for certain that did take place at Joymount was between the young Penn and Arran in which Penn eagerly sought and attained a recommendation from Arran to take over from Admiral Penn as commander of the fort at Kinsale, County Cork. The young Penn was clearly put out when his father, quite possibly offended by the suggestion, declined to answer Arran's letter on the matter. The somewhat wheedling tone of a follow-up letter from Penn to his father, a letter that surely shaded the truth somewhat, speaks to his youth and relative immaturity:

> Honourable Sir, when I was at Carrickfergus with my Lord of Arran, Sir George Lane, in my Lord Dunagle's house, called me aside, and told me, the character Lord Arran had pleased to give his father, obliged him to write you a letter on my behalf; which was, to surrender your government and fort. . . . To assure you of my lord's design, I saw the letter under his own hand, but am to seek whether Sir George Lane sent it or no, which I am to ask of yourself; my lord lieutenant telling me several times, he wondered you never answered his letter.[42]

It is hard to imagine that Arran was truly so concerned about the future of the young man that he would pester him about his father's lack of correspondence, nor does the younger Penn's ready willingness to cast aspersions on Sir George Lane, Ormonde's secretary and an influential Penn family friend, paint the young man in a particularly favorable light. Ten days later, his father responded, acknowledging that he had "received two or three letters" from his son to which he had not responded. Moving swiftly to the matter at hand, he wrote, "concerning the fort of Kinsale, I wish your youthful desires mayn't outrun your discretion."[43] Geiter reads this as evidence of the elder Penn's desire to retire and live off of his Irish estates more than as evidence of Penn's impetuousness, while Dunn sees the incident as indicative of the young Penn's "aggressive, argumentative, and contentious" character.[44] Penn, of course, would not take over command of Kinsale, nor was a military career in his future, even if the future would come to know him through the October 1666 portrait painted of him in military garb (figure 5.2). But his time in Ulster, and his brief encounter with the pluralist character of Carrickfergus, must have left more of a lasting impression

Figure 5.2 William Penn in armor, c. 1666. Artist unknown, Date unknown, Courtesy of the Philadelphia History Museum at the Atwater Kent, The Historical Society of Pennsylvania Collection. Gift of Granville Penn, 1833 (HSP.1833.1)

than generally acknowledged, albeit admittedly an impression for which there exists scant documentation.

Penn in County Cork, 1669–1670

The remainder of Penn's time in Ireland in 1666 and 1667 was divided between Dublin and Cork, documented principally through correspondence with his father, increasingly dominated by concern over Penn's religious activities.[45] Much more of our knowledge of Penn's Irish activities comes from the journal he kept of his later 1669–1670 sojourn, spent in an apparent whirlwind of visits with Quakers, tenants, and members of the elite. While most of his entries merely document these meetings and attendant meals, and the vagaries of travel, occasionally entries include observations that provide some insight into the wider cultural landscape. For example, on the 5th of December he notes in passing that in traveling from Tallow to the home of Captain Boles, a Penn family tenant, he and his companions "passed a great company of Irish gathered to the Mass upon a hill."[46] The relative nonchalance of his description could be taken as indicative of Penn's general toleration for Catholicism.[47] But it is additionally notable for what it reveals about the continuance of Catholic religious practice in Cork even after all priests were officially declared guilty of treason in 1653 and many were expelled, transplanted, or simply fled.[48]

The politics of the Restoration eased some of the harsh rhetoric, and as discussed earlier, transplantation ceased to be seen as a viable solution for a country dependent upon its Catholic workforce. Hence the 1667 decree by Lord Orrery (Roger Boyle), forbidding any Catholic religious services within the boundaries of Cork City but permitting worship out in the countryside, provides an explanation for the open-air meeting observed by Penn.[49] Penn described another encounter with a Catholic gathering in which he betrayed a rather less tolerant attitude than he had when viewing the outdoor Mass. This was on the 10th of April, when on the way to Rosscarbery he "overtook a burying, barbarous like the heathen."[50] Penn may have been referring to the *caoineadh*, or women's lament performed over the dead. Such "keening," as it was anglicized, was a practice that not only offended many English commentators but was also opposed by the Catholic Church.[51] While a decree of 1670 implored priests to "bring to an end the wailings and screams of female keeners who accompanied the dead to the graveyard,"[52] the *caoineadh* remained a common practice in Ireland until the twentieth century, notwithstanding continued church condemnation.

Whatever Penn did or did not think of Irish ritual practices, he, like other planters, was more than content to retain an Irish workforce and Irish tenants. Some acknowledgment of the traditional claim of Irish tenants to Penn lands is revealed in an entry from May 3: "The Irish inhabitants came. They had their houses and gardens as before."[53] Penn's journal also underscores not only continuity in Irish tenants but continuity in Irish economic practices, including those adopted by the New English of the plantation period. Cattle pastoralism was one such practice. When in April 1660 Penn sought to extract rent from a tenant by the name of Berry, he seized his cattle.[54] While Munster had a more mixed economy than the province of Ulster, cattle were as central to planter wealth as they had been in Gaelic society—so much so that, in gauging the productivity of land in the Munster plantation, officials resorted to enumerating cattle rather than tenants as the most accurate expression of value.[55] The ability of planters to accommodate the seemingly archaic practices and obligations of the Gaelic cattle economy with the economic imperatives of plantation demonstrates not just pragmatism but, crucially, an underappreciated ability to adapt to aspects of the unfamiliar culture of the demographically dominant Irish.

Penn's time in Ireland in 1669–1670 also brought him closer into the orbit of influential intellectuals and elites. Sir William Petty has already been mentioned, and is discussed in detail in chapter 4. Surprisingly less commented upon is Penn's engagement with the Gookin family, who appear on numerous occasions in his journal. In 1659, the two families may not have been on the best of terms, as Vincent Gookin Jr. had allegedly endeavored to put William Petty up for the seat of Bandon and Kinsale, which Lord Broghill (later Orrery) had intended for Admiral Penn.[56] A decade later, any rancor had clearly diminished. On several occasions Penn met and dined with Thomas Gookin, and while visiting at Rosscarbery he noted that "the young Gookins came," although he does not identify the children by name or parentage. Significantly, Thomas Gookin was half-brother to the Member of Parliament and opponent of transplantation Vincent Gookin Jr. Thomas himself was active in Cork civil life, serving as a burgess and as a corporation trustee for the town of Youghal.[57] Given Penn's penchant for discourse, it does not stretch the imagination to consider that the prominent Gookin family roles in Ireland and across the Atlantic, and particularly their attitudes toward cross-cultural engagements, arose in conversation between William and Thomas. This was the period when Penn was developing his own ideas of toleration, as set out in his *Great Case of Liberty of Conscience Once More Briefly Debated and Defended*.[58] What role did the Gookins play in shaping his thoughts, and vice versa? Later in Penn's life, one Charles Gookin (variously identified as Sir Vincent's son or grandson) became a Quaker and settled in Pennsylvania, a tantalizing hint of a reciprocal relationship.

Far surpassing the influence of the Gookin family on William Penn is the role played by the Boyle family. No discussion of Cork, or indeed Ireland, in the seventeenth century is complete without consideration of their influence. In short, the Boyle family controlled Munster, and the Gookins owed as much to their patronage as did William Penn.[59] In his time in Ireland in both 1666–1667 and 1669–1670, Penn engaged directly with three influential members of the Boyle family: Lord Orrery (Roger Boyle), Robert Boyle the scientist, and Francis Boyle (Lord Shannon). All three of these men (and their brother Richard, Lord Burlington and lord high treasurer of Ireland from 1660 to 1695), while different in temperament and intellect, owed their standing and success to their father, Richard Boyle. In 1602, the elder Boyle, born in England, acquired 42,000 acres of land originally granted to Walter Raleigh as part of the Munster Plantation. Boyle subsequently attained the title of first Baron of Youghal in 1616 and Earl of Cork in 1620. To Raleigh's 42,000 acres he added another 58,000 through the south of Ireland, and when he died, he was reputedly the wealthiest man in the three kingdoms of Ireland, Scotland, and England.[60] The elder Boyle was a man of his times: an adventurer, an entrepreneur, a master manipulator, and a mimic, and long considered an archetypal figure who embodied the transformative potential of English colonialism in Ireland.[61] Despite his successes, the world of Munster that he attempted to dominate was not an English world, it was Gaelic Irish and it was Old English. Incomers like Boyle negotiated such cultural realities through engaging with rather than rejecting the social networks of the local population. The demographic realities were clear. Out of a regional population of nearly one quarter million in 1641, New English planters accounted for a mere 7 to 8 percent of the regional population of roughly 250,000.[62]

Penn's daily life while in Munster was shaped by Boyle's activities in ways he may not even have appreciated, most notably in the extensive investments made by Boyle in bridge building and road construction.[63] What would later become known as the Boyle circle—those Enlightenment scientists and moralists who pivoted around Robert Boyle[64]—had its genesis in the political world of Richard Boyle, a world shaped by economic rivalries and religious, political, and cultural conflicts, fueled by preoccupations about how to engineer a society where English Protestant notions of civility and economy were accepted and practiced by all—notwithstanding the demographic realities. Penn's relationship with Boyle's offspring was crucial for his own standing, but it varied in character. Early on, he had overstepped his bounds in rashly turning to Orrery for assistance when arrested in Cork for his Quaker activities. An annoyed Orrery promptly informed Sir William of his son's insolence. The younger Penn seems to have had an easier relationship with Lord Shannon (Francis Boyle), as indicated by a lighthearted letter sent by Francis to William in August 1667 in which he laments his gout and alludes to some amorous activities on the part of Penn ("I left you in a young lady's company").[65] While seldom mentioned in Penn's early years, Robert Boyle would become increasingly important to William Penn. It was to Robert Boyle that he sent samples of ore and plants, and wrote extensively of his encounters with the Native people of Pennsylvania.[66] Robert Boyle had already demonstrated himself to be extremely concerned with issues surrounding the treatment and future of North American Native people. Boyle focused his efforts on religious education and conversion, much as family friend Daniel Gookin did. Boyle served as the first governor for the Society for the Propagation of the Gospel in New England.[67] When Daniel and his cousin Vincent Gookin advocated the importance of language in conversion and civilizing activities, Boyle provided the funds. In Ireland, he notably supported the 1685 publication of William Bedell's Irish Bible. A bequest from the Boyle estate would later be used to fund the Brafferton Indian School in Williamsburg, Virginia, associated with the newly founded College of William and Mary.

Conclusion: Penn, Ireland, and Pennsylvania

The context of cultural entanglement in the island of Ireland in the seventeenth century deserves a more prominent role in considerations of the formation of Penn's beliefs on toleration and the manner in which he sought to conduct his political discourse with Native people in the Pennsylvania colony. While the religious foundation for Penn's beliefs goes without questioning, the pragmatic responses to the position of the Irish in Ireland exemplified during the plantation period, as well as during the Interregnum and Restoration, must also be considered influential. Penn learned from his childhood and teenage exposure to the conflicts on the island, from his martial exploits at Carrickfergus, and from his firsthand experience engaging with Irish tenants and Gaelic elites. These formative experiences provided him with an entrée into his more adult conversations with those long experienced in addressing the challenge of intercultural relationships on the island, such as members of both the Boyle and the Gookin families, as well as his friend William Petty. Penn was exposed to understandings of the often overlooked thirty years of relative peace founded upon uneasy mutual toleration during the plantation period of the seventeenth century, and at midcentury, to the strongly worded arguments against transplantation and in favor of integration (Gookin) and transformation (Petty). At the very least both clearly provided much food for thought, if not outright models, for Penn.

All of Penn's engagements on the island of Ireland revealed the gap between colonial rhetoric and reality, a gap plugged by pragmatic accommodations on the part of all involved: Gaelic, Old English, New English, and Cromwellian newcomers. Discovering that the existing society and cultures resident in his newly granted territories in Pennsylvania were similarly characterized by intercultural accommodation and increasingly hybridized practices must have brought a sense of familiarity, if not necessarily comfort, in terms of the challenges that lay ahead in establishing his desired peaceable kingdom. Penn's insistence on using Native language in his engagement with the Lenni Lenape ("Let my letter and Conditions with my Purchasers about just dealing with them be read in their own tongue, that they may see, wee have their good in our eye, equal with our own interest")[68] clearly reflects the lessons of Ireland, where Vincent Gookin Jr. argued for the value of using Irish during the plantation period, Robert Boyle funded the translation of the Bible into Irish, and Daniel Gookin carried the same understanding to his engagement with the praying Indians of Massachusetts.

Coeducation was the model promoted by both of the Gookins, and despite the fallout from King Philip's War,[69] this model was not wholly abandoned in New England. In the 1720s, the Nipmuc of the Hassanimisco Praying town sold 7,500 acres of their lands to forty English families for a cost of sixteen hundred pounds, to be held in trust for the tribe by the overseers. Among other requirements, the forty families were required to set aside 20 acres for the construction of a school where "shall be received and taught as well Indians as English."[70] And just as the Gaelic and Old English elite encountered by the encroaching English in the sixteenth and seventeenth centuries demonstrated themselves to be active strategists rather than powerless colonial subjects, so too did the indigenous inhabitants of Pennsylvania. The Lenni Lenape approached their dealings with Penn and his agents in the 1680s with considerable knowledge of European cultures gained through extensive engagements with Swedish, Dutch, and English encroachment into their lands since the 1630s. As cogently argued by Jean Soderlund, the Lenape themselves had forged a society that, prior to Penn's arrival, had "created an inclusive, tolerant, decentralized society based on economic goals"; a society that incorporated Swedes, Finns, Dutch, and English but in which the Lenape remained sovereign.[71]

William Penn's experiences of Ireland occurred during the most formative and impressionable years of his life. As a child, he witnessed his parents' concerns and frustrations over the loss of their lands; the lands that his mother had once called home. As a teenager, he participated in the perhaps triumphant return of the family to Ireland, setting themselves up as members of the local Cork elite at Macroom Castle—only to have to surrender that estate in return for the more modest Shanagarry. Penn, of course, famously met Thomas Loe in Ireland, turned to Quakerism, and wrote what Andrew Murphy has considered was his most clearly articulated statement of toleration, the *Great Case*, while based at Shanagarry.[72] Before that, it was also in Ireland where, as a young man, Penn toyed with a career as a military servitor, contemplating his future while sitting around a table with Lords Arran and Donegall at Joymount, and gazed through the many windows of that mansion at the town and port of Carrickfergus, where Irish, English, Highland Catholics, and Lowland Presbyterians had rubbed shoulders for decades. As a landlord, Penn learned to negotiate a system heavily based on preexisting Gaelic economic activities, and he processed his own reaction to encountering alien cultural practices, such as the *caoineadh*. All these experiences together instilled an awareness not just of how quickly one's circumstances could change but also, crucially, of the value of pragmatic accommodation—itself the underpinning for Penn's ideas on toleration.

NOTES

1. Richard S. Dunn and Mary Maples Dunn, *The World of William Penn* (Philadelphia: Penn Press, 1986); Nicholas Canny, "The Irish Background to Penn's Experiment," in Dunn and Dunn, *World of William Penn*, 139–156. Canny's chapter focuses not on Penn's personal experiences but on the economic character of Cork at midcentury, drawing primarily on evidence from the 1641 depositions of planter losses. This theme is further expanded in Nicholas Canny, *Making Ireland British 1580–1650* (Oxford: Oxford University Press, 2001).

2. As noted by Albert Cook Myers, *Immigration of Irish Quakers into Pennsylvania 1682–1750* (Swarthmore: Published by the author, 1902), 82 and others; see, for example, Gary B. Nash, "The early merchants of Philadelphia: The Formation and Disintegration of a Founding Elite" in Dunn and Dunn, *World of William Penn*, 337–362.

3. Myers, *Immigration of Irish Quakers*, 82.

4. See Sean Connolly, *Divided Kingdom: Ireland 1630–1800* (Oxford: Oxford University Press 2008), 60–165; John Cunningham, *Conquest and Land in Ireland: The Transplantation to Connacht, 1649–1690* (Suffolk: Boydell and Brewer, 2011); and David Dickson, *Old World Colony: Cork and South Munster 1630–1830* (Madison: University of Wisconsin Press, 2005).

5. See Ted McCormick, "A Proportionable Mixture: William Petty, Political Arithmetic, and the Transmutation of the Irish," in *Restoration Ireland: Always Settling Never Settled*, ed. Coleman Dennehy (Aldershot: Ashgate 2008), 123–139.

6. For population figures see Toby Barnard, *The Kingdom of Ireland, 1641–1760* (Basingstoke, Hampshire 2004), 13, 29, 61; Brian Mac Cuarta SJ, ed., *Ulster 1641: Aspects of the Rising* (Belfast: Institute of Irish Studies, 1993).

7. T. C. Barnard, "Crisis of Identity among Irish Protestants 1641–1685." *Past and Present* 127 (1990): 39–83; Carla Pestana, *The English Conquest of Jamaica: Oliver Cromwell's Bid for Empire* (Cambridge, MA: Harvard University Press, 2017).

8. Vincent Gookin Jr., *The Great Case of Transplantation in Ireland Discussed* (London: John Crook 1655).

9. Barnard, "Crisis of Identity among Irish Protestants 1641–1685."

10. Vincent Gookin, "1633 Letter to Lord Wentworth," in *Calendar of State Papers Relating to Ireland of the Reign of Charles I and the Commonwealth Volume 18, 1647–1660 & addenda, 1616–1660*, ed. Robert Pentland Mahaffy (London: HMSO, 1908), 185.

11. Patricia Palmer, *Language and Conquest in Early Modern Ireland: English Renaissance Literature and Elizabethan Imperial Expansion* (Cambridge: Cambridge University Press, 2001).

12. Vincent Gookin Jr., *The Great Case of Transplantation*; T. C. Barnard, "Lord Broghill, Vincent Gookin and the Cork Elections of 1659," *English Historical Review* 88, no. 347 (1973): 352–365; Patricia Coughlan, "Counter-currents in Colonial Discourse: The Political Thought of Vincent and Daniel Gookin," in *Political Thought in Seventeenth-Century Ireland*, ed. Jane Ohlmeyer (Cambridge: Cambridge University Press, 2000), 56–82.

13. Vincent Gookin, *The Author and Case of Transplanting the Irish Connaught Vindicated from the Unjust Aspersions of Col. Richard Laurence* (London, 1655); T. C. Barnard, "Interests in Ireland: the 'Famntaic Zeal and Iregular Ambition' of Richard Lawrence," in *British Interventions in Early Modern Ireland*, ed. Ciaran Brady and Jane Ohlmeyer (Cambridge: Cambridge University Press, 2005), 299–314; Barnard "Crisis of Identity."

14. Granville Penn, *Memorials of the Professional Life and Times of Sir William Penn Knight*, vol. 2, 1644–1670 (London: James Duncan 1833), appendix H, 585.

15. Louise Breen, "Praying with the Enemy: Daniel Gookin, King Philip's War, and the Dangers of Intercultural Mediatorship," in *Empire and Others: British Encounters with Indigenous Peoples 1600–1850*, ed. Martin Daunton and Rick Halpern (Philadelphia: Penn Press, 1999), 101–122; Coughlan "Counter-currents."

16. Daniel Gookin, *Historical Collections of the Indians in New England* (Boston: Belknap and Hale, 1674), 81.

17. Kathleen Bragdon, "Crime and Punishment among the Indians of Massachusetts 1675–1750," *Ethnohistory* 28, no. 1 (1981): 23–32.

18. Gookin, *Historical Collections*, 81

19. Barnard, "Crisis of Identity," 70.

20. Granville Penn, *Memorials* vol. 2, 20; J. Coleman, "Admiral Penn, William Penn, and Their Descendants in the County Cork," *Journal of the Cork Archaeological and Historical Society* 14, no. 79 (1908): 9.

21. See James Lyttleton, *The Jacobean Plantations in Seventeenth-Century Offaly: An Archaeology of a Changing World* (Dublin, Four Courts Press, 2013) for an extended consideration of the Plantation activities of the Gaelic elite in Offaly.

22. Michael MacCarthy-Morrogh, *The Munster Plantation: English Migration to Southern Ireland 1583–1641* (Oxford: Clarendon, 1986), 197.

23. Dickson, *Old World Colony*, 23.

24. T. C. Barnard, "Lord Broghill, Vincent Gookin and the Cork Elections of 1659," *English Historical Review* 88, no. 347 (1973), 356.

25. William Hepworth Dixon *Life of William Penn* (Philadelphia: Blanchard and Lea, 1851), 40.

26. Denis Power, comp., *Archaeological Inventory of County Cork. Volume 2: East and South Cork* (Dublin: Stationery Office, 1994).

27. Granville Penn, *Memorials*, appendix N, 617.

28. William Penn, *My Irish Journal 1669–1670*, ed. Isabel Grubb (London: Longmans, Green and Company, 1952), 31.

29. Richard S. Dunn and Mary Maples Dunn, eds. *The Papers of William Penn, Volume 1, 1644–1679* (Philadelphia: Penn Press, 1981), 409.

30. Lord Lieutenant James Butler to Secretary Arlington, 25 May 1666, in Mahaffy *Calendar of State Papers*, 116.

31. Audrey Horning, *Ireland in the Virginian Sea: Colonialism in the British Atlantic* (Chapel Hill: University of North Carolina Press for the Omohundro Institute of Early American History and Culture, 2013), 61, 290, 296; Rachel Tracey, "From Garrison to Atlantic Port: Material Culture, Conflict & Identity in Early Modern Carrickfergus" (PhD thesis, unpublished, Queen's University Belfast, 2017).

32. John McCavitt, *Sir Arthur Chichester, Lord Deputy of Ireland 1605–1616* (Belfast: Institute for Irish Studies, 1998).

33. Ruairí Ó Baoill, "Archaeology of Post-Medieval Carrickfergus and Belfast 1550–1750" in, *The Post-Medieval Archaeology of Ireland 1550–1850*, ed. Audrey Horning, Ruairí Ó Baoill, Colm Donnelly, and Paul Logue (Dublin: Wordwell, 2007), 91–116.

34. Tracey, "From Garrison to Atlantic Port."

35. Kevin Forkan, "The Fatal Ingredient of the Covenant: The Place of the Ulster Scottis Colonial Community during the 1640s," in *Reshaping Ireland 1550–1700*, ed. Brian Mac Cuarta SJ (Dublin: Four Courts Press, 2011), 261–280, quote page 277.

36. Philip Robinson, *Carrickfergus: Historic Towns Atlas* (Dublin: Royal Irish Academy 1986), 2:5.

37. Declaration of the soldiers at the mutiny in Carrickfergus, in Mahaffy, *Calendar of State Papers*, 112.

38. Earl of Donegall to Lord Lieutenant, 23 may 1666, in Mahaffy, *Calendar of State Papers* 117.

39. "Memorandum on Nagle's Raid" 17 July 1666, in Mahaffy, *Calendar of State Papers*, 158.

40. Ó Baoill, "Archaeology of Post-Medieval Carrickfergus and Belfast," 80.

41. Rocheford 1666, quoted in S. McSkimin, *The History and Antiquities of the County of the Town of Carrickfergus* (Belfast: McCrum 1909 [1812]), 156–157.

42. William Penn to Admiral Penn 4 July 1666, in Dunn and Dunn, *Papers of William Penn* 41.

43. Admiral Penn to William Penn 17 July 1666, in Dunn and Dunn, *Papers of William Penn* 42.

44. Mary K. Geiter, *William Penn* (Edinburgh: Pearson Education, 2000), 27; Mary Maples Dunn, "The Personality of William Penn," in Dunn and Dunn, *World of William Penn*, 7.

45. See correspondence in Dunn and Dunn, *Papers of William Penn*, 39–56.

46. William Penn, *My Irish Journal*, 28.

47. Sandra Maria Hynes, "Changing Their Path: Quaker Adaptation to the Challenge of Restoration, 1660–1680," in Dennehy, *Restoration Ireland*, 87, suggests that Ireland's "religious heterodoxy" and Catholic majority allowed for greater toleration: "those who proved to be moderate enjoyed toleration even if it was not *de jure*."

48. Dickson, *Old World Colony*, 44.

49. Dickson, *Old World Colony*, 50.

50. William Penn, *My Irish Journal*, 48.

51. Patricia Lysaght, "Caoineadh os cionn coirp: The Lament for the Dead in Ireland," *Folklore* 108 (1997), 65–83.

52. Seán O Súilleabháin, *Irish Wake Amusements* (Dublin: Mercier, 1967), 138–140.

53. William Penn, *My Irish Journal*, 51.

54. William Penn, *My Irish Journal*, 49.

55. MacCarthy-Morrogh, *Munster Plantation*, 128–129; Martin Dowling, *Tenant Right and Agrarian Society in Ulster 1600–1870* (Belfast: Queen's University Belfast Institute for Irish Studies, 1999), 117–118.

56. Barnard, "Lord Broghill," 355.

57. Patricia Coughlan, "Sir Vincent Gookin" in *Dictionary of Irish Biography* Online (Cambridge: Cambridge University Press and Royal Irish Academy, 2017).

58. See Andrew Murphy, this volume; Andrew Murphy and Sarah A. Morgan, "Law and Civil Interest: William Penn's Tolerationism," in *Religious Tolerance in the Atlantic World*, ed. Eliane Glaser (Basingtsoke: Palgrave MacMillan), 111–133.

59. Barnard, "Lord Broghill."

60. David Heffernan, "Reconstructing the Estate of Richard Boyle, First Earl of Cork," *History Ireland*, 23, no. 2 (2015), 18–20; Terence O. Ranger, "Richard Boyle and the Making of an Irish Fortune, 1588–1614," *Irish Historical Studies*, 10, no. 39 (1957), 257–297.

61. Nicholas Canny, *The Upstart Earl: A Study of the Social and Mental World of Richard Boyle, First Earl of Cork, 1566–1643* (Cambridge: Cambridge University Press, 1982); David Edwards and Colin Rynne, "The History and Archaeology of the Irish Colonial Landscapes of Richard Boyle, First Earl of Cork c. 1595–1643," *Post-Classical Archaeologies* 7 (2017), 329–342; Audrey Horning, Shapeshifters and Mimics: Exploring Elite Strategies in the Early Modern Atlantic," in *The Colonial World of Richard Boyle, First Earl of Cork*, ed. David Edwards and Colin Rynne (Dublin: Four Courts Press, 2017), 27–42.

62. Dickson, 2005, 25.

63. Edwards and Rynne, "History and Archaeology," 336–337.

64. J. R. Jacob, "Boyle's Circle in the Protectorate: Revelation, Politics and the Millennium," *Journal of the History of Ideas* 38, no. 1 (1977): 131–140.

65. Lord Shannon to William Penn, 20 August, in Dunn and Dunn, *Papers of William Penn*, 48.

66. William Penn to Robert Boyle 5 August, 1683, in Albert Cook Myers, *William Penn's Own Account of the Lenni Lenape or Delaware Indians*, rev. ed. (Wilmington: Middle Atlantic Press, 1970), 44.

67. Breen, "Praying with the Enemy"; J. Patrick Cesarini, "What Has Become of Your Praying to God? Daniel Gookin's Troubled History of King Philip's War," *Early American Literature* 44, no. 3 (2009): 489–515; R. W. Cogley, *John Eliot's Mission to the Indians before King Philip's War* (Cambridge, MA: Harvard University Press, 1999).

68. William Penn, "Initial Plans for Philadelphia," 30 September 1681, in Dunn and Dunn, *Papers of William Penn*, 2:120.

69. Jill Lepore, "Dead Men Tell No Tales: John Sassamon and the Fatal Consequences of Literacy," *American Quarterly* 46, no. 4 (1984): 479–512.

70. Stephen Mrozowski and Heather Law Pezzarossi, *The Archaeology of Hassanamessit Woods: The Sarah Burnee/Sarah Boston Farmstead*, Cultural Resource Management Study 69 (Boston: Andrew Fiske Memorial Center for Archaeological Research, University of Massachusetts Boston, 2015); Jean O'Brien, *Dispossession by Degrees: Indian Land and Identity in Natick, Massachusetts, 1650–1790* (Lincoln: University of Nebraska Press, 1997).

71. Jean Soderlund, *Lenape Country* (Philadelphia: Penn Press, 2015), 149.

72. Andrew Murphy, this volume and *Liberty, Conscious and Toleration: The Political Thought of William Penn* (Oxford: Oxford University Press, 2016).

CHAPTER 6

The Roads to and from Cork

THE IRISH ORIGINS OF WILLIAM PENN'S THEORY OF RELIGIOUS TOLERATION

Andrew R. Murphy

William Penn was a quintessentially Atlantic figure, and scholars have long used the term to highlight his dual roles in both English and American public life, and the movement for religious freedom on both sides of the Atlantic to which he contributed. Although Ireland played a key role in Penn's development, both personal and public, scholars have less thoroughly explored the ways in which it served as a catalyst for Penn's career.[1] Penn received his first exposure to English colonization when he arrived at Macroom Castle in County Cork as a boy, taking up residence with his family on lands that Oliver Cromwell had granted to his father, a prominent naval commander. It was there that the young William Penn first met Thomas Loe, the itinerant Quaker who had been invited to preach to the Penn family, apparently at Sir William's invitation. (Years later, Penn would remember his father being moved to tears and himself, as a twelve-year-old, thinking, "What if they should all be Quakers?"[2]) During his next trip to Ireland, in 1666 and 1667, Penn received his first hands-on experience with the details of managing tenants, negotiating leases, and overseeing surveyors, working both with his father's tenants and in the halls of power in Dublin, where he secured letters patent to his father's lands in Shanagarry.

It was in Cork, of course, that Penn underwent his momentous Quaker convincement, thanks again to the preaching of Loe, whom he met again a decade after their first acquaintance, in late summer or early fall 1667. At that time, he also got his first taste of imprisonment for his faith, spending a few days in November 1667 in the Cork jail along with eighteen other Friends. On that occasion, Penn made his first public defense of religious liberty, insisting in a letter to the Earl of Orrery that there was "no way so effectual to improve or advantage this country as to dispense with freedom in things relating to conscience," and calling persecution a "malicious and injurious . . . practice to innocent Englishmen" and also "a bad argument to invite English hither [to Ireland]."[3] After his 1670 visit—which I shall explore in much more detail below—Penn returned to Ireland only once, in the summer of 1698, but his experiences there had provided him with rudimentary knowledge about the promise and peril of colonization.

More germane to the focus of this chapter, County Cork supplied the immediate context for Penn's first, and surely one of his most enduring, works of political theory: *The Great Case of Liberty of Conscience*. The composition of Penn's *Great Case* was undertaken against the backdrop of a series of particular events in Cork during the spring of 1670, but the arguments advanced in this early work formed the basis of Penn's political theory of toleration and liberty of conscience over the next forty-plus years.[4]

William Penn's Irish Journey 1669–1670

When his father sent William Penn to Ireland in autumn 1669, he had two main goals. He wanted to get his son out of England and hopefully out of trouble: William, not yet twenty-five, had already been imprisoned twice, once in the Tower of London and once in Ireland. And given his own declining health and the successful job his son had done managing the family's Irish affairs several years earlier, he hoped to further groom his son for the life of an English gentleman and landholder in Ireland by putting him in charge of negotiating new leases with his Irish tenants. The Penn lands comprised roughly twelve thousand acres that had been granted to Sir William by King Charles II shortly after the Restoration, as compensation for his surrender of Macroom Castle back to the Earl of Clancarty, a faithful supporter of the monarchy from whom Oliver Cromwell had seized it during the 1650s.[5]

One thing Sir William was, in all likelihood, not interested in doing, was encouraging his son's Quakerism. Although the overt strife that had poisoned their relationship in the wake of Penn's convincement had settled a bit, his parents remained deeply disappointed in their son's religious transformation. His father wrote to him in October 1669 that "if you are ordained to be another cross to me, God's will must be done."[6] As it turned out, Penn spent a great deal of time during his nine months in Ireland visiting persecuted Friends, attending Meetings, disputing with representatives of rival religious communities, and appealing to government officials across Ireland for leniency toward Quakers. Despite generally courteous treatment—he was, after all, the son of an English nobleman and naval hero—his efforts were largely unsuccessful. And yet, no matter what his name was, William Penn represented the Society of Friends, a despised and outlawed sect facing harsh legal disabilities and widespread popular hostility.[7]

These two dimensions of William Penn's identity—Quaker and English—would continue to frame his liminal existence during his time in Ireland. He had been a convinced Quaker for nearly two years by this point, and had become an active defender of Quakers and Quakerism, both in person and in print. During his 1669–1670 visit, he traveled a broad circuit between Cork and Dublin as a Friend, subject to arrest or fines at any time. As a Penn, on the other hand, he made the same circuit as a leading member of a colonizing elite that had dispossessed countless native Irish inhabitants in a centuries-long, exceedingly violent conquest.[8] The contrast between Penn the Quaker and Penn the English landlord was more visible on this trip to Ireland than in his previous one, since he had left Ireland shortly after his 1667 convincement. This second trip, which took place between October 1669 and July 1670, illustrated these tensions and paradoxes in Penn's public persona far more clearly.[9]

March 1670

On March 19, 1670, William Penn was staying at the home of Captain Richard Bent, a former officer in Cromwell's army then living in Castle Mary, near Cloyne in County Cork. Penn had been in Ireland just over four months. That day, he wrote in his journal, "I set about a book against persecution, called the Great Case of Liberty of Conscience debated and defended."[10] *The Great Case* would turn out to be something unique in Penn's fledgling career as Quaker controversialist: neither merely a defense of Friends against their critics nor a diatribe against the theological errors of others, it presented a systematic consideration of the foundations of liberty of conscience and a principled defense of guaranteeing rights of worship to Dissenters.

That said, *The Great Case* was a systematic treatise animated by two specific sets of events. First, and at a broader level, were a series of contentious debates during the late 1660s, in Parliament and the streets of London, leading up to Parliament's passage of the 1670 Conventicle Act, which outlawed unauthorized religious gatherings. Penn surely would have heard news about the progress of the legislation during his Irish journey, and the first edition of *The Great Case*, published in Dublin in 1670, referred explicitly to "the late Act" in its full title. Penn averred in the dedication that he was driven to present his work to the king "before the late Act has made too great a progress in [the country]."[11] The specific contexts in which the debates and ultimate passage of the Conventicle Act took place have been identified by a number of scholars as of central importance to understanding Restoration political and religious debates.[12] Second, and more immediately, March 1670 witnessed the outbreak of a particularly harsh episode of persecution of Quakers in Cork. The mid-March entries in Penn's journal are filled with references to the severe treatment unleashed on Friends in the city by Mayor Matthew Deane. "Friends imprisoned, great severity expressed"

(March 11); "Friends barbarously dealt with" (March 14); "a wickeder mayor or judge has not been in the city of Cork since truth came" (March 17).[13] Two days later, he began work on the book. Penn wrote at a brisk pace, recording in his journal that he "proceeded and almost finished my discourse against persecution" just four days after beginning it, and that he "sent one sheet" to the printers in Dublin less than a week later. He continued to work on *The Great Case* through early April, and it was published in late spring 1670, in Dublin.

Although the work of a young man whose career was still well ahead of him, all the arguments advanced in *The Great Case* would remain central to Penn's theory of toleration, which he continued to refine throughout the 1670s, attempted to implement in Pennsylvania, and later, alongside James II, worked tirelessly (and unsuccessfully) to bring to reality in England.

The Great Case: William Penn's Theory of Toleration

I have argued elsewhere that *The Great Case of Liberty of Conscience* was Penn's first attempt at, and the closest thing he ever produced to, a systematic treatise on liberty of conscience.[14] Its six substantive chapters synthesize the major arguments that had been advanced by tolerationists since the early seventeenth century, denouncing persecution as, above all, impious, but also as contrary to the spirit of Christianity, Scripture, nature and reason, principles of good government, and the testimony of dozens of statesmen, church leaders, and public figures since antiquity. And it was to this core set of arguments—laid out in a compact form, in just under 30 pages—that Penn would return a year later, in February 1671, in revising *The Great Case* while confined in London's Newgate prison.

This second edition of *The Great Case*, prepared while Penn was imprisoned, referred in its subtitle, not to the Conventicle Act, but more generally to "such late discourses, as have opposed a toleration." The second edition also added a clear definition of liberty of conscience:

> the free and uninterrupted exercise of our consciences, in that way of worship, we are most clearly persuaded, God requires us to serve Him in . . . which being matter of faith; we sin if we omit.[15]

Several pages later, Penn expanded on and clarified the parameters of this rather brief definition. By liberty of conscience, Penn argued, he meant

> not only a mere liberty of the mind . . . but the exercise of ourselves in a visible way of worship, upon our believing it to be indispensibly required at our hands. . . . Yet . . . not to . . . abet any contrivance destructive of the government and laws of the land, tending to matters of an external nature . . . but so far only, as it may refer to religious matters, and a life to come, and consequently wholly independent of . . . secular affairs.[16]

An expanded notion of conscience, of course, requires an expanded definition of persecution:

> By . . . Persecution, we don't only mean, the strict Requiring of us to believe this to be true, or that to be false . . . but . . . any coercive Let or Hindrance to us, from meeting together to perform those Religious Exercises which are according to our Faith and Perswasion.[17]

All the ingredients of a robust theory of religious liberty are present in these three brief passages.

First, Penn provides an expansive notion of conscience itself, the faculty that tolerationists sought so earnestly to liberate. Liberty of conscience includes the freedom not only of individual belief but also of action (i.e., religious exercise). The move from belief to action was significant, politically speaking. Even anti-tolerationists agreed that thought was free, and that anyone could believe anything he or she wanted to. Politically, however, they insisted that such individuals should keep unpopular or unorthodox religious views to themselves. As Thomas Hobbes put it in chapter 37 of *Leviathan*: "A private man has always the liberty (because thought is free), to believe, or not believe in his heart, those acts that have been given out for miracles." That said, Hobbes continued, "when it comes to confession of that faith, the private reason must submit to the public."[18] Surely the same could be said for a range of other religious teachings. The *political* question in Restoration Britain had to do not with the internal dimension of belief but rather with religiously inspired *behaviors* ("the products and effects of conscience in men's actings"[19]) and the degree to which they should be regulated by civil government.

Second, Penn understood conscientious religious exercise not merely as an individual right but as a collective one, as indicated in the plural pronoun in the phrase "the exercise of *ourselves* in a visible way of worship" (emphasis added). Liberty of conscience thus encompassed a wide range of actions falling under the broad rubric of "meeting together to perform those Religious Exercises which are according to our Faith and Perswasion." Like Locke's later *Letter Concerning Toleration*, Penn's *Great Case* was simultaneously a defense of individual conscience and a defense of independently gathered congregations and their right to worship as they saw fit, in the collective pursuit of their spiritual well-being.

Third, several specific types of collective rights—most particularly, freedoms of assembly, press, and speech—follow logically from liberty of conscience. Meeting with others, as mentioned earlier, serves an integral purpose to the exercise of individual conscience, since even the most theologically individualistic understandings of Christianity in the seventeenth century involved meeting with fellow believers in the process of pursuing salvation. In addition, some form of free speech seems implied as a dimension of liberty of conscience, since religious exercise involved preaching, the offering of testimonies of various sorts and, particularly in Quakerism's early years, evangelical attempts to turn others away from their erroneous religious views and to defend Friends' principles against their critics. The centrality of this cluster of related rights at the heart of modern politics has been recognized by political theorists both then and ever since, from John Milton to John Stuart Mill and down to Rawlsian liberals in our own time.[20]

Fourth, alongside the expanded notion of conscience, Penn also advanced a more expansive category of persecution. On his account, persecution includes not only political and legal sanctions for the exercise of conscience but any "coercive let or hindrance" to meeting for religious worship with like-minded others. To be concerned about persecution and toleration meant that one should attend not only to large-scale and graphic punishments like whipping, imprisonment, fining, and seizure of goods but also to the myriad ways in which early modern ecclesiastical and political authorities could interfere with Dissenters' religious exercise. Excluding those who dissented from the national church from holding public office, for example, as was the case under the Test Acts passed during the 1670s—or, more specifically to Penn and the Quakers, requiring oaths to be sworn in legal settings—punished individuals for their religiously held commitments and interfered with the exercise of conscience, less painfully perhaps, but as surely as fines and imprisonment.

Finally, this understanding of religion and conscience relied upon a bifurcation between "religious matters," which pertain to the "life to come," and those "matters of an external nature," which are properly the province of civil magistrates. Such a distinction served a rhetorically powerful function in emphasizing the compatibility between sectarian commitments like those held by Quakers and the requirements of social and political order, no small feat in Penn's time given the extraordinary public hostility directed at Friends from their earliest days. That said, many critics have pointed out (then and ever since) that such a dichotomy applies to some religious perspectives better than others, and that it runs the risk of misrepresenting the embodied nature of religion as a lived experience.[21]

The Case against Persecution

In these few sentences from *The Great Case*, Penn expanded the sorts of behaviors that ought to be understood as infused with conscientious justification. It was precisely this approach that so incensed critics of toleration like Samuel Parker, archdeacon of Canterbury and the author of the ferocious 1670 polemic *A Discourse of Ecclesiastical Politie*. In his *Discourse*, an extended, bitter, often ad hominem denunciation of those seeking toleration, Parker claimed that "to exempt religion and the consciences of men from the authority of the supreme power is . . . to expose the peace of kingdoms to every wild and fanatick pretender, who may, whenever he pleases . . . thwart and unsettle government without control."[22] As such, and to appreciate Penn's understanding of liberty of conscience, we must explore its many-sided nature, and the way he understood the political question before the nation. He stated that question by asking "Whether imposition, restraint, and persecution, upon persons for exercising . . . liberty of conscience . . . be not to impeach the honour of God, the meekness of the Christian religion, the authority of Scripture, the privilege of nature, the principles of common reason, the well-being of government, and apprehensions of the greatest personages of former and latter ages."[23] He then proceeded to answer his own question by specifying the particular ways in which persecution represented illegitimate governmental overreach.

Persecution was, at its most basic level, *impious*, an egregious interference with God's sovereignty over creation. To interpose human political authority between individuals and God—to decree which forms of worship are and are not to be allowed and to punish those who dissented from an established religion—"directly invade[s] divine prerogative . . . divest[s] the almighty of a due, proper to none besides himself . . . [and] enthrones man as king over conscience, the alone just claim and privilege of his creator."[24] John Owen, whom Penn knew from his student days at Christ Church College, Oxford, called conscience "God's great vice-regent" within the human soul and insisted that God "hath reserved the sovereignty of [our minds and consciences] unto himself, to him we must give account . . . at the great day."[25] Persecution puts humans in God's place as arbiters of proper religious beliefs and practices.

Penn further insisted that persecution was *fundamentally un-Christian*, contrary to the example of Jesus himself and of the early church more generally. The pattern laid down by the early Christians, on this view, illustrated that the true church does not persecute but rather emulates Jesus's own meek spirit (e.g., refusing to call down fire from heaven on critics, teaching that the first shall be last, and emphasizing the importance of peacemaking and Jesus's claim in John 18:36 that his kingdom was not of this world). Christianity "entreats all, but compels none," seeking spiritual goals only through the employment of spiritual weapons. *The Great Case* also offered a range of scriptural examples, from the parable of the tares and wheat and the Golden Rule, to Paul's exhortations to the Ephesians to bear meekly with others, and his remarks in Romans that each believer should be convinced in his own mind, and "whatsoever does not proceed from faith is sin" (Romans 14:5, 23). Persecution is not only impious, then, but more specifically represents "the overthrow of the whole Christian religion."[26] In making such references, Penn reflected broader tendencies in the tolerationist literature of the day.[27]

Of course, the movement for toleration in England was never simply about Christianity. It was always closely allied with the polity's Protestant identity and intertwined with long-standing English anti-Catholicism.[28] Protestants persecuting other Protestants, Penn lamented, "overturns the very ground of [their] retreat from Rome" and puts them in the place formerly occupied by their Catholic persecutors. Penn's formulation had the distinct advantage of allowing Quakers, as dissenters for the sake of conscience, to play the role of true Protestants: "for doubtless the papists said the same to you, and all that you can say to us: Your best plea was, Conscience upon principles, the most evident and rational to you: Do we not the like?" Calling those who differ in religion "heretics" is a "story . . . as old as the Reformation."[29] Denunciations of Roman Catholics were de rigueur among English tolerationists, who remained almost unanimous in their view that Catholics ought not to be tolerated. Penn shared his compatriots' deep distrust of Catholics, but in another work written during this same trip to Ireland, he attempted to step back from its harshest implications. In *A Seasonable Caveat against Popery*, Penn distinguished between ordinary Catholics and their leaders, admitting that "a great number of Romanists may be abused zealots, through the idle voluminous traditions of their church." Religious error alone was not sufficient to justify suppression, Penn insisted, and he maintained that Catholics whose political loyalty could be guaranteed might be granted toleration. Penn favored "a universal toleration of faith and worship" and insisted that his pursuit of toleration for Protestant Dissenters was not intended merely to shift the burden onto another group ("nor would I take the burden off my own shoulder, to lay it on theirs").[30]

Moving to a broader set of arguments against persecution, Penn maintained that punishment for the sake of conscience was unreasonable and contrary to human nature, that it was based on a misapprehension about the structure of human psychology and the way that humans understand and interpret the world. God "has given [humanity] both senses corporeal and intellectual, to discern things and their differences, so as to assert or deny from evidences and reasons proper to each."[31] Intellectual judgment is part of the process by which individuals understood and assessed the world around them. This act of judgment involves religious judgments as well: "As he that acts doubtfully is damned, so Faith in all acts of religion is necessary: now in order to believe, we must first will; to will, we must first judge; to judge anything, we must first understand."[32] For religion to be salvific for any individual, it must be the product of mature understanding and deliberate consideration.

Persecution was not only an affront to the functioning of the human mind, it was bound simply *not to work*. In other words, "the understanding can never be convinced, nor properly submit, but by such arguments, as are rational, persuasive, and suitable to its own nature. . . . Force may make an hypocrite, 'tis faith grounded upon knowledge, and consent, that makes a Christian."[33] The physical punishments delivered by punitive measures may induce behavioral changes, but they are powerless to effect the real inner change at the heart of true religion. This view of the workings of belief would later be put, most famously, by Locke in his *Letter Concerning Toleration*: "Such is the nature of the understanding, that it cannot be compelled to the belief of anything by outward force."[34]

Penn's theoretical case for toleration thus far in his *Great Case* had been rather negative. In other words, he provided a critique of persecution, reasons why state power ought not be turned against Dissenters. But there was always a positive vision as well: by criticizing what government was *actually* doing one simultaneously sketched a vision of what it *ought to be* doing. And so, in the work's fifth chapter, Penn argued that toleration is in the political interest of both rulers and ruled, that persecution was impolitic and destructive of principles of good government. Recall Penn's description of government, as concerned with things of an "external nature" and not with "the life to come." He defined it more explicitly as "an external order of justice, or the right and prudent disciplining of any society, by just laws."[35] If government is fundamentally about seeking justice, and if justice requires a kind of proportionality between crimes and punishments, persecution is ruled out as a kind of category mistake. In other words, "fines and prisons" are not "fit and adequate penalties for faults purely intellectual."[36]

In a straightforward political sense, all these issues—conscience, liberty, toleration—are ultimately about law (and more specifically about English law). Achieving tolerationists' goals would have entailed a significant revision in the legal status of religious dissent, as James II and Penn would be reminded, to their chagrin, in 1687 and 1688. Penn grounded his argument for liberty of conscience squarely in his English heritage; it was an argument aimed at English audiences and thus drew on widespread ideas about the normative force of antiquity and the "ancient constitution." To find reasons to denounce persecution, he wrote, one does not need to "scour the Corpus Civile of Justinian," but rather only to recommit oneself to the "good, old, and admirable laws of England."[37]

Key to this understanding of the laws of England was Penn's distinction between two types of law. Fundamental law (e.g., Magna Carta), as the name suggests, is "indispensable and immutable" and must not be abrogated under any circumstances. It functions to preserve essential liberties like liberty, property, and representation. Superficial laws, on the other hand ("temporary and alterable," passed by particular parliaments for the ordering of everyday life) are contingent, and must change with the times. Fundamental law forms the bedrock of society and must be maintained at all times, whereas superficial law may (and indeed must) be adjusted due to specific contingencies and circumstances, an argument that Penn made in more than one treatise.[38] Fundamental law secured Englishmen from the exercise of arbitrary power, and was like "Stars or compass for [rulers] to Steer the Vessel of this Kingdom by."[39] Penn's distinction between fundamental and superficial law enabled him to balance continuity with the need for change and evolution, and to argue that the changes he sought were not reckless innovations but rather a return to time-honored constitutional values.

From a tolerationist perspective, the Conventicle Act was a superficial law that was deeply incompatible with fundamental law, since the Magna Carta did not make civil liberty dependent on religious orthodoxy. In fact, English liberty and property were guaranteed by fundamental law, which predated Protestantism ("civil society was in the world before the Protestant profession"). The rights guaranteed by fundamental law could only be forfeited by clear violations of fundamental law and by established procedures for deciding when this had occurred (the classic case being the right to jury trial). In this regard, the persecutory framework of Restoration England itself was at issue, and one of Penn's contemporaries warned magistrates to "look, not so much whether they act regularly according to the late Act against Conventicles, as whether the Act itself be regular and according to the fundamental laws."[40] Simply passing legislation through Parliament was no guarantee of its legitimacy, since Catholics had passed anti-Protestant legislation in the past, legislation long denounced by Protestants as illegitimate.[41]

The important descriptors discussed earlier—government as external, as impartial, as dictated by the public interest and bound by fundamental law—indicate the significance of civil peace and prosperity to the conception of government Penn was articulating in *The Great Case*. Penal laws "are so far from benefiting the country, that the execution of them will be the assured ruin of it, in the revenues, and consequently, in the power of it; For where there is a decay of families, there will be of trade; so of wealth, and in the end of strength and power."[42] Penn attributed the prosperity of the Netherlands to its tolerationist stance toward religious difference.[43] If government is charged with promoting the common good, persecution undermines that goal, especially when considering how crucial Dissenters are to the nation's trade.[44]

Finally, Penn argued that further evidence of the happy coincidence between magistrates' interests and those of their people was provided by an extensive list of historical figures who tolerated Dissenters in their midst and reaped the benefits.[45] The first edition listed twenty-four such individuals, while the second edition added six more to the mix, from ancient statesmen like Cato and Hannibal down to English Kings James and Charles I. What made those statesmen, generals, and others so worthy of emulation is the way they grasped the importance of making prudential judgments informed by the proper ends of good government and respect for the rights of conscience.[46]

Penn never wavered in his conviction that the arguments arrayed in *The Great Case* presented an airtight argument for the religious, philosophical, psychological-epistemological, and political foundations of liberty of conscience. It was not only the proper policy for Christian rulers to adopt, it was the proper way to govern human beings, who are psychologically constituted in particular ways and gather in societies to seek shared goals. It is in the best interest of both rulers and ruled, and models from across human history and culture show how beneficial such a policy can be for the polities that adopt it. He summed up by asking, rhetorically, "[W]hat can be more equal, what more reasonable than Liberty of Conscience; so correspondent with the reverence due to God, and respect to the nature, practice, promotion, and rewards of the Christian religion; the sense of divine Writ; the great privilege of nature, and noble principle of reason; the justice, prudence, and felicity of government; and lastly, to the judgment and authority of a whole cloud of famous witnesses?"[47]

Conclusion

When William Penn sailed from Cork in late July 1670, he did not know that he would return only once, briefly, twenty-eight years later. Nor could he have foreseen that his subsequent travels on behalf of the Society of Friends would take him eastward into Holland and Germany (twice during the 1670s), and across the Atlantic to North America in the early 1680s. But his Irish experiences had shaped him and his thinking about toleration in important ways, and the searing experiences of persecution in Cork drove him to expand what had been, to that point, a public career focused largely on defending Quakers and attacking their rivals.[48] In *The Great Case*, Penn developed and defended a much broader vision as a proponent of religious toleration as a political approach to religious difference. The theory would be developed and elaborated, appropriate to changing political contexts, over the ensuing decades. Penn emphasized the importance of parliament in the governance of the realm, as reflective of the fundamental right of all Englishmen to representation, during the 1670s. During the early 1680s, Penn's explicit theorizing waned as he set about the difficult task of shaping Pennsylvania's institutions, in an attempt to bring the principles he championed as a Dissenter into practice as the ruling authority in a new society. He placed greater emphasis on the notion of civil interest as a kind of glue cementing together religiously diverse societies during the late 1680s, when he worked with James II (in spectacularly unsuccessful fashion) to repeal persecuting legislation. In each case—from the specific account of *The Great Case* offered in this essay to Penn's theorizing during the late 1680s and beyond—Penn's theory of toleration drew on long-standing themes and arguments in English political discourse and mobilized those arguments in particular political contexts.

The Great Case is worth lingering over not only for its systematic and synthetic presentation of arguments against persecution but also for the fact that it facilitated Penn's entry as a significant voice in the political debate over toleration. And his public profile would only continue to grow. When Penn returned to London from Ireland in summer 1670, he discovered that, under the terms of the Conventicle Act, the government had shuttered the Quaker meetinghouse on Gracechurch Street. As a result, on August 14, 1670, he and fellow Quaker William Mead began preaching in the street just outside the meetinghouse. The two were promptly arrested and charged with the common-law offense of disturbing the peace (i.e., riot) and addressing a tumultuous assembly. In their celebrated trial, the jury attempted to acquit Penn and Mead multiple times, in the face of a hostile and threatening court, finally finding the two men not guilty. Regardless of the quality of his arguments or the eloquence of his objections, Penn was sent to prison—not for preaching in the street, but for refusing to remove his hat in the presence of the judge. (He allowed his fines to be paid so that he could be released to be at his father's side in his final days.)

A purported transcript of the trial—entitled *The Peoples Ancient and Just Liberties Asserted*—was published anonymously shortly after its conclusion, while Penn was confined in Newgate prison, and went through nine printings in the last three months of 1670 alone. It recounts the contentious exchanges between the bench and the defendants, as well as between the bench and the jury, and includes a number of passages from historical documents and other sources vindicating Penn's and Mead's legal arguments. *The Peoples Ancient and Just Liberties Asserted* catapulted Penn to a national reputation by dramatizing the trial as a heroic confrontation between the defendants and the jury on the one hand, and an overbearing and oppressive court system on the other. It presents the trial as a morality play, with Penn and Mead as courageous Dissenters railroaded by a persecuting state–church system, and a conscientious jury punished for rendering their honest verdict. One of Penn's most impassioned "lines" in the trial refers us back to the centrality of fundamental law that he had laid out in *The Great Case*: "The question is not whether I am guilty of this indictment," Penn insists, "but whether this indictment be legal."[49]

As it turned out, the English legal system was not finished with William Penn. In February 1671 he was arrested again, for his presence at another Quaker meeting, in violation of the Five Mile Act, which forbade dissenting clergy from coming within five miles of any incorporated English town. (The fact that Quakers did not have clergy, per se, was a nuance with which Penn's judges were not concerned.) Unfortunately for Penn, persons accused under the Five Mile Act were not guaranteed a jury trial, and thus he went back to Newgate for six months. It was during this imprisonment that Penn revised *The Great Case* and published the second edition, which introduced his arguments in favor of toleration to an English audience and received a much broader circulation than the first.

When we put Penn's systematic recitation of arguments in *The Great Case* alongside his contentious and impassioned behavior in the courtroom in *The Peoples Ancient and Just Liberties*, we have a multifaceted picture of a young thinker and activist mobilizing long-standing political arguments as part of a broader movement for the toleration of conscientious religious dissent. Penn's career led him far from Cork, but his experiences there shaped his theory of toleration in deep and fundamental ways.

NOTES

This essay is based on, and expands, my keynote address to "The World of William Penn: Toleration and Migration," University College Cork, September 2016. My thanks go to Hiram Morgan and Ruth Canning for that invitation, and to the UCC audience for their constructive questions and comments. The UCC has recently posted, as part of its Corpus of Electronic Texts, a newly edited and annotated edition of Penn's "Irish Journal," along with a helpful bibliography, at https://celt.ucc.ie//published/E660001-002.html.

1. The exception that proves the rule is Nicholas Canny, "The Irish Background of William Penn's Experiment," in *The World of William Penn*, ed. Richard S. Dunn and Mary Maples Dunn (Philadelphia: Penn Press, 1986). On the more general Atlantic nature of Penn's theorizing, see my "'Livelie Experiment' and 'Holy Experiment': Two Trajectories of Religious Liberty," in *The Lively Experiment*, ed. Chris Beneke and Christopher Grenda (Lanham, MD: Rowman and Littlefield, 2015); and chs. 1 and 8 of my *Liberty, Conscience, and Toleration: The Political Thought of William Penn* (Oxford: Oxford University Press, 2016).

2. "An Account of the Convincement of William Penn," *Journal of the Friends' Historical Society*, 32 (1935): 22.

3. To the Earl of Orrery, in *Papers of William Penn [hereafter PWP]*, ed. Dunn and Dunn (Philadelphia: Penn Press, 1981), 1:51–52.

4. On the publication history of *The Great Case*, see Olive C. Goodbody and M. Pollard, "The First Edition of William Penn's *The Great Case of Liberty of Conscience*, 1670," *The Library* 16, no. 5 (1961): 146–149.

5. See Amy Wallis, "Who was Colonel Wallis?" *Journal of the Friends' Historical Society* 54 (1976), 12–13.

6. Sir William Penn to WP, October 6, 1669, in Granville Penn, *Memorials of the Professional Life and Times of Sir William Penn, Knt.* (London: James Duncan, 1833), 2:571–572. For more details on the bitter strife between father and son over William's Quaker conversion, see my *William Penn: A Life* (New York: Oxford University Press, 2019), ch. 3.

7. On the history of Irish Quakerism, and its later connection to Pennsylvania, see Albert Cook Myers, *Immigration of Irish Quakers into Pennsylvania, 1682–1750: With Their Early History in Ireland* (Swarthmore, PA, 1902).

8. See, e.g., Nicholas Canny, *Making Ireland British, 1580–1650* (Oxford: Oxford University Press, 2001).

9. For a comprehensive account of the journey, including details of Penn's travels and travails, see Murphy, *William Penn*, 66–75.

10. Penn's "Irish Journal" is reprinted in *PWP* 1:101–143; this quotation is at 121. Also helpful is the newly posted online version mentioned above; see https://celt.ucc.ie/published/E660001-002.html.

11. Penn, *The Great Case of Liberty of Conscience* (Dublin, 1670), title page, and "To the King."

12. For the broader context in which *The Great Case* appeared, see Gary S. de Krey, *London and the Restoration, 1659–1683* (Cambridge: Cambridge University Press, 2005), ch. 2; Tim Harris, *Restoration: Charles II and His Kingdoms, 1660–1685* (London: Penguin, 2005); and Andrew Murphy, *Liberty, Conscience, and Toleration: The Political Thought of William Penn* (Oxford: Oxford University Press, 2016), ch. 2.

13. *PWP* 1:120–121.

14. Murphy, *Liberty, Conscience, and Toleration*, ch. 2.

15. Penn, *The Great Case*, 2nd ed. (London, 1670), 4. The date on the title page of the treatise reads 1670, but the publication actually took place in February 1671 (which was listed as 1670 according to the Gregorian calendar, in which the new year began on March 25). Subsequent quotations from *The Great Case*, unless otherwise specified, will refer to this second edition.

16. Penn, *The Great Case*, 11.

17. Penn, *The Great Case*, 12.

18. Thomas Hobbes, *Leviathan* (London, 1652), ch. 37. In the Curley edition of *Leviathan* (Indianapolis: Hackett Publishing, 1994), the passage appears on p. 300.

19. Charles Wolseley, *Liberty of Conscience upon Its True and Proper Grounds Asserted and Vindicated* (London, 1668), 11.

20. John Milton, *Areopagitica* (London, 1644); John Stuart Mill, *On Liberty* (London, 1859), esp. ch. 1; and John Rawls, *A Theory of Justice* (Cambridge, MA: Harvard, 1971) and *Political Liberalism* (Columbia, 1993).

21. See, e.g., Talal Asad, *Genealogies of Religion: Disciplines and Genalogies of Power in Christianity and Islam* (Baltimore, MD: Johns Hopkins University Press, 1982).

22. Samuel Parker, *A Discourse of Ecclesiastical Politie* (London, 1670), 14–15.

23. Penn, *The Great Case*, 12.

24. Penn, *The Great Case*, 12, 13.

25. John Owen, *Indulgence and Toleration Considered in a Letter unto a Person of Honour* (London, 1667), 14; *A peace-offering* (London, 1667), 41.

26. Penn, *The Great Case*, 15; 21–22. Also Wolseley, *Liberty of Conscience*, 53.

27. Penn, *The Great Case*, ch. 3.

28. See, e.g., Slingsby Bethel, *The Present Interest of England Stated by a Lover of His King and Country* (London, 1671), 18–19, 22–23; John Corbet, *A Discourse of the Religion of England* (London, 1667), sec. 2–7.

29. Penn, *The Great Case*, 26, 32.

30. Penn, *A Seasonable Caveat against Popery* (London? 1670), 4, 32.

31. Penn, *The Great Case*, 19.

32. Penn, *The Great Case*, 20.

33. Penn, *The Great Case*, 22 (see also 23–24). See also Wolseley, *Liberty of Conscience*, 10, 29, 36, 49; Owen, *A peace-offering*, 20, 21, 39; Owen, *Indulgence and toleration*, 16.

34. John Locke, *Letter concerning toleration* (London, 1690).

35. Penn, *The Great Case*, 23.

36. Penn, *The Great Case*, Preface.

37. Penn, *The Great Case*, 3.

38. Penn, *England's Present Interest Considered* (London, 1675), 26.

39. Penn, *England's Present Interest Considered*, 52.

40. Anonymous, *The Englishman* (London, 1670), 12.

41. Penn, *The Great Case*, 35.

42. Penn, *The Great Case*, 27.

43. Penn, *The Great Case*, 41.

44. Owen, *Indulgence and Toleration*, 7, 8; Corbet, *A Discourse*, 26; Wolseley, *Liberty of Conscience the Magistrates Interest*, 8–10; Owen, *A peace-offering*, 37–38.

45. Penn, *The Great Case*, ch. 6.

46. Penn, *The Great Case*, ch. 6.

47. Penn, *The Great Case*, 44.

48. Penn had advanced some of his arguments for toleration in a lengthy letter to Lord Arlington while he was imprisoned in the Tower of London during June 1669. Then again, this was a piece of private correspondence and not a contribution to public debate. For the letter see *PWP* 1:89–95.

49. Penn, *The Peoples Ancient and Just Liberties Asserted* (London, 1670), 11.

PART III

Restoration Worlds

CHAPTER 7

New Worlds and Holy Experiments in the Restoration Literature of Milton, Bunyan, and Penn

Elizabeth Sauer

"My kingdom is not of this world" encapsulates Jesus's mission and "unworldly way of speaking," observes William Penn in his *Great Case of Liberty of Conscience* (1671).[1] Unlike Puritan colonists in the New World, who sought to found a "New English Canaan," English nonconformists, explains N. H. Keeble, lost hope in any significant change to their earthly existence.[2] Given that the coming of the kingdom was indefinitely deferred, what kind of society was conceivable, perhaps realizable, in the meantime, and what were the building blocks thereof? I address these questions by reviewing the literary evidence for the new worlds and holy experiments conceptualized by English tolerationists post-1660. In so doing, I take up, but reformulate, the challenge issued by Gary S. De Krey, who reclassifies works by Restoration nonconformists like Slingsby Bethel, John Humfrey, Philip Nye, John Owen, William Penn, and Sir Charles Wolseley. These dissenters made different claims to conscience and individual liberty, invoking natural law, interest theory, disestablishment, or prophecy in resisting the political, legal, and religious principles and policies of the church-state. Although their writings revealed their overlapping agendas, key figures and "better-known restoration authors," notably John Milton, John Bunyan, and William Penn have rarely been studied together in the *common* intellectual climate of the later seventeenth century, De Krey acknowledges. I would add that they have also been infrequently situated together in the cultural and literary milieu of the time, an oversight that this chapter aims, in part, to rectify.[3]

Focused less on the terms of dissent than on literary formulations of what Penn called his holy experiment, this chapter charts Milton's, Bunyan's, and Penn's errands into the wilderness as architects of new worlds founded on liberty of conscience. Particularly revealing is the company that their books keep on both sides of the Atlantic, the book being here the primary laboratory for holy experiments—literary, philosophical, legal. Examinations of the transatlantic reception of key writings by these authors unsettle some entrenched assumptions about each and about the historical and critical approaches applied to their works, here reconceived in the textual negotiations between the Old and New Worlds. A product of transnational exchanges, the received traditions of Milton, Bunyan, and Penn uncover more associations in the early modern literary landscape than have been typically imagined, while expanding the frontiers of literary production, troubling the notion of a coherent body of Restoration writings, and unsettling the concept of an insular English culture. This chapter thus invites literary scholars to enter the worlds of Penn in ways that Richard and Mary Maples Dunn's edited volume, *The World of William Penn*—dominated as it was by historians—did not.[4].

The English historian and essayist Thomas Babington Macaulay singled out Milton and Bunyan for their creative genius, while also mentioning the transatlantic translatability of their messages and influence. Milton was the "most devoted and eloquent literary champion," asserts Macaulay, as well as a champion of liberty, now exported to and nurtured in America, Macaulay adds. As for his contemporary, reports Macaulay, Bunyan derived great satisfaction from learning that "his Dream was the daily subject of the conversation of thousands" in New England.[5] Macaulay's tribute to these authors supports his own Whiggish agenda, of course, but the fact remains that he—a self-styled guardian of English culture and civility—saw fit to connect and commend the achievements of Milton and Bunyan above all other "creative minds" of the later seventeenth century: "One of those minds produced the *Paradise Lost*, the other the *Pilgrim's Progress*."[6] As for Penn, no national history is complete without him, Lord Macaulay decides, when, in *The History of England*, he credits Penn for framing his government on the principle of religious liberty, while also seizing the opportunity to indict the Quaker as an author of conspiracy and extortion—of popish proportion, in fact.[7]

The intersecting worlds of Milton, Bunyan, and Penn warrant examination in relation to the Anglo-American literary tradition. Though they may appear to be the strangest of traveling companions, Milton, Bunyan, and Penn conditioned their New World appeal and passage, and their books can productively be aligned along a transatlantic axis. "If a home in the American colonies possessed any books besides the Bible, they were likely to be *The Pilgrim's Progress* and *Paradise Lost*," according to Nancy Armstrong and Leonard Tennenhouse in *The Imaginary Puritan*.[8] How did the Baptist minister John Bunyan, and his "eminent . . . nonconformist contemporary," as N. H. Keeble refers to Milton,[9] make their way into the Anglo-American pantheon? Their favorable reception might be attributable to their shared interest in the pilgrimage, the ethic of suffering, and the trials of conscience, all of which were central for the dissenter Penn as well. Equally important is the transatlantic migration of *Paradise Lost*, *Pilgrim's Progress*, and Penn's *No Cross, No Crown*, his *Address to Protestants upon the Present Conjuncture*, and his *Truth Exalted* in the same period, as well as the ties to the motherland that all these writings represented for their exilic readers. A major goal of this recontextualization exercise is to consider the common places and spaces their books occupy and the ways in which they are used.

I

Louis Cazamian noted in his survey of English literature that *Paradise Lost*—the preeminent Restoration work—"is solitary [and] foreign to the movement surrounding it." Likewise, explains Cazamian in the same breath, *Pilgrim's Progress* "seems to belong to another world."[10] But as Milton was dislodged from the lonely eminence to which critical practice had raised him, Bunyan has reemerged, as Roger Sharrock observed, "not as an isolated heroic individual, . . . but as an exemplar of the Puritan culture, someone in a group with contemporaries whose works have analogues and rub together with the works of other men."[11] Certainly Milton's library confirms his immersion in a republic of letters,[12] though Bunyan's too shows an unexpectedly extensive community of the book. "If men are characterized by their company, why then may they not be by their choice of books?"[13] posits *The United States Democratic Review* in the nineteenth century. Bunyan's collection includes John Foxe's *Acts and Monuments* (which would later become prison literature for him); Arthur Dent's *The Plaine Mans Path-Way to Heaven*; Lewis Bayley's *The Practise of Pietie*; Lawrence Clarkson's *A Single Eye All Light, No Darkness* (1650); and Vavasor Powell's *Common-Prayer-Book No Divine Service* (1660, 1661), among numerous others. Bunyan would have read and refuted Penn's anti-doctrinal *The Sandy Foundation Shaken; or Those . . . Doctrines of one God subsisting in three distinct and separate Persons . . . Refuted* (1668)—the object as well of anti-Quaker nonconformist Presbyterian cleric Thomas Vincent's ire, as evidenced in *The Foundation of God standeth sure* (1668),[14]—and he censured English cleric Edward Fowler's *The Design of Christianity* (1671), along with works by Ranters and Quakers like Edward Burrough.[15] Bunyan may have consulted *A Key to Open Scripture Metaphors* (1682) by the Baptist Benjamin Keach, whose immensely popular works, including his anti-Quaker tracts, were transported across the Atlantic during the same time as Bunyan's and, for that matter, as Penn's Quaker defenses.[16]

Bunyan's textual life and afterlife developed alongside and intersected with both Milton's and Penn's. For example, seventeenth-century bibliophile Sir William Boothby, whose library holdings included Bunyan's *A Holy Life* and Thomas Sherman's counterfeit *Second Part of Pilgrim's Progress*, among other Bunyan-inspired productions, also possessed books by Milton, Baxter, Thomas Goodwin, Ferguson, John Owen, William Penn, and the aforementioned Thomas Vincent, with whom Penn contended, igniting a battle of books.[17] At the same time, the legacies of Milton, Bunyan, and Penn in the long eighteenth century were forged through acts of appropriation, sometimes amounting to censorship. Milton, Bunyan, and Penn were companions even in the adverse reception of their works. Material evidence thereof is found in the records of Restoration diarist and bibliophile Samuel Pepys, from whose diary references to Milton and Bunyan are missing, a conspicuous omission considering the stature of these two figures and the comprehensiveness of Pepys's record and book keeping.[18] Pepys's holdings, however, did include writings by the Penns. Pepys possessed a manuscript collection on naval affairs, assembled by Penn Jr., who had taken the material, as he reported, from "Sir William Penn's closet." As a closet compiler, Penn thus makes his way into the library of Pepys,[19] who had been Penn Sr.'s neighbor. Pepys designates as "ridiculous [and] nonsensical" the Quaker's first work *Truth Exalted*, which, Pepys confesses, he was "ashamed to read." In a slightly later entry, Pepys states, "I got my wife to read it to me," this time referring to "W. Pen's book against the Trinity." Pepys finds himself pleasantly surprised by his encounter with that anti-trinitarian book, namely the aforementioned *Sandy Foundation Shaken*, composed, the subtitle indicates, *By* W.P. j. *A Builder on that Foundation which cannot be moved* (1668): "I find it so well writ as, I think it is too good for him [Penn] ever to have writ it—and it is a serious sort of book, and not fit for every body to read. And so to supper," writes Pepys.[20] *The Sandy Foundation Shaken* had been illegally printed by Anabaptist John Darby. To Penn's dismay, Darby suffered the consequences for that impudent act at a time when few unlicensed printers actually did. As for Darby's connection with Bunyan, the former was employed by Nathaniel Ponder—publisher not only of tolerationist John Owen's works but also of Andrew Marvell's *Rehearsal Transpros'd* (at his and Darby's peril), and of Bunyan's *Pilgrim's Progress* and *Grace Abounding*.[21]

II

Transported across the ocean, Milton, Bunyan, and Penn would undergo a translation and naturalization as they undertook an errand into the "waste and howling" wilderness. To begin with Milton, the publication history of his epic *Paradise Lost* reveals how the poet would be drawn into America—"a country seeking national identity."[22] Thomas Goddard Wright in *Literary Culture of*

Early New England speculates, "If a poet of real ability had come to Boston, he would not have ceased to be a poet. If John Milton, for instance, had been driven over by the Restoration, I see no reason why he could not have developed '*Paradise Lost.*' . . . At least he would have found friends here," continues Wright, "Roger Williams; John Clarke; John Winthrop, Jr.," for example.[23] Nearly eighty years after Wright imagines a Boston setting for the production of *Paradise Lost*, Peter Ackroyd transports a pioneering, crusading Milton to America. "I leave England in order to save England," "I leave England in order to *be* England," "Providence is my guide," and "I shall be Milton among the Americans," prophesies John Milton, exilic Englishman, who is appointed Chief Magistrate of a new settlement, a city on a hill.[24] But Ackroyd's antihero is fated to confront his internal blindness, that is, his intolerance, with the result that a rather different holy experiment is conducted in New Milton, America, one that becomes known as "Paradise Lost."

As far-fetched as the attempted establishment of the paradisal, dystopian New Milton might sound, it depicts a likelier scenario than what the nineteenth-century humorist, Mark Twain, speculated about Milton's true literary pursuits and achievements. Upon learning, courtesy of Ignatius Donnelly's *Great Cryptogram: Francis Bacon's Cipher in the So-Called Shakespeare Plays* (Chicago, 1888), that Francis Bacon was Shakespeare's ghost writer, Twain credited John Bunyan for producing *Paradise Lost*, and Milton for realizing "his immortal *Dream*" in the composition of *The Pilgrim's Progress*.[25] As (the true) author of *Pilgrim's Progress*—designated by Isabel Hofmeyr as "a transnational and translingual text"—Bunyan became canonized in America, alongside Milton, the literary touchstone or "archetyp[al] . . . poet for New England."[26]

"Canonized" is an apt term, according the aforementioned *Democratic Review*, a highly influential American literary-political monthly. Indeed the transnational journeying of the printed *Pilgrim* was a success story. Its birthplace had been a prison, a venue where Milton and Penn had also done time. The "Denn" upon which Bunyan's narrator happens as he traverses the wilderness of this world in *Pilgrim's Progress* is marginally glossed "The Goal."[27] *Pilgrim's Progress* takes the form of an antipersecution narrative: "*What moved you at first to betake your self to a Pilgrims life?*" asks Piety of Christian (47). "I was driven out of my Native Country, by a dreadfull sound . . . That unavoidable destruction did attend me, if I abode in that place where I was" (48). The allegorical romance with its universal themes appealed to churchgoers and dissenters alike. Still, as W. R. Owens reminds us, the popularity of *The Pilgrim's Progress* did not instantly transform Bunyan's reputation as a "leading Dissenter and thus . . . a seditious opponent of church and state."[28] In 1681 Bunyan was accused of conspiring with other dissenters to "bind Kings in Chains . . . [and] bespatter great Ministers of State."[29] Penn himself would be cast a criminal,[30] though among the three figures, it was Milton who was the arch antimonarchist. Still, you had to choose your kings wisely or risk being branded as Jesuitical yourself.[31]

As the author of *Pilgrim's Progress*, Bunyan's own sectarian reputation did not become entwined with the prototypical, allegorical narrative of Christian's pilgrimage. The millenarian conclusion describes the dreamer's vision of Christian and Hopeful advancing toward the kingdom as they enter "the Country of *Beulah whose* Inhabitants called them, *The holy People, the redeemed of the Lord, Sought out*" (155). The "City . . . upon a mighty hill" (158) that the pair approaches is the final destination for those who make up "*the righteous Nation*" (161). The religious romance converts national election into personal election and grace for the formerly Graceless, the pilgrim's preconversion name and condition (46). The focus on the spiritual journey helps account for the popularity of the first edition of *Pilgrim's Progress*. The book's transnational significance and highly favorable reception is captured in the introductory verses appended to the Second Part of *The Pilgrim's Progress*. Here Bunyan sends off his book with an Envoye: "Go now, my little Book, . . . My *Pilgrims* Book has travel'd Sea and Land . . . / *Highlanders*, and *Wild-Irish* can agree / My *Pilgrim* should familiar with them be. / 'Tis in *New-England* under such advance, / Receives there so much loving countenance."[32]

Otherwise, however, Bunyan's writings register nothing but a passing interest in America. The same holds true for Milton. Notwithstanding J. Martin Evans's ground-breaking exploration of *Paradise Lost* as an epic strictly about America,[33] Milton's works in general avert a transatlantic or western orientation. Though lamenting in the Restoration era his failure to lay the foundation for a free English commonwealth,[34] Milton did not set his sights on the New World; and his extensive readings of such travel writings as Sir Walter Raleigh's *Discoverie of Guiana* (1596), Samuel Purchas's *Purchas His Pilgrimes* (1625), and Peter Heylyn's *Cosmographie* (1652) did not bring him closer to the Americas.[35] Instead, the promised land is providential. In the final books of *Paradise Lost*, Milton's angelic historian, Michael, envisions the "New heav'ns, new Earth, Ages of endless date / Founded in righteousness and peace and love."[36] The psychological, spiritual, and poeticized manifestation thereof is a "paradise within thee" (12.587) that Michael instructs Adam to cultivate, and which establishes the foundation of the true nation and the invisible church. In the meantime, the road to the new world is "Through the wild Desert, not the readiest way" (12.215). Adam and Eve, the two wayfarers (12.646), go forth "hand in hand with wand'ring steps and slow, / Through *Eden*" (12.648–649). These final verses recall the exiles' plight in Psalm 107:4: "They wandred in the wildernesse and strayed from the way: And found no citie where to dwell." Onto Israelite history, Milton in *Paradise Lost* maps an exodus story of "strangers and pilgrims."[37] Christopher Phillips observes in the *Epic in American Culture* that, "[w]hereas the present dominates the prophetic visions in Dante and Spenser, Milton inflects his narrative into the future tense."

In fact in *Paradise Lost* we witness for the "first time in the history of epic visions of futurity . . . that the vision moves temporally beyond the author's own era."[38] The postlapsarian pilgrims venture out into the modern world.

III

Penn's blueprints charted his own pilgrim's progress to the new world. While penning works to overturn weak foundations in the 1660s, much to Bunyan's disapproval, Penn championed liberty of conscience as a principle in such works as *The Great Case of Liberty of Conscience*, "A Postscript to *Truth Exalted*," and *An Apology for the Quakers*. Seeking to establish firm foundations, he composed constitutional writings to frame a government for a civil society that defended religious freedom.[39] In 1677 Penn and other influential Quakers were granted the colonial province of West New Jersey. Still in England, Penn announced to Robert Turner the christening of Pennsylvania: "God that has given it me through many difficultys will . . . bless & make it the seed of a nation."[40] Months later, he conceded to another Quaker, James Harrison, "There may be room there, tho not here, for such an holy experiment."[41] In the third chapter of the Book of Revelation "the Angel of the Church in Philadelphia" prophesied that the holy people of Philadelphia would populate the "Citie of my God, which is new Hierusalem."[42]

Upon his return to England following a near two-year stay in Pennsylvania from 1682 to 1684, Penn composed a farewell to the city on the hill, the fruit of his travels and tribulations: "Philadelphia, the virgin [settlement] of this province . . . w[ha]t travail have there been to bring thee forth."[43] The building materials for Penn's holy experiment were his anti-persecution and pro-toleration pamphlets. Among those now printed in the New World was *An Epistle to the People of God called, Quakers in the Province of Pennsilvania*, which was bound with *A General Epistle Given forth by . . . Quakers* (1686) and Frances Taylor's "An Epistle to Friends to be read in their Meetings," a tract that compares the Quakers to the Israelites en route to the promised land. The collection of pamphlets that constituted *A General Epistle* was printed by William Bradford in Philadelphia, when the first press was established in 1686. The final item in the collection is an inventory of books sold by Bradford, consisting mainly of titles by Penn, like his prison writing *No Cross, No Crown* (1668), as well as *A Brief Examination and State of Liberty Spiritual* (1681), *A Solemn Farewell to England* (1682), and, among others, *An Address . . . upon the Present Conjuncture*. As it nears its conclusion, *An Address* features a vision of a city on a hill, a trope so suggestive for Milton and Bunyan, as for Anglo-American writers from John Winthrop on. "Stand fast in the Liberty," urges Penn, quoting the Pauline epistles, "wherewith he has made you free, and be not entangled again into Bondage, for we are not come to that Mountain that we cannot touch . . . but [as] Christians are come to

Mount *Zion*, to *Jerusalem*, the Mother of Peace and Freedom," exclaims Penn (1:804). In listing causes of oppression, the appendix of *An Address . . . upon the Present Conjuncture* (1679)—which appears in a second edition as *An Address to Protestants of All Perswasions* (1692)—notes the refusal of the officials to acknowledge "the Kingdom of Christ is not of this World."[44] Again, the declaration is taken from John 18:36, and it served as the refrain of Penn's works, now printed in Pennsylvania, where the holy experiment would, in theory, deliver forth a civil society founded on liberty of conscience.[45]

Penn's writings thereafter included a history of another Quaker's pilgrimage—national and transatlantic. Penn had seen George Fox off to America in 1671, and welcomed him upon his return a year later. Several years after his death in 1691, Fox's journal, a composite project, was published, complete with a Preface by Penn. Fox was "no Man's *Copy*," Penn asserts admiringly in *A Journal or Historical Account of the Life, Travels, Sufferings, Christian Experiences and Labour of Love in the Work of the Ministry of . . . George Fox*, assembled by Quaker Thomas Ellwood, an amanuensis for Milton.[46] Ellwood assumed the responsibility of preparing the influential history of Fox's missions, life experiences, and sojourns, including his trips to Ireland and America. The 1694 *Journal* was a compilation of the experiences he recounted and dictated while in Worcester Jail. Ellwood organized the journal entries, supplemented them with manuscript letters and epistles, and documented the final fifteen years of Fox's life. Penn himself becomes a participant in the enterprise of bringing forth the narrative of Fox, and thus the *Journal* bound Fox, Ellwood, and Penn together textually.

In his Preface to Fox's *Journal*, Penn declares that his history "were fitter for a *Volumn* [*sic*] than a *Preface*," and later that year, he arranged for the separate publication of the Preface as *A Brief Account of the Rise and Progress of the People called Quakers*.[47] In his Epistle to the Reader in *A Brief Account*, Penn notes that narrative of Fox's life first appeared in Fox's *Journal*, but is now "republisht in a smaller Volume; knowing also full well that Great Books, especially in these days, grow Burthensome, both to the *Pockets* and *Minds* of too many."[48] Four of the six chapters, into which the Preface was now divided, review the dispensations of God up to the emergence of Quakerism. By Chapter 5, the way has been prepared for Fox, God's "First Instrument," infused with a "Divine, and not a Human Power" to witness to God's work in the world. His books and followers advance his mission, generate an afterlife for Quakerism, and connect the Old and New Worlds: "Thus he Lived and Sojourned among us . . . Recommending to some of us with him the *Dispatch* and *Dispersion* of an Epistle just before given forth by him to the Churches of Christ throughout the World, and his own Books: But above all, *Friends*, and of all Friends, those in *Ireland* and *America*, twice over. Saying, *Mind poor Friends in* Ireland *and* America."[49] Penn himself can't resist invoking the performance of his own treatise (which he identifies as a "Preface," a lingering reference from its earlier form as the front matter to Fox's *Journal*), which serves as a memorial and epitaph to Fox.[50]

IV

Books map and pursue their own course in their passages, translation, and repurposing. If, as book historian Hugh Amory maintains, consumption and reception are distinguishing factors in establishing the character of a body of literature,[51] then Milton's, Bunyan's, and Penn's works together have a stake in the development of an American literary culture—conceptual and material. Postmaster of the Massachusetts colony John Hayward had in his account a copy of *Pilgrim's Progress* (1682).[52] Acquisitions of Boston bookseller, John Usher, from a ship captain in 1683–1684 are itemized on a March 3rd invoice that features two copies of the Earl of Rochester's sultry *Poems* alongside four copies of Milton's *Paradise Lost*, eighteen copies of *Dr. Faustus*,[53] five of *Oxford Jests*, and three of *Present State of England*. An invoice dated May 29, 1684, lists the orders of ten copies of the *Second Part of the Pilgrims Progress*, alongside four of the *State of England*, two copies of *Two Journeys to Jerusalem*, and two copies of *Wonders of the Femall world*.[54] On April 13, 1685, *Miltons Logick* and the *History of Dr. Faustus* make their transatlantic journey together.[55] The hawkers' inventories at the time listed ballads, almanacs, Wigglesworth's *Day of Doom*, and *Pilgrim's Progress*.[56] The August 25, 1696 account of Boston bookseller Elkanah Pembrook included four copies of *The Pilgrim's Progress*.[57] That Bostonians were at this time aware of Penn is evident by references to his works made by Cotton Mather, who also cites Penn's disputant, Thomas Vincent.[58] At the end of the seventeenth century, Mather was finishing his Puritan epic jeremiad *Magnalia Christi Americana*, complete with quoted verses from book 6 of Milton's epic.[59] *Paradise Lost* thus helped Mather conceptualize his *Magnalia*, which exhibited the special place of the New World in the global narrative of Christian history and which, transported eastward across the Atlantic, would be published in London several years later.

In his travels, documented in *A Tour Thro' the Whole Island of Britain*, dissenter Daniel Defoe, whom Penn once tried to save from the pillory, takes the reader on a tour of key landmarks or "Monuments of *British* Worthies." After passing the statues of Sir Thomas Gresham and Indigo Jones, Defoe arrives at the Milton monument where he pays homage to the "sublime and unbounded Genius" of the poet, whose epic subject, based on the Genesis creation narrative, transported him "*beyond the Limits of this World*."[60] As the epic adventure continues, Defoe guides the reader across a covered bridge that offers a vision of New World prospects, mapping, and conquest. On the backside of the bridge's roof structure are alto-relievos, featuring representatives from the four quarters of the world presenting their products to *Britannia*, from which the rest of the world radiates. Bestowing order on newly discovered or possessed territories, the agents and instruments of British governance include "Sir *Walter Ralegh*, with a Map of *Virginia* in his Hand; and Sir *William Penn*, holding a Book styled *The Laws of* Pensylvania."[61]

Bunyan's books too were becoming (monumental) landmarks. A complete posthumous edition of Bunyan's works had been printed in two volumes, and Bunyan joined the ranks—on (and in) paper—of eminent contemporaries who had folio editions of their works: Richard Baxter, George Fox, Milton, and Anglican preacher John Tillotson.[62] And the material object did mean something for Bunyan, who declared "with very pardonable vanity," judges the aforementioned Thomas Macaulay, "that in New England his Dream . . . was thought worthy to appear in the most superb binding."[63] By now seventeen editions of the First Part of *Pilgrim's Progress* had been published in England, alongside six editions of the *Second Part*. And since imitation and other forms of repurposing offer evidence of influence and adaptability, it is noteworthy that Joseph Morgan soon thereafter drew on Bunyan in composing his allegorical *History of the Kingdom of Basaruah* (1715), which featured the American wilderness as the New Jerusalem.

The *Democratic Review* recognized, though with some dismay and skepticism, the acclaim that *Pilgrim's Progress* garnered: "Modern criticism, indeed, has ventured to assign to this work [*Pilgrim's Progress*] a rank even equal with that of Homer, [and] the sublime epic of Milton, and the mighty genius of the world's great poet!" Equally remarkable are, continues the article, the innumerable "copies of this extraordinary production . . . presented to the public in the several languages of the civilized world."[64] In the issue of the *Democratic Review*, *Paradise Lost* is described as a work "every body admires, but scarce any body reads."[65] Compare that to Samuel Johnson's admission—reported in the same issue of the *Democratic Review*—that *Robinson Crusoe* is a book "Nobody ever laid down . . . without wishing it longer."[66] Cultural value translated into something more or other than sublime, lofty epic poetry and literary sophistication, as the comparisons of Bunyan, Milton, Defoe in (Whig-infused) American literary criticism demonstrate.

Among the contributors to the *Review* were Nathaniel Hawthorne, and occasionally Quaker-inspired Transcendentalists Walt Whitman and Henry David Thoreau.[67] Their work showcased the connections between democratic impulses and a liberty-embracing literary tradition during the antebellum years. Further, it would claim to key literary achievements of English writers for an enlightened, civilized America. Though the periodical's first editor and columnist, John L. O'Sullivan asserted that Providence was the guide first and foremost of the "Anglo-American race,"[68] and saluted America as the model for and harbinger of the future,[69] the *Review* sustained tensions between professions of universalism and assertions of American exceptionalism. This was especially true in the sections on literary criticism. Titled "Nationality in Literature," a key article in the March 1847 issue of the *Review*, features as its epigraph Milton's famed *Areopagitican* description of London as a city on a hill: "Behold, now, this vast city: a city of refuge, the mansion-house of liberty. . . . What wants there to such a towardly and pregnant soil, but wise and faithful laborers, to make a knowing people, a nation of prophets, of sages, and of worthies?" Then, continues Thomas Prentice Kettell (editor, 1846–1851) seamlessly, "We are a nation of readers, thirty millions strong; but what are our books, and who are our writers?" given, he implies that national identity is a literary formulation and achievement.[70]

Tying "literary intelligence" to political and national interests, the *Democratic Review* published character sketches of historical champions of liberty to celebrate their feats of "Christian Heroism." Among the portraits composed by John Greenleaf Whittier, an American Quaker poet and abolitionist, and a prolific contributor to the *Democratic Review*, is one that sets Milton in apposition to Penn. The latter is commended for defending the rights of the English from his jail cell, while Milton, chained "like another Prometheus on his rock . . . still turned upon [his oppressor] with an eye of unsubdued defiance," enabling "Liberty [to] speak through him"—"nobly."[71]

"We learn, from other sources, that he continued to write and print in defence of his religious views up to . . . 1713," writes Whittier, this time about Thomas Ellwood, whose character portrait appears immediately after Bunyan's in Whittier's "Old Portraits and Modern Sketches" published in Boston in a collection of Whittier's prose writings. The sketch of Ellwood is important because he was, Whittier insists, "one of the firm confessors of the old struggle for religious freedom . . . the friend of Penn and Milton, and the suggester of *Paradise Regained*."[72] In his own *History*, Ellwood had decried the "diabologues" that Baptist Thomas Hicks composed to slander Quakers, and of which Bunyan signaled his approval.[73] Just before praising Penn's printed assaults on the Baptists, Ellwood had confronted Milton about the failure of his holy experiment: "Thou hast said much here of *Paradise Lost*; but what hast thou to say of *Paradise Found*?" asked Ellwood of Milton. "This is owing to you,"[74] Milton reputedly responded to Ellwood, who is credited with inspiring *Paradise Regained*, which maps the pilgrim's progress of the second Adam through the wilderness but no hint, however, of a kingdom come.[75]

Macaulay, observes Whittier, was justified in his declaration, cited earlier in this chapter, that "the two great creative minds of the seventeenth century" were those that produced *Paradise Lost* and the *Pilgrim's Progress*.[76] Whittier here recalls Macaulay's essays in which he aligned Bunyan and Milton as literary geniuses and defenders of liberty, defined as that "mighty principle" now embraced in America. For Whittier, the august company of Milton and Bunyan includes not only Locke but also Penn. Whittier doesn't demote Penn from the Whig Pantheon, as Macaulay needed to do. "What Milton and Penn and Locke wrote in defence of Liberty, Bunyan lived out and acted" in liberty's name; "There were giants in those days," Whittier adds admiringly in his biographical narratives, which align Old and New World freedom fighters.[77] The last sketch in "Historical Papers," the final section of volume 2 of Whittier's prose works, profiles Massachusetts Bay governor John Winthrop. Occupying the "noble[st] place" in the company of the first émigrés, the (relatively speaking) liberty-seeking Winthrop compares highly favorably with Sir Henry Vane and Milton as a gentleman, Puritan, and "enlightened statesman." As for the intolerance that darkened his time, Winthrop is hardly at fault for the error he shared with "the generation in which he lived."[78]

What can the history of the critical, literary, material, and transatlantic associations of *Paradise Lost* and *Pilgrim's Progress*, along with Penn's blueprints of his holy experiment, teach us? A study of the transmission and received tradition of these books pushes against the boundaries and protocols of periodization, here the early modern period and long eighteenth century, and reveals the interconnections of English and American national literatures. And, while it confirms that the British Atlantic world depended on the other for its cultural identity and complexion, this investigation shows how the New World context also helped redefine the contours of the discipline of English literature and letters, offering new paradigms for establishing literary intelligence, and exhibiting intersections of aesthetic, philosophical, political, and national values. Literary critical and cultural approaches reinvigorate readings of *Paradise Lost*, *Pilgrim's Progress*, and Penn's papers and the relationship among them. Put together along a transatlantic axis, the works offer a medium through which to explore the conceptions and constructions of holy experiments, all framing new worlds wrought out of book passages and textual transactions.

NOTES

I gratefully acknowledge my indebtedness to Andrew R. Murphy and the Rutgers British Studies Center at Rutgers University, New Brunswick, for inviting me to deliver a paper at the conference on "The Worlds of William Penn," which serves as the basis for the present chapter.

1. Penn, "To William, Prince of Orange," 26 February 1680; Penn, *The Great Case of Liberty of Conscience, A Collection of the Works of William Penn. In two volumes. To which is Prefixed a Journal of His Life. With many original letters and papers not before published*, 2 vols. (London: J. Sowle, 1726; rpt. New York: AMS Press, 1974), 2:27; 1:449. The quotation is based on John 18:36. See Andrew R. Murphy, "Persecuting Quakers? *Liberty and Toleration in Early Pennsylvania*," in *The First Prejudice: Religious Toleration and Intolerance in Early America*, ed. Chris Beneke and Christopher S. Grenda (Philadelphia: Penn Press, 2011), 147.

2. N. H. Keeble, *The Literary Culture of Nonconformity in Later Seventeenth-Century England* (Leicester: University of Leicester Press, 1987), 279.

3. Gary De Krey, "Rethinking the Restoration: Dissenting Cases for Conscience, 1667–1672," *Historical Journal*, 38, no. 1 (1995): 82.

4. Richard S. Dunn and Mary Maples Dunn, eds., *The World of William Penn* (Philadelphia: Penn Press, 1986).

5. Thomas Babington Macaulay, *Select Essays of Macaulay: Milton, Bunyan, Johnson, Goldsmith, Madame D'Arblay*, ed. Samuel Thurber (Boston: Allyn and Bacon, 1892), "Milton" (1823), 22; "Bunyan" (1854), 50.

6. [Thomas Babington Macaulay,] review of *The Pilgrim's Progress, with a Life of John Bunyan*, by Robert Southey, *Edinburgh Review, or Critical Journal*, 54, no. 108 (Edinburgh, December 1831): 461.

7. Thomas Babington Macaulay, *The History of England from the Accession of James II*, 5 vols. (Boston: Estes and Lauriat, 1880), 1: ch. 4, 457, 459.

8. Nancy Armstrong and Leonard Tennenhouse, *The Imaginary Puritan: Literature, Intellectual Labor, and the Origins of Personal Life* (Berkeley: University of California Press, 1992), 11.

9. N. H. Keeble, "Introduction," in *John Bunyan: Reading Dissenting Writing*, ed. N. H. Keeble (Bern: Peter Lang, 2002), 17.

10. Louis François Cazamian, *A History of English Literature: Modern Times (1660–1959)*, Part II of Émile Legouis and Louis François Cazamian, *A History of English Literature* (London J. M. Dent, 1961; rev. ed. 1964), 602.

11. Roger Sharrock, "Evaluation of Bunyan Studies," in *John Bunyan in England and Abroad: Papers delivered at the John Bunyan Tercentenary Symposium, Vrije Universiteit Amsterdam, 1988*, ed. M. van Os and G. J. Schutte (Amsterdam, the Netherlands: VU University Press, 1990), 53.

12. Jackson Campbell Boswell, *Milton's Library: A Catalogue of the Remains of John Milton's Library and an Annotated Reconstruction of Milton's Library and Ancillary Readings* (New York: Garland, 1975).

13. "The Pleasures of the Pen," *Democratic Review*, 20, no. 103 (Jan. 1847) (New York: J. & H. G. Langley): 33. Throughout this chapter, the title "The United States Magazine and Democratic Review" or "The United States Democratic Review" is cited as "Democratic Review."

14. Richard Greaves, *John Bunyan and English Nonconformity* (London: Hambledon Press, 1992), 39–41. On the controversy generated by *The Sandy Foundation*, see Mary Maples Dunn and Richard S. Dunn, eds. *The Papers of William Penn, Volume One 1644–1679* (Philadelphia: Penn Press, 1981), 72–73.

15. On Bunyan's books and reading materials, see Richard L. Greaves, *Glimpses of Glory: John Bunyan and English Dissent* (Stanford: Stanford University Press, 2002), 603–607.

16. English nonconformist Benjamin Keach's *The Grand Impostor Discovered: or, the Quakers Doctrine . . . found wanting*, for example, was printed in Boston by John Foster in 1678.

17. Greaves, *Glimpses of Glory*, 620n64.

18. Milton doesn't appear in Pepys's Diary and is only indirectly referenced in a letter of one of Pepys's correspondents, Daniel Skinner (Gamaliel Bradford, *Samuel Pepys* [London: Jonathan Cape, 1920], 151). See "Mr. Daniel Skinner to Pepys, Rotterdam, Nov. 19, 1676," in *The Life, Journals, and Correspondence of Samuel Pepys*, ed. Rev. John Smith, 2 vols. (London: Richard Bentley, 1841), 1:169–181. Skinner defends himself against being tainted by Milton's antimonarchism (1:178). Pepys's personal collection of books housed in the Pepys Library of Magdalene College, Cambridge, following his death in 1703 and containing over 3,000 volumes, including the diary, does have books by Milton and Bunyan. C. S. Knighton, ed., *The Catalogue of the Pepys Library at Magdalene College, Cambridge: Supplementary Series Volume 1: Census of Printed Books* (Cambridge: D.S. Brewer, 2004) lists entry #1430 (8) *Tenure of Kings and Magistrates* (1649); *Paradise Lost*, 1688 4th ed. Also listed are *Paradise Regained* and *Samson Agonistes* (entries #2699 1 and 2), 269. Entry #365 (41) is J. B. *The pilgrims progress to the other world; or, a dialogue between two pilgrims* (London, 1684).

19. *Facsimile of Pepys's Catalogue* (1991), ed. David McKitterick, vol. 7.2 of *Catalogue of the Pepys Library at Magdalene College Cambridge*, ed. Robert Latham et al., 7 vols. (Cambridge: D.S. Brewer, 1978–1994), 255.

20. 12 Oct. 1668; 12 Feb. 1669, Vol. 9 (1668–1669; pub. 1976) of Pepys, *The Diary of Samuel Pepys*, ed. Robert Latham and William Matthews, rev. ed., 11 vols. (London: Bell and Hyman, 1970–1983), 327, 446.

21. "Order of the Privy Council," 16 Dec. 1668, *The Papers of William Penn, Volume One 1644–1679*, 82. On Ponder, see F. M. Harrison, "Nathaniel Ponder: The Publisher of *The Pilgrim's Progress*," *The Library* 15 (1934): 257–294. *The Prose Works of Andrew Marvell: 1676–1678*, ed. Andrew Marvell, Martin Dzelzainis, Annabel M. Patterson, 2 vols. (New Haven: Yale University Press, 2003), 2:9.

22. George F. Sensabaugh, *Milton in Early America* (Princeton: Princeton University Press, 1964), ix.

23. See also Thomas Goddard Wright's breakdown of the types of books printed at Cambridge from 1638 to 1670 in *Literary Culture in Early New England, 1620–1730* (New Haven: Yale University Press, 1920).

24. Peter Ackroyd, *Milton in America* (London: Sinclair-Stevenson, 1996), 29, 142.

25. Notes for unwritten article in Notebook 27, *Mark Twain's Notebooks & Journals, Volume III (1883–1891)*, ed. Robert Pack Browning et al. (Berkeley: University of California Press, 1979), 324n73; 327, 326.

26. Isabel Hofmeyr, *The Portable Bunyan: A Transnational History of "The Pilgrim's Progress"* (Princeton: Princeton University Press, 2004), 1, 3; F. O. Matthiessen, *American Renaissance: Art and Expression in the Age of Emerson and Whitman* (New York: Oxford University Press, 1941), 103.

27. John Bunyan, *The Pilgrim's Progress from This World to That Which Is to Come*, ed. James Blanton Wharey, 2nd ed., rev. Roger Sharrock (Oxford: Clarendon Press, 1960), 8. Subsequent references to *The Pilgrim's Progress* are cited parenthetically.

28. W. R. Owens, "The Reception of *The Pilgrims Progress* in England," in *Bunyan in England and Abroad*, ed. Anne Laurence, et al., 94–104.

29. Cave Underhill and Vox Lachrymae, *A Sermon Newly Held Forth at Weavers-Hall, upon the Funeral of the Famous T.O. Doctor of Salamancha* (Frankfurt, 1681; rpt., London, 1682), 6–7.

30. J. R. Jones, "A Representative of the Alternative Society of Restoration England?" in *The World of William Penn*, ed. Richard S. Dunn and Mary Maples Dunn (Philadelphia: Penn Press, 1986), 57.

31. Such was the case with Penn, maligned as a "Jesuit in disguise," a code for the fear that the Quakers' and Baptists' support of James II's tolerationist policies was promoting the dangerous indulgence of Catholicism. [William Popple,] *Letter to Mr Penn* (London, 1688), 5–7. See also Scott Sowerby's "William Penn and James II," chapter 8 in this volume.

32. Bunyan, "The Authors Way of Sending Forth His Second Part of the 'Pilgrim,'" *The Pilgrim's Progress from This World*, 167, 169.

33. J. Martin Evans, *Milton's Imperial Epic: "Paradise Lost" and the Discourse of Colonialism* (Ithaca, N.Y.,: Cornell University Press, 1996).

34. Milton published the second edition of *The Readie and Easie Way to Establish a Free Commonwealth* in April 1660.

35. On this point, see Elizabeth Sauer, "Milton and the 'savage deserts of America,'" *Milton Studies* 58 (2017): 3–26.

36. Milton, *Paradise Lost*, in *John Milton: Complete Poems and Major Prose*, ed. Merritt Y. Hughes (New York: Macmillan, 1957), 12.549–550.

37. Exodus 6:4; Hebrews 11:13; The First Epistle of Peter 2:11.

38. Christopher N. Phillips, *Epic in American Culture: Settlement to Reconstruction* (Baltimore, MD: Johns Hopkins University Press, 2012), 65.

39. Article XXXV in Penn's *Frame of Government and Laws Agreed upon in England* (May 1682) lays out the terms for religious freedom: all occupants of Pennsylvania who acknowledge God's supremacy and "hold themselves obliged in Conscience to live peace-

ably and justly in *Civil Society*" won't be persecuted (Richard S. Dunn and Mary Maples Dunn, eds., *The Papers of William Penn, Volume Two 1680–1684* [Philadelphia: Penn Press, 1982], 225).

40. Letter to Robert Turner, 5 March 1681, Dunn and Dunn, *The Papers of William Penn*, 2:83. See Andrew Murphy's "'Livelie Experiment' and 'Holy Experiment': Two Trajectories of Religious Liberty," in *The Lively Experiment: Religious Toleration in American from Roger Williams to the Present*, ed. Chris Beneke and Christopher S. Grenda (London: Rowman and Littlefield, 2015), 47. The phrase appears in the first of Penn's Fundamental Constitutions of Pennsylvania (Summer 1681), an unpublished document that represented an early attempt at framing the colony's government. By contrast, Murphy further explains, Rhode Island's development of a "lively experiment" was authorized by Parliament in 1644 and by the Crown in the Royal charter of July 15, 1663.

41. Penn, "To James Harrison," 25 August 1681, Dunn and Dunn, *The Papers of William Penn*, 2:108. See A. R. Murphy, *Conscience and Community: Revisiting Toleration and Dissent in Early Modern England and America* (University Park: Penn State University Press, 2001), 180–185. As Murphy observes in his biography of Penn, "Pennsylvania was to be, in its founder's words, a bold 'Holy Experiment' in religious freedom and toleration, a haven for those fleeing persecution in an increasingly intolerant England and across Europe" (*William Penn: A Life* [Oxford: Oxford University Press, 2018]).

42. King James Bible, Revelation 3:7.

43. "To Thomas Lloyd, J. Claypole, J. Simcock, C. Taylor, and J. Harrison," 12 August 1684, Dunn and Dunn, *The Papers of William Penn*, 2:591.

44. Dunn and Dunn, *The Papers of William Penn*, 1:814.

45. As Stefano Villani noted in "'To Correct the Mistakes of the World . . .': Early Quaker Activity from 1654 to the Founding of Pennsylvania," Penn considered Philadelphia and Pennsylvania as a New Jerusalem, as announced in the Revelation of St. John (The Book of Revelation 3:7–12). Pennsylvania was a Promised Land, which was supposed to represent an example, a banner for all the nations of the world: a "holy experiment" (Paper presented at "The Worlds of William Penn," Rutgers University, New Brunswick, NJ, Nov. 2015).

46. George Fox, *A Journal or Historical Account of the Life, Travels, Sufferings, Christian Experiences and Labour of Love in the Work of the Ministry of . . . George Fox* (London, 1694), [H1r].

47. Penn, "The Preface, Being a Summary Account of the Diverse *Dispensations of God* to Men, From The Beginning of the World to That of our present Age, by the Ministry and Testimony of his Faithful Servant *George Fox*, as an Introduction to the ensuing *Journal*," in *A Journal or Historical Account of the Life, Travels, Sufferings, Christian Experiences and Labour of Love in the Work of the Ministry of . . . George Fox* (London, 1694), sig. A-Nv ([sig. C2r]); Penn, *A Brief Account of the Rise and Progress of the People called Quakers* (London, 1694).

48. Penn, "An Epistle to the Reader," *Brief Account of the Rise*, sig. A2v.

49. Penn, *Brief Account of the Rise*, 98.

50. Penn, "The Preface," in *A Journal or Historical Account of . . . George Fox*, Jv; Penn, *Brief Account of the Rise*, 99.

51. Hugh Amory, "Reinventing the Colonial Book," in *The Colonial Book in the Atlantic World*, ed. Hugh Amory and David D. Hall, vol. 1 of *A History of The Book in America* (Cambridge: Cambridge University Press, 2000), 28.

52. Worthington Chauncey Ford, *The Boston Book Market, 1679–1700* (Boston, 1917), 86.

53. The popularity thereof may have arisen because of the witchcraft controversies (Ford, *Boston Book Market*, 49).

54. Wright, *Literary Culture in Early New England, 1620–1730*, 122.

55. Wright, *Literary Culture*, 122

56. Wright, *Literary Culture*, 126

57. Ford, *Boston Book Market*, 155.

58. Wright, *Literary Culture in Early New England, 1620–1730*, 246, 249.

59. Mather, *Magnalia Christi Americana: or, The ecclesiastical history of New-England, from its first planting in the year 1620. unto the year of Our Lord, 1698* (London, 1702; Hartford, 1820).

60. Daniel Defoe, *A Tour Thro' the Whole Island of Great Britain. Divided into circuits or journeys. Giving a particular and entertaining account of whatever is curious, and worth observation; The Third Edition*, 4 vols. (London: Printed for J. Osborn, S. et al., 1742), 3:282 (my emphasis).

61. Defoe, *A Tour Thro' the Whole Island of Great Britain*, 3:285.

62. The 1692 folio edition of Bunyan's works was produced by Charles Doe. See also N. H. Keeble, "John Bunyan's Literary Life," in *The Cambridge Companion to Bunyan*, ed. Anne Dunan-Page (Cambridge: Cambridge University Press, 2010), 23; and W. R. Owens, "Reading the Bibliographical Codes: Bunyan's Publication in Folio," in *John Bunyan: Reading Dissenting Writing*, ed. N. H. Keeble, 59–77.

63. Thomas Babington Macaulay, "Bunyan" (1854), in *Select Essays of Macaulay: Milton, Bunyan, Johnson, Goldsmith, Madame D'Arblay*, ed. Samuel Thurber (Boston: Allyn and Bacon, 1892), 50.

64. "The Pleasures of the Pen," *Democratic Review*, 20, no. 103 (Jan. 1847) (New York: J. & H. G. Langley): 33.

65. "The Pleasures of the Pen," 34.

66. "The Pleasures of the Pen," 33.

67. Edward L. Widmer, *Young America: The Flowering of Democracy in New York City* (New York and Oxford: Oxford University Press, 1999), 66. The *Review* was initially edited by John O'Sullivan, who coined the phrase "Manifest Destiny" in 1845.

68. John L. O'Sullivan, "The Course of Civilization," *Democratic Review*, 6, no. 21 (Sept. 1839): 208–217 (211).

69. John L. O'Sullivan, "The Great Nation of Futurity," *Democratic Review*, 6, no. 23 (Nov. 1839): 427.

70. Thomas Prentice Kettell, "Nationality in Literature," *Democratic Review*, 26, no. 105 (March 1847): 264.

71. *Democratic Review*, 17, no. 85 (July–August 1845): 126.

72. John Greenleaf Whittier, "Thomas Ellwood," in *Old Portraits and Modern Sketches: Personal Sketches and Tributes: Historical Papers*, vol. 2 of *The Prose Works of John Greenleaf Whittier*, 3 vols. (Boston: Houghton Mifflin, Co., 1866, rpt. 1892), 2:68. The first two portraits in *Old Portraits* are of Bunyan and Ellwood.

73. Thomas Ellwood, *The History of the Life of Thomas Ellwood . . . To which is added, a Supplement by J[oseph] W[yeth]*, 2nd ed. (London, 1714), 313. The Philadelphia reprint date of the book is 1775. Bunyan, *Grace Abounding to the Chief of Sinners*, 6th ed. (London: Nathaniel Ponder, 1688), 58–59.

74. Ellwood, *The History of . . . Thomas Ellwood*, 246–247. See also Whittier "Thomas Ellwood," 54.

75. Milton, *Paradise Regained*, in *Milton: The Complete Shorter Poems*, ed. John Carey, 2nd ed. (New York: Longman, 1999), 1:192, 4:600.

76. Whittier, "John Bunyan," *Prose Works of John Greenleaf Whittier*, 2:36.

77. Whittier, "John Bunyan," *Prose Works of John Greenleaf Whittier*, 2:35.

78. Whittier, "John Winthrop," *Prose Works of John Greenleaf Whittier*, 2:436–437.

CHAPTER 8

William Penn and James II

Scott Sowerby

Politics can find no stranger bedfellows than James II and the Quakers. James was the most imperious of monarchs; the Quakers were the most obdurate of subjects. James believed in hierarchy; the Quakers believed in equality. James maintained a standing army, and Quakers refused to bear arms. James was not accustomed to asking for favors, and Quakers were not accustomed to granting them. An encounter between James II and a Quaker might have seemed likely to end in an imprisonment, not an alliance.

These differences might have been unbridgeable were it not for the fact that James, like the Quakers, worshipped outside the Church of England. The future king had converted to Catholicism in the late 1660s. His conversion had become publicly known when he resigned his post as lord high admiral in June 1673 after the passage of a Test Act forbidding Catholics from serving in public office. His open disavowal of the Church of England had provoked a spirited but ultimately unsuccessful political movement in the late 1670s to exclude him from the succession to the English throne.[1] James had ample reason to feel that he was being persecuted for his religious beliefs, and he shared this sense of grievance with Quakers who also felt unjustly exposed to the predilections of the Anglican majority. A common enemy might perhaps be enough to bring together these improbable allies.

The remarkable bond that formed between James and William Penn would be hard to explain without reference to the difficulties they both faced as religious minorities. A shared disdain of religious persecution was evident right from their first substantial conversation, which took place at St. James's Palace in late 1673 or early 1674. Penn went to the palace with a request in mind. He hoped that James, who was then the Duke of York, might intercede with his older brother, King Charles II, to procure the release from prison of the Quaker founder George Fox.[2] Penn arrived at the palace accompanied by his fellow Quaker

William Mead. The two men cannot have known how the duke would respond to their request, but they must have been pleased when he agreed to meet with them. Upon hearing their case, the duke was sympathetic, saying that "he was against all persecution for the sake of Religion. that It was true he had in his younger time been warm, especially when he thought people made it a pretence to disturbe goverment but that he had seen and considered things better, and he was for doing to others, as he would have others do unto him; and he thought it would be happy for the world if all were of that minde, for he was sure, he sayd, that no man was willing to be persecuted himself for his own Conscience."[3] The duke agreed to speak to the king about Fox. He noted that he had served in the navy with Penn's father, and that he had promised the elder Penn he would look out for his son. He invited Penn to come back and meet with him again in future. Thus was an unlikely friendship born.

From the late 1670s to the early 1680s, Penn cultivated a deepening relationship with the duke. As he later put it, James "declared to me it [liberty of conscience] was His Opinion; and on all occasions, when Duke, he never refused me the repeated Proofs of it, as often as I had any Poor Sufferer for Conscience sake to sollicit His help for."[4] After James's accession to the English throne in 1685, Penn became one of his unofficial advisers, especially on matters relating to religious toleration. When the king was asked why he enjoyed the Quaker's company, he replied that "Penn talked Ingeniously."[5]

From the start of the reign, the founder of Pennsylvania lobbied the king to liberate nonconformists.[6] After a year of delay, caused both by Anglican foot-dragging and by the king's irritation at nonconformist support for Monmouth's Rebellion, Penn finally received a positive response.[7] The king granted a general pardon in March 1686 releasing all those imprisoned for their religious nonconformity, including about fifteen hundred Quakers.[8] He then issued a proclamation in April 1687 declaring that the laws penalizing nonconformity were suspended entirely. This was his Declaration for Liberty of Conscience, also known as the Declaration of Indulgence.[9] The king and the Quaker conducted a joint speaking tour of the west of England in the summer of that year, with Penn speaking to large popular audiences in favor of the king's tolerationist agenda while James spoke to smaller groups of gentry.[10] Penn offered much advice to James over the course of his reign; when the king called for a new "Magna Charta for liberty of conscience," he may have been borrowing Penn's language.[11] The Quaker published five pamphlets in defense of the king's policies in 1687 and 1688.[12] He urged the king to call a parliament that might enact the proposed new Magna Carta into law, and James eventually did so, fixing November 1688 as the date for its session.[13]

Other Quakers also flocked to the English court, hoping to gain the king's ear and to improve the lot of their coreligionists. George Whitehead and Gilbert Latey met with James, first to lobby for the release of Quaker prisoners early in the reign and later to express their support for his Declaration for Liberty of Conscience.[14] Robert Barclay, a well-to-do Scottish Quaker theologian, had met with James in the late 1670s and early 1680s when he, like Penn, had been seeking the release of imprisoned Quakers.[15] In another parallel with Penn's career, Barclay had promoted emigration to America in the early 1680s, serving as governor of East New Jersey from 1682 to his death in 1690, although, unlike Penn, he never crossed the Atlantic to take up his governorship in person.[16] He offered advice to James during his reign, going so far as to accept a pension of £200 from the king in 1688 for his services.[17] In 1687 he shepherded an address to James from the Quakers of Scotland thanking the king for his Declaration for Liberty of Conscience.[18] Quakers in Bristol and Dublin sent similar addresses, and an address of thanks subscribed unanimously by the Quaker Yearly Meeting was delivered to the king by Penn himself.[19]

In 1688, Penn and several other nonconformist leaders sought to rally a popular tolerationist movement in support of the king's religious policies. They aimed to influence the composition of the parliament that James intended to summon that autumn.[20] Parliamentary elections began in late September, though they were soon canceled upon news of William of Orange's plans to invade England from the Netherlands.[21] In the interval that followed, the tolerationist movement fell apart.

With William in the ascendant and James's forces in disarray, Penn had overcommitted himself and found it difficult to regain his footing. Even while other nonconformists abandoned their king in the latter half of 1688, he chose to remain loyal. This was not a pragmatic stance for a man whose control of Pennsylvania would be vulnerable to forfeiture in a new reign; a cannier politician might have attempted to insure himself by steering a middle course between the king and the revolutionaries. In late October, he wrote a letter to William Popple that was published in six editions, including two printings by the Quaker Andrew Sowle that presumably had been authorized by Penn himself. Penn might have taken this opportunity to beat a hasty retreat and put out feelers to the Williamites. But instead of categorically disavowing the king, he used the letter to acknowledge the unusual degree of access he had had at Whitehall, while pleading that he had only ever visited the royal palace to advance the interests of Quakers and others who needed assistance.[22]

In the interregnum after James's flight from the capital in December 1688, Penn was accosted by two soldiers in Whitehall, who brought him before the council of peers administering London in the king's absence. The council asked the Quaker to explain his dealings with the now-fallen king. Rather than excuse his conduct, Penn stoutly defended it. All that he had done, he said, was to promote "an impartiall Liberty of Conscience to be Established by Law." He did not attempt to minimize his connection with James: "the King was always his Friend, and his Fathers Friend, and a Friend to those of his Persuasion; and in gratitude he was the Kings, and did ever as much as in him lay, influence him to his true Interest." Penn was released on bail but told to return to the Court of King's Bench at the start of the next term.[23] In the subsequent reign he was arrested four times on suspicion of plotting to restore James to the throne, and his proprietorship of Pennsylvania was stripped from him for about a year.[24] His friendship with James, which had powered his rise to prominence, had proved to be his downfall.

Penn and James in Historical Perspective

Penn's historical reputation has suffered from his affiliation with James. Historians have been bemused by the chasm between Penn's standing as one of the heroes of the Whig interpretation of British history and James's as one of the villains of that same interpretation. Relations between the two ought to have been frosty, not balmy. In the nineteenth century, Thomas Babington Macaulay sought to resolve this conundrum by demoting Penn from the Whig pantheon. He asserted that Penn's "enthusiasm for one great principle sometimes impelled him to violate other great principles which he ought to have held sacred," meaning that the Quaker had been too willing to overlook constitutional niceties in order to secure religious liberties. His "manners [had] been corrupted by evil communications, and his understanding obscured by inordinate zeal for a single object."[25] Quaker historians, meanwhile, sought to buttress Penn's bona fides as a tribune of liberalism by distancing him from James II's more notorious actions, such as his imposition of Catholic fellows on Oxford colleges, his prosecution of seven Anglican bishops, and his campaign to manipulate the parliamentary constituencies and pack a parliament that would repeal the laws that penalized nonconformity.[26] More recently, historians have asserted that whatever Penn's failings might have been, most of the Quakers remained suspicious of James (and, by some accounts, suspicious of Penn for his dalliances with the king). This interpretation left Penn isolated from his contemporaries and presented him as a controversial figure lacking a constituency—hardly a flattering portrait.[27]

One historian took a different tack. Vincent Buranelli argued in his 1962 book *The King & the Quaker* that Penn's positive appraisal of James should cause us to adopt a similarly favorable view of the king. James, in this reading, was not aiming to reimpose the Catholic faith in England by force but was merely seeking to advance religious toleration for his coreligionists and others. Thus Penn's choice to align himself with the monarch was not a sign of his nescience but of his prescience. The relationship between the two should cause us to elevate James in our estimations rather than to demote Penn.[28] Buranelli's provocative account attracted a swift barrage of criticism, dismissed as "puerile" by Joseph Illick and as a "polemic" by Mary Maples Dunn.[29] Its author was a journalist rather than a professional academic, he did not cite new archival sources to support his view, and his work had little impact on a debate that had begun over a century before.[30]

The historical profession, moreover, had been thoroughly inoculated against such unwelcome hypotheses. Macaulay's broadside was in effect an anticipatory rebuttal of the account offered by Buranelli. The line of argument that Macaulay was deflecting was the one that *The King & the Quaker* advanced: if Penn was good, and if he had good judgment in assessing the qualities of others, then his friendship with James suggested that the king might also have good qualities.

This debate may seem rather sterile to historians less invested than Thomas Babington Macaulay or Mary Maples Dunn in defending the rightfulness of the uprising of 1688–1689, the revolution still known as "glorious." But the alliance between William Penn and James II remains significant nonetheless, as it reveals a major fault line in the early Whig movement in England. Intellectual historians of the period have often affirmed that defenses of religious liberty and popular sovereignty went hand in hand, in Lockean fashion. A closer inspection of Penn's choices reminds us that in an age when the majority of the English population was wedded to religious intolerance, there were trade-offs to be made between championing the rights of parliament and championing the rights of marginalized groups.[31] Some of Penn's choices fell on the side of preferring religious liberty to popular sovereignty. His friendship with James was the most visible outcome of those preferences.

Penn, the Test Acts, and the Royal Prerogative

Despite the generally close relations between James II and William Penn, many historians have looked for signs of distance between the two. In particular, historians have suggested that Penn did not fully support the king's push for the repeal of the laws that barred Catholics and most Protestant nonconformists from holding public office. The Test Act of 1673 required all holders of civil or military office to take the oaths of allegiance and supremacy, to make a declaration against transubstantiation, and to receive the sacrament in the Church of England within three months of admission to office. This act ejected most Catholics and Protestant nonconformists from public office, with the exception of those possessing consciences flexible enough to enable them to comply with the requirements. A second Test Act in 1678 extended some of these restrictions to members of parliament, requiring them to make a declaration against transubstantiation and to take the oaths of allegiance and supremacy.[32] The Test Acts remained in force until their repeal in 1828 and 1829, apart from the brief period in 1687 and 1688 when James suspended them. In the 1680s, many moderate Anglicans were willing to loosen the laws penalizing nonconformist worship (the so-called penal laws), while opposing any weakening of the Tests, which were held to protect against a Catholic takeover of the government. This was the tack eventually taken by William and Mary's Act of Toleration in 1689, which retained the Tests while lifting the burden of the penal laws from all major Protestant groups, with the exception of the anti-Trinitarian Socinians.

The case for Penn's divergence from James on the Test Acts rests in part on a manuscript tract held in the archives of the Historical Society of Pennsylvania. The author of this unsigned tract argued that it was in the interest of Protestant nonconformists to repeal only the penal laws while retaining the Tests. The tract was uncovered by Joseph Illick, who attributed it to Penn and quoted the following passage from it: "I thinke it the true interest of all dissenters to repeale the penall Laws if they can, but to keepe up the Test, of the Papists to take of [off] both, & of the Church of England to preserve both . . . Roman Catholicks have no neede of the repeale of the Test dureing this Reign . . . I will rather lett the Penale Laws stand as they are then do any thing that may tend towards the repeale of the Test." Illick suggested that this "important essay" had been "neglected" by those who wished to depict Penn as an "apologist" for James. The manuscript, in his view, demonstrated that the Quaker was "not completely hoodwinked by James' tactics."[33]

Illick's eagerness to detect Penn's hand in this anonymous tract is puzzling. A note in pencil on its first page does indeed say "Wm Penn," but this might refer either to the author of the pamphlet or to its owner. The author writes from the standpoint not of a Quaker but of a moderate Anglican, using latitudinarian formulae, such as "the Dissenters may, & will have term's of accommodation from us; & we long for their Comprehension." The tract concludes with a critique of an unnamed man, whom the author charges with hypocrisy, stating that he would be better off employing "his time parts and money, to the relief of his distressed & undone friends in Pensylvania." The object of this critique could be none other than William Penn himself. On the verso of the final page are two endorsements in a seventeenth-century hand, reading "Received from Mr Cox about December 1687" and "Answering Mr. Pen and Care &c."[34] The pamphlet, then, was a response to the writings of Penn and his fellow repealer Henry Care that was passed along by a Mr. Cox.[35] Though it ended up in Penn's papers, its presence there need not mean that the Quaker wrote it.

Penn's views on the Test Acts are better discerned by an examination of tracts that can be attributed to him with confidence. In his published works, he derided the Tests. It was "ridiculous to talk of giving Liberty of Conscience (which yet few have now the fore-head to oppose) and at the same time imagine those Tests that do exclude men that Service and Reward, ought to be continued." He urged his readers not to "uphold Penal Laws against any of our Religious Perswasions, nor make Tests out of each others Faiths, to exclude one another our civil Rights."[36] He critiqued the Tests' arbitrary nature: "Should a Mans being of any

Religion, hinder him from serving the Country of his Birth? Does his going to a Conventicle naturally unqualifie him for a Constables Staff? or believing Transubstantiation, render him uncapable of being a good Clark? It were as reasonable to say, that 'tis impossible for a Phanatick to be a good Shoomaker, or a Papist a good Tayler. The very Notion is Comical."[37] The second Test Act was particularly objectionable, in his view, because it overrode the freedom of elections, preventing voters from choosing a Roman Catholic as their representative if that was their wish.[38] For these reasons, the Test Acts, in his view, were "fit to be Repealed."[39]

Penn was aware that some readers might disagree with his assessments. He noted the widespread concern that "if the Tests be repealed too, the Government is lost to the Romanists; for they may pack a Parliament of their own Religion."[40] Many Protestants feared that if Catholics were permitted to sit in parliament, the king would elevate scores of his coreligionists to the House of Lords and would use his powers over local officeholders to ensure that a largely Catholic House of Commons was returned. Such a parliament might then abolish Protestantism in England. Penn sought to allay these fears. In exchange for the Tests, he offered a constitutional instrument to provide all faiths with security. This was the "Magna Charta for Liberty of Conscience." Under the terms of this fundamental law, all religions would be protected, and no group could infringe on the liberties of another.[41] As he put it, "if we must have a Test, I shall pray that it may be translated from Transubstantiation to Persecution. That is to say, that no Man shall propose or consent to any thing in Government within this Kingdom, that may infringe the Conscience or Property of any man in it."[42]

Penn was not proposing the disestablishment of the Church of England: under his new scheme, the Church would continue to possess many of its privileges. The king had pledged that the Church would be maintained "as it is now by Law Established," and Penn took this to mean that her "Churches and Revenues" (i.e., buildings and tithes) would continue to belong to Anglicans alone.[43] Anglicans, in his view, would have little to fear from the repeal of the Tests as long as they relinquished the power to persecute others: "I am for having the Church of England keep the Chair, but let the rest subsist."[44] In his writings on behalf of James's toleration campaign, Penn did not mention the long-held Quaker goal of the abolition of compulsory tithes.[45]

Despite the vigor of his public rhetoric against the Tests, Penn appears to have had private misgivings about the campaign to repeal them. He expressed those concerns on several occasions to James Rivers, a spy for William of Orange at the English court. In a series of intelligence letters sent back to The Hague, Rivers reported on his contacts with Penn and other notables. He wrote that the king had announced that the Tests and penal laws "should stand or fall together so Mr Pen and Mr Stewart have lost all their hopes of separating them."[46] (James Stewart was one of the king's Scottish allies.) In another letter, Rivers noted that

"Pen and the other new protestant favourites hope to prevail with his Majesty to consent to the taking off the penal lawes without the Test."[47] A third letter recounted a conversation in which Rivers urged Penn to "join with moderate Catholics (of which there are many) to make the king take a single step, leaving aside the case of the Test." Penn assured Rivers that he was "working only for this."[48] In a fourth letter, the Williamite spy wrote that the Quaker leader was "more full of hopes then ever he was, that he will carry his busines I mean have the penall laws taken off and the test let alone whole or in part and for such parts of the test as shall be desired to be taken off; equivalents shall be offered that all the nation will accept of."[49] What remains unclear from these terse and second-hand accounts is whether Penn opposed the repeal of the Tests on principle, or whether he was worried that the campaign to repeal them might provoke a backlash that could jeopardize the more vital repeal of the penal laws. The latter interpretation would comport better with Penn's public rhetoric against the Tests; it also happens to be a fairly accurate reading of the political situation in England in the spring of 1688, when such a backlash was certainly brewing.[50]

Rivers also reported that Penn was promoting an alternative program whereby Catholics would be barred only from the House of Commons but not the Lords, while the public offices of the kingdom would be divided into thirds among Catholics, Anglicans, and Protestant nonconformists.[51] This proposal was unlikely to satisfy Anglicans, who represented over nine-tenths of the population but would have been left with only one-third of the offices. The device was reminiscent of previous theorizing by Penn about balancing different religious factions. In a pamphlet from the previous decade, he had advised the monarch to govern "upon a Ballance, as near as may be, towards the several Religious Interests."[52] In 1685, he had noted that religious toleration could benefit the monarch since "either the conforming or non-conforming Party may be undutiful; the one is then a Ballance to the other."[53] Intriguingly, James later proposed a quota system for the higher offices of state in a memorial of advice for his son, composed in the 1690s. Were he ever to rule England, James advised, his son should appoint one Protestant and one Catholic secretary of state, along with five commissioners of the Treasury: three Anglicans, one Catholic, and one Protestant nonconformist. Perhaps the exiled king was harkening back to conversations he had had with Penn a few years before.[54]

The Quaker leader, then, was not wedded to a wholesale repeal of the 1673 and 1678 Test Acts. But neither was the king. In the summer of 1688, the English privy council discussed the fears of many Protestants about the future state of the Church of England. James agreed to a scheme whereby Catholics would continue to be barred from the House of Commons, though they would be readmitted to the Lords. Protestants would thus exercise a veto over any legislation. The new proposal was announced in a royal proclamation on September 21, 1688: "We are willing the Roman Catholicks shall remain incapable to be Members of the

House of Commons, whereby those Fears and Apprehensions will be removed, which many Persons have had, That the Legislative Authority would be Engrossed by them, and turned against Protestants."[55] This proclamation was issued only two days before the king learned, via a letter from the English ambassador at The Hague, that William's war preparations were directed at him, and only seven days before he canceled his planned parliament entirely.[56] Few royal proclamations have been as stillborn. Although it quickly became a dead letter, the announcement reflected discussions that had been under way at court for months. James's concessions would have gone some way to assuaging Penn's concerns about the speed with which he was moving and may have reflected the Quaker's influence.

Whatever his true feelings about the Tests, Penn expressed few qualms about the use of the royal prerogative to proclaim toleration by fiat. In a pamphlet from 1687, he described the king's proclamation in favor of liberty of conscience as "his Great and Gratious Declaration." Delivering an address of thanks to the king for the edict, he gave a short speech praising James for the "Noble Resolution" that had led him to proclaim it.[57] He defended the king's use of his suspending power by alluding to the royal prerogative in ecclesiastical affairs, a prerogative that might be controversial when deployed by a Catholic monarch but that had been exalted by Anglican clerics when it had been in the hands of monarchs of whom they approved.[58]

Though Penn supported the king's use of his prerogative powers in this instance, he, like James himself, was eager to see the tolerationist policy underwritten by a parliamentary repeal of the acts that the king had merely suspended.[59] The Quaker did not scruple from acting personally in the campaign to regulate the parliamentary constituencies. This campaign of regulation, in which James employed his powers under borough charters to remodel civic governments, was seen by many as a threat to the independence of parliament. In some boroughs, only the town's magistrates held the parliamentary franchise; by replacing those officials, the king could completely remodel the electorate in those places. In other boroughs, all of the freemen could vote, but James's newly appointed magistrates could (and sometimes did) add hundreds of new freemen to swamp the polls. As it happens, James only remodeled the governments of about half of the parliamentary boroughs, which was probably not enough for him to gain the pro-repeal parliament he desired. But there were also widespread, if unsubstantiated, fears that James might nominate corrupt returning officers who would ignore the voting entirely and substitute their own tallies.[60]

Penn's participation in the regulating campaign was direct. He wrote to a friend in the parliamentary borough of Huntingdon asking him to provide a list of names of magistrates who should be removed from the town's government and another list of nominees for their replacements. He explained that these measures would help to elect an assembly sympathetic to toleration: "for when a few Towns are done we may expect to hear of a Parliament to render our Ease legal, that our poor Posterity may be preserved from the Cruelty of wicked Persecutors."[61] At the Yearly Meeting in London in June 1688, Penn pressed for the establishment of a committee to offer advice to Quakers about accepting appointments to civic office. His unconventional proposal was overridden by George Fox, who believed that such discussions should be held informally, without the imprimatur of the Yearly Meeting.[62]

Penn's attitude toward established electoral procedures was somewhat cavalier at times. He told James Rivers that the Parliament of 1685 had been monopolized by the Anglicans and that the planned Parliament of 1688 would be "chosen as fairly as that." He went on to note that since the Anglicans had violated electoral procedures in the past, they could hardly complain if others imitated them, though he added that he himself would do his best to prevent such abuses from occurring.[63] In print, he denied that the king's efforts represented a "packing" of parliament. Instead, he described the toleration campaign as "Unpacking for the Good of the Whole, that which hath been so long Packt for the sole Good of a Party," meaning the Church of England.[64] When it came to matters of religious liberty, Penn elevated the *salus populi* above the *vox populi.* As he had suggested in 1687, the majority should not always rule, and some principles should not be put to a vote: the "major vote in things not to be voted" ought not to be respected.[65]

Despite his public endorsement of James's religious policies, Penn did not always approve of the king's attacks on the Church of England. In the spring of 1688, James had issued an order commanding the reading of his Declaration for Liberty of Conscience in church on two successive Sundays. Seven bishops, including the archbishop of Canterbury, signed a petition declining to obey the order. When their petition was subsequently published and spread around London, James accused them of promoting sedition. The bishops were imprisoned for a week in the Tower of London and were tried for seditious libel in King's Bench, where a largely Anglican jury acquitted them.[66] Penn believed, with good reason, that this defeat had been self-inflicted. In a meeting with the king before the trial, he had urged him to abandon his prosecution and release the bishops. Such an act of clemency, Penn had believed, would restore James to the good graces of his people.[67] When the king had refused the opportunity to show mercy, furious jockeying had ensued at court, with Penn joining Robert Barclay and the king's chief minister, the Earl of Sunderland, in seeking to avert the looming disaster.[68] Meanwhile, Barclay visited the bishops in the Tower in an attempt to distance the Quakers from the proceedings. Some unspecified persons had been saying that the king's treatment of the bishops was their just deserts for the widespread persecution of Quakers over the previous generation. That persecution had led to the deaths of more than 320 Quakers in prison from hardship or illness. The bishops, upon getting wind of these charges, had complained that they had nothing to do with these deaths. Barclay assured them that the Quakers had no intention of imputing to them any bloodguilt, especially since they "through change of circumstances were now under oppression" themselves.[69]

Penn and Jacobitism

Penn's prudence in the affair of the seven bishops did little to mollify his critics. His support for the king had made him notorious. His pamphlets defending James had attracted a string of rebuttals, libels, and critiques.[70] Seeking to neutralize his influence, his opponents had spread rumors that he had secretly converted to Catholicism and even had joined the Jesuit order.[71] In October 1688, Penn felt compelled to announce that "I am not only no Jesuit, but no Papist. . . . I am so far from having been bred at St. Omers and having received Orders at Rome, that I never was at either Place; nor do I know any body there; nor had I ever a Correspondency with any one in those Places."[72] In 1686 he had averred to John Tillotson that "I am no Roman Catholick, but a Christian."[73] Despite these denials, a newsletter of December 1688 slyly referred to him as "Father Pen."[74]

The rumors of Penn's supposed Catholicism continued after James's overthrow.[75] It is remarkable that Penn remained persona non grata after 1688 when so many other nonconformists who had participated in the repealer movement were successfully rehabilitated in the next reign.[76] Perhaps he had been too visible an ally of the exiled king to avoid being cast into purgatory for a spell. But he also did not try as hard as he could have to ingratiate himself with King William III in the years immediately following the revolution. There were many who suspected that Penn at this time was a Jacobite, actively conspiring to promote James's restoration. Though he was never put on trial for treason, he was arrested four times and kept under watch. His name was included on a list of those who were purportedly planning to travel to France (presumably to visit James), but whether he ever took such a journey is unclear.[77]

The most perilous episode for Penn occurred in 1691, when he was implicated by two witnesses in a plot led by Lord Preston to restore James to the English throne. One of those witnesses was Preston himself, who indicated that he had evidence of Penn's complicity.[78] The other was a Jacobite agent, Matthew Crone, who deposed that he had met with Penn to discuss James's restoration and that the Quaker had written a letter of advice to the exiled monarch proposing methods to recover his kingdom.[79] On his way to France, Preston had been captured along with a packet of letters intended for James, and the peer later deposed that one of the letters was Penn's. A government minister believed that a second letter was also in Penn's hand.[80] Penn requested an interview with the minister, Viscount Sydney, to address the charges against him, on condition that the interview be done in a clandestine fashion and that he not be taken into custody. At the interview, Penn denied any hand in a treasonous design against William and Mary, protesting "in the presence of God that he knew of no plot." He would not, however, answer Sydney's queries about the letters found with Preston, saying only that he would disclose what he knew more fully if he were to be granted an interview with the king.[81] (No such interview was granted.) Penn's evasiveness seems damning, since a firm denial, had he felt able to issue one, would have done much more to protect him from future prosecution.

Under the English law of treason, Penn could have been convicted and executed on the testimony of the two witnesses, Preston and Crone.[82] A proclamation was issued for his arrest, but Preston wavered in his willingness to testify, and Penn successfully went into hiding for about two years until the whole affair had blown over.[83] In late 1691 King William described Penn as "one of his greatest enemies," but the king's ministers did not behave as though that were truly the case. The government's lack of zeal in apprehending Penn suggests that his prominent status as the founder of Pennsylvania and a leader of the Quakers afforded him some degree of protection.[84] He was permitted to rehabilitate himself in November 1693 when, after a plea made on his behalf by three lords, the king indicated that he would not be prosecuted. By August 1694, he had recovered his proprietorship of Pennsylvania.[85]

The friendship of William Penn and James II cannot be written off as a marriage of convenience, for by 1689 it had become entirely inconvenient, at least for one of the two parties. Despite the risks to his reputation and standing, Penn's sympathies appear to have remained with the fallen king in the years immediately following the revolution, although it is difficult to assess to what extent he acted on those sentiments. At one point early in William and Mary's reign, Penn was dragged before the authorities. He made a bold and somewhat reckless avowal of his personal attachment to James: "since he had loved King James in his prosperity, he should not hate him in his adversity, yea, he loved him as yet for many favours he had conferred on him." At the same time, he disavowed any treasonous designs: he "had never the vanity to think of endeavouring to restore him that Crown which was fallen from his head."[86] Robert Barclay made a similar declaration of sympathy around the same time: "I must own nor will I decline to avowe That I Love King James, That I wish him well, That I have been and am sensibly touched with a feeling of his misfortunes, And that I cannot excuse my self from the duty of praying for him."[87] In the months after the revolution, a Quaker prophetess traveled around East Anglia offering prayers for "king James" and proclaiming "that he shall cum againe and that people shall Lay housd on frinds scirts for shelter [lay hands on Friends' skirts for shelter]."[88] Quakers were not wont to hide their true feelings, even when they were impolitic.

Partners against Persecution

The alliance of James II and William Penn, then, is not so much of a puzzle. The two men shared similar attitudes on several key questions. They both opposed religious persecution, and they both were willing to see royal powers used to promote toleration, even when that meant countermanding the expressed will of previous parliaments. Macaulay was correct that Penn was willing to sacrifice other principles, including the rule of the majority, to his overriding aim of religious liberty. During the quarter century between the Restoration of Charles II and the accession of James II, the Quakers had learned that the English parliament, when dominated by the Anglican majority, was not their friend. Many turned to a monarch who offered much more.

Other Protestant nonconformists had refused to enter into an alliance with a Catholic potentate, fearing that James was merely seeking to divide the Anglicans from the nonconformists before conquering them both. But Penn, unlike many of his dissenting contemporaries, was not strongly animated by a fear of Catholic power during James II's reign; instead, he argued that English Catholics were too few in number to pose a genuine threat to the Protestant religion in England.[89] He appeared to share the king's frustrations with the "fears and jealousies" of many anti-popish Englishmen.[90] The king and the Quaker had come to share a set of antagonists, the anti-popish Anglicans who, in rallying to the defense of the Church of England as by law established, would not give an inch to the repealers.

Penn's pamphlets of 1687 and 1688 represented a shift in his rhetoric regarding Catholicism and "popery"; before 1685, he had often espoused anti-Catholic ideas in his published works.[91] While James may have been influenced by Penn's political philosophy, Penn also learned something from James: Protestant critiques of popery did not always account for the actual diversity of Catholics, some of whom (like James) had disavowed persecution.[92] This realization, in turn, led to Penn's signal contribution as a political theorist: he was willing to support the extension of toleration to Catholics at a time when many others, including John Locke, adopted an accommodating stance toward the exclusion of Catholics from full citizenship. Abandoning the Catholic exception enabled Penn to put forward a more expansive and full-throated rationale for toleration and a more radical mechanism for enforcing it—the Magna Carta for liberty of conscience. This proposed fundamental law anticipated modern theories of constitutionalism and liberal democracy. John Stuart Mill would not have disagreed with Penn's insight that majority rule did not always promote the freedoms of minorities and that, for a people to be truly free, democracy must be underpinned by a constitutional order guaranteeing liberty of conscience. As Mill later wrote, "the people, consequently, may desire to oppress a part of their number; and precautions are as much needed against this as against any other abuse of power."[93]

In the view of Penn and other Quakers, the king had been inspired by God to espouse religious tolerance. As George Whitehead put it, referring to the king's decision to issue his Declaration for Liberty of Conscience, "it appeared that the Lord had opened His Understanding therein."[94] Since for Quakers salvation involved attending to the Inner Light, not accepting a particular creed, to say that James was attending to God's inspiration was, for them, to suggest that he might be destined for heaven.[95] They would not have called James a Quaker. But then, Quakers did not call *themselves* Quakers. They were the Religious Society of Friends. When they called James a friend, or said that they loved him, they were welcoming him into their society.

NOTES

1. Ronald Hutton, *Charles the Second: King of England, Scotland, and Ireland* (Oxford, 1989), 301–302.

2. On Fox's arrest in mid-December 1673, see William C. Braithwaite, *The Second Period of Quakerism* (London, 1919), 427.

3. American Philosophical Society [hereafter APS], 974.8 P365, vol. 1, pp. 114–116 (William Penn's "Apology for himself"), published in Richard S. Dunn and Mary Maples Dunn, eds., *The Papers of William Penn*, 5 vols. (Philadelphia, 1981–1987) [hereafter *PWP*], 3:338–339. In this quotation, as in others to follow, thorns and abbreviations have been lengthened.

4. [William Popple], *A Letter to Mr Penn with his Answer* (London, 1688, Wing P2964A), 7; see also *PWP*, 1:360, 369; 2:95, 115, 604, 606.

5. Gerard Croese, *The General History of the Quakers* (London, 1696, Wing C6965), book 2, p. 106.

6. *PWP*, 3:30, 32, 117; Library of the Society of Friends, London [hereafter LSF], Meeting for Sufferings Minutes, vol. 4, pp. 125, 134; [William Penn], *Considerations Moving to a Toleration* (London, 1685, Wing P1269), 5–8; [William Penn], *A Third Letter from a Gentleman in the Country* (London, 1687, Wing P1381), 9–10.

7. APS, 974.8 P365, vol. 1, p. 121 (William Penn's "Epistle Generall to the people of God called Quakers"), published in *PWP*, 3:269; Scott Sowerby, *Making Toleration: The Repealers and the Glorious Revolution* (Cambridge, MA, 2013), 26.

8. *A Proclamation of the Kings Majesties most Gracious and General Pardon* (London, 1686, Wing J363); *Calendar of State Papers, Domestic, James II, 1686–87*, 71, 138, 303; LSF, Book of Cases, I (1661–1695), pp. 161–171, 179–180; *Historical Manuscripts Commission, Downshire*, 1:139; George Whitehead, *The Christian Progress* (London, 1725), 587–591; *London Gazette*, no. 2245 (23–26 May 1687).

9. James II, *His Majesties Gracious Declaration to all his Loving Subjects for Liberty of Conscience* (London, 1687, Wing J186).

10. *PWP*, 3:163; Sowerby, *Making Toleration*, 41–43.

11. Sowerby, *Making Toleration*, 40–44. On Penn's contacts with James at this time, see *Historical Manuscripts Commission, Portland*, 3:403, newsletter from September 1687; Samuel M. Janney, *The Life of William Penn*, 2nd ed. (Philadelphia, 1852), 298; and Charlwood Lawton, "A Memoir of Part of the Life of William Penn," *Memoirs of the Historical Society of Pennsylvania*, vol. 3, part 2 (1834–36), 213–231.

12. [William Penn], *A Letter form* [sic] *a Gentleman in the Country, to his Friends in London, upon the Subject of the Penal Laws and Tests* (n.p., 1687, Wing P1318); idem, *A Second Letter from a Gentleman in the Country* (London, 1687, Wing P1361); idem, *A Third Letter from a Gentleman in the Country* (London, 1687, Wing P1381); idem, *Good Advice to the*

Church of England, Roman Catholick, and Protestant Dissenter (London, 1687, Wing P1296); idem, *The Great and Popular Objection against the Repeal of the Penal Laws & Tests Briefly Stated and Consider'd* (London, 1688, Wing P1298A).

13. West Yorkshire Archive Service, Leeds, WYL156/51/53, Nathaniel Johnston to Sir John Reresby, 24 Jan. 1688; Nottingham University Library [hereafter NUL], Portland MSS, PwA 2129/1, James Rivers to [Hans Willem Bentinck], 13/23 Jan. 1688; James II, *By the King, A Declaration* (London, 1688, Wing J158), dated 21 Sept. 1688.

14. Whitehead, *Christian Progress*, 570–580, 587–593, 610–611, 615–624; "A Brief Narrative of the Life of Gilbert Latey," in *Friends' Library, Consisting Principally of Journals and Extracts from Journals and other Writings of Members of the Society of Friends*, 16 vols. (Lindfield, 1832–38), 9:77–85.

15. Robert Barclay to Princess Elizabeth of the Rhine, 12 Sept. 1677, printed in John Barclay, ed., *Diary of Alexander Jaffray* (London, 1833), 412–413; *Reliquiae Barclaianaie* (London, 1870), 52, 55, 57; Charles Wright Barclay, Hubert F. Barclay, and Alice Wilson-Fox, *A History of the Barclay Family*, 3 vols. (London, 1924–34), 3:145; *Historical Manuscripts Commission, Buccleuch and Queensberry (Drumlanrig Castle)*, 1:215; *PWP*, 1:367; Historical Society of Pennsylvania, Penn-Forbes Collection, vol. 2, p. 15, Robert Barclay to William Penn, 31 Jan. 1679/80.

16. John E. Pomfret, *The New Jersey Proprietors and Their Lands* (Princeton, 1964), 36, 39, 43; Maxine N. Lurie, "The Barclay Record Book and Its East Jersey Minutes: An Early Look at Context and Content," *Journal of the Rutgers University Libraries*, 43 (2007), 11–12.

17. *PWP*, 2:95, 115; LSF, Temp MSS, 285, no. 42 (Notebook of Robert Barclay), pp. 42, 49; *A Genealogical Account of the Barclays of Urie* (Aberdeen, 1740), 56; *Historical Notices of Scottish Affairs, Selected from the Manuscripts of Sir John Lauder of Fountainhall*, 2 vols. (Edinburgh, 1848), 2:847.

18. Address of Quakers in Scotland to James II, in *London Gazette*, no. 2252 (16–20 June 1687); William F. Miller, "Gleanings from the Records of the Yearly Meeting of Aberdeen, 1672–1786," *Journal of the Friends' Historical Society*, 8 (1911), 62–64.

19. Address of Bristol Quakers to James II, in *London Gazette*, no. 2287 (17–20 Oct. 1687); address of Dublin Quakers to James II, in *London Gazette*, no. 2273 (29 Aug.–1 Sept. 1687); address of the Quaker Yearly Meeting in London to James II, in *London Gazette*, no. 2245 (23–26 May 1687); LSF, Yearly Meeting Minutes, vol. 1 (1668–93), 178; *The Speech of William Penn to His Majesty, upon his Delivering the Quakers Address* (London, [1687], Wing P1372A). See also an earlier address of London Quakers to James II, printed in the *London Gazette*, no. 2238 (28 April–2 May 1687), which was said by Robert Yard to have been signed by over six hundred hands: Lilly Library, Indiana University, Albeville MSS, Yard to Marquis d'Albeville, 29 April 1687.

20. Sowerby, *Making Toleration*, 28–34.

21. James II, *By the King, A Proclamation* (London, 1688, Wing J260); on the elections, see Sowerby, *Making Toleration*, 212–215.

22. [Popple], *A Letter to Mr Penn*, 6–7. The six editions are numbered in Donald Wing's *Short-Title Catalogue* as P2961, P2962, P2963, P2964, P2964A, and P2964B, with the last two printed by Sowle.

23. *The Entring Book of Roger Morrice, 1677–1691*, ed. Mark Goldie, John Spurr, Tim Harris, Stephen Taylor, Mark Knights, and Jason McElligott, 7 vols. (Woodbridge, 2007–2009), 4:384–385, 5:94–95; *The English Currant*, no. 2 (12 Dec. 1688); Robert Beddard, *A Kingdom without a King: The Journal of the Provisional Government in the Revolution of 1688* (Oxford, 1988), 76–77. See also the briefer notices of Penn's apprehension in George Agar Ellis, ed., *The Ellis Correspondence*, 2 vols. (London, 1829), 2:356; Narcissus Luttrell, *A Brief Historical Relation of State Affairs*, 6 vols. (Oxford, 1857), 1:486; Boston Public Library, Ms. Am. 1502, vol. 7, no. 61, newsletter dated 20 Dec. 1688; and *The London Mercury*, no. 1 (15 Dec. 1688).

24. Mary K. Geiter, *William Penn* (Harlow, 2000), 66–70; Edwin B. Bronner, *William Penn's "Holy Experiment": The Founding of Pennsylvania, 1681–1701* (New York, 1962), 157–170.

25. Thomas Babington Macaulay, *The History of England from the Accession of James II*, ed. C. H. Firth, 6 vols. (London, 1913–15), 1:503, 2:950.

26. W. E. Forster, *William Penn and Thomas B. Macaulay: Being Brief Observations on the Charges Made in Mr. Macaulay's History of England, Against the Character of William Penn* (London, 1849); Samuel M. Janney, *The Life of William Penn*, 4th ed. (Philadelphia, 1876), 308–335; Braithwaite, *Second Period of Quakerism*, 139–144, 148–149.

27. Douglas R. Lacey, *Dissent and Parliamentary Politics in England, 1661–1689* (New Brunswick, NJ, 1969), 203, 215; Steve Pincus, *1688: The First Modern Revolution* (New Haven, 2009), 204; Geiter, *William Penn*, 57. Geiter cited as evidence of Quaker disillusionment with Penn a letter from the Clarendon state papers that she believes was intended as criticism of him: see Bodleian Library, MS Clarendon, vol. 89, fols. 175r–176v (letter to Penn written at Dublin in Sept. 1688). The letter, however, is unsigned and its contents do not suggest that it was written by a Quaker. It is, moreover, highly laudatory; if there is any criticism of Penn in it, it is buried too deeply in the subtext for this reader to detect. Geiter argued that the letter's reference to "a great Courtier, a much greater favorite with his King, then with his god," was meant to apply to Penn. This seems implausible, given that the letter-writer was appealing to Penn to protect English Protestants in Ireland from the ascendancy of Irish Catholics. A much clearer reading would be that the "great Courtier" was the Earl of Tyrconnell, the Roman Catholic peer who had been installed by James as lord deputy of Ireland in 1687.

28. Vincent Buranelli, *The King & the Quaker: A Study of William Penn and James II* (Philadelphia, 1962), 117–120, 127–135, 204–212.

29. Joseph E. Illick, *William Penn the Politician: His Relations with the English Government* (Ithaca, 1965), 80; Mary Maples Dunn, review of *The King and the Quaker* in *Pennsylvania Magazine of History and Biography*, 87, no. 1 (Jan. 1963), 89–90.

30. In her review, Dunn referred to the book's author as "Mr. Buranelli," presumably unaware of his 1951 doctoral thesis from Cambridge on "The Aristocratic Opposition to Monarchical Absolutism in French Political Thought during the Reigns of Louis XIV and Louis XV."

31. On this point, see Andrew R. Murphy, *Liberty, Conscience, and Toleration: The Political Thought of William Penn* (Oxford, 2016), 194–198.

32. 25 Car. II. c. 2; 30 Car. II. stat. 2. c. 1.

33. Illick, *William Penn*, 90–91.

34. Historical Society of Pennsylvania, Ferdinand J. Dreer Autograph Collection, box 321, folder 26 ("Off the Penal and Tests"), 5–8.

35. Mr. Cox may have been Nehemiah Cox, the Baptist minister in Westminster who actively supported James's toleration campaign, although he was usually known as "Dr. Cox": see Sowerby, *Making Toleration*, 136. Alternatively, Mr. Cox may have been the Presbyterian by that name who presented an address to James in 1687: see *The Humble Address of the Presbyterians* (n.p., 1687, Wing A2912), 1.

36. [Penn], *Good Advice to the Church of England, Roman Catholick, and Protestant Dissenter* (London, 1687, Wing P1296), 58–59.

37. [Penn], *A Third Letter from a Gentleman in the Country* (London, 1687, Wing P1381), 14.

38. [Penn], *Third Letter*, 17.

39. [Penn], *Good Advice*, 61.

40. [Penn], *A Second Letter from a Gentleman in the Country* (London, 1687, Wing P1361), 13–14; see also [Penn], *Third Letter*, 11–12; [Penn], *The Great and Popular Objection against the Repeal of the Penal Laws & Tests Briefly Stated and Consider'd* (London, 1688, Wing P1298A), 7.

41. [Penn], *Great and Popular Objection*, 6, 8, 10, 22; see also [Penn], *Second Letter*, 18; [Penn], *Good Advice*, 45.

42. [Penn], *Third Letter*, 18–19.

43. For James's pledge, see *An Account of What His Majesty Said at His First Coming to Council* (London, 1684/5, Wing J150); for Penn's interpretation of it, see his *Good Advice*, 16.

44. [Penn], *Second Letter*, 17.

45. For Quaker agitation about tithes during James II's reign, see the address of the Yearly Meeting to James II, printed in *London Gazette*, no. 2354 (7–11 June 1688); LSF, Yearly Meeting Minutes, vol. 1 (1668–93), 201–202; LSF, Meeting for Sufferings Minutes, vol. 6, pp. 178, 180, 183; and Religious Society of Friends Historical Library, Dublin, Sharp MSS, S6, fols. 30–31, George Fox to William Edmundson, 28 Nov. 1687, fols. 32–34v, same to same, 3 Feb. 1688. For James II's opposition to the abolition of tithes, see *The Diary of Dr. Thomas Cartwright, Bishop of Chester*, Camden Society, old series, vol. 22 (London, 1843), 66.

46. NUL, Portland MSS, PwA 2113, James Rivers to [Hans Willem Bentinck], 8 Dec. 1687.

47. NUL, Portland MSS, PwA 2100, James Rivers to [Hans Willem Bentinck], 17 Nov. 1687.

48. NUL, Portland MSS, PwA 2127/1, James Rivers to [Hans Willem Bentinck], 19 Jan. 1688. The original passage in French reads: "qu'il falloit se joindre aux Catholiques moderés (il y en a de tels) pour faire que le Roi fiit un seul pas en laissant l'affaire du Test à part. Il m'a assuré qu'il ne travaille qu'a cela."

49. NUL, Portland MSS, PwA 2142, James Rivers to [Hans Willem Bentinck], 5/15 Feb. 1688.

50. On the backlash, see Sowerby, *Making Toleration*, 153, 169–173, 207–211.

51. NUL, Portland MSS, PwA 2129/1, James Rivers to [Hans Willem Bentinck], 13/23 Jan. 1688.

52. Penn, *England's Present Interest Discover'd* (n.p., 1675, Wing P1280), 38.

53. Penn, *A Perswasive to Moderation to Dissenting Christians* (London, 1685, Wing P1337A), 32.

54. J[ames] S[tanier] Clarke, *The Life of James the Second King of England*, 2 vols. (London, 1816), 2:641–642.

55. James II, *By the King, A Declaration* (London, 1688, Wing J158).

56. For the consternation at court on 23 September about William's intentions, see Samuel Weller Singer, ed., *The Correspondence of Henry Hyde, Earl of Clarendon*, 2 vols. (London, 1828), 2:189; Archives du Ministère des Affaires Étrangères, Paris, Correspondance Politique, Angleterre, vol. 166, Barrillon to Louis XIV, fol. 258, 23 Sept./3 Oct. 1688; British Library, Add. MS 34512, fol. 103v, van Citters to States General, 25 Sept./5 Oct. 1688. For the letter that caused this uproar, see British Library, Add. MS 41816, fol. 207, marquis d'Albeville to Earl of Middleton, 20/30 Sept. 1688. For the subsequent recall of the parliamentary writs, see James II, *By the King, a Proclamation* (London, 1688, Wing J260).

57. [Penn], *Second Letter*, 14; *The Speech of William Penn to His Majesty, upon his Delivering the Quakers Address* (London, 1687, Wing P1372A), 1. Penn had also approved of Charles II's Declaration of Indulgence of 1672: see his *Perswasive to Moderation*, 33–34.

58. [Penn], *Third Letter*, 4–5; on this point, see Jacqueline Rose, *Godly Kingship in Restoration England: The Politics of the Royal Supremacy, 1660–1688* (Cambridge, 2011), 61–67.

59. [Penn], *Third Letter*, 6; [Penn], *Great and Popular Objection*, 13.

60. Sowerby, *Making Toleration*, 92–93, 126, 206, 216–217.

61. British Library, Add. MS 70518, fol. 261, William Penn to [Richard Jobson?], 19 Jan. 1688, printed in *PWP*, 3:175–176.

62. LSF, Yearly Meeting Minutes, vol. 1 (1668–93), 199; Braithwaite, *Second Period of Quakerism*, 144–145. For Quakers who became town magistrates in 1688, see Sowerby, *Making Toleration*, 143, 320–321.

63. NUL, Portland MSS, PwA 2129/1, James Rivers to [Hans Willem Bentinck], 13/23 Jan. 1688. The letter was mostly written in French: "[Penn said that] le dernier Parlement etoit de l'Eglise Angli[ca]ne: que celui ci should be chosen as fairly as that. Je lui dis, que de 500 personnes, il n'y en avoit pas eu 200 bien elus dans le dernier Parlement. Il dit si l'Eglise Anglicane avoite violé les Elections, il n'avoient rien à dire à ceux qui les imiteroient; mais pour lui, il feroit son mieux pour prevenir cela."

64. [Penn], *Great and Popular Objection*, 14.

65. [Penn], *Third Letter*, 18; for similar anti-majoritarian positions being taken by other repealers at the time, see Sowerby, *Making Toleration*, 60–61, 69–70.

66. Sowerby, *Making Toleration*, 176–192.

67. Lawton, "A Memoir of Part of the Life of William Penn," 230–231.

68. *The Correspondence of Henry Hyde . . . with the Diary of Lord Clarendon*, ed. Samuel Singer, 2 vols. (London, 1828), 2:178; Archives du Ministère des Affaires Étrangères, Paris, Correspondance Politique Angleterre, 165, fols. 330v–333, Barrillon to Louis XIV, 3 June/24 May 1688; J. P. Kenyon, *Robert Spencer, Earl of Sunderland, 1641–1702* (London, 1958), 194–199.

69. *Diary of Alexander Jaffray . . . [and] Memoirs of the Rise . . . of the People Called Quakers, in the North of Scotland*, ed. John Barclay (London, 1833), 445; on the 320 Quaker deaths in prison, see Whitehead, *Christian Progress*, 580.

70. *Some Queries Concerning Liberty of Conscience, Directed to William Penn and Henry Care* (n.p., [1688], Wing S4559); Thomas Comber, *Three Considerations Proposed to Mr. William Pen[n], Concerning the Validity and Security of his New Magna Charta for Liberty of Conscience* (n.p., [1688], Wing C5496); *A Letter from Father La Chaise, Confessor to the French King, to Father Peters, Confessor to the King of England . . . to which is Added a Letter from Will Penn to Father la Chaise* (n.p., [1688], Wing L1465); *A Dialogue between Father P—rs and William P—n* (n.p., [1688], Wing D1310).

71. BL, Add. MS 34727, fol. 157, anonymous letter sent to William Penn in late 1687 or 1688 by a former member of parliament.

72. [William Popple], *A Letter to Mr Penn with his Answer* (London, 1688, Wing P2964A), 6–7.

73. *PWP*, 3:80.

74. BL, Egerton MS 2717, fol. 416, newsletter dated 13 Dec. 1688. For earlier versions of these innuendos and Penn's responses to them, see *PWP*, 1:534 (Penn's speech to a committee of parliament, 22 March 1678), and *PWP*, 1:545 (letter from John Gratton to Penn, 19 Dec. 1678).

75. Henry Cadbury, "Gossip in Yorkshire about William Penn," *Friends' Historical Association of Philadelphia Bulletin*, 23 (1934), 95–96.

76. On this process of rehabilitation, see Sowerby, "Forgetting the Repealers: Religious Toleration and Historical Amnesia in Later Stuart England," *Past and Present*, 215 (May 2012), 107–114.

77. Mary K. Geiter, "William Penn and Jacobitism: A Smoking Gun?" *Historical Research*, 73 (2000), 217. Edward Corp suggested that Penn visited St Germain in the early 1690s: see his "James II and Toleration: The Years in Exile at Saint-Germain-en-Laye," *Royal Stuart Papers*, 51 (1997), 7. To substantiate this claim, Corp relied on an enigmatic set of references to Penn in François Ravaisson, ed., *Archives de la Bastille: Documents Inédits*, 18 vols. (Paris, 1866–1903), 9:328–330.

78. *Calendar of State Papers, Domestic Series, May 1690–Oct. 1691*, 228, 244; for Preston's deposition implicating Penn, see *Historical Manuscripts Commission, Finch* (London, 1957), 3:316–317.

79. *Historical Manuscripts Commission, Finch,* 3:47, 321, 325, 330, 333, 338, 344.

80. *Historical Manuscripts Commission, Finch,* 3:309, 316; *Calendar of State Papers, Domestic Series, May 1690–Oct. 1691*, 228. For a third letter that Penn may have sent to the Jacobite court, see *PWP*, 3:664–666.

81. The National Archives, SP 8/8/103, Viscount Sydney to William III, 27 Feb. 1691, transcribed in *PWP*, 3:293–294.

82. *Historical Manuscripts Commission, Finch*, 3:128.

83. *Calendar of State Papers, Domestic Series, May 1690–Oct. 1691*, 246. On government discussions about whether to prosecute Penn, see *Historical Manuscripts Commission, Finch*, 3:393, 397, 401, 404. On Preston's unwillingness to testify, see BL, Add. MS 32681, fol. 418v, Earl of Nottingham to Viscount Sydney, 4 Aug. 1691; *PWP*, 3:663.

84. *PWP*, 3:332.

85. *PWP*, 3:330–331, 382–384; Braithwaite, *Second Period of Quakerism*, 162–171; Geiter, *William Penn*, 66–68, 72–74; Bronner, *Founding of Pennsylvania*, 170.

86. Gerard Croese, *The General History of the Quakers* (London, 1696, Wing C6965), book 2, p. 113; see also *PWP*, 3:235–236, 252.

87. Swarthmore College, Safe 1006, Box 34, MSS 050 (Robert Barclay's "Vindication of his apology"), 6–7, printed in John Pomfret, "Robert Barclay and James II: Barclay's 'Vindication,' 1689," *Bulletin of Friends Historical Association*, 42 (1953), 39.

88. LSF, Portfolio 15, no. 104, Isaac Sadler to John Knight, 2 July 1689.

89. [Penn], *A Letter form* [sic] *a Gentleman*, 8; [Penn], *A Second Letter from a Gentleman*, 10, 14; [Penn], *Good Advice*, 49.

90. For James II's critiques of anti-popery, see Sowerby, "Opposition to Anti-Popery in Restoration England," *Journal of British Studies*, 51 (2012), 31, 39.

91. Paul Douglas Newman, "'Good Will to all men . . . from the King on the throne to the beggar on the dunghill': William Penn, the Roman Catholics, and Religious Toleration," *Pennsylvania History*, 61 (1994), 460–467.

92. On this point, see Sowerby, "Opposition to Anti-Popery," 42–43.

93. John Stuart Mill, *On Liberty and The Subjection of Women*, ed. Alan Ryan (London, 2006), 10. On the Quaker embrace of constitutionalism, see Jane E. Calvert, *Quaker Constitutionalism and the Political Thought of John Dickinson* (Cambridge, 2009), 59–63.

94. Whitehead, *Christian Progress*, 628.

95. For Robert Barclay's view that even "those commonly called Heathens" could be saved by following their own Inner Light, see his *Universal Love Considered* (n.p., 1677, Wing B741), 37.

CHAPTER 9

William Penn, German Pietist(?)

Patrick M. Erben

Scholarship on the life and work of William Penn has long followed a declension narrative. Accordingly, Penn emerged as a champion of religious dissenters in England and the Continent in the 1660s and '70s, fighting tirelessly for religious toleration and civic anti-authoritarianism, eventually realizing his dream of a "Holy Experiment" in the founding of Pennsylvania. Yet, as the narrative goes, he was soon bogged down in ruling his proprietary colony like a feudal lord, becoming embroiled in Pennsylvania's factional politics, boundary disputes with Lord Baltimore, and imperial wrangling for power in Britain. After his death, his own sons betrayed his legacy by converting to Anglicanism, ruling the proprietary colony as absentee landlords, and trading in their father's pacifist dealings with the indigenous people of Pennsylvania for the treachery of the "Walking Purchase." Perhaps Penn's own principles and aspirations were always so deeply divided—between worldly ambition and spiritual introversion—that only a many-faces approach to his life and world could truly make sense of such contradictions. This scholarly and popular paradigm by and large squared with the historiography on Penn's eponymous colony, which still juxtaposes utopian beginnings with secularization and a waning of religious zeal among Quakers. Even this present volume strives to make sense of the multifaceted nature of the man and his colony by moving from the formerly singular *World of William Penn* to the plural *Worlds*.[1]

This chapter does not attempt to create an artificially unified image of Penn. Rather, it tries to account for the astounding fact that for much of his life and long after his death, German (radical) Pietists on both sides of the Atlantic considered William Penn a veritable early-modern rock star—a celebrity dissenter on whose name and image a host of spiritual, millenarian, radical Protestant, Philadelphian, and broadly dissenting expectations and visions could be pinned. This conceptualization was hardly grounded in an actual knowledge of Penn himself but a construction akin to the promotion of early America itself. A number of crucial factors converged in this discursive construction of "William Penn" as a brand, a dream, and an embodiment of a vision attractive to most German dissenters: Penn's early writings on religious toleration and Christian virtue, his travels and "missionary" journeys through Holland and Germany, and the transmission of his promotional writings by translators, colonial agents in Europe, and German-immigrant champions in America. The textual apotheosis of William Penn by German Pietist and Separatist publishers, promoters, and writers on both sides of the Atlantic to some degree relied on common articles of belief between English Quakers and German dissenters, although individuals closer to the Lutheran and Reformed orthodoxy rejected Quaker principles, such as the concept of the Inner Light, as anti-Christian. Nevertheless, Francis Daniel Pastorius, the Pietist founder of Germantown, carried on the banner of Penn-veneration in his German-language descriptions of Pennsylvania as well as his manuscript poetry.

The image of Penn as peacemaker and champion of freedom of conscience in America became so popularized among German immigrants that even later generations of Pennsylvania Germans wielded it rhetorically during the imperial wars of mid-eighteenth century North America. The Pennsylvania-German printer Christoph Saur deployed this image of Penn as central to the founding myth of Pennsylvania in order to oppose efforts by Benjamin Franklin and various provincial governors to institute military service or raise taxes for wartime expenses (and thus integrate Pennsylvania more fully into British imperial interests). "William Penn" became more and more removed from physical, historical, and biographical reality and elevated into the realm of the founding father of early American religious liberty. German Pietists were instrumental in this historical and cultural process.

Quakers and Pietists

Quakerism and Pietism alike sprung from a rising dissatisfaction among spiritually inclined Protestants in Britain and on the Continent with the outcome of the Reformation. During the seventeenth century, the Anglican Church on the British Isles, as well as the Lutheran and Reformed Churches on the Continent, had increasingly turned toward a confessionalization and orthodoxy, that is, an entrenchment of theological and ecclesiastical policies becoming more and more akin to the strict hierarchies and dogmatism of the Catholic Church. Religious warfare eventually led to political and religious settlements that clamped down on religious dissenters and established mainstream Protestant churches as state-sponsored institutions. In response, Quakerism and Pietism emerged in the mid- to late seventeenth century as complementary, though also significantly differentiated, spiritualist movements.

Pietism began not as a unified movement but as a simultaneous awakening among individual ministers and theologians, laypeople, and mystical visionaries who shared a desire for a greater inwardness of religious experience and practical, lived piety.[2] An inward change of faith should translate into a turn away from a worldly lifestyle, pursuit of personal pleasure and financial gain, jockeying for high office, and proud disputes over church doctrines. Pietists promoted a religion of the heart through a personal and emotional relationship to Christ and thus a more direct access to the divine spirit. Moderate Pietists worked within established church structures to change worship, faith, and piety. Other groups, called "radical" by their critics, identified the orthodox Protestant churches as "Babel," thus extending the earlier association of the fallen or unregenerate church that had been applied to Catholicism. Some radical Pietists, including the Frankfurt group Penn met in 1677, believed in the imminent arrival of the millennium and eventually pitched emigration as a potential escape from the apocalyptic punishments to be inflicted on Europe.

Pietist groups differed with regard to their opinion about the church ordinances and the nature of Jesus Christ. Most Pietists distanced themselves from the Quakers' eschewal of baptism and communion, as well as the Quakers' spiritualized notion of Christ and supposed disregard for his physical suffering and the doctrine of atonement.[3] Similar to Quakers, however, Pietists criticized "orthodox" Protestants for hearing sermons and receiving the sacraments without an inward spiritual change and altered outward behavior. Both movements advocated for the reflection of inner, spiritual conviction of faith in practical piety and concrete acts of love toward fellow humans. Francis Daniel Pastorius, the German Pietist founder of Germantown and admirer of William Penn, demonstrates the fluidity between related Protestant dissident movements like Quakerism and Pietism as well as the distinctiveness of specific practices and ideas in each tradition. After the Frankfurt Pietists failed to follow Pastorius to the land they had bought from William Penn in Pennsylvania for building a settlement, Pastorius quickly embraced Penn and other prominent Quakers as role models of an idealized Christian community and converted to the Society of Friends himself. He became a great apologist for the Quakers among his erstwhile coreligionists in Germany—all via Penn as the conduit for praise and affection.

Pietists and Quakers alike probed how individuals and groups seriously committed to a renovation of their faith should behave toward the society and the dominant church in which they lived. Emigration increasingly gained in importance as individuals and groups who shared common concerns for a renovation of Christianity pondered not just how but where their goal could be achieved. In the late seventeenth century, the emerging concept of Philadelphianism linked various Protestant groups in England and Germany in a common concern for Christian renewal and an exodus from the societies and confessional churches they considered the Babel of the current age. Philadelphian notions—especially a common belief in universal spiritual renewal, the unity of Christian churches and believers, and the brotherhood of all human beings—gave Quakers and radical Pietists a common purpose.

William Penn and the Promotion of Religious Liberty in Germany

William Penn emerged as the foremost international Quaker spokesperson during the early 1670s with his first missionary trip to Holland and Germany. During his 1671 visit to Herford, Germany, Penn made his first contact with a spiritualist religious group akin to Pietism, the Labadists. The French minister Jean de Labadie had gathered a separatist religious group in Amsterdam in 1669 and removed as a result of persecution to the estate of Princess Elizabeth of the Palatinate in Herford, Germany.[4] Penn's visit, however, was stunted, as the group feared the Quakers' influence and did not allow them to meet together.[5] Yet his passionate writings about and defenses of religious liberty during the 1670s caught the widespread attention of religious dissenters on the Continent and paved the way for his much more successful journey through Holland and Germany in 1677. Penn had already advocated freedom of worship and a cessation of state-sanctioned oppression of Protestant dissenters in Restoration England. He now expanded his activism by assisting outlying Quaker communities in Europe in writing petitions to their worldly oppressors, arguing for religious toleration. A letter Penn had originally sent in Latin to the magistrates of Emden and Danzig (Dansk) was published in English as *Christian Liberty* (1674) and in German as *Send-Brieff an die Bürgermeister und Raht der Stadt Danzig* (1675). The popularity of this tract among German-speaking dissenters is evidenced by its addition to the 1681 German translation of Penn's first promotional tract on Pennsylvania.[6]

Penn first pointed out the inconsistency between the oppression of religious dissenters within Protestant principalities and their own former struggle against Papal authority in the past. He displays a firm knowledge in the history of the Reformation in the German states, citing their vehement advocacy for "the Cause of Liberty of Conscience," their resistance against "Popes Bulls and the Spanish Inquisition," and their declaration as "Antichristian all Force on Conscience, or Punishment for Non-Conformity."[7] The tract even mentions specific petitions in favor of religious toleration made at the Imperial Diets of Nürnberg and Speyer ("Nurimberg and Spira") and concludes with the scolding accusation that all these examples "are pregnant Proofs in the Case: and your Practice doth not lessen the Weight of their [i.e., their own forefathers'] Reasons; on the contrary, it aggravates your Unkindness, let me say, Injustice."[8] German-speaking dissenters—among them German Quakers, Anabaptists, and the emerging

Pietists—witnessed Penn advocating religious toleration in general but also demonstrating that his principles were informed by the history of the Reformation in their own country. Though Penn had elsewhere used English Common Law as a further sanction of religious freedom, he omits this approach entirely in *Christian Liberty*. In sum, Penn's original letter had displayed a culturally aware rhetorical approach to the issue that increased his popularity and credentials among German-speaking dissenters.

William Penn's 1677 Missionary Journey

The most significant journey for shaping William Penn's image among German dissenters—specifically the newly emerging Pietist movement—occurred in 1677. Penn was accompanied by an illustrious cast of "Friends," including George Fox, Robert Barclay, George Keith, and Benjamin Furly. These Quakers created international and interdenominational communication networks between dissenters in England and Europe, while establishing the structures that Penn and his agents harnessed to promote the settlement of Pennsylvania a few years later.[9] The English "Friends" explored, renewed, cemented, or established compatibilities among related religious groups, including Dutch Quakers, Mennonites, Pietists, and Labadists.[10] In keeping with the fundamental Quaker doctrine of the Inner Light working in all human beings, the "missionaries" were on a quest to create spiritual community among like-minded individuals. Thus the particular meetings and exchanges Penn recorded in his *Journal* describe a process of mutual "opening." On his journey to visit Pietist and other spiritualist and reformist Protestants in Holland and Germany, Penn searched for outward evidence of the inward breaking down of a fallen, human self-will or self-determination.

For Penn, this search for reciprocal inwardness was especially successful among several German noblewomen—Princess Elizabeth of the Palatinate, Anna Maria von Schurman, Anna Maria van Hoorn, and Johanna Eleonora von Merlau—who had already been in correspondence with Quakers and practiced a form of "inner, ascetic religion."[11] Labadie had removed his group to Altona, freeing the women to entertain visitors like the Quakers. Robert Barclay and Benjamin Furly had visited Herford in 1676 and begun an extensive communication and exchange of religious materials with her, Schurman, and Hoorn.[12] Penn's journal entries of his personal visit to the Princess in 1677 reveal his attempt to establish a deeply spiritual communication that could serve as precedent for his contact with other radical Protestant individuals and groups in Germany. Penn describes a particularly effective meeting that evidences his apparent ability to reach out to the German-speaking women he met during his journey with a mix of personal charisma and emotive religious conversation that broke down barriers of linguistic, social, and denominational differences: "[T]he Princess came to me, & took me by the hand . . . & went to speak to me of the sense she had of that power & presence of god, that was amongst us; but was stopd: & turning herself to the window broke forth in an extraordinary [passion], [illegible deletion] crying out, *I can not speak to you, my heart is full; clapping her hand upon her breast.* It melted me into a deep & calm tenderness, in wh^{ch} I was moved to minister a few words softly to her."[13] The passage constructs a spiritual reciprocity between the Princess and Penn, mediated by a set of physical and emotional gestures that ultimately dissolve the borders between "self" and "other." Throughout his travels in Germany, Penn re-created such moments of spiritual union with congenial individuals and groups, thus setting the foundation of an idealized perception of himself and the "Holy Experiment" he would attempt to build in America.

Penn made the greatest impact among the so-called Saalhof Pietists in Frankfurt, where he visited after departing from Elizabeth at Herford. Originally organized as one of Spener's Pietist conventicles, during the late 1670s the Frankfurt Pietists moved toward a more radical chiliastic and mystical orientation under the leadership of Johann Jakob Schütz, Johann Wilhelm Petersen, and his (later) wife Johanna Eleonora von Merlau.[14] Most likely, Penn's visit with the Frankfurt Pietists disposed this group to regard Pennsylvania as a direct answer to their Philadelphian visions and purchase fifteen thousand acres from Benjamin Furly with the original intention to relocate, as a group, to America. In 1677, though, the emphasis of Penn's visit lay on exploring common ideals between Quakers and Pietists, especially the idea that an opening to the divine spirit must be precipitated by an erosion of human self-will. Penn elaborated on the workings of this principle in describing his meetings with two prominent Pietist women, Johanna Eleonora von Merlau and Juliane Bauer von Eysseneck, "who had a deep sense of that power & presence of god, that accompanied our Testimony: & their hearts yearned strongly towards us."[15]

According to Penn, the two women wished for a combination of spiritual perfection and worldly suffering akin to Quakerism. Penn felt most connected to Merlau, with whom he initiated a lively correspondence. In a September 11, 1677, letter written after his departure, Penn advises her (and the other Pietists) to continue in the "sensible feeling of his daily divine visits, shinings, & breathings upon your spirits." He thus defined Merlau and the rest of her community as a mystical society receiving divine communications binding them to God and to each other: "For this know, it was the life in your selves, that so sweetly visited you by the ministry of life through us."[16] Rather than Penn instilling in the Pietists a Christian faith, they opened an awareness of the spirit within themselves.

For Penn and the German Pietists, letter writing served to cement spiritual bonds already established through physical acquaintance but also to prepare new ties. Certain letters Penn wrote to individuals and groups were eventually printed or distributed in manuscript form, thus further disseminating the spiritual bonds established in person or through correspondence. In turn, Penn's promotional tracts on Pennsylvania were eventually circulated in manuscript or even letter form among the networks established during these journeys, thereby harnessing the seemingly impersonal medium of print to facilitate spiritual relationships. After visiting a Lutheran congregation with Pietist leanings in Worms, Penn immediately sent them books in order to continue and deepen the impact of the personal spiritual fellowship."[17] Penn thus deepened and extended the impression left by his personal presence by deploying Quaker books that had already been translated and printed for readers on the Continent. This strategic joining of personal presence and textual communication created a crucial linkage: whereas German Pietists and other dissenters would later on learn about Penn's colony and its visionary promises primarily through translated and printed texts rather than from Penn directly, these treatises were nevertheless endowed with the residue of Penn's personal visits as well as the intimacy of continuing correspondence flowing through the networks established in the 1670s.

William Penn's Promotion of Pennsylvania and His Promotion in German Tracts

The promotional writings that William Penn published and disseminated after receiving the charter for Pennsylvania in 1681 appealed to Pietist readers in Germany not primarily because of the promise of material abundance but because of the expectation of freedom of conscience promised by Penn and the continuation of the kind of spiritual fellowship he had created during his journeys and in his correspondence. Even among groups and individuals whom Penn had not met in person during his travels, promotional writings on Pennsylvania would have a similar effect, because they continued to speak the language of spiritual communion and cast Penn as the foundation of these spiritualist expectations. When promotional literature slipped into a more conventional discourse of colonization, Quaker agents like Benjamin Furly ensured its appeal to radical Protestant groups on the Continent.[18] The moment Penn began to publicize and promote Pennsylvania to a variety of investors across Britain and Continental Europe, his projection as a champion of religious tolerance flipped from his own agency and personal involvement to a discursive construction in texts received, edited, modified, and eventually written by Quaker intermediaries like Furly and Pastorius. Rather than Penn wooing Pietists, German dissenters now created an idealized version of Penn and his colony in their writings, letters, and communications. Pastorius's letters and reports to Germany featured his personal interactions with Penn in Pennsylvania and thus authenticated the expectations German dissenters pinned on the proprietor and his colony.

In his first promotional tract, entitled *Some Account of the Province of Pennsilvania* (1681), Penn specifies as the target audience "those of our own, or other

Nations, that are inclin'd to Transport themselves or Families beyond the Seas."[19] The German edition—entitled *Eine Nachricht wegen der Landschafft Pennsilvania*—follows the general structure of Penn's *Some Account*; its departures and additions, however, address the shortcomings of the English original as a promotional tool for a German, radical Protestant audience.[20] Surprisingly, Penn nowhere mentions the cherished principle of religious toleration: "[As] soon as any are ingaged with me, we shall begin a Scheam or Draught together, such as shall give ample Testimony of my sincere Inclinations to encourage Planters, and settle a free, just and industrious Colony there."[21] Adapting the tract to the sensibilities of German dissenters, the editor or translator of *Eine Nachricht* added the following clause to Penn's sentence: "and also there to institute the freedom of conscience for anyone to practice their faith and to worship publicly."[22] In grafting the clause on religious liberty onto *Some Account*, the translator or editor was drawing from the precedent Penn had set with his writings on religious freedom before his acquisition of Pennsylvania, such as the letters to the cities of Emden and Danzig in the 1670s.

How important a written guarantee of religious toleration in Pennsylvania was for European dissenters emerges from Furly's critique of subsequent changes made in several drafts of the *Frame of Government*. The first *Frame of Government of the Province of Pennsilvania in America*, published in May 1682, was the result of some intense political and textual wrangling over the specific rights of the proprietor and the new settlers. The drafting process produced at least twelve preliminary documents and involved Penn's collaboration with several other interested individuals.[23] Benjamin Furly severely criticized the changes made between the initial draft, "The Fundamentall Constitutions of Pennsilvania," and the *Frame* of 1682. "Fundamentall Constitutions," the most liberal of all the drafts, opened with a proclamation of religious freedom.[24] In the *Frame* published in 1682, however, liberty of conscience was downgraded from the prominent status of a preamble to an almost insignificant position as item number 35. In a letter to Penn, Furly expressed his indignation over the changes.[25] Furly objected to the less prominent position of religious toleration as well as to the absence of any regulation against excessive litigation,[26] communicating to Penn his insight into the interpenetration of legal and religious sensibilities of German and Dutch immigrants: "Consider further that there are many Christians in holland [*sic*] & Germany that look upon it as unlawfull to sue any man at the Law, as to fight wth armes[.] These then having no other fence but their prudence in intrusting none but honst [*sic*] men."[27] Furly also claimed that inheritance laws and a xenophobic naturalization policy disadvantaged non-English immigrants.[28] At this crucial moment, Furly lobbied for Pennsylvania to live up to the promises Penn had made to dissenters in Holland and Germany.[29] Furly's editorial emendations of tracts intended for radical Protestants on the Continent nevertheless continued the mythos of a utopian experiment under the patronage of a spiritually enlightened proprietor.

Penn and Pastorius

With the textual changes made by Furly and other translators or editors, the German versions of English promotional accounts of Pennsylvania catered to the expectations of those German religious dissenters whom Penn had visited during his mission trip down the Rhine in 1677. When a strong demand made printed volumes scarce, German promoters circulated handwritten transcriptions among their friends.[30] For instance, Furly sent both personal letters and printed accounts to the Frankfurt Pietists whom Penn had visited in 1677 or to interested individuals such as the Lübeck pastor Jaspar Könneken.[31] In turn, these groups or individuals produced manuscript transcriptions of printed texts or personal letters. Könneken, for instance, assembled an impressive manuscript collection of primary accounts from Pennsylvania, including letters or tracts by Penn, Pastorius, and other English, German, and Dutch writers. Passing through this network, the promotional discourse was not only adapted to the social and political situations of local audiences, but it also gained a personal dimension. Penn's presence in these accounts was paired with the social and spiritual bonds among local communities.

Manuscript circulation of promotional tracts on Pennsylvania throughout Germany may have rivaled the spread of printed material on this issue. For example, manuscript copies of Penn's *Letter . . . to the Committee of the Free Society of Traders* in German combined the formality and authority of printed accounts with the intimacy of direct communication. A manuscript entitled "Ein Brief von William Penn Eigenthumbs Herrn und Befehlshabern in Pennsylvania" (A Letter from William Penn, Proprietor and Governor in Pennsylvania), for example, contains no introductory matter or title page but immediately starts with the title and the address "Meine werthen freunde" ("My dear friends"), speaking directly to the readers of the manuscript in Germany.[32]

Pastorius's retrospective account of his decision to emmigrate to Pennsylvania demonstrates the crucial role played by the transmission of Penn's tracts along the personal connections he had forged during his early journey through Germany. Having just returned from a two-year "Grand Tour" accompanying a German nobleman, Pastorius describes the community of Pietists at the "Saalhof" in Frankfurt as the conduits for Penn's news of the colony, encouraging him to move with them to Pennsylvania:

> And forasmuch as I after this my Return was glad to enjoy the ancient familiarity of my former Acquaintances (rather than to be with the aforesd. von Bodeck feasting, dancing, &c.) especially of those Christian Friends who frequently assembled together in a house, called the Saalhof, viz. Dr. Spener, Dr. Schutz, Notarius Fenda, Jacobus van de Walle, Maximilian (bynamed the pious) Lersner, Eleonora von Merlau, Maria Juliana Baurin, &c. who some-

> times made mention of William Penn & of Pennsilvania, and moreover communicated unto me as well some private letters from Benjamin Furly, as also a printed Relation concerning the sd province, and finally the whole Secret could not be withholden from me, viz. that they purchased 15000. Acres of land in this remote part of the world, some of 'em entirely resolv'd to transport themselves, families & all; this begat such a desire in my Soul to continue in their Society, and with them to lead a quiet, godly & honest life in a howling wilderness, (which I observed to be a heavy Task for any to perform among the bad examples & numberless Vanitates Vanitatum in Europe).[33]

The local community of Frankfurt Pietist had remained connected to Penn and Furly through the correspondence of individual members, and they subsequently became a community of readers in the textual promotion of Pennsylvania. Penn's printed tract and his personal image were thus enhanced by the local community of Pietist sympathizers.

Pastorius's hopes to transplant to Pennsylvania the affection he had found in the Pietist community in Frankfurt were dashed by the group's failure to follow their agent into this "howling wilderness."[34] While retaining his official assignment to promote and administer a German settlement in the province, Pastorius found personal and spiritual affinity in relationships with many English Quaker immigrants, particularly William Penn. Though Pastorius had not been part of the original Frankfurt Pietist group inspired by Penn's personal visit, his meetings with Penn in America ironically reaffirmed his decision to seek spiritual renewal in Pennsylvania. For Pastorius, Penn became the physical incarnation of the textual and oral construction of the proprietor he had witness among his Pietist friends in Frankfurt. In turn, Pastorius's own reports of his interactions with Penn rehearsed and intensified the dissemination of Penn's textual idealization in Germany.

Pastorius's first published report to his Frankfurt friends (written in March 1684)—later printed and distributed as a promotional tract entitled *Sichere Nachricht* (*Positive Information*)—ostensibly evaluates the chances of an exclusively German community, but his exuberant appraisal of Penn values intellectual and spiritual consanguinity over national affiliation in the construction of community in Pennsylvania.[35] According to *Sichere Nachricht*, the affection between the two men relied on common visions for the spiritual and social development of the province but also on bonds of a common intellectual heritage including the mastery of Latin and French.[36] Pastorius reported that Penn "often invites me to his table and has me walk and ride in his always edifying company; and when I lately was absent from here a week . . . and he had not seen me for that space of time, he came himself to my little house and besought me that I should at least once or twice a week be his guest."[37] Passing by the house Pastorius had built in Philadelphia, Penn read and was pleased by the Latin motto from

Virgil's *Aeneid* above the door: "Parva domus sed amica bonis, procul este prophani" ("A little house, but a friend to the good; remain at a distance, ye profane."[38] Penn and Pastorius shared the cosmopolitan heritage of the late Renaissance, epitomized by their common knowledge of classical languages and literature.[39]

If the congeniality provided by an elite European education was beyond the reach of most immigrants, a shared vision of spiritual renewal under Pennsylvania's motto of "brotherly love" could attract religious dissenters from any class or social standing. Pastorius's praise of Penn thus moves Christian fellowship to the center of communal bonding in the province:

> I, on the following day, delivered to William Penn the letters that I had, and was received by him with amiable friendliness; of that very worthy man and famous ruler I might properly . . . write many things; but my pen . . . is much too weak to express the high virtues of this Christian—for such he is indeed. . . . He heartily loves the [*Germans*], and once said openly in my presence to his councillors and those who were about him, I love the [*Germans*] and desire that you also should love them. Yet in any other matter I have never heard such a command from him. . . . I can at present say no more than that William Penn is a man who honors God and is honored by Him, who loves what is good and is rightly beloved by all good men. I doubt not that some of them will come here and by their own experience learn, that my pen has in this case not written enough.[40]

Just as Penn had engendered the Pietists' eagerness to immigrate to Pennsylvania, Pastorius now deployed his experience of the proprietor to chide his Frankfurt friends for failing to close the cycle of spiritual affinity. Pastorius's invocation of bi-weekly dinners with Penn and joint walks or rides through the woods exchanges the "ancient familiarity" with his "Christian Friends" in Frankfurt for similar affection for the English proprietor.

Though Pastorius called out the Frankfurt Pietists for their spiritual fruitlessness, they nevertheless recognized the value of his congenial accounts of Penn as advertisements for *other* radical Protestant immigrants. In fact, the Frankfurt Pietists deployed the Christian friendship between Penn and Pastorius as a promotional device in later publications. In 1700, they published a collection of Pastorius's reports as *Umständige Geographische Beschreibung* (*Circumstantial Geographical Description*), which included an excerpt from Penn's 1683 *Letter . . . to the Committee of the Free Society of Traders* (in German translation) and a letter from Penn to Pastorius's father. Penn's appraisal of Pastorius mirrors Pastorius's own paean to the proprietor. Penn wrote: "Your son was recently among the living and is even now in Philadelphia. This year he is justice of the peace, or was so very lately. Furthermore, he is called a man sober, upright, wise, and pious, of a reputation approved on all hands and unimpeached."[41] Penn's testimony allowed prospective immigrants from Germany to picture themselves vicariously in a similar position, as the recipients of Penn's praise and affection. Similarly, the excerpt from Penn's *Letter . . . to the Committee of the Free Society of Traders* reemphasized the mutuality between Penn and German settlers, signaling to readers that in Pennsylvania many voices joined in a single purpose. Though originally sent to business investors in England, the German translation is introduced as if it had been expressly sent to Penn's friends in Germany: "In conclusion follows a description written by the proprietor and head of this province himself and sent to his friends."[42]

Throughout his reports from Pennsylvania, Pastorius anchored his spiritual vision in the symbolically uniting figure of William Penn, who stands as the safeguard of religious liberty: "And notwithstanding the aforesaid William Penn belongs to the sect of the Tremblers, or Quakers, yet he constrains no one to any religion, but leaves to each nation freedom of belief."[43] Although Pastorius here seems to solidify the association of national heritage with a particular faith, Penn, as political and spiritual figure head, makes such distinctions obsolete. Virtually cribbing Penn's *Letter . . . to the Committee of the Free Society of Traders*, Pastorius writes of Penn's original arrival in Pennsylvania and his reception by established European colonists: "Penn was received as their ruler by these people with especial tokens of affection, and they most willingly discharged their obligation of submission to him. All that he required of them in return was: A temperate life and neighborly love. On the other hand, he promised to protect them in both spiritual and temporal matters."[44] For Continental immigrants used to a strong state power encapsulated in the territorial prince, Penn embodied the ideal of the good Christian ruler. Penn could somehow accomplish the impossible: unite members of various nations and denominations in a spiritual and political harmony *without* curtailing their free exercise of religion. When critics in England and Pennsylvania not only impeded Penn's exercise of power but also questioned his ability as spiritual leader, Pastorius continued to assert Penn's primacy in both arenas.[45] In his letter to his father dated May 30, 1698, Pastorius writes:

> William Penn is and remains lord of the proprietary and sanctioned prince over Pennsylvania, and although he has not been here with us for some years, nevertheless he has done us more service in England through his presence there, than probably might have been the case if he had remained here all the time. The estimable man has very many enemies on account of his religion, who however rather overdo matters, since they, for their part, are not surely informed, much less can they see into another's heart. We expect his arrival in this country without fail, this summer, or next autumn, if no ill-health or other hindrance occurs.[46]

Certainly, Pastorius's insistence on Penn's prerogative to rule Pennsylvania and his personal and spiritual attachment to Penn seem naïve and founded on nostalgic memories of their early fellowship. Although Penn indeed returned to the province in 1699, Pastorius's failsafe belief in his arrival reads like grasping at straws; behind Pastorius's urgent desire for Penn's return stood a decade of political and religious disputes among Pennsylvania's Quakers and other groups, of which the Keithian schism was the most extreme manifestation. Read in light of Pastorius's earlier assertion that the persecution of Pietists and Quietists in Europe was a certain sign of Christ's immanent second coming, however, such hopes make sense. Just short of linking the "return" of Penn to the Second Coming, Pastorius invests both events with eschatological hopes in the restoration of a divine order.

The Keithian Controversy: Rejection and Vindication

The schism among Pennsylvania Quakers that arose in the early 1690s, however, deeply shook the faith of Pastorius and other German-speaking Pietist immigrants in the salubrious effects of Penn's "holy experiment," some of them even declaring it broken. Some followers of the mystical Pietist Johannes Kelpius, who had appeared in Pennsylvania in 1694 to found a quasi-monastic order, joined the Keithians in their critique of William Penn and orthodox Quakers, whereas Pastorius rushed to their defense. To a certain degree, German immigrants reenacted the linguistic and spiritual confusion of the Keithian controversy. Troubled by the extreme partisanship of the religious, civic, and political divisions created or precipitated by the Keithian controversy, Pastorius never abandoned his veneration of Penn. Pastorius issued printed works defending Penn and the Quakers to the Pietists in Germany, while composing personal poems and paeans sent directly to the proprietor. Although Penn's image among German-speaking dissenters suffered as a result of the controversy, Pastorius's vouching for Penn specifically and the original Quaker vision of religious toleration and spiritual inwardness more generally carried over into the radical Pietist vision of Pennsylvania culture and politics that German printer Christoph Saur promoted from the 1730s onward.

Although historians debate a variety of causes for and meanings of the Keithian controversy, it is by and large recognized as a theological debate that exposed and exacerbated ecclesiastical, civic, and political fractures among American Quakers.[47] In the late 1680s and early '90s, George Keith, one of the leading figures of late seventeenth-century Quakerism, began arguing with other prominent Quakers over what constituted acceptable religious testimony. Valuing a personalized faith over a set of doctrines, Quakers regarded any inspired religious testimony as a reflection of an indwelling divine light or presence of God. Keith, however, was appalled by his fellow Quakers' supposed ignorance of Scripture and the basic tenets of Christianity. The Quaker elite initially refused to comment on the doctrinal issues raised by Keith but objected to his vociferous attacks. Eventually, the Quakers rebutted, claiming that Keith denied the sufficiency of the Inner Light for Christian salvation. In 1692, Keith and his followers established a separate meeting and dubbed themselves "Christian Quakers." The "orthodox" Quakers rejected the new meeting and disowned Keith, yet the controversy spread into print and dragged on for years, with opponents on both sides accusing each other of libel and deeply scarring a society of "friends."

Pastorius tried to remain neutral but was aghast at witnessing the disruption that Keith and his followers wrought upon the spirit of affection. The German Pietist mystic Johann Gotfried Seelig, who had arrived in Pennsylvania in the immediate aftermath of the schism even described the Quakers in a post-Babel state of confusion, claiming that the "pieces of their established Meetings lie scattered all over."[48] The Keithian controversy exposed underlying differences among Pietist immigrants, who differed widely in their relative proximity to or distance from Protestant orthodoxy. The German Lutheran theologian Heinrich Bernhard Köster had followed the mystically inclined Kelpius to Pennsylvania as an expression of his millenarian leanings; in Pennsylvania, however, he sympathized with the Keithians' trenchant criticism of the Quakers' alleged heresies, undergoing a personal shift back to a much more dogmatic position. When Köster and several English Keithians disrupted a Quaker meeting at Burlington in 1696, Pastorius issued a strongly worded pamphlet. Entitled *Four Boasting Disputers Briefly Rebuked*, Pastorius's tract lambasted Köster for breaking the Quaker peace principle and creating further spiritual divisions.[49] In a German-language tract sent to his former Pietist sponsors and friends, entitled *Ein Send-Brieff Offenhertziger Liebsbezeugung an die so genannte* Pietisten *in Hoch-Teutschland* (a letter of open-hearted affection to the so-called Pietists in Germany), Pastorius explicitly rejected the abuse that some Keithians heaped upon Penn in particular:[50]

> God, who is a god of peace as well as war, gave William Penn (who is also derisively called a Quaker and now in his absence is being railed at and reviled with various kinds of epithets by some of the abovementioned new arrivals) this province to govern as his property, which he received from the King of Great Britain almost 17 years ago. God has preserved us, a defenseless people, amidst all the war and calls of war in distant as well as in neighboring countries until this present time in a state of happy retirement and has thereby strengthened our faith all the more, because he alone can avert our outward and inward enemies from us and give us physical and spiritual peace, as long as we trust only in Him as our mighty protector.

While initially flattering the German Pietists as part of a larger European movement toward a general renovation of the Christian church, Pastorius used this letter to represent his view of the Keithian controversy, refute Köster's specific allegations, and vindicate his newly adopted religious community. For Pastorius, this letter was a public coming out moment: he declared in print to the Pietists that he had joined the Quakers. According to Pastorius, raillery against

Penn was not merely an affront against a person he admired but a downright heresy, because the province of Pennsylvania was indeed his God-given property. That Pennsylvania had been spared from the imperial wars raging in Europe and around the Atlantic was thus a result of the order and peacefulness God had imparted through the person of the proprietor.

Pastorius also dedicated a significant portion of his manuscript writings—poetry, letters, and German translations—to honoring and personally encouraging Penn. In a 1699 manuscript poem sent to Penn directly (recorded in Pastorius's "Bee-Hive" commonplace book and poetic miscellany), Pastorius celebrates Penn's second arrival in Pennsylvania "for which good Patriots these sev'ral years did long, / And which Occasions this his German's English Song, / Who'f old could talk with him but in the Gallic Tongue." While their common education and knowledge of French had originally served to unite the two men in spirit and action, the situation has changed upon Penn's return to the province. Pastorius has gained knowledge of Penn's native tongue through his involvement in the community.[51] In other poems recorded in the "Bee-Hive," Pastorius satirized the Keithians but lauded the forbearance and bemoaned the suffering of prominent Friends, such as Thomas Lloyd and William Penn:

> We understood what things in Pensilvania were
> Of good or evil use, to follow, or t'avoid,
> The wisest of us all was honest Thomas Lloid.
> Some lent their itching Ears to Kuster, Keith & Budd,
> And miserably fell into the Ditch of Mud,
> Where they may stick & stink; For as a sightless whelp,
> So stark-blind Apostates do grin at profer'd help:
> They spend their Mouths, & fain with words would ensnare,
> Or if this will not do, scold, back-bite, bug-bear, scare;
> Hereof, brave William Penn, me thinks, thou hadst thy share.[52]

The poem could change nothing about the events that Pastorius, Lloyd, and other Pennsylvania Quakers witnessed or participated in; yet it differentiates the individuals who broke the peace, those who stayed the course, and those who suffered from the alleged vituperation of the Keithians. Pastorius thus departed from a dominant strain in Pennsylvania religious and political discourse that largely blamed Penn for the disorder in the province. In this poem, Penn is not merely a person but he is metonymically linked to the land he is given as proprietary: framing the first and last line of this section of the (longer) poem, Pennsylvania and William Penn together offer residents a range of choices for their actions within the community—the free will implicit in freedom of conscience. The choice of the Keithians to "scold, back-bite, bug-bear, scare" thus not only hurts Penn but abuses Pennsylvania as both a place and a communal ideal.

After trying to engage publicly in the destructive debates of the Keithian controversy and privately expressing his affection for Penn, Pastorius turned his energy toward educating Pennsylvania's youth both in the Germantown school and in the English Quaker schools of Philadelphia. Lacking instructional books, Pastorius published one language primer and produced several other manuscript textbooks on topics from math to grammar. Once again moving William Penn to the center of his vision for Pennsylvania, Pastorius translated several Quaker classics into German, including Penn's *A Key* (published in 1692 as a defense of Quaker principles) and his earlier and widely popular book of Quaker spirituality, *Fruits of Solitude* (1682).[53] Pastorius and his students also created a manuscript collection dedicated to the birth of William Penn's son John. Entitled "Genetliacum or An hearty Congratulation," the collection contains so-called Onomastical Considerations, brief moral and religious reflections associated with a specific name, in this case "John."[54] Pastorius inculcates Penn's authority as ruler of the province and his newborn son's legitimacy as his successor. The manuscript's title page thus addressed Penn as "*Patri Patriæ*, The Father of this Province, and lately also the Father of John Penn, an innocent & hopeful Babe, by whose Nativity & Names sake they were first contrived." Confronting the doubters and haters, Pastorius declared Penn the once-and-future ruler of Pennsylvania. Pastorius's image of Penn's benevolent paternalism probably raised eyebrows—even in 1700s Pennsylvania. Yet the historical and communal mythos of Penn as sole guarantor of the province's special freedoms and privileges, as well as its peace, enjoyed lasting purchase among German-speaking immigrants, especially radical Pietist and Separatist settlers like the first Pennsylvania-German printer, Christoph Saur, who arrived with his family in America in 1724, a few years after Pastorius's death in 1719.[55]

Posthumous Penn: Pietist Politics and the Mythologizing of the Proprietor

In the late 1730s, Christoph Saur established a printing press and publishing house whose most widely recognized and distributed organs, his newspaper and almanac, influenced German-speaking immigrants far beyond Pennsylvania.[56] Saur's radical Pietist and Sectarian religious attitudes, as well as his knowledge of the arbitrary power of German territorial princes made him an avowed spokesperson for German immigrant liberties in Pennsylvania, especially the treasured freedom of conscience and right *not* to bear arms. Saur and the thousands of German-speaking immigrants who arrived in Pennsylvania around the middle of the eighteenth century were, though they differed considerably in their specific religious beliefs, unified by their aversion to forced military service. Saur thus considered any call to arms from Pennsylvania governors and the province's foremost citizen, Benjamin Franklin, a breach of William Penn's Charter of

Liberties (1701) and a violation of the bonds established between the first generations of English Quaker and German Pietist and sectarian immigrants who founded Pennsylvania. Tellingly, Saur issued the first German translations of the Charter in the 1740s, precisely at a moment when he and other pacifist Sectarians, Anabaptists, and Pietists feared they might once more be pressed into military service in violation of their consciences.[57]

Saur specifically harnessed the image of William Penn as progenitor and once and future protector of Pennsylvania's peace principle at the moment that Franklin proposed in his widely read pamphlet *Plain Truth* (1747) the establishment of a voluntary militia for the defense of Pennsylvania. With the Quaker-led Assembly refusing funds for defense as a violation of their faith, Franklin published the pamphlet *Plain Truth*, calling for the establishment of a voluntary militia or "Association" for the defense of the city and province.[58] *Plain Truth* was immediately translated into German as *Lautere Wahrheit* by Franklin's German acquaintance Joseph Crellius and published by Franklin's German printing partner, Gotthard Armbrüster. Both versions of the pamphlet were distributed free of charge.[59]

Saur denounced the Association throughout its existence and dissuaded his German readers from participating in the organization. According to Franklin's own testimony in a letter to his friend Peter Collinson in England, most Germans heeded Saur's advice and refrained from joining the militia, causing him to doubt the loyalty of these non-English residents.[60] The success of Saur's campaign against the Association stemmed from his ability to present Pennsylvania as a unique place where different national and denominational groups were joined by the absence of political or religious coercion. Even a voluntary militia, Saur feared, would establish the willingness to bear arms as a standard of communal cohesion that, in turn, would cast pacifists as antisocial delinquents. Recognizing Franklin's tacit charge of disloyalty against German immigrants, Saur launched a communal model for Pennsylvania based on William Penn's founding promise of religious liberty and freedom from oppressive military service.

German radical Pietists and Sectarians like Saur were not alone in invoking the precedent Penn had set in establishing a peaceful policy toward Native Americans and renouncing the participation in imperial warfare. The anonymous English writer of *A Treatise*, for instance, contrasted the account of other English-led colonization projects with the famed policies of Pennsylvania's founder:

> I think proper to begin here, treating on the Manner or Method taken by WILLIAM PENN, in Order to perfect the Settlement of this Province, and as he was a great, wise, and good Man, so accordingly he proceeded in this weighty Affair, consulting the Article of GOD: and we have just Reason to believe, that his Proceedings were pleasing to divine Providence; who blessed his Under-

> takings with admirable Success, in that of coming to a legal Bargain or agreement, and Purchaser of this Province of the owners (as a Part of the Creation, assigned them by Providence) the Indians.[61]

Such peaceful dealings even affected a change in the very nature of an otherwise "barbarous and cruel People." With the dominance of the Quaker point of view now under attack in the 1740s, Christoph Saur in particular deployed short history lessons in order to remind readers of the reasons for a sixty-five-year record of peacefulness in the province—all predicated upon the central figure of William Penn.

Saur understood relationships between English and German residents as a direct continuation of the interdenominational relationships promoted and established by William Penn and the first generation of English Quaker and German Protestant immigrants. An especially central role in this history was played Penn's missionary journeys through Germany, where he had forged lasting ties to Pietist groups:

> King Charles the second gave William Penn this land as a present for the faithful service that his father had rendered him in his unlucky condition. And because William Penn was a man who loved a quiet and godly life, he wanted to have this country settled only with pious and godly people. And since at that time there were a number of pious people who were serious about their life with God, this godly Penn traveled through England, Scotland, Ireland, and Germany and sought out such people who were being oppressed for Christ's sake and were not being tolerated. He not only gave much to such poor people but even paid their passage to this country if they were unable to do so. . . . At the time when he was traveling through Germany to seek out such pious people, a company of wealthy pious people in Frankfurt bought a large tract of land from him, and 25,000 acres of this tract were to be distributed to poor people without pay. But, through the trickery of lawyers, the land came into the hands of ruthless people, so that not a single poor person received even an acre of land, but anyone who obtained a piece of that land had to pay dearly for it.
>
> But as William Penn realized that any pious person could very well become wicked if the evil spirit comes back into the heart along with 7 others and, on the other hand, an ungodly person can become quite pious and godly, he allowed that good and bad people would live amongst each other, just as God allows them to exist together on earth.
>
> Since among the first inhabitants most were pious, godly, cordial, faithful, loving, and brotherly, they named their city Philadelphia, that is brotherly love, and William Penn befriended the Indians and paid them for the land so that they voluntarily withdrew and it is still happening in the same manner. Those who remember this country 40, 30, or 20 years ago, will admit that it was a

> blessed land full of righteous people, and even though many hundred and thousand people from Ireland and the Palatinate &c. have come here from places where the most vicious godlessness rules, many who have a good and honorable master or neighbor let of somewhat or a lot from their uncouth cursing, swearing, lying, cheating, dancing, gaming &c. through the assistance of better company; and through shame or conviction of conscience many have come to fear God or even to experience the Love of God.[62]

Saur's historical account of the settlement of Pennsylvania begins with Penn's founding concept of populating the province with pious and virtuous people. Significantly, Saur stresses that Penn, during his travels through various nations, discriminated exclusively on the basis of religious oppression. Thus Saur rehearses the founding myth of Pennsylvania as a haven established by William Penn for the oppressed and persecuted of Europe. Earlier betrayals of this founding idealism included the affairs of the Pietists' Frankfurt Land Company, whose business was taken over from Francis Daniel Pastorius by a German adventurer who employed English lawyers such as David Lloyd to disown most of the company's original landholders. This anecdote is particularly important for Saur's present purpose of deriding the proponents of the Association, for it exemplifies how people without conscience may take advantage of poor German immigrants. While mentioning Penn's pacifist dealings with the Indians in passing, Saur finally arrives at his current vision of society in Pennsylvania. In spite of a massive influx of immigrants from countries with degenerating morals, an adherence to Penn's principles of brotherly love and godliness as well as a sober lifestyle can convert even the most corrupted.

Throughout much of the eighteenth century, therefore, Christoph Saur's press promoted a Pennsylvanian exceptionalism focused on the central figure of William Penn and the original Quaker founders. For much of the Atlantic world, Benjamin Franklin had replaced Penn as the prototypical citizen of the New World, replete with the insignia of natural philosophy and science—the beaver fur cap and the kite and key—that complemented Enlightenment conceptualizations of America. Yet, for German-speaking immigrants—radical and orthodox Protestants alike—Saur kept alive the venerated figure of William Penn as the guarantor of religious liberty and his colony as virtually the sole remaining refuge from almost universal warfare. In the very first issue of his newspaper, published August 20, 1739, Saur confronted his Pennsylvanian readers with an account of America treacherously entangled in the imperialist machinations of Europe: "And because Holland, England, Denmark, France, and Spain all have their territories here in America and none of them would like to lose it; it is clear as daylight that at the moment there is war almost on the entire surface of the earth, and cries of war can be heard everywhere. Thus, anyone can draw his own conclusions from what follows."[63] Yet the frontispiece engraving at the begin-

Figure 9.1 Cover page from Christoph Saur, *Der Hoch-deutsch americanische Calender* . . . (Germantown, Pa., 1761). Courtesy, American Antiquarian Society.

ning of his popular almanac hinted at a different model: Pennsylvania was a haven shielded from engulfing storm clouds (and the banner "Krieg und Kriegsgeschrey," i.e., war and screams of/for war) by a central tableaux: a Quaker figure, dressed in a plain, long waistcoat and a broad-rimmed hat handing a letter to a rustically dressed man, likely a recently arrived German-speaking immigrant (figure 9.1). Out of place for the 1760s, the dress worn by both figures harkened back to the late seventeenth century and the founding of the colony. For German immigrants, this scene embodied the central myth of Pennsylvania: the engraving pictured a figure akin to the proprietor handing the poor German migrant the title to land and liberty. Though the envelope was shielded from their eyes and the identity of the Quaker benefactor shrouded, previous generations of German immigrants had made it clear: William Penn was one of them, and it was he who fulfilled their vision of America.

NOTES

1. Exemplary for the declension narrative in biographies written for a more general audience is Hans Fantel, *William Penn: Apostle of Dissent* (New York, 1974). Tellingly, Fantel titles the last chapter of his biography "Twilight." Though the book and its approach are outdated from a scholarly perspective, the frequent citations of Fantel's book in the Wikipedia article of William Penn reveals the power of such narratives to continue to shape popular perception (https://en.wikipedia.org/wiki/William_Penn. June 24, 2017). In historiography, Gary Nash's classic *Quakers and Politics: Pennsylvania, 1681–1726* (Boston,

1968; 1993) stands at the head of a dissension as well as declension narrative about Penn, Pennsylvania Quakers, and the fate of the so-called Holy Experiment. More recently (and more usefully), John Smolenski has replaced the notion of decline and contentiousness for Penn and his colony with the concept of creolization and accounts for the surprising ability of Penn and Pennsylvania Quakers to factious society that nonetheless proved immensely successful in its negotiation of unprecedented pluralism (*Friends and Strangers: The Making of a Creole Culture in Colonial Pennsylvania*, Philadelphia: Penn Press, 2010). Richard S. Dunn and Mary Maples Dunn, *The World of William Penn* (Philadelphia, Penn Press, 1986).

2. In Germany, Philipp Jakob Spener is commonly considered the founder of the Pietist movement, marked by the publication of his manifesto, *Pia Desideria* in 1675. Though giving German Pietism its most distinguishable impulse, Spener's drew from earlier mystic and spiritualist religious authors, especially Johann Arndt and Jakob Böhme. For the most accessible recent overviews on the topic of Pietism on the Continent in English, see Hans Schneider, *German Radical Pietism*, trans. Gerald MacDonald (Lanham, MD: 2007); Douglas A. Shantz, *An Introduction to German Pietism: Protestant Renewal at the Dawn of Modern Europe* (Baltimore: 2013); Jonathan Strom, Hartmut Lehman, and James Van Horn Melton, *Pietism in Germany and North America, 1680–1820* (Burlington, VT: 2009).

3. For general background literature on the Quakers (or, Society of Friends), especially their early period in England, see William Braithwaite, *The Beginnings of Quakerism*, 2nd ed. (Cambridge, 1961); Braithwaite, *The Second Period of Quakerism*, 2nd ed. (Cambridge, 1961); Richard Bauman, *Let Your Words Be Few: Symbolism of Speaking and Silence among Seventeenth-Century Quakers* (Cambridge, 1983); Melvin B. Endy, *William Penn and Early Quakerism* (Princeton, 1973); Rosemary Moore, *The Light in Their Consciences: Early Quakers in Britain, 1646–1666* (University Park, 2000); Kate Peters, *Print Culture and the Early Quakers* (Cambridge, 2005); Nigel Smith; *Perfection Proclaimed: Language and Literature in English Radical Religion, 1640–1660* (Oxford, 1989).

4. Trevor J. Saxby, *The Quest for the New Jerusalem: Jean de Labadie and the Labadists, 1610–1744* (Dordrecht, 1987). William I. Hull, *William Penn and the Dutch Quaker Migration to Pennsylvania*, reprint ed. (Baltimore, 1970), 2–19.

5. Penn, "To John de Labadie's Company. Herwerden. 8^{m} [October 16]71." *The Papers of William Penn*, vol. 1 (Philadelphia, 1981), 215–219. William I. Hull, *William Penn: A Topical Biography* (Freeport, 1937, 1971), 121.

6. Penn, *Eine Nachricht Wegen der Landschaft Pennsilvania in America* (Amsterdam, 1681).

7. Penn, *Christian Liberty As it was Soberly Desired in a Letter, To Certain Forreign States, Upon Occasion of their late Severity to several of their Inhabitants, meerly for their Different Perswasion and Practice in Point of Faith and Worship towards God* (London, 1674), 3–4.

8. Penn, *Christian Liberty*, 4.

9. Richard S. Dunn and Mary Maples Dunn, eds., *The Papers of William Penn*, 5 vols. (Philadelphia, 1982), 1:425–508. The manuscript version was published as *An Account of William Penn's Travels in Holland and Germany: anno MDCLXXVII [. . .]* (London, 1714). On the networks established by Penn's journey and later connections to dissenting groups on the Continent, see Rosalind J. Beiler, "Bridging the Gap: Cultural Mediators and the Structure of Transatlantic Communication," in *Atlantic Communications: The Media in American and German History from the Seventeenth to the Twentieth Century*, ed. Norbert Finzsch and Ursula Lehmkuhl (Oxford, 2004), 45–64; "Distributing Aid to Believers in Need: The Religious Foundations of Transatlantic Migration," *Pennsylvania History: A Journal of Mid-Atlantic Studies* 64 (Summer 1997): 73–87. For an extensive account of Penn's journey and contacts with "Quakers" in Europe, see Hull, 1–177.

10. Dunn and Dunn, *Papers* 1:425.

11. Lucinda Martin, "Female Reformers as the Gatekeepers of Pietism: The Example of Johanna Eleonora Merlau and William Penn," *Monatshefte*, 95, no. 1 (2003), 39.

12. On Barclay and Furly's correspondence with these women, see Hull, 22–35.

13. Dunn and Dunn, *Papers*, 1:445.

14. On the origins and development of the Frankfurt Pietists (also known as "Saalhof Pietists" for the name of their meeting location), see Andreas Deppermann, *Johann Jakob Schütz und die Anfänge des Pietismus* (Tübingen, 2002). For Philipp Jakob Spener's founding of the Frankfurt group as a Pietist conventicle or "Collegium Pietatis," see Martin Brecht, "Philipp Jakob Spener, sein Programm und dessen Auswirkungen," *Der Pietismus vom siebzehnten bis zum frühen achtzehnten Jahrhundert*, ed. Martin Brecht (Göttingen, 1993), 281–328.

15. Dunn and Dunn, *Papers*, 1:447.

16. Dunn and Dunn, *Papers*, 1:470–471.

17. Dunn and Dunn, *Papers*, 1:454.

18. See Albert Cook Myers, ed., *Narratives of Early Pennsylvania, West New Jersey and Delaware* (New York, 1912), 405.

19. William Penn, *Some Account of the Province of Pennsilvania in America [. . .]* (London, 1681), 1. For an overview of Penn's accounts of Pennsylvania and their spread on the Continent, see Hull, 311–316.

20. William Penn, *Eine Nachricht wegen der Landschaft Pennsilvania in America* (Amsterdam, 1681). The Dutch translation of this tract was made by Furly, but no translator of the German is listed. Hull speculates that it was Jan Claus (*Dutch Quaker Migration*, 312).

21. Penn, *Some Account*, 5.

22. Penn, *Eine Nachricht*, 10.

23. In my appraisal of the process that led to the first and second *Frame of Government*, I am following the documents selected in *The Papers of William Penn*, vol. 2.

24. The draft's commitment to religious toleration is unequivocal, granting to any person residing in Pennsylvania "the Free Possession of his or her faith and exercise of worship towards God, in such way and manner As every Person shall in Conscience believe is most acceptable to God" (Dunn and Dunn, *Papers*, 2:140).

25. Dunn and Dunn, *Papers*, 2:235.

26. Furly's letter to Penn includes an itemized comparison of changes made between the first draft and the *Frame*.

27. Dunn and Dunn, *Papers*, 2:232.

28. Furly demanded that lands purchased by foreigners who deceased before occupying their possessions in the province (by dying at sea, for example) should be passed on to their heirs instead of being forfeited and returned to the proprietor. The *Frame* also added a clause that mandated a general observance of the Sabbath (or Sunday), which would, Furly argued, abridge complete liberty of conscience and "prove a vile snare to the conscience of many" (Dunn and Dunn, *Papers*, 2:234) by endowing a human institution (a holiday) with religious significance.

29. Besides his direct correspondence with Penn regarding the alterations in the *Frame*, Furly drafted a detailed response; see, Julius Friedrich Sachse, *Benjamin Furly, an English Merchant at Rotterdam, who promoted the First German Emigration to America* (Philadelphia, 1895), 23–32.

30. Hull, 311ff.

31. Jaspar Balthasar Könneken (or: Casper Balthasar Köhn), bookseller in the northern German city of Lübeck and later pastor in the town of Behlendorf, was one of the individuals who received the most recent reports from Pennsylvania through Furly, copied the tracts or letters, and passed them on to interested individuals throughout Germany. Könneken's manuscript collection concerning Pennsylvania comprises thirteen different texts and is today located in the collection "Geistliches Ministerium" in the "Archiv der Hansestadt Lübeck" (Archive of the Hanseatic City of Lubeck), MS. Fol. 356–372. Among the reports collected in the "Könneken manuscript" are letters and reports by William

Penn, Benjamin Furly, Francis Daniel Pastorius, Thomas Paschall (German spelling: Paskell), and Jacobus van der Walle. See: Julius Friedrich Sachse, *Letters relating to the Settlement of Germantown in Pennsylvania, 1683–4. From the Könneken Manuscript in the Ministerial-Archive of Lübeck* (Lübeck and Philadelphia, 1903).

32. Penn, "Ein Brief von William Penn Eigenthumbs Herrn und Befehlshabern in PENNSYLVANIA," photostat copy, "Learned Collection," Historical Society of Pennsylvania. The manuscript does not reproduce the introductory matter added by Furly in the 1684 German translation published as *Beschreibung.* Since Furly's preface is extremely useful for a German audience, it seems plausible that the transcription was not prepared from the printed text of *Beschreibung.* Possibly, the model could have been either the English original or the Dutch translation of Penn's tracts. The German text of the manuscript copy may thus represent an original translation independent from the text presented in *Beschreibung* (1684). The assumption that both texts are different translations is also corroborated by the fact that the section of *Beschreibung* reproducing Penn's original letter is entitled "Sende-Schreiben von William Penn, Eygenthümer und Gouverneur von Pensylvania," while the manuscript transcription translates the title of the letter as "Ein Brief von William Penn Eygenthumbs Herrn und Befehlshabern."

33. These details are included in a biographical and genealogical narrative, written in English, Pastorius included in his "Bee-Hive" manuscript after his immigration to Pennsylvania. In spite of the fact that he had already become estranged from the Frankfurt Pietists and converted to Quakerism at this point, he nevertheless remembered as an ideal the spiritual community experienced among the Frankfurt Pietists at this point. See, Francis Daniel Pastorius, "Bee-Hive," Ms. Codex 726, Rare Book and Manuscript Library, University of Pennsylvania, 221.

34. The reorganization of the Pietists' Pennsylvanian investments in 1686 confirmed Pastorius's suspicions. Renamed from the original "German Society" to "Frankfurt Land Company," the group now pursued an exclusively economic agenda in America. See: Frankfurt Land Company. "Im Nahmen und zur Ehre Gottes! . . . Welcher gegeben zu Franckfurt am Mayn, den 12, Novemb. anno 1686" (Frankfurt, 1686).

35. A unique printed copy is extant in the Stadtbibliothekt Zürich. Pastorius, *Sichere Nachricht auß America, wegen der Landschafft Pennsylvania / von einem dorthin gereißten Teutschen / de dato Philadelphia, den 7. Martii 1684.* For a photostat reproduction of this print, see Marion Dexter Learned, *The Life of Francis Daniel Pastorius* (New York: Philadelphia: Campbell, 1908), 8 unnumbered pages inserted between 128 and 129. All subsequent quotations from Pastorius's *Sichere Nachricht* are taken from the English translation entitled "Positive Information" by Gertrude Selwyn Kimball.

36. In a poem written upon Penn's return to Pennsylvania in 1699, Pastorius claims that, upon his own arrival in the province in 1683, he could "talk with him [Penn] but in the Gallic Tongue" (*Bee-Hive* 177).

37. Pastorius, *Circumstantial Geographical Description of Pennsylvania*, trans. Gertrude Selwyn

Kimball, in *Narratives of Early Pennsylvania, West New Jersey and Delaware*, ed. Albert Cook Myers (New York, 1912), 396; *Sichere*, 2.

38. Pastorius, *Positive*, 404; *Sichere*, 5.

39. For detailed studies of Pastorius's education in Europe, see Learned, *Life of Pastorius*, Rosamund Rosenmeier, "Francis Daniel Pastorius," *Dictionary of Literary Biography 24*, and John David Weaver, "Franz Daniel Pastorius (1651-c.1720): Early Life in Germany with Glimpses of his Removal to Pennsylvania" (Diss. U of California, Davis, 1985).

40. Pastorius, *Positive*, 396–397 (*Sichere* 2); emphasis added.

41. Pastorius, *Circumstantial*, 445 (*Umständige*, 97). Penn's original letter to Pastorius's father is in Latin; *Umständige Geographische Beschreibung* provides a German translation. The English translation is by Gertrude Selwyn Kimball.

42. Pastorius, *Umständige Geographische Beschreibung*, 121.

43. Pastorius, *Circumstantial*, 387; *Umständige*, 33.

44. Pastorius, *Circumstantial*, 379; *Umständige*, 20–21.

45. On Penn's waning reputation in England and Pennsylvania and his embroilment in both imperial and provincial politics, see Mary Maples Dunn, 132–193; Geiter, 141–159; Nash, 89–343.

46. Pastorius, *Circumstantial*, 436; *Umständige*, 82.

47. For various scholarly interpretations of the Keithian controversy, see Jon Butler, "'Gospel Order Improved': The Keithian Schism and the Exercise of Ministerial Authority in Pennsylvania," *William and Mary Quarterly*, 3rd ser., 31 (1974): 431–452; Butler, "Into Pennsylvania's Spiritual Abyss: The Rise and Fall of the Later Keithians, 1693–1703," *Pennsylvania Magazine of History and Biography* 101 (1977), 151–170; Butler, "Power, Authority, and the Origins of American Denominational Order: The English Churches in the Delaware Valley, 1680–1730," *Transactions of the American Philosophical Society* 68, no. 2 (1978): 32–39; Butler, "The Records of the First 'American' Denomination: the Keithians of Pennsylvania, 1694–1700," *PMHB* 120 (1996): 89–105; Edward Cody, "The Price of Perfection: the Irony of George Keith," *Pennsylvania History* 39 (1972): 1–19. J. William Frost, *The Keithian Controversy in Early Pennsylvania* (Norwood, PA: 1980); Frost, "Unlikely Controversialists: Caleb Pusey and George Keith," *Quaker History* 64, no. 1 (1975): 16–36; Michael Goode, "*A Colonizing Peace: The Quaker Struggle for Gospel Order in Early America*" (book manuscript in progress); David L. Johns, "Convincement and Disillusionment: Printer William Bradford and the Keithian Controversy in Colonial Pennsylvania," *Journal of the Friends' Historical Society [Great Britain]* 57, no. 1 (1994): 21–32; Ethyn Williams Kirby, *George Keith (1638–1716)* (New York, 1942); Clare J. L. Martin, "Controversy and Division in Post-Restoration Quakerism: The Hat, Wilkinson-Story and Keithian Controversies and Comparisons with the Internal Divisions of Other Seventeenth-Century Non-Conformist Groups" (Diss., The Open University, 2003); Andrew R. Murphy, *Conscience and Community: Revisiting Toleration and Religious Dissent in Early Modern England and America* (University Park, 2001), 187–207; Smolenski, 149–177.

48. Seelig, *Copia Eines Send-Schreibens auß der neuen Welt [. . .] Germandon in Pennsylvania Americæ d. 7. Aug. 1694* ([Halle; Frankfurt?] 1695), 9.

49. Francis Daniel Pastorius, *Henry Bernhard Koster, William Davis, Thomas Rutter &Thomas Bowyer, four Boasting Disputers Of this World briefly Rebuked [. . .]* (New York, 1697).

50. Pastorius, *Ein Send-Brieff Offenhertziger Liebsbezeugung an die so genannte Pietisten in Hoch-Teutschland* (Amsterdam, 1697).

51. For a detailed discussion of this poem, see Oliver Scheiding, "The Poetry of British America: Francis Daniel Pastorius, 'Epibaterium, Or a hearty Congratulation to William Penn' (1699) and Richard Lewis, 'Food for Criticks' (1731)." *A Handbook of American Poetry: Contexts—Developments—Readings*, ed. Oliver Scheiding (Trier, 2014), 23–36.

52. Pastorius, *Bee-Hive*, 108.

53. Unfortunately, none of these manuscript translations seems to be extant, and only the list of books Pastorius owned documents their existence. See Pastorius, *Res Propriæ;* Learned, *Life*, 275–276. The titles Pastorius translated into German include William Penn's *Key* ("Wm Penns Schlüssel von mir übersetzt") and Penn's *Fruits of Solitude* ("Wm Penns Früchte der Einsamk, von mir verteutscht").

54. Francis Daniel Pastorius, "A few Onomastical Considerations" (Ms. AM 1.3, German Society of Pennsylvania, Joseph Horner Memorial Library. Photostat copy of the original at Friends' House, London). John Penn (1700–1746), was the son of William Penn and Hannah Penn, and he was the only one of William Penn's children born in America.

55. For information on Christoph Saur and his son Christoph Saur II, see Donald F. Durnbaugh, "Christopher Sauer, Pennsylvania-German Printer: His Youth in Germany and

Later Relationships with Europe," *PMHB* 82 (1958): 316–340; Stephen L. Longenecker, *The Christoph Sauers: Courageous Printers Who Defended Religious Freedom in Early America* (Elgin, IL: 1981); Anna Kathryn Oller, "Christoph Saur, Colonial Printer: A Study of the Publications of the Press, 1738–1758" (Diss., University of Michigan, 1963). For Saur's publications, also see Karl John Richard Arndt and Reimer C. Eck, eds. and Gerd-J. Bötte and Werner Tannhof, comp., *The First Century of German Language Printing in the United States of America: A Bibliography Based on the Studies of Oswald Seidensticker and Wilbur H. Oda, Vol. 1 (1728–1807)* (Göttingen, 1989); Karl John Richard Arndt and May E. Olson, *German-American Newspapers and Periodicals, 1732–1955: History and Bibliography* (Heidelberg, 1961).

56. *Der Hoch-Deutsch Pensylvanische Geschicht-Schreiber, Oder: Sammlung Wichtiger* Nachrichten, aus dem Natur-und Kirchen-Reich. Ed. and publ. Christoph Saur. Aug. 20, 1739–Oct. 1777 (changed name to *Pennsylvanische Berichte*); *Der Hoch-Deutsch Americanische Calender, Auf das Jahr Nach der Gnadenreichen Geburt unsers Herrn und Heylandes Jesu Christi 1739 [. . .] Eingerichtet vor die Sonnen Höhe von Pennsylvanien: jedoch an denen an grentzenden Landen ohne mercklichen Unterschied zu gebrauchen. Zum ersten mahl herausgegeben.* Germantown: Christoph Saur, [1738].

57. See, *Der neue Charter oder Schrifftliche Versicherung der Freyheiten, welche William Penn, Esq: den Einwohnern von Pennsylvanien und dessen Territorien gegeben. Aus dem englischen Original übersetzt* (Germantown, 1743). On the history and development of the so-called Pennsylvania peace churches, see Jan Stievermann, "A 'plain, rejected little flock': The Politics of Martyrological Self-Fashioning among Pennsylvania's German Peace Churches, 1739–65." *William and Mary Quarterly*, 3rd ser., 66, no. 2 (April 2009): 287–324.

58. On the Association debate, see Barbara Gannon, "The Lord is a Man of War, The God of Love and Peace: The Association Debate, 1747–1748," *Pennsylvania History* 65 (1998): 46–61; Sally F. Griffith, "'Order, Discipline, and a Few Cannon': Benjamin Franklin, the Association, and the Rhetoric and Practice of Boosterism," *PMHB* 116 (1987): 131–155; Bennett J. Nolan, *General Benjamin Franklin: The Military Career of a Philosopher* (Philadelphia, 1936); Peter Silver, *Our Savage Neighbors: How Indian Wars Transformed America* (New York, 2008), 31–34.

59. Franklin's Pennsylvania Gazette announced the publication of the pamphlet in its issue of November 12, 1747. Benjamin Franklin, *Plain Truth: Or, Serious Considerations On the Present State of the City of Philadelphia, and Province of Pennsylvania. By a Tradesman of Philadelphia* (Philadelphia, 1747); Franklin, *Die Lautere Wahrheit, Oder Ernstliche Betrachtung des gegenwärtigen Zustandes Der Stadt Philadelphia und der Provintz Pensylvanien. Von einem Handwercksmann in Philadelphia. Aus dem Englischen übersetzt durch J. Crell* (Philadelphia, [1747]). On Franklin's attempt to set up a series of German printing partners to counter the influence of sectarian printer Christoph Saur, see Ralph Frasca, "'To Rescue the Germans Out of Sauer's Hands': Benjamin Franklin's German-Language Printing Partnerships," *PMHB* 121 (1997): 329–350.

60. Benjamin Franklin, "To Peter Collinson, May 9, 1753." *The Papers of Benjamin Franklin*, 4:485. The variations in the text are based on differences between several manuscript copies of the original, non-extant, letter. See editorial note in *Papers*, 4:477–479.

61. Anonymous, *A Treatise Shewing The Need we have to rely upon God as sole Protector of this Province; And The Reason of Man's degenerating from his State of Purity and the Means whereby he may be reestablished again . . . Together with Something in Answer to a late Performance, intituled Plain Truth; discovering the Falsity therein contained, with Remarks on the Authors Irreligion . . .* (Philadelphia, 1748), 15; emphasis in original.

62. Christoph Saur, *Christliche Wahrheiten und Kurtze Betrachtung Über das kürtzlichherausgegebene Büchlein, Genannt: Lautere Wahrheit. Aufgesetzt zur Überlegung, Von einem Handwercksmann in Germanton* (Germantown, 1748), 14–16.

63. *Der Hoch-Deutsch Pensylvanische Geschicht-Schreiber*, August 20, 1739.

PART IV

American Worlds

CHAPTER 10

"*Rancontyn Marenit*"

LENAPE PEACEMAKING BEFORE WILLIAM PENN

Michael Goode

In June 1654, ten Lenape sachems gathered at Tinicum Island to make peace with Johan Risingh, the governor of the New Sweden colony. Their timing was auspicious. Risingh had arrived that year to replace Johan Printz as governor. During the previous decade, Printz had worked to stabilize New Sweden, a fledgling colony in the lower Delaware Valley that was perpetually vulnerable to attack by Dutch colonists from New Netherland. The Lenape called Printz "Big Belly," owing to the fact that he weighed around four hundred pounds, but the nickname also captured his domineering personality. Printz was bellicose by nature, but he knew that with "hardly thirty men" to defend New Sweden he was not in a position to war against the Lenape. Early in his tenure as governor, the Lenape had murdered five colonists, including two soldiers. Printz had no choice but to accept the offer of peace from local sachems who claimed the killings "happened without their knowledge." Although he received their gifts of wampum and beaver skins, he remained skeptical of the sachems' intentions, noting that "they do not trust us and we trust them still less." Printz, a hardened veteran of the Thirty Years' War, told the Swedish Privy Council that maintaining "a couple of hundred soldiers" in the colony would be necessary "until we broke the necks of all of [the Indians] in this River."[1]

Fortunately for the Lenape at Tinicum, Risingh, the new governor, was eager to broker a treaty. More bookish than his predecessor, Risingh admired Dutch commercial power and understood the strategic value of trade with Native Americans.[2] While Printz was governor, the Dutch had attempted to cut off New Sweden from the Indian trade by building two forts in the region. The first, named Beversreede ("Beaver's Road"), was located on the Schuylkill River at the entrance to the Great Minquas Path, a vital Susquehannock fur trading route that connected the Delaware River to the Susquehanna Valley. The second, Fort Casimir, was a mere seven miles south of Fort Christina, the primary Swedish settlement in the Delaware Valley. Though lacking soldierly experience, Risingh managed to capture Fort Casimir shortly after arriving as governor. The move would ultimately provoke the Dutch conquest of New Sweden, but in that moment it afforded Risingh an opportunity to work out an alliance with the Lenape.[3]

The Lenape, in turn, were also ready to make peace. Unlike New Sweden, however, they had the upper hand, at least for the time being. Peacemaking for them was a strategic choice. In their treaty encounters with Europeans, the Lenape engaged in a matrix of peacemaking practices rooted in an indigenous context and worldview. Native understandings of peace were defined through reciprocity, a "right ordering" of relationships that were ideally mutually beneficial. Kinship was central to this process. Indians extended the ties of fictive kinship to European partners through the ritual exchange of gifts, which was often performed at treaties. Indians offered land and resources with the expectation that wealth would be shared, not appropriated by Europeans outright. Native peoples intended that alliances would be periodically renewed as a means to maintain the bonds of fictive kinship. Indian peacemaking was also based on self-interest. It was a survival strategy and a means to generate wealth. But more than that, it was an expression of "ought-ness." To achieve their peace, the Lenape deployed words, speeches, skins and furs, wampum, ceremonies, myths, metaphors, gestures, trade, and more.

Peace language at treaties could paper over conflicts in ways that allowed the Lenape and their Euroamerican allies to look past old grievances, but it also engendered future conflicts by emboldening colonial authorities to extend their version of peace, one that attempted to subordinate Indians, or to displace them from their lands altogether. Yet indigenous peacemaking strategies helped the Lenape adapt to and resist colonization. Because the Lenape remained numerically dominant until the late seventeenth century, their peacemaking, in word and deed, influenced European diplomacy in the Delaware Valley. At first, Lenape peacemaking worked to keep Swedish and Dutch colonization in check. Over time, peacemaking enabled the Lenape to adapt to the changing colonial context. By the time of Pennsylvania's founding, however, the rapid pace of English colonization posed an unprecedented threat to Lenape sovereignty. Threatened with the loss of their lands, Lenape chiefs doubled down, drawing on and inverting William Penn's own words to pressure Pennsylvania governors to honor their agreements.

At the Tinicum treaty, Governor Risingh and the Lenape sachems worked out an alliance that ultimately strengthened relations between the primarily Swedish and Finnish, but also Dutch, German, and even English colonists that constituted "New Sweden." The treaty itself did not herald a new era so much as confirm what was already happening in the lower Delaware Valley. New Sweden, like many early seventeenth-century colonies in North America, suffered from a serious gender imbalance, with men heavily outnumbering women. With limited marriage prospects, New Sweden's bachelors found it easier to maintain conjugal relationships with Lenape women. The Lenape welcomed these relationships as a way to offset the alarmingly high mortality rates in their own communities, deaths that were attributable in part to the spread of smallpox and other European diseases. Over time, these relationships, mostly hidden from and beyond the control of colonial officials, forged a tenuous yet stable middle-ground existence, with the European settlers learning to grow Indian corn and engaging in joint hunting and fishing expeditions with their Lenape neighbors. More crucially, the Lenape adopted at least some of these colonists as fictive kin, deepening New Sweden's dependence on Indians for its social and material well-being.[4]

The Tinicum treaty outlined a practical framework for the maintenance of peace. Both parties agreed that each would warn the other of any impending enemy attack. Risingh needed the Lenape to confirm New Sweden's earlier land purchases. The sachems, "with a common sound," gave their affirmation. In return, Risingh promised to "do no harm to them or their plantations," while he expected the Lenape would "not kill our swine or cattle, nor tear down our fences or ruin our grain and fields."[5] Euroamericans in the Delaware Valley, like colonists elsewhere in North America, allowed their livestock to trespass and forage on Indian farms. The Lenape sometimes retaliated by killing the animals, and they also occasionally tore down the fences that symbolized the colonists' unwelcome transformation of Indian landscapes.[6] While no one at the treaty conference admitted it, the conflict over livestock and fences was symptomatic of a more fundamental conflict over land.

Peace meant different things to Indians and colonists. Securing the peace from the Swedish view of the treaty meant eliding the incompatibility of Indian and Euroamerican claims to sovereignty in the Delaware Valley. Risingh hoped Tinicum would secure the alliance he needed to preserve New Sweden against Dutch and Indian enemies. He could ill afford to admit his longer-term plans to turn New Sweden from a trading outpost into a bustling colony, where "trade and produce would develop, and our own goods and the profits of them would remain in our own hands and not be chased into the purses of strangers." In his report to company directors the following year, Risingh advocated turning New Sweden into a commercial hub for Swedish merchants to warehouse "West Indian merchandise" on their way to European markets.[7]

The Tinicum treaty also captured a particular Lenape approach to peace. Although the Lenape, like their Euroamerican partners, understood "peace" to mean, among other things, a cessation of violence between two parties and the resumption of an alliance, the treaty also revealed a Lenape understanding of harmony rooted in the maintenance of "right" relationships. Naaman, one of the sachems present at the meeting, recalled the past "good friendship" between the Lenape and the Swedes, who were "one body and one heart during the time of *Meschatz*, i.e., large stomach [Printz]." During his speech, Naaman deliberately ignored past tensions and conflicts, including the Lenape killing of five colonists, in favor of a more peaceful interpretation of the past, one that could be more usefully linked to a promising future. To solemnify his words, Naaman struck his breast, and the published version of the treaty noted he "stroked himself down his arm a few times" and "grasped about his head and twisted around with his hands." Naaman indicated that the final gesture represented the "round growth" of a calabash, "without a fissure or cut." Like the calabash, Naaman suggested, "so should we hereafter also be like one head without a fissure."[8]

Although Risingh understood Naaman's words and gestures to mean that the Lenape would accept the proposed alliance, the treaty nevertheless evidenced the colonists' contempt for Indian speech and culture. Peter Lindestrom, the military engineer for New Sweden who was present during the negotiations, published an account that derided Naaman's calabash metaphor as "ridiculous." Toward the end of the meeting, one of the other sachems alongside Naaman requested a boat to meet with Tentackan, a respected Lenape elder. The sachem informed Risingh that he wanted to implore the elder to take away a bad *Manitou* [spirit] that surrounded the governor's ship, which he likened to a fire. The governor's interpreter, Gregorius van Dyck, unwisely dismissed this as "nothing else but the salt water which thus sparkled." The sachem shot back by calling the interpreter an "old fool." Van Dyck, not wanting to derail the proceedings, conceded that the sachem "may indeed be right, I did not believe you to be so intelligent, I am in this matter not so wise."[9]

There were other cultural barriers evident during the treaty. Lindestrom's account noted that one sachem was seated in the middle of a table, while the other Lenape chiefs were on the floor. This probably struck the Swedish delegation as odd, even amusing. Lindestrom offered no explanation for the gesture, but it is possible that the sachem may have been elevating himself to a position of equality among the colonists, who remained standing throughout. The Indians' consumption of alcohol also bred contempt, despite the fact that hard liquor was commonly served at treaties and both Europeans and Indians drank. To celebrate the new alliance, Risingh fired a salvo of cannon fire from his fort and then served his Indian guests wine and brandy. Lindestrom, in recalling this event, later remarked that "one must carefully see to it that he does not get too much of that kind, for then he becomes entirely mad." The comment betrayed a common belief among colonists that Indians had trouble controlling themselves, particularly with alcohol.[10]

Despite the cultural distance separating the two sides, the colony owed its success to Lenape peacemaking. As Risingh knew, his Indian partners had the upper hand. New Sweden normally had less than two hundred colonists, while the Lenape, despite suffering losses from disease, still numbered around four thousand in the lower Delaware Valley.[11] Friend or foe, Indians had the numbers on their side to demand, and receive, respect from their European counterparts. Ironically, the success of Lenape peacemaking partly depended on threats of violence. A year after the Tinicum conference, Risingh admitted in a letter to the Swedish government that the Lenape "threaten not only to kill our people in the land and ruin them, before we can become stronger and prevent such things, but also to destroy even [our] trade." Risingh begged Swedish authorities for more supplies and tradesmen, else the colony "go to pieces." Commercial trade with Indians was critical to the colony's continued survival. Risingh may have exaggerated the extent of Lenape threats, but he understood Native business acumen. As his report acknowledged, Lenape traders acquired trade goods from New Sweden on credit, exchanged them with local Susquehannocks for skins and furs, then sold them to Dutch traders in Manhattan, who can "pay more for them than we do, because more ships and more goods arrive there."[12]

The Lenape also had good reasons to trade with, rather than destroy, the New Sweden colony. In the Delaware Valley, Indians generally benefited from having Dutch, English, and Swedish colonists competing for native trading partners. Dealing with several European allies at once, and pitting them against each other, gave the Lenape and the Susquehannocks significant bargaining leverage. When Stuyvesant met with Lenape leaders in 1651 in order to obtain lands for Fort Casimir, Mattahorn, one of the sachems, informed him that "all Nations coming to the River were welcome to them."[13] The Lenape welcomed Europeans to trade because it materially benefited them. It also gave them a strategic advantage with other Native groups further inland, who would have to deal with the Lenape if they wanted to access European trade goods flowing into the Delaware Bay. In the 1620s, the Susquehannocks warred against the Lenape to gain access to European trade goods. Once they were in a position to trade at Fort Christina and Kent Island in the Chesapeake, the Susquehannocks worked out a mutually beneficial alliance with the Lenape that allowed both groups to prosper as Indian brokers in the region.[14]

While they welcomed trade, the Lenape resisted colonization schemes that threatened their lands and sovereignty. Decades earlier, in 1631, the Sickoneysincks massacred thirty-two Dutch colonists at Swanendael, a short-lived colony at the mouth of the Delaware Bay at Cape Henlopen. The Dutch West India Company hoped that Swanendael, a whaling and agricultural venture, would gain them a foothold in the lower Delaware Valley. Instead, the Sickoneysincks killed all of the settlers and destroyed the colony within a year of its founding. The immediate catalyst for the massacre was the murder of a sachem who made tobacco pipes out of a tin sign the Dutch had put up to mark the colony's boundaries, but the underlying cause was more likely related to the

Sickoneysinck resentment of the Dutch for using more land than they had negotiated for. When reports of Swanendael's demise reached Amsterdam, the Dutch West India Company sent David de Vries to repair relations with the Lenape.[15]

De Vries arrived, "well armed," the following year, in 1632. He encountered the Sickoneysincks within a few days of discovering Swanendael's ruins and finding the "skulls and bones" of the colonists murdered there. The Sickoneysincks this time seemed eager to make peace. De Vries presented their sachems gifts of "duffels [a coarse, Belgian-made cloth], bullets, hatchets, and various Nuremberg trinkets." According to De Vries, his Indian hosts seemed to be filled "with great joy of us, that we had not remembered what they had done to us, which we suffered to pass, because we saw no chance of revenging it."[16] As with the Tinicum treaty later on, peacemaking depended on a willful forgetting of past conflicts.

By early January 1633, De Vries had sailed up the Delaware River to Fort Nassau, which the Dutch had abandoned for several years. There, he encountered more Lenape communities. Although De Vries had gifted most of his trade goods to the Sickoneysincks "for the purpose of making the peace," he offered the local Indians some cloth and kettles for Indian corn. One Lenape woman cautioned De Vries and his crew not to stray too far from the area because her people "intended to make an attack" on them. More alarmingly, she admitted that they had recently killed some Englishmen in a shallop. The next day, De Vries had more cause to be suspicious when about forty Mantes arrived wearing English jackets. Sensing the tension, the Mantes played "tunes with reeds" to signal their intentions to trade, and their sachem offered "an armful of beaver-skins . . . in order to tempt us." De Vries, however, threatened to "shoot them all" unless they kept their distance on shore. Giving "the Indians too much liberty," he later rationalized in his journal, left an opening for "accidents [to] occur, which otherwise, with friendship, might be prevented."[17]

A few days later, De Vries finally got his chance at making friends at Fort Nassau, despite running short of trade goods to barter with. Upon returning to the fort, which was "full of Indians, and more and more constantly coming," nine sachems approached De Vries's ship in a canoe. Once aboard, the sachems formed a seated circle and reassured De Vries that they "came to making a lasting peace with us, whereupon they made us a present of ten beaver-skins, which one of them gave us, with a ceremony with each skin, saying in whose name he presented it; that it was for a perpetual peace with us, and that we must banish all evil thoughts from us, for they had now thrown away all evil." Significantly, the sachems refused to accept the few remaining trade goods De Vries had left, "declaring that they had not made us presents in order to receive others in return, but for the purpose of making a firm peace."[18]

In his journal, De Vries identified a phrase in Delaware jargon for Lenape peacemaking, *rancontyn marenit*.[19] Delaware jargon was a pidgin language European and Indian traders used to communicate with each other. It was based on a simplified form of Unami, the Lenape language predominantly spoken in the Delaware Valley. In Delaware jargon, *rancontyn* is associated with the Unami term *walankjnti-n*, "peace is made, or exists (between two sides)." The word *marenit* refers to the Unami verb "to make." Taken together, the phrase *rancontyn marenit* connotes "to make peace." Although Delaware jargon evolved out of the Lenapes' early encounters with Europeans, the expression has Unami roots, reflecting a more indigenous vernacular. De Vries explicitly referred to the term in his journal, when he recalled the Sickoneysincks came to "make a firm peace, which [the Lenape] call rancontyn marenit." As a term of peacemaking, its usage was widespread. De Vries found the Munsees using it as far north as Long Island.[20]

European ethnographic accounts in the seventeenth and eighteenth centuries frequently depicted the Lenape as peaceful Indians. William Penn touted the Lenape as model Indians whom potential colonists migrating to Pennsylvania had little reason to fear. He found Unami to be "of more sweetness or greatness, in Accent and Emphasis" than European languages." The Lenape, by his estimation, were exceedingly generous. "Give them a fine Gun, Coat, or other thing, it may pass twenty hands, before it sticks." More importantly, the proprietor maintained, their sachems have declared "that the Indians and English must live in Love, as long as the Sun gave light," and they vowed to "live in Peace with me, and the People under my Government."[21] In a separate tract promoting colonization to Pennsylvania, Penn claimed the Lenape "generally leave their guns at home, when they come to our settlements; [and] offer us no affront, not so much as to one of our Dogs."[22] Other promotional tracts touting the wonders of Pennsylvania offer similar characterizations. Gabriel Thomas's promotional tract, published around the same time as Penn's, characterizes the Lenape as "Exceeding[ly] Liberal and Generous" and "Kind and Affable."[23] In the following century, the Moravian missionary John Heckewelder insisted that "every person who is well acquainted with the true character of the [Lenape] will admit that they are peaceable, sociable, obliging, charitable, and hospitable among themselves." Heckewelder even went so far as to claim that the Lenape live "as peaceably together as any people on earth."[24]

Of course, Europeans had their own reasons to portray the Lenape as peaceful. Penn's and Thomas's tracts, published in the 1680s, promoted Pennsylvania to investors and potential colonists. It was in their interest to represent the Lenape as peaceable neighbors and allies, imbued with childlike innocence and amenable to colonization. Heckewelder's account, published in 1819, was retrospective, coming at the tail end of a century's worth of colonization that led to the Lenape's dispossession of their lands, culminating with the Gnadenhutten massacre of 1782, when Pennsylvania militia butchered ninety-six Lenape Christians at Gnadenhutten, a Moravian missionary village in Ohio. David Zeisberger, who founded Gnadenhutten, mentored Heckewelder and appointed him to serve as a missionary to the Lenape in Ohio. Heckewelder had ample reason to portray the Lenape as peaceable in order to heighten their victimization at the hands of colonizers. He admitted that listening to "these descriptions of their hard sufferings" made him feel "ashamed of being a *white man*."[25]

The Unami origins of *rancontyn marenit*, "to make peace" in Delaware jargon, and its widespread use in the Delaware and Hudson Valleys, suggests, however, that Lenape peacemaking was more than a European fantasy. The Lenape, in the words of historian Jean Soderlund, "gained a reputation among Native Americans and Europeans as a peaceful nation, but they were neither faint-hearted nor weak."[26] Even before the advent of colonization, violence was a part of life in the Delaware Valley, as the archaeological evidence of war clubs and fractured bones attests. When warfare occurred, however, it was usually small scale and decentralized. Most Lenape wars were blood feuds, typically when warriors avenged the death of their kin by killing or capturing the rival kin group deemed responsible. As the Lenape explained to Lindestrom, blood feuds usually involved an aggrieved party dispatching warriors "to the [offending] nation and stealthily has one of them killed."[27]

Lindestrom, who served as a military engineer for the New Sweden colony, was struck by the lack of palisades or fortifications in Lenape communities. By comparison, farther west, the Susquehannocks fortified their principal town in the Susquehanna Valley. Their location near the Susquehanna River afforded the Susquehannocks access to vital Indian trading networks that extended from the Great Lakes to the Chesapeake Bay, but it also rendered their town vulnerable to attack from outside enemies. In the 1660s, for example, Iroquois raids severely battered the Susquehannocks. The Delaware Valley afforded the Lenape a measure of protection from invasions until the late seventeenth century, when English colonization began to overwhelm the Lenape. Because the Lenape engaged in only small-scale warfare, there was little apparent need to build walls to protect against large-scale enemy attack.[28]

If the Lenape had no need for fortifications, it was partly because they had a talent for turning enemies into allies. In the 1770s, the Lenape told Zeisberger that the Iroquois, whose territory was centered in present-day upstate New York, had warred against their people "before the coming of the white man." According to the Lenape version of events, the Iroquois elected to seek a negotiated peace because they realized the Lenape were too powerful to defeat. Both groups convened a council in which the Iroquois and Lenape agreed that the latter would become symbolically "women," who "shall not go to war, but endeavor to keep peace with all."[29] As fictive women, the Lenape would interposition themselves between warring parties. The Iroquois diplomat Canasatego would later turn the gendered metaphor into a marker of submission, telling the Lenape in 1742 that "We conquer'd You, we made Women of you."[30] But as Gunlög Fur argues, the

Lenape had always insisted that the "female role was one that involved responsibilities as peacekeeper or broker of peace in the complicated relations between different Native and European peoples."[31]

The metaphor accorded with the fact that through the early eighteenth century, Lenape women in the Delaware Valley had peacemaking authority, in addition to having the power to make decisions about land. In the 1660s, for instance, a coalition of Lenape women compelled Esopus warriors in the Hudson Valley to end their destructive war with the Dutch.[32] According to Zeisberger, when the Lenape first agreed to be "women," the Iroquois invited them to a feast, during which they symbolically dressed them "in a woman's long habit, reaching down to your feet, and adorn you with ear-rings, meaning that they should no more take up arms." The Iroquois also symbolically hung "a calabash filled with oil and medicine" upon their arms "to cleanse the ears of other nations, that they may attend to good and not to bad words . . . that they may return to their senses and incline their hearts to peace."[33] Although Governor Risingh was not aware of it, Naaman's calabash metaphor, comparing the Lenape alliance with the Swedish to a smooth gourd "without a fissure or cut," invoked the feminine authority of Lenape women and men as peacemakers.

In forging their alliance with the Lenape, the Iroquois also positioned themselves as "uncles," while the Lenape accepted the role of maternal "nephews." The Lenape and the Iroquois were matrilineal societies, and accordingly Indian men maintained close relations with the nephews of their sisters. The bonds between uncles and maternal nephews were just as strong, if not more so, than the bonds between parents and their children. The uncle–nephew relationship connoted the intimacy of close-knit family members. The Lenape acceptance of the role of "women" and "nephews" to the Iroquois signaled their willingness to use kinship roles as a strategy for peacemaking.[34]

Among the Lenape and Iroquois, gift exchange cemented kinship ties. Indian economies for both groups were redistributive, rather than merely acquisitive. Native households contributed land, food, clothing, and other material resources to community members according to need. Material exchange among Indian households and kin groups took the form of "gifts." Gifting was an action that bound the giver and receiver together, committing each to a reciprocal set of obligations that ideally promoted group harmony and minimized the potential for violent conflict. Native leaders established their authority not by hoarding and conspicuously displaying their wealth, as a European monarch would, but rather by becoming a conduit through which goods flowed to the community. By extending the circles of kinship to outsiders through the medium of gift exchange, Indian leaders also mitigated the kind of endemic violence brought on by blood feuds, which always had the potential to spiral outward into endless cycles of retaliatory warfare. Extending kinship ties through ritual exchange was especially effective in a world where Indian communities retained a good deal of autonomy and where the authority structure within those communities was relatively decentralized.[35]

Because Native leaders governed through persuasion and prestige, and not by force, important decisions about peace and war were made by consensus. Native authority was further complicated by the existence of war and peace chiefs. War chiefs, who were exclusively male, mobilized Indian communities for war through a complex process of persuasion, convincing warriors within a particular or extended kin group, usually younger men, to go on a campaign. Paradoxically, the process of going to war utilized the very same kinship networks that mitigated the potential for violence. The limited authority of war chiefs, dependent as they were on the consent of their people, also acted as a restraint on the number of wars a particular Indian community would likely engage in.[36]

For the Iroquois, the need for captives was a powerful motivator for war. By the mid-seventeenth century, disease epidemics and nearly continuous warfare with New France and their Indian allies had battered Iroquois populations. In what historians now call the "mourning wars," the Iroquois went to war against their Algonquin enemies in the Saint Lawrence Valley and Great Lakes region and against the Susquehannocks in the Susquehanna Valley. The goal was to secure captives for ritual torture or adoption. Male captives, usually enemy warriors, faced ritual torture, while women and children were typically adopted into Iroquois households. Mourning war captives compensated Iroquois families for their dead kin, but they also facilitated destructive cycles of violence, as Algonquin warriors, equipped with French muskets, raided Iroquois territory to avenge their lost kin.[37]

By the end of the seventeenth century, the Iroquois began to pursue diplomacy as a means to end the destructive cycle. Accordingly, peace chiefs wielded more influence within Iroquois communities. Peace chiefs, like war chiefs, governed through persuasion, but their role was made easier at times when the costs of war mounted and the political will shifted in favor of diplomacy. For peace chiefs, extending fictive kinship to outsiders by including them in ritual gift exchange networks that bound different peoples together in a web of mutual obligations was their most powerful diplomatic tool.

The Iroquois achieved this first through binding their five constituent nations together into a loosely knit confederacy. The origins of the Great League of Peace, which began in the fifteenth century, were captured by the epic of Deganawidah. According to Iroquois tradition, a supernatural being named Deganawidah, the Peacemaker, visited Hiawatha in the forest and promised him an end to wars if only the Iroquois would heed his message. Hiawatha's first convert was Tadadaho, an Onondaga warrior chief whose lifetime of killing left him with writhing snakes for hair and other physical deformities. Hiawatha healed Tadadaho by rubbing wampum on his body, and the two eventually succeeded in uniting the Five Nations together in a Great League of Peace. To commemorate this mythic event, the Iroquois chose Onondaga as the site for their Grand Council, where representatives from the Five Nations met annually to exchange gifts and repeat Deganawidah's sacred words of condolence. In the words of Iroquois historian Daniel Richter, the ritual ceremonies associated with the Great League of Peace "sought to replace the mourning-war with what might be termed the mourning-peace."[38]

The Lenape, whose peoples were made up of many different autonomous communities that stretched from the Delaware to the Hudson River valleys, did not form their own League of Peace, but their strategic alliances with the Swedes continued long after the Dutch defeat of New Sweden in 1655. European diseases in the Delaware Valley had diminished the Lenape's numbers, but by the 1680s they still outnumbered colonists. When Printz was governor, the Lenape occasionally conducted mourning-war attacks, though they sought to kill a limited number of colonists rather than take them captive. But Lenape women preferred forming intimate partnerships with Swedish and Finnish men as a way to compensate for the loss of their kin.[39]

After the demise of the New Sweden colony, the Lenape alternated between peacemaking, threats, and, occasionally, attacks on the colonists' property, as a means to resist aggressive colonization. Because of their unprecedented numbers, English colonists were their greatest threat, particularly Quakers who first settled on the east bank of the Delaware River, to form the West Jersey colony in the late 1670s, then especially on the west bank after 1682, after Pennsylvania's founding. According to Thomas Budd, a founding member of the Philadelphia Yearly Meeting, the Lenape informed Quaker colonists in West Jersey that "they were advised to make war upon us, and cut us off whilst we were but few."[40]

They had good reason for concern. Less than a year after receiving his charter for Pennsylvania, William Penn wrote a letter "to the King of the Indians," informing Lenape sachems that "I have sent my Commissioners to treat with you about land and a firm league of peace." Penn closed his letter by reassuring his would-be Indian neighbors of his "resolution to live Justly peaceably and friendly with you."[41] While Penn's words were undoubtedly sincere, his colonization scheme, Pennsylvania, represented the greatest threat to Lenape autonomy since the Dutch first arrived in the Delaware Valley in the 1620s. The Lenape were already well aware of what English colonizers meant when they came to "treat about land." They had to look no further than to New England or the Chesapeake to know that the English might pull off what the Swedes or Dutch could only have dreamed about—filling the Delaware Valley with colonists.

Penn's peace was a colonizing peace, and within two decades of his assurances to the Lenape that his Quakers would "Winn and gain your Love and friendship by [their] kind, just and peaceable life," the colonization of Pennsylvania would overwhelm the Lenape and set in motion their gradual migration to the Susquehanna Valley. If there was a lesson in this, it was that English ships loaded with Quakers and words of peace could, from an indigenous point of view, be just as destructive as cannon fire and musket.[42]

In the decade before the great Quaker migration to Pennsylvania, Lenape councils were divided between war chiefs and peace chiefs. By the turn of the eighteenth century, however, the peace chiefs won out, if only for a time. There was no choice. By then, the Lenape had lost their numerical advantage in the Delaware Valley. The resort to targeted killings, while still potentially effective, was no match for the numbers of colonists pouring into the region, many of whom were increasingly non-Quaker and less beholden to Penn's vision of living peaceably with Indian neighbors.

To combat this, the Lenape drew on the peacemaking strategies they developed over the seventeenth century, enabling them to adapt and survive in the face of rapid demographic changes in the Delaware Valley. Lenape leaders, once again playing the role of "women," extended their fictive kinship networks to include Quakers and other Pennsylvania colonists, enmeshing them in gift exchange networks they hoped would temper the onslaught of colonization, or at least somehow bend it to their advantage.

One key strategy early on was to turn the provincial government's desire for land into opportunities for gift exchange, and to receive valuable trade goods in return for shared usage rights to land, rather than just simply yielding up their territory altogether. This was, as historian Amy Schutt put it, a "notion of land as process rather than commodity."[43] The Lenape expected that negotiations for land would be periodically renewed, a strategy that allowed them to insist on ritually renewing their relationships, both with Indians and colonists. As the Lutheran missionary Israel Acrelius observed in 1759, if Lenape sachems signed land deeds "in the presence of a number of their people, then the purchase was valid."[44]

In their treaties with Pennsylvania colonists, the Lenape also demonstrated a willingness to reinvent the past as a way to move forward on their terms. As a peacemaking strategy, it was not new. Decades earlier, Naaman, and before him, the Sickoneysincks, had used it with Dutch and Swedish colonists. When the Lenape chief Sassoonan told Governor Gookin in 1715 that he had come to Philadelphia to "renew the former bond of friendship that William Penn had, at his first coming," he omitted the fact that Quaker colonization had compelled him to abandon his home along the Schuylkill River for lands farther west in the Susquehanna Valley.[45] Instead, he invoked what would increasingly become a popular trope among the Lenape and with many other Indian nations, including the Iroquois—the myth of William Penn as the Great Peacemaker.

Penn himself promoted this myth in order to secure more lands for his colony, but in the eighteenth century, the Lenape turned the myth on its head as a way to remind or even shame provincial authorities to honor past treaty agreements and to pressure them to resolve current differences in good faith. In time, Pennsylvania governors also found the myth of Penn useful to validate their own authority or pressure the Lenape or other Indian nations to accede to their demands. In Pennsylvania, these two conflicting narratives of William Penn—in essence, conflicting indigenous and colonial peace narratives—would shape Indian and provincial debates over land and trade in the eighteenth century. Fittingly, it would be a debate mostly fought on treaty grounds, where colonial and indigenous peacemaking both intersected and clashed.

NOTES

1. "Report of Governor Printz, 1644," in *Narratives of Early Pennsylvania, West New Jersey, and Delaware, 1630–1707*, ed. Albert Cook Meyers (New York: Charles Scribner's Sons, 1912), 101–103; Amandus Johnson, *The Swedish Settlements on the Delaware, 1638–1664*, vol. 2 (Philadelphia: Swedish Colonial Society, 1911), 688–689; Jean Soderlund, *Lenape Country: Delaware Valley Society before William Penn* (Philadelphia: Penn Press, 2015), 70–71.

2. Mark Thompson, *The Contest for the Delaware Valley: Allegiance, Identity, and Empire in the Seventeenth Century* (Baton Rouge: Louisiana State University Press, 2013), 130.

3. Paul A. W. Wallace, *Pennsylvania: Seed of a Nation* (New York: Harper & Row, 1962), 21; Soderlund, *Lenape Country*, 76–77, 79; on the Great Minquas Path, see Paul A. W. Wallace, *Indian Paths of Pennsylvania* (Harrisburg: Pennsylvania Historical and Museum Commission, 1965), 64–65.

4. Soderlund, *Lenape Country*, 58, 65–69.

5. "Treaty between the Swedes and the Indians at Tennakonck," in *Early American Indian Documents: Treaties and Laws, 1607–1789*, ed. Alden Vaughan, vol. 1: *Pennsylvania and Delaware Treaties, 1629–1737*, ed. Donald H. Kent (Washington, DC: University Publications of America, 1979), 25–27; Soderlund, *Lenape Country*, 81.

6. Virginia DeJohn Anderson, *Creatures of Empire: How Domestic Animals Transformed Early America* (Oxford: Oxford University Press, 2004).

7. "Report of Governor Rising, 1655," in Meyers, *Narratives of Early Pennsylvania*, 161.

8. "Treaty between the Swedes and the Indians at Tennakonck," 26.

9. "Treaty between the Swedes and the Indians at Tennakonck," 26–27.

10. "Treaty between the Swedes and the Indians at Tennakonck," 26; James O'Neil Spady, "Colonialism and the Discursive Antecedents of Penn's Treaty with the Indians," in *Friends and Enemies in Penn's Woods: Indians, Colonists, and the Racial Construction of Pennsylvania*, ed. William A. Pencak and Daniel K. Richter (University Park: Penn State University Press, 2004), 24; Peter Mancall, *Deadly Medicine: Indians and Alcohol in Early America* (Ithaca: Cornell University Press, 1997).

11. On the Lenape and colonial population in the Delaware Valley, see Soderlund, *Lenape Country*, 17–18, 65–67.

12. "Report of Governor Risingh, 1655," in Meyers, ed., *Narratives of Early Pennsylvania*, 156–157, 160; Soderlund, *Lenape Country*, 92; Amy C. Schutt, *Peoples of the River Valleys: The Odyssey of the Delaware Indians* (Philadelphia: Penn Press, 2007), 55–56.

13. Samuel Hazard et al., eds., *Pennsylvania Archives*, 2nd ser., 5 (Harrisburg, 1877): 248; Soderlund, *Lenape Country*, 77.

14. Daniel K. Richter, *Before the Revolution: America's Ancient Pasts* (Cambridge: Harvard University Press, 2011), 150; Soderlund, *Lenape Country*, 43–44.

15. Soderlund, *Lenape Country*, 36–42.

16. "David de Vries's Notes," in Meyers, *Narratives of Early Pennsylvania*, 15–18.

17. "David de Vries's Notes," in Meyers, *Narratives of Early Pennsylvania*, 18–20.

18. "David de Vries's Notes," in Meyers, *Narratives of Early Pennsylvania*, 20–21.

19. The phrase appears in De Vries's journal, when he tells a Sickoneysinck party aboard his ship that once their sachem arrives "we would then make a firm peace, which they call *rancontyn marenit*;" see "David de Vries's Notes," in Meyers, *Narratives of Early Pennsylvania*, 16.

20. Ives Goddard, "The Delaware Jargon" in *New Sweden in America*, ed. Carol Hoffecker, Richard Waldron, Lorraine Williams, and Barbara Benson (Newark: University of Delaware Press, 1995), 139–140, 147, f. 18.

21. "Letter from William Penn to the Committee of the Free Society of Traders, 1683," in Meyers, *Narratives of Early Pennsylvania*, 230, 233, 236.

22. "A Further Account of the Province of Pennsylvania, By William Penn, 1685," in Meyers, *Narratives of Early Pennsylvania*, 276.

23. "An Historical and Geographical Account of Pennsylvania and of West New-Jersey, by Gabriel Thomas, 1698," in Meyers, *Narratives of Early Pennsylvania*, 335.

24. John Heckewelder, *History, Manners, and Customs of the Indian Nations* (1819, rpt. Philadelphia: Historical Society of Pennsylvania, 1876), 330.

25. Quoted in Andrew Newman, *On Records: Delaware Indians, Colonists, and the Media of History and Memory* (Lincoln: University of Nebraska Press, 2012), 2.

26. Soderlund, *Lenape Country*, 34.

27. Peter Lindestrom, *Geographia Americae with an Account of the Delaware Indians Based on Surveys and Notes Made in 1654–1656*, trans. Amandus Johnson (Philadelphia: Swedish Colonial Society, 1925), 205; quoted in Schutt, *Peoples of the River Valleys*, 10; Herbert Kraft, *The Lenape-Delaware Indian Heritage: 10,000 B.C.—A.D.* 2000 (Stanhope: Lenape Books, 2001), 251.

28. Lindestrom, *Geographia Americae*, trans. Amandus Johnson, 241; Schutt, *Peoples of the River Valleys*, 10; Richter, *Before the Revolution*, 151.

29. Arthur Butler Hulbert and William Nathaniel Schwarze, eds., *David Zeisberger's History of the North American Indians* (Ohio State Archaeological and Historical Society, 1910), 34; Heckewelder, *History, Manners, and Customs of the Indian Nations*, 59, f. 3.

30. Samuel Hazard, et al., eds., *Minutes of the Provincial Council of Pennsylvania* (Harrisburg: Theo Fenn, 1851), 4:579.

31. Gunlög Fur, *A Nation of Women: Gender and Colonial Encounters among the Delaware Indians* (Philadelphia: Penn Press, 2009), 169.

32. Fur, *A Nation of Women*, 171–172.

33. Heckewelder, *History, Manners, and Customs of the Indian Nations*, 59, f. 3.

34. Fur, *A Nation of Women*, 170.

35. Daniel Richter, *The Ordeal of the Longhouse: The Peoples of the Iroquois League in the Era of European Colonization* (Chapel Hill: University of North Carolina Press, 1992), 22–23; for a discussion of gift exchange as both an economic and a noneconomic practice and as a simultaneous action of giving and taking, see David Murray, *Indian Giving: Economies of Power in Indian–White Exchanges* (Amherst: University of Massachusetts Press, 2000).

36. Wayne Lee, *Barbarians & Brothers: Anglo-American Warfare, 1500–1865* (Oxford: Oxford University Press, 2011), 132–150.

37. Daniel Richter, "War and Culture: The Iroquois Experience," *William and Mary Quarterly* 40, no. 4 (October 1983): 528–559.

38. Richter, *Ordeal of the Longhouse*, 30–32, 38–40; quotation on p. 40.

39. Soderlund, *Lenape Country*, 70, 148; Soderlund suggests that the Lenapes' killing of five colonists in the 1640s was possibly a "mourning war to atone for the deaths of family members from European diseases;" quotation on p. 70.

40. Thomas Budd, *Good Order Established in Pennsilvania & New-Jersey in America* ([Philadelphia], 1685), 32; Soderlund, *Lenape Country*, 143.

41. William Penn, "To the King or King of the Indians," October 18, 1681, reprinted in Daniel Richter, *Trade, Land, Power: The Struggle for Eastern North America* (Philadelphia: Penn Press, 2013), 136–137.

42. Penn, "To the King or King of the Indians," in Richter, *Trade, Land, Power*, 136.

43. Schutt, *Peoples of the River Valleys*, 40.

44. Israel Acrelius, "Account of the Swedish Churches in New Sweden, 1759," in Meyers, *Narratives of Early Pennsylvania*, 72; Schutt, *Peoples of the River Valleys*, 35.

45. "Council of Gov. Gookin and Council with Chiefs of Delaware and Schuylkill Indians," June 14, 1715, in Vaughan, *Early American Indian Documents*, 154; Schutt, *Peoples of the River Valleys*, 64.

CHAPTER 11

William Penn, John Winthrop, and Colonial Political Science

Alexander Mazzaferro

New World colonialism has long enjoyed a positive association with innovation. The societies established in the Americas during the seventeenth and eighteenth centuries command interest in part because the new cultural, political, and economic formations that attended them figure powerfully in a story of progress that culminates with the modern world of its own narrators. Such a story fails to account, however, for the fact that "innovation" was a pejorative term during the settlement period. From antiquity through the early nineteenth century, the word was a loose synonym for "rebellion" and "heresy" that functioned to undermine departures from precedent. Believing that change of almost any kind inevitably led to civil disturbance, early modern writers of various ideological stripes found in the idiom of innovation a handy brush with which to tar their opponents. But when this ethos was exported to the New World, the novelty of colonial society became a significant philosophical and representational problem.[1]

Despite their frequent portrayal as literal and figurative pioneers, Pennsylvania proprietor William Penn and Massachusetts Bay governor John Winthrop made frequent use of the pejorative idiom of innovation. Penn argued, for example, that Quaker meetings might "Lawfully and Christianly deny . . . Communion" to "dissenting or innovating Person[s]," and Winthrop was even more energetic in expelling those "affecting . . . Innovation" from his colony.[2] Yet both figures also endorsed political innovation by another name, arguing that divinely inspired, elite-led political change might sometimes be legitimate in unique circumstances. Using Winthrop as a point of comparison, this chapter examines Penn's ambivalent relationship to innovation, arguing that he legitimized certain new policies and institutions by engaging with an empirical approach to political knowledge that Winthrop's career exemplifies. I call this inductive, experiential approach "political science" in order to distinguish it from the deductive, rationalist discourse of "political philosophy" associated with more canonical thinkers like Thomas Hobbes.[3] I contend that this overlooked political scientific tradition—at once a defense against innovation and a mechanism for producing it—found special purchase in the Americas, where certain political novelties seemed as desirable as others seemed detrimental. And I show that several factors, especially theological affiliations and imperial circumstances, impacted the relationship between novelty and empiricism in different strains of Anglo-American political thought.

The colonial endeavors that Penn and Winthrop famously called a "holy experiment" and a "City upon a Hill" were undertaken with a heightened awareness of what we might call the innovation prohibition.[4] Both figures arrived in North America intending to put relatively unfamiliar conceptions of civil and ecclesiastical organization into practice, and both imagined their colonies serving as correctives to conventional assumptions and as new models for emulation; but they also insisted that they were simply recovering prior arrangements, not inventing new ones.[5] Respectively steeped in Puritan primitivism and in the Whig ideology of England's ancient constitution, the two founders formally denounced political novelty even as their ideals led them to create societies with few analogues in recent memory. They were able to do so, I argue, because they utilized the key method of empirical political science: the inductive interpretation of first- or second-hand observations.[6] Colonial elites turned to empiricism because the challenges they encountered in the Americas were unprecedented and undiscussed in the canonical works of ancient and early modern political thought. They appealed to the emergent epistemological category of experience in order to substantiate the claim that the New World was somehow exceptional and thus that the societies they founded there would need to be, in both Penn and Winthrop's words, "extraordinary" by Old World standards.[7] Yet they also maintained that their primary aims were restorative. To adapt a pointedly paradoxical phrase of Penn's, both he and Winthrop wished to "secure . . . the Execution of our Ancient Laws by New Ones."[8]

The succeeding analysis builds on scholars' occasional descriptions of Penn as an "empirical" political thinker. But where they have taken Penn's attention to historical particulars as evidence of his inferiority to "more sophisticated and profound thinkers like Thomas Hobbes," I will demonstrate that this tendency constitutes an equally sophisticated response to exceptional political situations: from metropolitan constitutional crises like the Glorious Revolution to the precarious status of Quakers to the uncertain project of New World settlement. Likewise, where historians have intimated that Penn was "uncomfortably aware" that his methods "might result in a break with the past," I will offer a more nuanced account of how his engagement with colonial political science facilitated his circumvention of the innovation prohibition.[9]

For a variety of reasons, Penn's political thought was less empirical than Winthrop's, however. Winthrop engaged directly in the forms of observation, reportage, and induction that Sir Francis Bacon had promoted as a sound basis for political knowledge, whereas Penn gravitated more toward the protoempirical practice of generalizing from history on display in the writings of Niccolò Machiavelli.[10] Routinely drawn back toward rationalist deduction by his ideological and theological affiliations, by his commitment to theoretical concepts like "fundamental law," and by the vagaries of his career, Penn oscillated between Winthrop's colonial particularism and the metropolitan habits of abstraction found in Hobbes's *Leviathan* (1651). In what follows, I demonstrate that Penn's ambivalent relationships toward political innovation and political science were mutually reinforcing, and I hazard some explanations for why he did not participate in the empirical tradition as fully as did Winthrop. In so doing, I suggest that the disappointments of Penn's political career, in both England and America, derived in part from his hesitance about the kind of experientially derived improvisation that secured the orthodoxy's hegemony in Puritan New England.

There are obvious reasons to put Penn and Winthrop into conversation, even as that conversation tends to be a study in contrasts rather than similarities. Richard Dunn put the case succinctly when he titled a 1987 article on the two leaders "An Odd Couple."[11] Because of their very different relationships to their colonies, because of their dissimilar intellectual backgrounds, and because Pennsylvania was founded a full fifty years after the Massachusetts Bay colony, Penn and Winthrop faced distinct challenges. Winthrop served as elected governor and magistrate and resided exclusively in New England following his arrival there in 1630. He oversaw the colony before and during the English Civil Wars, when the Crown and Parliament were too preoccupied with one another to seriously interfere with the Bay's government. And he enjoyed the remarkable autonomy that resulted from the unprecedented transportation of his colony's charter to the New World and from the decentralized nature of English imperialism in the first half of the seventeenth century, when "metropolitan authorities governed by hearsay."[12]

Penn, by contrast, was a proprietor rather than an elected official. He resided in his colony only from 1682 to 1684 and 1699 to 1701 and was otherwise preoccupied in England with his efforts on behalf of Quakerism, on behalf of the colony, and on behalf of the principle undergirding its founding, liberty of conscience. He not only governed at a distance and contended with an increasingly centralized imperial apparatus, he was also distracted by his active involvement in English politics during the late Restoration and Glorious Revolution.[13] Finally, Penn was a member of a sect that Puritans like Winthrop had actively persecuted: Quakers numbered among the theological groups that Philip Gura and others call the "radical spiritists," Protestants who insisted upon an "utter dependence on the power of the Holy Spirit" often thought to be heterodox and seditious.[14] Despite his efforts to counter the rebellious, sectarian, and individualist impulses latent in Quakerism, Penn's theology existed on a spectrum with the heretical antinomians driven out of Massachusetts by Winthrop in the 1630s, some of whom eventually became Quakers.[15] These dissimilarities notwithstanding, Penn and Winthrop were united in their inclination toward experiential political knowledge and their attendant openness to certain forms of political change. The intimate connection between colonial political science and the innovation prohibition thus provides a framework for revisiting a familiar scholarly preoccupation with the relationship between theory and practice in the two founders' respective careers.[16] Indeed, it allows us to plot that distinction along an Old World–New World axis and to consider how questions of form and genre shaped a tradition of political thought to which colonials were more significant contributors than we have yet recognized.

Winthrop's political empiricism is especially apparent in a 1644 pamphlet entitled *A Short Story of the Rise, Reign, and Ruin of the Antinomians*, the Massachusetts Bay orthodoxy's quasi-official account of the outbreak of heresy and sedition that historians call the "Antinomian Controversy" or, more recently, the "free grace controversy."[17] Between 1636 and 1638, the controversy divided the colony between two different strains of Calvinist soteriology. The orthodoxy, which included Winthrop and most of the colony's ministers and magistrates, sought to balance human agency and divine sovereignty by arguing that, even though salvation was effected entirely by God's grace, it took place through natural means and could therefore be apprehended empirically. This view positioned scripture and clergy as crucial mediators between the individual and the divine and rendered obedience to moral law a sturdy sign—though not the cause—of election, which, Calvinists insisted, could not be earned. Centered in the Boston Church, the heterodox antinomian party included a handful of magistrates, the minister John Wheelwright, the Puritan nobleman Sir Henry Vane the Younger, and the lay spiritual leader Anne Hutchinson. Drawing on the theology of the renowned New England minister John Cotton, as well as ideas circulating in old England's theological underground, the antinomians stressed the elect individual's utter passivity in the face of overwhelming grace and God's direct communication with the believer. Because this position devalued scriptural and clerical mediation and obedience to moral law as forms of quasi-Catholic "salvation by works" at odds with the Protestant emphasis on unmerited grace, and because its adherents' claims to intimacy with the divine were believed to countenance rebellion, the orthodoxy regarded antinomianism as deeply subversive. Accordingly, the colony's leaders brought the newly minted apparatuses of church and state power to bear on the heretics, suppressing their dissent through disenfranchisement, excommunication, and banishment.

Authored by Winthrop and other Bay elites and geared toward a metropolitan audience, the *Short Story* seeks to justify the magistrates' and ministers' handling of the controversy.[18] The text's empirical method is essential to this project. Drawing unmistakably on what Jim Egan calls "the rhetoric of experience," the pamphlet's subtitle stakes its credibility on its compiler's status as "an eye and ear-witness" to the controversy.[19] Throughout the text, Winthrop marshals observed particulars to evidence the threat the heretics posed to the new settlement. The first section enumerates and refutes "A Catalogue of . . . [eighty-two] erroneous [theological] opinions," fleshing out the antinomians' alleged views in elaborate detail.[20] Subsequent sections provide forensic accounts of the trials of Hutchinson and others before the Massachusetts Bay General Court and the Boston Church. Most significantly for our purposes, the text includes an eyewitness description of a "monstrous" stillborn fetus delivered by the antinomian Mary Dyer and alludes to another "monstrous" birth delivered by Hutchinson herself following her banishment. Winthrop's interpretation of these "monstrous births" as providential manifestations of divine displeasure with the heretics depends upon his adherence to the stylistic protocols of empiricist reportage common to both natural and political science. These techniques allow him to denounce the antinomians' heresy as an "innovation" and, simultaneously, to legitimize a variety of elite innovations in the colony's political and ecclesiastical structure.[21]

Bearing out scholarly arguments for the affinities between Protestantism and empirical science, Winthrop's account of the "monstrous birth" provides evidence not only of the antinomian threat to religious uniformity and civil peace but also of the broader exceptionality of New World political challenges.[22] In a passage adapted from his journal he writes,

> At Boston in New England, upon the 17. day of October 1637. the wife of one William Dyer . . . was delivered of a large woman child, it was stillborn, about two months before her time, the child having life a few hours before the delivery, but so monstrous and misshapen, as the like hath scarce been heard of: it had no head but a face, which stood so low upon the breast, as the ears (which were like an Ape's) grew upon the shoulders. . . . The eyes stood far out, so did the mouth, the nose was hooking upward, the breast and back were full of sharp prickles, like a Thornback, the navel and all the belly with the distinction of the sex, were, where the lower part of the back and hips should have been, and those back parts were on the side the face stood. . . . The arms and hands, with the thighs and legs, were as other children's, but instead of toes, it had upon each foot three claws, with talons like a young fowl. . . . Upon the

> back above the belly it had two great holes, like mouths, and in each of them stuck out a piece of flesh. . . . It had no forehead, but in the place thereof, above the eyes, four horns, whereof two were above an inch long, hard, and sharp, the other two were somewhat shorter.[23]

This relentlessly detailed testimony, adapted from Dyer's midwife, receives collective corroboration from the other "women who were present" at the birth.[24] To adapt a phrase from the historian of science Steven Shapin, these witnesses serve as "extensions of [Winthrop's] own senses," just as Winthrop, as credible reporter, serves as an extension of his metropolitan reader's senses.[25] After questioning the women about the fetus, which had been buried in secret months earlier, Winthrop engages in what is arguably the text's most brutally empiricist act and orders that it be exhumed and "viewed."[26] This material evidence confirms the ocular reports he had compiled, and again, this corroboration is collective, having been "seen . . . [by] above a hundred persons."[27] In this way, he stakes his claims about the heretics on emergent scientific standards of truth telling. Winthrop's empiricism was not without its liabilities: his text gave voice to anticolonial dissidents and provided ammunition for English Presbyterians eager to prove that Congregationalism was inherently disorderly. But it served him well in New England.

The utility of Winthrop's observational political epistemology proceeds from its dialectical relationship to innovation: novelty demands empiricism, and empiricism authorizes new courses of action. It is no coincidence then that the criticism of the antinomians leveled in the more polemical sections of the *Short Story* centers on their theological novelty. Much as he describes Dyer's "monstrous birth" as unprecedented ("the like hath scarce been heard of"), Winthrop refers disparagingly to the heretics' "new opinions," "new tenets," and "new sprung errors"; and throughout, this novelty is linked to the threat of "sedition" and "civil disturbances."[28] The antinomians' heresy-as-innovation calls for observation and induction, which ratify the exceptional nature of New World political challenges and in turn provide Winthrop with a warrant to depart from precedent in the pursuit of civil and ecclesiastical order. The top-down innovations he oversaw included the restriction of freemanship to church members, the limitation of the freemen's powers, resistance to the codification of the colony's laws, and a controversial order forbidding new immigrants from residing in the colony for more than three weeks without official approval (a measure designed to prevent an influx of additional antinomians). Although scholars have often emphasized the colony's liberal, democratic, and republican attributes, the archive presents a countervailing tendency toward absolute magisterial authority, not only during moments of crisis like the free grace controversy but throughout the exceptional early period that Winthrop termed the "infancy of plantations."[29] In primitivist fashion, the Bay governor claimed strict adherence to scriptural precedent, but because the Bible was silent on a variety of issues and because Old Testament judges had often enjoyed the right to alter or mitigate positive law, Winthrop found there a powerful argument for magisterial "discretion."[30]

Criticism of the magistrates' powers as "a sinful innovation" soon followed.[31] The non-antinomian New England dissident Thomas Lechford was especially astute in recognizing the dynamic whereby empirically observed contingency and the trump card of biblical primitivism were used to justify "arbitrary" or innovative proceedings. Thus he attacked the Massachusetts Bay government for "slight[ing] all former laws of the Church or State, [and] cases of experience and precedents, to go hammer out new [ones], according to several exigencies; upon pretense that the Word of God is sufficient to rule us."[32] Yet in a moment of minimal imperial oversight such a critique found little traction. Even as the democratization of the Bay colony's political process proceeded apace, Winthrop and others exploited the authority granted by eyewitness experience in order to undermine nonelite political innovations and legitimize their own.

In many ways William Penn shared John Winthrop's investment in a political epistemology grounded in experiential particulars rather than deduced axioms, a commitment exhibited by many other colonial writers, including John Smith, William Bradford, William Strachey, and Richard Ligon. While Penn appealed, in rationalist fashion, to abstract concepts like England's ancient constitution, he also grounded his interpretations in a careful reading of history—a protoempirical hermeneutic found in Machiavelli's *Discourses on Livy*, which Penn cited with approval despite the Florentine's widespread condemnation in the period.[33] And while Penn is not primarily known for producing political texts as committed to eyewitness reportage as Winthrop's *Short Story*, he nonetheless resembled the Massachusetts governor in regarding "Fact and Experience" as "the best and greatest Evidence."[34] He lamented that it was "the Infelicity of Governors to see and hear by the Eyes and Ears of other Men," and he sought to remedy this problem by promoting careful witnessing and candid reportage as correctives to the "Mis-intelligence" that so often caused political turmoil.[35] Thus, in the opening pages of *The Peoples Ancient and Just Liberties Asserted* (1670), he invokes rampant "misrepresent[ation]" to justify publishing a report on his recent trial for "Disturbance of the Peace," arguing that "Judicious Intelligence" is "impossible" "without due Observation."[36] The text then proceeds to offer the closest thing to Winthrop's report that Penn was to produce: an argument for liberty of conscience rooted in a detailed, forensic account of a topical event.[37]

If the firsthand reportage found in *Peoples* is not exactly typical of Penn's corpus, the appeal to history is. Indeed, his tracts are studded with historical examples intended to evidence his fundamental claim that enforced religious uniformity does not work. Penn devotes an entire chapter of *The Great Case of Liberty of Conscience* (1670), for instance, to the recitation of extracts and examples from the "Wisest . . . Persons" and "best States . . . of Ancient and Modern Times" demonstrating the futility of exerting "Force upon Conscience"—from the ancient "Jews, Romans, [and] AEgyptians" to the modern "French" and "Hollanders," and from "Cato, Livy, and Tacitus" to "Grotius, Rawleigh, . . . and King Charles the First."[38] In *England's Present Interest Considered* (1675), he rehearses an "Ancient Chronicle" of "William of Normandy" to demonstrate that fundamental English rights preexisted and survived the Norman Conquest.[39] And in *A Perswasive to Moderation to Church-Dissenters* (1686), he argues for toleration based on its existence not only in England's past but also in Greco-Roman antiquity. Citing "Plutarch, Strabo," and others, he demonstrates how "far . . . those Ages, which we have made as the Original [i.e., which we regard as the origin] of Wisdom . . . [were] from thinking Toleration an Error of State, or dangerous to the Government."[40] Drawing on another source of "Experience" elsewhere in the text, he contends that "the down-right Toleration [practiced] in most of the Kings Plantations abroad, prove[s] the Assertion, That Toleration is not dangerous to Monarchy."[41] But perhaps the best illustration of the self-defeating nature of religious persecution is "our late Lamentable Civil Wars."[42] Inverting the conventional interpretation of the Civil Wars as caused by the political rebelliousness inherent to theological dissent, he argues that revolt was the *effect* of spiritual persecution and thus presents toleration as an underappreciated bulwark of monarchical power. In each case, Penn's use of precedent isn't normative—proof of a transhistorical and independently deduced truth—so much as prescriptive, the fruit of induction from experience accumulated across a diverse and dynamic period of time.

While Penn's appeals to the secondhand experience of history, like his appeals to nature and reason, might seem to bespeak a conventional belief in the dangers of political innovation, his approach in fact presupposes that the past might sometimes counsel the *inapplicability* of precedent. That is, his attention to preexisting ways of political life paradoxically leads him to mitigate the innovation prohibition in significant ways. As Andrew R. Murphy notes, Penn tempered precedent's force by drawing "a crucial distinction" between "Fundamental" laws, which are "Immutable," and "Superficial" laws, which are "alterable."[43] Penn explained that, "when any . . . Fundamental Law of this Realm is altered . . . dangerous Inconveniences do follow," whereas "Laws Superficial" are "suited [only] to the present Conveniency and Emergency of State."[44] This allowed him to argue that, just as the Catholic aspects of the English state had proven "abrogable," so was the Anglican establishment "no Essential Part of the old English Government."[45] State-imposed religious uniformity was a "Superficial" law, whereas English rights to property, judicial and legislative participation, and freedom of worship are so "Fundamental" that "there can be no just Ground for infringing, much less abrogating the Laws that secure them."[46] In short, differentiating between what is long established but merely "Superficial" and what is more deeply "Fundamental" opens up a space for legitimate, albeit limited, political change. In Murphy's summary, this "distinction . . . enabled [Penn] to balance continuity with the need for change and evolution, and to argue that the changes he sought were not reckless innovation but rather a return to time-honored traditional constitutional values."[47]

Penn had insisted, in *The Peoples Ancient and Just Liberties Asserted*, that the riot he was accused of fomenting "was no New Thing"—that it was a "Peaceable" assembly rather than an innovative or rebellious one.[48] And he had followed dissidents in both old and New England when he condemned the court's proceedings against him as "Arbitrary," a commonplace used to describe innovative forms of rule based on personal whim rather than adherence to the norms and precedents laid out in an established constitution.[49] Nonetheless, Penn ultimately advocated something akin to innovation as the necessary response to unprecedented circumstances. In *England's Present Interest*, he writes, "However Advisable it may be, in the Judgment of some Worldly Wise Men, to prevent, even by Force, the arising of any New Opinion . . . England's Circumstances are greatly changed, and they require new Expedients and another Sort of Application."[50] The passage associates Penn's opponents not only with a dangerous reverence for outmoded precedents but also with a nonempirical relationship to present "Circumstances," which prevents them from recognizing when those "Circumstances" are "greatly changed." Careful witnessing reveals that there are in fact precedents for change.

Far from exhibiting a straightforward "antipathy to change," then, Penn worked to temper the innovation prohibition.[51] In *A Perswasive to Moderation*, he makes this argument for the value of political change explicit: "to tie the Magistrate to old Measures, is to be regardless of Time, whose fresh Circumstances give Aim to the Conduct of Wise Men in their present Actions. Governments, as well as Courts, change their Fashions: The same Clothes will not always serve: And Politicks made Obsolete by new Accidents, are as unsafe to follow, as antiquated Dresses are ridiculous to wear. . . . This justifies the Government's change of Measures from the change of Things."[52] Here, Penn spells out the danger of persisting in conventional courses amidst unconventional circumstances; to do so, he claims, is far more "unsafe" than innovation was traditionally held to be. As with Winthrop's insistence that the Bay's departures from precedent were appropriate only to that particular time and place (the "infancy of plantations"), Penn mitigates innovation's capacity for exponential disturbance by restricting it to one cultural arena, arguing that "State Religions have been changed without the Change of the States."[53] And like Winthrop, Penn develops his argument for novel policy through empirical, rather than rationalistic, methods: "Finding then by sad Experience, and a long Tract of Time, that the very Remedies applied to cure Dissension, increase it," he writes, "[we] should, methinks, put an End to the Attempt" and try something "new."[54] Penn's creative citation of a wide cross-section of history permits him to argue that England's special circumstances demand legal guarantees of liberty of conscience that recover the freedoms of the ancient constitution. In this way, he hopes to "secure . . . the Execution of our Ancient Laws by New Ones."[55]

The project of founding an American colony only intensified this complex relationship to political change. Penn felt no strong compulsion to uphold precedent to the letter in the New World. Indeed, he announced in *The Frame of the Government of the Province of Pennsylvania* (1682), "I do not find a model [of government] in the world, that time, place, and some singular emergencies have not necessarily altered; nor is it easy to frame a civil government that shall serve all places alike."[56] And yet he also seems to have hoped that Pennsylvania's novel political structure, once settled, would never be changed. Summarizing the contradictory combination of these two impulses in private correspondence with fellow Quakers in April 1681, Penn acknowledged in patently Winthropean terms that he sought to implement "that which is extraordinary" in Pennsylvanian "matters of liberty and privilege"; but he added that he hoped "to leave myself and successors no power of doing mischief" through arbitrary change.[57] On the one hand, then, we find Penn obsessed with getting the details of the founding just right. Thus, for example, the signatories to one of the colony's many early constitutions agreed to "preserve [the document] . . . inviolably," since it was "the ground and rule of all future laws and government in that country."[58] On the other hand, this ambition would prove impractical. That very document was soon superseded, in part because it lacked any provision for amendment, and later constitutions reflect Penn's willingness to adjust the colony's political structure to shifting circumstances.[59] He remained ambivalent about who would do the adjusting, however. *The Charter of Pennsylvania* (1681) "empowers the proprietor to enact ordinances in emergencies without the consent of the Assembly," thereby granting him extensive discretionary powers comparable to Winthrop's.[60] But Penn was eventually forced to accept that members of Pennsylvania's General Assembly might amend the constitution themselves.[61] In short, the constitutional debates that took place during the colony's early years attest to the tremendous ambiguity of political change in this moment: unchanging law was at once a guarantor of and an infringement upon fundamental liberties; and political change was at once the essence of rebellion and the ruler's best means of preserving a polity subject to contingency.

William Penn's political career was not as successful as John Winthrop's.[62] To be sure, the early history of Massachusetts is rife with persecution and conflict, whereas Pennsylvania became a thriving colony largely committed to liberty of conscience. But Winthrop is remembered primarily for his ability to steer his fledgling settlement through a series of crises, whereas Penn is held to have lost control of his colony, which succumbed to political factionalism and theological dissension before stabilizing itself without him. When matters like his border dispute with Maryland proprietor Lord Baltimore called Penn back to England for the remaining fifteen years of his life, unanticipated problems arose, leading to a powerful anti-proprietary movement that demanded substantial changes to the *Frame of Government* adopted at the colony's founding.[63] These ostensible innovations were precipitated, the colonists insisted, by Penn's own attempts at "'changing' the government" by delegating his authority to commissions and governors, including the extremely unpopular New England Puritan John Blackwell.[64] As Mary Maples Dunn notes, Penn "experimented with authoritarian measures" à la Winthrop during these years.[65] In fact, the colony's best-known instance of political-theological unrest, the Keithian schism (1692–1694), resulted in a 1693 pamphlet whose title—*New England's Spirit of Persecution Transmitted to Pennsylvania*—emphasizes the similarities between the forms of discipline deemed expedient in Penn and Winthrop's colonies.[66]

Yet this approach secured Penn few of his northern predecessor's advantages. Tellingly, Maples Dunn's explanation for this is fundamentally epistemological: "because the proprietor was separated from the colonists by time and distance, and . . . distracted by English affairs, his understanding of local Pennsylvania problems was incomplete," and he was ultimately forced to capitulate to the colonists' demands by signing the 1701 Charter of Privileges.[67] That is, Penn's ability to govern effectively was impeded by the nonempirical relationship to his colony dictated by the brevity of his residence there and by the British Empire's increasing centralization, which complicated his proprietary authority. By contrast, Winthrop's power to alter legal norms at his own discretion in order to frustrate rebellion—to innovate in order to thwart innovators—derived from the firsthand knowledge of the Bay's unique circumstances facilitated by his permanent residence there, by the unique character of his colony's charter, and by the lack of metropolitan oversight in the period. In short, Penn in the 1680s became one more unfortunate "Governor" forced "to see and hear by the Eyes and Ears of other Men," whereas Winthrop in the 1630s enjoyed so much autonomy that one dissident satirized him as the region's "King."[68]

Much the same can be said of Penn's ill-fated decision to ally himself with James II in a bid for toleration on the eve of the Glorious Revolution.[69] In both cases, an insufficiently experiential approach to events on the ground meant that Penn was denied the enabling flexibility that Winthrop enjoyed. Beyond the geopolitical conditions and historical contingencies responsible for Penn's incomplete commitment to empirical political science I would submit two other explanations. First, his reliance on abstract concepts like the ancient constitution sometimes confined the wisdom of experience within a more deductive framework that limited his capacity to improvise. Second, Penn's Quakerism may have conditioned an imperfect commitment to empiricism. Quakerism shared with the antinomianism confronted by Winthrop a "radical spiritist" emphasis on God's direct communication with humanity. This belief served to align antinomians and Quakers with intuitive rationalism rather than with the empiricism that undergirded orthodox Puritan hermeneutics. Where Puritan providentialism required that truth be mediated by nature, scripture, or clergy and confirmed by collective eyewitnessing, radical spiritism entailed a more personal experience of truth that was resistant to empirical verification.[70] Indeed, Anne Hutchinson and her supporters not only criticized Winthrop's political theology but also voiced a more fundamental rejection of the experiential epistemology at its core. Believing that revelation—whether about political matters or matters of personal salvation—took place immediately (i.e., without mediation), they rejected the notion that one might read earthly signs like the "monstrous births" as God's "means" of expressing his will.[71] Radical spiritism, in short, tended to entail anti-empiricism. And if, as David S. Lovejoy argues, "Hutchinsonian enthusiasm . . . differed only in voltage from [Quaker founder] George Fox's inward light," then Penn may well have inherited some of this anti-empiricist strain.[72] Oscillating between colonial political science and a political rationalism resembling the Quaker notion of truth "writ in one's heart," Penn hesitated to exploit the capacity to innovate granted by Winthrop's experientially derived discretionary power. Persisting in the pursuit of what he had disparagingly called a "Politicks made Obsolete by new Accidents," he was ultimately unable to realize the "holy experiment" he had originally imagined.[73]

NOTES

1. See "innovation, n." *OED Online*, esp. definitions 1b and 2b; and Benoît Godin, *Innovation Contested: The Idea of Innovation over the Centuries* (London: Routledge, 2015).

2. William Penn, *Judas and the Jews Combined against Christ and His Followers* (London: 1673), 11; John Winthrop, *The Journal of John Winthrop, 1630–1649*, ed. Richard S. Dunn, James Savage, and Laetitia Yeandle (Cambridge: Harvard University Press, 1996), 674. I have preserved my early modern sources' original spelling, capitalization, and punctuation except to silently eliminate italics in quotations and to standardize the capitalization of texts' titles.

3. On Hobbes's preference for rationalist deduction over experiential particularism see Noel Malcolm, *Aspects of Hobbes* (New York: Oxford University Press, 2002), 53–79. My distinction between (colonial) "political science" and (metropolitan, Hobbesian) "political philosophy" owes much to Susan Scott Parrish, "Richard Ligon and the Atlantic Science of Commonwealths," *William and Mary Quarterly*, 3rd ser., 67, no. 2 (2010): 209–248, esp. 213–214.

4. William Penn, "To James Harrison," 25 August 1681, in *The Papers of William Penn*, ed. Richard S. Dunn and Mary Maples Dunn (Philadelphia: Penn Press, 1981–1987), 2:108; John Winthrop, "A Modell of Christian Charity," in *American Sermons: The Pilgrims to Martin Luther King Jr.*, ed. Michael Warner (New York: Library of America, 1999), 42. Winthrop may not have used the phrase himself, but scholars often describe Puritan New England as an "experiment"; see, for example, Francis J. Bremer, *The Puritan Experiment: New England Society from Bradford to Edwards* (Hanover, NH: University Press of New England, 1995).

5. This claim would seem to reinforce Perry Miller's influential argument that the settlers of Puritan New England imagined their venture as an "Errand" to reform the Old World through their own example. But my account of Winthrop's—and Penn's—engagement with the innovation prohibition in fact builds on one of the most pronounced critiques of the "Errand" thesis, T. Dwight Bozeman's examination of Puritan primitivism in *To Live Ancient Lives: The Primitivist Dimension in Puritanism* (Chapel Hill: University of North Carolina Press, 1988). See Perry Miller, "Errand into the Wilderness," in *Errand into the Wilderness*, rpt. (Cambridge: Harvard University Press, 1993), 1–15.

6. The empirical political tradition is woefully understudied. Exceptions to its critical neglect include Barbara J. Shapiro, "Empiricism and English Political Thought, 1550–1720," *Eighteenth-Century Thought* 1 (2003): 1–33; Barbara J. Shapiro, *Political Communication and Political Culture in England, 1558–1688* (Stanford: Stanford University Press, 2012), 54–76; and Parrish, "Richard Ligon and the Atlantic Science of Commonwealths."

7. William Penn, "To Robert Turner, Anthony Sharp, and Roger Roberts," 12 April 1681, in Dunn and Dunn, *Papers of William Penn*, 2:89; Winthrop, "A Modell of Christian Charity," in *American Sermons*, 40. On the rise of "experience" and its relationship to New World colonialism see Jim Egan, *Authorizing Experience: Refigurations of the Body Politic in Seventeenth-Century New England Writing* (Princeton: Princeton University Press, 1999).

8. William Penn, *England's Great Interest, in the Choice of This New Parliament . . .* (1679), in *The Political Writings of William Penn*, ed. Andrew R. Murphy (Indianapolis: Liberty Fund, 2002), 384–391, quotation on 385.

9. Mary Maples Dunn, *William Penn: Politics and Conscience* (Princeton: Princeton University Press, 1967), 48, 50.

10. On Bacon's political empiricism see B.H.G. Wormald, *Francis Bacon: History, Politics and Science, 1561–1626* (Cambridge: Cambridge University Press, 1993); and Sir Francis Bacon, "Of Seditions and Troubles," in *The Essayes or Counsels, Civill and Morall*, ed. Michael Kiernan (Cambridge: Harvard University Press, 1985), 43–50. For Machiavelli's protoempirical approach, see Niccolò Machiavelli, *Discourses on the First Ten Books of Titus Livy*, trans. Julia Conway Bondanella and Peter Bondanella (New York: Oxford University Press, 1997).

11. Richard S. Dunn, "An Odd Couple: John Winthrop and William Penn," *Proceedings of the Massachusetts Historical Society*, 3rd ser., 99 (1987): 1–24.

12. Jonathan Beecher Field, *Errands into the Metropolis: New England Dissidents in Revolutionary London* (Lebanon, NH: Dartmouth College Press, 2009), 14. On colonial reportage and imperial knowledge-making more generally, see Ralph Bauer, *The Cultural Geography of Colonial American Literatures: Empire, Travel, Modernity* (Cambridge: Cambridge University Press, 2003). On the Bay charter, see Edmund S. Morgan, *The Puritan Dilemma: The Story of John Winthrop*, 3rd ed. (New York: Pearson, 2007), chapter 7, esp. 78, 82–84; and Perry Miller, *Orthodoxy in Massachusetts, 1630–1650*, 2nd ed. (Boston: Beacon Press for Harvard University Press, 1959), 229–230, and passim.

13. For an account of how increasing imperial centralization impacted Penn's charter, see Stephen Saunders Webb, "'The Peaceable Kingdom': Quaker Pennsylvania in the Stuart Empire," in *The World of William Penn*, ed. Richard S. Dunn and Mary Maples Dunn (Philadelphia: Penn Press, 1986), 173–194.

14. Philip F. Gura, *A Glimpse of Sion's Glory: Puritan Radicalism in New England, 1620–1660* (Middletown, CT: Wesleyan University Press, 1984), 30.

15. The antinomian Mary Dyer, who delivered the "monstrous birth" reported by Winthrop, famously became a Quaker and was hanged in 1660 for repeatedly disobeying a Massachusetts law forbidding Quakers from entering the colony. On Penn's efforts to temper Quakerism's subversive impulses see Hugh Barbour, "The Young Controversialist," in *The World of William Penn*, ed. Richard S. Dunn and Mary Maples Dunn (Philadelphia: Penn Press, 1986), 15–36.

16. For representative examples of this preoccupation see Andrew R. Murphy, "Introduction," in *The Political Writings of William Penn*, ed. Andrew R. Murphy (Indianapolis: Liberty Fund, 2002), viii, xii; Gary B. Nash, "The Framing of Government in Pennsylvania: Ideas in Contact with Reality," *William and Mary Quarterly*, 3rd ser., 23 (1966): 183–209; and Maples Dunn, *William Penn: Politics and Conscience*, esp. vii, viii, 3, 46, 193.

17. Michael P. Winship renames the "Antinomian Controversy" the "free grace controversy" is his illuminating book-length study, *Making Heretics: Militant Protestantism and Free Grace in Massachusetts, 1636–1641* (Princeton: Princeton University Press, 2002). The secondary literature on the controversy is vast. Other major studies informing my argument include William Stoever, *A Faire and Easy Way to Heaven: Covenant Theology and Antinomianism in Early Massachusetts* (Middletown, CT: Wesleyan University Press, 1978); and Gura, *A Glimpse of Sion's Glory*, chapter nine. For primary texts see David D. Hall, ed., *The Antinomian Controversy, 1636–1638: A Documentary History*, 2nd ed. (Durham, NC: Duke University Press, 1990).

18. For the text's complex composition and publication history see David D. Hall, *Ways of Writing: The Practice and Politics of Text-Making in Seventeenth-Century New England* (Philadelphia: Penn Press, 2008), chapter two and passim. For Hall, the *Short Story* is a prime example of "social authorship" (*Ways of Writing*, 66), but for the sake of convenience, I will refer to Winthrop as its primary author and compiler.

19. Egan, *Authorizing Experience*, 20; *A Short Story of the Rise, Reign, and Ruin of the Antinomians, Familists & Libertines, that Infected the Churches of New-England . . .* (London: 1644), title page.

20. John Winthrop, "A Short Story of the Rise, Reign, and Ruine of the Antinomians, Familists & Libertines," in Hall, ed., *The Antinomian Controversy, 1636–1638: A Documentary History*, 2nd ed. (Durham, NC: Duke University Press, 1990), 201–310, quotation on 219.

21. Winthrop, "A Short Story," in *The Antinomian Controversy*, 276. On monstrous births as a subject of quasi-scientific inquiry, see Lorraine Daston and Katharine Park, *Wonders and the Order of Nature, 1150–1750* (New York: Zone Books, 1998), especially chapter 5.

22. Representative examples of scholarship on Protestantism and empiricism include Charles Webster, *The Great Instauration: Science, Medicine and Reform 1626–1660* (New York: Holmes & Meier, 1975); Peter Harrison, *The Bible, Protestantism, and the Rise of Natural Science* (Cambridge: Cambridge University Press, 1998); and Sarah Rivett, *The Science of the Soul in Colonial New England* (Chapel Hill: University of North Carolina Press, 2011).

23. Winthrop, "A Short Story," in *The Antinomian Controversy*, 280–281. For the journal passage see Winthrop, *Journal*, 253–255.

24. Winthrop, "A Short Story," in *The Antinomian Controversy*, 281.

25. Steven Shapin, *A Social History of Truth: Civility and Science in Seventeenth-Century England* (Chicago: University of Chicago Press, 1994), 258.

26. Winthrop, "A Short Story," in *The Antinomian Controversy*, 282.

27. Winthrop, "A Short Story," in *The Antinomian Controversy*, 282.

28. Winthrop, "A Short Story," in *The Antinomian Controversy*, 248, 264, 301, 280, 213.

29. Winthrop, *Journal*, 167. Recent scholarship emphasizing New England's liberal, democratic, and republican character includes David D. Hall, *A Reforming People: Puritanism and the Transformation of Public Life in New England* (New York: Knopf, 2011); and Michael P. Winship, *Godly Republicanism: Puritans, Pilgrims, and the City on a Hill* (Cambridge: Harvard University Press, 2012). For the debates about legal codification see Mark D. Cahn, "Punishment, Discretion, and the Codification of Prescribed Penalties in Colonial Massachusetts," *American Journal of Legal History* 33, no. 2 (1989): 107–136. And for the anti-immigrant order, see Winthrop, *Journal*, 219.

30. On Puritan primitivism see Bozeman, *To Live Ancient Lives*. On "discretion" and the Puritan assimilation of Machiavellian "reason of state" see George L. Mosse, *The Holy*

Pretence: A Study in Christianity and Reason of State from William Perkins to John Winthrop (New York: Howard Fertig, 1968).

31. Winthrop, *Journal*, 390.

32. Thomas Lechford, *Plain Dealing; or Newes from New-England: A Short View of New-England's Present Government Both Ecclesiastical and Civil, Compared with the Anciently-Received and Established Government of England* (London: 1642), 28.

33. For Penn's reference to "N. Machiavel in his Discourses upon Livy," see William Penn, *England's Present Interest Considered . . .* (1675), in *The Political Writings of William Penn*, ed. Andrew R. Murphy (Indianapolis: Liberty Fund, 2002), 22–76, quotation on 52. The best introduction to the ideology of England's ancient constitution remains J.G.A. Pocock, *The Ancient Constitution and the Feudal Law: A Study of English Historical Thought in the Seventeenth Century* (Cambridge: Cambridge University Press, 1957).

34. William Penn, *A Perswasive to Moderation to Church-Dissenters . . .* (1686), in *The Political Writings of William Penn*, ed. Andrew R. Murphy (Indianapolis: Liberty Fund, 2002), 289–329, quotation on 294.

35. William Penn, *The Great Case of Liberty of Conscience . . .* (1670), in *The Political Writings of William Penn*, ed. Andrew R. Murphy (Indianapolis: Liberty Fund, 2002), 79–119, quotations on 79.

36. William Penn, *The Peoples Ancient and Just Liberties Asserted, in the Trial of William Penn and William Mead . . .* (1670), in *The Political Writings of William Penn*, ed. Andrew R. Murphy (Indianapolis: Liberty Fund, 2002), 3–21, quotations on 6, 5.

37. Andrew Murphy has argued that Penn's *Peoples* provides a substantive discussion of political principles not through the literary strategies of canonical political thought (i.e., the deduction of general principles from accepted premises) but rather through a fine-grained, embodied, even performative account of politics on the ground. See Andrew R. Murphy, "Trial Transcript as Political Theory: Principles and Performance in the Penn-Mead Case," *Political Theory*, 41, no. 6 (2013): 775–808.

38. Penn, *The Great Case of Liberty of Conscience*, in *The Political Writings*, 105.

39. Penn, *England's Present Interest Considered*, in *The Political Writings*, 29.

40. Penn, *A Perswasive to Moderation*, in *The Political Writings*, 295.

41. Penn, *A Perswasive to Moderation*, in *The Political Writings*, 303.

42. Penn, *England's Present Interest Considered*, in *The Political Writings*, 66.

43. Andrew R. Murphy, *Liberty, Conscience, and Toleration: The Political Thought of William Penn* (New York: Oxford University Press, 2016), 49; Penn, *England's Present Interest Considered*, in *The Political Writings*, 26.

44. Penn, *England's Present Interest Considered*, in *The Political Writings*, 47; Penn, *The Great Case of Liberty of Conscience*, in *The Political Writings*, 96.

45. Penn, *England's Present Interest Considered*, in *The Political Writings*, 45, 53.

46. Penn, *England's Present Interest Considered*, in *The Political Writings*, 48.

47. Murphy, *Liberty, Conscience, and Toleration*, 49.

48. Penn, *The Peoples Ancient and Just Liberties Asserted*, in *The Political Writings*, 16.

49. Penn, *The Peoples Ancient and Just Liberties Asserted*, in *The Political Writings*, 10. Winthrop was so often accused of "arbitrary" proceedings that he wrote a treatise defending himself from the charge; see John Winthrop, "Discourse on Arbitrary Government," in Edmund S. Morgan, ed., *Puritan Political Ideas* (Indianapolis: Bobbs-Merrill, 1965), 149–160.

50. Penn, *England's Present Interest Considered*, in *The Political Writings*, 55.

51. Maples Dunn, *William Penn: Politics and Conscience*, 97.

52. Penn, *A Perswasive to Moderation*, in *The Political Writings*, 322.

53. Penn, *A Perswasive to Moderation*, in *The Political Writings*, 294.

54. Penn, *England's Present Interest Considered*, in *The Political Writings*, 23.

55. Penn, *England's Great Interest*, in *The Political Writings*, 385.

56. *The Frame of the Government of the Province of Pennsylvania . . .* (1682), in Jean R. Soderlund, ed., *William Penn and the Founding of Pennsylvania, 1680–1684: A Documentary History* (Philadelphia: Penn Press, 1983), 120–128, quotation on 121.

57. William Penn, "To Robert Turner, Anthony Sharp, and Roger Roberts," 12 April 1681, in Dunn and Dunn, *Papers of William Penn*, 2:89.

58. *The Fundamental Constitutions* (1681?), in Jean R. Soderlund, ed., *William Penn and the Founding of Pennsylvania, 1680–1684: A Documentary History* (Philadelphia: Penn Press, 1983), 96–108, quotation on 108.

59. Soderlund, *William Penn and the Founding of Pennsylvania*, 96.

60. Soderlund, *William Penn and the Founding of Pennsylvania*, 40.

61. See Richard Alan Ryerson, "William Penn's Gentry Commonwealth: An Interpretation of the Constitutional History of Early Pennsylvania, 1681–1701," *Pennsylvania History* 61 (1994): 393–428.

62. See Caroline Robbins, "William Penn, 1689–1701: Eclipse, Frustration, and Achievement," in *The World of William Penn*, ed. Richard S. Dunn and Mary Maples Dunn (Philadelphia: Penn Press, 1986), 71–84.

63. According to Caroline Robbins, these changes effectively "reversed much of [Penn's] original plan." See Robbins, "William Penn, 1689–1701," in Dunn and Dunn, *The World of William Penn*, 72. See also Maples Dunn, *William Penn: Politics and Conscience*, 160. For the process of drafting and revising Pennsylvania's constitution, see Soderlund, *William Penn and the Founding of Pennsylvania*.

64. Maples Dunn, *William Penn: Politics and Conscience*, 157.

65. Maples Dunn, *William Penn: Politics and Conscience*, 158.

66. On the Keithian schism see Andrew R. Murphy, *Conscience and Community: Revisiting Toleration and Religious Dissent in Early Modern England and America* (University Park: Penn State Press, 2001), chapter 5.

67. Maples Dunn, *William Penn: Politics and Conscience*, 151. Soderlund concurs: Penn's "departure in 1684 . . . and his prolonged absence from Pennsylvania severely damaged his effort to guide the colony" (*William Penn and the Founding of Pennsylvania*, 9). On Penn's conflicts with the colonists more generally, see Soderlund, *William Penn and the Founding of Pennsylvania*, chapter 11.

68. Penn, *The Great Case of Liberty of Conscience*, in *The Political Writings*, 79; Winthrop, *Journal*, 538.

69. See Maples Dunn, *William Penn: Politics and Conscience*, 133; Murphy, *Conscience and Community*, 126, 136.

70. On the differences between Quakerism and Puritanism more generally, see Melvin B. Endy Jr., "Puritanism, Spiritualism, and Quakerism: An Historiographical Essay," in *The World of William Penn*, ed. Richard S. Dunn and Mary Maples Dunn (Philadelphia: Penn Press, 1986), 281–301.

71. See for example Winthrop, "A Short Story," in *The Antinomian Controversy*, 215.

72. David S. Lovejoy, *Religious Enthusiasm in the New World: Heresy to Revolution* (Cambridge: Harvard University Press, 1985), 88.

73. Penn, *A Perswasive to Moderation*, in *The Political Writings*, 322.

CHAPTER 12

Religion and Revolution in New England

1689

Sarah A. Morgan Smith

In the late 1680s, William Penn found himself estranged not only physically but psychologically from his own colony, struggling to assert his prerogatives and vision as the proprietor against an increasingly factious local Assembly and Council. At the same time, he was deeply involved in the political storm brewing in England over James II's policies, serving as a royal confidante and even spokesperson, particularly on the question of religious toleration. By 1689, Penn would be under arrest for his Jacobite sympathies and would see a new king and queen on the throne as a result of the Glorious Revolution.

In contrast to the disappointment and disorientation Penn must have felt as his colonial vision and hopes for an expansive religious toleration settlement in England simultaneously disintegrated during these years, 1689 was a "happy" year for many in the empire, a time for the confirmation and celebration of English liberties. This chapter focuses on one specific colonial incident—the overthrow of the Dominion of New England in April 1689—as an example of not only the successful transference of traditional English political commitments to a new world environment but also their transformation in the articulation and defense of a particular *new* English civic identity against an intrusive external government. Although they were never able to recover the degree of autonomy they had enjoyed prior to the Stuart Restoration, New Englanders experienced 1689 not primarily as bystanders to a metropolitan-focused event but, rather, as an assertion of their own quasi-independent status as a community with a unique identity stemming largely from their shared religious commitments and heritage.[1] New Englanders—even while being drawn into the empire—consistently maintained their own civic identity, rooted in both the principles of "English rights" and the principles of their revolutionary founding. Although a minor incident in Penn's career as well as from the imperial perspective, the effort by New Englanders to assert a vision of a political community characterized by religiously informed principles of personal liberty and popular participation that culminated in the "April Revolution" represents a significant moment in the formation of the *American* political tradition, a foreshadowing of the arguments about legitimate popular dissent that would recur in 1776 and beyond.

Background

Although the Declaration of Breda (1660) had promised charity toward those who had overthrown his father's reign, Charles II's policies toward New England following his restoration to the throne in April 1661 struck some in the Bay Colony as punitive. Charles often cloaked his criticisms of the colony's government in terms of his promise of instating religious toleration through his realm, but New Englanders' perceived royal demands for institutional reform as thinly veiled attacks against a religious movement the king closely associated with his father's political and actual demise.

Relations between crown and colony grew increasingly strained over the course of the next two decades, although pressing international concerns distracted Charles from pursuing the matter in earnest until July 1683, when he issued a Quo Warranto against the colony's charter. Dubious of the king's professed intention to "to respect all private interests and properties" should the colony submit speedily, the General Court responded in December 1683 by authorizing an agent in London to protest the legality of the writ. Among the many issues raised by the court in their instructions to the attorney was the question of whether a charter granted for operation in America could legitimately be subject to examination and recall by the English courts. Without saying so directly, the General Court suggested that their de facto separation from England geographically also implied a degree of de jure separation that would significantly limit (if not negate) the king's ability to oversee the colonial government.[2]

No matter how delicately framed, such an argument had overtones of rebellion with political and theological consequences. The General Court therefore invited the advice of the local clergy on legitimacy of further resistance. The clerical response, "Arguments Against Relinquishing the Charter," clearly expounded a position born out of the tradition of Reformed resistance theory with which English Puritanism in particular had long been associated—indeed, the very same theory that had motivated the founders of New England in 1630.[3]

As the clergymen assessed the situation, the people of Massachusetts had "no reason to believe that their religion and the court's pleasure will consist together," or that the king would leave their civil liberties secure. Indeed, the king's actions against the charters of other corporations suggested that any alterations would be aimed at the abolition of the consent-based politics upon which the civic identity of Massachusetts depended, and which were in direct conflict with the king's program of absolutism. To submit would be "destructive to the life and being of their charter." It would also, therefore, be a sin, for to do so would be the equivalent of political suicide: "men may not destroy their political any more than their natural lives," the ministers asserted. It was, therefore, both prudent and pious for New Englanders to fight for their charter privileges.[4]

If further persuasion was necessary, the ministers admonished New Englanders to follow the brave example of their fathers, who had resisted earlier encroachments by the Crown, and from whom they had received their "civil liberties" as a "part of the[ir] inheritance." It would be the height of ingratitude and disrespect, not only to the founders but to God, to "give that inheritance away."[5] As they had advised the court at an earlier point in the conflict with the crown, it was the "undoubted duty" of the people to "abide by what rights and privileges the Lord our God in his merciful providence hath bestowed upon us."[6] If, in other words, God had granted a people freedoms (as was the case in New England when He called the founding generation to establish a new political community), then it was unquestionably their responsibility to defend those freedoms.

In the course of their arguments, the ministers noted in passing that since the government in Massachusetts depended upon the consent of the people, it could only be "resign[ed] to the pleasure of the court" with their consent, something they were sure "the generality of the freemen and church members throughout New England will never consent hereunto. Therefore, the government may not do it."[7] The clerical position proved to be either prophetic, or persuasive: throughout the colony, town meetings were held on the question, the majority of which voted against surrendering the charter.

Increase Mather recorded his participation in a town meeting held in Boston on January 21, 1684, to discuss the question of "whether we shall make a full submission and entire resignation of our charter and the privileges of it [to] the king's pleasure." He spoke vehemently against submission, essentially summarizing the clergy's "Arguments" and exhorting the freeman not to "give away the inheritance of [their] fathers."[8] He reported with satisfaction a few days later, "God was gracious in giving [the] freemen to be unanimous in declaring they durst not give away their liberties."[9] Boston's example "had a great influence on the country," such that "many other towns follow[ed]" it, also voting to support the General Court in their fight of the Quo Warranto.[10]

When the General Court declined to send representatives to London to argue their case, the charter was declared void, and Charles immediately began preparations for a new phase of colonial governance, one that would be much more closely tied to the desires of the crown. To help curb the colonial governments' tendency to act as if they enjoyed sovereignty of their own right, Charles consolidated the previously independent colonies of Massachusetts, Plymouth, New Hampshire, Maine, and Rhode-Island into one larger administrative unit known as the Dominion for New England. Negotiating the details of the government to be put in place over the Dominion took time, and a variety of factors further delayed the actual selection and installation of a royal governor and council throughout 1684–1685. In the meantime, Joseph Dudley, the colonial agent for Massachusetts then serving in London, a known royal sympathizer, was sent back to Boston to serve as interim governor, assisted by a small, unelected council—the first nonelected government in Massachusetts Bay's history.[11] Dudley would be replaced in December 1686 by Sir Edmund Andros: authoritarian, autocratic, and, perhaps worst of all, Anglican.[12]

The imposition of the Dominion government—which had no provision for representation at any level—was deeply resented by New Englanders in principle, and things only became worse after Andros proved to be corrupt and arbitrary in his management of colonial affairs, ignoring existing land claims, denying town meetings, and silencing political dissent. These rights, as the minsters had articulated in their advisory statement to the General Court earlier in the conflict, were not only among the traditional rights of Englishmen but were, in a significant sense, religious rights, derivable from specific points of Reformed theology. In His providence, they believed, God had led the founding generation to a land where they had been free to establish a political community in conformity to scriptural principles. Andros's attacks on private property, consent-based government, and personal liberty were understandable, therefore, as attacks on the theological underpinnings of the Puritan polity.

Andros infringed upon the more obviously religious rights of the people as well, coopting one of the Boston meetinghouses for the use of the town's small Anglican congregation despite the offensiveness of this practice to both the property rights of the "host" congregation and their religious sensibilities. Moreover, although Puritans did not scruple to swear oaths, there were some who objected to the practice of swearing "on the book," preferring instead to "swear with an uplifted hand, agreeable to the ancient custom of the colony."[13] Under Andros, these men were ineligible to serve on juries or in other civic capacities requiring an oath and were sometimes fined and even imprisoned for their refusal. Although this issue has received less attention than some of the other more obvious rights violations, to New Englanders, the imposition of book swearing was a serious infringement upon their rights of conscience and an illegitimate restraint upon their ability to participate in the life of the community. Increase Mather and Samuel Willard each published a short tract outlining the ways in which such action would or would not constitute a violation of biblical teachings. Mather, for example, objected to it on the grounds that it was derived from "popish superstition" and akin to idol worship.[14]

After enduring Andros's maltreatment of their religious and political principles for the better part of a year, New Englanders must have been quite relieved in the fall of 1687 when word of James's Declaration of Indulgence (also known as the Declaration for Liberty of Conscience) reached the Bay Colony. Increase Mather encouraged the clerical consociation to draft an address thanking the king for his actions. Later in the season, upon learning of the favorable impact of this first effort, he "moved that our churches (and not the ministers only) might thank the king" and that this time, the address be delivered by a specially selected emissary, someone who, while in England, could "obtain an interest in such nonconformists as have the king's ear."[15] Mather professed to have been surprised when the nomination fell upon him, but on the grounds of duty and with a sense of divine calling he agreed to make the journey.

When word of the plan became public, the Andros government attempted to detain Mather on a trumped-up defamation charge; unfortunately for their plan, the jury was comprised of commonwealth men who cleared Mather of all charges, and he sailed for England in April 1688.[16] After an uneventful crossing, he wasted no time in making arrangements for a royal audience, and on the morning of May 30, 1688, presented the thanksgiving address to James II, noting that it was "subscribed by twenty ministers in New England in the name of their several congregations."[17] Flattered, the king replied "I am glad my subjects in New England are sensible of any ease or benefits by my declaration. And it shall continue. I hope by a parliament to obtain a magna carta for liberty of conscience."[18] After this successful interview, Mather reported he ended the day by attending a meeting of nonconformists at William Penn's house, thus launching the second element of his two-pronged attempt to secure the civil and religious liberties of Massachusetts by developing an allegiance with other religious dissenters.[19]

Mather's plan was to link Massachusetts's historically and theologically grounded resistance to the attack on the 1629 Charter to the king's declared interest in promoting toleration. In Penn, Mather had found a potent advocate for New English concerns, at least insofar as those concerns paralleled Penn's own cause célèbre, toleration for religious nononformity. Although neither of them was likely able to muster a wholehearted approval (or a full-throated trust) of the other given Mather's association with the harshly anti-Quaker government of Massachusetts, for the time being, their interests were allied. Penn's concept of religious toleration was much more expansive than Mather's, but both sought to utilize the personal politics of royal influence to secure freedom of worship for their preferred sects. Interestingly (and against many of their contemporaries'—as well as their own—distrust of royal prerogative), both men were more than willing to accept James's patronage as a workable (if less than ideal) means to an end.

As a royal confidante, Penn's support was essential to the success of Mather's strategy to regain some measure of local, consent-based government for Massachusetts. Mather cultivated their relationship assiduously over the course of the next six months, meeting with Penn several times at Whitehall as well as in more private settings to discuss the plight of New England.[20] Reflecting on these meetings later in life, Mather would write in his *Autobiography*, "to give Mr. Penn his due, he did in my hearing in the king's closet (when no one has been present besides the king, Penn, and I) advise King James to be kind to his subjects in New England."[21] Penn seems also to have spoken to James about the matter on his own time: he told Mather in a conference at Whitehall on June 18, 1688, that "they" (he and the king?) "had been considering the NE affair," and had determined that "[Lieutenant Governor of the Dominion of New England, Francis] Nicholson should be removed, and something sent to Andros which would nettle his nose, and that if he did not comply with them, he should be turned out of his government." The "true reason" for these actions, Penn confided, "was that the state of affairs is now changed in England," but he assured Mather, "they in New England will think you are the only cause of it, and that will make them afraid of thee."[22] Mather was understandably pleased by this proposal, perhaps because it suggested some sort of practical relief was at hand, and also because Penn and the king seemed willing to allow him to take the credit for the arrangement. Unfortunately, what Mather did not know was that the "change" in England's state of affairs to which Penn alluded would ultimately prevent the scheme from coming to fruition: less than two weeks after this episode, on June 30, 1688, William of Orange would receive his much-anticipated invitation to come to the "relief" of England.

Although Mather would continue to meet with Penn and James through the end of 1688, nothing further came of the proposal to remove Andros. Mather's diary reveals his growing sense of frustration: again and again, he left Whitehall with promises and assurances from James that something would be done for New England . . . again and again, he was forced to return and plead his case anew.

And so it continued until James was out of government, Penn was out of influence, and "the change" in English affairs had been completed, all of which forced Mather to begin his negotiations anew with the untested but prickly new monarch, William of Orange. On January 9, 1689, he met William the first time and wasted no time in "requesting a restoration of charters" for New England.[23] On March 14 of the same year, he secured the King's promise to relieve New Englanders of Andros's oppressive government and recall the royal governor to England to give "an accounting" of his actions.[24] Once again Mather had secured the promise of royal intervention on behalf of New English interests, and once again, circumstances would change before that promise could be realized.

In Defense of Protestantism and the People

On the morning of April 18, 1689, "drums beat through the town" as the citizens of Boston took up arms against the Dominion of New England, rounding up the leaders of the government and putting them in the local prison.[25] At noon, a member of the resistance read a "Declaration of the Gentlemen, Merchants, and Inhabitants of Boston, and the Country Adjacent," aloud to the assembled public, listing not only the grievances against the Andros regime but also the rationale for taking up arms at that moment. Shortly thereafter, a messenger was dispatched to the fort to demand Andros's surrender.

By midafternoon, news of the unfolding political drama in Boston had spread to the neighboring towns, and another "twenty companies" of militia men arrived to support the revolutionaries. Approximately another fifteen hundred men were unable to cross into the town proper but remained on the outskirts, possibly in anticipation of taking part in some sort of military action should Andros refuse to surrender, or worse, call for reinforcements from the English frigate then anchored in the harbor. Fortunately, as the day drew to a close, Andros decided to turn himself and the fort over to the leaders of the popular movement. Within the next two days, a provisional government, headed by Simon Bradstreet and consisting largely of those who had previously served as members of the general court under the Charter government, had assumed responsibility for the "safety of the People, and the Conservation of the Peace" and for the resumption of the status quo ante-Andros.

The leaders of the uprising took steps throughout to ensure that their revolution was framed in the imperial context of William and Mary's accession as well as within the local context of inherited, religiously derived civic principles so clearly articulated by Mather and others during the initial conflict over the Quo Warranto. Prominently listed among the members of the revolutionary movement were the venerable Simon Bradstreet and Thomas Danforth, two of the few surviving members founding generation, and, even more importantly, the last freely elected governor and deputy-governor of the colony.[26] Their participation therefore provided a living connection to the aspirations of Massachusetts Bay's founding and to its last legitimate (because consent-based) government. In settling these two relics back into their previous positions of authority, the leaders of the rebellion sent a message to the people of the commonwealth that the outcome of the April Revolution would be in conformity with the traditional ideals and liberties of the commonwealth.

While the 1689 Revolution in England was to be known to history as "Glorious," that in New England was described by apologists Samuel Sewall and Edward Rawson in 1691 as "happy," for it brought about the "rescue [of] the nation from Slavery as well as Popery." Drawing on their inherited religiously informed principles of dissent and resistance, the Boston revolutionaries fought for the reestablishment of "their Ancient Charter-Government," which was itself the product of the founders' dissent from an established order and so a revolutionary document. Those who joined the Massachusetts Bay Company renounced their past civic associations in order to commit to the difficult task of establishing a new society on the foundation of a shared commitment to three essential principles: the moral equality of persons, the importance of industry as a personal and public virtue, and a deep and abiding sense of civic love, or communion.[27] The "happy revolution" then, not only "exploded" the false doctrines of "*passive obedience* and *non-resistance*" (emphasis in the original), but it did so in the name of *preserving* these inherited political aspirations.[28] As Cotton Mather would describe it, the April Revolution was both "just and fair," for New Englanders were "not resisting an ordinance of God but restraining a cursed violation of his ordinance" which, in fact, favored individual liberty.[29]

The apologetic pamphlets published by New Englanders both internally and externally develop this idea of resistance on the grounds of principle and demonstrate how ordinary citizens and public leaders could share a sense of responsibility for the inherited civil order. Although the principles being asserted were broadly derived from the English tradition, the rhetorical use to which they were being put strongly differentiates New Englanders from others within the empire. The focus is on asserting an identity for New Englanders (collectively) based on their shared heritage of a colonial founding against the perceived threat of an *external* government, and against the judgments of outsiders. This is particularly evident in the discourse around the revolution prepared for the "home audience," as it tended to draw more openly on the religious heritage of the colony, and to more boldly assert the popular nature of the politics of Massachusetts.

We see this clearly in the aftermath of the April 18 Revolution, when the provisional government of the "Council for the Safety of the People, and the Conservation of the Peace" quickly became the subject of a popular referendum. Although there were some who argued that the Council should maintain control until the events of the revolution could be communicated to London, and the king could signal his wishes for the future of the colony, the majority of the freemen of Massachusetts believed the Council should quickly turn over its political and military authority to a duly elected government.[30]

The Council, although comprised primarily of respected members of the colony's last government under the charter, was nevertheless, an unelected, unrepresentative body. Within two weeks of the revolution, "there being some agitation in council of the necessity of settling some forms of government, and several gentlemen appearing out of the country moving the same thing," the Council voted to solicit the "farther consultation and advice of the people for the directing to the exercise of that power and authority which is necessary in the present exigence" through a meeting of specially elected deputies.[31]

On the appointed day, "sixty-six persons as representatives of forty-four towns and villages" of Massachusetts joined the members of the council in Boston. The following day, these men (styling themselves the "Chamber of the Country Representatives") passed a resolution providing that for the remainder of the year, "the governor, deputy governor, and assistants chosen and sworn in May 1686 according to our Charter Rights, and the deputies then sent by the freemen of the several towns to be the government now settled in our abovesaid Colony."[32] In other words, these representatives of the people of Massachusetts were asserting their constituents' right to resume their previous charter privileges—including most importantly, the right to freely elect their governor and legislators.

With some towns from the colony having declined to send representatives to the meeting, however, the members of the Council asked that the matter be referred back to the freemen directly in their town meetings, the results of which were to be communicated to the Council via a second convention. In this appeal for broader popular input into the post-Andros government settlement, we see the relatively dialogical nature of the interactions between the assistants and the deputies, as well as that between Boston and the rest of the towns in Massachusetts politics during this period. Although technically, the results of the earlier convention could have been allowed to stand, despite the incomplete nature of the returns, the political leaders of the colony had both principled and prudential reasons for attempting to garner a more fully representative mandate in support of the new government.[33]

Over the course of the following two weeks, at least three anonymous broadsides appeared discussing the theoretical implications of the proposed vote. Directed exclusively at an internal audience that shared a core understanding of the intent of the April Revolution as the restoration of the colony's religiously shaped civic heritage, the authors nevertheless have slightly different understandings of precisely what such a restoration would require. Taken together, these documents offer an intriguing glimpse at the internal discourse of the citizens of Massachusetts Bay over the meaning of their inherited civic ideals and institutions, most particularly on the nature and degree of consent necessary for legitimate politics.[34]

The first broadside, signed N. N., offered a cautious interpretation of what a "restored" government in Massachusetts would look like. It opens with a reference to "Deliverance to God's Israel" who—like their forefathers, who fled to New England to escape persecution—have drawn together with a unified spirit in order to "escape" once again from those who would limit their freedom.[35] By framing the recent revolution as not only a political act but also a reflection of the community's shared religious identity, N. N. reminded New Englanders that the sovereignty of the people was not unbounded; rather, it was the result of their covenantal relationship with God. He therefore exhorted the people to adopt a policy of restraint and peaceableness in the matter of settling the new government.

It would be unwise, he argued, for New England to assert too boldly its right to select its own style of government and governors, which might only serve to antagonize the new king and queen. The best course of action would be to eschew a new election and to simply reinstate (or, "reassume") the 1686 government: this was the option best suited to respect the people's right to government by consent *and* the least likely to be seen as a radical statement by those outside the colony. After all, he reminded the public, "the Magistrates and Deputies Chosen in '86 were chosen for the Year, but were by force hindered; and that quickly from Discharging their Duty." They were thus "a standing Court, and adjourned," although their adjournment had been prolonged by the imposition of the Andros regime.[36] To restore to the last freely elected representatives of the people the political power usurped from them would give the postrevolutionary government a veneer of continuity with all the previous governments under the 1629 charter. This, in turn, would help to legitimize the claims being made to English audiences about the limited aims of the revolution in New England: a restoration of the previous government was less likely to be seen as a radical attempt to assert the colony's independence from the (new) monarchy.

The second broadside, signed Philo. Angl., denied that prudence ought to overcome principle for "in violent changes the people can as well authorize civil as military government; and in the meantime are not (neither can they be) tied to any other laws than what agree with the present necessity." If the good of the people was indeed the supreme law, and it required them to overthrow their existing government, under no circumstances could they be induced to accept the idea that they were bound to reassume any other particular form simply as a matter of tradition or custom. In the end, however, because the existence of Massachusetts as a political entity was dependent upon the 1629 charter with its extensive grant of self-government to the people of the colony, Philo. Angl. agreed with N. N. that reassuming the 1686 government in continuity with the 1629 charter *was* the course best suited to securing the public good.[37]

In contrast, the third broadside argued that the only legitimate way to settle the government of the colony in the aftermath of the revolution was to hold entirely new elections. The author, known only as S. I., asserted that "the main essential thing [to] be attained" by the revolution was not simply the end of the Andros regime but, rather, "that an election or choice of government be made" by the people of the colony.[38]

In other words, if the legitimation of the April Revolution depended on the claim that Andros's government had been illegitimate and arbitrary because it was unrepresentative and destructive of individual rights, then in the aftermath of the revolution, lacking any settled government, the political power of the community had returned to the people at large. The people as constituted in 1689 were a new political entity, different from the people who had elected the government in 1686: they now held their sovereignty directly as they had at the time of the founding, and they must therefore directly give it up through the process of new elections.

The recent revolution, S. I. argued, had made the "country" of Massachusetts "more united" and more interested in protecting their liberties than ever before.

Moreover, circumstances had provided a slate of potential candidates for office, a group of "honorably worthy gentlemen, that have hazarded their lives for the obtaining our liberties." With such a selection of worthies, he continued, "we shall not find ourselves puzzled in nomination of fit persons to manage the affairs of our government, if we can but have opportunity to manifest our minds by election. . . . We say therefore, we are in the fittest posture for Choice that ever we were in." To regain their right to choose their own government was the "one main thing aimed at in the Motion of the Army" in deposing Andros. To deny the people their right to choose would be "an occasion (as we may plainly foresee) of dividing a country, at this time so heartily united," and therefore, to waste all of the political momentum and goodwill that might otherwise be put to good purpose in advancing the public welfare.[39]

Although in some ways the most outspoken defender of the political rights of New England's freemen, S. I. closed his letter with a statement recognizing that the colony's future was not entirely within their control. Acknowledging that Massachusetts was in a state of "dependence" on England, he expressed his hope that William would "consult our peace and prosperity, and once again restore to us our dear lost liberties and patent-privileges, and set up our hedge of government about us, that we may sit under our vines and fig-trees, and there may be none to make us afraid."[40] He reinforced these Old Testament metaphors for the providence of God in the daily affairs of His people with a final prayer that the God who had "made us know [t]he worth of [our liberties] by the want" of them, might even now, intervene to ensure that these were secured.[41]

From Puritan to Protestant: Massachusetts Post-1689

Interestingly, all three authors agreed that the theoretical implications of the recent crisis of political legitimacy required the colony to expand the franchise to include non-church members. At this critical juncture, the policy put in place by the founding generation of restricting political participation to the recognizably godly was more of a liability than an asset in terms of rallying domestic support to the side of the rebellion. It was far more important to the perpetuation of New England's founding principles that the "generality" of the people (most of whom were at best, halfway members of their local churches) be persuaded that their interests and the interests of the colony were aligned than that some elusive standard of purity be maintained. In all four documents surrounding the second town convention, it is clear that the ideal of civic communion now necessitated the expansion of freemanship to include all reputable freeholders. This would not only be "a great expedient to our peace and security, and to the settlement of our charter-privileges,"[42] it would also make the government in the colony "the most easy and most safe Government in the World."[43] By expanding the franchise, the political leaders of Massachusetts in 1689 effectively resolved the civil crisis associated with restrictive church membership practices in the previous generation and ensured that all who had the means to evidence their material interest and membership in the colony could do so in political matters as well.[44]

In May 1689, the Council for the Safety of the People sent an address to William and Mary both congratulating them on the "the late glorious enterprise . . . for the relief and deliverance of the distressed kingdoms," and framing the April Revolution as a response to, or continuation of, those events and William's declarations "encouraging the English nation to cast off the yoke of a tyrannical and arbitrary power."[45] New Englanders, they explained, "being themselves under alike (if not worse) evil," and with the added fear of an "invasion" from neighboring French colonies, had been "excited to imitate so noble and heroic an example."[46] They ended the address with an expression of their hope "that under the shadow of your imperial crown we may again be made to flourish in the enjoyment of our former rights and privileges, being the sole encouragement unto our fathers, and predecessors, at their own great cost, and expense to settle this colony to the enlargement of the English dominions, and so much for the glory of that crown."[47] Although the language here is conciliatory, it is not submissive: the Council has succinctly asserted the legitimacy of their actions in overthrowing Andros and reassuming self-government, not only on the basis of William's declarations but also on the grounds of their historic charter and their forefathers' investment in the colony.

Similarly, in a second address to William and Mary prepared on June 6, 1689, the newly elected government told the monarchs that although "several weeks" had passed since they had requested the Crown's advice about settling the government, no such orders had been received. In the absence of external direction, and "finding an absolute necessity of civil government," they explained, they had been forced to accede to the popular demand for a more permanent, elected government.[48] Although they were careful to classify their own sense of their authority as only a partial resumption of the 1629 charter,[49] the authors were nevertheless bold in their assertion that Charles and James had acted "unrighteously and injuriously" in revoking the colony's charter. That had been an especially grievous abuse of power, they argued, because the "royal charter [was] the sole inducement, and encouragement unto our fathers and predecessors to come over into this wilderness and here to plant, and settle the same at their own cost, and charges, which through the blessing of God, was a flourishing plantation enlarging your majesties dominion to the glory of the English crown; though since the alteration of that government, greatly impoverished and brought low."[50] In both of these addresses, the acting government adopted a tone of limited and incomplete deference toward the monarchy: they seem to want to align their cause with that of the English towns and corporations that had appealed to William and Mary as the defenders of the "Protestant interest" while simultaneously maintaining the relatively independent and sovereign status of New England within the empire.

These questions would plague New Englanders as they attempted to preserve the colony's founding aspirations and the sense of a separate New English identity in the face of an imperial policy of consolidation and Anglicization. In London, Increase Mather would be joined by Samuel Sewall, Elijah Cooke, and Thomas Oakes as colonial agents working to secure the return of the 1629 charter or a close approximation thereof. In pursuit of this goal, Mather would publish a number of pamphlets defending New England's actions in the April Revolution and asserting the legitimacy of their claims to self-government. In Boston, his son Cotton became the unofficial spokesman for the new administration, preaching the first "election" sermon given in the post-Andros era, as well as several more on topics of political significance over the course of 1689 to 1692. Together, the Mathers and other pamphlet writers would help to preserve New Englanders' sense of civic identity by focusing on the applicability and sustainability of the colony's religiously inspired commitments to moral equality, industry, and civic communion within their new imperial framework.

New Englanders were too prone to turn every dispute into a question of principle, the younger Mather observed, to draw lines between groups rather than to look for commonalities. In their pursuit of a godly polity, the founders had gone too far, excluding non-church members from the full exercise of their civil liberties. The internal divisions thus created left the colony vulnerable when external threats appeared, as the second and third generations had learned to their chagrin in the recent tangle with the Crown. Mather urged his fellow citizens to continue in the more irenic approach they had adopted by expanding freemanship in the wake of the April Revolution to other areas of civic life. Although "we have hitherto professed ourselves *a country of puritans*," he observed, the time had come to "have the wisdom to be first pure, then peaceable."[51] The combination of these two attributes would lead individuals to look for areas of agreement and compromise, rather than stubbornly insisting on promoting their own understandings of the "best" course of action in any circumstance. Only then would New England be able to fully realize its potential as a place known both for the government of the godly and for godly government.

If Increase Mather spoke with William Penn again after James fled England, neither man left an account of their conversation. Yet, perhaps by offering Mather his assistance, Penn also furthered his own tolerationist agenda by helping Mather to recognize the political utility of a more ecumenical approach to questions of conscience. The colony's alleged intolerance of Quakers, Baptists, and other dissenters as well as Anglicans had been a significant factor in Charles's decision to issue the Quo Warranto in the first place. Although the General Court had robustly defended their actions against the Quakers as necessary for the maintenance of public order, and denied the charge that nondisruptive variation in worship was subject to persecution, Massachusetts refused to separate political rights from membership in a recognized church until the crisis of 1689. Then, forced by the unpleasant experience of Andros's oppressive practices to revisit the sense of persecution that had driven the founders to New England in the first place, they were also forced to confront their inconsistent application of their principles.[52] The expansion of freemanship to non-church members and the concessions to religious toleration under the new charter were the logically necessary extension of the founding commitments of Massachusetts.

In 1691, after having labored in London for three years, the elder Mather finally secured a new charter for the colony, which, he argued in some measure, granted even greater privileges to New England than had the 1629 charter.[53] Under the new charter, "religion is secured; for Liberty is granted to all Men to Worship God after that manner which in their Consciences they shall be persuaded is the most Scriptural way. The General Court may by Laws Encourage and Protect that *Religion* which is the general Profession of the Inhabitants there. . . . No bad Counselor, Judge, or Justice of the Peace, can now be imposed on them. These things are as a Wall of Defense about the Lord's Vineyard in that part of the World."[54] Note that Mather maintained his position that New England was a place marked by its religious commitments, a "vineyard" where the Lord was extending His providential care and governance of the world. Far from leading to increased secularization, the new charter offered robust protection for the colony's founding religious commitments, extending them to their logical conclusions and thereby broadening their potential adoption by those beyond the borders of Massachusetts.

NOTES

1. My interpretation of the event runs counter to the majority of the scholarship which interprets 1689 as the turning point toward secularization in Massachusetts: see David S. Lovejoy, *The Glorious Revolution in America* (New York: Harper and Row, 1972) and Craig Yurish, *Settlers, Liberty, and Empire* (New York: Cambridge University Press, 2011) Chapts. 1–2, especially; Theodore B. Lewis, "A Revolutionary Tradition, 1689–1774: 'There Was a Revolution Here as Well as in England,'" *NEQ*, 46, no. 3 (September 1973), 424; Stephen Carl Arch, "The Glorious Revolution and the Rhetoric of Puritan History," *Early American Literature*, 27, no. 1 (1992): 61–74; and Ian K. Steele, "Origins of Boston's Revolutionary Declaration of 18 April 1689," *NEQ* 62, no. 1 (1989): 81. More recently, Owen Stanwood has presented an intriguing analysis of the April Revolution that takes into consideration its religious dimensions and roots in the New English experience, but which ultimately links those to imperial and even international ambitions; see "The Protestant Moment: Antipopery, the Revolution of 1688–1689, and the Making of an Anglo-American Empire," *Journal of British Studies* 46, no. 3 (2007): 481–508.

2. See entry 1159 for July 20, 1683, *Calendar of State Papers, Colonial Series: America and West Indies, Vol. 6, 1681–1685* (London: 1898), 456; *Records of the Governor and Company of the Massachusetts Bay in New England, Volume 5, 1674–1686* (Boston: 1854), 421, 424–425, 430–431.

3. "Arguments Against Relinquishing the Charter," *Collections of the MHS*, 3rd Ser., 1 (1801): 74–81; Increase Mather, *The Autobiography of Increase Mather: Proceedings of the*

American Antiquarian Society, October 1961, ed. Michael G. Hall (Worcester, MA: American Antiquarian Society, 1962), 307.

4. "Arguments Against Relinquishing the Charter," 74–76, 81.

5. The reference here is to the 1638 Quo Warranto, a document not so much resisted as ignored and, ultimately, voided by the events of the English Civil War. "Arguments Against Relinquishing the Charter," 77, 81.

6. They cite a report given to the General Court on January 4, 1680; "Arguments Against Relinquishing the Charter," 78.

7. See, "Arguments Against Relinquishing the Charter," 79.

8. I. Mather, *Autobiography*, 308.

9. I. Mather, *Diary*, January 21 and 23, 1684, Microfilm edition of the Increase Mather papers, a joint publication of the Massachusetts Historical Society and the American Antiquarian Society.

10. I. Mather, *Autobiography*, 308.

11. On Dudley's motivations, and his role in the settlement of terms for the Dominion government, see Michael G. Hall, "Randolph, Dudley, and the Massachusetts Moderates in 1683," *New England Quarterly*, 29, no. 4 (1956), 513–516; on his use of his brief stint as governor to further his own interests, see Theodore B. Lewis, "Land Speculation and the Dudley Council of 1686," *William and Mary Quarterly*, 31, no. 2 (April 1974), 255–272.

12. See Mary Lou Lustig, *The Imperial Executive in America: Sir Edmund Andros, 1637–1714* (Cranbury: Fairleigh Dickinson University Press, 2002).

13. See, for example, Samuel Sewall's diary entry for June 11, 1686, which records that he took his oath as an officer in the Artillery Company "holding the book in my Left hand and holding up my Right Hand to Heaven," and that his acquaintance, a "Captain Hutchinson" refused to swear at all. Diary of Samuel Sewall in *Collections of the Massachusetts Historical Society*, vol. 5 (Boston: 1878), 143.

14. "Declaration," in *Andros Tracts*, 1:48; I. Mather, *A brief discourse concerning the unlawfulness of the common prayer worship and of laying the hand on and kissing the booke in swearing* (Cambridge: 1686), 19–21. See also Samuel Willard, *A brief discour[se] concerning the ceremon[y] of laying the hand on the Bible in swearing* (London: 1689).

15. I. Mather, *Autobiography*, 320.

16. See I. Mather, *Diary*, March 27, 28, 30, and April 1, 1688; as well as the account of the proceedings in Cotton Mather, *Parentator* (Boston: 1724), 106–107.

17. For a complete account of Mather's activities on behalf of New England while in London, see "Representing Massachusetts in London (1688–1691)," in Michael G. Hall, *The Last American Puritan: The Life of Increase Mather, 1639–1723* (Middletown, CT: Wesleyan University Press, 1988), 212–254.

18. IM, *Diary*, May 30, 1688.

19. IM, *Diary*, May 30, 1688.

20. See entries in Mather's *Diary* for May 31, June 13, June 18, July 10, and September 26, 1688.

21. IM, *Autobiography*, 326.

22. IM, *Diary*, June 18, 1688; Mather repeats his account of this conversation in his autobiography as well, see previous citation.

23. IM, *Diary*, January 9, 1689.

24. IM, *Diary*, March 14, 1689.

25. My description of the facts of the actual overthrow are drawn from Nathaniel Byfield's *An Account of the Late Revolution in New-England* (London: 1689). The tract was published from a letter written by Byfield to friends in England in the immediate aftermath of the revolution, on April 29, 1689.

26. See Francis J. Bremer, "Bradstreet, Simon (bap. 1604, d. 1697)," *Oxford Dictionary of National Biography* (Oxford: Oxford University Press, 2004), http://www.oxforddnb.com

/view/article/37215, accessed 9 Nov 2015; Roger Thompson, "Danforth, Thomas (bap. 1623, d. 1699)," *Oxford Dictionary of National Biography* (Oxford: Oxford University Press, 2004).

27. See *The Revolution in New England Justified, and the People There Vindicated from the Aspersions cast upon them by Mr. John Palmer* (Boston: 1691) in W. H. Whitmore, ed. *The Andros Tracts: Being a Collection of Pamphlets and Official Papers . . .*, 3 vols., Prince Society, V–VIII (Boston: 1868–1874; rpt. 1971), 1:71–72 [Hereafter: *Andros Tracts*]. Whether similar goals of individual liberty drove the revolution in England has been the subject of much debate: see the summary provided by Lois G. Schwoerer in her introduction to *The Revolution of 1688–89: Changing Perspectives* (New York: Cambridge University Press, 1992), 1–20.

28. *The Revolution in New England Justified . . .* in *Andros Tracts*, 1:71.

29. CM, *Parentator*, 117–118.

30. The reason for keeping the Council in place seems to have been strategic: at least one pamphlet argued that to replace the emergency government with one formally elected following the model of the 1629 Charter would appear presumptuous and cause the King to look unfavorably on the colony. See the anonymous and undated "Opinion Against Resumption of the Charter" in Lovejoy, *Glorious Revolution*, 359–360.

31. Council Records for 1–2 May 1689 in Lovejoy, *Glorious Revolution*, 64–65.

32. Declaration of the House of Representatives, 10 May 1689 in Lovejoy, *Glorious Revolution*, 71.

33. Council Records for 10 May 1689 in Lovejoy, *Glorious Revolution*, 71–72. On the negotiated nature of this appeal, see Richard C.Simmons and S. I., "The Massachusetts Revolution of 1689: Three Early American Political Broadsides," *Journal of American Studies*, 2, no. 1 (April 1968): 1–6.

34. Simmons and S. I, "Three Early American Political Broadsides," 1–12.

35. Simmons and S. I, "Three Early American Political Broadsides," 7.

36. Simmons and S. I, "Three Early American Political Broadsides," 7–8.

37. Simmons and S. I, "Three Early American Political Broadsides," 8, 9.

38. Simmons and S. I, "Three Early American Political Broadsides," 10.

39. Simmons and S. I, "Three Early American Political Broadsides," 10.

40. Simmons and S. I, "Three Early American Political Broadsides," 10.

41. Simmons and S. I, "Three Early American Political Broadsides," 10.

42. Simmons and S. I, "Three Early American Political Broadsides," 10.

43. Simmons and S. I, "Three Early American Political Broadsides," 8, 9

44. "At a Convention of the Representatives of the Several Towns and Villages," Lovejoy, *Glorious Revolution*, 394–395.

45. "The Humble Address of the President and Council for the Safety of the People, and Conservation of the Peace," 20 May 1689, Lovejoy, *Glorious Revolution*, 77.

46. "Humble Address," 20 May 1689, Lovejoy, *Glorious Revolution*, 78.

47. "Humble Address," 20 May 1689, Lovejoy, *Glorious Revolution*, 78–79.

48. "Humble Address and Petition of the Governor, and Council, and Convention of Representatives of the People of Your Majesty's Colony of the Massachusetts in New England," 7 June 1689, Lovejoy, *Glorious Revolution*, 89.

49. At this stage in the postrevolutionary restructuring of government, the administration was styling itself a "convention of the governor, council and representatives of the Massachusetts Colony," rather than using the more traditional terminology of the General Court, consisting of the governor, assistants, and deputies. On June 7, 1689, the representatives passed a resolution urging the governor and his council to cease insisting on the "partial" nature of their powers and instead to recognize they, as the people's agents, had duly empowered them to "accept government according to our charter rules" and using the former titles. See "Declaration of the Representatives from the Several Towns," 7 June 1689, Lovejoy, *Glorious Revolution*, 90–91.

50. “Humble Address,” 7 June 1689, Lovejoy, *Glorious Revolution*, 90.

51. C. Mather, *The Way to Prosperity: A Sermon to the Governor, Council, etc., May 23, 1689* (Boston: 1690), 31.

52. See entry for 11 June 1680, *Records of the Governor and Company of the Massachusetts Bay in New England*, 5:287.

53. I. Mather, *A brief account concerning several of the agents of New-England, their negotiation at the Court of England with some remarks on the new charter granted to the colony of Massachusets shewing that all things duely considered, greater priviledges than what are therein contained, could not at this time rationally be expected by the people there* (London: 1691), in *Andros Tracts*, 3:271–296.

54. I. Mather, *Brief Account*, in *Andros Tracts*, 3:288–289.

PART V

Quaker Worlds

CHAPTER 13

William Penn as Preface Writer, Historian, and Controversialist

Catie Gill

When George Fox's *Journal* appeared in print in 1694, three years after the Quaker leader's death, its preamble included a lengthy work by William Penn. In its first outing, it was termed "The Preface," but this work was also issued separately in the same year under a different (and lengthy) title: *A Brief Account of the Rise and Progress of the People, Call'd Quakers In Which Their Fundamental Principle, Doctrines, Worship, Ministry, and Discipline Are Plainly Declared to Prevent the Mistakes and Perversions That Ignorance and Prejudice May Make to Abuse the Credulous* (1694). Penn used Fox's death as a moment of reflection not only on the man himself but on the movement he helped to build. This verbose subtitle represented what Penn was really trying to achieve with this separate publication. He sought to provide an explanation of the "fundamental Principle[s], Doctrines, Worship, Ministry and Discipline" of the movement.[1] It was into this portrait of the evolving practices of Quakerism that the memorializing, and fond, reflections on Fox, the "Faithful Servant" were embedded.[2] Penn's *A Brief Account* (as I will hereafter refer to it) is indicative of Penn's affection toward Fox, but it also provides insight into his concerns about how Quakerism could retain its appeal as it moved into a second phase.

More than simply establishing Fox's legacy for future generations of Quakers was at stake in the writing of this memorial. Attacked consistently, sometimes by ex-followers, but often devastatingly in this period by members of the Anglican Church, the Quaker movement was persistently identified as the magnet for enthusiasts and enthusiastical ideas even before Fox's death. With the *Journal* providing the most intimate portrait to date of the deceased leader's mindset, including candid accounts of the miracles he worked as part of a wider pattern of responding to premonitions of God's will, the text's publication led to an intensification of debate about the values that the movement most cherished.[3] Penn's work, especially when appended to the *Journal* rather than featured as a stand-alone comment on Quaker history, seemed designed to chime with the visionary insight of the former leader.[4] This can be ascertained from the reverent manner in which Penn referred to Fox's calling as a religious leader, which is indicative of a desire to preserve and protect the Quakers' radical traditions as children of the Light.

While *A Brief Account*'s attention to a shared heritage seems to anticipate the interests of readers from within the movement, his rhetorical approach provides readers less familiar with the unique practices of God-inspired Quakers with instruction as to this religious body's significance, and its former leader's character. The extended title of *A Brief Account* insists the document can be consulted "by way of introduction." Not a testimonial written only for those familiar with Fox, Penn's endeavor was for his work to engage productively with non-Quakers. As can be demonstrated from closely attending to this work's rhetorical strategies, Penn coins apt phrases that clarify Quaker ideas, describes the movement's history with concision, and in the process, sometimes implicitly, gestures toward the future. *A Brief Account* therefore offers itself as the volume to consult for an authoritative account of Quakerism at this point in the movement's history.

There are two strands to articulating what Penn achieved. The first is arrived at by assessing the text as a composition with spokesmanly confidence, in command of the formal and rhetorical qualities that make this work so readable. In any discussion of this text's reception, it will be important to remember that *A Brief Account* was often turned to and reprinted, and so had considerable appeal.[5] Yet the most productive way to approach the text is to highlight the difficulties of writing a history, given that Quakerism moved forward from schism to schism and had the potential to divide opinion. Penn's decision to combine memorial (to Fox) with history would have made these tensions fairly clear to many readers familiar with the way the society fractured in the years before the Quaker leader's death. Though Penn is drawn to ameliorating, where possible, the most divisive aspects of Quaker history, it will be an important part of this discussion to bring to the fore the underlying strains. The second strand of analysis is an extension of the first and is arrived at by thrusting Penn, the memorialist, into the role of controversy writer. My focus is on the external reception of the work by the non-Quaker community, and by Anglicans specifically. Material that is on the face of it hostile to Quakerism often offers the best evidence about the significance of the medium of print. This feature has previously received some attention but can be revisited afresh as part of the wider assessment of Penn's achievements that this volume provides.[6]

The Reception of Fox's *Journal*

Within a few short years of Fox's death, the deceased Quaker leader had been denounced and his legacy derided. In an effort to undermine the reception of this text, cherished by the Quaker John Whiting as an "excellent Journal," adversaries of the movement reduced the leader to ignominy.[7] Fox's reputation was not enhanced by the publication of his memoir: according to these highly critical readers, the *Journal* made his ignorance, self-delusion, and hypocrisy palpably clear.[8] In turn, the high regard in which the *Journal* appears to have been held exposed the Quakers to a different sort of criticism. Non-Quakers soon noticed that Fox's *Journal* was prominent in the curriculum of newly established Quaker schools.[9] The prediction made by a long-standing opponent of Quakerism, John Faldo, that one author (i.e., Fox) would "fill the mouths of many" looks particularly apt when considered in the light of the possible filtering down of his ideas through the new school system.[10] George Whitehead, a Quaker who, with Penn, became a leader in the years following Fox's death, observes another key feature of the opprobrium. It was common to speak of the publication of the *Journal* as a crime against the established church.[11] Indeed, one of the key participants in this debate felt so strongly about the possible ramifications that he called Anglicans "tame" for not opposing the Quakers' fraudulent publications, especially the *Journal*, more strenuously.[12] According to Quaker opponents, therefore, the *Journal* should be rendered unpalatable to future readers as an act of public morality.

Given the interdependence of *A Brief Account* on the *Journal* it is not surprising that Penn himself would also be criticized for his role in the creation of Fox's legacy. The reception of this work shows how far from being a neutral act of memorialization was the writing of this text. Antisectarian pamphleteers of the period instinctively grasped that an attack on Fox was an attack on what Quakerism had historically represented, while a critique of Penn could undermine the movement's newer orthodoxies and perhaps threaten its survival. The Anglican writer Charles Leslie produced the most pointed critique of the *Journal* and Penn's role in establishing its significance, and he will therefore be the main focus of analysis in this chapter.[13] William Kolbrener argues that antagonists to sectarianism knew how to mobilize long-standing prejudices in order to cause alarm.[14] Leslie's approach to the Quaker menace had a good deal of the sensationalism that was standard in antisectarian literature. Yet Leslie does not only appeal to his readers' manipulable anxieties: as I will show, he seeks to provoke a reasoned rejection of sectarianism.

The first of the texts produced by Leslie was titled *A Snake in the Grass*. His imagery suggests that Quakerism was coiled, venomously, threatening the stability of the 1690s. As a tagline with considerable potential, not only for what it says about the approach of anti-Quaker antagonists but also for its transmutation in the course of debate, the snake denominator is worth pursuing a little further. Owing to the fact that Leslie's first publication did not have his name on the title page, he became known popularly as "Mr. Snake."[15] While using the snake as a symbol of Quakerism was not a unique coinage, this deployment is nevertheless interesting because it took on a life of its own.[16] By 1700, the printer who set the title page could draw attention to the fact that Leslie had submitted yet another work into the now six-year-old controversy about Fox's *Journal* by advertising *Five Discourses by the Author of the Snake in the Grass* (1700), which suggests this reptilian designation for Leslie has become commoditable, worth advertising. As David Manning has observed, the precise significance of the parallel would be apparent to readers who knew 2 Corinthians 11:13–14, a biblical passage that identifies the errors of false apostles by equating them to a snake.[17] Thus, while Leslie clearly meant to inflame suspicion of the Quakers and of Fox's ungodly ministry, the name, instead, became attached to him.

Leslie established the terms of the debate through *The Snake in the Grass*, and thereafter produced four more thoroughgoing anti-Quaker works between 1696 and 1700.[18] Other non-Quaker writers who intervened by publishing works in this series of controversy texts were John Faldo, in a reissuing of a 1675 text brought in, presumably, to support the Leslian line (1698), and Samuel Young under the nom de plume Trepidantium Malleus (1697). The influence of Leslie could be observed in the latter.[19] As was typical when the press seized on an aspect of Quaker identity, Friends replied, seeking to clear the truth. George Whitehead, *Antidote Against Venome* (1697), Richard Scoryer, *Truth Owned* (1698), and Joseph Wyeth, *Angius Flagellatus: Or a Switch for the Snake* (1699) contributed to an ever-burgeoning affray. In these pamphlets, the discussion could range widely as writers came to articulate some key aspects of Quaker theology and discipline. Christo-presentism was a particular point of interest in the argument as it diversified and grew to consider ever more theologically engaged topics. Something of a snowball effect pertains with controversy writing as it gathers pace. In order not to lose the original point of focus of Leslie's engagement with Fox's legacy, only "Mr. Snake's" response to the *Journal* need be of concern in my account. Discussion of this matter in any case provides a snapshot of Leslie's theological objections to Christo-presentist Quakerism.

Penn as Memorialist

Cecile M. Jagodzinski has noted that during the seventeenth century autobiography became a respected genre in which to reflect on an individual's significance, because it "moves into the approved and authorized sphere of public witness."[20] While Jagodzinski provides a best-case scenario for memorial and autobiography, the hostile reception of the *Journal*, shows how far it diverged from the "approved" form of discourse that was so typical. In all other aspects of Jagodzinski's criteria, *A Brief Account* is a very accomplished work of "public witness." In Penn's summary, Fox emerges in a vivid character study designed to honor the Quaker leader as a man who "excellest" all.[21] In his organizational roles, Fox is represented as a capable leader to whom the movement owed much of its prosperity.[22] In the manner of providing a concise overview, these aspects are quickly passed over in *A Brief Account* as Penn leads up to his most moving tribute, which is also a prime example of Penn's pithy prose style. Penn's vignette depicts Fox as sober, humble, but able to move his listeners with "admiration," or wonder.[23] He was a charismatic preacher, "nearer to the Lord than other men," in sum.[24] This character sketch by Penn is notable for pointing readers toward the exceptionality of Fox as a religious leader.

The anti-Fox writer, Leslie, sought to diminish Fox by challenging the hagiographic mode of address that Penn developed through the elegantly written character sketch that venerates the deceased leader and his ministry. In addition to declaring Fox close to God, *A Brief Account* insists that Fox's distinctive singularity meant that the Quaker was "no man's copy."[25] Leslie observes Penn's striking phrasing closely, because it provides an opportunity to assign a different significance to the words than Penn intended, and thus to attack this hagiography. In *Primitive Heresie Revived*, Leslie's approach is to play on the idea that a "copy" can be corrupt, rather than reliable. This diminishing of Fox through an attack on Penn's phrasing begins with the *Journal*. In his memoir, Fox explains simply that he was motivated by God to act when called, and to avoid actions when "he [God] forbad me."[26] Leslie, however, believes a more logical explanation to be possible: the Quaker leader follows Judas, not God.[27] *Primitive Heresie Revived* consequently declares that Fox is now "depriv'd of the *Glory* of being an *Original*, and to be *No Man's Copy*, as is Boasted of him (emphasis in the original)."[28] Because Leslie has proven Fox to be diabolically led, not religiously dutiful, his "copy" (of Judas) has now been revealed. Leslie's economy in slandering two Quakers simultaneously is notable. The way Leslie constructs this phrase makes Penn no less reprehensible than Fox. *A Brief Account*, by this measure, has engaged in empty, unthinking, hero worship of a false idol by terming Fox "no man's copy."

Penn was a seasoned-enough writer of Quaker discourse to know how to preempt the negative scrutiny of the reading public. Though, ultimately, foreknowledge does not sufficiently guard him against attack, he is primed and ready for controversy. "An Epistle to the Reader" provides this insight, from the 1694 edition of *A Brief Account*, and subsequent editions published separately: in it, Penn rails against a spate of "unjust" criticism.[29] Given that Leslie had not at this point in 1694 entered the pamphlet debate, Penn is clearly not referring to his animadversions. Even so, "An Epistle to the Reader" takes this opportunity to make revealing comments as to the enemies Penn had in mind. Complaining of the misjudgments of "[people] that once walked under the profession of Friends,"

Penn seems to invoke the Keithian controversy.[30] This ex-Quaker was a chief scourge of the movement in the 1690s. Penn's considerable efforts to anticipate debate show that he understands the exposure he is risking by entering into the public forum of print on behalf of Fox.

The "Epistle to the Reader" expands even further on the theme of being resolute in the face of adversity and criticism. Penn deploys common tropes of steadfastness, and this feature of his prose again shows him commenting on the broader implications of hostile accounts of Quakerism. Claiming that the controversy Quakers met with makes their continued adherence to their religion more necessary, Penn's "Epistle to the Reader" explains that he hopes to overcome "the ill usage we have met with, being the realities of religion, an effectual change before our last and great change: that all may come to an inward, sensible, and experimental knowledge of God."[31] The faithful here are represented as misunderstood, but undeterred, even when they are reviled. The adversarial role of the defender of Quakerism is, indeed, something that Penn's *A Brief Account* also both anticipated and even embraced. Since, according to Penn, the first stirrings of the movement produced a reaction "not unlike those Jews of old, that rejected the Son of God," their perseverance in the face of contradiction had a glorious antecedent.[32] Penn is referring here to the persecution and misunderstanding that the first Christians faced in order to parallel their treatment to the reviling of the religious in his own age. In turn, the reference to primitive Christianity enables him to indicate that standing up to the opposers of truth is one duty of the faithful.[33]

In fact, the distinction being drawn seems to be between the act of writing, which is prompted by writerly motivations of one kind, and the anticipation that the text will be received in a different way. Engagement with opponents is, in other words, a feature of the text's life in the public sphere of pamphlet debate, something Quakers did regularly through controversy. But provoking controversy was not necessarily one of the aims that Penn consciously formulated in writing *A Brief Account*. The authority that is conferred on Penn as the writer of *A Brief Account* is, primarily, that of a codifier of the movement's aims, whose act of retrospectively tracing its origins, and the role of its founder, is inherently more conducive to the writer of a moderate, and reflective, piece than it is to the ire of the controversialist.[34] In the broader framework of seventeenth-century writing, a similar attempt to condense a complex social process into a narrative also produced a text with a degree of neutrality. The work of David L. Weaver-Zercher on writings in the Anabaptist tradition confirms that even controversial or emotive subjects (such as martyrdom) were subject to a law of transmission: the tendency for writers to downplay distinctive matters of doctrine in favor of conveying general aspects of theology.[35] This observation by Weaver-Zercher is instructive as to the way that texts construct a literary heritage. At the point of codifying a faith into a document, the act of remembrance precludes drawing attention to the possibility that the movement being recorded is still debating its significance with outsiders. The account has to appear to fix even present-day disagreements over doctrine, so as not to open the body of believers to further attack.

In order that his principles as a writer with a tendency to codify faith may be further explored, *A Brief Account*'s method when defining and memorializing Quakerism will be compared to other texts in the Penn oeuvre. According to Michael Graves, William Penn was "an active and significant memorialiser" of deceased Quakers.[36] Graves's focus is on the "epideictic genre of public address," whereby the individual being commemorated is made an example for others to follow, and the placing of his or her life in the broader scope of religious history is established. Graves further draws on the work of Celeste Michelle Condit in order to emphasize that these elements are conducive to "shaping and sharing a community."[37] The priorities of the writer of a testimony, like those of the history writer who seeks to memorialize a movement, are concurrent in many ways. Just as Graves drew out the lessons for the wider Quaker community that were distilled in a memorial written by Penn in 1688, a similar explicatory approach informs Penn's *A Brief Account*. His message focuses on what Quakers of the 1690s might learn from the disunity of the past, specifically in relation to unifying around the leadership, since disunity was detrimental.

This is evident in the way that *A Brief Account* seeks to minimize (but notably, not omit altogether) a feature of Fox's leadership: the opposition that he faced. While Penn's main aim was to offer both a record of Fox's life and also a summary of the traits in which he "abundantly excelled," he is drawn also to comment on infighting.[38] His language evokes the biblical antecedent that I have cited earlier: the Apostles' and first Christians' resilience in the face of combatants (the "Jews of old").[39] Penn insisted that Fox be regarded as a defender of the cause "as in primitive times, some rose up against the blessed apostles of our Lord Jesus Christ . . . so this Man of God had his share of suffering."[40] There was, Penn observes, "no person the discontented struck so sharply at."[41] In the manner of a testimony writer and memorialist, and in the instinctive spirit of a conveyor of religious history, Penn neither names nor expands on this infighting. Yet he anticipates the way in which the *Journal* and inevitably also his "Preface" might be received, by drawing attention to the fact that in his later years, particularly, the critique of Fox hampered the movement.

Penn's method in *A Brief Account* was without doubt more focused on accommodating difference than revealing the causes of contention, but it nevertheless still included material that would infuriate rival churchmen such as Leslie. Because of the necessity of establishing Quakerism as a curative to the failings in the Anglican religion, Penn's writing on other faiths was potentially inflammatory. Penn derided "the lifeless ways and teachers," before practiced, and the "little fruit" their ministry produced.[42] The extensive anticlericalism that is scattered within Quaker writings finds its way into a denunciation of the teachers who, in an evocative phrase in widespread usage, are said to have forms of godliness but not the power (2 Timothy 3:5).[43] Associated with a formal worship that denied the efficacy of the spirit to move the believer, Church of England ministers seemed to be rigid, dogmatic, and earthly, in comparison to the Quaker ministry and faith. Assertions by Penn in *A Brief Account* were therefore predicated on the contentious precept that the movement's origin was directly linked to the established church's failures to provide religious guidance. Leslie was drawn to the controversy in order to challenge the Quaker belief that they freed the people from a false worship within the Church of England. There appears to be real feeling in Leslie's refutation, when he responds "how freely they [Quakers] had *Branded* all the Christian World (for they have greater Tenderness towards the *Heathen*, whom they make the next True *Christians* to themselves) as *Apostates, Blasphemers, Devils, Conjurers, & c.*"[44]

Penn's memorializing work was, hence, received as polemic rather than as an accurate account of the rise of Quakerism and the authority of its leaders, including Fox. According to Justin Champion, seventeenth-century historians were in the process of redefining their discipline in order to stress its empirical basis; however, despite these efforts, this form of writing remained subject to intense scrutiny and accusations of bias.[45] Leslie's instruction to Penn was that in order to "prevent the deceiving of after-Generations" he should print material enabling readers to "examine into matters of fact," so as to achieve a perspective on how Quakers drew conclusions.[46] In effect, Leslie was delineating a problem of resources and reliability, so applying a skeptical and rationalistic framework. Noting Quaker claims to an especially intimate relationship with God were based on miraculous or providential events, *The Snake in the Grass* demystifies the faith. Demanding "Mr Penn wou'd Now *Publish* his Register of Quaker Prophecies, or for ever after hold his Peace," Leslie deplores the Quaker assertion that they are God's people, and Fox his minister.[47] His request for verifiable evidence is therefore an example of how provocatively he pursued his goal of critiquing the Quaker religion.

Penn and the Future of Quakerism

Penn's social status meant that he held an unusual place in the Quaker movement. More the patrician than the mechanic preacher, even Penn's enemies recognized him as a man of learning. In *The Second Period of Quakerism*'s account of the Penn–Leslie controversy, William Braithwaite avers that because of his social advantages, Penn gets "off more lightly than other Quakers."[48] In the linking of Fox and Penn that occurs through the publication of *A Brief Account*, distinctions of status and social position inform parts of the discussion. While it is the case that in general Fox's background makes him an easy target, critics almost invariably pointing out that this religious leader started life as a Leicestershire shoemaker, Penn's own class position could be problematical. How able was Penn to elide the differences between rank and background in writing about the deceased leader? And how much of an advantage was Penn's high social position, given that it enabled critics like Leslie to see him as a class traitor? An especially revealing strand of the Penn–Leslie controversy, then, is its negotiation of the intricacies of status.

Awareness of the differences of rank between Penn and others informs this pamphlet war. Penn himself implicitly acknowledges a distinction when, in *A Brief Account*, "low and mechanical" ministers are praised for their role in establishing Protestantism as the credible alternative to Catholicism.[49] The "low" as much as the "mechanical" of Penn's phrasing shows that, though he venerates these ministers, he is not akin to them. For Leslie, this social difference between Penn and the majority of his coreligionists could be used as a lever to suggest a further point of dissension in the Quaker community. According to Leslie, early Quakers were little more than a "*Mechanic Gang*"; Penn, meanwhile, was patently a man of "*Sense and Breeding*."[50] Leslie could be deploying a gentleman's code of speaking with respect to an equal in complimenting Penn, but evidence points to a different motivation.

It is more likely that the complex set of assumptions that undergird Leslie's comment on Penn's superior "breeding" are an instance of false praise, not peer recognition. "Let them [Quakers] either justifie what is plainly Quoted out of their Books: or freely disown and condemn the Blasphemous Errors of *G. Fox* their first *Apostle*, and others of their Party," he insists.[51] Leslie's identification of the misguidedness of Quakerism begins with his denunciation of Fox. Leslie's broader point is that the Quaker mechanic preachers need to be held in check. *The Snake in the Grass* positions Penn as now the only Quaker able to interrogate the former leader's "Nonsense" and "Blasphemy": the decision about how to do so now "lies upon Mr Penn's Shoulders."[52] In this way, the social advantage that Penn possesses as someone of higher rank and education than the majority of Quakers buys him credit only to a degree. It makes him in fact directly responsible for reforming the movement, because he is assumed to be capable of achieving critical distance that the "mechanic" cannot. This also makes him culpable, as a man born for leadership, should this endeavor fail.

Leslie asks for nothing short of a rethinking of Quakerism's ontological assumptions and the shelving of its central insight: that God's substance can be comprehended in the Light. It is difficult to assess whether *The Snake in the Grass* feels that, by rational argument, the Quakers might be convinced to take a position on spiritual illumination more broadly in line with Anglicanism, or whether the extent of the Quaker misunderstanding is so great that they are beyond any appeal based on rational criteria.[53] Leslie did seek to make Anglican piety exist as a viable alternative to Quakerism: "whatever the Quakers think, the Ch. of

England has always Acknoweleg'd the Influences and Inward Operation of the B. Spirit of God upon our Hearts."[54] *The Snake in the Grass* may have believed that Anglicanism, the via media of religion, could incorporate dissenters, because of its position of the Church for all believers. However, the provocative "whatever Quakers think" makes Friends seem resistant to such an appeal to logic, or even too stubborn to turn. It is here that Penn's role in the future of Quakerism becomes crucial in closing the gap between these two versions of Protestantism. For Leslie, it remained to men like Penn (whom he specifically names in this respect) to "make it appear [i.e., prove] that the Quakers and every one of them in Particular, have this Light more than other Men."[55] Forcing on Quakers the burden of proof, Leslie is setting an exceptionally high threshold for truth in expecting clarification to come from "every one of them [Friends]" about their experience of the Light. When writing like this, Leslie is not the irenic thinker capable of seeing a time of comprehension within the Church of England. He is setting up the Quakers to unsatisfactorily engage in a debate where the odds are stacked against their ability to defend their theology.

The position that Leslie constructs for 1690s Quakers is therefore one that insists they perversely maintain their first principles while being dimly aware that their theology is ontologically unsound. According to Leslie, the Quaker principle of spiritual illumination as a light distinct from nature, and originating in God himself, needs to be wholly rejected. Penn operates as the focus for this aspect of the critique because Leslie accepts that he can be reasoned with. As a consequence of Leslie's desire to prove Penn wrong in his defence of Fox, the *Journal* becomes an ontological battleground. *The Snake in the Grass* accuses Penn of evincing "over-Charity" when he seeks to explain away Fox's belief that he has unity with the godhead: "Mr Penn's Excuse . . . [is Fox's] extreme Ignorance," Leslie observes.[56] The implication here is that in explaining Fox's theological position, Penn not only makes matters worse for the Quakers, by slowing the process of them coming to a better realization of theological matters, but he is also compromising his own intelligence in so doing. Malleus, a facetious writer in terms of what he contributed to discussions of theology, rendered the issue thus: "you [Penn] cannot believe the Fables you relate of him [Fox]."[57] This baldly worded statement is arguably highlighting what is being implied in Leslie's account of the relationship between Fox and Penn.

A further detail of the circumstance when Penn's *A Brief Account* was going to press suggests that there was also disquiet closer to home, in that at least one Quaker had some reservations about Penn's suitability as a preface writer. The evidence is inconclusive, and brief, and it is to be found in the Society's Minutes and the extant copies of 1694's edition of Fox's *Journal*. Question was made during the Second Day Meeting, which oversaw Quaker publications, of the appropriateness of prefacing Fox's *Journal* with *A Brief Account*. Fox's son-in-law, William Meade, is on record stating that he "refuses to hear [the Preface] Read being Resolved it shall not be printed with the Journall if he can help it."[58] The Library of the Society of Friends, London, possesses seven copies of the 1694 *Journal*, and four of these contain Penn's preface while three do not.[59] It is possible that one reason why we do not know how Penn responded to Leslie is that other Quakers took up this controversy in place of him. Though the disquiet felt by Meade was not in the end a barrier to publication, it may be the case that Penn's further involvement beyond writing *A Brief Account* was unwelcome.

The textual account alone therefore represents Penn's best answer to the matter of whether, in Malleus's words, "you cannot believe" *A Brief Account*'s hagiographic response to Fox. Some of the text's phrases seem to suggest Penn feels some anxiety as he offers Fox's *Journal* to a 1690s readership, such as when reflecting on how "abruptly and brokenly" Fox spoke.[60] There are, then, moments when Penn emerges as a social superior to Fox. Another example is when Penn prepares genteel readers for what they will find in the prose style of Fox: "no art nor parts had any share in the matter or manner of his ministry."[61] Penn tries to elide the differences between the social ranks and does not always completely achieve this, as his higher status is glimpsed. Yet more pervasively, Penn's spiritual egalitarianism is apparent, and hence his approval of Fox and his methods shows through. Quite simply, Fox's ministry, "greatly confirmed me [Penn] that it was of God."[62] Rather than valuing Fox less because he was of humble parents, Penn values him more. In Penn's work of memorialization, the mechanic preacher's unstudied eloquence is the paradigm for explaining true righteousness.

To this extent, Penn grounds his assertion of Fox's significance in what he saw of the leader's ministry and his power to move others. Leslie doubted that Penn believed the hagiography that he wrote of Fox. While Penn refuses in *A Brief Account* to engage with theology, he rests his not inconsiderable claims for the piety of Fox on his personal charisma instead. Detractors such as Leslie might protest, but Penn had shown his support for Fox clearly through this characterization.

Conclusions

Penn had been clear in *A Brief Account* that he wanted to speak to persons "not of our communion"—to non-Quakers as much as to Quakers.[63] Penn's involvement in the construction of Fox's legacy had, however, drawn the opprobrium of non-Quakers such as Leslie in the process. The Anglican assault on *A Brief Account* was at once flattering about Penn's intellectual capability and dismissive. Penn emerges in this debate as the man who possesses the requisite ability to define the Quaker Inner Light but who squanders this by engaging in hero-worship of a deluded minister, Fox. Controversy writing often reflects the prejudices of a given society, and it can be a very low form of public address. It can resort to scaremongering and insult hurling, so controversy may appear unproductive. In Leslie's critique, there is an element of "railery" when he is up against the Quakers' more "ridiculous" ideas (as he saw them).[64] Setting aside the name-calling, cross-factional discussion can be a more incisive mode of discourse. Leslie is a key example of a writer whose intervention in public debate asks serious questions of the remaining Quakers of how they wish to proceed. *The Snake in the Grass* shows Quakers that they have a chance to reform their movement in the wake of Fox's death. Leslie maintains that the man of wit, Penn, has "refin'd" some of the Quakers' "gross notions," and will continue to do so; yet he feels bound to observe that the process is yet incomplete as superstitious Quaker ways are only "coming off by degrees."[65] Penn's slightly unusual position in Quakerism made him an interesting person to appeal to. Ultimately, it seems unlikely that Leslie thought Penn capable of as thoroughgoing a reassessment as *The Snake in the Grass* presents as necessary. Many of Leslie's rhetorical observations seem designed to present Penn as a lost cause.

In his role as the writer of Fox's biography, Penn gives a heavy steer to the reader to accept his concise and public-focused overview of the Quaker leader's life and character as a valid representation. *A Brief Account* constructs a historical memoir by describing the chief developments in Fox's life and mapping these onto the development of Quakerism. The hagiographic element emerges in the way that Penn supplies examples of Fox's exceptionality as a minister "nearer to the Lord than other men."[66] Penn's text fulfills a useful purpose for print at this point in Quaker history, in commemorating and endorsing Fox's spiritual beliefs and setting him out in the best possible light. However, in so decisively endorsing Fox's legacy, Penn must have been aware that the image of the charismatic preacher he was presenting would be unpalatable to some readers. It is possible to discern in the approach of *A Brief Account* a concerted effort to secure a reader's approval. Both in the sense that he explicitly appeals for unity, and in the sense that his rhetorical approach seems designed to make the reader see *A Brief Account* as a balanced record of the period, Penn places a lot of emphasis on securing his readers' consent. His work remains controversial in its subject matter and its opinions, not because his prose is ineffective. The circumstances inevitably made it so.

Penn addressed the "sober and considerate Reader" at the opening of *A Brief Account*.[67] Such a person might indeed discern in the movement, and its founder, the true principles of the Quaker religion. It has been clear through this overview that a section of the readership of this text was less than convinced by Penn's efforts at codifying the movement's key practices and beliefs. However, at a fundamental level, the basis of the character sketch of Fox in *A Brief Account* is personal throughout. Penn declares that his portrait is drawn "not only by report of others, but from my own long and most inward converse, and intimate knowledge of him" not just because this secures his authority as a memorialist.[68]

More than that, by asserting that history and biography are more reliable when based on experience, Penn establishes an advantage over his many non-Quaker adversaries. Whatever else *The Snake in the Grass* could observe, Leslie would always lack a priori knowledge possessed by Penn. *A Brief Account* remains an invaluable account of this period of Quakerism's history, and Fox's ministry, precisely because it is firsthand.

NOTES

1. "The Preface, Being a Summary Account of the Diverse Dispensations of God to Men from the Beginning of the World to that of our Present Age, by the Ministry and Testimony of his Faithful Servant George Fox, as an Introduction to the ensuing Journal," in *A Journal or Historical Account of the Life [of] George Fox* (London: Thomas Northcott, 1694), sigy. A-B2[r] (A[r]). For more on the text's publishing history, see below. I will refer to Penn's text by its second title, *A Brief Account* because this is a more distinctive denominator than the "Preface." I quote from the Bronner edition, in *The Peace of Solitude and Other Writings*, ed. by Edwin B. Bronner (London: J. M. Dent, 1993), 267–320 (298). This is based on *A Collection of the Works of William Penn*, ed. Joseph Besse (London: J. Sowle, 1726).

2. The term "Faithful Servant" is from the extended title to *A Brief Account*. Bronner "suspects that WP had in mind a separate publication of this essay from the beginning." See Edwin B. Bronner and David Fraser, *The Papers of William Penn: William Penn's Published Writings, 1660–1726, An Interpretive Bibliography* (Philadelphia: Penn Press, 1986), 5:411. I do not speculate on this matter, as my essay is concerned with the effect of Penn's work being published alongside the *Journal*.

3. See "Introduction," Henry J. Cadbury, in *George Fox's Book of Miracles* (Cambridge: Cambridge University Press, 2012).

4. In the sense of the effect on the original reader of seeing the two works, *A Brief Account* and the *Journal*, bound together.

5. The publication history is as follows:

1. *A Brief Account* prefaced editions of Fox's *Journal* for three centuries. After its first printing in 1694, the *Journal* was thereafter reissued in the following years: 1695, 1709, 1765, 1827, 1836, 1852.
2. *A Brief Account* was first issued as a separate printing in 1694. It was then reprinted in 1695 and 1708. This printing is erroneously referred to as the fourth edition. Bronner explains that this indicates that the versions that appeared as appended to the *Journal* are being included in this count. The final edition to appear in the eighteenth century says it is the tenth edition (1794).
3. *A Brief Account* also appeared in Penn's *Works* (1726, 1782).

Individual copies varied, and the discrepancies in the editions of the *Journal* are discussed below.

6. The focus in criticism is often split. It either emphasises the relationship between Fox and Penn, or the publishing context, missing the fact that both aspects require assessment. Specifically, see this approach to personalities in Geoffrey F. Nuttall, "Reflections on William Penn's Preface to George Fox's Journal," *The Journal of the Friends' Historical Society*, 57, no. 2 (1995): 113–117; Melvin Endy, "George Fox and William Penn: Their Relationship and their Roles in the Quaker Movement," *Quaker History*, 93, no. 1 (1994): 1–39. By contrast, see William Braithwaite, *The Second Period of Quakerism* (York: William Sessions, 1979 [1919]), 288–499, 495. *SPQ's* overview focuses on the controversy between Quakers and Anglicans in the 1690s but does not appreciate that this doctrinal dispute offers vital clues to the reader response and the publishing context of Fox's and Penn's work.

7. John Whiting, *Persecution Expos'd* (London: J Sowle, 1715), 212. Whiting notes in passing that the *Journal* is "well known," 212.

8. It is beyond the remit of this chapter to summarize the discussion that ranged across all of the texts produced in response to the publication of the *Journal*. By focusing on Fox's religious disposition, I am however able to touch on the assassination of his character as well as his religious beliefs—and hence make compressed reference to Fox's reputation for ignorance and delusion. Their main way of undermining Fox was as follows: to comment on the simplicity of his writing; to pinpoint errors; to identify points of self-exaltation; to focus on his relatively humble background. This chapter cannot consider another essential feature of the anti-Quaker discourse: criticism of Fox's leadership. His enemies charge Fox with being an authoritarian leader. They therefore suggest that in his support for the principle of spiritual equality he is merely hypocritical.

9. Charles Leslie, "Some Gleanings," appended to *Satan Dis-Rob'd* (London: Charles Brome, 1697), 20. The same fact is repeated in Trepidantium Malleus [Samuel Young], *The Foxonian Quakers* (London: W. Marshall, 1699), 34.

10. John Faldo, *The Snake in the Grass Further Discovered* (London: J.F., 1698), 232.

11. George Whitehead, *An Antidote Against the Venome of the Snake in the Grass* (London: Tho. Northcott, 1697), 253.

12. Leslie, "Some Gleanings," in *Satan Dis-Rob'd*, 11.

13. For a brief overview of his life and work, see Robert D. Cornwall, "Charles Leslie," in *Oxford Dictionary of National Biography* 2004–2016.

14. William Kolbrener, "The Charge of Socinianism: Charles Leslie's High Church Defense of 'True Religion,'" *Journal of the Historical Society*, 3 (2003): 1–23.

15. Malleus, *The Foxonian Quakers*, 11.

16. Further work could be done in tracing this usage. However, for the purposes of this chapter, it is most significant that John Faldo's work refers to snakes and Satanism in the 1670s. Faldo's work was republished during the 1690s to coincide with the interest that Fox's death generated in his earlier reputation. See *XXI Divines* (London: J. D., 1675), 27.

17. David Manning, "Accusations of Blasphemy in English Anti-Quaker Polemic, c. 1660–1701," *Quaker Studies*, 14 (2009): 27–56 (35).

18. The texts by Leslie that offer the fullest account of Quakerism, and that received the most comment from Quakers in their refutations are *The Snake in the Grass* (1696), *Satan Disrob'd* (1697), *Primitive Heresie Revived* (London: Charles Brome, 1698), and *Five Discourses by the Author of the Snake in the Grass* (London: Charles Brome, 1700).

19. Faldo, *The Snake in the Grass Further Discussed*, is a reissue of *Quakerism no Christianity* (1675); William Penn took part in the 1670s refutation of this text. For Malleus's acknowledgment of his debt to Leslie, see *The Foxonian Quakers*, 55. The dispute also prompted discussion from a Church of England minister, Edmund Elys, *Reflections Upon Some Passages* (London: T. Sowle, 1700), and another, Anon, *A Parallel between the Faith and Doctrine of the Present Quakers* (London: John Nut, 1700).

20. Cecile Jagodzinski, *Privacy and Print: Reading and Writing in Seventeenth-Century England* (Charlottesville and London: University Press of Virginia, 1999), 65.

21. Penn, *A Brief Account*, in Bronner, *The Peace of Solitude*, 307.

22. Fox as the movement's founder, see Penn, *A Brief Account*, in Bronner, *The Peace of Solitude*, 299–300, and for Penn's reference to Fox as the Lord's "chosen vessel" to reform religion see 276. For organization, see 304, and Penn's comment in the section of *A Brief Account* on discipline as the "first instrument," 294. For Fox's ministry, see 302; for comments and on the qualities of "experimental preachers," see 278.

23. Penn, *A Brief Account*, in Bronner, *The Peace of Solitude*, 303.

24. Penn, *A Brief Account*, in Bronner, *The Peace of Solitude*, 303.

25. Penn, *A Brief Account*, in Bronner, *The Peace of Solitude*, 302.

26. Fox, *Journal*, 24

27. Leslie, *Primitive Heresie*, 17.

28. Leslie, *Primitive Heresie*, 17.

29. Penn, *A Brief Account*, in Bronner, *The Peace of Solitude*, 267.

30. Penn, *A Brief Account*, in Bronner, *The Peace of Solitude*, 267.

31. Penn, *A Brief Account*, in Bronner, *The Peace of Solitude*, 267–268.

32. Penn, *A Brief Account*, in Bronner, *The Peace of Solitude*, 276.

33. Penn, *A Brief Account*, in Bronner, *The Peace of Solitude*, 268. The author was motivated by three goals: (1) testifying to the truth, (2) testifying that the Quaker movement established the principles of primitive Christianity, (3) producing an account of Fox's life. See Penn, *A Brief Account*, in Bronner, *The Peace of Solitude*, 267.

34. For Penn as a writer of "moderate," considered prose, see Neil Keeble, "The Politic and the Polite in Quaker Prose," *Prose Studies*, 17 (1994), 112–125.

35. David L. Weaver-Zercher, *Martyrs Mirror: A Social History* (Baltimore: Johns Hopkins University Press, 2016), 41.

36. Michael Graves, "Travelers Here in This Vale of Tears: William Penn Preaches a Funeral Sermon," *Quaker Studies*, 12 (2007): 7–25 (12).

37. Graves, "Travelers," 18; citing Condit "The Functions of the Epideictic: The Boston Massacre Orations as Exemplar," *Communication Quarterly*, 33 (1985): 284–299 (289).

38. Penn, *A Brief Account*, in Bronner, *The Peace of Solitude*, 298.

39. Penn, *A Brief Account*, in Bronner, *The Peace of Solitude*, 276.

40. Penn, *A Brief Account*, in Bronner, *The Peace of Solitude*, 304.

41. Penn, *A Brief Account*, in Bronner, *The Peace of Solitude*, 305.

42. Penn, *A Brief Account*, in Bronner, *The Peace of Solitude*, 278, 279.

43. Penn, *A Brief Account*, in Bronner, *The Peace of Solitude*, 280.

44. Leslie, "Some Gleanings," in *Satan Dis-Rob'd*, 6.

45. *The Pillars of the Preistcraft Shaken: The Church of England and its Enemies 1660–1730* (Cambridge: Cambridge University Press, 1992), 21.

46. Leslie, *The Snake in the Grass*, sigy. Lxxi.

47. Leslie, *The Snake in the Grass*, sigy. Lxxi.

48. Braithwaite, *The Second Period of Quakerism*, 489.

49. Penn uses this phrase of preachers from the first phases of Protestantism—possibly Puritans. He observes of Fox that his speech sounds "uncouth and unfashionable"; his approach was untutored hence connecting him to these mechanics. Penn, *A Brief Account*, in Bronner, *The Peace of Solitude*, 274, 302.

50. Leslie, *The Snake in the Grass*, 35, 34.

51. Leslie, *The Snake in the Grass*, 266.

52. Leslie, *The Snake in the Grass*, sigy. Ccxliii. "Nothing less will serve their turn, than down right to Acknowledge the Folly and Wickedness of their Former Prophets," *The Snake in the Grass*, sigy. Cxcvi.

53. Contemporaneously, Leslie was attacking the other thinkers, causing religious disquiet in the 1690s: deists; Charles Leslie, *A Short and Easie Method with the Deists* (London: Charles Brome, 1699). He refers to Quakers in passing in this pamphlet, 34.

54. *A Defence of a Book Intituled A Snake in the Grass*, 27. Similar assertions are made in *The Snake in the Grass*, sigy. Xlvi, and p. 82, where he says Anglicanism's construction of the private spirit is very similar to Quakerism's. See also his summary of the Anglican position in *Satan Dis-Rob'd*, 34.

55. Leslie, *The Snake in the Grass*, 158.

56. Leslie, *The Snake in the Grass*, 59, 57.

57. Malleus, *The Foxonian Quakers*, 9.

58. London Second Day's Morning Meeting (LSMM), 1692–1700, vol. 2, 51–52. Entry for 2 April (2nd month). Melvin Endy speculates that Meade's antagonism toward Penn had a personal basis, perhaps stemming from a familial affiliation to his wife and father-in-law—

or that the Morning Meeting thought Penn too controversial a figure to represent Quakerism. See "George Fox and William Penn," 15–16, 18.

59. http://quaker.adlibhosting.com/Details/fullCatalogue/27622. [Accessed June 9, 2017].

60. Penn, *A Brief Account*, in Bronner, *The Peace of Solitude*, 302.

61. Penn, *A Brief Account*, in Bronner, *The Peace of Solitude*, 302.

62. Penn, *A Brief Account*, in Bronner, *The Peace of Solitude*, 302.

63. Penn, *A Brief Account*, in Bronner, *The Peace of Solitude*, 317.

64. Leslie, *The Snake in the Grass*, 12.

65. Leslie, *The Snake in the Grass*, 5.

66. Penn, *A Brief Account*, in Bronner, *The Peace of Solitude*, 303.

67. Penn, *A Brief Account*, in Bronner, *The Peace of Solitude*, 267.

68. Penn, *A Brief Account*, in Bronner, *The Peace of Solitude*, 298.

CHAPTER 14

Quakers, Puritans, and the Problem of Godly Loyalty in the Early Restoration

Adrian Chastain Weimer

Thomas Venner's armed revolt against the newly restored monarchy on the first Sunday of 1661 led to an era of intense prosecution and surveillance of Quakers and other English nonconformists. Venner and his followers took up arms and occupied St. Paul's Cathedral in London on behalf of King Jesus. The revolt ended quickly after troops arrived. Its aftermath, however, extended for years. An anti-sectarian reaction included arrests, searches and seizures of private homes and goods, raids on religious meetings, and mob violence.[1] The reaction against nonconformists was so strong that the restored king Charles II himself tried to moderate it, insisting that local officials have a warrant unless an actual second revolt were under way. Efforts to "disarm and secure the fanatics" led to a period of concentrated reflection among Quakers about the meaning of godly loyalty.[2] The most well-known outcome of this reflection was a consolidation of what would later be called the Peace Testimony, a repudiation of carnal, or worldly, weapons. However, Quakers also wrote extensively about the nature of their political relationships. A vocal contingent of Quaker polemists and missionaries found the most effective way to affirm Quaker loyalty was to juxtapose it with others' disloyalty. Quakers repeatedly claimed to serve the king in their role as discerners of hearts.

Close attention to how Quakers and other nonconformists addressed the problem of godly loyalty contributes to a richer history of the Restoration, one in which the colonial periphery plays a significant role. It is easy to dismiss transatlantic nonconformist communities' rhetoric about loyalty as hypocritical, if necessary, political posturing. However, there is evidence that Quakers and others were genuinely wrestling with the meaning of loyalty after the nominally Anglican king claimed his father's throne in 1660. Both Quakers and Congregationalists were intensely concerned with the spread of falsified reports about their disloyalty to the king or his predecessors. While some Friends thought the Peace Testimony would be enough to allay fears about their potential for rebellion, others went in a different direction, claiming to serve the king through their ability to distinguish between his true and false supporters. They alone could identify those men and women in his far-flung realms who gave him lip service but were secretly antagonistic. As they tried to come to terms with the Restoration of the monarchy, Quakers adroitly articulated their innocence through their role as spiritual judges, informing the king about the true affections of his far-flung subjects.

"So Far as They Do Rule for God and His Truth": Allegiance and Its Limits

Investigations into the Venner uprising revealed its Fifth Monarchist rather than Quaker origins. Quakers, however, knew that convincing the new government of their allegiance would still be a difficult task. Their rejection of loyalty oaths was only the beginning. George Fox had been imprisoned in June 1660 as "an Enimie to our Soveraigne Lord the King" and a leader of "insurrections" intended "to embroile the whole kingdome in blood." Though Fox denied any involvement in plots, the language he used to articulate loyalty probably raised more questions than it answered. Even after his arrest, he wrote boldly to the king that the Restoration was an act of the Lord's power, rather than a result of deft political maneuvering or divine-right entitlement. The kingdom might be advanced by Charles II's rule, especially because he gained power without bloodshed. However, his return to the throne was thanks to a divine gift, not because the office was his by right.[3] For Fox as for most early Quakers, rulers and systems of government were ultimately grounded in immediate divine action, rather than reason, the Bible, or natural law. And so, Fox argued, the Lord would overthrow Charles II's kingdom if he did not show mercy and stop arresting the righteous.[4]

The prominent Quaker leader Margaret Fell also articulated the theological limits on obedience in a 1660 letter to the king: "we do Love, Own, and Honour the King and these present Governours, so far as they do rule for God and his Truth."[5] Fell had access to the king because of her rank and would often plead with him in person to release Quaker prisoners. She would have known how traditional statements of allegiance were framed. For example, Parliament had proclaimed "heartily, joyfully, and unanimously" that Charles II was king "by Inherent Birth-right . . . Lineally, Justly, and Lawfully . . . And that by the Goodness and Providence of Almighty God, hee is . . . the most Potent, Mighty, and undoubted King, Defender of the Faith, &c. And thereunto Wee most humbly and faithfully do submit and oblige our Selves, our heirs and posterities for ever."[6] Quakers could not agree to these proclamations. If the king ruled wickedly, they would cease to own him. Though unwavering on the qualified nature of Quaker allegiance, Fell did carefully articulate her affection for the king, warding off possible concerns about feigned love or mixed intentions. For example, she wrote, "my love is deare unto you all & not for any outward end (the lord knowes)," and in another letter, "in deare & tender bowelles of Love doe I write unto you, not in feignednes or dissembling for an end, but in sincerity of heart, & true Love to you[,] the Lord knowes that searches the secrets of all hearts." Fell did not, however, back down on the point that Quaker fealty and affection were circumscribed by the godliness of the king's decrees; the state was subservient to the church. Through the interventions of Fell and another Quaker leader, Anne Curtis, in combination with Fox's own protestations that he was "innocent & clean & pure as a child," he was released in late September or early October 1660.[7] Convincing judges of Quaker innocence and affection would become even more difficult after Venner's revolt.

Immediately after the January uprising, Fox, Francis Howgill, Richard Hubberthorne, and other Quaker leaders gathered to draft a statement for the king from "Harmles" Quakers "Against All Plotters and Fighters in the World." This rejection of worldly weapons, or Peace Testimony, was a natural development within Quakers' apocalyptic theology. Quakers understood themselves as having immediate access to Christ's supernatural power, a power far beyond human weapons that could bring about the Kingdom of God on earth.[8] In 1660 the Peace Testimony was also a political necessity. Many Quakers had been Cromwellian soldiers. Their tendency to reject oaths and tithes, and to publicly confront priests and magistrates, made them prime suspects for rebellion.

In this 1661 statement the Quaker leaders argued that seeking peace was central to Quaker principle and practice. They accurately anticipated non-Quakers' objections: Friends repudiated carnal weapons now, but what if Christ guided them to sell their coats and buy swords? Because onlookers saw that Quaker politics was ultimately grounded in their religious convictions, they worried that if the Light of Christ led Friends to militance, their previous commitments would disappear. The Quaker authors responded: "That Spirit of Christ by which we are guided, is not changeable, so as once to command us from a thing as evil, & again to move unto it."[9] They argued for the permanence of the Peace Testimony by grounding militance in the sinful impulses of lust and covetousness, and peacefulness in the principle of loving enemies. However, these arguments by implication put Anglican royalists on morally shaky ground.

Other nonconformists also scrambled to protest their loyalty that January of 1661. Closely associated with the 1649 regicide, Congregationalists, or Puritans, had perhaps the most daunting task in proclaiming any kind of convincing allegiance. While Charles II had declared a general pardon in the Declaration of

Breda, he made a priority of executing and mutilating the bodies of the judges who had condemned his father to death, many of whom were Congregationalists. But at least they could appeal to the language of the Savoy Declaration of 1658. In Congregationalists' 1661 letter to the king, they quoted the section "Of the Civil Magistrate" from the Savoy Declaration at length. One part addressed subjects' duty to obey even an ungodly ruler: "to pray for Magistrates, to honor their persons, to pay them Tribute and other dues, to obey their lawful commands, and to be subject to their Authority for conscience sake. Infidelity, or difference in Religion, doth not make void the Magistrates just and legal Authority, nor free the people from their obedience to him."[10] This part mirrored the Westminster Confession. Its qualifications of obedience only to "lawful commands" and "for conscience sake" left some room for resistance, but at least authority was not dependent on orthodoxy and the magistrates' persons were to be honored. Calvinists had spent the last hundred years developing theories justifying the resistance of lesser magistrates to ungodly rulers.[11] As J. Sears McGee has pointed out, "implicit or explicit in most puritan writing, was the conviction that the truly godly man could perform cheerful, complete obedience only to equally godly magistrates."[12] However, the Savoy Declaration language proved somewhat useful to English Puritans in this crucial moment. It was an "artifice of Satan," they said, that they were being charged as Vennerites. The revolt's "diustrbance [*sic*] and destruction of those States which yet by Christ do Reign" was a "daring madness," on par with the barbarous inhumanity of Münster. The Kingdom of Christ, the new Heaven and new Earth, they proclaimed, is "never to be set up by outward Violence."[13] Repudiating violent millennialism of the Fifth Monarchist variety, Puritans tried to ground their loyalty in biblical and creedal mandates to obedience. While both Quakers and Puritans could decry plotting and eschew violent methods, neither professed the kind of unqualified loyalty the king or his supporters wanted to hear.

Both Puritans and Quakers were trying to proclaim loyalty in the face of deeply rooted antagonism. A bitter Cavalier Parliament was already trying to overturn the king's Declaration of Breda, convinced that nonconformists could not truly be loyal subjects. Many in this Parliament were high Anglicans, embracing formal liturgy and hierarchy in the church. Their assumptions about the incompatibility of nonconformity and political stability emerged from the experience of the Interregnum as well as long-standing religious norms. Traditionally Anglicans considered obedience to the ruler to be a central part of religious devotion, and they distrusted the piety of individuals who made a habit of evaluating their rulers' wisdom. Thus, in Jacqueline Rose's words, "Anglican royalists positively reveled in their claims to be the *only* upholders of true Christian obedience" in stark contrast with nonconformists.[14]

And pious obedience was more than a commitment not to rebel; it encompassed submission of the whole person, including thoughts and affections.[15] As seen earlier, the 1660 proclamation by Parliament used the language "heartily" and joyfully" to describe obedience.[16] These theological assumptions about affectionate obedience had long been incorporated into English law. When the definition of sedition was clarified and developed as a legal category under Elizabeth, it involved not only slanders or libels on public officials but also speech that alienated the rulers from "the sounde and well affected parte of the subiectes." Sedition was at least in part an interior category, a category of the heart as well as speech and action. One of the preeminent legal minds behind the early modern English framework for sedition, Sir Edward Coke partially derived his understanding of libel and sedition from Ecclesiastes 10, which, in the King James Bible, reads "The indignacion of the harte is treason." It was clear to Coke from this verse that libel was libel, and "a greate offence," even if it was true.[17] The harm was in alienating others' affections from the magistrate or monarch.[18] True loyalty meant a loyalty of the heart.

The brilliant young Quaker preacher and pamphleteer Edward Burrough took on the challenge of proving Quakers' sincere allegiance. Slow to embrace the Peace Testimony, he may have seen that it raised as many problems as it solved. In wartime, those who did not take up arms would have a very hard time proving themselves loyal citizens. He had urged soldiers to serve the cause of God and contend for "liberty, both in Spiritualls and Temporalls."[19] Burrough may have been especially attuned to shoring up Friends' reputation with the new king because he had issued some statements in the late 1650s that could be taken as distinctly antimonarchical in flavor. Burrough had looked forward with excitement to the rule of the [Quaker] saints, who would "bind Kings in chains and Nobles in fetters of iron," overturning them as Pharaoh in Egypt.[20] Most of England's kings, Burrough had claimed, had rejected the Lord's word and his wisdom. They lacked the Spirit, and so lacked true authority. Therefore, "they are as the Potsherds of the Earth that the Iron Rod must break in pieces."[21] This dramatic language required some explaining post-Restoration. So did Burrough's 1659 letter to the Committee of Safety and Council of Officers, where he had declared himself "an Ambassadour from the only Heir of the Government, whose Right alone it is to Rule: And by special Authority and Commission from him [Jesus], this is sent unto them, that they may . . . deliver up the proper Right of the only King unto him."[22] Burrough's claim to ambassadorship, on a divine mission to tell England's leaders to acknowledge Jesus as King, sounds less overblown when we remember that Burrough, like other Quaker prophets, was speaking not as an autonomous subject, but "as heteronomous agent for Christ." This agency was sustained by an overwhelming sense of the power of God and an "assertion of a subjective continuity with that power."[23] As Quakers viewed their own prophetic role as directly empowered by God, so they believed individual magistrates' power derived directly from divine mandate. Burrough's challenge was to maintain the primacy of divine authority while assuring the king that Quakers were his most loyal subjects of all.

In May 1660, just after the Restoration of the monarchy and about half a year before Venner's uprising, Burrough had sketched a preliminary Quaker theory of sovereignty and subjecthood by way of responding to a set of queries by a supposed friend of the king. Though young, Burrough was already an accomplished polemicist, having engaged in debate with John Bunyan and Richard Baxter.[24] He began in conciliatory terms, identifying Quakers as those who suffered but did not oppress and who desired the "good of all." He then addressed the burning question: do Friends "adjuge it Reasonable and Equitable that" Charles II should "inherit the Nations of which is born the right Heir?" Burrough answered "yes" in a particular sense: his restoration was "through the purpose of the Lord," which was always reasonable and just. Though Quakers, he added, were waiting to see if he would indeed reign with justice. Burrough went forward with painful honesty to recall the "very great Oppressions and Vexations" of the reign of Charles I, who was displaced because the "Lord was offended" at his rule.[25] The legitimacy of a ruler, he argued, was conditional on pleasing God.

In a separate, appended treatise, Burrough directly answered an objection regarding "the Kings Supremacy": whether Quakers would accept Charles II as "Lawful King, and own his Supremacy, and will obey him willingly or unwillingly, and be Subjects in Conscience, or against our Consciences?" This was a very difficult question, and Burrough answered it in a way that was consistent with Quaker principles but would no doubt have confused a royalist. Quakers, he said, would obey any authority over them "either by doing and fulfilling their just Commands, or by suffering under their Commands which have been unjust." Friends' willingness to suffer the penalties for breaking unjust laws (such as those requiring tithes or oaths) demonstrated their long-term commitment to the well-being of the state. Conscientious objection, willingness to suffer the consequences of disobeying unjust laws, was itself a form of obedience. In other words, Quakers' allegiance to their own conscience was ultimately in the best interest of the regime and so should not be considered seditious. And Quakers could accept the king in the sense of "believing that he is set to Rule in this Nation, not without, but by, and according to the purpose of the Lord." Earthly power did not exist apart from divine mandate. Quakers would make this point repeatedly in the years to come: if the Lord withdrew his blessing, Charles II would be overthrown. Yet even with these caveats, Quakers who maintained upright lives honored the king more than all those who proclaimed his sovereignty with "Drinking Healths, and Bonfires."[26] Much more than partying royalists, it was Quakers who would keep the king on the throne. While it made sense within a Quaker cosmos, Burrough's understanding of the moral and spiritual contingency of kingship was more likely to incense than placate already-suspicious royalists after Venner's uprising.

In a post-Venner 1661 tract Burrough made it a point to affirm that Quakers "do acknowledge Government, and Rule, and Magistracy to be an Ordinance of God." However, he maintained his earlier position that Charles II's government, though established by God's will, was in effect "for the Cause, and End, and Time, and Purpose, known to Himself, and not to mortal man." Burrough further clarified: God was giving the king time to prove that he was able to rule with "Truth, Justice and Righteousness, Mercy and Peace"—if he succeeded "God may establish" Charles II's reign "for long continuance." Quakers would obey righteous laws actively and wicked laws passively, like the biblical Daniel obeying God rather than men. When they broke the law, however, Quakers were not doing so in "Contempt" or "Rebellion against the Kings Person or Government" but rather for "good Conscience sake."[27] In keeping with Coke's definition of sedition, intentionality mattered. Quakers might disobey, but they did so for the king's own good. Even so, Charles II's right to the throne was probationary, not secure.

Burrough, Endicott, and the "Interest of Caesar"

After Venner's revolt Burrough also developed a more circuitous, but perhaps more effective practice of reading others' statements of allegiance to the king and countering them in print. Quakers could demonstrate their loyalty and value to the realm by informing the royal government of the true state of his other subjects' hearts. The leaders of Massachusetts Bay were an obvious target. They had recently executed three Quaker missionaries, William Robinson, Marmaduke Stephenson, and Mary Dyer, who had returned to the colony after banishment on pain of death. Further, unlike London Congregationalists, colonists could not come quickly to their own defense.[28] Letters could take six weeks or more to reach London from Boston, if they were not lost at sea. And so, rather than continuing to compete with other religious groups' arguments based on divine-right monarchy or unqualified obedience to English law, Burrough set out to affirm Quakers' loyalty by way of contrast to those rebellious Congregationalists overseas.

Evaluating Massachusetts governor John Endicott's February 1660/1 letter to the king, Burrough offered to clear all doubt from the king's heart on the matter of which group really feared God and honored the king. Endicott's letter was a belated attempt to congratulate the king on his restoration to the throne and, above all, to plead for continuance of the Massachusetts Bay charter. In his denunciation of Endicott's letter, Burrough insisted that he had "no desire for Revenge" or "to incense the King against" New England. He was trying to be consistent with Quakers' stated priority of loving enemies. Yet, Burrough continued, "duty to God and the King teacheth me, and love constraineth me . . . to spread our denyal of their bitter and malicious Accusations." While New

Englanders sought "to cover themselves, and to hide their Wickedness before thee," Burrough would reveal their true nature as fawners and flatterers.[29]

Massachusetts Bay's treatment of Quakers was itself evidence that Puritan hearts were disloyal to the king. Burrough explained, "Is not this derogating from the Honour and Authority of the King, for the subordinate Magistrates of New-England to usurp such Authority over free-born People of England, as to prevent them from Egress and Regress in lawful occasions in any part of the Kings Dominions?" By regulating who could enter and leave the colony, Massachusetts was usurping royal authority and overreaching their charter: "I suppose this will be found contrary to their Patent and Prescription, delivered them by Charles the First."[30] Through claiming that the General Court had violated, and therefore nullified, their charter, Burrough in effect declared Massachusetts Bay seditious and politically illegitimate. Massachusetts Bay's "contempt and derision" of Quakers, Burrough argued, was actually a form of contempt for the king. And so he expressed Quakers' own affectionate loyalty for the king by proving Massachusetts Bay's falsity of both affection and action.

In the post-Venner letter Burroughs was reading, Endicott had struggled to profess loyalty to a king who was known to seek Catholic allies. Mustering genuine affection for Charles II had been both necessary and near-impossible. The best he could do was to declare New England's inadequacy: "We forget not our Ineptness as to these approaches, we at present owne such impotencie, as renders us unable to excuse our impotencie of speaking unto our Lord the King." This powerlessness to speak to the king encompassed both physical and emotional distance. Endicott could not approach the king as rulers ought to be approached, in person and with heartfelt loyalty. How could he maintain integrity without putting the Massachusetts Bay charter in further jeopardy? Endicott found his way to an expression of loyalty through an identification with the king as an outcast and exile. It was through connection with this "aspect of Majestie" that he could "present this script, the transcript of our loyall hearts into your Royall handes." However, Endicott quickly moved to comparing his own community's support for the king with Quakers' enmity. Colonists were the defenders of order and the civil state, he averred; Quakers were "open enemies to Government it self, as established in the hands of any but men of their own Principles." Quakers' practice of publicly cursing magistrates and repeatedly defying laws made them, in Endicott's view, dangerous subversives. It was Quakers, not Puritans, who were "seditious to the Interest of Caesar."[31]

Burrough decided that given Endicott's attack, he had to work even harder to communicate Quaker loyalty and puritan hypocrisy. Quaker practice, he wrote in March 1661, had never been "to vilifie nor rebel against any Government or Governours."[32] Burrough was on thin ice here, speaking about a group who regularly interrupted court sessions, cursing ministers and magistrates to their face. Yet disobedience for conscience's sake, as he had argued consistently, was the truest form of loyalty because it helped the king reign with justice. The ultimate act of godly disobedience was martyrdom, and so Burrough turned to defending the recent Quaker martyrs' sacrifice, which, in his view, was ultimately for the good of the realm. Endicott had argued that by returning to Massachusetts Bay after being banished on pain of death, the Quaker martyrs ran themselves into the sword, dying as foolish criminals. Having written a version of Mary Dyer's martyrology and edited one of her letters, Burrough knew the details of her story well.[33] However, he chose not to respond with emotion to Endicott's claims but rather to simply point out that Endicott's "poor Evasions . . . ought not to cover them from the Justice of God, nor from the Justice of the King." Burrough might have stopped here, but he felt the need to defend Dyer's decision to return twice after banishment: "for it's to be considered, that where God commands one thing, and men another, God ought to be obeyed rather than men." Burrough was in the awkward position of having to convince the king that Quakers were right to defy the law when they acted by direct inspiration of the Holy Spirit. "[I]t is fully believed by us that these Sufferers did not go into new-England in their own cause, but in Gods Cause, and in the Motion of his Holy Spirit."[34] The Holy Spirit moved Dyer to return to Massachusetts Bay after banishment, and might also move Quakers to disobey the laws of England.

Burrough thus addressed a profound paradox in Quakers' understanding of civil disobedience, a paradox that was at the core of their argument to be the king's best subjects. Even if it led them to break the law, faithfulness to God's cause would, in the end, shore up the current regime. When Puritans broke the law, they did so without love or the Spirit, and so they were the true rebels. Moved only by their own self-interest, Puritan colonists who disobeyed the law were subject to legitimate punishment. For Endicott to claim that Quakers were seditious was "back-biting and slandering in the highest degree," Burrough claimed, and so "punishable by the Laws of God and Men." By claiming "Absolute Power" the Boston court assumed a "usurped Authority."[35] Their contempt and presumption constituted the true danger to the realm.

Burrough also brought as evidence a Puritan letter from the mid-1650s (probably from Richard Bellingham to John Gurdon) that grouped Charles (the son) with Quakers and "the Popish Princes of Germany" as those dangerous parties who might "trouble and overcome" Cromwellian England.[36] It was not hard to find anti-Stuart phrases in old Puritan correspondence. Burrough was realizing that proving others' disloyalty might be a more direct path to the kings' favor than proclamations of the Lord's power over all. Like Endicott, Burrough struggled to express his own affection to the king. However, he was able to adroitly advise the king on how he might best elicit the affection of his people. By punishing seditious and schismatic New England the king would "engage the hearts of many honest People unto Thee" across his realm.[37] Quaker insight into his subjects' hearts could ensure the king's success more than anything New England could offer.

With all the condemnations of the violence and turbulence of the Interregnum circulating in print in the early 1660s, nonconformists felt the need to distance their sect from the civil wars. Burrough and Endicott were no exception. Burrough did so not by pointing to the chronology of the Quaker faith, which by most accounts dated to midcentury. Perhaps he did not want to emphasize his sect's newness, or his own youth (he had been in his early teens in the 1640s). Rather, he argued by way of moderation and intention: Quaker converts who had fought against the king in the Parliamentary army did so "not in rebellion against him or his Father, as that we fought their destruction as men." So even if they took up arms against royalist troops, they did not seek regicide. Further, they joined the army "upon Sober & Reasonable Principles" rather than for riches or honors.[38] Though fighting against the king's army, those men who would become Quakers did so with pure intentions and moderate actions, Burrough claimed. Endicott dealt with the problem of the civil wars in more general terms by claiming New England was grateful to have stayed neutral. "Our Lot after the example of the Good Old Non Conformist," he argued, "hath been only to Act a Passive part throughout these late Vicissitudes and successive Overturnings of State." He wrote this statement knowing that many colonists went back to England in order to fight or serve as chaplains.[39] For both Quakers and Puritans, proving their loyalty involved creative maneuvering to work around the number of civil war veterans still active in both religious communities.

Endicott and Burrough also shared concerns about falsified or unfavorable information that was reaching the king's court, though they expressed it in different ways. Endicott wrote in a formal and learned style: "Touching complaints put in against us, our humble Request only is, that for the Interim wherein we are dumb, by reason of absence, Your Majesty would permit nothing to make an Impression upon your Royal heart against us, until we have opportunity and license to answer for our selves." He then quoted a line attributed to the fourth-century Roman emperor Julian: "Few will be nocent, said that Impleader, if it be enough to denie; few will be innocent, replyed the then Emperour, if it be enough to accuse."[40] By invoking Julian, commonly known as Julian the Apostate, Endicott may have been making a backhanded point that fellow Puritans would appreciate more than royalist intelligentsia.

A farmer in rural Westmorland before his career as a Quaker preacher, Burrough was not in a position to quote learned sources, and probably would have avoided them in any case. With regard to false reports, Burrough simply requested that Friends might know of any "Informations and Accusations" that petitioners or detractors brought to the king. Like Puritans, Quakers were worried that they might "suffer prejudice or suspition in the Kings mind" before

Quaker apologists could counter false charges. However, he concluded his plea on a powerful note of supernatural confidence: "for there is not any thing, whereof we can be accused, concerning either Civil or Religious Matters, but I hope we can make our Defence clear, and prove Gods Innocency, with which we are cloathed."[41] Quaker innocence was a supernatural innocence, as their authority to discern hearts was a supernatural authority.

Burrough would die in prison in 1663, confident to the end that the Quaker witness would usher in England's commitment to justice.[42] Rather than emphasizing the Peace Testimony, he argued creatively and passionately for Quaker allegiance by explaining the paradox that even when Quakers broke the law, they had the best interests of the realm at heart. Friends were the king's best subjects because their righteousness would extend his reign. After Venner's revolt, Burrough continued with these arguments but also focused his attention on contrasting Quakers' heartfelt loyalty with Endicott and other colonial Congregationalists' mundane, power-hungry intentions. Though Puritan New England seemed like it had the most value to the realm in terms of potential tax revenue and militia recruits, Quakers' righteousness and their ability to discern English subjects' true hearts would in the end bring the king a long and happy rule.

Christiansen and Rotten Hearts

Burrough's method of proving Quaker loyalty through their role as discerners of hearts was taken up in the colonies by Quaker missionaries. The little-known story of Wenlock Christiansen and his argument with Boston magistrates over who had more true affection for the king provides a glimpse of Quaker discernment of true subjecthood in a more spontaneous context. In early 1661 Christiansen dramatically appeared at court on the day of William Leddra's trial. Leddra, a Quaker missionary, had previously been banished on pain of death in Massachusetts Bay. He then continued his missionary work in Plymouth colony, where he was imprisoned for ten months. After his release Leddra returned to preach in Boston, knowing a death sentence awaited him. Christiansen had also been banished on pain of death, and so the court now had two potential martyrs on their hands. According to the Quaker chronicler Joseph Besse, Christiansen's appearance struck the court with "a sudden Damp and Consternation, so that for some Time there was a general Silence."[43] Christiansen knew that his performance at court had more than one audience. His mission was to convince the court of their unjust laws. He sought to encourage the Quakers in prison and the local Quaker community, based mostly in Salem. He also desired to make a public statement about Quaker allegiance and Puritan disloyalty.

A divided General Court had good reason to retreat into silence, faced with the prospect of adding another martyr to the Quaker rolls. Endicott spoke up first, asking Christiansen point blank "why he might not die"—meaning, why should the Court not sentence him to death? Christiansen answered calmly that he had "done nothing worthy of death." Referring to a Bible verse from 1 Samuel, another magistrate said that Christiansen had "come in amongst us . . . in Rebellion, which is as the Sin of Witchcraft, and ought to be punished." Christiansen retorted, "I came not in among you in Rebellion . . . but in obedience to the God of Heaven, not in contempt to any of you, but in love to your Souls and Bodies." Intentionality and the higher law mattered more than obedience to human law. Christiansen's acts, though illegal, were the furthest things from rebellion because they were not done in contempt. Interrupting their court session in order to call the magistrates to a higher standard of justice, for Christiansen, was an act of loyalty and Christian love, because his goal was to prepare them for the "Righteous Judgements of God." Christiansen followed up this ominous warning with prophetic judgment: "God doth but wait, till the measure of your Iniquity be filled up, and that you have run your ungodly race, then will the Wrath of God come upon you to the uttermost."[44] Divine wrath, he prophesied directly to Major-General Humphrey Atherton, was hanging over his head, as if in a bucket, just about to be poured out at the moment he least expected it. This vivid rhetoric was normative for Quaker prophesy. But Christiansen then went in a different direction as he pursued a public statement of contrasting loyalties. He pressed the magistrates on the limits of their patent and the status of their hearts toward the king.

Like Burrough, Christiansen had read Endicott's 1660/1661 letter to Charles II in which he tried to affirm the colonists' loyalty and plead for protection of the charter. He pressed the Boston magistrates on the nature of their subjecthood—were they truly the king's subjects? Stunned at the question, Edward Rawson replied, "What good will that do you?" Christiansen then made his point, "in your Petition to the King, you desire that he would protect you, and that you may be worthy to kneel amongst his Royal Subjects." When they acknowledged the petition, Christiansen continued: "So am I; and for anything I know, am as good as you, if not better; for if the King did but know your hearts, as God knows them, he would see that your hearts are as rotten towards him, as they are towards God."[45] He then demanded to be tried by English rather than colonial law. Elizabeth Hooton, Edward Wharton, and others would similarly accuse the Massachusetts magistrates of disloyalty to or abuse of the king, in contrast to Quakers' faithfulness.[46]

Thus Burrough's method of serving the king by revealing the duplicitous nature of other nonconformists' expressions of loyalty was picked up by Quaker missionaries in the colonies. It was also highlighted and developed by Quaker polemicists. The chronicler of Christiansen's story, George Bishop, added a note in his text's margins at the point where the Boston magistrates accused Christiansen of coming in rebellion: "But are you of the same mind now, who are turned rebels to the King?" Bishop concluded his narrative by contrasting Christiansen's sincerity with Massachusetts agent John Leverett's duplicity, affirming that Congregationalists "seemed to Kneel before" the king with their "lips" though their "hearts were far from him."[47] While Quakers could not state their allegiance in traditional fashion, they could serve the king by discerning who were his true subjects, who served him with loyal hearts.

The Rhode Island Debate in Context

Over the next decade the Cavalier Parliament instituted laws, known as the Clarendon Code, that severely limited freedom of worship and political rights for English nonconformists. Thousands of Quakers, Puritans, and Baptists were imprisoned for refusing to pay tithes or take loyalty oaths or for meeting in groups of more than five. Hundreds died of disease and malnutrition in prison. In the midst of these very difficult years, the competition over heartfelt subjecthood continued. Awarded a generous charter by Charles II in 1663, Rhode Island became a place of extraordinary freedom for Quakers, who soon gained control of the government. It is not surprising, then, that Rhode Island became an important stage for the Quakers' effort to prove their loyalty and others' disloyalty.

A decade after Venner's revolt, Quakers and Roger Williams engaged in the most heated effort yet to prove their worth in the eyes of the king. In this case, Roger Williams was arguing on behalf of New England. Despite his earlier banishment, Williams maintained close relationships, as well as business partnerships, with leaders in Connecticut and Massachusetts Bay. While he did not reconcile to Congregationalist theories of government, he was an orthodox Calvinist on most counts. Because he believed magistrates had no spiritual authority to do otherwise, he allowed Quakers to settle in Rhode Island. However, he considered their theology spiritually dangerous and morally detestable. And so he took it upon himself to defend Protestant New England against the Quaker menace through an open debate. Most scholarly treatments of the 1672 debate focus on either on the complex theological differences raised or the breakdown of decorum. However, the larger audience on both sides was understood to be the Stuart government.[48] One of the main points under discussion was Williams's contention "that the Spirit of their [Quaker] Religion tends mainly . . . To a sudden cutting off of People, yea of Kings and Princes opposing them." The debate thus gave Quakers a platform to expand their efforts to prove their loyalty and to serve the king by disclosing Puritan New Englanders' true affections.

The debate was originally supposed to be between Roger Williams and George Fox, who had visited Rhode Island on his 1672 colonial tour. However, Williams's invitation somehow arrived after Fox departed. An aging Williams instead spent four days debating Quaker missionaries William Edmundson, John Burnyeat, and John Stubbs. The debate was ostensibly about theological divergence between

Quakers and other Protestants. However, Williams himself noted that "your Majestyes Name is often mentioned and concerned in these Concertations."[49] And as both sides wrote their versions of the event, continuing their argumentation in printed works, the politics of godly loyalty emerged as central to the episode.

In his account of the debate, *George Fox Digg'd Out of his Burroughs*, Roger Williams added an epistle dedicatory to Charles II. Williams styled himself as writing on behalf of "your New-English Subjects" in order to inform the king of the serious religious disagreements between "the Protestants and the Quakers." Williams prayed that God would "preserve your Royal Spirit" from the "Cheatings," of both Quakers and the Pope, "that is from the Oracles of Hell in their mouths."[50] Quakers only pretended to be meek, according to Williams. In reality, "G. Fox sets up his Saints . . . to be the higher Powers, as knowing who Worship God aright, and who not, and only able to judge of Powers, and Magistrates, Kingdomes and Churches."[51] Williams thus recognized and deliberately set out to undermine the Quaker mission to serve as the king's discerners of hearts.

Soon after Williams's treatise was printed, George Fox and John Burnyeat gathered at William Penn's home in order to craft their own competing account, *N.E. Fire-Brand Quenched*. In it they argue that Williams "goes about to flatter the King, (but the Lord knoweth his heart, and the hearts of you New England Professors were and are manifest)." It is Williams, not the Quakers who "abuse the King. . . . But does R.W. think, that the King will not see through his flatteries and vain applauses?" New Englanders are not "a Glory to the Protestant Name" as Williams boasted. Rather, they are worse than "Papists" in their persecutions (neither side seemed to be aware of Charles II's Catholic leanings). Roger Williams's very prayer was "unmerciful, unnatural and wicked"—"Here the King and his Councel may see, what Spirit the New-England Priests are of, by Roger Williams their great Oratour." As Burrough had for Endicott, Fox and Burnyeat took the time to scour Williams's earlier writings for anti-Stuart rhetoric. In a 1652 epistle to Lady Vane they found Williams's statement that God had "Crowned the Memory of those his Second Zealous Servants in King Henry the Seventh his Days with a most Eminent, Blessed succession of such Names and Spirits at this Day, Cromwel and Lambert." This particular example gained punch from the fact that Lady Vane was the wife of Sir Henry Vane the Younger, executed in 1662 for treason. Fox and Burnyeat also found a statement in Williams's 1652 *Bloudy Tenant* that Charles I's ruin was due to his willingness "to oppress the Consciences of others."[52] In Quakers' estimation, Williams, like all the New England clergy, were enemies to the Stuart monarchy.

How exactly the king's name or interest was used in the actual debate is unknown, though it is unsurprising that it was frequently invoked.[53] To say that the debate was in part about demonstrating loyalty is not to deny that it was a sincere, if raucous, attempt at theological persuasion. It is very difficult to splice religion from politics in this era. The debaters, and then Williams, Fox, and

Burnyeat in their treatises, turned their attention to the problem of authentic, godly political allegiance because it was still a live issue and would have enormous repercussions on the king's colonial policy.

Conclusion

Nonconformist leaders knew well that Venner's revolt altered the landscape of English politics and necessitated creative, careful statements with regard to royal authority. The Restoration era would see a deluge of indictments for seditious speech emerging from discontent with the government and the Church of England. Even insiders admitted at times that an intense conversion experience made sincere affection for the king problematic.[54] Given their unique theological commitments, Quakers could not affirm the king's legitimacy on the same grounds as Anglicans or even Puritans.[55] Continuing to withhold tithes and interrupt church services and court meetings, Quakers viewed their disobedience as ultimately an act of loyalty because it averted divine judgment that might overthrow the regime.

While Quakers and Puritans diverged significantly, they had more in common with each other than they did with high Anglicans. These commonalities become more clear when their attempts to profess loyalty are read side by side. Both eschewed violence as a path to the millennial kingdom. Both avoided effusive, saccharine praise, hewing close to an ethic of plainness. Both worried about false or exaggerated news and tried to distance their veterans from the worst excesses of the Parliamentary army. And both argued that their success—moral and practical—would contribute to the success of the realm.

Though they continued to preach the Peace Testimony, most Quakers realized they would need additional methods of proving themselves good subjects. Attending to other nonconformists' inadequacies, falsities, and anti-Stuart pasts served as a powerful deflection. As they suffered disproportionately under the Clarendon Code, Quakers' critique of other nonconformists' narratives took attention off their own inability to say, without equivocation, that the king deserved or belonged on the throne. Edward Burrough and others knew well that for the king to believe one group meant disbelieving the other. While perhaps not a zero-sum game, the extent and intensity of Quaker–Puritan polemics would have made it difficult to believe both sides at once. Burrough, Christiansen, and eventually Fox and Burnyeat found a promising way to respond to concerns about their political loyalties by disclosing New Englanders' flattering, rotten hearts. Providing the king with valuable information about colonial deceit positioned them as loyal subjects of the realm even as they routinely defied its laws.

Historically, Fox and other Quaker prophets at various times had hoped for a godly prince to usher in a reign of righteousness, and they struggled to interpret "the experience of defeat" with the fall of the Cromwellian regime.[56] On a practical level, reining in the insurgent fringe was the most difficult task of all for Quakers. Members of the group probably *were* involved in plots to overthrow Charles II; the commitment to nonviolence took hold in different ways regionally, and not every Quaker complied.[57] Aware of these issues, Quaker performances in print, courtrooms, and debates addressed both internal and external challenges. As they demonstrated loyalty by calling out its opposite, they also encouraged recalcitrant Quakers to accept the monarchy. Aware that their version of true subjecthood might look like rebellion, Quakers developed multiple paths toward making their peace with the king.

NOTES

1. Even the home of John Owen (former dean of Christ Church at Oxford, leading Congregationalist, and friend of the young William Penn) was raided. Richard Greaves, "Owen, John," *Oxford Dictionary of National Biography.*

2. Secretary Nicholas to Sir Henry Bennet, *Calendar of State Papers, Domestic, 1660–1661* (London, 1860), 476; Richard Greaves, *Deliver Us from Evil: The Radical Underground in Britain, 1660–1663* (New York: Oxford University Press, 1986), 56. The years between 1659 and 1662 showed an outpouring of Quaker works to the government or addressing the nature of godly government. "Appendix: Types of Quaker Writings by Year—1650–1699" in Hugh Barbour and Arthur O. Roberts, eds., *Early Quaker Writings, 1650–1700* (Grand Rapids, MI: Eerdmans, 1973), 567–569.

3. George Fox, *The Journal of George Fox,* ed. Norman Penney (Cambridge: Cambridge University Press, 1911), 1:371, 361–362, 370. On Quaker repudiation of divine-right monarchy, and their subordination of reason to collective spiritual intuition, see Jane Calvert, *Quaker Constitutionalism and the Political Thought of John Dickinson* (New York: Cambridge University Press, 2009), 67–78. However, Andrew Murphy makes a compelling case for William Penn's embrace of reason alongside the Inner Light in his political philosophy. Andrew Murphy, *Liberty, Conscience, and Toleration: The Political Thought of William Penn* (New York: Oxford University Press, 2016), 8, 49–52, 125–133. On Burrough's use of reason in his theological argumentation, see also Pink Dandelion and Stephen Angell, "Outcasts of Israel: The Apocalyptic Theology of Edward Burrough and Francis Howgill," *Early Quakers and Their Theological Thought* (New York: Cambridge University Press, 2015), 124–125.

4. Richard L. Greaves, "Shattered Expectations? George Fox, the Quakers, and the Restoration State, 1660–1685," *Albion*, 24, no. 2 (Summer, 1992), 237–239; Larry Ingle, *First among Friends: George Fox and the Creation of Quakerism* (New York: Oxford, 1996), 8, 189–191; Hugh Barbour, *Quakers in Puritan England* (New Haven: Yale University Press, 1964), 203–205; 218–223; Kate Peters, *Print Culture and the Early Quakers* (New York: Cambridge University Press, 2005), 205–206.

5. Margaret Fell, *A Declaration and an Information from us the People of God called Quakers* (London, 1660), 4; Elsa F. Glines, *Undaunted Zeal: The Letters of Margaret Fell* (Richmond, IN: Friends United Press, 2003), 277, 282.

6. Parliament of England and Wales, *A Proclamation of Both Houses of Parliament* (London, 1660), 1.

7. Fox, *Journal,* 1:371, 361–362, 370. See also Ingle, *First among Friends,* 190–192.

8. For more on the early theology and practice of nonviolence see Meredith Weddle, *Walking in the Way of Peace: Quaker Pacifism in the Seventeenth Century* (New York: Oxford University Press, 2001), chaps. 1–3.

9. George Fox et al., *A Declaration from the Harmles & Innocent People of God, Called Quakers, Against All Plotters and Fighters in the World* (London, 1660), 1–3, 5–6. See also George Fox, *A Word in the Behalf of the King* (London, 1660), 5, 9.

10. Joseph Caryl et al., *A Renuntiation and Declaration of the Ministers of Congregational Churches . . . Against the Late Horrid Insurrection* (London, 1661), 8–9, 3, 5; "Savoy Declaration," in Williston Walker, *Creeds and Platforms of Congregationalism* (New York: Scribner, 1893), 394. Nathaniel Mather, Thomas Weld, and John Oxenbridge were also signers. The Savoy Declaration was a revision of the work of the Westminster Assembly and would be adopted in modified form in New England as part of the Reforming Synod of 1679–1680, and Connecticut's Saybrook Platform in 1708 (Walker, *Creeds and Platforms*, 350–353).

11. Robert Kingdon, "Calvinism and Resistance Theory" in *The Cambridge History of Political Thought, 1450–1700* (New York: Cambridge University Press, 1991), 210; John Coffey, *Politics, Religion and the British Revolutions: The Mind of Samuel Rutherford* (New York: Cambridge University Press, 1997), 176–183.

12. J. Sears McGee, *The Godly Man in Stuart England: Anglicans, Puritans, and the Two Tables, 1620–1670* (New Haven: Yale University Press, 1976), 120–122.

13. Caryl et al., *A Renuntiation and Declaration*, 3, 5. Crawford Gribben argues that John Owen's use of the Savoy Declaration in his 1667 *A Peace-offering* may have done more harm than good because "it rooted the development of Independent theology in the events of the revolutionary period" and because the Savoy Declaration, unlike the Westminster Confession, did not confirm "religious obedience to the king." In the third section of the chapter "Of the Civil Magistrate," the Savoy Declaration departed from the Westminster Confession by limiting the king's role in determining and enforcing doctrine. Gribben, *John Owen and English Puritanism: The Experiences of Defeat* (New York: Oxford, 2016), 231; Walker, *Creeds and Platforms*, 393.

14. McGee, *The Godly Man in Stuart England*, 142–152; Jacqueline Rose, *Godly Kingship in Restoration England: The Politics of Royal Supremacy, 1660–1688* (New York: Cambridge, 2011), 12.

15. McGee, *Godly Man in Stuart England*, 149.

16. Parliament of England and Wales, *A Proclamation*, 1.

17. Paul Seaward, *The Cavalier Parliament and the Reconstruction of the Old Regime, 1661–1667* (New York: Cambridge University Press, 1988), 33; McGee, *The Godly Man in Stuart England*, 116–117; "An Advertisement touching seditious wrytings," PRO, SP 12/235/81, quoted in Roger B. Manning, "The Origins of the Doctrine of Sedition," *Albion*, 12, no. 2 (Summer, 1980): 100, 115.

18. This is one reason why scholars have noted that Habermas's public sphere as a "realm of rational debate" sits uneasily with the formation of local political communities in the mid-seventeenth century. The emotions, or better, passions, were central to the political speech and performance. John Staines, "Compassion in the Public Sphere of Milton and Charles" in *Reading the Early Modern Passions: Essays in the Cultural History of Emotion* (Philadelphia: University of Pennsylvania Press, 2004), 92–93.

19. Edward Burrough, *To the Whole English Army* (London, 1659), 1.

20. Edward Burrough, *The vvofull cry of unjust persecutions* (London, 1657), 18–19.

21. Edward Burrough, "To the Present Distracted and Broken Nation of England" in *The Memorable Works of a Son of Thunder and Consolation* (London, 1672), 603–604. See also Rosemary Moore, *Light in Their Consciences: Early Quakers in Britain, 1646–1666* (University Park: Penn State University Press, 2000), 168. In 1659 Burrough wanted Quakers restored to their positions as "officers and Souldiers," expecting the sect to play a prominent role in government. Barry Reay, "The Quakers and 1659: Two Newly Discovered Broadsides by Edward Burrough," *Journal of the Friends' Historical Society*, 54, no. 2 (1977), 110.

22. Edward Burrough, "A Message to the Present Rulers of England" in *The Memorable Works of a Son of Thunder and Consolation* (London, 1672), 588.

23. Hillary Hinds, *George Fox and Early Quaker Culture* (Manchester: Manchester University Press, 2011), 80–81; on Quaker self-transcendence see also Phyllis Mack, *Visionary Women: Ecstatic Prophesy in Seventeenth-century England* (Berkeley: University of California Press, 1992), ch. 4 and 183–186.

24. Edward Burrough, *The true faith of the gospel of peace contended for . . . . Or, an answer to his book called, Some Gospel truths opened* (London, 1656); John Bunyan, *A vindication of the book called, Some Gospel-truths opened . . . the opposition made against it by Edward Borrough . . . examined and confuted* (London, 1657); Catie Gill, "Burrough, Edward," *Oxford Dictionary of National Biography.*

25. Edward Burrough, *A visitation and presentation of love unto the King, and those call'd Royallists* (London, 1660), 3, 7, 13.

26. Burrough, *A visitation and presentation*, 21, 37. For an extended discussion of why civil disobedience was "based on a strong sense of political obligation," see Calvert, *Quaker Constitutionalism*, 63 and chs. 1–2. Phyllis Mack argues that "Righteous and sober Quakers were, in fact, more obedient citizens than the members of some other radical sects." Mack, *Visionary Women*, 132.

27. Edward Burrough, *A just and righteous plea* (London, 1661), 21, 23–25.

28. Jonathan Beecher Field, *Errands into the Metropolis: New England Dissidents in Revolutionary London* (Hanover: University Press of New England, 2009), 107.

29. Edward Burrough, *A declaration of the sad and great persecution and martyrdom of the people of God, called Quakers, in New-England for the worshipping of God . . . . Also, some considerations, presented to the King, which is in answer to a petition and address, which was presented unto him by the general court at Boston: subscribed by J. Endicot, the chief persecutor there; thinking thereby to cover themselves from the blood of the innocent* (London, 1661), 3–11.

30. Edward Burrough, *A declaration of the sad and great persecution*, 3–11.

31. Massachusetts General Court, *The Humble Petition and Address of the General Court sitting at Boston in New-England, unto The High and Mighty Prince Charles the Second* (London, 1660), 5–6.

32. Burrough, *A declaration of the sad and great persecution*, 11.

33. Johan Winsser, "Quieting Mary Dyer: Edward Burrough and Dyer's Letter to the Massachusetts General Court, 26 October 1659," *Quaker History*, 105, no. 1 (2016): 22–47. Burrough moderated Dyer's language, deciding "that it was too audacious to publish as originally written" (24).

34. Burrough, *A declaration of the sad and great persecution*, 11.

35. Burrough, *A declaration of the sad and great persecution*, 11. Bellingham was the deputy governor for Massachusetts Bay, and Gurdon was the Suffolk MP John Gurdon. The letter is also mentioned in Francis Howgill, *Popish Inquisition Newly Erected in New-England* (London, 1659), 68.

36. Burrough, *A declaration of the sad and great persecution*, 11, 14–15.

37. Burrough, *A declaration of the sad and great persecution*, 11, 14–15. Even in an earlier letter titled *A visitation and presentation of love unto the King, and those call'd Royallists* (London, 1660), Burrough did not directly profess affection outside the title. In another tract Burrough pleaded for a cessation of fines and imprisonments of Quakers by arguing that those who conformed either "against their Consciences" or "in the ignorance thereof . . . . will neither be true and faithful in Church nor State . . . and their hearts will be disengaged in love and affection to you-wards." Edward Burroughs, *The case of free liberty of conscience in the exercise of faith and religion presented unto the King and both Houses of Parliament* (London, 1661), 10, 4.

38. Burrough, *A declaration of the sad and great persecution*, 10.

39. Massachusetts General Court, *Humble Petition and Address*, 5. On remigration see Susan Hardman Moore, *Pilgrims: New World Settlers and the Call of Home* (New Haven: Yale University Press, 2007).

40. Ammianus Marcellinus, *Ammianus Marcellinus*, trans. J. C. Rolfe, vol. 1 (Cambridge, Harvard University Press, 1950), XVIII, 1:4; Massachusetts General Court, *Humble Petition and Address*, 5.

41. Burrough, *A declaration of the sad and great persecution*, 32.

42. Barbour, *Quakers in Puritan England*, 224.

43. Joseph Besse, *Collection of the Sufferings* (London, 1753), 2:221.

44. 1 Samuel 15:23 (King James Version): "For rebellion is as the sin of witchcraft, and stubbornness is as iniquity and idolatry." George Bishop, *New England Judged. The Second Part* (London, 1667), 32.

45. Bishop, *New England Judged*, 33. See also William Sewel, *History of the Rise, Increase, and Progress of the People called Quakers* (London, 1722), 278–280; Joseph Besse, *Collection of the Sufferings*, 2:222–223; Nathaniel Shurtleff, *Mass. Records* (Boston, 1854), IV, Part 2:20–21. Christiansen was released.

46. Adrian Chastain Weimer, "Elizabeth Hooton and the Lived Politics of Toleration in Massachusetts Bay," *William and Mary Quarterly*, 3rd ser. 74, no. 1 (2017): 43–76; Besse, *Collection of the Sufferings*, 2:232.

47. George Bishop had been an intelligence agent for the Council of State and served as a well-connected mentor among Friends; he mediated the relationship between his old military colleague Sir William Penn and his son after the younger William Penn embraced Quakerism around 1667. George Bishop to Sir William Penn, in *The Papers of William Penn*, ed. Richard S. Dunn and Mary Maples Dunn (Philadelphia: Penn Press, 1981), 1:54–55. Bishop, *New England Judged*, 32, 38; Sewel, *History of the Rise, Increase, and Progress*, 279–280; Besse, *Collection of the Sufferings*, 2:222. The actual letter from the king arrived with Samuel Shattuck in November.

48. David S. Lovejoy, "Roger Williams and George Fox: The Arrogance of Self-Righteousness," *New England Quarterly*, 66, no. 2 (June 1993): 199–225; Leon R. Camp, "Roger Williams vs. 'The Upstarts': The Rhode Island Debates of 1672," *Quaker History*, 52, no. 2 (Autumn 1963): 69–76; J. William Frost, "Quaker versus Baptist: A Religious and Political Squabble in Rhode Island Three Hundred Years Ago," *Quaker History*, 63, no. 1 (Spring 1974): 39–52. Robert J. Lowenherz, "Roger Williams and the Great Quaker Debate," *American Quarterly*, 11, no. 2, part 1 (Summer 1959): 157–165. Lowenherz puts the debate in the context of Rhode Island politics.

49. Roger Williams, *George Fox Digg'd Out of his Burroughs* (London, 1676), 5.

50. Williams, *George Fox Digg'd*, Epistle Dedicatory.

51. Williams, *George Fox Digg'd*, 5, 318. Lovejoy highlights Williams's need to defend Rhode Island from charges that they abetted Quaker activity ("Roger Williams and George Fox," 206).

52. Fox, *N.E. Fire-Brand Quenched*, 1:4–5; 2:241. The epistle to Lady Vane began Roger Williams's *Experiments of spiritual life & health and their preservatives* (London, 1652). "Second" in the original reads "2" and "Henry the Seventh" in the original is "Henry the 8th." Also in the original Cromwell and Lambert's names are in the margins rather than the text. That Fox and Burnyeat chose the latter statement about Charles I's ruin as an example of disloyalty, when Burrough had pointed out Charles I's oppression directly in his 1660 *A visitation and presentation of love*, indicates how much Quakers had modulated their political critique.

53. Lowenherz says Fox and Burnyeat were working primarily with "a stenographic record of the debate, Burnyeat's recollections, and a copy of Williams's book" ("Roger Williams and the Great Quaker Debate," 157). Henry Cadbury writes that other Quakers at Penn's home that month were also involved in the book's authorship. Cadbury, "George Fox's Later Years" in George Fox, *The Journal of George Fox*, rev. ed. John L. Nickalls (Cambridge: University Press, 1952), 721. Thomas Clarkson in his biography of William Penn speculates that Penn also "assisted" with the book. Clarkson, *Memoirs of the Private and Public Life of William Penn* (Philadelphia, 1814), 1:139.

54. Tim Harris, "Understanding Popular Politics in Restoration Britain," in Alan Craig Houston and Steven Pincus, eds. *A Nation Transformed: England after the Restoration* (New York: Cambridge University Press, 2001), 126–127, 146–147; Buchanan Sharp, "Popular Political Opinion in England 1660–1685," *History of European Ideas* 10 (1989): 13–17; Michael Winship, "Defining Puritanism in Restoration England: Richard Baxter and others respond to *A Friendly Debate*," *Historical Journal*, 54, no. 3 (2011): 694; McGee, *Godly Man in Stuart England*, 134.

55. Greaves, "Shattered Expectations?" 239; Barbour, *Quakers in Puritan England*, 223.

56. Adrian Chastain Weimer, *Martyrs' Mirror: Persecution and Holiness in Early New England* (New York: Oxford, 2011), 104; Christopher Hill, *The Experience of Defeat: Milton and Some Contemporaries* (New York: Viking, 1984).

57. Richard Greaves, "Seditious Sectaries or 'Sober and Useful Inhabitants'?: Changing Conceptions of the Quakers in Early Modern Britain," *Albion*, 33, no. 1 (Spring 2001): 29; Weddle, *Walking in the Way of Peace*, chaps. 3, 9–10.

CHAPTER 15

From Puritan to Quaker

MARY DYER AND PURITAN–QUAKER CONVERSION IN THE SEVENTEENTH-CENTURY ATLANTIC

Rachel Love Monroy

In the spring of 1660 Mary Dyer returned to Boston. She had spent the previous winter on Shelter Island, a small landmass tucked between two peninsulas on the eastern edge of Long Island.[1] Prior to arriving on Shelter Island, Dyer had narrowly escaped death at the hands of Massachusetts puritan magistrates witnessing the executions of her fellow missionaries Marmaduke Stephenson and William Robinson.[2] The former puritan merchant turned Quaker, Nathaniell Sylvester, and his wife Grizzell, welcomed Dyer to Shelter Island along with other Quaker friends, including John Taylor, a former sugar merchant from Barbados, and Grizzell's sister and brother-in-law Sarah and William Coddington. Together the group led meetings and ministered to local Manhassett Indians. Dyer's time on Shelter Island served as a respite, a renewal of sorts that would prepare her for one last journey to Boston.[3]

Dyer's execution in June 1660 quickly became a watershed event in Quaker history, defining later understandings of puritan and Quaker confrontations. Carla Pestana has argued that, while contemporary accounts of Dyer's death reiterated her passionate apocalyptic warnings in the face of puritans' devout stand against heresy, as the radicalism of early Quaker missionaries faded into the pacifism of the eighteenth century, accounts of the first generation were retold to align with contemporary trends. While an eschatological impulse colored the behavior of early Quakers, making them zealous defenders of their faith, a shift toward pacifism in the eighteenth century calmed Quaker urgency and lessened their threat to opposing faiths. The arrival of the Restoration stilled fears and anxieties surrounding the world's end and undermined prophetic language of the previous generation. At the same time, George Fox's journey throughout the

American colonies provided a structure for the growing sect and articulated a new adherence to quietist teachings. Together, these influences encouraged a recasting of the violent Quaker past into a history that reinforced eighteenth-century Quaker values.[4] Mary Dyer's narrative lay at the center of this initiative, and her death helped provide a powerful cornerstone upon which Quaker architects could reposition their faith. Her aggressive and confrontational attributes were replaced with a passive martyrdom tailored to mimic Jesus as the sacrificial lamb being led to the slaughter. This "mythic past" allowed Quakers to depict Dyer as a Christlike figure who quietly succumbed to an unjust death under puritan persecution. Thus Dyer and her fellow Quakers who had died in Boston fit neatly in the tradition of Christian martyrdom depicted both in Scripture and in Fox's *Book of the Martyrs*.

The paradigm of puritan–Quaker opposition has since become an essential historiographical trope in colonial history. In reshaping accounts of early Quaker behavior to align with eighteenth-century religious ideals, Quaker historians set off a flood of scholarship grounded in the dichotomy between puritan and Quaker belief. More recently scholars have begun peeling away the historical layers to reveal the sectarian responses as related reactions to what David Como has labeled the antinomian underground.[5] Birthed out of a milieu of denominational reactions to spiritual discontent with the establishment, both puritanism and Quaker faith shared many characteristics. Geoffrey Nuttall, in his classic *The Holy Spirit in Puritan Faith and Experience*, laid the framework for revisionist scholarship by seeing Quaker faith as a heretical outgrowth of puritan doctrine based on the exaggeration of the Holy Spirit.[6] Building on Nuttall's argument that Quakerism emerged from within the puritan faith through a theological misinterpretation, Tolles argued that Quakerism "cannot be understood unless it is seen as one of the variant expressions of the dominant and all-pervading Puritanism of the age."[7] He too believed that Quakerism, if aberrant from mainline puritan doctrine, emerged from it. In his foundational work on early Quakerism Hugh Barbour also recognized Quakers shared an inheritance with puritanism saying that Quakerism "actually stemmed from the same traditions, and most of their critical doctrines were the same."[8]

Rather than viewing the two belief systems as opposite each other on two ends of the religious spectrum, we can understand their differences as a matter of spiritual progression. They were birthed from the same movement and traveled in the same direction, at least for a time, although Quakers seemed to take that path much farther, where puritans dared not venture. The English Civil War and Interregnum set off an explosion of religious sects and seekers that left English shores and settled throughout the Caribbean and eastern North America.[9] Untethered to a central religious authority, puritans who made their way to the colonies naturally developed their faith according to their own lights, following local leadership and adjusting to the challenges encountered on the colonial frontier.[10]

The Massachusetts Bay colony served as the sole exception, placing strict governance on theology and doctrine and developing a local religious structure to control deviant behavior. In the historiography, puritanism has mistakenly been equated with Massachusetts, leading many to question the authenticity of puritan faith exercised in colonies outside of New England. Rather than viewing Roger Williams and Thomas Hooker as peculiar puritans whose aberrant conduct placed them outside of the Massachusetts devout, we should see their behavior as consistent with a larger expression of puritanism throughout the Atlantic world. It was this strand of Atlantic puritans that Quakers found uniquely appealing in their missionary efforts. They likely saw in the network of believers a weak structure of religious authority, inconsistent access to spiritual resources, and a wealth of untapped connections to similar puritans throughout the Atlantic world. The Quaker missionaries that arrived in the middle of the seventeenth century merely continued a movement that had already been set in motion. Just as Hooker and Williams had left the Massachusetts Bay colony to practice their faith as they saw fit, the congregants of the Ancient Church, leaving England and later Amsterdam in the middle of religious tumult and schism, also sought to practice their faith according to personal convictions. Conversion to Quaker belief offered the ultimate path toward individual faith, an ability to receive divine revelation through the Inner Light.

As people of the book, puritans centered their faith upon Scripture. The doctrine of *sola scriptura* dictated the need to filter any knowledge of the divine through God's written revelation in the Bible. Thus natural revelation, God's voice and actions in the world around them, as well as the witness of the Holy Spirit, God's inner promptings to the believer, were to follow the lead of Scripture and be measured against it for accuracy. The Bible constantly mediated puritans' knowledge of the Divine. Their God was seen and understood through the written words in Scripture, those of Yahweh to Moses on Mount Sinai and Jesus's rebuke of the disciples at Gethsemane. The prompting of an inner voice, a vision that came through a dream, or the sign of a natural wonder were by themselves untrustworthy, for the Holy Spirit did not work apart from Scripture and never challenged God's written revelation.[11]

The Quakers' rejection of Scriptural authority naturally placed them at odds with their puritan neighbors. Denying the necessity of God's Word as a safeguard against unchecked divine revelation through the natural world and the unfettered work of the Holy Spirit, for the orderly puritan, seemed to open a Pandora's box of heretical possibilities. While mature Quaker faith and orthodox puritanism were clearly opposed in their orientation of Scripture, in practice the line was not so clear. Intermittent neglect of Scriptural authority, perhaps through extempore prayer or a puritan's vision of God through a dream, allowed puritans a taste of Quaker experience.[12] Their full journey down the Quaker road may have been spurred on by a lack of spiritual leadership or available resources in remote locales throughout the Atlantic World. While the path between puritan faith and Quaker conversion was not neatly marked by a series of spiritual steps, regulated by an episcopacy, or documented through conversion narratives, many believers made this journey during the middle of the seventeenth century. Perhaps in their desire to follow the promptings of divine providence they had found wanting any hope of supreme assurance. Caught between the aching desire for confirmation of their election and the unknowable reaches of God's will, a number of Atlantic puritans began to embrace what seemed to them a closer, more personal manifestation of the Holy Spirit in George Fox's Inner Light.

While Dyer's death once marked the distance between puritan and Quaker belief, her example can also serve to connect the two faiths and their corresponding historiographies. Dyer's stay on Shelter Island, at the home of former puritan turned Quaker Nathaniell Sylvester, links her to a network of Atlantic puritan communities that underwent widespread Quaker conversion during the middle of the seventeenth century. Examining the full breadth of the puritan Atlantic alongside Quaker missionary work and successful conversion reveals that the two movements did not exist in isolation. Quaker conversion in the Atlantic World was uniquely dependent upon the previous expansion of puritan networks and their proven ability to navigate the geographical, commercial, and political boundaries within the New World. At the same time, Quaker success in converting former puritans relied on a combination of the failure of these puritan networks to maintain a strong connection with a central spiritual authority and the Quakers' ability to tap into an existing movement toward the individual exercise of faith. I argue that what once thrived as the puritan Atlantic during the early seventeenth century was targeted by Quaker missionaries and transformed into a successful network of Quaker believers that capitalized on puritan successes while learning from and improving upon their failures.

Studying the continuum between puritan faith and Quaker conversion reunites Quaker and puritan history, once artificially separated by religious categories. Neither the puritan or the Quaker Atlantic can be properly understood when studied separately, because the individuals at the center of each passed from one faith into the other. An isolated study of Quaker history apart from its puritan past, or the reverse, erases dynamic relationships between puritan fathers and their Quaker children, glosses over the new Quaker convert's struggles to maintain ties to his puritan business colleagues, and ignores the passionate separatists' turn to pacifism. A long view of Quaker history reintroduces this human element. It reveals the complexity of relationships separated along lines of faith, the adaptability of personal conviction, and the spiritual struggles individuals faced in attempting to align commercial pursuits, familial relationships, political interests, and spiritual belief within the seventeenth-century Atlantic world. Studying the Quaker Atlantic apart from its puritan counterpart abbreviates the story as Atlantic Quaker networks seem to materialize from nothing while puritan communities fade away into the colonial backdrop. Reuniting these two histories around the story of the individuals that brought them together reveals a different account of balancing spiritual convictions, familial interests, business pursuits, and political ties in the ever-shifting Atlantic world.

George Fox's 1671 American journey provides a mechanism for studying the widespread transition from puritan to Quaker faith in the seventeenth-century Atlantic. His route draws a clear line between once puritan communities transformed into flourishing centers of Quaker movement. Beginning his journey in Barbados, Fox encountered Nathaniell Sylvester's former puritan business partner, Thomas Rous, a successful Quaker merchant and previous member of the puritan Atlantic. On his way to the Chesapeake, he stopped in Jamaica before arriving in Virginia to meet Nathaniel Basse, a former puritan and business partner of Richard Bennett, the once puritan turned Quaker governor of Virginia. In Maryland Fox came upon the exiled remnant of a puritan settlement from Nansemond, Virginia, that left under Governor Berkeley and converted to Quaker faith after the arrival of missionary Elizabeth Harris. His journey took him northward by way of Indian trails to New Jersey and Rhode Island, where Fox led a meeting with William Coddington, a converted puritan and the Governor of Rhode Island, as well as the brother-in-law of Nathaniell Sylvester. Perhaps at the promptings of Coddington, Fox continued to Long Island and visited Nathaniell Sylvester's plantation, Shelter Island, aptly named as a place of protection and rest for Quaker missionaries, where Dyer once stayed before returning to Boston.

In arriving on Shelter Island, George Fox reunites Mary Dyer's death with the puritan Atlantic that preceded it. Rather than looking to Pendle Hill where Fox was first awakened to the promptings of the Inner Light as the origin of the Quaker Atlantic, historians can now trace the beginnings to the small prison cell where Henry Barrow wrote puritan pamphlets in secret during the winter of 1590–1591. The beginnings of the puritan Atlantic can now mark the origins of the Quaker Atlantic.

When George Fox arrived in the colonies the flourishing puritan settlements of the early seventeenth century had been replaced by centers of Quaker activity. In order to understand fully the impact that the puritan Atlantic had on the birth of Quakerism that followed, this chapter traces the formation of Atlantic puritan networks out of the diaspora of the Ancient Church. I then follow the transition of puritan settlements toward the Quaker faith beginning after the arrival of Quaker missionaries to the colonies in the 1650s. In following the spread of the Ancient Church throughout the colonies and into the Quaker faith we begin to see the continuity between the two faiths, which are usually studied separately. We see families who moved from meeting in conventicles on the south side of the Thames, to worshipping among nonconformists in

Amsterdam travel across the Atlantic to Virginia, Maryland, New York, and Barbados, suffer through the persecution under Anglican majorities, and finally find comfort in Quaker teachings. The once separate and often opposing studies of puritan and Quaker faith can be viewed instead as waypoints of spiritual expression on a religious journey taken by many seventeenth-century nonconformists.

The antecedents of many puritan communities outside of New England found a common origin in the Ancient Church, a separate puritan congregation that began in Southwark, London, under the leadership of Henry Barrow and John Greenwood.[13] After a remnant of the congregation migrated to Amsterdam a later diaspora of the Ancient Church spread adherents throughout the Atlantic colonies from Barbados, to Virginia, Maryland, and Long Island, while leaving some of the remaining congregants in the Netherlands. The initial division was spurred on by pamphlets released by a former member of the church, Christopher Lawne, and the pastor's brother George Johnson. In his 1612 publication, *The Prophane Schism of the Brownists*, Lawne detailed the ghastly sins of his fellow congregants, including "Adulterie, Incest, Murder, Treason, Drunkennesse, Perjurie, and Blasphemie," while hinting at a latent popery within the congregation.[14] Encouraged by his predecessor Lawne, George Johnson released a tell-all pamphlet entitled *A Discourse of Some Troubles and Excommunications in the Banished English Church at Amsterdam* listing the faults of his brother Francis Johnson, and former teachers and elders Henry Ainsworth and Daniel Studley.[15] Lawne followed up his publication by recruiting one hundred equally disgruntled members of the congregation to follow him to Virginia. They left England in March 1619 aboard the *Marigold* and arrived in Virginia on May 20th.[16] Edward Bennett, one of Lawne's congregational rivals, followed him to Virginia in 1621, eventually recruiting as many as six hundred individuals, largely from the Ancient Church congregation, to join him. Bennett, a member of the Virginia Company, along with his nephew Richard, helped to provide substantial financial and political backing for the puritan community in Virginia.[17] Nathaniel Basse, also from the Ancient Church, established a separate settlement known as Basse's Choice and brought an additional one hundred settlers to Virginia. Henry Jacob, a former member of John Robinson's church in Leyden settled at Lawne's plantation between 1622 and 1624. Another elder of the Ancient Church, Francis Blackwell, brought 180 members of the congregation to Virginia, but only 50 survived the journey.[18]

At the same time that many former members of the Ancient Church traveled to Virginia the Sylvester family remained in Amsterdam, eventually establishing puritan roots on Long Island and Barbados. Giles Sylvester, his wife Mary, and their five sons helped to build and strengthen Atlantic puritan networks through their extensive trading interests. Also members of the Ancient Church, the family owned a number of vessels and traded in tobacco, wine, sugar, slaves, and other goods in Virginia, Barbados, New York, Spain, and France.[19] His sons, specifically Nathaniell and Constant Sylvester, followed their father into the business, with Constant managing the family's interests in Barbados and Nathaniell heading up an initiative to establish a provisioning plantation on Shelter Island, New York, which would provide the necessary foodstuffs for their sugar plantations in Barbados. The family also likely purchased tobacco from former members of the Ancient Church on their regular trips to Virginia.[20] While schism threatened to destroy the Ancient Church in Amsterdam, separation and subsequent migration eventually established an extensive network of puritans stretching throughout the Atlantic; a network that would soon become a useful tool in Quaker missionary hands.

In the years following colonial migration, the former members of the Ancient Church strengthened their hold in local communities while maintaining connections with former puritan congregants throughout the Atlantic. In Virginia, Edward Bennett advocated for a Virginia Company tobacco monopoly against Spain to defend puritan tobacco interests, while his nephew Richard pursued a political career alongside former congregant John Utie.[21] The initial transplanted puritan community grew with the addition of other puritans, such as the Irish cattle merchant and planter Daniel Gookin. Their presence on the south side of the James River became so pronounced that Anglican Governor Berkeley eventually saw them as a religiopolitical threat and sought to eradicate the community. When John Winthrop sent ministers to the Virginia puritans from Massachusetts Berkeley ordered them out of the colony. In 1649 nearly three hundred of the Virginia puritans traveled to the Severn and Patuxent Rivers in Maryland under the promised protection of Maryland's governor William Stone.[22] By the middle of the seventeenth century former members of the Ancient Church had built puritan communities in Nansemond, Virginia; Providence, Maryland; Barbados, and Shelter Island, New York. Constant Sylvester's original property holdings had grown significantly while he had also placed himself within the inner circle of Barbados's powerful sugar merchant elite through his marriage to Grace Walrond. Nathaniell Sylvester had stretched puritan networks through his union with Grizzell Sylvester, establishing ties with his brother-in-law William Coddington, a fellow puritan and the governor of Rhode Island. Nathaniell's close proximity to John Winthrop Jr. allowed him to maintain a relationship with the son of the powerful governor of Massachusetts Bay. Quaker missionaries who first arrived in Patuxent, Maryland, entered upon a community of interconnected puritan believers whose conversion held the key to exponential growth of the Quaker movement throughout the Atlantic and up the North American coastline.

When George Fox landed in Barbados in 1671, nearly twenty years had passed since the first Quaker missionaries had arrived on the shores of the British colonies. Little remained of the vibrant puritan Atlantic that had once thrived during the first half of the seventeenth century. Inconsistent colonial spiritual leadership outside of Massachusetts, augmented by the geographical distance placed between former members of the Ancient Church and Governor George Berkeley's persecution of the Virginia settlement left the puritan Atlantic in a vulnerable spiritual state. Somewhere along their journey from England, to Amsterdam, and throughout the colonies the intensity of their original convictions had been diluted to a cocktail of beliefs that appeared more like Quakerism than its original puritan roots. While sources do not indicate the precise theological journey these individuals took from puritan to Quaker faith, it is likely that they began on the path toward Quakerism while still in England.

Henry Barrow's leadership placed the Ancient Church on the fringe of puritan circles. His dismissal of praying the Psalms and encouragement of extempore prayer augmented the role of the Holy Spirit and placed a tiny crack in the structure of *sola scriptura*. Over the years this crack continued to spread under the pressure of competing doctrines, internal factions leading to schism, the want of spiritual guidance and leadership within the colonies, and the strain of persecution from the Anglican majority. Without the guidance of regular teaching, access to religious texts, and insistence of scriptural authority, Atlantic puritans probably gradually dismissed their elevation of Scripture over natural or personal revelation. When they could not find trained ministers to travel to Virginia lay pastors sufficed.[23] When Berkeley broke up the conventicles, private study by necessity replaced communal worship and teaching. And in the quiet of Scriptural meditation, the mind drifted to a still, small voice, perhaps a divine whisper, and a word from God apart from Scripture.

The transition was likely slow and unconscious. In the spiritual desert a word through prayer, a vision experienced in a dream, or a sign in the natural world quenched the puritan's spiritual thirst. Slowly and inductively they may have come to accept that God could speak to them outside of the written Scripture, and that the Holy Spirit assumed other roles apart from inspiration. They likely still clung to *sola scriptura*, testing divine apparitions, counsel, and guidance with the Bible. But with the allowance of competing revelation, apart from God's Holy Word, Atlantic puritans had already begun a journey toward Quaker belief. Perhaps through negligence or overt disobedience, daily Scriptural meditations may have become less common. Intermittent puritan teachings, shifting communal ties, and threats of persecution probably all contributed to a movement away from corporate and individual biblical studies. When Scriptural study no longer remained part of their daily routines, Atlantic puritans likely still uttered prayers between daily duties, debated spiritual convictions among friends, and spent time in extended prayer and fasting during times of particular distress. Almost without notice, *sola scriptura* was surpassed by a personal connection with the divine through the Holy Spirit, nurtured in prayer.

When Quaker missionaries first arrived on the banks of the Chesapeake the first Atlantic puritans they encountered were probably unknowingly practicing a faith akin to Quakerism. Unfamiliar with the term "Inner Light" and likely surprised at missionaries' egalitarian language, Atlantic puritans were probably at ease with many of the core convictions of Quaker faith. Although Elizabeth Harris and her fellow Quaker missionaries gave Atlantic puritans a name for their spiritual adaptation, the conversion from puritan to Quaker probably occurred as a slow process over the first half of the seventeenth century.

Within a short period of time a burgeoning movement of Atlantic Quakers seemed to sprout from the puritan ashes. With Elizabeth Harris's 1656 arrival to Maryland, Mary Fisher and Henry Fell's ministry in Barbados, Josiah Coale and Thomas Thurston's work in Virginia, along with other missionaries' efforts in Rhode Island and Shelter Island, Quaker faith replaced puritanism at the center of seventeenth-century networks. Quakerism spread like an infection throughout the colonies, as former puritans used ties to fellow believers in facilitating conversion. Singular conversions were rare if unheard of, with the faith moving along community lines; claiming families, neighborhoods, and business networks for the Quaker cause. In Salem, Massachusetts, 75 percent of the first-generation Quakers had spouses who also embraced their faith, and only six out of the original sixty-seven Quaker converts within the town did not have another family member among the Quakers.[24] The accounts of conversion in former puritan settlements throughout the colonies suggest a similar pattern. George Fox's efforts would serve to strengthen a zealous yet disjointed Quaker following, bringing them all under the leadership of the London office and setting them on track for a longevity their puritan predecessors never enjoyed.

Following Fox's American Journey

Nearly a month and a half after leaving London George Fox and his company spotted dolphins on the horizon, flying fish breaking the surface of the ocean, and "a bird called Booby, as bigge as a wilde goose." As their time at sea lengthened Fox and his followers began to notice a change in the water; perhaps the deep blue began to lighten into the paleness of Carlisle Bay, signaling their proximity to land. John Hull reported that they "saw early in the morning the Iland of Barbados, and about the ninth hourse at night or tenth wee anchored in Carlile Bay."[25] Once they had landed, John Rous brought Colonel Chamberlaine's coach to deliver the group to Thomas Rous's house, the home of John Rous's father.

The connection between George Fox and the Rous family illustrates a deeper link between Atlantic puritans turned Quakers on the island of Barbados. In 1652, prior to his Quaker conversion, the elder Rous was an established Barbadian planter and original investor, alongside Thomas Middleton, Constant Sylvester, and Nathaniell Sylvester, in a venture on Shelter Island; the same island where Dyer later stayed before her return to Boston. The four had purchased the

Island outpost from Stephen Goodyear, paying "sixteen hundred pounds of good merchantable muscovado sugar." They then signed the "Articles of Agreement" in 1652 allowing Constant, Middleton, and Rous to return to Barbados while their fourth partner, Nathaniell, managed the provisioning plantation in New York. Their original contract stipulated that the pastures, orchards, gardens, estuaries, and mill on Shelter Island were all to be held in common among the partners.[26] The four men purchased Shelter Island in the early years of what Russell Menard has labeled the sugar boom on Barbados. While the plantation eventually served as a source of provisions for the Sylvesters' interests in Barbados, its purchase was also likely tied to the royalist coup on Barbados and the need for the puritan brothers and business partners to pursue business interests elsewhere. With Barbados's forced submission to the Commonwealth government at the hands of parliamentary commissioner and former member of the Ancient Church Richard Bennett, Rous, Middleton, and Constant Sylvester were able to safely return to the Island of Barbados.[27] Rous did not remain long a partner with Middleton and the Sylvester brothers, but his business ties and participation within the puritan Atlantic provide an example of the path from puritan to Quaker in the Caribbean.

Prior to his collaboration with the Sylvesters, Rous had become a successful merchant planter on the island of Barbados. In 1641 Rous purchased "all that parte and pcell of ground or plantacon now in the occupation of the sd Walter Fenton scituate lying and being the pish of St. George in the Island of Barbados aforesd conteyning three score acres of land fallen & unfalne" for "the sume or quantity of seventeen thousand pounds of good merchantable and well cleared cotton by the sd Tho Rous."[28] His purchase included "all houses edifices buildings thereupon" along with the timber, and the "services of eight men servtantas wtall ye house hold stuffes utensells armes tooles & necessaries & all & evry the Severne dunghill fowles to the said plantacon." He purchased another eight servants in December of 1641, including "John Brigden, William Godoby, George Oaker, Thomas Rutter, John Hall, Roger Lugne, Andrew Bockley, and Thomas Hatch."[29] In May 1693 when Thomas Rous drafted his will he reported a considerable amount of property.[30]

When Fox docked in the blue waters of Carlisle Bay, the Rous family, both John and his parents Thomas and Mary, had been faithfully serving the Quaker cause for over fifteen years. The family was likely converted by the first Quakers to arrive on Barbados, Ann Austin and Mary Fisher. Henry Fell, another Quaker missionary on the island, wrote that Thomas Rous and his wife "are convinced & are very loving and truly he hath been serviceable." Fell also developed an affinity for their son, John Rous, who grew "very deare" to Henry Fell because of his desire to participate in the ministry traveling "among these friends here." He reported by April 1657 that they were having "four or 5 Meetings a weeke."[31] The younger Rous became an important resource for the Quaker cause with a particular passion for the apostasy of Barbados. In 1656 John Rous published a *Warning to the Inhabitants of Barbados Who live in Pride, Drunkennesse, Covetousness, Oppression and deceitful dealings*.[32] Rous dismissed subtlety in his impassioned plea for conversion, proclaiming "Barbadoes! Barbadoes! Who excels in wicknedness, pride and covetousness, oppressing, cheating and cozening." Rous warned, "the Lord who is a consuming fire and everlasting burning will render to every one of you according to your wayes." Not sparing any from his indictment the recent convert singled out "you covetous ones, who strive to get you care not how; who enlarge your Estates by vilence, and increase your wealth by wickedness; the cry of the oppressed is entred into the ears of the Lord of Sabbath, who will Speedily come to pour forth his plagues upon you, you wicket ones."[33] John Rous made a personal plea to those like himself, sons and daughters of wealthy planters, urging them not to follow in their fathers' footsteps exhorting them, "all you young men and young women, who have not yet acted in the same excess of wickedness, as you Parents have done" should "not do wickedly because your Elders do so; but in the time of your youth seek after the Lord." In doing this, "you shall be examples to those that be old; and keeping to that which is just, in moderation and sobriety, you shall exceed those who have lived many yeers, and have spent their time in vanity."[34] Rous's impassioned plea to fellow Barbadians likely stemmed from his own family's ambiguous situation on the island. As the son of wealthy planters, Rous's involvement in the Quaker community placed him at odds with many of the elites.

Other individuals expressed Quaker leanings in their wills. George Foster gave "unto Friends Stock namely the people of God called Quakers six thousand pounds of Sugar to be paid yearely by one thousand pounds a yeare" leaving to "ye Judgement of my friends hereafter named to dispose of it either for the use of the people called Quakers here or to them in England were these shall be most need."[35] Elizabeth Barnes gave twenty pounds sterling per year to the "people called Quakers in this Island."[36] She also gave the remainder of her estate for the Quakers "to build an Allmshouse for poor aged friends men and women."[37] The planter Ronald Holton of Saint Phillips Parish left "to the poor people amongst them called Quakers in this Island . . . seven acres of land being part of that my plantation at the foul bay to be laid out adjoining the lands of Capt Thomas Rawlins for the space of ten years."[38] Another Quaker, Henry Gallop, left the care of his children upon his widow's death to his Quaker friends.[39] The widow Martha Hooton left instructions that "my body may have a decent and Christian Internment according to the manner & method of my friends, the People of God called Quakers."[40] While the ownership of slaves was still common among Quaker planters in Barbados Hooton also gave instructions to "acquit Discharge Relase Manumitt and set free a negroe girl named Maria Two yeares after my decease from all manner of servituer and slavery."[41] Elisha Mellowes wrote in his will that "my funeral bee performed without any manner of formaillity Church Ceremonyes, Priest black cloth scarfes or any other thing relating thereto but that it be excuted according to the usuall manner of the people of God called Quakers."[42] He then gave "unto the poor of the people called Quakers of this Island forty pounds of current money."[43] As expressed in these Quaker wills, a number of other citizens of considerable means in Barbados had come to the Quaker faith. The Rouses' ties with the Sylvester family formed a unique bridge that may have precipitated Nathaniell's eventual conversion. Ultimately connections such as these allowed for a largely successful effort of Quaker missionaries to convert former Atlantic puritans, transforming the puritan Atlantic into a web of Quaker connections.

Quaker conversion on the island of Barbados cut across planters' designs to engender a sense of solidarity among elites and poor white farmers and combat the fear of a growing black majority. As the first English colony to write a comprehensive slave code, Barbados led the way in developing ideas around race within the seventeenth-century Atlantic. Quakerism, through its inclusivity toward African slaves, challenged a forming consensus among white planters, and placed converts such as the Rous family at odds with their peers. Russell Menard identifies Barbadian racial ideology as a product of the island's changing demography accentuated by the adoption of sugar cultivation and fears associated with the rapid growth of a "hostile and angry slave population."[44] Despite Richard Ligon's assurances that planters maintained social control, attempted uprisings in 1675, 1682, 1683, and 1686 suggested otherwise.[45] In a 1664 letter to Lord Clarendon, William, Lord Willoughby expressed his anxiety over the declining white population, fearing that the slaves would grow too difficult to manage. In response to this crisis and a failed attempt to recruit more white servants to the island planters endeavored to create a white identity and persuade white servants and small planters to defend the island against slave insurrection.[46]

By 1660 persons of African descent had become a majority of the population of Barbados, and a year later the legislature passed a code governing the treatment of servants and slaves and describing Africans as "an heathenish, brutish and uncertaine dangerous kind of people," such that they could not be trusted with the laws Englishmen enjoyed. In contrast, servants of European descent were in need of protection and encouragement to achieve their full potential.[47] Certain legal provisions were granted to servants, restricting discipline and allowing white servants to appeal to the courts on grounds of mistreatment. In 1676 the Assembly restricted blacks from skilled crafts, while a later act blamed African slaves for driving poor whites off the island.[48] Emergent racial ideologies converged with religious interests as planters attempted to preserve Christianity as a privilege of the whites. In 1681 the Assembly wrote to the governor, saying, "we are ready to do anything for the encouragement of Christian servants . . . but as to making the Negroes Christians, their savage brutishness renders them wholly incapable. Many have endeavored it without success."[49] While the majority of white planters had decided that African slaves were incapable of conversion, Quakers contradicted normative behavior by bringing their slaves to meeting. Their actions resulted in severe fines, which proved ineffective and ultimately led the governor to order the provost marshal to dismantle the Quaker meeting house in Bridgetown, pulling down the seats and stalls and nailing the windows shut.[50]

While the majority of Barbados's planter class sought to accentuate racial differences, Quakers exhibited a dangerous, deviant behavior. Through the 1660s poor white children were granted education privileges, excluding the education of children of African descent. At the same time the primary objective of the militia was expressed as the "regulation and policing of Negroes."[51] The Quakers' role at the cross-section of developing racial ideology is evident in George Fox's early discussion of whiteness published in his 1672, *To the Ministers, Teachers, and Priests*. Menard identifies this mention as the first reference to a Barbadian of European descent as white. Ultimately puritan to Quaker conversion in Barbados placed the Rous family at odds with their fellow planters and Anglican neighbors. While the theological underpinnings of their impetus toward Quaker faith can only be speculated, their decision was clearly not one of expedience.

From Barbados, George Fox continued on to Jamaica, where he wrote that "wee travailed many hundreds of miles and sett up a matter of 7 meetings" and from there traveled to Maryland.[52] The party "sailed leeward toward the gulfe of fflorida where the same day wee were over against Alligator poind and Manatee valley."[53] From there they "sailed a week backwards and forwards" before passing out of sight of Jamaica and then passed by the Caymen Islands, "by grand Caimanus the Islands of Turkles Alligators & sharks & Crockadills."[54] After a vilent storm followed by "great ffogs & mists" they saw the land of Virginia, came to Cape Henry, and "cast Anchor in the bay of Petuxant River."[55] On the banks of the Patuxent River, Fox encountered "James Prestons on Potoxen."[56] Before arriving on land in Maryland, George Fox and his company suffered "a great Storme and a boat was cast upon us for shelter." The result of the tempest was that "the boat was lost and 500 li worth of goods."[57] Because Fox and his fellow travelers could not get to land they "had a fine meeting with them on the Sea."[58] When they finally arrived on land "there was a meeting which helf 4 days & there came to it 5 or 6 Justices of peace and a speaker of Parliament & one of the councell and severall other considerable men of the world."[59]

James Preston was the son of Richard Preston, who had traveled with his wife and family, alongside Richard Bennett and a number of other Nansemond puritans, after Berkeley's persecution and Governor William Stone's invitation to Maryland. The patriarch, Richard Preston, had previously received two grants, one for 150 acres and the other for 500 acres, in Norfolk County, Virginia. Having lived alongside Richard Bennett and other puritan sympathizers initially in Virginia and later in Maryland, the Prestons were likely of the puritan fold as well. In Maryland Richard Preston claimed land on the north side of the Patuxent River. After William Claiborne and Richard Bennett used their power as parliamentary commissioners to depose William Stone as governor, Richard Preston became one of six Maryland commissioners. When Stone was reappointed governor, Preston joined the Council and drafted men for an expedition against the Indians.[60] Richard Preston and his son-in-law, William Berry, were later fined for harboring Josiah Coale and Thomas Thurston, two itinerant Quaker ministers who had been expelled from the colony. The Preston family, closely tied to the puritans who had once lived south of the James River in Virginia, had now become important figures in Maryland's Quaker community.

While George Fox was likely drawn to the shores of the Patuxent knowing that Quaker missionaries Josiah Coale, Thomas Thurston, and Elizabeth Harris had experienced considerable success convincing former puritans in the region, the original impetus for the arrival of Quaker missionaries to the northern reaches of the Chesapeake, if not tied to the networks of puritan communication from Barbados to the Chesapeake, was likely linked to these relationships. puritan networks fostered the creation of a like-minded religious community stretching across the Atlantic, whose presence during the second half of the seventeenth century allowed for Quaker missionaries to easily track and trace potential outposts for likely conversion. Fox's arrival in Anne Arundel County, Maryland, occurred nearly twenty years after the first Quaker missionary, Elizabeth Harris, had first landed in the colony. Her success in converting puritan leaders in the region, including Richard Bennett, laid the foundation for the Quaker stronghold Fox visited nearly twenty years later.

In 1656 Elizabeth Harris left her husband and infant son behind in England to evangelize the puritan remnant in Maryland.[61] Nicholas Wyatt was one of the first Marylanders to be convinced by Elizabeth. He had moved from the Lower Norfolk Region to Maryland in 1650.[62] Edward and Ann Dorsey, formerly puritans of the Elizabeth River region, became Quakers under the instruction of Elizabeth Harris as well.[63] Also among the former Virginians convinced was Thomas Marsh, one of the men that journeyed with the itinerant puritan minister William Durand in 1648 to the Severn area. Settling on "Marsh's Seat" his family became Quaker, and his daughter Elizabeth Taylor became a prominent Quaker on the Eastern Shore after Marsh's death.[64] Richard Owens, together with Thomas Meers, Edward Lloyd, Thomas Marsh, and John Norwood, once a nonconformist from Nansemond, also became a Friend, along with his wife Mary Norwood. The two had traveled to Maryland in 1650.[65] Other Maryland converts of the puritan settlement in Nansemond included Richard Galloway and Anne Chew. Chew had been the only daughter of William Ayres of Nansemond, and after the death of her husband she devoted the rest of her life to Quaker ministry.[66]

Harris's success produced both quantitative and qualitative results with surprising success among the puritan leadership. Among her converts was the former commander of the puritan forces at Severn, William Fuller, who at the time was serving on the governor's council.[67] She converted William Durand, a lay minister who taught the Virginia puritans from a book of notes he had compiled while attending John Davenport's sermons in England. In Maryland, Durand served beside Fuller on the governor's council.[68] Harris also convinced Henry Catlyn, one of the first commissioners of Anne Arundel County and a former vestryman of the Elizabeth River Church in Virginia.[69] Some of the earliest puritan settlers of the Severn area, including the former church warden in Virginia and his wife, became Friends as well.[70] Virginia's commonwealth governor, Richard Bennett, eventually joined the Quakers although there is some debate over exactly when his convincement occurred.[71] Regardless of the debate, Bennett remained a friend of the Quakers for the rest of his life and practiced as a Quaker on his deathbed, willing two thousand pounds of tobacco to each of four of his Nansemond Quaker neighbors. Bennett's daughter Anne followed her father into the Quaker faith.[72]

Thomas Thurston and Josiah Coale, the first Quaker missionaries in Virginia, continued Harris's work in Maryland. George Rofe, an English Quaker who had spent much time behind bars as a result of his sectarian faith, also ministered throughout the South and Maryland. Writing of his ministries to a fellow Quaker he rejoiced at having been made "an instrument of good in those countries." Rofe had "visited Maryland, Virginia, New England, and the islands thereabout, also the island of Bermuda, in all of which places there are many Friends." He eventually "settled in the fruitful island of Barbadoes, which may be called the nursery of truth" as "a meeting is held there every day, and sometimes two or three."[73]

Apart from facilitating conversion, missionaries provided new converts with the necessary spiritual resources. The newly convinced Robert Clarkson wrote, "We have disposed of the most part of the books which were sent, so that all parts where there are Friends are furnished and every one that desires it may have benefit of them; at Herring Creek, Rhoad River, South River, all about Severn, the Brand Neck, and thereabouts the Severn Mountains and Kent."[74] According to Clarkson's testimony, the former puritan settlement of the Anne Arundel region served as the locus of Quaker faith within the Maryland region. The new believers worked outward from this central location to spread the message through the dissemination of Quaker tracts.

By the year 1658 the Quaker faith had proliferated with such ease that the government began to take notice. That year the upper house reported an "alarm" from "the increase of the Quakers" in the region of Patuxent.[75] In the minutes of their proceedings they wrote, "The Councell considering that these contempts of Acts of Assembly, breach of Articles, & disobedience to Proclamacons could not but tend to the embroileing of this Province in further troubles Ordered That a warrent should Issue for the apprehending the said Thurston and Cole to answer theyr misdemeanours."[76] Authorities had taken notice of the missionaries' success. Coale and Thurston continued to agitate local government through their refusal to take an oath and encouragement of others to do the same.[77] Their followers included Michael Brookes of Calvert County, who following conversion refused to swear an oath and was fined for his disobedience.[78] Thus the message of the Quaker Inner Light had been firmly planted within the Patuxent region and began to spread among the former puritan community. Missionaries William Robinson, Christopher Holder, and Robert Hodgson followed up initial efforts with a visit to the colony in 1659 resulting in a "large convincement." Coale later wrote in February 1661, "As concerning Friends in the Province of Maryland, I left them generally very well and fresh in the truth."[79] The considerable amount of conversions alongside the recent political attention focused on the Quakers highlighted Harris and her fellow missionaries' widespread success in convincing former puritans in Maryland.

Leaving from Maryland, George Fox's group hired Indian guides to lead them through the wilderness to New Jersey and from there to Oyster Bay, where Fox wrote, "we stayed for a winde to goe to Rhode Island."[80] On March 28th the winds were favorable and they set sail for Rhode Island, about two hundred miles by water, arriving on March 30th.[81] John Stubbs wrote to Margaret Fell about their time in Rhode Island, saying that William Coddington had hosted a four-day men's meeting preceded by the general meeting and followed by the women's meeting.[82] Coddington also held a marriage at his home and later wrote to John Winthrop Jr., saying, "George Fox being at my house (who saw thee in England) spake to me to write thee, viz. that Samuel Winthrop, thy brother, was with him at Barbadoes, came hither to visit him, and G.F. could wish that thou was like him, and that thou wouldst stave off persecution."[83]

George Fox's fellowship with the Coddingtons, including his protracted stay through multiple meetings and the wedding that followed, highlights another key connection between the puritan network and the Quaker Atlantic that followed. William Coddington, once a leader among Atlantic nonconformists became a pillar of the Quaker movement. Coddington initially arrived in Boston, Massachusetts, in 1630, sympathizing with the dissenters and defending Anne Hutchinson against her accusers. In 1638 he left Boston to lead a dissenting group to Aquidneck, the island portion of Rhode Island, where he was the judge and acting governor from 1640 to 1647. Coddington later founded Newport, and it was on a trip to England in 1650 to secure another charter for Rhode Island, placing himself at the helm, that Coddington met and married Grizzell Sylvester's elder sister, Anne Brinley. The following year Coddington took his new wife back to Rhode Island, along with her younger sister, the then Grizzell Brinley, in hopes that she would find a suitable husband in the colonies.[84] While their exact conversion date is unknown, Coddington and his family had become Quakers before 1665, slightly later than his fellow Atlantic puritans in Barbados and the Chesapeake. Their ties to the Sylvesters, across the Long Island Sound on Shelter Island, and their subsequent ties to Barbados and the Chesapeake through their membership in the puritan Atlantic further illustrate the role at outlying puritan settlements played in the creation of a Quaker Atlantic.

When it was still daylight, Fox and his party left Rhode Island, taking the sloop and passing by "point Juda, & by blocke Iland, & from thence to ffishers Illand as before. Fox wrote,

> Wee went at night upon the shore, & wee were not able to stay for the Muscatoes, soe wee went in the sloope again, & putt off from the shore, & cast Anchor, & stayed all yt night; and ye next day we went into the Sound, & our sloope was not able to live in ye water & wee turned in againe, for we cold not passe, & soe came to Anchor agine at fishers Iland 2: nights, & there was Exceedinge much raine, whereby wee were much wett being in an open boate; and we passed over the 2: horseraces waters (soe called) & by Garners Iland & ye Gulls Iland, & soe came to Shelter Iland which was 27: leagues from Roade Iland.[85]

George Fox and his company had arrived on Shelter Island to visit the Sylvester family, but Fox was also concerned about the local Manhassett population. He recorded "a Meetinge at Shelter Iland amonge the Indians, & the Kinge & his Councell, with about 100: more Indians with him." Fox described the event, how "they sate about 2: hourse & I spoke to them by an Interpreter, that was an Indian, yet could speake English very well." Pleased with the Manhassett response he thought them receptive as "they appeared very Loveinge, & they saide all was truth, & did make a confession after ye Meetinge of it."[86] Fox's success in preaching to the local Indians allowed him to "set up a meettinge amonge them once a fortnight and a friend Joseph Silvester is to reade the Scriptures to them."[87] Following his success with the Manhassett, "on the first day after there was a great Meettinge, being at Shelter Iland & many of ye world, & Preists people yt never heard friends before, was there, & they was very much satisfield." Fox wrote, "I could not goe away until they had seene mee, & spoke to mee after the Meettinge, and I went downe to them, & they was taken with ye truth, & great desires there is, & a great love & satisfaction were among the people."[88]

Like Barbados and Maryland, Shelter Island had developed into a celebrated epicenter of Quaker activity, uniquely positioned across the Long Island Sound from New Haven and relatively close to the Massachusetts Bay colony. Nathaniell Sylvester exhibited Quaker sympathies as early as 1654 when local government records show that he made offensive statements concerning the Sabbath.[89]

In 1660 the court responded to a letter from Nathaniell Sylvester, "written with his owne hand . . . professing to be a Quaker."[90] The court accused Nathaniell of being a "frequent harbourer to give entertainemt to yt cursed sect, who fro his island have frequently taken opportunity to come amongst or people, soweing the seeds of their pnitious doctrines, & sometimes by grosse affronts, publiquely to make disturbances at Southold." As punishment for his actions the court ordered "100 li of ye said Nathaniels estate within this jurisdiction be attached & seised, & not to be released vntill this court of magistrates have received satisfaction from him for these & such like offences." Nathaniell Sylvester was also summoned to a court of magistrates to be held in New Haven on October 17, 1661.[91] Nathaniell was called a total of three times to present himself to court but never appeared.[92] The accusations of Nathaniell's tendency to harbor Quakers on Shelter Island seem to have been correct. The Quaker missionary John Taylor first arrived on the island in 1659 writing of his experience:

> I came late into an Indian Town, where my guide led me into a Wigwam or House; such kind of Hutts that they live in, which are round, made like Arbours with small Polls, &c. And being received kindly, and directed to my Lodging upon some Matts and Rushes, I laid down to Sleep. This was a great man's House next to the King, and he was very Ill; but by and by, came in a great many lusty proper Men, Indians all, and sat down, and every one had a short Truncheon Stick in their hands pretty thick, about two foot long. So they began to Pow-wow as they called it.

The Manhassett Indians asked Taylor to cure the sick man, and although he was unable to do so himself he sent someone back that could care for the man. When Taylor returned that way the man was once again well, and the other Indians were "exceeding joyful to see me," providing him "an opportunity to declare the Truth to them, and to turn them from Darkness to the Light of Christ Jesus . . . and they heard me soberly, and did Confess to the Truth."[93] Taylor stayed on Shelter Island until his ship was loaded and ready to sail for Barbados. He wrote, "and there came several Friends from other Parks in New-England, to see us: One was Mary Dyer, who afterwards was put to Death by the Cruel Persecutors and Professors of New-England."[94] In Taylor's description Dyer was "a very Comely Woman and a Grave Matron" who "shined in the Image of God." The two held "several brave Meetings there together, and the Lord's Power and Presence" came to meet them there. Dyer sailed for Boston before Taylor left for Barbados and Taylor recounted his departure saying: "And when we were all ready, I, in much Love and tenderness took leave of Nathaniel Silvister, his Wife and Family, and all Friends there, leaving them to the Grace of God, and ingrafted Word, that is able to save their Souls."[95]

While Taylor's visit clearly strengthened the Sylvesters' faith, it was likely that their conversion occurred before his arrival because of Taylor's warm welcome.

The Quaker missionary Joan Brocksopp had also visited Shelter Island, and her husband wrote of the "tender love and fatherly care" given to his wife while visiting the Island.[96] Lawrence and Cassandra Southwick, Quaker exiles from Salem, Massachusetts, fled to Shelter Island too, where they died a little over a year later.[97] Nathaniell and Grizzell Sylvester's conversions further demonstrate the relationships between puritan Atlantic networks and the growth of Quaker faith throughout the Atlantic. As Fox traveled from Barbados to Maryland, Rhode Island, and up to Shelter Island he did so knowing, like the Quaker missionaries before him, that former puritan settlements were ripe for Quaker conversion, and the ties between those settlements would likely precipitate convincement. Thomas Rous's former business connections with Nathaniell Sylvester had now blossomed into shared religious convictions. While it is not clear if either Thomas Rous or John Rous reached out to the Sylvesters to encourage their conversion, their relationship and subsequent conversions were probably not coincidental.

George Fox's arrival on Shelter Island and his successful ministry among the Indians and Europeans unravels a deeper web of puritan contacts that eventually birthed the Quaker Atlantic. Rather than sailing from New England, Fox and his party traversed back toward the Chesapeake along a land route through Maryland and on "ye 5th day of ye 9 moth wee sett sayle towards Virginia, the 6 day wee Rowed & sailed about 80: miles, the weather beinge stormie, & winde & ffoggs and raine, and at night wee putt to the shore, & in ye woods we made us a fire with much adoe, all things being wett, and there stayed all night by it." When they woke the next morning Fox wrote "wee went on ye water, & sailed all ye day."[98] That night in the dark and rain they came upon a ship from Plymouth and stayed. They began sailing again at daybreak and came to Nansemond on the seventh day of the ninth month.[99]

Fox's journey to Nansemond, Virginia, placed him near the home of Richard Bennett, and many of the original puritan settlers to arrive in the colonial Chesapeake. When Fox visited the then Quaker settlement, Bennett was likely a more fragile shell of the puritan commissioner and governor he had once been. Although he had traveled with fellow puritans from Virginia to Maryland following Berkeley's persecution, he had returned to Virginia sometime after considering that his will, written on March 15, 1674, referred to himself as "Richard Bennett of Nansemond river in Virginia."[100] In her writings Elizabeth Harris reported that a governor had been convinced, more than likely referring to Bennett, who had been appointed governor by Cromwell in 1652, serving until 1655. Bennett also owned tracts of land in the Lower Norfolk region of Virginia along with his property near the Severn River, the two main loci of Harris's missionary efforts. When tensions arose between the Commonwealth government and the newly settled puritans in Maryland, Richard Bennett and William Claiborne exercised a considerable amount of influence on the Puritan community in

Maryland, albeit against Cromwell's direction.[101] Bennett's influence in the region may also have led a number of former puritans turned Quaker to refer to him as governor, even though he had officially served as the governor of Virginia.

Bennett's 1674 will reveals further Quaker ties, as he bequeathed two thousand pounds of tobacco to four of his Quaker neighbors, including Thomas Jordan of Chuckatuck Creek, the same Jordan who hosted Fox on his visit.[102] Fox's travels through the Lower Norfolk region brought him to the homes of many former puritans in the colony. Passing through the "woods, & over many boggs & swamps" Fox and his company came to Bennett's Creek, "& there wee lay [at his house], and the woman of ye house lent us amatt, & wee lay on it by ye fire side."[103] From Richard Bennett's Fox traveled to the home of Nathaniel Basse, who recounted the story of a woman healed by Fox.[104] Fox later wrote of Nathaniel Basse and Richard Bennett explaining how he had left an epistle to be read by Basse to the Tuscaroras' emperor and kings.[105]

Prior to Fox's arrival, the former puritan stronghold had transformed into a center of Quaker activity, attracting a considerable amount of Atlantic attention. Elizabeth Harris's visit there in the late 1650s, coupled with the work of Thomas Thurston, Josiah Coale, and William Robinson, resulted in a number of early conversions. Coale, speaking of Thurston's ministry in Virginia, wrote, "The living power of the Lord goes along with him, and there is like to be a great gathering." Other missionaries followed Thurston and Coale to the lower Norfolk Region. These early Quakers included William Robinson and Christopher Hodgson. Robinson recounted their missionary work saying, "there are many people convinced, and some in several parts are brought into the sense and feeling of truth."[106] Coale similarly remarked, "I left Friends in Virginia generally very well and fresh in the truth. I believe I shall be in Virginia again."[107] George Rofe also spoke of his missionary work within the colony of Virginia, that God had made him "an instrument of good to many through these countries"[108]

Their success did not go unnoticed by Governor Berkeley, who established a commission, on June 27, 1663, that "the abominate seede of ye Quakers spread not."[109] Quakers were fined two hundred pounds of tobacco apiece for their "unlaweful meetinge" and many were arrested at the home of Richard Russell.[110] News of the spread of Quaker faith in the Chesapeake also attracted heretical teaching from within the Quaker fold. John Perrot, who had formerly traveled to Rome in hopes of converting the Pope, made his way to the settlement in Lower Norfolk to raise controversy concerning Quaker form and ceremony, specifically the wearing of hats and the holding of meetings. John Burnyeat arrived in 1665 to discover the "bewitchment" of John Perrot, who had encouraged Quakers to "forsake their meetings" and to become "loose and careless." Burnyeat quickly went to work restoring the Nansemond area to its original Quaker ideas. He reported that soon "Friends were revived and refreshed, and raised up into a service of life through the Lord's goodness and renewed visitation." William

Edmundson followed Burnyeat to Virginia where he held "powerful meetings," "settling men's minds in the truth."[111]

The fruits of their combined missionary efforts had resulted in the convincement of a number of former puritan leaders of the community. Along with Richard Bennett, former puritans, Captain Francis Emperor, and his wife Mary Emperor, had also become Quakers, like their relatives the Oistins in Barbados.[112] Nathaniel Basse, mentioned by Fox, was formerly a prominent puritan in the region having served as one of Christopher Lawne's original backers in 1619.[113] Bennett's colleague William Claiborne became a Quaker too and George Fox passed by his home "where wee hade service" on his travels from Maryland to Virginia.[114]

George Fox's arrival in Virginia completed a journey that traced a line connecting the remnant of the Ancient Church with an emerging Quaker Atlantic. His travels from Barbados to Maryland, Rhode Island, Shelter Island, and Virginia brought Fox into contact with a number of puritans who had recently experienced Quaker conversion. The names that dot the pages of his journal, many of them leaders within the Quaker faith, had once belonged to puritan communities. Through his journey, Fox highlights the geography of Atlantic puritan–Quaker conversion. His travels connect two accounts of spiritual origin previously kept separate. Individuals like Nathaniell Sylvester, William Coddington, Richard Bennett, and Richard Preston, among others, demonstrate how, although the religious categories to which they belonged changed, the relationships that bound them to each other did not. While some families were divided along lines of religious conviction, it was more often that conversion followed bonds of kinship, friendship, and partnership. Quaker missionaries like Elizabeth Harris targeted leaders of the puritan Atlantic who, once converted, assisted in leading their relatives, friends, and colleagues into the Quaker faith. Ultimately, this Quaker missionary approach, coupled with the interconnected nature of Atlantic puritan networks, allowed the Quaker message to spread like wildfire throughout the puritan Atlantic. Within a few short years of the arrival of Quaker missionaries little remained of the former puritan Atlantic, while the Quaker movement was gaining momentum in the colonies.

In rejoining the previously separate histories of the puritan and Quaker Atlantic we gain a more complete understanding of each movement. We reintroduce the individuals that bound each faith to the other and recapture the ways in which they negotiated spiritual convictions, familial bonds, and community ties within the Atlantic world. The widespread transition from puritan to Quaker underlines the significance of faith and membership within a community of believers while also highlighting the ways in which missionaries used existing business, familial, and community networks to achieve conversion. Although the puritan Atlantic's collapse into Quaker belief may provide insight on puritan belief in the seventeenth-century Atlantic, perhaps it reveals more about

Quaker ingenuity and successful missionary efforts in the seventeenth-century Atlantic.

Mary Dyer's short stay on Shelter Island, after being exiled from Boston and before returning again to her eventual death, continues to bring both the puritan and the Quaker Atlantic into deeper conversation. Like the Quaker missionaries that had arrived before her, Dyer knew she would be welcomed among the Sylvester family. Dyer also saw herself as connected to a larger Atlantic movement and likely perceived her efforts in Massachusetts Bay as a continuation of the successful conversions experienced among puritans in Barbados and up the eastern coastline. Having heard word of the harvest of souls Elizabeth Harris was reaping in Maryland among puritans exiled from Virginia, along with news of Thurston and Coale's efforts in the Chesapeake and Henry Fell's ministry among the Rous family following Ann Austin and Mary Fisher's success on Barbados, Dyer was likely mindful of former puritans' susceptibility to Quaker conversion. She was also keenly aware of the risk. The female Quaker missionaries that had gone before her such as Ann Austin, Mary Fisher, and Elizabeth Harris had experienced hardship, persecution, and separation from their families through imprisonment. Her previous visit to Massachusetts Bay, along with Marmaduke Stephenson and William Robinson, was met with ardent opposition. Whereas her fellow missionaries had reported success from Barbados, to Virginia and Maryland, Dyer's attempts at the colonial nucleus of puritan faith barely seemed to scratch the rigid shell of Massachusetts orthodoxy. While her return to Boston is often painted as an act of martyrdom rather than a belief that her actions would solicit heartfelt conversion, an understanding of Quaker convincement throughout the puritan Atlantic suggests an alternate interpretation. Although Dyer likely knew that her unwelcome arrival in Boston could result in death, her stay on Shelter Island also laid the hope for a different outcome. As puritans turned Quaker, the Sylvesters' conversion, alongside the conversion of their former puritan colleagues in Barbados, Virginia, Maryland, and Rhode Island, suggested that puritans often found solace in Quaker conversion. Widespread puritan to Quaker convincement revealed what many Quakers had likely suspected. Disconnected from a strong religious organization, with little access to a continuing flow of spiritual nourishment, and common roots in Henry Barrow's radical separate tendencies, the remnant of the Ancient Church and the puritan networks they formed had gradually drifted toward Quaker belief. Having traveled to the colonies to worship in a manner they saw fit these puritans, bereft of consistent religious instruction, had likely allowed personal study and private prayer to replace corporate worship and teaching where inaccessible. What began as an occasional word from God in prayer, or a prompting from the spirit in a dream, probably expanded to a more constant flow of divine revelation to the individual believer. Thus, on the eve of Quaker arrival, what remained of the Ancient Church and the networks its members had established, probably looked very similar to Quaker belief in practice. When Mary Dyer's predecessors arrived in the colonies they most likely encountered former puritans who practiced a faith very similar to Quakerism, making their conversion more of a semantic formality than a significant shift in religious thought or teaching. Mary Dyer's connection to a network of Atlantic Quaker missionaries conditioned her for a similar response and outcome. When she arrived in Boston Common, at the center of colonial puritan activity, Dyer probably hoped for a taste of the success experienced by her fellow Quaker missionaries. Far from a foolish mission or a predetermined martyrdom, Dyer's actions were likely laced with a hope for conversion among Boston's puritan population, if only because she had witnessed similar spiritual awakening among the Sylvesters. While her hopes were never achieved, Dyer's work should be understood as an attempt to continue successful Quaker missions to puritan outposts throughout the Atlantic rather than a remarkable case of Quaker martyrdom that engraved a perceived separation between puritan and Quaker faith and the historiography that has followed.

NOTES

1. Mac Griswold, *The Manor: Three Centuries at a Slave Plantation on Long Island* (New York: FSG Books, 2013), 209–210.

2. I have left puritan lowercase in recognition of the many different groups that called themselves puritans who shared some, but not all beliefs and attitudes towards their faith. I present the term in lowercase, as Karen Kupperman has done before, to indicate the lack of precision while preserving the reality of the movement. Karen Kupperman, *Providence Island, 1630–1641: The Other Puritan Colony*, New York: Cambridge University Press, 1993), xiii.

3. These letters can be seen in Ruth Talbot Plimpton, *Mary Dyer: Biography of a Rebel Quaker* (Boston: Branden Books, 1997).

4. Carla Gardina Pestana, "The Quaker Executions as Myth and History," *The Journal of American History* 80, no. 2 (Sep., 1993): 441–469.

5. David Como, *Blown By the Spirit: Puritanism and the Emergence of an Antinomian Underground in Pre-Civil-War England* (Stanford, CA: Stanford University Press, 2004).

6. Geoffrey Nuttall, *The Holy Spirit in Puritan Faith and Experience* (Chicago: University of Chicago Press, 1946).

7. Frederick Tolles, *Meeting House and Counting House: The Quaker Merchants of Colonial Philadelphia, 1682–1763* (Chapel Hill: The University of North Carolina Press, 2011), 52.

8. Hugh Barbour, *The Quakers in Puritan England* (New Haven, CT: Yale University Press, 1964), 2, 133–159.

9. Carla Gardina Pestana, *Protestant Empire: Religion and the Making of a British Atlantic World* (Philadelphia: Penn Press, 2010); John Donoghue, *Fire under the Ashes, An Atlantic History of the English Revolution* (Chicago, IL: University of Chicago Press, 2013).

10. Karen Ordahl Kupperman, *Providence Island, 1630–1641: The Other Puritan Colony* (New York: Cambridge University Press, 1995).

11. For more on Puritan dreaming see Ann Marie Plane, *Dreams and the Invisible World in Colonial New England: Indians, Colonists, and the Seventeenth Century* (Philadelphia: Penn Press, 2014).

12. This is seen among the Puritans of the Ancient Church through the leadership of Henry Barrow who encouraged extempore prayer, Henry Barrow, *A Brief Discoverie of the False Church* (1590), 65.

13. In his discussion of Coleman Street Ward and the Atlantic dimensions of the English Revolution, John Donoghue identifies the Ancient Church, which he calls the Southwark Congregation, as tied to a network of independent Puritans centered around Coleman Street Ward. What he labels "extreme independents" participated in an expanding community of Puritans that eventually spread their ideas about Protestantism and the English Revolution throughout the Atlantic World. John Donoghue, *Fire under the Ashes: An Atlantic History of the English Revolution* (Chicago: The University of Chicago Press, 2013), 188, 313.

14. Christopher Lawne, *The Prophane Schisme of the Brownists or Separatist* (1612), 15–16.

15. George Johnson, *A Discourse of Some Troubles and Excommunications in the Banished English Church at Amsterdam* (1603), 185.

16. Lawne's trip was sponsored by Richard Wiseman, one of Richard Bennett's business partners, and Nathaniel Basse, a fellow member of the Ancient Church. They settled on the lower side of the James River, an area known by the Indian name Warresqueak, in current Isle of Wight County, Virginia. The area was eventually known as Lawne's Neck and Lawne's Creek after its original settler. Lawne did not survive long in Virginia and died shortly after his arrival. His patent was conferred to the remaining holders, including Basse and Wiseman. While Lawne's settlement was plagued with the disease frequent in Virginia's early years it became the center of a community of Puritan settlers in Virginia. H. R. McIlwaine, ed., *Minutes of the Council and General Court of Colonial Virginia 1622–1632, 1670–1676 With Notes and Excerpts from Original Council and General Court Records in 1683, Now Lost* (Richmond: Virginia State Library, 1924), 90; Martha W. McCartney, *Virginia Immigrants and Adventurers, 1607–1635: A Biographical Dictionary* (Baltimore, MD: Genealogical Publishing company, 2007), 50; Susan M. Kingsbury, ed., *The Records of the Virginia Company of London* (Washington, DC: G.P.O., 1906), 1:414, 255.

17. Kingsbury, *Records of the Virginia Company*, 1:466; Edward Bennett, *A Treatise Divided into three parts, touching the inconveniences, that the Importation of Tobacco out of Spain, hath brought into this land*, (ca. 1620).

18. Kingsbury, *Records of the Virginia Company*, 1:561; D. Reid Ross, "Edward Bennett and his family in early seventeenth century Virginia and Maryland," *Virginia Tidewater Genealogy* 39, no. 2 (2008): 27–29, 16.

19. Dutch Notarial Archives 848/97; 134, folio 173v; 141/folio 48v-49v; 149/102v; 720/46.

20. For more on the Sylvester trade networks see Dutch Notarial Archives 601/32v; 1570/91, 237; 848/903; 1289 folio. 101v-102v/ 1294/68; 849/123. For more on Constant Sylvester's property management in Barbados see Barbados Department of Archives RB3/2, 68, 192, 635, 782–783, 57. For Nathaniell Sylvester's management of the provisioning plantation on Shelter Island see Shelter Island Historical Society, Middleton et al. "Articles of Agreement," 1652.

21. Bennett, *A Treatise*; Kingsbury, *The Records of the Virginia Company*, 1:446, 554, 562, 3:63; "Isle of Wight County Records" *William and Mary Quarterly*, 7, no. 4 (April 1899): 217; William Bennett Boddie, *Seventeenth century Isle of Wight county, Virginia: a history of the county of Isle of Wight, Virginia, during the seventeenth century, including abstracts of the county records* (Baltimore: MD: Genealogical Publishing Company, 1973), 276; Richard Bennett served on the Governor's Council alongside former congregant of the Ancient church, John Utie. PRO, C.2/Ch.I/T.24/64; McIlwaine, *Minutes of the Council*, 19.

22. Babette May Levy, *Early Puritanism in the Southern and Island Colonies* (Worceter, MA: American Antiquarian Society, 1960), 132–133; Daniel R. Randall, *A Puritan Colony in Maryland* (Baltimore, MD: Genealogical Publishing Company, 1886), 17; Jon Butler, ed. "Two 1642 Letters from Virginia Puritans" *Proceedings of the Massachusetts Historical Soci-*

ety, 3rd Ser., 84 (1972): 106; John Winthrop, *The History of New England from 1630 to 1649*, ed. James Savage (Boston, 1853), 2:94; John Winthrop, *Journal*, ed. James Kendall Hosmer, *Original Narratives of Early American History* (New York, 1908), 2:167–168; Edward Johnson, *The Wonder-Working Providence of Sion's Saviour in New England*, ed. J. Franklin Jameson, *Original Narratives of Early American History* (New York, 1910), 3:265–267.

23. The Virginia Puritans attempted to recruit three ministers from New England in 1642, but they did not stay long in the colony because of Governor William Berkeley's attempt to eradicate any nonconformity. Later William Durand served as a lay minister for the community. John Butler, ed. "Two 1642 Letters," 106; John Winthrop, *The History of New England from 1630 to 1649*, ed. James Savage (Boston, 1853), 2:94; John Winthrop, *Journal*, 2:167–168; Edward Johnson, "The Wonder-Working Providence," 3:265–267: Kingsbury, *Records of the Virginia Company*, 1:534.

24. Pestana, *Quakers and Baptists in Colonial Massachusetts* (New York: Cambridge University Press, 1991), 68–69.

25. "John Hull's Account of the Voyage," in George Fox, *The Journal of George Fox*, ed. Norman Penny (New York: Octagon Books, 1973), 2:185–186.

26. Shelter Island Historical Society, Middleton et al. "Articles of Agreement," 1652.

27. "Surrender of Virginia to the Parliamentary Commissioners, March, 1651–2 an excerpt from the British Museum Library. E 665. 3. Page, 1604–1607," *The Virginia Magazine of History and Biography* 11, no. 1 (1903):32–41.

28. Barbados National Archives, RB3/1, 314–316.

29. Barbados National Archives, RB3/1, 314–316.

30. Barbados National Archives, RB6/3, 169.

31. Larry Gragg, *The Quaker Community on Barbados* (Columbia, MO: University of Missouri Press, 2009), 39.

32. John Rous, *A Warning to the Inhabitants of Barbados* (London, 1656).

33. Rous, *A Warning to the Inhabitants of Barbados.*

34. Rous, *A Warning to the Inhabitants of Barbados,* 3.

35. Barbados National Archives RB6/8, 330.

36. Barbados National Archives, RB6/8/566.

37. Barbados National Archives, RB6/8/566.

38. Barbados National Archives, RB6/14, "Will of Ronald Holton" Entered July 24, 1680.

39. Barbados National Archives, RB6/14, "Will of Henry Gallop" Entered September 1, 1680.

40. Barbados National Archives, RB6/16, 188–189.

41. Barbados National Archives, RB6/16, 188–189.

42. Barbados National Archives RB6/11, 68–72.

43. Barbados National Archives RB6/11, 68–72.

44. Russell R. Menard, *Sweet Negotiations: Sugar, Slavery, and Plantation Agriculture in Early Barbados* (Charlottesville: University of Virginia Press, 2014), 115.

45. Richard Ligon, *A True and Exact History of Barbados*, ed. Karen Ordahl Kupperman (Indianapolis, IN: Hackett Publishing Company, 2011), 46; Michael Craton, *Testing the Chains: Resistance to Slavery in the British West Indies* (Ithaca, NY: Cornell University Press, 2009), 109–114, 335.

46. Menard, *Sweet Negotiations*, 116.

47. Menard, *Sweet Negotiations*, 117.

48. Menard, *Sweet Negotiations*, 118.

49. Quoted in Winthrop D. Jordan, *White Over Black: American Attitudes toward the Negro, 1550–1812* (Chapel Hill, NC: University of North Carolina Press, 2012), 185; Menard, *Sweet Negotiations*, 118.

50. Menard, *Sweet Negotiations*, 188; Richard S. Dunn, *Sugar and Slaves: The Rise of the Planter Class in the English West Indies, 1624–1713* (Chapel Hill, NC: University of North

Carolina Press, 2000), 104; Thomas E. Drake, *Quakers and Slavery in America* (New Haven, CT: Yale University Press, 1965), 5–7.

51. Menard, *Sweet Negotiations*, 118.

52. George Fox, *The Journal of George Fox*, ed. Norman Penny (New York: Octagon Books, 1973), 206–207.

53. Fox, *The Journal of George Fox*, 207.

54. Fox, *The Journal of George Fox*, 207.

55. Fox, *The Journal of George Fox*, 209.

56. Fox, *The Journal of George Fox*, 232.

57. Fox, *The Journal of George Fox*, 209.

58. Fox, *The Journal of George Fox*, 209.

59. Fox, *The Journal of George Fox*, 209–210.

60. Samuel Troth, "Richard Preston, Sr. Puritan Quaker of Maryland, Grandfather of Samuel Preston," *Pennsylvania Magazine of History and Biography*, 16, no. 2 (July 1892), 211.

61. For a long time historians believed that Harris arrived first in Virginia because of a letter written by Robert Clarkson to George Fox about Harris. In the letter he referred to the area she ministered in as "Virginia." J. Worall Jr. supported the position that Harris arrived first in Virginia, but Rufus M. Jones and J. Reaney Kelly both argued that she arrived in Maryland first and traveled later to Virginia. In speaking of Virginia, Clarkson could have been referring to the larger area of Maryland and Virginia, especially considering the fact that he references "two missionaries," probably Thurston and Coale, who had not yet arrived. Thus, Harris probably began her missionary work in Maryland and Thurston and Coale followed her there after working for a while in Virginia. J. Worrall Jr., *The Friendly Virginians, America's First Quakers* (Athens, GA: Iberian Publishing Co.,1994), 2; Rufus M. Jones, *The Quakers in the American Colonies* (New York: Macmillan Co, 1923 [orig. publ. 1911]), 266–268; J. Reaney Kelly, *Quakers in the Founding of Anne Arundel County Maryland* (Baltimore, Maryland: Maryland Historical Society Press, 1963), 2.

62. Letter dated the 20th of the 2nd month, 1658, from Thomas Hart, of London to Thomas Willan and George Taylor, embodying a copy of a letter from Robert Clarksonne of Severn to Elizabeth Harris in London dated ye 14th of ye 11th month, 1657. Swarthmore Collection, Friends Historical Library, London. Quoted in Rufus M. Jones, *The Quakers in the American Colonies* (New York: Macmillan Co, 1923 [orig. publ. 1911]), hereafter referred to as the Hart-Clarkson-Harris letter.

63. Alice Granberry Walter, ed. *Lower Norfolk County Virginia Court Records* (Baltimore, MD: Genealogical Publishing Company, 1994), 71a, 126a, 133a, Hart-Clarkson-Harris Letter.

64. Anne Arundel Wills, Hall of Records, Annapolis,10 ff., 82, 1ff., 494–497 cited in Kelly, *Quakers in the Founding of Anne Arundel County Maryland*, 47.

65. Kelly, *Quakers in the Founding*, 27.

66. Kelly, *Quakers in the Founding*, 43–44.

67. Hart-Clarkson-Harris letter.

68. Hart-Clarkson-Harris letter.

69. Hart-Clarkson-Harris letter; Kelly, 21.

70. Kelly, *Quakers in the Founding*, 22.

71. The debate arises over a letter that was written by Gerard Roberts to George Fox in July 1657 (Hart-Clarkson-Harris letter). In the letter he talks of Elizabeth Harris saying "The Friend who went to Virginia is returned in a pretty condition. There she was gladly received by man who met together, and the Governor is convinced." Rufus M. Jones argued that in saying "Governor" Roberts used it in a "loose and untechnical sense," and thus he was referring to Robert Clarkson, who was a citizen of Maryland and a Burgess for Ann Arundel County (*The Quakers in the American Colonies*, 266–267). Jay Worall Jr. disagrees with Jones

in saying that the governor convinced could only be Richard Bennett. This seems probable, considering that Bennett still owned tracts of land in Nansemond and the Severn region to which he might have returned at the end of his term as governor on April 1, 1655. Also, both areas were regions where Harris ministered on her journey (Jay Worall Jr., *The Friendly Virginians, America's First Quakers*, 6); J. Reaney Kelly provides a third interpretation of the letter, saying that the "Governor" might have referred to Captain William Fuller as he was often called by the name of Governor and served as leader for the colony in 1658 (J. Reaney Kelly, *Quakers in the Founding of Anne Arundel County Maryland*, 18).

72. J. Worrall Jr., *The Friendly Virginians, America's first Quakers*, 6–7, convinced by William Edmundson, Kelly, 7. Although Harris did not remain long in the colony, her legacy persisted in Maryland as both her husband, William Harris, and their son Will emigrated from England after the death of Elizabeth's father to live in Anne Arundel County. While Elizabeth remained in jail through the end of her husband's life, she moved to their settlement "Harris's Mount" in 1672. Later that year she greeted George Fox who had come to the colonies to give structure and organization to the newly formed Quaker communities (Worrall, 9–10).

73. George Rofe's letter is summarized in C.F. Smith, *Steven Crisp and His Correspondents, 1657–1692* (London, 1892), 30.

74. Quoted in Jones, *Quakers in the American Colonies*, 268.

75. Liber H. H., *Proceedings of the Council of Maryland, 1657–1660*, reproduced in William Hand Browne, Edward C. Papenfuse, et. al. eds., *Archives of Maryland*, 215+ volumes, (Baltimore and Annapolis, Md., 1883–), 3: 347 (hereinafter cited as *Archives of Maryland*).

76. *Archives of Maryland*, 348.

77. *Archives of Maryland*, 348.

78. *Archives of Maryland*, 358.

79. Quoted in Jones, *Quakers in the American Colonies*, 279.

80. Jones, *Quakers in the American Colonies*, 212.

81. Jones, *Quakers in the American Colonies*, 212.

82. Jones, *Quakers in the American Colonies*, 205.

83. Fox, *Journal of George Fox*, 377.

84. Griswold, *Manor*, 120–122.

85. Griswold, *Manor*, 224.

86. Griswold, *Manor*, 224.

87. Griswold, *Manor*, 224.

88. Griswold, *Manor*, 224–225.

89. Charles J. Hoadly, *Records of the Colony or Jurisdiction of New Haven, from May, 1653* (Hartford, 1858), 93.

90. Hoadly, *Records of the Colony or Jurisdiction of New Haven*, 364.

91. Hoadly, *Records of the Colony or Jurisdiction of New Haven*, 364.

92. Hoadly, *Records of the Colony or Jurisdiction of New Haven*, 412.

93. John Taylor, *An Account of Some of the Labours . . . By Sea and Land of John Taylor* (London, 1710), 6–7.

94. Taylor, *An Account of Some of the Labours*, 8.

95. Taylor, *An Account of Some of the Labours*, 8.

96. Griswold, *Manor*, 205.

97. Griswold, *Manor*, 205.

98. Griswold, *Manor*, 233.

99. Griswold, *Manor*, 233.

100. "The will of Richard Bennett" in William Bennett Boddie, *Seventeenth century Isle of Wight County, Virginia: a history of the county of Isle of Wight, Virginia, during the seventeenth century, including abstracts of the county records* (Baltimore: MD: Genealogical Publishing Company, 1973), A:286.

101. "Surrender of Virginia to the Parliamentary Commissioners, March, 1651–2 an excerpt from the British Museum Library. E 665. 3. Page, 1604–1607," *Virginia Magazine of History and Biography* 11, no. 1 (1903), 32–41.

102. "Surrender of Virginia to the Parliamentary Commissioners"; Fox, *Journal of George Fox*, 233.

103. Fox, *Journal of George Fox*, 234.

104. Fox, *Journal of George Fox*, 234.

105. George Fox, *Epistles*, 1698, 336.

106. Quoted in Jones, *Quakers in the American Colonies*, 273.

107. Jones, *Quakers in the American Colonies*, 273.

108. Smith, *Stephen Crisp*, 30.

109. Alice and Walter Granberry, ed. *Lower Norfolk County Antiquary, Virginia Court Records Book A and B* (Baltimore, MD: Genealogical Publishing Company, 1994), 3: 78.

110. Granberry, *Lower Norfolk County Antiquary,"* 3: 79–110, 109, 36.

111. Caroline Nicholson Jacob and Henry J., ed., *The journal (abridged) of Wm. Edmondson, Quaker apostle to Ireland and the Americas, 1627–1712* (Philadelphia, PA: Philadelphia Yearly Meeting of the Religious Society of Friends, 1968), 58–59.

112. G. Andrews Moriarity Jr. "The Emperour Family of Lower Norfolk," *Virginia Magazine of History and Biography*, 21, no. 4 (October 1913), 419.

113. Kingsbury, *Records of the Virginia Company*, 1:414, 255.

114. Fox, *Journal of George Fox*, 242.

PART VI

Imperial Worlds

CHAPTER 16

Pennsylvania's Religious Freedom in Comparative Colonial Context

Evan Haefeli

Pennsylvania is famous above all else for its religious tolerance. William Penn's most enduring legacy to America is often seen as inaugurating America's eighteenth century. Pennsylvania symbolizes the new era of commercially prosperous colonies, full of ethnically and religiously diverse immigrants, expanding westward and questioning slavery. The year 1680 has become the significant turning point in recent overviews of colonial history, displacing the once crucial 1688. For Jon Butler, it is when the colonies start to "become America." Ned Landsman, whose survey of "American Thought and Culture" also begins in 1680, has a different thesis: where Butler sees colonial America's development as "the Revolution before 1776," Landsman sees it going "from colonials to provincials."[1] Either way, Pennsylvania's religious liberty is seen as a decisive moment when pluralism and associated questions about modernity became fixtures of a distinct American destiny, setting it on a different, more liberal, course from Europe, and, implicitly, the other, earlier, American colonies like Massachusetts and Virginia. To understand just how exceptional Pennsylvania's religious tolerance was is to understand just how exceptional Pennsylvania was—or was not.

Louis XIV's revocation of the Edict of Nantes just a few years after Pennsylvania's founding only reinforces the impression that, with Pennsylvania, America left behind a Europe caught in the repressive grasp of an intolerant, conservative Old Regime. Europeans agreed. While some commentators praised Pennsylvania's toleration from the beginning, Pennsylvania's international reputation was sealed once French philosophes held it up as a model of the sort of tolerant society they desired. Most famously, J. Hector St. John de Crèvecoeur amazed over how, in America, religious hostility simply "burns away in the open air, and consumes without effect." Crèvecoeur's "Letters from an American Farmer" are not set in Massachusetts or Virginia: they are set in Pennsylvania, and the adjacent parts of New York and New Jersey that he knew.[2] More than just a model for European society, Pennsylvania has occasionally been seen as a model for colonization more broadly. Thus, at the dawn of the twentieth century, an English aristocrat writing a history of India claimed that, until recently, "the white man had brought no blessing to the darker nations of the earth," existing as a "despoiler, the enslaver, the exterminator of simpler races. The bright and brief episode of Pennsylvania stands out against a grim background of oppression and wrong."[3] It is not just Americans who see Pennsylvania as distinctive.

The uses to which Pennsylvania's reputation for peaceful religious coexistence has been put over the past three centuries would make a worthy study in its own right. Yet it should be recognized as such: a reputation, an image built up and used by an array of different figures, from American Quakers to French philosophes and others, each for their own reasons. Pennsylvania was an extraordinary place for many reasons. However, as this chapter will show, it was not extraordinary in its offer of religious liberty. That had been done before in a number of different colonies—in fact, a remarkable number of other English colonies had some form of religious toleration in 1680. The emphasis on Pennsylvania inaugurating a new era of religious pluralism overshadows those other examples, leading us to misunderstand the context out of which Pennsylvania emerged. Yes, it had a remarkable amount of religious freedom, but, as stated, in this it was not alone. And, like all other forms of toleration, Pennsylvania's had distinct limits and preferences. For the first few decades it appealed mostly to Quakers, and indeed helped consolidate their hegemony in the Delaware Valley. Pennsylvania represents an important stage in the history of religious tolerance, but its significance is due for a reassessment.

If we expand our perspective a bit, Pennsylvania appears less as the dawn of a new era than the last gasp of an earlier imperial order, one in which radical experiments with religious toleration were possible in a way they would not be after 1688. Even in North America, Pennsylvania was not the first colony to offer some form of religious liberty: Rhode Island, Maryland, and New Jersey had already pioneered a strategy of avoiding a formal church establishment. Carolina and New York had some sort of religious establishment, but each permitted a degree of pluralism years before Pennsylvania began. If we expand the frame a bit further, it is clear that, far from pioneering a new, eighteenth-century idea of colonization with religious freedom, Pennsylvania represented the culmination of a seventeenth-century pattern of strategic religious liberty designed to protect the interests of certain groups over others. A quick look at subsequent colonial religious arrangements confirms that Pennsylvania was the last experiment in religious freedom, followed by a century of a more limited Protestant hegemony. It was this position as the last, most vibrant, prosperous, and best-advertised example of colonial religious liberty that guaranteed Pennsylvania's fame, not its newness or uniqueness.

Indeed, Pennsylvania's religious liberty seems a bit conservative compared to some of the other possibilities on hand in 1680: it was neither the most radical, nor the most inclusive, nor even the first experiment in religious liberty in the region. This chapter begins with a quick look at regional precedents for religious liberty before pulling out to survey the range of religious tolerance available in the English colonies at the time of Pennsylvania's founding, and the particular religious atmosphere they created and fostered. Some of these cases, like Rhode Island, are well known. Others, like the Bahamas or Jamaica are not. Yet all need to be taken into account in any discussion of the power of William Penn's religious vision. The result demonstrates that Pennsylvania was not as unique as is generally thought: it was but one of a spectrum of possibilities. However, only when we consider the colony's religious system within the context of its time can we really grasp what, if anything, was distinctive about Penn's "Holy Experiment."

Significantly, Pennsylvania differed from many of its neighboring colonies in that it was not the first colony established on its territory. Six other colonies had been attempted in the Delaware Valley, and holdovers from each still lived there when Penn claimed ownership. The toleration Penn offered them was not the first they had experienced. The Dutch colonies of New Netherland and New Amstel, as well as the Swedish colony of New Sweden all had envisioned some type of religious tolerance for the area. The Swedes, who had a Lutheran Church establishment, had offered a limited toleration to the Dutch Reformed, and the Dutch Reformed offered a limited toleration to the Swedish Lutherans as each battled the other for control. More remarkable were the possibilities that emerged after the city of Amsterdam took over the region, turning it into the colony of New Amstel. None of these possibilities foreshadowed Pennsylvania's tolerance. Indeed, most were downright hostile to Quakers. Penn was not the first person to imagine religious pluralism for the Delaware River Valley, but he was the first to make it friendly to Quakers.[4]

Generally, the Dutch and Swedes strove to restrict pluralism as much as possible while favoring their respective church establishments. The Swedes colonized the area first, in 1638, only to be conquered by the Dutch of New Netherland in 1655. The Dutch allowed the Swedes to retain the services of just one of their Lutheran pastors: a limited toleration, but more than they were willing to grant the Lutheran community of the Hudson River Valley. However, the West India Company that owned New Netherland could not afford to administer the whole colony, which stretched from Connecticut to Maryland. By 1660, it sold all its rights in the Delaware Valley to the city of Amsterdam. Initially, Amsterdam's burgomasters looked as if they would promote the Dutch Reformed Church in their colony of New Amstel as much as the West India Company did in New

Netherland. Dominie Henricus Selijns, writing from Manhattan, claimed it was "very necessary" to send a Dutch Reformed minister to the Delaware River because "of the abominable sentiments of various persons there, who speak very disrespectfully of the Holy Scriptures," since it had not enjoyed steady preaching from an orthodox Dutch Reformed minister, allowing the local Swedish Lutherans to do "great damage among the sheep, who have so long wandered about without a shepherd." Amsterdam did send two ministers along with a few hundred colonists. The first died after two years of work; his replacement died on the voyage over. A few months after Selijns wrote, New Netherland fell to the English. New Amstel's small flock of Dutch Reformed had to wait decades for a new minister. The Dutch Reformed colonists who stayed on in the area were still seeking one at the time they were incorporated into Pennsylvania.[5]

Amsterdam's enthusiasm for the hegemony of the Reformed Church in its colony proved short-lived. In the early 1660s, two separate Catholic priests were given permission to administer to Catholics in the region (Maryland was right next door), provided they did so discreetly and privately (it is not clear if they ever went). Inspiration for even more radical forms of toleration came from the Collegiants, a small but influential group of religious Seekers who did not quite exist as an organized church but resembled Quakers in some ways. Instead of religious rituals, their services simply involved reading a chapter out of the Bible and discussing it. They were open to a range of visitors and sympathizers: Mennonites, mystics, philosophers, and freethinkers, including two men, Franciscus van den Enden and Pieter Corneliszoon Plockhoy, who proposed radical social and religious experiments for New Amstel.[6]

Franciscus van den Enden, a former Jesuit, brought the influences of Spinoza, Descartes, and the Collegiants together in his plan for an American colony. He had been a Jesuit in his native Spanish Netherlands before moving to Amsterdam. Born in Antwerp in 1602, he had distinguished himself as a teacher of Latin grammar, poetics, and rhetoric but ran into trouble teaching theology. Expelled from the order in 1633, he settled in Amsterdam, where he practiced medicine, sold artistic prints, and opened a Latin School for those who did not wish to attend the official, Reformed Protestant, Latin School of Amsterdam. Through this school, he instructed several great figures of the Dutch Enlightenment, including Spinoza. Most important for Van den Enden's relationship to America was his acquaintance with Pieter Corneliszoon Plockhoy around 1661. That February, the States General in conjunction with the West India Company passed an act opening New Netherland to "all Christian people of tender conscience in England or elsewhere, oppressed." They especially targeted "English, good Christians" who might not want to face life in the recently restored monarchy. Without giving further specifics, it guaranteed settlers "full liberty to live in the feare of the Lord," as well as concessions on land, taxes, and trade.[7]

Soon after the passage of this act, the city of Amsterdam considered at least three proposals for settlements in New Amstel. First was a proposal by the aforementioned Franciscus van den Enden. His idea involved a wide-ranging vision of a just society that, among other things, came out strongly against slavery and for reason: "in so far as the Christian Religion is a reasonable Religion, that it consequently is also in conflict with it and with sure Reason, to hold humans as permanent slaves." With regard to religion, he wanted a pluralistic "Society of different people with conflicting sentiments" resembling nothing so much as a gathering of Collegiants. Preachers of all sorts would be kept out, for they "are feeders and stiffeners of everyone's particular opinion." If "preachers from one sect were chosen, it would be impossible for so many people of different humors and inclination to agree with it." The alternative, "to appoint particular Preachers for each sect," would be both impractical and "an unavoidable ruinous pest of all peace and concord." Instead, colonists would rely on the "very most peaceful and also cheapest Preacher, the Holy Scripture." Coming together for joint worship services at a set time on Sundays and other Dutch Holy days, they were to listen to an appropriate chapter of the Bible, singing psalms before and after the reading for mutual edification, and then leaving, as they had gathered, with consideration and modesty. The absence of a chance to discuss the day's reading—a notable difference from the Collegiants—may have been part of Van den Enden's scheme to ban religious conflict by preventing confrontation. While "nobody" was "in one way or another allowed to be molested on account of whatever assertion in matters of religion or opinion," Van den Enden's desire to maintain "peace and unity" and avoid "all private quarrels and violent sectarianism concerning religious matters" in his colonial community led him to exclude most of his contemporaries from his "Christ-civil Society." These included "all intractable people, such as obstinate Papists narrowly devoted to the Romish Chair, usurious Jews, obstinate English Quakers, Puritans and reckless, stupid believers in the millennium, together with all obstinate contemporaries claiming revelations, etc." It was both an extraordinarily ecumenical and extraordinarily limited vision of pluralism.[8]

Van den Enden wanted a society founded on "Divine reason," but it is not clear if he ever intended to go to America to create it. His vision fit better into the urban milieu of Amsterdam than the forests of America. The other proposals considered by the Amsterdam city council involved people who clearly intended to emigrate. First was a group of twenty-five Mennonite families in April 1662. Then, a month later, came Pieter Corneliszoon Plockhoy's proposal. Unlike Van den Enden, he actually created a small community on the Delaware River, possibly with some of those Mennonite families. Plockhoy was not as deeply rooted in Amsterdam as Van den Enden. He had been out of the country for several years before 1661. While his connections to Amsterdam's various radical circles were tenuous, he had spent the previous five years or so on an international quest to build an ideal community. He had the experience and persistence that an intellectual like Van den Enden lacked to actually create a settlement.[9]

A relatively unknown but extraordinary figure in the history of Dutch tolerance and colonization, Pieter Corneliszoon Plockhoy was not a child of privilege and education. An artisan's son who lost his father at a young age, he spent his whole life working for a living. Beginning as a Mennonite in Zeeland, he embarked on a spiritual as well as physical journey that took him to England in the late 1650s before he settled in Amsterdam around 1661, where he attended Collegiant meetings. In between he had developed a connection to Samuel Hartlib and his circle of international, ecumenically inclined Protestants, and had presented to Oliver Cromwell a plan for universal religious toleration that involved the abolition of churches and ministers throughout England, Scotland, and Ireland to be replaced with "one general Christian assembling or meeting-place," in which "all people" could "orderly confer together concerning the Doctrine and Instruction of their Lord and Master Christ." Another tract of his proposed the founding of an egalitarian community to "eschue the yoke of Temporal and Spiritual Pharaohs who have long enough domineered over our bodies and souls, and set up again (as in former times) Righteousness, love and Brotherly Sociableness, which are scarce any where to be found." People from all walks of life would live together, mutually sharing in any mercantile profits while at the same time communally underwriting all capital investments. Medical care would be free and available to all, and widows and orphans would be cared for in a community centered on the life of the family. Such social and economic concerns had not received much attention in Van den Enden's proposal.[10]

Plockhoy had come close to setting up his ideal ecumenical community in Ireland when the Restoration of Stuart rule threw everything into doubt. After first contemplating a move to the Calvinist County of Wied along the Rhine River, which was granting extensive religious freedom and civil rights to foreigners of any faith to develop the new trading town of Neuwied, Plockhoy turned to America, hoping to set up his utopian community on the Delaware along the lines of what he had proposed in Britain. The idealistic community's existence was brief and tragic. Thirteen months after twenty-five families totaling forty-one people landed at the mouth of the Delaware in July 1663, their homes were thoroughly plundered by conquering English troops. Plockhoy, his family, and most, if not all, of his fellow colonists returned to Amsterdam, where he soon died (although his blind son eventually returned to die decades later in Germantown).[11]

New York governed the Delaware Valley for a decade and a half before Pennsylvania arrived, yet it was not the first English colony planned for the area. Chartered the same year as Maryland, the colony of New Albion had been granted to a loyal and wealthy member of the Catholic gentry: landowner and lawyer, Sir Edmund Plowden. Had New Albion succeeded, the middle colonies never would have existed. Its grant encompassed the entire Mid-Atlantic, from today's New York to Delaware. Alas for Plowden, a unusual combination of difficulties at home and in America consigned his efforts to oblivion. Unlike Calvert, Plowden had been a recusant his whole life and had never been able to develop powerful political connections. Family troubles and political opposition (especially from members of the government connected to the Virginia Company) delayed his departure by almost a decade. When he and a party of relatives and indentured servants finally arrived on the Delaware River in 1642, they encountered New Sweden, whose governor sent Plowden to Virginia, where he sat out the English Civil War. When he returned to England for reinforcements in 1648, his efforts were swallowed up by the revolution that killed his king and conquered Ireland, leaving New Albion's claims to languish until they were eventually supplanted by the 1664 charter for New York.[12]

New Albion's failure is a useful reminder that flexibility on religious and even political matters was no guarantee of colonial success. The major source of information on Plowden's religious proposals is his promotional pamphlet of 1648. The *Description of the Province of New Albion* makes clear that this was a dynastic enterprise aimed to transform the Plowdens from beleaguered gentry into people who could almost look a peer of the realm in the eye. It said nothing about Plowden's Roman Catholicism, nor did it make a special appeal to Roman Catholics, but it did say a good deal about his "ancient family" and boasted that only Plowden had "a special creation of an Earle Palatine," unlike the other colonial proprietors. The titles the Earl Palatine bestowed on his family, such as the "Baron of Mount Royall" and the "Baronesse of Princeport," make his royalist sympathies clear."[13] Meanwhile, the Catholic tinge to his dream appears in his proposal to rename the island of Manhattan "Syon," after the wealthy and famous Bridgettine convent that had existed just west of London before the Reformation.[14]

However, in the revolutionary circumstances of 1648, Plowden played down his Catholic and aristocratic pretensions in favor of having a "Parliament or Grand Assembly." Regarding religion, since he could not follow the current example of England, where religion was "yet unsettled," Plowden proposed an ambitious system of tolerance modeled after that of the Dutch. After New Albion's "Parliament" passed an act "to settle and establish all the Fundamentals necessary to salvation, as the three Creeds, the Ten Commandements, Preaching on the Lords day, and great days, and Catechising in the afternoon, the Sacrament of the Altar and Baptisme," Plowden would permit "no persecution to any dissenting." They would be allowed to have "free Chapels" as the Walloons did in Holland. Eschewing coercion, New Albion's religious settlement would take hold through "argument or perswasion ... acted in mildenesse, love and charity, and gentle language, not to disturb the peace or quiet of the inhabitants," as long as they obeyed "the Civill Magistrate." Prosecution was reserved only for those who were "seditious" and would "bitterly rail and condemn others."[15]

It is unclear if William Penn was aware of New Albion, although he was well aware of Dutch tolerance, having passed through the country on a preaching tour, where he denounced it. Regardless, there were a number of other English examples of colonial religious tolerance on hand at the time Penn received the charter for Pennsylvania in 1681. In North America alone, six colonies already permitted an extraordinary amount of religious liberty: Rhode Island, Maryland, Carolina, New York, East Jersey, and West Jersey. Rhode Island and Maryland had begun before the English Civil Wars began, but had had their charters reconfirmed shortly after the Restoration in 1660, at a time when the new regime was still sorting out its religious settlement at home and overseas. Neither Rhode Island nor Maryland had ever had any sort of church establishment, albeit for very different reasons. Rhode Island's intensely biblical culture allowed radical Protestants of various stripes to flourish, but especially Baptists, while in Maryland the lack of an official establishment allowed its Catholic elite to make Roman Catholicism more or less the unofficial religion in the colony. Most of Maryland's Anglicans were poor and depended on the occasional visit from a Virginia minister. The colony's mix of Quakers and Presbyterians were allowed to go their own way, albeit in different corners of the colony from where the Catholics lived. Maryland and Rhode Island were both pluralistic, but not in the same way.[16]

Meanwhile, several of the Caribbean colonies founded before the Restoration also permitted religious toleration to some degree. The Bahamas had begun in 1648 without an established church, but the colony virtually collapsed after the shipwreck of its version of the *Mayflower.* The few people who stayed on were incorporated in 1670 into the proprietary colony of the Bahamas the king granted to the Carolina Proprietors. Although no Fundamental Constitutions were drawn up for the Bahamas, the charter permitted the proprietors "to grant indulgences and dispensations with regard to religious worship." As in Carolina, the assumption was that ultimately the prevailing religion should be that of the Church of England. Eventually, by the 1730s, that was the case.[17]

Jamaica, acquired in the 1650s, had, like Rhode Island, begun its existence as an English colony with much religious fervor but without a formal established church. As in Rhode Island, Baptists, Congregationalists, and Quakers thrived in the absence of an established church. However, unlike Rhode Island, after the Restoration Jamaica was divided up into parishes and the Church of England effectively established. The many Protestant dissenters living on the island became a tolerated minority as the Church of England grew steadily in strength. In 1682 Jamaica's governor reported that the "Quakers and Independents" (i.e., Congregationalists) who were "the chief sects" on the island were "very submissive to the civil government and enjoying toleration.[18]

A similar situation existed on Barbados. The Church of England had been established at the colony's founding, and its parishes have ever after formed the island's political units. However, there had been a good deal of sympathy for the Puritan cause on the island, and during the revolutionary years of the 1640s and 1650s the episcopal Church of England was replaced by a variety of Protestant inclinations, most notably Quakerism, which spread from Barbados across the Caribbean and up to North America in the 1650s, and the English Atlantic's first recognized Jewish community. The Restoration of the monarchy brought back the Church of England establishment, albeit with a certain degree of religious liberty for Protestant dissenters. However, by the time Pennsylvania was being established, Barbadian Quakers were facing stepped up harassment, primarily for bringing slaves to religious services and refusing to serve in the militia. They were not banished from the island—indeed, a number had been banished *to* the island in the 1660s—but gradually they began to leave. By the eighteenth century, Pennsylvania had supplanted Barbados's position as a cornerstone of the Quaker Atlantic, and Barbados' Quaker population was in terminal decline.[19]

The other American colonies with religious toleration, Carolina, New York, and the Jersies, were creations of the Restoration regime. The first, and most capacious vision of tolerance, was Carolina, created in 1663. Its Fundamental Constitutions, drafted in part by John Locke, allowed for the public exercise of any religion on which "seven or more persons" could agree, with just three restrictions. First, everyone had to belong to a church and every church had to keep a strict record of its membership. Second, no one could "use any reproachful, reviling, or abusive language against any religion of any church or profession," a rule that could be used to restrain aggressive proselytizing (at the time an issue primarily associated with Quakers). Finally, the constitutions allowed for the eventual establishment of the Church of England by the colonial assembly; no other church could ever receive official funds. Although proposing a remarkably wide-ranging form of tolerance, these requirements also excluded certain people, most obviously those "that doth not acknowledge a God, and that God is publicly and solemnly to be worshiped." The proprietors knew that this opened Carolina to "Jews, heathens, and other dissenters from the purity of Christian religion." However, they hoped that, "by good usage and persuasion" these individuals might "be won over to embrace and unfeignedly receive the truth," in other words, that they would eventually join the Church of England. The Fundamental Constitutions were never made law, but Carolina remained without an established church until the early eighteenth century, when the Church of England became the church of the colony. Significant congregations of dissenters, especially Quakers and Congregationalists, remained, but now as minorities enjoying an indulgence rather than as fellow equals.[20]

New York—originally the entire territory of the Dutch colony of New Netherland plus the eastern half of Maine and the various islands off the New England coast, like Martha's Vineyard—had yet another system, created after the 1664 English conquest. The Dutch population was allowed to continue worshipping as Dutch Reformed as before. However, now they had to pay for it themselves, losing the governmental funding that had previously paid for their ministers. Moreover, the groups they had denied the right to worship openly, Lutherans and Quakers, gained that right under the English. Elsewhere, outside the Dutch settlements and the towns of New York and Albany, there were several different congregations permitted; the new law code of 1665, the Duke's Laws, provided for a mix of religious tolerance and establishment. Every village and town was required to have an established religion, but what that would be depended on a majority vote of the householders. Thus there was a right to choose one's religion, but it resided in the town, not with the individual. The Duke's Laws specified that no one could be "molested fined or Imprisoned for differing in Judgment in matters of Religion who profess Christianity" (unlike Carolina there was no allowance for Jews or other non-Christians). However, no alternative source of religious sacraments was permitted apart from the local minister.[21]

New York's bias toward an organized establishment reflected the systems in place in Virginia and New England. Indeed, New Hampshire, which had a similar, if smaller, mix of English Protestants, ended up with a system similar to New York's, albeit after much contention, and not codified until the 1680s.[22] A Quaker community existed, but intermittent harassment encouraged a number of them to move across the river to New Jersey. The most outstanding element in New York's religious mixture was its Jewish community, the only one in English North America. With roots stretching back to the Dutch colony of New Netherland, the Jewish community had faded away in the years after the English conquest. However, by 1682 enough Jews had arrived to form a stable congregation capable of holding religious services. New York's strong governor helped protect them from the occasional attack by the legislature. No Jewish communities were established in colonial New Jersey, and a Jewish community did not emerge in Pennsylvania until the mid-eighteenth century, when a few from the New York community moved down to Philadelphia. In the 1680s, that same executive power allowed a small Catholic community to emerge in New York, where some even became officeholders, including the governor and Irish soldier Thomas Dongan. The Church of England was weak until the 1690s, when, after the suppression of the Catholics, the governor used the establishment clause to establish it in the counties in and around New York City.[23]

Pennsylvania was thus simply the latest in a series of colonies that officially permitted religious tolerance. Indeed, it was not even the only Quaker colony around. Soon after the conquest of New Netherland, New Jersey had been created. Then, after 1674, it was split into two colonies, East and West, both largely controlled by Quakers. The original New Jersey colony had been granted by the Duke of York to two of the Carolina Proprietors, who had not established the

Church of England, preferring to leave the mixed population of Dutch Reformed, Quakers, and Baptists living in northern New Jersey to worship as they pleased, even though the original proprietors Berkeley and Carteret were both conservative Anglicans. Their "Concessions and Agreements of the Lords Proprietors of the Province of New Jersey," which applied to the colony between 1665 and the Dutch conquest of 1673, echoed the sentiments in the law codes of New York and Carolina, but with a stronger opposition to established religion. Settlers were authorized to "at all times truly and fully have and enjoy his and their Judgements and Conciences in matters of Religion throughout all the said Province" and no one could be "any waies molested punished disquieted or called in Question for any difference in opinion or practice in matters of Religious concernments" as long as they behaved "themselves peaceably and quietly and" did not use "this liberty to Licentiousness, nor to the civill injury or outward disturbance of others." Harassment, discrimination, and aggressive proselytizing were prohibited, "any Law Statute or clause conteyned or to be conteined usage or custome of this Realme of England to the contrary thereof in any wise notwithstanding." Well into the eighteenth century, colonists would invoke this religious liberty.[24]

These provisions were further sharpened after Berkeley, more in need of money than a colony, sold his half of New Jersey to two Quakers: John Fenwick and Edward Byllynge. Fenwick had been a Parliamentarian cavalry officer during the civil war. He witnessed the execution of Charles I, then served in the guard troops of the Cromwellian regime before becoming a Quaker around 1660.[25] Byllynge's origins are more obscure. He also served in the cavalry but never rose above the rank of cornet. Byllynge and his wife were converted in 1657 by George Fox in Scotland, where Byllynge was stationed. Leaving the army, Byllynge moved to Westminster, where he became a prolific pamphleteer for the Quaker cause and a fairly prosperous brewer. He developed contacts with leading Quakers, including William Penn, and a number of important government officials, like Samuel Pepys, Henry Bennett, Lord Arlington, and Berkeley, who sold him his share of New Jersey. However, Byllynge also had many debts. On the verge of bankruptcy when he purchased West Jersey, Byllynge partnered with the more fiscally sound Fenwick in a financially complicated sale that ultimately gave Fenwick one-tenth of the colony's land.[26]

West Jersey was the first colony to build a Quaker society from the ground up. After a vigorous promotional campaign in Quaker circles, the first Quaker immigrants arrived in 1675, led by John Fenwick, but not until 1676 did Carteret and Byllynge agree to split New Jersey into two colonies. Thereafter, colonists, almost all of them Quakers, arrived at a steady pace until by 1681 some 1,400 lived in West Jersey, transforming the Quaker population of the Delaware Valley from nothing to roughly the same size as the existing non-Quaker population, if not more.[27]

West Jersey protected its largely Quaker population with a principled statement about religious liberty in its constitution. The Concessions and Agreements of West Jersey claimed that "no Men nor number of Men upon Earth hath power or Authority to rule over mens consciences in religious matters," proclaiming that "no person or persons whatsoever within the said Province at any time or times hereafter shall be any waies upon any pretence whatsoever called in question or in the least punished or hurt either in Person Estate or Priveledge for the sake of his opinion Judgment faith or worship towards God in matters of Religion." If any member of the Assembly should "designedly willfully and Maliciously move or excite any to move any matter or thing whatsoever that contradicts or any wayes subverts any fundamentall of the said Laws . . . they shall be proceeded against as Traitors."[28] These principles were reiterated and clarified in a new Fundamental Agreement drawn up in 1681. The new constitution reiterated that liberty "of conscience in matters of faith and worship towards God" was granted to all "who shall live peaceably and quietly therein," and reinforced Quakers' right to hold colonial office with the provision that "none of the free people of the said province shall be rendered uncapable of office in respect of their faith and worship."[29] There was no more radical endorsement of religious freedom than that of West Jersey.

West Jersey's religious freedom was designed by and for Quakers, the vast majority of the population. Its promotional materials assumed it was a colony of, by, and for Friends. George Fox in 1677 reminded "My Dear Friends, in New Jersey, and you that go to New Jersey," that much was expected of the colony, "For many Eyes of other Governments or colonies will be upon you; yea, the Indians also. . . . And therefore, let your lives, and Words, and Conversations, be as becomes the Gospel."[30] William Penn and two other Quakers who served as financial Trustees of Byllynge's interest in the colony, clarified the Quaker nature of the colony, saying "we would not have any to think, that it is promised or intended to maintain the liberty of the exercise of religion by force and arms; though we shall never consent to any the least violence on conscience; yet it was never designed to encourage any to expect by force of arms to have liberty of conscience fenced against invaders there of." Although they would not coerce people's beliefs, they hoped "that nothing which hurts or grieves the holy life of truth in any that goes or stays, may be adhered to; nor any provocations given to break precious . . . of friends where they live."[31]

Very little is known about the religious life of West Jersey before 1690, but it was clearly something of a Quaker paradise. A set of promotional letters from Quaker colonists published in 1676 stressed the bounty of the land, the healthiness of the climate, its affordability, but also the spiritual contentment it offered. One woman wrote, "I have more comfort in one day here, than I had in many dayes in England, which is great joy to my soul." A man believed "the Lord is making way to exalt his name and truth," assuring his wife that in West Jersey "we may live very quietly and Peaceably, where we shall have no vexation, nor tearing nor rending what we have from us," referring to the harassment, imprisonment and seizure of Quakers' property to pay fines and legal costs back in England. Another woman was more explicit: "here is liberty for the honest hearted that truly desire to fear the Lord; here is liberty from the cares and Bondage of this World." West Jersey had religious freedom—for Quakers.[32] It remained almost completely a Quaker affair until Edward Byllynge died in January 1687. Then his heirs sold his remaining shares, along with the right to govern the colony, to Dr. Daniel Coxe, an Anglican speculator with good court connections.[33]

East Jersey faced greater political and religious challenges. Colonization had begun before it became New Jersey, and it had difficulty gaining independence from New York. Philip Carteret, New Jersey's first governor, had been forced to return to England in 1672 to clarify his powers. Returning in 1674, Carteret continued to face opposition on issues relating to land, taxes, and political power until the Duke of York formally surrendered his rights over New Jersey in August 1680. But the proprietor, Sir George Carteret, had died six months earlier, prompting his family to auction off their rights to East Jersey to a new group of twelve Quaker proprietors headed by William Penn in February 1682. These twelve proprietors then agreed to take on twelve additional associates, for a total number of twenty-four proprietors of East Jersey. Five of the additional proprietors were Quakers, two from Dublin and three from Scotland. The rest were Quaker associates from London and Scotland. Thus, while not entirely Quaker, the East Jersey proprietors were mostly so, and the rest clearly were happy to support their influence.[34]

Already religiously diverse, East Jersey soon became much more so once William Penn brought Scots into the enterprise. In 1683, the leading Scottish Quaker, Robert Barclay, and a mixed group of fellow Scottish Quakers and Episcopalians (both of whom were persecuted minorities in Presbyterian Scotland) acquired a controlling share of East Jersey. Barclay was appointed governor, sending over several Quaker deputy-governors to represent him until his death in 1690. The Scots developed a wedge of settlement running south and east from Perth Amboy, sending over six hundred Scots in four expeditions between 1683 and 1685. For the Scottish proprietors, Scottishness rather than a specific religious affiliation was the key asset. Scottish Quakers were too few to populate a colony, being only about one thousand people out of one million Scots. Instead, most of the Scottish colonists were Presbyterians, including about a hundred Cameronians, radical Presbyterians who refused to recognize the legitimacy of Charles II's government. The rest were a mix of Episcopalians, Quakers, and even a handful of Catholics. One Scottish Catholic, William Douglas, was elected to the Assembly in 1680, only to be expelled after admitting his religion. East Jersey was pluralistic, with an unusually diverse group of Scots living alongside

English Quakers, Congregationalists, Baptists, and Jersey Islanders brought over by Philip Carteret, joined by a few French, probably immigrants from New France, including the French boy baptized by the Superior of the Maryland Jesuits at Woodbridge in 1683.[35]

In East Jersey, Quaker liberties required the embrace of the colony's religious diversity. The advent of the Scottish proprietors prompted the drafting of a new "Fundamental Constitution for the Province of East New Jersey" in 1683. Like the Fundamental Constitutions of Carolina, most of its provisions proved too complex to implement in America. The religious provisions continued New Jersey's initial pledge not to disturb any peaceable citizens over matters of conscience, only the new Fundamental Constitutions went further to explicitly protect Quakers from the sort of discrimination they were currently suffering in New York and elsewhere. No one was to "be compelled to frequent and maintain any religious worship, place, or ministry whatsoever," and officials had to swear that they would not "endeavor alteration in the government" or seek "the turning out of any in it or their ruin or prejudice, either in person or estate, because they are, in his opinion, heretics or differ in their judgment from him." Finally, the religious purpose of the law was emphasized with the clarification that it was not "intended that any under the notion of this liberty shall allow themselves to avow atheism, irreligiousness," or to indulge in the coarse habits of popular culture, such as "cursing, swearing, drunkenness, profaness, whoring, adultery, murdering . . . stage plays, masks, revels, or such like abuses."[36]

As with West Jersey, there is little evidence on the experience of religious life in East Jersey. Promotional materials made much of the fertility of the soil, the potential for harbors and trade, but also stressed that "the Constitutions of the Country" drawn up by Berkeley and Carteret provided for "Liberty in matters of Religion and Property in their Estates." Colonists enjoyed not only the safety of their property, but "an uninterrupted Exercise of their Particular perswasions in matters of Religion." The new proprietors boasted that these liberties led to the colony being already "considerably Peopled, and that much from the adjacent Countries" and expressed their willingness to make "such farther additions and supplements to the said Constitutions" as would help settle the colony "with a sober and Industrious People."[37] Their proposal for the town of Perth Amboy set aside "Four Acres for a Market-place, Town-house, etc." but made no mention of constructing a church.[38] Nonetheless, a "Brief Advertisement" published in Scotland in 1685 encouraged those who "upon accompt of their not going that length, in [religious] conformity required of them, by the Law do live very uneasie," to move to East Jersey with their ministers.[39]

Between them, West and East Jersey had established the most radical forms of religious tolerance available in English America at the time of Pennsylvania's founding. They went beyond the provisions for liberty of conscience in Carolina and Rhode Island to explicitly defend the privileges of Quakers to both serve in government and be free from harassment over their beliefs, such as pacifism. And Quakers were much safer in New Jersey than most other colonies, as they were both a majority of the population and dominated both its governments of halves in the 1680s.

From this perspective, Pennsylvania's religious freedoms did little more than follow the lead of the other Quaker colonies. Like the other Quaker colonies, it owed its existence to close connections to indebted courtiers. Penn's connection was strengthened by a debt of about sixteen thousand pounds King Charles II had never paid his father. The debt provided the excuse for granting Penn a colony. However, it had a political purpose as well. Charles did not feel obliged to compensate Penn until 1680: the height of the exclusion crisis that had brought England's government to a standstill. Several months before Penn petitioned for a colony, he had supported the election of Algernon Sidney to Parliament. Sidney, a revolutionary aristocrat who would be executed for treason in 1683, was a determined Calvinist, a republican, and a bitter opponent of the Restoration regime. Finally granting Penn his wish for an American colony was, the historian Mary Geiter has concluded, part of Charles's strategy of "dividing his opponents" by "appealing to moderate elements among them." His new colony gave Penn and all those who invested in the colony—many of them connected to the opposition in London—a reason to support the Crown. Until then, overseas trading companies had been an Anglican prerogative. Pennsylvania opened up a rare opportunity for non-Anglicans to form their own trading company. After months of negotiation, interwoven with the ongoing political crisis, Penn's charter was granted at the beginning of March 1681, just three weeks before the final Exclusion Parliament met. Missing from the opposition in that final Parliament was the backing of a number of influential London merchants, particularly Protestant dissenters. With their king having just opened up a new opportunity to them and their friend William Penn, they had a strong incentive to drop their support for Exclusion.[40]

Pennsylvania was thus closely associated with a range of powerful people: a significant difference from the other Quaker colonies. When Penn drew up a constitution for his colony, he added some distinctive flourishes indicating he was not imagining Pennsylvania to be a place for Quakers only. Like the other Quaker colonies, he ensured that government would be by moral Christians who could, by the wording, be anything from Quaker to Catholic. All officers and all electors were to "be such as profess faith in Jesus Christ, and that are not convicted of ill fame or unsober and dishonest conversation." It also reiterated that particularly Quaker concern that none shall "be compelled at any time to frequent or maintain any religious worship, place, or ministry whatever." However, his religious requirement for immigration was considerably broader, open to all those "who confess and acknowledge the one almighty God to be the creator, upholder, and ruler of the world." In theory this could include all monotheists, including Jews, although it was clearly targeted primarily at Christians. Colonists merely needed to "hold themselves obliged in conscience to live peaceably and justly in civil society," and they would "in no ways be molested or prejudiced for their religious persuasion or practice in matters of faith and worship."[41]

By the eighteenth century, Pennsylvania would have large communities of German Lutherans, Scots and Irish Presbyterians, as well as substantial numbers of Anglicans, but they were not what Penn initially had in mind.[42] Instead, similar to Van den Enden and Plockhoy, he hoped Pennsylvania could be a place for ecumenical understanding among like-minded, albeit not uniformly affiliated, members of a range of Protestant sects, although he intended Quakers to be the "socially dominant faith."[43] For years he had cultivated friends and contacts among pietistic and mystical-leaning Protestants across Europe, and it was them he hoped to lure to his colony. In his first promotional letter from Pennsylvania, he wrote how he "found Love and Respect enough where I came; an universal kind Welcome, every sort in their way. For here are some of several Nations, as well as divers Judgments."[44] Two years later, Penn's second open letter promoting the colony continued his emphasis on diversity, harmony, order, and dutiful coexistence. Pennsylvania was not an English refuge, but a European phenomenon, containing "a collection of divers nations in Europe: as, French, Dutch, Germans, Sweeds, Danes, Finns, Scotch, Irish and English." He admitted that the number of English was "equal to all the rest," most of them Quakers.[45]

Penn's expectation of harmonious coexistence is evident in his description of the mixed group of colonists populating his colony in the 1680s. They were "of one kind, and in one place and under one allegiance, so they live like people of one country, which civil union has had a considerable influence towards the prosperity of that place." They shared a desire for "the suppression of Vice, and encouragement of Vertue and Arts; with Liberty to all People to worship Almighty God, according to their Faith and Perswasion." It was a deliberately social, commercial, and religious vision, but one without a particular confessional affiliation. Nevertheless, in his town planning, he was more explicit about the need for religious gathering spaces than the proprietors of East Jersey, allotting land for townships with a view toward "Society, Assistance, Busy Commerce, Instruction of Youth, Government of Peoples manners, Conveniency of Religious Assembling, Encouragement of Mechanicks, distinct and beaten roads."[46]

Something of Penn's religious predilections for Pennsylvania can be gleaned through his friendship with Francis Daniel Pastorius. A Lutheran lawyer of pietistic inclinations and associate of the famous Frankfurt pietist Philipp Jakob Spener, Pastorius traveled to Pennsylvania on the same ship as Penn in 1683. He served as leader and agent of Germantown community, founded by a dozen Mennonites and Dutch Quakers who worshipped for several years in a common meetinghouse. The Latin inscription Pastorius carved above his first little house: "Parva domus sed amica bonis, procul este prophani: It's a little house, but welcoming to good people: Profane men keep your distance" won Penn over instantly.[47] Pastorius shared Penn's expectations for the colony, criticizing the one Lutheran preacher in the area, an old German who had been serving the Swedes for the previous decade, as a drunkard who failed "to show the Swedes the way to heaven" as he should have: "like a statue of Mercury." He celebrated the religious diversity he encountered in Pennsylvania. The ship that carried him (and Penn) over had people "of such different religions and behaviors that I might not unfittingly compare the ship that bore them hither with Noah's Ark." The Philadelphia household where he first lodged contained "those who hold to the Roman, to the Lutheran, to the Calvinist, to the Anabaptist, and to the Anglican Church, and only one Quaker." For Pastorius, like Penn, this diversity was laudable, for what mattered was the quality of people's religious devotion, not the specific confessional allegiance.[48]

Another effective articulation of the appeal of the toleration available in Pennsylvania and the Quaker colonies in the 1680s comes from Penn's friend and sympathizer Thomas Tryon. Tryon was something of an eccentric Protestant pietist. In 1640, at the age of six, he had experienced a religious vision that forever changed his life, leading him on a hard-working but prosperous journey from the Gloucestershire countryside to London, where he became such a successful hatter he retired at the age of 48 and became a writer of advice books on religion and, especially, health, having lived much of his life as an ascetic vegetarian. He had been to Barbados, but never North America. In his 1684 *Planter's Speech to his Neighbours & Country-men of Pennsylvania, East & West-Jersey, and to all such as have transported themselves into New-Colonies for the sake of a quiet retired life*, he warned the colonists not to forget the reasons why they emigrated in the first place. If they simply enriched themselves with trade, they would not be "one Inch the nearer your proposed Happiness in America, than in Europe; and have travelled some Thousands of Miles to as little purpose as the Jesuits into Japan and China, or foolish Pilgrims in their tedious vain Journeys to Compostela, Loretto, or Jerusalem."[49]

Tryon understood the emigrants' religious motives to be, in essence, the hope of building a society along Quaker lines. In America they could live in peace (without government harassment as in England) and "Worship God and Obey his Law with freedom, according to the Dictates of the divine Principle, unencumbred with the Mouldy Errors and Fierce Invasions of Tradition, Politick Craft, Covetous or Ambitious Cruelty." They left behind the "Ungodly Company" of England to "avoid both being grieved with the sight and Infections, as well as odious Examples of Horrid Swearings, Cursings, Drunkenness, Glutony, Uncleanness, and all kinds of Debauchery continually committed with greediness; and also escape the Judgments threatened to every Land polluted with such

Abominations." In America, "under the bountiful Protection of God, and in the Lap of the least adulterated Nature" they could "bring forth more plentious Fruits to the Glory of God, and publick Wellfare of the whole Creation." Although he did not name Quakers by name, it is clear that they and their friends were the people he had in mind, for he hoped that by their "Holy Doctrine, and the Practical Teachings of our Exemplary Abstemious Lives, transacted in all Humility, Sobriety, Plainness, Self-denial, Virtue, and Honesty," all key terms of Quaker religiosity, that they "might gain upon those Thousands of poor dark Souls scattered round about us, (and commonly, in way of Contempt and Reproach call'd, Heathens) and bring them not only to a state of Civility, but real piety." Quakers were not simply seeking a refuge. They wanted a pious society constructed on Quaker terms that was capable of converting non-Christians. Pennsylvania and the other Quaker colonies thus promised to fulfill an age-old desire of European expansion as well as secure Quakerism.[50]

Pennsylvania did not introduce a new idea of religious liberty to English America. That had already existed for decades. In Carolina and West Jersey it was arguably more radical than what Penn proposed for his colony. Moreover, potential immigrants understood the difference between these religious arrangements. Not all who sought religious liberty in the 1680s went to Pennsylvania, much less West Jersey. Huguenots and Jews preferred New York and Carolina; Catholics Maryland; Baptists Rhode Island. Anglicans became a recalcitrant minority in Pennsylvania who, after insisting on having oaths sworn in Court, found themselves opposed by the majority of colonists and Penn himself, who saw in this maneuver an infringement of liberty of conscience. The "Church of England Men" complained that Penn and his allies "stigmatized" them "with the grim and horrid titles of treacherous and perfidious fellows," who were "Introuders and Invaders in the Province" as well as "dissenters & Shismaticks from the Establish't Religion," which in Pennsylvania, the Anglicans claimed, "is Quakerism."[51]

The Glorious Revolution of 1688 ended this extraordinary era of colonial experiments in religious ecumenism. Quakers, and all the colonies that had resisted the growth of the Church of England, were looked on with suspicion. Now, a broad, church-based Protestant hegemony that permitted a different, more limited religious tolerance (it explicitly excluded Catholics from the benefits they'd enjoyed in places in the 1680s, for example) became the rule until the American Revolution. It favored the expansion of churches linked to some sort of establishment, be it the Congregational Church in New England, Presbyterianism, or the Church of England. The range of toleration constricted as the Church of England expanded into all the American colonies, where it gained formal recognition in some, like Maryland and Carolina, and partial recognition in others, like New York. Never again would Quakers, Baptists, or other religious minorities have the upper hand in organizing a colony's religious life.[52]

With some luck, Pennsylvania survived to thrive in the eighteenth century. If religious liberty alone had made such a feat possible, then we would be talking much more about Rhode Island, yet Rhode Island did not change the American religious landscape as Pennsylvania did. The last in a long series of religious experiments in religious liberty, Pennsylvania was distinguished above all by William Penn's connections, wealth, and spirit of enterprise. Roger Williams lacked anything like Penn's valuable and politically influential networks. Spanning England and western Europe, they enabled Penn to draw on far more resources than any of the other colonies that had already implemented religious liberty. Pennsylvania also laid claim to a great deal of land, which encouraged a steady flow of immigrants to help it grow and prosper. Other colonies had embarked on comparable Holy Experiments of religious toleration before, but none managed to attract so many people and so much capital. That material support made Pennsylvania not the first, but rather the biggest of the colonial experiments in religious liberty. Without all of that support from Europe, Pennsylvania could have floundered and failed like many of the other colonial experiments in religious liberty that had preceded it.

NOTES

1. Jon Butler, *Becoming America: The Revolution before 1776* (Cambridge, MA: Harvard University Press, 2000); Ned Landsman, *From Colonials to Provincials: American Thought and Culture, 1680–1760* (Ithaca: Cornell University Press, 2000).

2. J. Hector St. John Crèvecoeur, *Letters from an American Farmer and Sketches of Eighteenth-Century America* (New York: Penguin, 1986), 75–76.

3. Sir William Wilson Hunter, *The India of the Queen and Other Essays*, ed. Lady Hunter, intro. Francis Henry Skrine (London: Longmans, Green, and Co., 1903), 213.

4. Evan Haefeli, "The Pennsylvania Difference: Religious Diversity on the Delaware before 1683," *Early American Studies* 1, no. 1 (2003): 28–60.

5. Edward T. Corwin, ed. *Ecclesiastical Records: State of New York*, 7 vols. (Albany: James B. Lyon, 1901–1916), 1:549–550; 2:823. Evan Haefeli, *New Netherland and the Dutch Origins of American Religious Liberty* (Philadelphia: Penn Press, 2012), 233–237.

6. Haefeli, *New Netherland*, 238–239.

7. Edmund B. O'Callaghan, and Berthold Fernow eds. *Documents Relative to the Colonial History of the State of New York*, 15 vols. (Albany: Weed, Parson & Company, 1853–1887), 3:37–39; Haefeli, *New Netherland*, 239–240.

8. Haefeli, *New Netherland*, 241–247.

9. Haefeli, *New Netherland*, 247.

10. Haefeli, *New Netherland*, 248–250.

11. Haefeli, *New Netherland*, 250–251.

12. Louis H. Roper, "New Albion: Anatomy of an English Colonization Failure, 1632–1659," *Itinerario* 32, no. 1 (2008), 1–15.

13. Beauchamp Plantagenet, *A Description of the Province of New Albion* (Middelburg? 1648), 7, 8, 9–12.

14. *CSPC, 1574–1660*, 154.

15. Plantagenet, *Description*, 6, 13, 27–28.

16. Evan Haefeli, "How Special was Rhode Island? The Global Context of the 1663 Charter," in Chris Beneke and Chris Grenda, eds. *The Lively Experiment: Religious Toleration in America from Roger Williams to the Present* (Lanham, MD: Rowman and Littlefield, 2015), 21–36.

17. *CSPC, 1675–1676*, 122–23, 147; Michael Craton and Gail Saunders, *Islanders in the Stream: A History of the Bahamian People*, 2 vols, vol. 1 *From Aboriginal Times to the End of Slavery* (Athens: The University of Georgia Press, 1992), 131.

18. *CSPC, 1681–1685*, 314.

19. *CSPC, 1661–1668*, 7, 29, 49, 142–43, 269; *CSPC, 1669–1674*, 506–7; *CSPC, 1675–1676*, 331, 422–24, 426, *CSPC, 1677–1680*, 223, 502–4; Larry Gragg, *Englishmen Transplanted: The Colonization of Barbados, 1627–1660* (Oxford: Oxford University Press, 2003).

20. "Fundamental Constitutions of Carolina, March 1, 1669/70," in Mattie Erma Edwards Parker, ed. *North Carolina Charters and Constitutions* (Raleigh, 1963), 181–183; W. L. Saunders, ed. *The Colonial Records of North Carolina*, 26 vols. (Raleigh, NC: Printer to the State, 1886–90), 1:156, 202–204; L. H. Roper, *Conceiving Carolina: Proprietors, Planters, and Plots, 1662–1729* (New York: Palgrave, 2004), 128–131.

21. Northrup A. Judd et al., eds. *The Colonial Laws of New York from 1664 to the Revolution*, 5 vols. (Albany: J. B. Lyon, 1894), 1:19–20, 24–26, 32, 45–46, 59, 78.

22. David E. Van Deventer, *The Emergence of Provincial New Hampshire, 1623–1741* (Baltimore: Johns Hopkins University Press, 1976), 181–190.

23. Haefeli, *New Netherland*, 169–185; Joyce D. Goodfriend, *Before the Melting Pot: Society and Culture in Colonial New York City, 1664–1730* (Princeton: Princeton University Press, 1992), 46; Jacob R. Marcus, *The Colonial American Jew, 1492–1776*, 3 vols. (Detroit: Wayne State University Press, 1970), 1:305–308; 2:863–865; Eli Faber, *A Time for Planting: The First Migration, 1654–1820* (Baltimore: Johns Hopkins University Press, 1992), 38–41; John H. Kennedy, "Thomas Dongan: Governor of New York (1682–1688)" (PhD., diss. The Catholic University of America, 1930), 86–87; Thomas Hughes, *History of the Society of Jesus in North America, Colonial and Federal: Text*, 2 vols. (London: Longmans, Green, and Co., 1907–1917), 2:142–149; John G. Shea, *History of the Catholic Church in the United States*, 4 vols. (New York: Edward O. Jenkins' Sons, 1866), 1:87–89.

24. William A. Whitehead et al., eds. *Archives of the State of New Jersey*, 1st ser., 43 vols. (Newark, NJ, 1880–1949), 1:30. A 1747 petition to incorporate a Dutch Reformed Church invoked the religious liberty granted by Berkeley and Carteret, see Dutch Church Patent, Second River, Newark, NJ, 1747 in Van Cortlandt Family Papers, Case for Oversized Mss., New York Historical Society.

25. John Fea, "Fenwick, John (1617/18–1683)," *Oxford Dictionary of National Biography* (Oxford: Oxford University Press, 2004) [http://www.oxforddnb.com/view/article/71092].

26. Caroline Robbins, "William Penn, Edward Byllynge and the Concessions of 1677," in n.a., *The West Jersey Concessions and Agreements of 1676/77: A Round Table of Historians* Occasional Papers Number 1 (Trenton: New Jersey Historical Commission, 1979), 17–23.

27. John E. Pomfret, *The Province of West New Jersey, 1609–1702: A History of the Origins of an American Colony* (Princeton: Princeton University Press, 1956), 75, 106–107. There were about eight hundred Swedes, four hundred Dutch, and maybe two hundred non-Quaker English.

28. Richard S. Dunn and Mary Maples Dunn, eds. *The Papers of William Penn*, 5 vols. (Philadelphia: Penn Press, 1981–1987), 1:396–397.

29. Fundamental Agreement of the Governor, Proprietors, Freeholders, and Inhabitants of West New Jersey, November 25, 1681, in *Foundations of Colonial America: A Documentary History*, ed. W. Keith Kavenagh, 3 vols. (New York: Chelsea House Publishers, 1973), 2:1101.

30. Cited in Edwin B. Bronner, "The English Setting," in n.a., *West Jersey Concessions and Agreements*, 15.

31. Epistle Respecting West Jersey, 1676, in Albert Cook Myers, ed. *Narratives of Early Pennsylvania, West New Jersey and Delaware, 1630–1707* (New York: Scribner's, 1912), 184, 185.

32. *A Further Account of New Jersey in an Abstract of Letters Lately Writ from thence by several Inhabitants there Resident* (1676), 1, 3, 4, 6, 8. See also John E. Pomfret, "West New Jersey: A Quaker Society," *William and Mary Quarterly* 8 (1951), 494–519.

33. Coxe was a doctor and natural philosopher who conducted chemical experiments with vegetables. He sold his interests in West Jersey in 1692, and then acquired the title to the Carolana colony and attempted to explore and colonize the mouth of the Mississippi River. Michael Hunter, "Coxe, Daniel (1640–1730)," *Oxford Dictionary of National Biography* (Oxford: Oxford University Press, 2004) [http://www.oxforddnb.com/view/article/37319].

34. John E. Pomfret, *The Province of East New Jersey, 1609–1702: The Rebellious Proprietary.* (Princeton, NJ: Princeton University Press, 1962); John E. Pomfret, *Colonial New Jersey: A History* (New York: Scribner's, 1973), 29–35, 49–50.

35. Pomfret, *Colonial New Jersey*, 50–54, 57; Ned Landsman, "William Penn's Scottish Counterparts: The Quakers of 'North Britain' and the Colonization of Early New Jersey," in *The World of William Penn*, ed. Richard S. Dunn and Mary Maples Dunn (Philadelphia: Penn Press, 1986), 241–258; William Whitehead, *East New Jersey under the Proprietary Government* (Newark, 1875), 410–472; Ned C. Landsman, *Scotland and Its First American Colony, 1683–1765* (Princeton, NJ: Princeton University Press, 1985), 17–194; John G. Shea, *History of the Catholic Church in the United States*, 4 vols. (New York: Edward O. Jenkins' Sons, 1866), 1:90. For Catholics from New France, see Evan Haefeli and Kevin Sweeney, *Captive Histories: English, French, and Native Narratives of the 1704 Deerfield Raid* (Amherst: University of Massachusetts Press, 2006), 134, 138–139.

36. W. Keith Kavanagh, ed. *Foundations of Colonial America: A Documentary History*, 3 vols. (New York: Chelsea House Publishers, 1973), 2:1107; Pomfret, *Colonial New Jersey*, 51.

37. William Penn et al., *A Brief Account of the Province of East-Jersey in America, published by the present Proprietors thereof* (London, 1682), 4–5. See also George Scot, *The Model of the Government of the Province of East-New-Jersey in America* (Edinburgh, 1685).

38. *Proposals by the Proprietors of East-Jersey in America for Building a town on Ambo-point* (London, 1682), 2.

39. *A Brief ADVERTISEMENT, Concerning East-New-Jersey, in AMERICA*, National Archives of Scotland, Edinburgh, RH 18/1/93.

40. Mary K. Geiter, *William Penn* (London: Longman, 2000), 33–48; Mary K. Geiter, "The Restoration Crisis and the Launching of Pennsylvania, 1679–81," *EHR* 112, no. 446 (1997): 300–318; Mary K. Geiter, "London Merchants and the Launching of Pennsylvania," *Pennsylvania Magazine of History and Biography* (hereafter *PMHB*) 100 (1997), 101–122.

41. "Laws Agreed Upon in England," in *William Penn and the Founding of Pennsylvania: A Documentary History*, ed. Jean R. Soderlund (Philadelphia: Penn Press, 1983), 132.

42. On the challenges to Penn's vision of coexistence posed by the growth of Anglicans, Presbyterians and other non-sectarian Christians, see Sally Schwartz, *"A Mixed Multitude": The Struggle for Toleration in Colonial Pennsylvania* (New York: New York University Press, 1987).

43. Andrew R. Murphy, *Conscience and Community: Revisiting Toleration and Religious Dissent in Early Modern England and America* (College Park.: Pennsylvania State University Press, 2001), 185. See also, J. William Frost, "Pennsylvania Institutes Religious Liberty," *PMHB* 113 (1988), 323–348 and Edwin Bronner, "The Failure of the 'Holy Experiment' in Pennsylvania, 1684–1699," *Pennsylvania History* 21 (1954), 83–108; Schwartz, *A Mixed Multitude,"* 12–35.

44. William Penn, Letter to the Committee of the Free Society of Traders, 1683, Albert Cook Myers, ed. *Narratives of Early Pennsylvania, West New Jersey and Delaware, 1630–1707* (New York: Scribner's, 1912), 225.

45. Subsequent growth in the Quaker population was due to a combination of conversions among existing colonists and natural reproduction, Richard T. Vann, "Quakerism: Made in America?" in *The World of William Penn*, ed. Richard S. Dunn and Mary Maples Dunn (Philadelphia: Penn Press, 1986), 157–172.

46. William Penn, "A Further Account of the Province of Pennsylvania, 1685," in Myers, *Narratives of Early Pennsylvania*, 260, 263, 276.

47. Anthony Grafton, "The Republic of Letters in the American Colonies: Francis Daniel Pastorius makes a Notebook," *American Historical Review* 117, no. 1 (2012): 4.

48. Francis Daniel Pastorius, "Positive Information from America," in Soderlund, *William Penn and the Founding of Pennsylvania*, 355, 356. For more on Penn's ecumenical vision, and some of the Germans who shared it with him, see Patrick M. Erben, *A Harmony of the Spirits: Translation and the Language of Community in Early Pennsylvania* (Chapel Hill: The University of North Carolina Press for the Omohundro Institute of Early American History and Culture, 2012).

49. Thomas Tryon, *The Planter's Speech to his Neighbours & Country-men of Pennsylvania, East & West-Jersey, and to all such as have transported themselves into New-Colonies for the sake of a quiet retired life* (London, 1684), 8.

50. Tryon, *The Planter's Speech*, 5–6. Quakers had a strong testimony against fleeing persecution. Pennsylvania had to be an opportunity rather than a refuge, J. William Frost, "William Penn's Experiment: Promise and Legend," *PMHB* 107, no. 4 (1983), 588, 591.

51. William Stevens Perry, ed. *Historical Collections Relating to the American Colonial Church*, 5 vols. (Hartford: Church Press Company, 1870–), 2:4.

52. On the changes in colonial religious policy, see Evan Haefeli, "Toleration and Empire: The Origins of American Religious Diversity," in *British North America in the Seventeenth and Eighteenth Centuries*, ed. Stephen Foster, supplemental volume, William Roger Louis, ed. *Oxford History of the British Empire* (Oxford: Oxford University Press, 2013), 103–135.

CHAPTER 17

William Penn and Security Communities

A CAREER

Patrick Cecil

On a dreary, overcast day in May 1666 Captain Richard Rooth stood on the deck of *HMS Dartmouth*, cruising the Irish coast off the seaport of Carrickfergus and watching smoke and commotion arise from the town. The English garrison, short on food and awaiting nine months of back pay, mutinied and seized the small urban center and its castle. After several days of monitoring the situation, Rooth witnessed four companies of loyal troops approaching the town under the command of the Earl of Arran, son of the Viceroy of Ireland, the Duke of Ormonde. To his surprise, Rooth found his twenty-one-year-old cousin William Penn among the ranks. Rooth watched with pride as his cousin charged forward alongside his comrades in arms and squelched the mutiny by force. Writing a letter in July to his uncle, Admiral Sir William Penn, Rooth accounted how his cousin "was pleased to accompany his lordship" at Carrickfergus, "to his no small reputation."[1] The younger Penn's future and career looked promising. As an up-and-coming son of one of England's most famous admirals, Penn had begun to cultivate relationships with influential men such as Arran and Ormonde. With their support, and having proven himself in his first taste of battle, Penn appeared to be on the path to a military career.[2]

This short-lived account of William Penn's military promise has generated almost no attention compared to his better-known legacy of being the founder of Pennsylvania and the champion of liberty of conscience and the rights of Englishmen. And, echoing the oversight to Penn's military career, scholars have given little analysis to the factors that fashioned his approach to conflict resolution and maintaining peace between entities. This article fills this historiographical void by presenting William Penn's view on security between groups, and how he arrived at this understanding emphasizing the active pursuit and practice of peace.

In this discussion "security" is defined as stability in diplomatic, military, and trade relations between different entities, whether persons or groups. This stability is an understanding of and respect for the relationship dynamic in its current state. By not upending the status quo with a singular instance of violence or a series of antagonizing events in a short timeframe, those entities enjoying this stability gain assurance for peace moving forward. This beginning of a collective purpose for keeping peace is practiced consistently over time. Emanuel Adler notes that the foundations for the construction of this relationship can begin with trade and social interactions. Though participants may not be actively aware of what they are establishing, they are providing for the basis of new bonds and new understandings to be formed.[3]

A sense of integration, or rather community, begins to build upon the initial interactions between groups. These transactions and agreements, while not necessarily promoting equality, establish how things are in the relationship. With practice and repetition these interactions take on a greater meaning within the reality in which participants find themselves. Adler argues this emphasis on historical, cultural, and political contexts within a relationship is a learning process. Peace is constructed in society. It is a slow progression, spanning generations. With regular practice, members of this growing and strengthening community "diffuse their 'lessons' and expectations to one another through various processes of communication," such as through gift giving or meetings.[4] What results is a security community, where members have become integrated and have bought into peace as being the desirable status in their relationship. When conflict does arise, they have practiced and thus turn to "deeply entrenched habits for conflict resolution" in order for peace to be maintained.[5]

William Penn pursued his own security communities in multiple arenas. He understood that security could be achieved when different groups actively pursued peace together, ranging from its earliest stages of a trade agreement or social interaction to the more intentional practice of conflict resolution. The sources for Penn's security perspective are found in his early professional development in Ireland, the immediate aftermath of his Quaker conversion and subsequent literary defense, and the situation present in the Delaware River Valley prior to his colonizing ventures. These early arenas informed Penn's outlook on keeping peace in society. As his public career matured, he sought to implement his security philosophy in active colonizing ventures in the Delaware River Valley and ultimately in idealistic theories and proposals for the greater Atlantic World. It is evident throughout William Penn's public career that he understood that the way to stability, prosperity, and ultimately lasting peace came through the establishment of a security community among differing peoples.

As a leading figure within the Society of Friends (commonly known as the Quakers), a proponent of civil liberties, and an American colonizer, Penn has rightfully attracted discussion from scholars with a variety of interests. However, these scholars have not considered the formative experiences and ideas that fashioned his security approach in tandem with its implementation in Pennsylvania and the Atlantic World. Of Penn's biographies, Edward Beatty's *William Penn as Social Philosopher* examines Penn's life through his social ideas and approaches his subject thematically in several chapters associated with security: "Builder of a New Utopia," "Founder and Governor," "Patriot and Imperialist," and "Friend of the Indians."[6] Beatty notes Penn's strategy to treat Indians with justice. However, there is no deeper discussion offered in how Penn understood stability in society, or in how to maintain it.

Like Beatty's chapter on Penn's Indian relations, scholars have used the proprietor's interactions with Indians in North America as a window into how Penn aided in promoting the notable long period of peace in Pennsylvania. Francis Jennings's essay in Richard and Mary Dunn's *The World of William Penn* considers both Penn's and Indian perspectives regarding land purchases.[7] He sees sincerity in Penn's dealings with Indians, as well as pragmatic considerations over trade and boundary disputes. Jennings begins to delve into Penn's interactions that assist in providing a basis for peace, but does offer commentary on how Penn arrived at this understanding. Daniel Richter's *Trade, Land, Power* examines a letter from Penn to Indians and also highlights Penn's just attitude.[8] While noting the importance that Indians, and for that matter Penn, placed on diplomacy, Richter also does not develop the factors that influenced Penn's approach for emphasizing stability. Jean Soderlund's *Lenape Country* examines the relationship between Lenape Indians and the Swedish, Dutch, and English settlers in the Delaware River Valley during the seventeenth century.[9] Her study demonstrates how the Lenape traded and negotiated with Europeans, yet also maintained their position of power through diplomacy and occasional violent prods. In treating Penn and the arrival of Quakers, Soderlund finds the Friends' commitment to religious liberty and friendly relations with Indians found a favorable political situation already present, but she too does not delve into the factors that shaped Penn's security outlook. In these three works, Penn's arrival brings a newcomer to the Delaware River Valley that could potentially disrupt the status quo. His background and experiences, however, point to an awareness of how to achieve and maintain stability, and thus secure his colony.

Beyond Pennsylvania and Indian relations, scholars have examined William Penn's proposals for multiple government entities working together to secure common goals of defense, economic prosperity, and a more just society. His *Essay towards the Present and Future Peace of Europe*, "Briefe and Plaine Scheam," and meeting with North American governors in 1700 offer evidence of Penn's security perspective, yet they have been analyzed in political and intellectual approaches. William Hull and Mary Dunn treat these proposals as examples of Penn's political acumen, while John Moretta emphasizes the imperial context surrounding Penn in order to understand his political decisions and proposals.[10] Caroline Robbins's essay in *The World of William Penn* uses the three proposals to demonstrate Penn's intellectual capability when faced with obstacles and setbacks in life.[11] But in analyzing the proposals from perspectives of political skill or intellectual determination, scholars have not explicitly discussed Penn's approach to achieve security, or stability, between groups and the factors of his background that informed this understanding. Quaker pacifism or fair treatment of Indians in and of themselves cannot explain how Penn understood the methods to keep peace between groups. In a violent Atlantic World in which Penn was heavily invested, it is necessary to examine the beginnings of Penn's security approach and how he came to consistently practice peace in order to achieve stability.

Before William Penn's security community outlook took shape, he received valuable military experience that would contribute to part of a well-rounded understanding of military force and its relationship to securing peace. As the son of Admiral Sir William Penn, the younger Penn gained instruction in military and naval affairs from his father. Twenty-year-old Penn went aboard ship with his father in the spring of 1665 as the English fleet prepared for the Second Anglo-Dutch War. Under his father's watch, Penn gained a charge to present an account of the fleet and to relay messages from the Duke of York, Lord High Admiral, to Charles II. Penn arrived at Whitehall Palace at the end of April and noted that the king came down from his chambers "only in his gown and slipers."[12] Charles inquired about Sir William Penn several times, and after interrogating young Penn for over half an hour about the state of the fleet and Sir William's messages, bid that the Penns go about their business. Having witnessed the fleet's organization alongside his father, and required to relate his observations and instruction before the king, Penn gained an early exposure and understanding to outward symbols of defense.

William Penn's hands-on lessons on defense matters continued in Ireland. Sir William gained lands in southern Ireland for service to Parliament and the Stuarts, but because of his role with the navy, he sent his son to tend to affairs on family lands. In addition to this very real need to manage his estate, Sir William also wanted to expose his son to the Irish Court and allow him to establish connections. Penn the younger soon developed a friendship with the Earl of Arran. When the English garrison at Carrickfergus mutinied in May 1666, Penn stood by his friend as they charged into battle and helped squelch the uprising. This experience signaled the possibility of a military career. The Duke of Ormonde, Arran's father and the Viceroy of Ireland, observed Penn's "forwardnesse on the occasion of repressing the late Mutiny among the Souldiers," and suggested that Sir William resign his post as commander of the company of Kinsale in favor of the admiral's son.[13]

Penn displayed his eagerness at the prospect of a military career when Sir William delayed his response to Ormonde's suggestion. He wrote to his father on July 4, 1666, about the proposed commission and asked him to acknowledge Ormonde's and Arran's kindness and consideration. While waiting for his father to respond, Penn sat for a portrait depicting him in military armor. Tellingly, this would be the only one he ever sat for. Both the letter and the portrait illustrate Penn's enthusiasm to be a soldier in his early twenties. Sir William, however, put an end to these aspirations. He warned his son against "youthful desires" outrunning "discretion," and wrote to Ormonde thanking him for the kindness he had shown to his son. He also informed Ormonde that he intended to settle back in Ireland and collect on the Kinsale captain's annual salary of £400.[14] Observing the fleet and the action at Carrickfergus served as good experiences for the young Penn. Penn had taken part in military action and understood how it had resolved a matter that endangered the local area and could potentially explode into something larger, especially with the Cromwellian conquest of Ireland having just concluded the previous decade. But Sir William envisioned his son becoming a lawyer or statesmen. Despite having his aspirations dashed by his father's veto, the young William Penn retreated from a military career with lessons learned about military and naval affairs and combat experience.[15]

While Ireland provided military experience, it also served as the first arena for the development of how Penn envisioned a security community. Letters from Sir William in the spring of 1667 demonstrate that the younger Penn gained experience in business transactions, managing estates and tenants, and exercising a degree of autonomy. While traveling in Ireland between 1669 and 1670, Penn kept a journal detailing his meetings and noting the status of lands. On November 25, 1669, he ended business with "the Inhabitants of Corke."[16] The following month he described a farm managed by a Captain Boles to be "well Improv'd" and went "about admeasureing C[apt. John]. W[akeham's]. land" and later agreed on rent rates.[17] Penn began to absorb insights into different peoples and cultures while traveling through the countryside, conducting business, and interacting among the Irish population. He also learned about being an English colonial landlord over a native population where relations still simmered since Cromwell's conquest. Treating the Irish Catholics as equals was not in the cards, but Penn also did not seek to aggravate the state of affairs. By conducting business dealings in a cordial and professional manner, peace had a chance to grow following war.

Ireland also allowed for Penn to sharpen his understanding of the relationship between stability, peace, and the use of force. His travels brought him into contact with numerous military-minded men. One of his first meetings noted in his Irish Journal occurred with a former colleague of his father, Sir George Ascue, who had retired from naval service after rising to the rank of rear-admiral. On November 20 he met with Robert Sandys, a colonel of a company of foot at Kinsale, and on May 19 Penn met "wth old R[obert]. S[outhwell].—disputed wth him. ended wth C[ousin Ensign William]. Penn. Din'd wth my C[ousin Richard]. Disputed much at table. return'd to Cork."[18] It is important to note Penn's disputes. By this time he had converted to Quakerism and in coming to grips with his newfound faith, Penn engaged in debate with men of military backgrounds. Having a background in military and naval affairs but being pulled in another direction by Quaker tenets, Penn, through these debates, continued to forge his understanding of the relationship between military force and peaceful endeavors to achieve stability. Ireland provided the perfect venue for an overlord trying to achieve peaceful prosperity and steady income. Penn's previously established connections also provided influence. On June 4, 1670, he dined with the Earl of Arran, Lord Shannon, Major Thomas Fairfax, Henry Bulkeley, Colonel Hugh Leeson, and Edmund Sheffield. Fairfax, Bulkeley, Leeson, and Sheffield all had military backgrounds. Furthermore, not only did Penn have a friend in Lord Arran, but both Leeson and Sheffield had served as comrades in arms with Penn and Arran in suppressing the Carrickfergus mutiny, a story no doubt revisited in the discussions held over dinner and wine. Over the course of several years in Ireland, and with numerous hands-on experiences ranging from warfare, business transactions, dinners, and debates, William Penn gained an education in the role that diplomacy and military strength played in building security in Ireland.[19]

William Penn's conversion to Quakerism is estimated to have occurred in Cork during the summer of 1667 after he heard the itinerant Quaker preacher Thomas Loe. With this conversion, Penn learned about Quaker ideas of pacifism and new ideas of community. Pacifism has become one of the hallmarks for the Society of Friends. Early Quaker history, however, shows that the tenet has not always been definitive. The peace testimony developed over a gradual and complicated process with both spiritual and political motivations. Some early Quakers, notably soldiers from Oliver Cromwell's army, did not reject war. George Fox, the founder of the Society of Friends, tried to reassure Cromwell in 1655 that he used only spiritual weapons to combat the evils in the world. Growing spiritual hostility toward violence coincided with the political realities of the Stuart restoration. In June 1660 the Quaker leader Margaret Fell articulated to Charles I and Parliament the sect's aversion to strife, wars, and contentions. After the government crushed the insurrectionist plot of Thomas Venner's Fifth Monarchists, Fox and other Quakers released *A Declaration from the Harmlesse & Innocent People of God Called Quakers Against All Plotters and Fighters in the World* on January 21, 1661. This marked the official declaration of the peace testimony, and, combined with Robert Barclay's *Apology for the True Christian*

Divinity (1678), laid the foundation for pacifism to grow within the Quaker community. Quakers also developed a sense of spiritual unity. Persecuted for their beliefs, especially under the Stuarts, members offered support and hospitality to one another. Quakers steadily adhered to the peace testimony as brothers and sisters suffered as they did. While the Quaker belief in the Inner Light highlighted individual revelation, the sect developed a strong and cohesive sense of community.[20]

Penn struggled early to adhere to a shifting peace testimony, but he came to embrace the communal resistance against persecution. In the fall of 1667 Penn attended a Quaker meeting in Cork, where he observed a soldier causing a disturbance. Still young in his newfound faith and coming to grips with the peace testimony, Penn could not check his growing impatience with the soldier. He seized him by the collar and physically removed the troublemaker from the meeting. With the rush of adrenaline and anger, Penn prepared to throw the soldier down a set of steps. The congregation, however, stopped him from harming his fellow man. His pride hurt, the soldier returned with reinforcements, arrested Penn, and hauled the Quakers before the magistrate. Penn remained dedicated to defending his faith. He resided in the Tower of London from December 1668 through July 1669 on the charge of blasphemy, found himself on trial in London in September 1670 for preaching, and sat in a Newgate prison from February to July 1671, also for preaching. But in the course of increasing his resolve on behalf of Quakers, Penn's conflict with the peace testimony receded. When Penn did not want to give up wearing his sword, the weapon that had saved his life in a duel in Paris and that marked his status as a gentleman, George Fox trusted that the Inner Light would work its own revelation for Penn and advised him to wear it as long as he could. According to Mary Brailsford, the sword had disappeared the next time Penn and Fox met. Penn became part of the Quaker community in the course of his imprisonments and public preaching. In so doing, he grew in his understanding of the restraint and patience practiced by his fellow believers.[21]

William Penn's imprisonments helped launch another arena, found in the literary defense of religious toleration and the rights of Englishmen. He tried over the course of his career as an author to emphasize the importance of building a sense of civic community that could encompass multiple religious communities in England. In June 1669 Penn wrote from the Tower of London to Henry Bennet, the Lord Arlington, against the charge of blasphemy that had imprisoned him. He argued for liberty of conscience: "it's not the property of Religion . . . to persecute & compel Religion; which should be embrac'd freely for her selfe, not by force."[22] He continued on the theme of liberty of conscience when he published *The great case. Of liberty of conscience once more debated & defended* the following year. As a dissenting Quaker Penn attempted to align his sect within the greater Protestant community. Self-interest is present, but Penn believed religious toleration built security and stability for all. He argued that inhibiting a person's religious beliefs served to undermine the Christian faith and that religious persecution destroyed natural affection.[23] With fellow Quakers suffering at the Isle of Ely, Penn cited the history of religious violence in Europe to show that persecution "hatches & brings forth Warrs," and that toleration naturally brought about happiness.[24] In defending his religious beliefs and those of his fellow Quakers, Penn maintained that religion should not be a tool of force. Penn provided insight into how he believed society could prosper by arguing that religiously inspired persecution broke down affection between differing peoples and faiths. A peaceful and stable society grew from toleration, both with regard to religion and in respecting a person's fundamental rights.

In addition to illustrating the hypocrisy of religious persecution, William Penn's defense of the rights of Englishmen also shows his views on security and peace in society. When he published *England's present interest* (1675) Penn combined the contemporary ideas of John Locke and the natural rights of man with the historical precedent of the rights of Englishmen to argue that a stronger community and peace arose from toleration: "Charitable Connivance and Christian Toleration often Dissipates [men's passions]."[25] Disrespecting a man's honor and private beliefs only emboldens him, as Penn had demonstrated as he dug in his heels when authorities attacked his Quaker beliefs. Penn argued that the strength of a community and its governing force rested in the consent of the governed. He reasoned in *One project for the good of England* (1679) that "where People are sure of their own, and are Protected from Violence or Injury, they chearfully yield their Obedience, and pay their Contribution to the support of that Government."[26] Penn's vision for maintaining a peaceful and prosperous society rested in toleration and justice. He utilized common law to support his case for the rights of Englishmen. His emphasis on toleration built upon this, as the active decision to respect another person's faith allowed for civic community to build.

Though William Penn's experiences in Ireland and England shaped his thoughts on how community building could enhance security, the implementation of his outlook relied in part on becoming a player in the colonial efforts in the Delaware River Valley and recognizing the relationships and methods of conflict resolution already in place there. Lenape and Susquehannock Indians had tolerated small numbers of Europeans into the Delaware River Valley. The slaughter at Swanendael in 1631, where a group of Lenape wiped out a Dutch outpost, demonstrated the power dynamic in the area between Native Americans and the first Europeans. Thereafter both Indian groups competed for European allies, viewing the newcomers as subordinates who could be incorporated as trading partners. Dutch and Swedish settlers enjoyed trading profits but kept their investment in the region limited. They approached the dispersed Indian polities in a restrained manner rather than risk losing trade or their own lives.

Both sides saw value in each other and resorted to dialogue to smooth over isolated murder cases. Over the course of several decades this practice developed into a shared understanding of how to manage security in the area. After conquering New Netherland in 1664, the English remained dependent upon local Dutch and Swedish magistrates who were already familiar with local practices for conflict resolution. Hans Block, Israel Helme, Peter Rambo, Peter Cocke, and Peter Alrichs (Aldrick) were specifically named as potential counselors to "be called to Advise and direct what is best to be done in all cases of difficulty which may arise from the Indians" as well as "to give their Councell and orders for the arming of the severall plantacons and Planters."[27] New to governing the Delaware River Valley, English authority relied on the experience and inroads forged within Indian diplomacy and trade made by Dutch and Swedish settlers.[28]

This approach toward maintaining security in the Delaware River Valley averted war as Dutch, Swedish, and Lenape restraint tamed English aggression following incidents of local violence. When Indians murdered servants of the local magistrate William Tom in the summer of 1668, New York Governor William Lovelace initially showed patience and asked Dutch and Swedish officials to resolve the tension. Tom and Peter Alrichs asked Lovelace to make peace with the Lenape and recognize their authority. The Lenape had used moments of violence to remind European settlers who stood at the top of the hierarchical relationship. When the Lenape killed two of Peter Alrichs's servants in 1671 to avenge a murder, Lovelace's patience ran out. He directed local officials to prepare for war and strike if the opportunity arose. Leaders in the Delaware River Valley, however, dragged their feet. They understood that other means, based on years of tradition and understanding, remained at work in bringing a resolution. Cooperation between Indian sachems and their Dutch and Swedish allies paid off in December 1671 when Lenape leaders executed one of the murderers, and Alrichs offered gifts as a token of thanks. Their renewed alliance and understanding of local security averted the outbreak of large-scale violence.[29]

Quaker travels to the New World prior to the establishment of West New Jersey and Pennsylvania provided William Penn the necessary insight into the Delaware River Valley, the inhabitants, and how things were practiced with regard to security. His friend Josiah Coale visited North America and stayed among the Susquehannock Indians in 1658. In a letter to fellow Quaker George Bishop, also a friend to the Penn family, Coale described the Indians' kindness and how they accompanied the European travelers to Dutch settlements along the Delaware River. Quakers considered making a land purchase from Indians in the Susquehanna River Valley based on Coale's reports. George Fox made a trip to North America and interacted with Indians as he traveled along the Susquehanna and Delaware Rivers from 1672 to 1673. Penn's relationships with Coale, Bishop, and Fox offered him insights into the realities present in the Delaware River Valley. Fortunately for Penn, his previous experiences in Ireland

and emphasis on toleration and justice to achieve peace molded conveniently with the ways in which people there had created peace and security.[30]

William Penn's first opportunity to put his ideas about community and security into practice occurred on the east bank of the Delaware River in West New Jersey. Penn became one of three trustees for the colony while arbitrating a dispute between two Quakers over lands in West New Jersey.[31] The West New Jersey Concessions, signed in 1676, addressed security matters by recognizing the past relationship and instances of tension and violence between local Indians and Europeans. Its approach and tone regarding these issues point to the influence of Penn's past experiences, particularly in Ireland where Penn sought to keep the relationship dynamic but also respected a culture different from his own. Penn believed that colonial charters entitled him and other Europeans to the right to land. He also recognized the past precedent established by Europeans in the Delaware River Valley and maintained that lands be "contracted for with the Natives" in order to maintain justice, reciprocate goodwill, and promote peace.[32] Aware of the political situation and the emphasis on dialogue, as opposed to warfare, Penn and the trustees wanted to keep lines of communication open and gave reassurances to sachems that justice would be done in cases of Indians being wronged. In an interesting example the Concessions stated that juries were to be divided in half between Indians and Europeans in trial cases involving Indians. While it is highly unlikely that Indians served on juries, this reflects Penn's emphasis on community and his awareness of the local political situation.[33]

As a newcomer armed only with a piece of paper stating he was entitled to lands west of the Delaware River and beyond, William Penn understood that the future of Pennsylvania's security depended on the first meetings with inhabitants. After receiving his charter in March 1681, Penn sent agents to represent him and instructed them on the need to establish good relations with Indians: "soften [the natives] to mee and the people, lett them know that you are come to sit downe Lovingly among them. Let my Letter and Conditions wth our own Interest, and after reading my Letter and the said Conditions, then present their Kings wth what I send them, and make a Frien{d}ship and League wth them."[34] Pennsylvania's security relied on the Lenape's willingness to accept the influx of new settlers onto their lands and to accept them as allies and trading partners. Penn's letter to the Lenape on October 18 demonstrated his desire to enjoy the land with their "Love and Consent, that we may always live together as Neighbours and friends."[35] He offered presents to show his intent to live in peace as a friend. He followed a similar approach with the Iroquois in order to gain their friendship and trade favor, instructing his agents to present gifts to illustrate that their relationship would be built on honesty and justice.[36] Penn's strategy of pleasantries and providing gifts to the Indians reflected his awareness of interpersonal dynamics and the importance of trusted intermediaries. Penn relied on his experiences in Ireland and his belief in respecting the beliefs and practices of other peoples. His instructions, goodwill messages, and astute choice in intermediaries built upon the foundation stones of a security community in the Delaware River Valley laid by the Indians and Europeans. Trade goods, coupled with Penn's outlook, acted as tokens of friendship, a bonding element for a favored status in trade and alliance, and secured peace and stability in a frontier environment.

Penn also made good use of his arguments for toleration in dealing with those Europeans already present. He assured them that they "shall be govern'd by laws of y^{r} own makeing, & live a free & if you will, a sober & industreous People. I shall not usurp the right of any, or oppress his person." He continued, "w^{t}ever sober & free men can reasonably desire for the security & improvem^{t} of their own happiness I shall heartely Comply wth."[37] Penn did not want to fix something that was not broken. He understood that the Dutch, Swedish, and other European settlers already living in the area had developed practices regarding security, and saw no need to change them. Adamant in wanting to win over the native European population and develop a sense of community with them, Penn made the effort to have a letter of introduction written in Swedish in order that the Swedish clergy could relay his message to the congregation. Through presents, letters of introduction, and assurances, Penn demonstrated his security community approach and established relationships before he set foot on Pennsylvania soil.[38]

When William Penn arrived in North America in October 1682, his ideas about how to build a safe and secure community drew upon his experiences on both sides of the Atlantic. With his personal development in Europe and the political and security environment present in the Delaware River Valley, Penn promoted friendship and did not seek to unravel the relationships between Europeans and Indians. For European colonials already present they found Penn had liberal policies for naturalization. Penn assured Augustine Herrman that his property in the Lower Counties (modern Delaware) would not be disturbed: "I come a man of peace yet fear noe warr . . . & hope to act suitable to my duty & not unworthy of his Just favour."[39] When local officials presented Penn with the keys to the fort at New Castle, an installation that had changed hands and names multiple times as a result of European hostilities, Penn did not rely on military symbols to show strength and security. Instead he actively promoted the present stability and peace and kept the fort's doors open and accessible.[40]

Penn's naturalization policies and spirit of toleration extended to newly arriving Europeans, notably the Germans and Welsh. Germantown local leader Francis David Pastorious noted how Penn encouraged them to build up their settlement and offered toleration to their religious beliefs and respect for their ethnic identity. Welsh Quakers received a tract of land where their customs and language could be practiced in a self-contained barony with its own administrative and court system. This active promotion of peace allowed for community to blossom. By the end of 1682 the Lower Counties had petitioned for an act of union with Pennsylvania, and in a letter to Lord North in July 1683, Penn commented on the growing sense of community as people enjoyed fair and weekly markets to sell produce.[41]

The active promotion of peace also solidified friendship, trade, and alliance with surrounding Indians. William Penn's cousin and deputy, William Markham, had purchased lands from the Lenape in April 1862 with goods valued at £21,644. He also made agreements with Indian sachems to allow for uninhibited passage between respective lands and to uphold justice by bringing complaints to respective leaders. When Penn arrived in Pennsylvania, he too secured land purchases from the Lenape in what became part of Bucks and Philadelphia Counties. When he sought to secure rights to the Susquehanna River in order for his colony and its economy to grow, he demonstrated his knowledge of Indian diplomacy, politics, and power by acknowledging the Iroquois influence over the Susquehannocks and sent agents to the Five Nations to negotiate the purchase of lands along the Susquehanna River. Penn's background from Ireland is present here, particularly with his interpersonal skills. He recognized the diplomatic and trade practices established by earlier generations. But he also did not seek to upend the status quo either for his expanding colony or for certain Indian groups, such as the Iroquois. Dwindling Indian populations and the availability of lands west and north of European settlement areas assisted Penn's ability to make agreements, build alliances, and avoid unnecessary tension.[42]

Aside from land agreements, Penn actively engaged in the development of community with surrounding Indians. In a letter to the Free Society of Traders dated August 16, 1683, Penn noted his growing familiarity with the Lenape language and his observations of Indian practices during negotiations. In addition to his respect for Indian culture and customs, Penn also noted in the letter his awareness that alcohol could potentially subvert peace by escalating violent behavior. He helped draft legislation that imposed heavy fines for selling alcohol to Indians to guard against alcohol-related violence. Germantown's Francis Pastorius reflected on Penn's early dealings with the Indians: "It is to be remarked that William Penn did not drive forth the naked native inhabitants of the land with military authority, but brought with him upon his arrival especial clothing and hats for the principal Indians, and thereby secured their goodwill, and purchased their land."[43] Whether through gifts and just land agreements, or in exercising toleration and respect for customs and practice, William Penn secured an alliance with the Lenape and built a Chain of Friendship in order that new settlers could live peaceably alongside them in a spirit of community.[44]

William Penn's fight to retain Pennsylvania provided the impetus for his idealistic theories and proposals that promoted security through community. His first sojourn to his colony remained short-lived when border disputes with

Maryland's Lord Baltimore forced him to return to England in August 1684 to defend his claim. Penn found a target fixed to his back several years later with the events of the Glorious Revolution. Sympathetic to the Stuart kings, Penn fell out of favor with William and Mary on suspicion of being loyal to James II. Accusations of high treason and Jacobitism forced Penn into hiding. The proprietor's low profile and absence from his colony did not help with the perception in England that Pennsylvania, suffering from factionalism and disagreement between the Assembly and the governor, appeared ill defended and ripe for the taking in war against France. On October 12, 1691, the Lords of Trade recommended that Pennsylvania be placed under royal control. Penn understood the reasoning for losing his colony, pointing to his absence, government disorders, and the threat of French invasion as reasons for the crown to place Pennsylvania under the care of Colonel Benjamin Fletcher, the governor of New York. With England caught up in the Nine Years War and himself out of favor at court, Penn saw an opportunity to demonstrate that he held England's interests at heart in order to gain favor with the Crown and regain his colony. Relying upon his writing prowess and security community approach that stressed respect for other peoples and cultures and seeking out peaceful resolutions to conflict, Penn argued for multiple government entities working together to secure common goals of defense, economic prosperity, and a more just society.[45]

In the ten years from Pennsylvania being placed under royal control and the proprietor's second journey to the colony, William Penn offered three idealistic theories and proposals that reflect his plan for a security community. The first, and most famous, appeared in 1693 with the publication of *An Essay towards the Present and Future Peace of Europe by the Establishment of an European Dyet, Parliament, or Estates*. Often likened as the forerunner to the United Nations, Penn's "Essay" and the European governing body that he put forth centered on developing a sense of community among the princes of Europe in order to achieve peace and allow society to prosper. War in Europe, Penn argued, demonstrated the satisfaction that could be achieved by actively seeking and promoting peace: "As if we could not taste the Benefit of Health, but by the Help of Sickness; nor understand the Satisfaction of Fulness without the Instruction of Want; nor, finally, know the Comfort of Peace but by the Smart and Penance of the Vices of War."[46] He continued his reasoning by discussing the relationship between justice and warfare. Taking a page from his contemporary John Locke and his own arguments for liberty of conscience, Penn built upon the idea of proper balance between people and their government in the prevention of civil tumult and applied it to the international community. Penn's ideal European body would see ambassadors, representing the princes of Europe, meeting at regular intervals or whenever necessary in order to discuss and resolve differences as a community in a just manner. No one state could withstand the power of the greater body. As had been the case in his defense for religious toleration and for the rights of Englishmen, and from his own efforts in the New World, Penn believed that respecting others served as an avenue for peace and security.[47]

In addition to the idealized European parliament's purpose for achieving peace in Europe, Penn's description of its makeup and the fruits it would bear also illustrate his communal approach for security. He envisioned ambassadors meeting in a round room with multiple entrances into the chamber, inviting members to peacefully resolve their differences. Members included Russia and the Turks. Penn argued that incorporating frontier neighbors and giving them representation would enhance the pan-European government's stature by representing "the Best and Wealthiest Part of the Known World; where Religion and Learning, Civility and Arts have their Seat and Empire."[48] More voices in debates and final decisions increased the overall sense of community. And by including the Muslim Turks, Penn believed that the military threat to southeast Europe could be removed and stop the considerable loss of life and destruction to Christendom. Membership in the European body did not require total disarmament. Penn allowed for states to keep a small force within their borders to repel any surprise invasion, yet small enough not to endanger their neighbors.[49] Stalemate would force members to resort to diplomacy and reach agreements based on justice. The resulting peace would yield surpluses to be enjoyed by princes and their subjects as well as improve Christianity's reputation, as the Christian states would stop fighting one another and their Muslim counterparts and would embrace each other in community. Like his arguments for religious toleration, self-interest is present for Christianity, but Penn's proposal would bring peace and security for all.[50]

William Penn's second idealistic proposal for multiple governments working together for their prosperity and security resulted from the circumstances facing himself and England's growing involvement in the Atlantic. When he submitted "A Briefe and Plaine Scheam" to the Board of Trade on February 8, 1697, Penn envisioned an intercolonial governing body bounded together by mutual defense, trade, and justice.[51] Similar to how accusations of Jacobitism and treason spurred him to write his "Essay" for Europe, Penn offered this "Scheam" to assure the government of his ability to administer Pennsylvania. Penn regained his colony in August 1694 after agreeing to return to Pennsylvania as soon as possible and to provide a quota of troops for New York's defenses. Still in the midst of the Nine Years' War, known as King William's War in North America, England's Board of Trade had entertained ideas of a unified military command for its American colonies to address the French threat in Canada. The Board of Trade also sought to rein in illegal trade and piracy, which cost the Crown an estimated £50,000 each year of critical revenue that could be used in the war against France. Penn, himself under pressure to enforce the Navigation Acts and provide military assistance from his colony, and understanding the problems facing England, put forward his inter-colonial union in order to assist the Crown and achieve peace and safety for the colonies.[52]

Like the "Essay," Penn's "Scheam" stressed community among the different English colonies and their increasingly diverse European-American populations in order to achieve greater security and prosperity. Just as the ambassadors of Europe would meet regularly, representatives from the colonies would meet at least once a year at the intercolonial congress in order to "hear and Adjust all matters of Complaint or difference Betweene Province and Province."[53] Justice featured heavily in the proposal. He identified how "Offenders fly [the] Justice" of one colony in order to avoid paying their debts, and that "Justice cannot well be had upon such offenders in the Provinces that entertain them."[54] Discussion of civil problems among colonial deputies offered not only to strengthen the sense of community among colonies themselves but would also begin to address the problems of illegal trade and piracy that plagued the Board of Trade.[55]

Of the problems facing the colonies, however, Penn devoted most of his attention to the French security threat. The colonial congress would allow for consideration "of wayes and meanes to support the Union and safety of these Provinces against the Publick Enemies."[56] He proposed New York as the meeting site for the congress because of its importance as "a Fronteir" in the fight against France and that New York's royal governor act as commissioner of the congress and commander of military forces.[57] As a community linked together for the promotion of security, the delegates could debate appropriate troop quota levels and discuss defense "with more freedome and satisfaction, and better adjust and ballance their affaires in all respects for their Common safety."[58] This defensive union served to bind the colonies militarily and strengthen their collective security, and above all would be accomplished through a community of representatives charged with "[debating and resolving] such Measures, as are most adviseable for their better understanding, and their Publick Tranquility and Safety."[59]

While William Penn's "Essay" and "Scheam" appear as more idealistic in their proposals, his lesser-known meeting with the governors of New York and Virginia in 1700 offered the best chance of fomenting community and cooperation among colonial governments. When Penn returned to Pennsylvania in 1699 he continued to nurture positive Indian relations and addressed government infighting. He also pursued greater unity and cooperation among the colonies despite the Board of Trade rejecting his "Scheam." Richard Coote, the Earl of Bellomont, had endorsed the "Scheam" while on the Board of Trade and now served as governor of New York. Penn wrote to Coote, Governor Francis Nicholson of Virginia, and Governor Nathaniel Blakiston of Maryland stating his desire for a meeting to promote "a good Understanding among the Governours of the Provinces under the Crown of England for their Reputation at home, & the Prosperity of the Respective Provinces" and that they be "Dutiful to the

Crown, Careful of its Revenues, & the good of Mother Country, and very friendly to our Neighbour Colonies."[60] Penn, Coote, and Nicholson met in Albany sometime in late September and early October 1700.[61] In an extension from his "Scheam" that sought to establish an intercolonial union, Penn hoped a meeting and discussion among governors could address problems facing their colonies and England's imperial infrastructure. Correspondence with the Board of Trade shows that even though the meeting did not call explicitly for a colonial governing body, the heads discussed by the governors illustrate their intent to work together for improved economic ties, mutual defense, and a peaceful society.

Penn's report of the meeting that he sent to the Board of Trade touched upon a variety of subjects, including commerce, security, and ways to integrate new European migrants into the colonies. To make commerce "more easy & certain," the governors proposed a standard currency throughout the colonies. Penn explained that a "piece of Eight" went in Boston for six shillings, where as in Virginia it went for five shillings.[62] A centralized mint in New York City would also guard against "Clipping and filing" of coins.[63] In addition to binding the colonies closer together, standardized currency stemming from a central mint could combat against fraud and illegal trade in the imperial system as well as enhance colonial government and landlord power, both of which would benefit Penn. With regard to security, peace with France and its allied Indians offered an opportunity English and French commissioners to establish fixed boundaries. Fixed borders offered stability, peace, and the promotion of trade. Not taking the opportunity to make agreements and avoid further infringement upon lands risked a "great and Irreparable" loss.[64] The governors, as executives of colonies with diverse populations, also treated the issue of immigration and the naturalization of foreigners. They recommended that "a general Law of Naturalization pass in England, that Such foreigners as come to Inhabit in any of the Kings Colonies" in order to allow for successful integration of migrants and to encourage harmony in society.[65] Not only would foreigners be accepted within the colonies but they would enjoy the same rights and privileges as natural-born Englishmen. Penn's security community outlook is apparent throughout. He promoted cooperation among colonies in order that societies could enjoy prosperity and security. Furthermore, as he had demonstrated with European settlers in his own colony, Penn extended his liberal naturalization policies to newly arriving immigrants along the Atlantic seaboard in order that they be treated as new Englishmen to promote the spirit of community.

Reaction by the Board of Trade to the proposals of the 1700 meeting indicated the possibility for further unity and cooperation among the colonies, but ultimately it suffered a tragic ending. Coote's letters and report arrived first in England and did not appear to sway the Board members. However, the arrival of Penn's materials in April 1701 witnessed a change in sentiments. A letter from the Board of Trade to Penn dated April 15, 1701, described the discussion heads as maybe being "of very good use for the general benefit of H.M. Plantations" and encouraged continued correspondence among the governors. The Board enjoyed seeing correspondence coming from William Penn, a proprietary governor once suspected of treason and whose colony had been under scrutiny for illegal trade and security, and the greater attention given to enforcing the Navigation Acts and considering imperial defense. This momentum, however, faltered with the death of Coote on March 5 after a severe case of gout. The delay in sea traffic did not allow the Board to realize this when they sent off their letter to Penn in April. The loss of Coote and Penn's final departure from Pennsylvania the following year removed the two leading proponents of intercolonial cooperation. For Penn himself, the meeting acted as the last of his idealistic theories and proposals and had continued in the same vein of establishing a security community to attain stability and peace.[66]

Over the course of his public career William Penn maintained that achieving security in society rested in respecting other peoples and cultures, understanding a relationship's dynamic, and actively pursuing peace. Instead of simply viewing peace as a lofty goal, he understood that stability and prosperity resulted from the building of a security community and actively seeking it. Regular trade and interactions establish the relationship, deepen the sense of how things are, and with regular practice become habits that participants turn to in order to deescalate and resolve conflict and keep peace. Penn developed, implemented, and maintained this security community approach over the course of a varied public career across the Atlantic World. Whether as a business man, a defender of social justice, colonizer and proprietor, courtier, or idealistic visionary, William Penn consistently maintained that peace and security derived from justice and a fundamental respect for people, their beliefs and way of life, and their desire for peace.

NOTES

1. Granville Penn, *Memorials of the Professional Life and Times of Sir William Penn, Knt.* (London: James Duncan, Paternoster Row, 1833), 2:430.

2. Penn, *Memorials*, 2:429–431; Mary Richmond Brailsford, *The Making of William Penn* (Freeport: Books for Libraries Press, 1970), 163–165; See footnote in Richard S. Dunn and Mary Maples Dunn, eds., *The Papers of William Penn* (Philadelphia: Penn Press, 1981), 1:41. Hereafter: *Penn Papers, Vol. 1.*

3. Emanuel Adler, "Condition(s) of Peace," *Review of International Studies* 24 (December 1998): 165–168, 178.

4. Adler, "Peace," 175.

5. Adler, "Peace," 175. See also Karl W. Deutsch et al., *Political Community and the North Atlantic Area: International Organization in the Light of Historical Experience* (New York: Greenwood Press, 1969), 5–7; Klaus Schlichtmann, "Linking Constitutional Laws of Peace and Collective Security," *Indian Journal of Asian Affairs* 17, no. 2 (December 2004): 1–2; Jeffrey Kimball, "Alternatives to War in History," *OAH Magazine of History* 8, no. 3 (Spring 1994), 5–9.

6. Edward C. O. Beatty, *William Penn as Social Philosopher* (New York: Octagon Books, 1975). For scholarship discussing William Penn with regard to politics and religion, as well as general biographies, see Joseph E. Illick, *William Penn the Politician: His Relations with the English Government* (Ithaca: Cornell University Press, 1965); Mabel Richmond Brailsford, *The Making of William Penn* (Freeport: Books for Libraries Press, 1970); Melvin B. Endy, Jr., *William Penn and Early Quakerism* (Princeton: Princeton University Press, 1973); Hans Fantel, *William Penn: Apostle of Dissent* (New York: William Morrow & Company, Inc., 1974); Harry Emerson Wildes, *William Penn* (New York: Macmillan Publishing Co., Inc., 1974); Richard S. Dunn and Mary Maples Dunn, ed., *The World of William Penn* (Philadelphia: Penn Press, 1986); Mary K. Geiter, *William Penn* (Harlow: Parson Education Limited, 2000). For the political turmoil and breakdown of the holy experiment among Pennsylvania settlers in the first decades of the colony's formal existence, see Edwin B. Bronner, *William Penn's "Holy Experiment": The Founding of Pennsylvania, 1681–1701* (New York: Temple University Publications, 1962). See also Gary B. Nash, *Quakers and Politics: Pennsylvania, 1681–1726* (Princeton: Princeton University Press, 1968).

7. Francis Jennings, "Brother Miquon: Good Lord!" in *The World of William Penn*, ed. Richard S. Dunn and Mary Maples Dunn (Philadelphia: Penn Press, 1986), 195–214.

8. Daniel K. Richter, *Trade, Land, Power: The Struggle for Eastern North America* (Philadelphia: Penn Press, 2013).

9. Jean R. Soderlund, *Lenape Country: Delaware Valley Society before William Penn* (Philadelphia: Penn Press, 2015).

10. William I. Hull, *William Penn: A Topical Biography* (London: Oxford University Press, 1937); Mary Maples Dunn, *William Penn: Politics and Government* (Princeton: Princeton University Press, 1967); John A. Moretta, *William Penn and the Quaker Legacy* (New York: Pearson Education, Inc., 2007).

11. Caroline Robbins, "William Penn, 1689–1702: Eclipse, Frustration, and Achievement," in *The World of William Penn*, ed. Richard S. Dunn and Mary Maples Dunn (Philadelphia: Penn Press, 1986), 71–84.

12. William Penn, "To Sir William Penn," (May 6, 1665), *Penn Papers, Vol. 1*, 34.

13. Sir William Penn, "Sir William Penn to Sir George Lane," (February 8, 1666), *Penn Papers, Vol. 1*, 39–40; Brailsford, *Making of William Penn*, 157–161. See Ormonde to Admiral Penn from Carrickfergus, May 29, 1666, in the footnote of *Penn Papers, Vol. 1*, 42.

14. Sir William Penn, "From Sir William Penn," (July 17, 1667), *Penn Papers, Vol. 1*, 42; Penn, *Memorials*, 2:432–433; Brailsford, *Making of William Penn*, 157, 164–165.

15. Penn, *Memorials*, 2:433–434; Brailsford, *Making of William Penn*, 157, 166.

16. William Penn, "My Irish journall," (September 1669—July 1670), *Penn Papers, Vol. 1*, 108.

17. Penn, "Irish journall," 112.

18. Penn, "Irish journall," 127.

19. Penn, "Irish journall," 106, 108, 127, 129. See footnotes for bibliographical information on those whom Penn met in his Irish travels in Dunn and Dunn, ed., *Penn Papers, Vol. 1*, 131–143.

20. Dunn and Dunn, ed., *Penn Papers, Vol. 1*, 49; Howard Brinton, *Friends for 300 Years: The History and Beliefs of the Society of Friends since George Fox Started the Quaker Movement* (New York: Harper & Brothers, 1952), 118, 130, 160–161; Peter Brock, *Pioneers of the Peaceable Kingdom* (Princeton: Princeton University Press, 1968), xi, xiii; Douglas V. Steere, ed., *Quaker Spirituality: Selected Writings* (New York: Paulist Press, 1984), 12, 22, 88–89, 105–106; Peter Brock, *The Quaker Peace Testimony, 1660–1914* (York: Sessions Book Trust, 1990), 10, 15, 21, 25, 31; Meredith Baldwin Weddle, *Walking in the Way of Peace: Quaker Pacifism in the Seventeenth Century* (Oxford: Oxford University Press, 2001), 7–11; Robert L. Greaves, "Seditious Sectaries or "Sober and Useful Inhabitants"? Changing Conceptions

of the Quakers in Early Modern Britain," *Albion: A Quarterly Journal Concerned with British Studies* 33, no. 1 (Spring 2001): 29–30, 33–35; Hilary Hinds, *George Fox and Early Quaker Culture* (Manchester, UK: Manchester University Press, 2011), 25. See also Peter Brock, *Pacifism in the United States: From the Colonial Era to the First World War* (Princeton: Princeton University Press, 1968).

21. Dunn and Dunn, ed., *Penn Papers, Vol. 1*, 24–26; Geiter, *William Penn*, 18–19; Brailsford, *Making of William Penn*, 175–176, 207.

22. William Penn, "To Lord Arlington," (June 19, 1669), *Penn Papers, Vol. 1*, 93.

23. William Penn, *The great case. Of liberty of conscience once more debated & defended*, (1670), *Early English Books Online*, http://eebo.chadwyck.com.libdata.lib.ua.edu/search/full_rec?SOURCE=pgimages.cfg&ACTION=ByID&ID=V33078 (accessed February 13, 2013).

24. William Penn, "Narrative of the Sufferings of Quakers in the Isle of Ely," (November? 1671), *Penn Papers, Vol. 1*, 226.

25. William Penn, *England's present interest discover'd with honour to the prince, and safety to the people*, (1675), *Early English Books Online*, http://eebo.chadwyck.com/search/full_rec?SOURCE=pgimages.cfg&ACTION=ByID&ID=V93329 (accessed February 17, 2013), 49–50.

26. William Penn, *One project for the good of England* (1679), *Early English Books Online*, http://eebo.chadwyck.com.libdata.lib.ua.edu/search/full_rec?SOURCE=pgimages.cfg&ACTION=ByID&ID=V60052 (accessed February 17, 2013), 2.

27. "[Resolutions and Directions for the Settlement of the Government in Delaware]," (April 21, 1668), in *Books of General Entries of the Colony of New York, 1664–1673: Orders, Warrants, Letters, Commissions, Passes and Licenses by Governors Richard Nicolls and Francis Lovelace*, ed. Peter R. Christoph and Florence A. Christoph (Baltimore: Genealogical Publishing Co., Inc., 1982), 158. Hereafter: *Entries, 1664–1673*. The same resolutions provided that local civil government continue as it had before, that a supplied military garrison of twenty soldiers and one officer be lodged in the fort, and that no offensive war be made against any Indians, both in order to avoid trade disruption and because the thin colonial population could not effectively fight against a scattered Indian opponent.

28. "Instructions to Sir Robert Carr for the Reducing of Delaware Bay, and Settling the People there, under his Majesties obedience," *Entries, 1664–1673*, 60; "Articles of Agreement between the Honourable Sir Robert Carr Knight on the Behalf of his Majesty of Great Britain, And the Burgomasters on the Behalf of themselves, and all the Dutch and Swedes Inhabiting in Delaware Bay and Delaware River," (October 1, 1664), *Delaware Papers (English Period): A Collection of Documents Pertaining to the Regulation of Affairs on the Delaware, 1664–1682*, vols. 20–21, ed. Charles T. Gehring (Baltimore: Genealogical Publishing Co., Inc., 1977), 2. Hereafter: *Delaware Papers (English)*. Gehring, ed., *Delaware Papers (English)*, xiii. For an authoritative social and political history of the interactions between Delaware Indians and European colonists in the Delaware River Valley during the seventeenth century that stressed peaceful resolutions to conflict, respect for differing cultures and beliefs, and trade, see Soderlund, *Lenape Country* (2015).

29. "[William Tom and Peter Alrichs to Gov. Lovelace about Indian Affairs]," (March 9, 1670), *Delaware Papers (English)*, 11; "[Letter Concerning the Murder of Settlers by Indians]," (August 24, 1670), *Entries, 1664–1673*, 366–367; "[Letter to Captain Carr Concerning the Murders on Matiniconck Island]" (September 28, 1671), *Entries, 1664–1673*, 448; "Lettre from the Governor to Capt. Carr at Delaware, Dated November 9th 1671," (November 9, 1671), *Entries, 1664–1673*, 453; "Copy of the Lettre from Mr. Tom of Dellaware to his Honor the Governor," (December 15, 1671), *Entries, 1664–1673*, 455–456; "An Order for Capt. Nicolls to summon a Part of his Troop to attend the Governor to Delaware," (March 8, 1671/2), *Entries, 1664–1673*, 471; "Instructions for Mr. Garland about making preparacions for his Honors Voyage to Delaware," (March 12, 1671/2), *Entries, 1664–1673*, 473; Soderlund, *Lenape Country*, 7, 127–128.

30. James Bowden, *The History of the Society of Friends in America* (London: Charles Gilpin, Bishopsgate Street Without, 1850), 1:123–124; Brailsford, *Making of William Penn*, 347–348. George Bishop and Admiral Penn both shared parliamentary military service in the 1640s and 1650s before Bishop converted to Quakerism in 1654. Following William Penn's release from his Cork imprisonment in late 1667, the younger Penn visited Bishop on his way to see his father. Utilizing the younger Penn as a messenger, Bishop wrote to his old friend and appealed to the admiral to be open to his son's religious experience. For Bishop, see Dunn and Dunn, ed., *Penn Papers, Vol. 1*, 50, 55. For Penn lamenting the loss of his friend Josiah Coale, see William Penn, "To Lodowick Muggleton," (February 11, 1669), *Penn Papers, Vol. 1*, 87–88.

31. In 1664 the Duke of York granted proprietorship of New Jersey to Sir John Berkeley and Sir George Carteret. Berkeley offered to sell his half interest (West New Jersey) in March 1674 to his friend Edward Byllynge, a Quaker, for £1,000 so that Byllynge could sell off the land in order to recoup his finances. Because of his poor economic stance, Byllynge had fellow Quaker John Fenwick purchase Berkeley's share in trust. An argument between Byllynge and Fenwick developed when Fenwick demanded a share of the land and a cash payment of the £1,000 he spent. Byllynge did not want to surrender the land, nor could he repay the debt. Quaker leaders feared that the dispute would go to court and discredit the Society; they persuaded the two to submit to arbitration under William Penn. Utilizing his experience from Ireland, Penn negotiated an agreement that was formalized in a legal indenture, where Byllynge transferred ten of his one hundred shares in West New Jersey to Fenwick, as well as payment of £400. The remaining ninety shares were placed in trust with three Quaker trustees, who were empowered to sell Byllynge's shares to pay off his debts, and then return the remaining shares when he was solvent. Two of the three trustees were Gawen Lawrie and Nicholas Lucas, creditors of Byllynge, with the third being William Penn. See Gawen Lawrie, Nicholas Lucas, and William Penn, "The Epistle of Penn, Lawrie, and Lucas, Respecting West Jersey," (1676) in *Narratives of Early Pennsylvania, West New Jersey, and Delaware, 1630–1707*, ed. Albert Cook Myers (New York: Barnes & Noble, Inc., 1959), 182–185; Dunn and Dunn, ed., *Penn Papers, Vol. 1*, 383; Geiter, *William Penn*, 105.

32. "The West New Jersey Concessions," (ca. August 1676), *Penn Papers, Vol. 1*, 389; Beatty, *Penn as Social Philosopher*, 266–267, 275–277, 281; Geiter, *William Penn*, 165; Jennings, "Brother Miquon," 197.

33. "West New Jersey Concessions," *Penn Papers, Vol. 1*, 401.

34. William Penn, "Initial Plan for Philadelphia," (September 30, 1681), in *The Papers of William Penn*, vol. 2, ed. Richard S. Dunn and Mary Maples Dunn (Philadelphia: Penn Press, 1982), 120. Hereafter: *Penn Papers, Vol. 2*.

35. William Penn, "To the Kings of the Indians," (October 28, 1681), *Penn Papers, Vol. 2*, 128.

36. William Penn, "To the Emperor of Canada," (June 21, 1682), *Penn Papers, Vol. 2*, 261.

37. William Penn, "To the Inhabitants of Pennsylvania," (April 8, 1681), *Penn Papers, Vol. 2*, 84.

38. For Penn's letter to the Swedish community, see the following, where he notes the enclosure: William Penn, "To William Markham," (April 8, 1681), *Penn Papers, Vol. 2*, 126–127

39. William Penn, "To Augustine Herrman," (November 2, 1682), *Penn Papers, Vol. 2*, 309.

40. "John Moll's Account of the Surrender of the Three Lower Counties to William Penn," (1682), *Penn Papers, Vol. 2*, 306.

41. William Penn, "The Surveying of Germantown," (October 12, 1683), *Penn Papers, Vol. 2*, 490; Francis Daniel Pastorius, "Circumstantial Geographical Description of Pennsylvania," 1700, in *Narratives of Early Pennsylvania, West New Jersey, and Delaware, 1630–1707*, ed. Albert Cook Myers (New York: Barnes & Noble, Inc., 1959), 375–381; William

Penn, "Warrant to Survey a Welsh Barony," (March 13, 1684), *Penn Papers, Vol.* 2, 527; "Petition for an Act of Union," (December 6, 1682), *Penn Papers, Vol.* 2, 318; William Penn, "To Lord North," (July 24, 1683), *Penn Papers, Vol.* 2, 414–415; Dunn and Dunn, ed., *Penn Papers, Vol.* 2, 526–527.

42. "Deed from the Delaware Indians," (July 15, 1682), *Penn Papers, Vol.* 2, 261–269; "Deed from the Delaware Indians," (June 23, 1683), *Penn Papers, Vol.* 2, 404–405; William Penn, "Commission and Instructions to James Graham and William Haige," (August 2, 1683), *Penn Papers, Vol.* 2, 423

43. Pastorius, "Description of Pennsylvania," 374.

44. William Penn, "To the Free Society of Traders," (August 16, 1683), *Penn Papers, Vol.* 2, 442–455; "Tavern Regulations," (ca. March 23, 1683), *Penn Papers, Vol.* 2, 367–369; Jennings, "Brother Miquon," 197, 201.

45. William Penn, "Breviate of Petition to Queen Mary and the Privy Council" (ca. July 4, 1694), in *The Papers of William Penn*, vol. 3, ed. Marianne S. Wokeck and others (Philadelphia: Penn Press, 1986), 395. Hereafter: *Penn Papers, Vol. 3*. Nash, *Quakers and Politics*, 183.

46. *The Political Writings of William Penn*, ed. Andrew R. Murphy, *An Essay towards the Present and Future Peace of Europe, by the Establishment of an European Dyet, Parliament, or Estates* (Indianapolis: Liberty Fund, 2002), 402.

47. Penn, *Essay towards the Present and Future Peace of Europe*, 402–406.

48. Penn, *Essay towards the Present and Future Peace of Europe*, 409.

49. It is interesting to note that Penn did not make mention of any naval forces. As he developed his security community outlook, Penn still retained the lessons learned from his father, especially on a fleet's organization and the projection of naval power. A reduction in land forces would greatly benefit England and its traditional naval power. England could continue to rely on its fleets to defend its shores and to promote its sea-going trade. Restricting armies on the continent would as a result restrict any intentions of France or Spain. By reducing the power of continental states, Penn stood to gain favor with William III and recover Pennsylvania. See Penn, *Essay towards the Present and Future Peace of Europe*, 411.

50. Penn, *Essay towards the Present and Future Peace of Europe*, 412–414.

51. The full title of the "Scheam" is as follows: "A Briefe and Plaine Scheam How the English Collonies in the North Parts of America viz[t]. Boston, Conetticut, Road Island New York, New Jerseys, Pensilvania, Maryland, Virginia and Carolina may be made more usefull to the Crowne, and one anothers Peace and safety with an Universall Concurrence." See William Penn, "Draft of A Breife and Plaine Scheam" (February 8, 1697), *Penn Papers, Vol.* 3, 482.

52. Penn, "Scheam," 482; Wokeck and others, eds. *Penn Papers, Vol.* 3, 442, 479; "Commissioners of Customs to the Lords of the Treasury" (November 16, 1696), *Calendar of State Papers, Colonial Series, America and the West Indies*, ed. J. W. Fortescue, Vol. 15, May 15, 1696—October 31, 1697 (London: Mackie and Co. LD., 1904), text-fiche; J. W. Fortescue, ed. *Calendar of State Papers, Colonial Series, America and the West Indies*, Vol. 15, May 15, 1696—October 31, 1697 (London: Mackie and Co. LD., 1904), text-fiche, x; Nash, *Quakers and Politics*, 189; Moretta, *Penn and the Quaker Legacy*, 201.

53. Penn, "Scheam," 482.

54. Penn, "Scheam," 482.

55. Penn, "Scheam," 482.

56. Penn, "Scheam," 482.

57. Penn, "Scheam," 482.

58. Penn, "Scheam," 482.

59. Penn, "Scheam," 482.

60. William Penn, "To Francis Nicholson" (December 12, 1699), *Penn Papers, Vol.* 3, 578; William Penn, "To Nathaniel Blakiston" ([December 13, 16]99), *Penn Papers, Vol.* 3, 579; William Penn, "To the Earl of Bellomont" (January 30, 1700), *Penn Papers, Vol.* 3, 583.

61. Governor Blakiston fell ill en route to Albany and returned to Maryland. See footnote, William Penn, "To the Board of Trade" (c. October 1700), *Penn Papers, Vol. 3*, 619.

62. Penn, "To the Board of Trade," 618.

63. Penn, "To the Board of Trade," 618.

64. Penn, "To the Board of Trade," 618.

65. Penn, "To the Board of Trade," 619.

66. *Board of Trade Journals: 1675–1782*, vol. 13, 1700–1701 (London: 1895), 428–430, 443; "Council of Trade and Plantations to Mr. Penn" (April 15, 1701), *Calendar of State Papers, Colonial Series, America and the West Indies*, ed. Cecil Headlam, vol. 19, 1701 (London: His Majesty's Stationary Office, 1910), 161–162.

BIBLIOGRAPHY

PRIMARY SOURCES

Board of Trade Journals: 1675–1782. Vol. 13, 1700–1701. London: 1895.

Bowden, James. *The History of the Society of Friends in America*. Vol. 1. London: Charles Gilpin, Bishopsgate Street Without, 1850.

Calendar of State Papers, Colonial Series, America and the West Indies. Edited by J. W. Fortescue. Vol. 15, May 15, 1696—October 31, 1697. London: Mackie and Co. LD., 1904. Text-fiche.

———. Edited by Cecil Headlam. Vol. 19, 1701. London: His Majesty's Stationary Office, 1910.

Christoph, Peter R., and Florence A. Christoph, eds. *Books of General Entries of the Colony of New York, 1664–1673: Orders, Warrants, Letters, Commissions, Passes and Licenses by Governors Richard Nicolls and Francis Lovelace*. Baltimore: Genealogical Publishing Co., Inc., 1982.

Gehring, Charles T., trans. and ed. *Delaware Papers (English Period): A Collection of Documents Pertaining to the Regulation of Affairs on the Delaware, 1664–1682*. Vols. 20–21 Baltimore: Genealogical Publishing Co., Inc., 1977.

Myers, Albert Cook, ed. *Narratives of Early Pennsylvania, West New Jersey, and Delaware, 1630–1707*. New York: Barnes & Noble, Inc., 1959.

Penn, Granville. *Memorials of the Professional Life and Times of Sir William Penn, Knt*. Vol. 2. London: James Duncan, Paternoster Row, 1833.

Penn, William. *England's present interest discover'd with honour to the prince, and safety to the people*. 1675. *Early English Books Online*. Accessed February 17, 2013. http://eebo.chadwyck.com/search/full_rec?SOURCE=pgimages.cfg&ACTION=ByID&ID=V93329.

———. *The great case. Of liberty of conscience once more debated & defended*. 1670. *Early English Books Online*. Accessed February 13, 2013. http://eebo.chadwyck.com.libdata.lib.ua.edu/search/full_rec?SOURCE=pgimages.cfg&ACTION=ByID&ID=V33078.

———. *One project for the good of England*. 1679. *Early English Books Online*. Accessed February 17, 2013. http://eebo.chadwyck.com.libdata.lib.ua.edu/search/full_rec?SOURCE=pgimages.cfg&ACTION=ByID&ID=V60052.

———. *The Papers of William Penn*. Edited by Richard S. Dunn and Mary Maples Dunn. Vol. 1, 1644–1679. Philadelphia: Penn Press, 1981.

———. *The Papers of William Penn*. Edited by Richard S. Dunn and Mary Maples Dunn. Vol. 2, 1680–1684. Philadelphia: Penn Press, 1982.

———. *The Papers of William Penn*. Edited by Marianne S. Wokeck, Joy Wiltenburg, Alison Duncan Hirsch, and Craig W. Horle. Vol. 3, 1685–1700. Philadelphia: Penn Press, 1986.

———. *The Political Writings of William Penn*. Edited by Andrew R. Murphy. *An Essay towards the Present and Future Peace of Europe, by the Establishment of an European Dyet, Parliament, or Estates*. Indianapolis: Liberty Fund, 2002.

SECONDARY SOURCES

Adler, Emanuel. "Condition(s) of Peace." *Review of International Studies* 24 (December 1998), 165–191.

Beatty, Edward C. O. *William Penn as Social Philosopher*. New York: Octagon Books, 1975.

Brailsford, Mabel Richmond. *The Making of William Penn*. Freeport: Books for Libraries Press, 1970.

Brinton, Howard. *Friends for 300 Years: The History and Beliefs of the Society of Friends since George Fox Started the Quaker Movement*. New York: Harper & Brothers, 1952.

Brock, Peter. *Pacifism in the United States: From the Colonial Era to the First World War*. Princeton: Princeton University Press, 1968.

———. *Pioneers of the Peaceable Kingdom*. Princeton: Princeton University Press, 1968.

———. *The Quaker Peace Testimony, 1660–1914*. York: Sessions Book Trust, 1990.

Bronner, Edwin B. *William Penn's "Holy Experiment": The Founding of Pennsylvania, 1681–1701*. New York: Temple University Publications, 1962.

Deutsch, Karl W., Sidney A. Burrell, Robert A. Kann, Maurice Lee Jr., Martin Lichterman, Raymond E. Lindgren, Francis L. Loewenheim, and Richard W. Van Wagenen. *Political Community and the North Atlantic Area: International Organization in the Light of Historical Experience*. New York: Greenwood Press, 1969.

Dunn, Mary Maples. *William Penn: Politics and Government*. Princeton: Princeton University Press, 1967.

Dunn, Richard S., and Mary Maples Dunn, ed. *The World of William Penn*. Philadelphia: Penn Press, 1986.

Durham, Geoffrey. *The Spirit of the Quakers*. New Haven: Yale University Press, 2010.

Endy, Melvin B., Jr. *William Penn and Early Quakerism*. Princeton: Princeton University Press, 1973.

Geiter, Mary. *William Penn*. Harlow: Pearson Education Limited, 2000.

Greaves, Richard L. "Seditious Sectaries or "Sober and Useful Inhabitants"? Changing Conceptions of the Quakers in Early Modern Britain." *Albion: A Quarterly Journal Concerned with British Studies* 33, no. 1 (Spring 2001), 24–50.

Hinds, Hilary. *George Fox and Early Quaker Culture*. Manchester, UK: Manchester University Press, 2011.

Hull, William I. *William Penn: A Topical Biography*. London: Oxford University Press, 1937.

Illick, Joseph E. *William Penn the Politician: His Relations with the English Government*. Ithaca, NY: Cornell University Press, 1965.

Kimball, Jeffrey. "Alternatives to War in History." *OAH Magazine of History* 8, no. 3 (Spring 1994), 5–9.

Moretta, John A. *William Penn and the Quaker Legacy*. New York: Pearson Education, Inc., 2007.

Nash, Gary B. *Quakers and Politics: Pennsylvania, 1681–1726*. Princeton: Princeton University Press, 1968.

Richter, Daniel K. *Trade, Land, Power: The Struggle for Eastern North America*. Philadelphia: Penn Press, 2013.

Schlichtmann, Klaus. "Linking Constitutional Laws of Peace and Collective Security." *Indian Journal of Asian Affairs* 17, no. 2 (Dec. 2004), 1–22.

Soderlund, Jean R. *Lenape Country: Delaware Valley Society before William Penn*. Philadelphia: Penns Press, 2015.

Steere, Douglas V., ed. *Quaker Spirituality: Selected Writings*. New York: Paulist Press, 1984.

Weddle, Meredith Baldwin. *Walking in the Way of Peace: Quaker Pacifism in the Seventeenth Century*. Oxford: Oxford University Press, 2001.

Wildes, Harry Emerson. *William Penn*. New York: Macmillan Publishing Co., Inc., 1974.

CHAPTER 18

William Penn's Imperial Landscape

IMPROVEMENT, POLITICAL ECONOMY, AND COLONIAL AGRICULTURE IN THE PENNSYLVANIA PROJECT

Shuichi Wanibuchi

What was William Penn's relationship with the British empire?[1] Historians have answered this question by scrutinizing Penn's political relationship with kings and imperial bureaucrats. The so-called imperial school of historians placed Penn's colonial enterprise within the political sphere of Restoration England and saw him as a pragmatic courtier at the courts of Charles II and James II as well as an intent Whig polemicist in the Restoration public sphere. Beginning with the monumental work of Charles M. Andrews, these imperial interpretations have revealed how Penn acquired a vast tract of land in America from Charles II, who was meanwhile tightening control over England's American colonies. With their keen interest in micropolitical processes, they have opened the possibility of understanding the Pennsylvania project within the broader context of British imperial history.[2] This line of scholarship, however, has limited itself to political processes in a strict sense; imperial historians have failed to capture the intellectual and ideological aspects of Penn's commitment to the Restoration empire. On the other hand, the insistent emphasis on his religious motivation for the founding of Pennsylvania has discouraged historians from looking to the imperial aspect of Penn's thought and understanding his colonial enterprise in the context of Restoration English imperialism. This chapter therefore examines Penn's imperial ideology and reconsiders his vision of colonization in the intellectual climate of his time, particularly in the emerging discussions of political economy and natural philosophy.

Perhaps not surprisingly, Penn is absent in recent studies on the intellectual history of the early modern British empire.[3] The imperial aspect of Penn's thought has long been ignored with the sole exception of James Oglethorpe, who canonized Penn as one of the patron saints of Britain's colonial empire in a tract anonymously published when Oglethorpe launched a campaign for establishing Georgia in the 1730s.[4] In the same way, despite Penn's connections with leading natural philosophers as well as major political theorists of the day, historians of early modern science and empire have yet to discover the importance of imperial science in Penn's colonization project. Although Frederick B. Tolles once explained Penn's inclination to the "New Philosophy" by employing the so-called Merton thesis on the relationship between Puritanism and experimental science, he did not correlate Penn's scientific interest with his colonial enterprise.[5] As I shall argue, if we see Penn's imperialism as a fabric, its vertical threads are woven by a century-long accumulation of English colonization schemes from Elizabethan colonizers to his rival, the first Earl of Shaftesbury, while its horizontal threads are composed of contemporary discourses of political economy and natural philosophy. In other words, while inheriting the core ideological traits of English imperialism from his predecessors, Penn aggressively employed new forms of knowledge for his colonial enterprise. This perspective sheds new light on Penn's colonial writings and practices by contributing to the expanding literature on science and empire.

This chapter first traces the formation of Penn's imperialism in his youth, particularly focusing on Penn's connections with Anglo-Irish improvers and scientists in post-Cromwellian Ireland. The second section scrutinizes Penn's vision of colonization and commerce in the context of the mercantile political economy of Restoration England. The third section examines the role of natural philosophy in Penn's colonization by focusing on Penn's relationship with the Royal Society and Robert Boyle. Finally the chapter discusses Penn's involvement in colonial agriculture and winemaking as imperial projects. I argue that Penn's colonization project cannot be fully understood through only his religious motivation. Instead, we must restore his fuller imperial visions, which were equally informed by material and economic goals.

Fashioning Imperialism

William Penn formed a vision of empire through his educational and travel experiences in his youth. Although historians have pointed out that Penn's involvement in land management in Ireland and co-proprietorship in West New Jersey gave him economic and financial lessons for his own colonial enterprise, we need to take into account his earlier career in order to properly appreciate his intellectual commitment to the British empire.[6] In this section, I argue that Penn's imperialism was shaped by three intellectual elements—humanist learning, cosmopolitanism, and the ideology of improvement. Penn's travel experience, especially in Ireland, played an important role in shaping these elements.

Born in 1644, as the only son of the most celebrated naval hero in Commonwealth and Restoration England, Penn had a formal education typical for sons of aristocrats and gentlemen at the time. He received a classical education at Chigwell School[7] and Christ Church College, Oxford, where he was expelled for his religious nonconformity, and later a legal training at Lincoln's Inn. In fact, Penn had full command of Latin and classical knowledge and used his broad knowledge of classics for his writings.[8] As a Quaker convert with humanist learning, Penn drew on classical texts not only in his religious and political pamphlets but also in the promotional literature of his colony. In *Some Accounts of the Province of Pennsilvania in America* (1681)—his first publication on the Pennsylvania project—he begins with the justification of colonization by referring to the "fame" and "reputation" of the ancient Greeks who "planted many parts of Asia" and the Romans who "moraliz'd the manners of the nation they subjected," as well as the church fathers, such as Moses and Joshua, who conquered and settled in Canaan.[9] This short passage explicitly shows his inheritance of humanist discourse on colonization. As we shall see in the next section, Penn's humanist learning served as a foundation of his political economy.

If a classical education bestowed on Penn a theoretical vindication of colonization, travel experiences taught him cosmopolitanism: a practical skill to communicate and make a good relationship with cultural aliens. Penn was an avowed traveler through his life. His father Admiral Penn ensured multiple opportunities to travel outside England after his childhood. After a mission in the Caribbean ended up in failure in the Anglo-Spanish War, the admiral was exiled to his estate in Ireland with his family when the younger Penn was fifteen. And after being expelled from Oxford in 1662, Penn was sent to the continent by his father and spent two years abroad, mainly in France. Returning from this Grand Tour, Penn went again to Ireland twice as his father's deputy in 1666 and 1669, and journeyed not only all over England but also to Holland and Germany frequently between 1671 and 1677 as an emissary of the Society of Friends. These travel experiences seemed to prepare his cosmopolitan nature before he left for America. While he socialized with French courtiers and German Pietist groups, Penn learned different manners and customs of locals, including the Irish peasants he met on his father's estate. In 1669, for example, Penn recorded in a calm manner in his journal that "[w]e pas'd by a great company of Irish gather'd to the mass upon a hill."[10] Such a cosmopolitan nature and neutral habit of observing others kept Penn free of the religious and racial dogmatisms against Catholicism and indigenous peoples, which prevailed in England in his time.[11]

Such a cosmopolitan outlook, however, did not prevent Penn from being a zealous exponent of improvement. Having originally meant to merely raise rents on landholdings, the concept of improvement spread in seventeenth-century

England in order to mark a broad range of material progress the English experienced in agriculture, industry, economy, landscape, and material life in general.[12] While the word was applied in both domestic and overseas situations, it carried an assimilationist connotation when used in the context of English colonial expansion in Ireland and North America. The historian T. C. Barnard points out that "[i]mprovement, of course, meant making Ireland more like England; or rather, and this was unspoken, like lowland England." Associating with preconceptions about civility, English improvers saw the indigenous landscape as a wild and undeveloped one, and found the potential for the reformation and exploitation of the land and resources there.[13] Penn shared this ideology with his contemporaries and showed his sense of value when he moved to English plantations in Munster, Ireland. After narrowly passing through a torrential river on horseback, Penn "came by Lismore, the Earl of Cork [Richard Boyle]'s great seat, and so to Talloe [Tallow], a road well improv'd and much English, where we lay at the signe of the George."[14] In an English colonial countryseat in southern Ireland, he saw an anglicized landscape as an "improved" one. Penn frequently applied this adjective to English settlements in Ireland and later in Pennsylvania, but never to indigenous settlements in both lands.

In Ireland, Penn witnessed the culture of improvement in an English settler society. His father's estate in Shanagarry was located near Cork, the center of English plantations in southern Ireland. The peopling of this region by English settlers had begun in the reign of Elizabeth I, almost at the same time as that of North America. Among the New English, Richard Boyle, the first Earl of Cork, acquired large tracts of land in Munster and developed his estates through land leases with both English and Irish tenants. After the outbreak of the war in 1649, his son, the second Earl of Cork, launched the reform of land management and introduced a series of projects—iron and cloth making, reclamation, mineral mining, and agricultural experiments—under the influence of Protestant scientific reformer Samuel Hartlib and his circle.[15] As we shall see, the cult of improvement went hand in hand with scientific pursuit, but profit was always a powerful driving force of improvement for landowners and settlers. William Petty, the surveyor general of Ireland and a former member of the Hartlib circle, wrote to his friend and antiquarian John Aubrey in 1674 that "[a]s with the New World where Sir William Penn, my Lord Baltimore, and others have encouraged you to settle, Ireland offers wild prospects and great returns."[16] Improvers and projectors rushed into colonial Ireland as an economic vacuum. In the Restoration era, Ireland became a laboratory for improvement.

Penn personally knew some of these improvers in Ireland. The Earl of Orrery, brother of Richard Boyle, was a vigorous Protestant warrior-projector who pioneered the manufacture of linen and supported industrial and agricultural experiments in his estate in Cork.[17] He was close with the Penns since the family moved to the estate near Cork in 1655. According to Penn's journal, they met

Figure 18.1 Isaac Fuller, Portrait of William Petty, c. 1650. © National Portrait Gallery, London.

regularly when Penn was in Ireland and had already become Quaker, and he then learned Orrery's business enterprise.[18] Another improver whom Penn knew well was William Petty (figure 18.1). In terms of his enthusiasm in both scientific pursuit and profit seeking under England's colonial rule of Ireland, Petty embodied the spirit of improvement in this period. While renowned as one of the founders of political arithmetic, Petty made enormous profits from his various projects, such as ironworks and fishery in his Irish estates. Penn met Petty first in Dublin in 1669, and their friendship continued until Petty's death in 1687. Petty might have given advice to Penn about land management in his father's Irish estate as the responsible person of the Down Survey and the 1659 Census, on which every landowner in Ireland, including Penn, had to consult for land problems and management.[19]

Furthermore, Penn's relationship with Petty provided a direct link between his Irish experience and the Pennsylvania project. In later years Petty appeared as a practical adviser to Penn's colonization scheme as well as a potential purchaser of land in Pennsylvania. Petty drafted several manuscript proposals on various subjects from land distribution to manufactures to land use to the management of population and marriage in Pennsylvania in the form of his political arithmetic throughout the 1680s. Although these documents are now archived in the Petty papers in the British Library, Penn must have obtained their copies from Petty, who typically circulated his politico-arithmetic proposals in manuscript form. Petty's advice on the colonial enterprise was based on his expertise as surveyor and political economist and on accumulated data about the population and economy of Ireland and New England.[20] Petty's primary concerns were land distribution and population management, and his surviving letter to Penn clearly shows his advice on these two subjects: "I advice you to take a perfect accompt of every soul within your teritory [*sic*] and jurisdiction, and then, to sett out a peece of land . . . ought to bee chosen for its situation, healthfulness and fertility, and to bee defenceable by nature as much as may bee." Petty also emphasized that the accurate understanding of natural resources would make Penn's colonial undertaking a success: "a perfect survey," he wrote, "with description of the animals, vegitables and minerals," gives "great light to your plantation & forraign commerce."[21] Thus the improvers whom Penn knew in Ireland provided useful examples for his Pennsylvania project.

The Pennsylvania Project in the Political Economy of Empire

Soon after Penn acquired the charter of his colony from Charles II and his Privy Council on March 4, 1681, he set out the promotion of his colonial venture and published a series of tracts thereafter. Penn and his fellow promoters astutely arranged multiple editions of pamphlets with slight variations to appeal to different kinds of audiences. Among them, *Some Account of the Province of Pennsilvania in America* is the first of those editions printed with similar titles by the London printer Benjamin Clark and the only edition that contains the section called "the benefit of Plantations or Colonies in general."[22] Though Penn seemed to distribute the other editions to his fellow Quakers and other radical sectarians who were persecuted in England and other parts of Europe, the first edition seemed to be intended to attract big investors for the financial setup of the new colony. In its early stage, as Gary Nash and Mary Geiter point out, Penn's colonial enterprise heavily relied upon the merchant community in London, which constituted the main part of the Free Society of Traders, a joint-stock company formed for the purpose of speculation in colonial ventures such as the fur trade, lumbering, agriculture, and mining in Pennsylvania.[23] Therefore, there is little wonder that Penn's argument in the tract reflected the contemporary mercantile discourse proliferating in the public sphere of Restoration England. But it does not only mirror the interest of London merchants, it also expresses Penn's own view of the political economy of empire.

In order to consider this point, we need to understand the political backdrop of England's commercial and colonial policies at this period. Despite the political fluctuations from the Interregnum to the Glorious Revolution, the basic tone that characterized England's colonial policies over the second half of the seventeenth century was the expansion and consolidation of imperial structure through wars and the state regulation of trade. A set of imperial policies designed by Oliver Cromwell in the 1650s—the conquest of Ireland, a series of the Navigation Acts, the Anglo-Dutch War, and the Western Design in the Caribbean—laid the foundation for Britain's commercial empire in North America until the late eighteenth century.[24] The career of Benjamin Worsley, for instance, vividly shows the continuity of imperial policies in this period. While engaging in Cromwell's land survey project in Ireland as a leading physician and experimental scientist (as well as a political enemy of William Petty) in the Commonwealth, Worsley played a vital role in designing the 1651 Navigation Act and establishing the Council of Trade, which aimed to control the American colonies, especially Virginia, in the 1650s. Even after the Restoration, Worsley continued to take a seat in the Privy Council's Committee of Trade and Foreign Plantations, where he exercised his expertise on trade and colonial issues. Worsley's career suggests that expertise and knowledge became more and more important in commerce and imperial governance after the mid-seventeenth century.[25]

In the age of commerce and empire building, a number of theorists envisioned the future of the English empire and proposed relevant commercial and colonial policies. Political economists showcased a variety of opinions about commerce, land, population, and manufactures, and some of them, such as William Temple and Josiah Child, actually got involved in the government's policy making. Applying the methods of natural philosophy to socioeconomic problems, they argued how to increase England's national wealth and power in order to compete with European powers, especially the Netherlands and France.[26] In particular, William Petty developed methods of analyzing nations' socioeconomic situations using mathematics and statistics, which he called "political arithmetick." Petty explained the difference between traditional discourses and his own methods as follows: "The method I take to do this, is not yet very usual; for instead of using only comparative and superlative words, and intellectual arguments, I have taken the course (as a specimen of the political arithmetick I have long aimed at) to express my self in terms of number, weight, or measure."[27]

The central concerns of these political economists in the Restoration period were the balance of trade and the size of population in England and its colonies. The balance of trade theory is known as the core element of mercantilist thought; it assumes that the increase of export surplus against importations in a country becomes the source of the nation's wealth. According to this theory, imports of foreign goods decrease the wealth of a nation and thus should be reduced. Instead, the country should produce more goods for consumption and export in order to strengthen national power, notably through the accumulation of money, preferably specie. On the premise of the importance of correctly adjusting the balance of trade, Charles Davenant wrote "Gold and Silver are indeed the measures of trade, but the Spring and Original of it in all countries is the Natural and Artificial Product of the Country, that is to say, what their Land, or what their Labour and Industry produces."[28] Such theorists therefore welcomed overseas colonies as a means of achieving a favorable balance of trade. Early colonial endeavors in the first half of the seventeenth century proved that their productions, such as tobacco, fish, and sugar, were substituted for import goods from Spain, the Netherlands, and the Baltic. For mercantilist thinkers, the more England's colonial trade increase, the more favorable the nation's balance of trade would be.[29]

From the viewpoint of population, however, overseas colonization was not a favorable solution for the increase of England's wealth and power. Population was an important element in the mercantilist thought that put an emphasis on the production of domestic goods and thus saw people as a labor force. "People are the Wealth of a Nation," Sir Dalby Thomas wrote, "it is only meant, Laborious and Industrious People, and not such as are wholly unemploy'd, as Gentry, Clergy, Lawyers, Servingmen, and Beggers, etc."[30] After England experienced the devastating civil war, migrations to Ireland and North America, and the great fire and plague of 1666, the fear of depopulation spread widely among elites and intellectuals, and there appeared many attempts to determine the cause of decline in terms of its negative effects on the national economy. Thus, as Dalby's remark shows, the classification and management of population became great concerns in the mercantilist paradigm, urging theorists such as Petty and John Graunt to develop a statistical method of calculating the population in England and its plantations.[31] But colonial enterprises also required more labor force in the land with scarce population. In 1662, the Council of Foreign Plantations stated "[i]t being universally agreed that People are the foundation and Improvement of all Plantations, and the people are increased principally by sending servants thither. It is necessary that a settled course be taken for furnishing them with servants."[32]

In the conflicting demands for human labor both in England and within overseas colonies in the Restoration era, many political economists kept a skeptical attitude toward the transplanting of English men and women into the colonies.[33] These views appeared even across the border of political factions. Among them, the most radical opinion came up from the Tory critic Roger Coke. Coke's logical statement is clear: "lesser numbers of people diminish trade," and "the peopling the American plantations subject to the crown of England, has caused lesser numbers of people in England." "Therefore," he continues, "peopling of the American plantations, hath diminished the valuable trades of England, and the fishing trade, which was to be demonstrated."[34] An influential Whig writer, William Petyt, also decried that "England never was so populous as it might have been, and undeniably must now be far lesse populous then ever, having so lately peopled our vast American Plantations and Ireland."[35] Other economic writers of the day, such as Samuel Fortrey and Carew Reynell, were less hostile, but their priority was not capital investment in colonial ventures but in domestic industry. In 1674, Reynell warned his contemporaries "not to waste men in large and unprofitable Territories, which ruin'd the Spaniard."[36]

Penn unfolded his own view on colonization within this ideological climate. He refuted anticolonial opinions that foreign plantations decreased England's population and wealth by employing a humanist discourse:

> Nor did any of these ever dream it was the way of decreasing their people or wealth: for the cause of the decay of any of those states or empires was not their plantations, but their luxury and corruption of manners: for when they grew to neglect their ancient discipline, that maintained and rewarded virtue and industry, and addicted themselves to pleasure and effeminacy, they debas'd their spirits and debauch'd their morals, from whence ruine did never fail to follow to any people: With Justice therefore I deny the vulgar opinion against Plantations, that they weaken England; they have manifestly inrich'd, and so strengthened her; which I briefly evidence thus.[37]

Claiming the benefit of plantations, Penn attributed the cause of a nation's decline to people's "luxury and corruption of manners." This view no doubt came from the civic humanism that Penn seemed to learn through the work of James Harrington and other republican writers, who argued the nature of government in terms of people's manners.[38] In that sense, Penn's defense of colonial empire has common ground with what J.G.A. Pocock calls the neo-Machiavellian political economy, whose exponents during the Restoration period were mainly Tory theorists, such as Josiah Child. This fact indicates that, unlike his political thought, Penn's political economy was not the Whig's one, but more akin to that of the court of James II, Penn's close friend and political ally.[39]

For Penn, plantations did not absorb the population of England. Rather, they served as a solution for domestic problems, such as poverty and unemployment.

Penn states that in England the neglect of husbandry and the decay of rural manufacture due to urban migration "causes the more industrious to go abroad to seek their bread in other countries, and gives the lazy an occasion to loiter and beg or do worse, by which means the land swarms with beggars."[40] He instead offers the economic prospect of settling foreign plantations: "[T]he plantations employ many hundreds of shipping, and many thousands of seamen; which must be in diverse respects and advantage to England, being an Island, and by nature fitted for navigation above any Country in Europe. This is followed by other depending trades, as shipwrights, carpenters, sawyers, hewers, trunnel makers, joiners, slopfellers, dry salters, iron workers, the Eastland merchants, timber fellers, victuallers, with many more trades which hang upon navigation.[41]" Penn here insists that settling in overseas colonies produces a lot of domestic employment in trade and related businesses. Moreover, even migrants in the colonies contribute to the domestic market as both producers and consumers. "And when they are there," Penn writes, "they are not (as I said before) lost to England, since they furnish then with much cloths, household stuff, tools, and the like necessaries and that in greater quantities than here their condition could have needed, or they could have bought, being there well to pass, that were but low here, if not poor."[42]

As the quotations in the preceding paragraph reveal, Penn's vision of political economy was based on his understanding of the emerging Atlantic economy. The newly opened colony should be established with the active traffic of commercial relations with the metropole. "[F]or the laws of navigation so strictly observed," Penn wrote in a letter, "as they are in, this province, must make England the mart of all our industry, as well as that our supplyes come only from her. I wave to be particular, but timber, iron, flax & hemp, will be of no small import to that kingdom, & some of these, to say nothing of tobacco (already planted) we are in hand with."[43] Here, the Navigation Act provides the commercial framework of colonial productions. James Claypoole, a wealthy merchant and chief promoter of the Free Society of Traders, shared this assumption about the imperial market: "I believe what goes or comes from Pennsylvania must be entered in England because of the Act of Navigation."[44] In 1685, a leading colonist Thomas Budd also showcased his prospect of finding "a good Market" for their agricultural and dairy productions in the West Indies. From its inception, therefore, Pennsylvania was embedded within the Atlantic economy.[45]

Penn's mercantile political economy can also be found in his vision of colonial economy. At the end of March in 1682, when he was still in London, Penn signed the charter for the Free Society of Traders in Pennsylvania, a joint-stock company formed by nine wealthy merchants and professionals "for the better improvement of trade."[46] According to Gary Nash, Penn and those who invested heavily in the Pennsylvania project expected the Free Society of Traders to play "a controlling role in the economic development of Pennsylvania." Penn gave it special privileges, including a twenty-thousand-acre manor with a reduced rate of quitrent, their own jurisdictions, and the right to send three representatives to the provincial council. Initially, they attracted more than two hundred investors with approximately six thousand pounds and planned to send two hundred indentured servants to the colony for agriculture, the manufacture of hemp and linen, fisheries, mining, the establishment of "factories," and the fur trade. But the ultimate goal of the Free Society of Traders was the control of economic activities in Pennsylvania by the proprietor and its trustees.[47] The constitution of the corporation states that, "This Union of Traffique prevents Emulation; for every One is Interested in every Ones prosperity; and the Profit must be greater and surer; and Navigation, Manufacture, and Arts better Improved, than by the Force of private and divided Stocks."[48] This manifestation of a monopolistic slant, especially against open competition, seems to correspond to the Tory mercantile political economy with its preference for the well organized and regulated trade and state-protected monopolistic ventures such as the East India Company and the Royal African Company. Again, Penn's view of political economy has a substantial overlap with that of James II and his economic adviser Josiah Child rather than that of Whigs, and Penn envisioned creating a well-ordered economy on a colonial scale.[49]

Natural Philosophy and Colonization

Not only did Penn use the rhetoric of political economy, he also employed natural philosophy in his colonial enterprise. A year after he landed in Pennsylvania, Penn wrote to John Aubrey, an antiquarian, natural philosopher, and one of the first purchasers: "I am a Greshamist throughout; I love inquiry, not for inqury's sake, . . . yet I love that inquiry should be modest and peaceable."[50] The word "Greshamist" then meant a natural philosopher or devotee of Baconian experimental science who had some connection to the Royal Society of London. Indeed, evaluating the role of natural philosophy in Penn's colonial enterprise requires an examination of his relationship with the Royal Society. Established in 1662, the Society represented English scientific activities in the Restoration era not only because it was "an amalgamation of the scientific groups of the interregnum" but also because it self-consciously promoted a new mode of natural philosophy based on the Baconian programs of empirical natural inquiry.[51] Penn personally knew many leading members in the Society, such as John Aubrey, William Petty, and Robert Boyle, although Penn was of course not a natural philosopher in the sense that his friends were. Penn was elected as a fellow of the Society in November 1681, but he never joined the Society's meetings, even when he stayed in London.[52] From this fact, we may conclude that Penn was merely one of many typical gentlemen virtuosi who wanted to receive the title F.R.S. (Fellow of the Royal Society), because scientific activities were prominent during the Restoration period.[53]

Penn's relationship with the Society, however, should be understood in imperial as well as intellectual contexts. The Society was more than a place of pure scientific pursuit; quite the contrary, it was embedded in the web of political, economic, religious, and imperial interests in Restoration England. Inheriting the agenda of the protestant reformer Samuel Hartlib's Invisible College, it functioned as a kind of intelligence agency on England's domestic and colonial conditions of trade and industry. While engaging in agricultural improvement for gentleman farmers in the English countryside, it also gathered information on the geography and natural history of overseas territories to exploit profitable natural resources. Alchemist and governor of Connecticut John Winthrop Jr.'s relationship with the Society in the 1660s illustrates this imperial aspect of the Society. While Winthrop exchanged information about alchemy and natural history with the Society's members in London, Winthrop sought to win political patronage and solicited investment from the leading members, such as Robert Boyle.[54] It seems no coincidence that Penn was elected as a fellow at the same year of his acquisition of the land in North America. As proprietor and governor Penn was expected to contribute to the Society by collecting and reporting on the natural history of the colony as his plans moved on. The only thing Penn did for the Society was to send a map of Pennsylvania, just published by cartographer John Seller in 1681.[55]

Despite the fact that he never engaged in the Royal Society's official activities after he moved to Pennsylvania, Penn continued private correspondence with his scientist friends. Not to speak of the correspondence with Petty and Aubrey, Penn sent some letters from Philadelphia to Robert Boyle, the most important member of the Society at that time. A surviving letter dated August 5, 1683, mainly refers to Penn's observation of the Delaware Indians, but he also tells Boyle that "some chemists intent an observation upon" local medicinal plants and herbs and sent several kinds of ores discovered in the colony for Boyle's examination.[56] Although no account remains about the fate of those mineral samples, for Boyle as natural scientist this sort of information was of value for the purpose of data accumulation. Data gathering was an essential foundation of Boyle's and the Society's methodological development of Baconian natural philosophy, and the Society sought all sorts of information about natural phenomena from travelers and seamen all over the world. The Society compiled and catalogued the information and things they collected to make a fuller natural history of the world.[57] As for Pennsylvania, William Petty drafted inquiries about the natives, which seemingly were never implemented.[58] Penn undoubtedly shared such enthusiasm with other philosophical travelers. Although at this time

Penn sent letters to several people in London with descriptions of the geography and natural resources in the Delaware Valley, Penn's letter to Boyle reveals that Penn saw the collection and observation of natural products in the colony in terms of scientific activities as well as economic opportunities.

From this point of view, Penn seemed to write *A Letter . . . to the Committee of the Free Society of Traders* (1683) in the form of a scientific travel narrative, probably in order to increase the credibility of his description of Pennsylvania. For the promotion of distant colonies such as the West Indies and North America in the early modern period, it was always problematic whether the descriptions of places were trustful. The promoters of Pennsylvania had to pay much attention to their pamphlets' truthfulness and credibility. As Steven Shapin has argued, what guaranteed the truthfulness of empirical claims in seventeenth-century natural science was the testimony from the gentlemen whose gentility and sociability qualified them as trustworthy observers.[59] As a celebrity author-gentleman at the time, Penn was in the best position to authenticate his empirical claims on the colony as a scientifically accurate account. This was, however, not a straightforward process. Penn's first articulation after he sailed to Pennsylvania was to prove that he successfully survived the voyage across the Atlantic and to deny the rumor that he was a Catholic ("Jesuit"), which would have tremendously reduced his reputation as a dissenter. Far away from England, Penn had to secure credibility by his own voice.[60]

While he attested to his identity, Penn sought to increase the credibility of his description of the colony by following the guidelines prepared by the Royal Society for travelers and seamen to write a complete natural history of a place. Robert Boyle had laid out for such a description a decade before Penn launched the Pennsylvania project in an article, titled "General Heads for a Natural History of a Country, Great or small." In this article, which appeared in the premiere issue of the *Philosophical Transactions* in 1666, Boyle set multiple "heads of inquiry," beginning with "the *Air*, the *Water*, the *Earth*," and then the "*Productions* of the Earth" with "a careful account given of the *Inhabitants* themselves, both *Natives* and *Strangers*," and the "*External*" and "*Internal* Productions of the Earth." The last head, "Subterraneal," means minerals and stones.[61] The format of Penn's *Letter . . . to the Committee of the Free Society of Traders* almost exactly follows Boyle's outline of heads. Penn divides "the general Condition" of the colony into italicized heads: I. the *Soyle* (earth), II. the *Air*, III. the *Water*, IV. the *Seasons*, V. the *Natural Produce*, VI. The *Artificial Produce*, VII-VIII. *Animals*, IX-X. *Plants* and the *Woods*, XI-XXVI. the *Natives*, XXVII-XXIX. the *First Planters*, XXX-XXXIII. (the English) *Settlement*.[62] This is to say that Penn wrote his most informative promotional tract in the manner of a scientific travel account.

Colonial Agriculture, Experiments, and Winemaking in Pennsylvania

For Penn, colonial agriculture was the field in which his interests in political economy and natural knowledge merged and took specific shape. Like other colonial proprietors and investors in British America, Penn wanted his colony to produce the goods that Englishmen had long desired for filling the needs of domestic consumption and foreign export, notably in order to reduce imports from France and the Netherlands and therefore improve their balance sheet of international trade. As Joan Thirsk has pointed out, the economic movement to amend this situation in England began at least from the late sixteenth century, and it extended to overseas colonies in Ireland and North America in the seventeenth century.[63] In a tract published in London in 1681, Penn listed the goods he hoped to produce in Pennsylvania. As he was informed by "several knowing persons," "there may be *Silk*, and *Wine*, if not *Oyle*; and for *Flax, Hemp, Wood, Madder, Liquorish, Pot-ashes*, and *Iron*, there needs to be no question."[64] All these items were nothing less than a list of goods in which English people wished to achieve self-sufficiency without dependence on imports. In order to yield these goods in his colony, Penn made agricultural experiments with knowledge of contemporary agricultural innovations. Penn's engagement in colonial agriculture, particularly winemaking, reveals how his colonial enterprise acted in concert with Britain's imperial rivalry against European powers.

The link between agriculture and colonization was first formulated as a scheme by Sir Francis Bacon in "of Plantations," which was included in the 1625 edition of his *Essays*. Following the economic success of Virginia, Bacon warned of a risk of relying exclusively on Indian trade or precious metals, and encouraged cultivation in plantations. For Bacon, colonization should be a long-term process that requires patient investment. His scheme consisted of the following: (1) Maintain peaceful relations with indigenous inhabitants. (2) Transplant industrious settlers of diverse occupations. (3) Investigate the produce of the land. (4) Gain a profit from agriculture. (5) Establish an aristocratic government.[65] Bacon's text was widely read at the later stage of English colonization of North America. Penn must have been familiar with Bacon's essay on plantations because the essay was reprinted in the religious promotional tract written by the Quaker writer William Loddington; Penn might have assisted in its publication.[66]

The concept of improvement played the most important role in colonial agriculture. English colonizers believed that they could claim property right over land through cultivating its soil. They considered that Indians could not improve their land as the English did, therefore they could not possess the land. Puritans in New England employed this rhetoric to justify their domination of the land, as their English predecessors, such as Edmund Spenser and Francis Bacon, had done in Ireland.[67] The ideology of improvement thus functioned as a tool of English imperialism through the seventeenth century. Penn shared this ideology, but in a milder tone than other settlers in the British Atlantic. In the Delaware Valley, not only Indians but also the Dutch and Swedish settlers had already established their own ways of life through the combination of agriculture and hunting gathering. English colonizers, as latecomers, made efforts to distinguish themselves from natives as well as European predecessors by employing the discourse of agrarian improvement. Penn described the Dutch and the Swedes as "plain, strong, industrious people, yet have made no great progress in culture, or propagation of fruit trees, as if they desired rather to have enough that plenty of traffic."[68]

Despite having obtained the charter of the colony from Charles II, Penn believed that the title of his colony should be secured not only by purchasing land from Indians but also by improving the land through settlers' labor. As Francis Jennings pointed out, Penn understood that the Indians possessed "a native right of land ownership" and that he could not exercise his lordship over them because the Indians were not the conquered subjects of the English as the indigenous people in Ireland were. Thus he had to negotiate and purchase the right of land from sachems along the Delaware River before he sold and distributed it to his purchasers.[69] After the purchase, settlers should improve the land, whose title was secured by both the English king and "Indian kings." Before Penn left England, he made an agreement with principal purchasers about conditions for land selling. "That every man shall be bound to plant," he insisted in it, "or man so much of his share of Land as shall be set out and surveyed within three years after it is so set out and surveyed."[70] This clause shows his expectation for the effective use and development of land in his colony. Furthermore, he had no intention of excluding all Indians from Pennsylvania if they accepted English standards of civility. "That the Indians have liberty to do all things relating to improvement of their Ground," the agreement says, "and providing sustenance for the families, that any of the planters shall enjoy."[71] For Penn, the improvement of land through cultivation meant the development of the colony, and even Indians could contribute to it through accepting the English way of husbandry.

The Interregnum (1649–1660) witnessed the progress of knowledge in agriculture and horticulture as the era's most advanced science in England. "Husbandry and gardening" became the central concern for the Hartlib circle to pursue a Baconian program for the advancement of useful knowledge.[72] At the same time, English farmers sought alternative agriculture and, due to the downturn of grain prices in the mid-seventeenth century, began introducing industrial crops such as silk, dye stuffs, and vines for winemaking with other fruits and vegetables. Joan Thirsk has pointed out that the proliferation of agricultural treatises in England since the 1650s reflected these farmers' demand for more profitable crops.[73] For example, the publication of Richard Weston's manuscript by Samuel Hartlib in 1652 introduced a set of by then unknown farming methods and crops, such as clover, into England.[74] According to Thirsk, the diffusion of these agricultural innovations into the rural society in England happened slowly after the 1660s.[75]

Penn must have been familiar with such agricultural innovations in England. He held several agricultural and horticultural treatises written by Hartlibian agronomists and gardeners in his estate in Pennsylvania. The University of Pennsylvania library owns a copy of the aforementioned Hartlib's treatise that has Penn's armorial bookplate of 1703. And the account of goods at Pennsbury Manor in 1687 contains eight books on horticulture and agriculture, including John Evelyn's translation of *the French Gardener* and John Worlidge's *Systema Agriculturae*.[76] Penn had likely studied these treatises before the launch of his colony. He mentions the potential for the cultivation of many new crops in the soil of Pennsylvania in his promotional writings, and repeatedly advocates those industrial crops to be planted in any land suitable for "English Husbandry." Penn reported in his 1685 pamphlet about agricultural experiments he conducted in order to transplant those plants in the garden of his estate on the bank of the Schuylkill River, and that in the colony they grew better than or as well as in England.[77]

Penn made his garden a laboratory for agricultural experiments in planting commercial crops in the soil of Pennsylvania. During his first two years in the colony, he compared native plant species with European counterparts sown and grown in the same piece of land. In 1683, he was still wondering "whether it be best to fall to refining the fruits of the country, especially grape, by the care and skill of art, or send for foreign stems and sets, already good and approved." Two years later, however, he wrote, "[u]pon trial we find that the corn and roots that grow in England thrive very well there."[78] In particular, Penn made a careful experiment with "English grass seed."[79] In the sixteenth and seventeenth century, the improvement of pasture was essential in the development of dairy farming. In the earliest phase of settlement in New England, according to William Cronon, the invasion of European grass species happened accidentally because immigrants and their livestock brought those species through hay and their feces. By the 1640s, however, colonists learned to transplant hardy European species by themselves for the improvement of meadows for dairy farming.[80] It is not certain that Penn knew this happened, but he "made an experiment" in order to "confute the Objections that lie against those Parts, as of that, first, English grass would not grow; next, not enough to mow; and lastly, not firm enough to feed, from the levity of the mould."[81] At the same time, a leading Quaker colonist Thomas Budd also saw the utility of this plant: cattle breeding would be improved "by draining of low rich Land, and by plowing of it, and sowing it with English-GRASS-seed, which here thrives very well."[82]

Among his agricultural experiments, Penn held the greatest expectations for winemaking. While winemaking in seventeenth-century England was never beyond gentlemen's hobby in their countryseats, early English colonizers thought North America would be a perfect place to cultivate vines for winemaking because the most of English colonies, where native vines grew abundantly, were on the same latitude as the southern part of France and Italy, the countries from which England imported wine and other Mediterranean products, such as silk and olive oil. Captain John Smith reported in 1612 that the Virginia settlers tried winemaking in Jamestown. The dream of silk and wine continued to attract many colonial investors and proprietors, including the first Earl of Shaftesbury, who sent John Locke to France in order to learn skills of producing these goods in South Carolina.[83]

Penn shared this desire for winemaking. In his first pamphlet on Pennsylvania, he did not forget to emphasize the southern boundary of the colony (at the 40th degree) "is about the Latitude of Naples in Italy, or Mompellier in France."[84] And, in early 1682, he sent a Huguenot vigneron named Andrew Doz to set up his two-hundred-acre vineyard on the bank of the Schuylkill River, in the manor of Springettsbury.[85] Using native and European vines, Penn had Doz conduct experiments in the vineyard, hoping "the consequence will be as good Wine as any European Countries of the same Latitude do yield."[86]

But how could Penn believe it possible to cultivate vines in the climate of Pennsylvania, with its "sharp Frosty weather" in the winter and "extraordinary Heats" in the summer? While emphasizing that his colony had the same latitude as France and Italy, Penn understood that geographical characteristics in North America made a difference in the climate. For the coldness of the winter, he explains, "the reason of this cold is given from the great Lakes that are fed by the Fountains of Canada."[87] But Penn believed in the contemporary theory of climate amelioration. According to this theory, "climate was a product of local physical features, including the degree of cultivation and settlement."[88] In other words, the more one cleared the forest and cultivated the land, the warmer and milder the climate would be. Even if the present climate was not like that of France, it would be improved through the progress of settlement in the Delaware Valley. That is why Penn wrote, "as the Woods come by numbers of People to be more clear'd, that [the air] it self will Refine."[89] For Penn, the progress of colonization would improve the environment itself, making it suitable for winemaking. Penn states, "upon experience of some French People from Rochel and the Isle of Rhee, Good Wine may be made there, especially when the Earth and Stem are fin'd and civiliz'd by culture."[90]

Penn seemed to have had prospects for commercial winemaking before he left for the colony. "I am desired by William Penn," James Claypoole wrote in a letter to his associate merchants in Bordeaux at the beginning of January 1682, "to write to get about 1,500 or 2,000 vine plants to carry with him to Pennsylvania."[91] After he landed on the Delaware Valley, Penn began active promotions for both investors and settlers. In the end of the *Letter . . . to the Free Society of*

Traders, Penn explicitly endorsed the winemaking project: "and though I am ill at Projects, I have sometimes put in for a Share with her Officers, to countenance and advance her Interest. You are already informed what is it for you further to do, whatsoever tend to the Promotion of Wine, and to the Manufacture of Linnen in these parts, I cannot but wish you to promote it; and the French People are most likely in both respects to answer that design: To that end, I would advice you to send for some Thousands of Plants out of France, with some able Vinerons, and People of the other Vocation.[92]" Penn thus expected winemaking, as well as a linen industry, to be among the main economic activities in his colony. Not only promoted among merchants who invested in the Free Society of Traders, Penn also encouraged settlers to cultivate vines. "And since the Governor, William Penn, holds it of the first importance to establish weaving and the cultivation of the Vine," Francis Daniel Pastorius, a leader of a German Pietist group and a founder of Germantown, wrote at the end of November 1684, "it would be well for the Company to send out here a quantity of vine-stocks, together with all sorts of field and garden-seeds."[93]

A key factor in this project's success was a particular reservoir of skilled labor: Huguenots. Regardless of whether they possessed skills of winemaking and linen manufacture, colonial proprietors desperately sought them as migrants to the colonies. Penn competed with Carolina proprietors for recruiting persecuted Huguenots in Pennsylvania.[94] He began negotiations with Huguenot leaders in London in 1682, and had Benjamin Furly, his agent in Amsterdam, publish the French translation of promotional tracts as well as the German edition in 1684. Furly did not forget to insert the word "vignerons" in the sections on "those persons that providence seems to have fitted for Plantations" in the French edition.[95] Penn's offers of religious freedom and economic prospect were supposed to attract Huguenot refugees into Pennsylvania. In 1685, Penn confidently foresaw the developing landscape of vineyards with Huguenot immigrants: "If wine can be made by Andrew Dore [Doz], at the vineyard, it will be worth to the province thousands by the year—there will be hundred of vineyards, if it takes. I understand he produced ripe grapes by the 28th of 5 mo., from shoots of fifteen or sixteen months, planting. Many French are disheartened by the Carolinas (for vines,) as not hot enough!"[96]

When Penn laid out his plan of colonial adventure, he shared a vision of expansive empire in Restoration-era England. Even if his primal motive for the establishment of the colony was to solve his financial problems or to create a religious haven for his fellow sectarians, his "holy experiment" was never an isolated program in the moment of English imperial expansion. Rather, it was part of this expansion, at least in Penn's blueprint of Pennsylvania. Penn's personal connections in Ireland show the continuity of ideology and theory between the colonization of Ireland and that of Pennsylvania. His political economy shows no inconsistency with the Tories' mercantile economic policies in the court of James II. His interest in natural philosophy rather reflects the imperial aspect of scientific activities in this era. And his devotion to agricultural improvement and winemaking in Pennsylvania reveals his engagement in England's imperial economy through his colonial enterprise. In his vision, his personal motivation and religious cause could never be inconsistent with England's imperial design. Rather, Pennsylvania could be an active participant in the emerging English empire in America.

Despite Penn's expectations, however, the development of Pennsylvania followed an entirely different course through the late seventeenth and eighteenth centuries. Due to the conflict with Lord Baltimore over his colony's border, Penn himself had to leave Pennsylvania and was away from 1684 until 1699. The Free Society of Traders caused resentment among merchants and settlers in the colony, and as a result the general assembly rejected to approve the charter with its privileges in December 1682.[97] At the same time, individual merchants, many of them moving from other colonies in North America and the West Indies and not belonging to the corporation, such as Samuel Carpenter and Jasper Yeates, began to dominate the commerce of the colony. As the corporation's budget dried up, the Free Society of Traders ceased to act. The collectivism of the Free Society thus collapsed in the early stage of colonization.[98] As for winemaking, despite Andrew Doz's continued effort, Pennsylvanians never succeeded in it on a commercial scale until the end of the eighteenth century. Huguenot refugees did not choose Pennsylvania as their destination. "The report reaches this place with that disgrace," Penn lamented in 1686, "that we have lost I am told, 15000 persons this fall, many of them men of great estates that are gone & goeing for Carolina."[99]

Penn's imperial visions thus ended with mixed success, regardless of the colony's economic triumph in the eighteenth century, when the colony depended on the intensive cultivation of grain for export to the Atlantic market. While historians have much appreciated Penn's religiopolitical legacy—needless to say, religious freedom, they have not paid enough attention to his imperial legacy. But both these two legacies made possible the social and economic development of Pennsylvania throughout the eighteenth century. While religious freedom helped Pennsylvania attract diverse groups of immigrants from various parts of continental Europe, the empire incorporated the nascent colony into the Atlantic market, which enabled the colony to find the destination of its agricultural products. Penn himself saw being an essential part of the burgeoning system of empire as the key to the success of his colony. Penn's ideological and intellectual commitment to the empire was thus essential for the formation of the Pennsylvania project.

NOTES

1. The "British empire" did not officially exist during the years Penn was actively involved in his colonial enterprises in North America. The "English empire" is more appropriate to describe the object accurately before the Act of Union between England and Scotland in 1707. But this chapter uses the terms "British" and "English" interchangeably for both thematic and historiographical expediencies, particularly concerning the continuity of its imperial ideology throughout the early modern period. See, for instance, David Armitage, *The Ideological Origins of the British Empire* (Cambridge: Cambridge University Press, 2000).

2. Charles M. Andrews, *The Colonial Period of American History, vol.3: The Settlements* (New Haven: Yale University Press, 1937), 268–328; Joseph Illick, *William Penn, the Politician: His Relations with the English Government* (Ithaca, NY: Cornell University Press, 1965); Stephan Saunders Webb, "'The Peaceable Kingdom': Quaker Pennsylvania in the Stuart Empire" in *The World of William Penn*, ed. Richard S. Dunn and Mary Maples Dunn (Philadelphia: Penn Press, 1986), 173–195; Mary K. Geiter, "The Restoration Crisis and the Launching of Pennsylvania, 1679–81," *English Historical Review*, 112 (1997): 300–318; Geiter, *William Penn* (London: Longman, 2001).

3. I am thinking here of works such as Armitage, *The Ideological Origins of the British Empire*; Andrew Fitzmaurice, *Humanism and America: the Intellectual History of English Colonization, 1500–1625* (Cambridge, UK: Cambridge University Press, 2003); Richard Drayton, *Nature's Government: Science, Imperial Britain and the "Improvement" of the World* (New Haven: Yale University Press, 2000); Sarah Irving, *Natural Science and the Origins of the British Empire* (London: Routledge, 2008); Philip J. Stern and Carl Wennerlind, eds., *Mercantilism Reimagined: Political Economy in Early Modern Britain and Its Empire* (New York: Oxford University Press, 2013); Joyce E. Chaplin, *Subject Matter: Technology, the Body, and Science on the Anglo-American Frontier, 1500–1676* (Cambridge, MA; Harvard University Press, 2001); Susan Scott Parrish, *American Curiosity: Cultures of Natural History in the Colonial British Atlantic World* (Chapel Hill: University of North Carolina Press, 2006); Walter W. Woodward, *Prospero's America: John Winthrop, Jr., Alchemy, and the Creation of New England Culture, 1606–1676* (Chapel Hill: University of North Carolina Press, 2010).

4. [James Oglethorpe,] *Select Tracts relating to Colonies* (London, 1732), 26–30. In this pamphlet, Oglethorpe reprinted a passage from Penn's *Some Account of the Province of Pennsilvania* under the title of "The Benefit of Plantation, or Colonies," with the texts of other theorists of empire, such as Machiavelli, Francis Bacon, John De Witt, and Josiah Child.

5. Frederick B. Tolles, *Meeting House and Counting House: the Quaker Merchants of Colonial Philadelphia, 1682–1763* (New York: W. W. Norton, 1948), 205–213. On the Merton thesis, see Robert K. Merton, "Science, Technology, and Society in Seventeenth-century England," *Osiris* 4 (1938): 360–632.

6. Richard S. Dunn, "Penny Wise and Pound Foolish: Penn as a Businessman," in *The World of William Penn* , ed. Richard S. Dunn and Mary Maples Dunn (Philadelphia: University of Pennsylvania Press, 1986), 38–40; Nicholas Canny, "The Irish Background to Penn's Experiment," in *The World of William Penn*, 139–156.

7. Cf. Geiter, *William Penn*, 14. She guesses that Penn learned mathematics and other "practical" subjects rather than Latin at Chigwell School because of his father's preference.

8. On classical influence on Penn's political thought, see Mary Maples Dunn, "William Penn: Classical Republican," *Pennsylvania Magazine of History and Biography* (hereafter *PMHB*) 81 (1957): 139; Richard Mott Gummere, "Apollo on Locust Street," *PMHB*, 56 (1932), 70–74.

9. William Penn, *Some Account of the Province of Pennsilvania in America* (London, 1681), 1–2.

10. "My Irish Journal," in *The Papers of William Penn* (hereafter *PWP*), ed. Richard S. Dunn and Mary Maples Dunn (Philadelphia: Penn Press, 1981–1987), 1:110.

11. Mary Maples Dunn argues that Penn's nature as restless traveler made him keep emotional distances from other people. Dunn, "The Personality of William Penn" in *The World of William Penn*, 11. Also, J. R. Jones comments "Penn was one of the very few Englishmen of his generation who escaped becoming trapped in a rigid, unchanging, and corrosive antipapist ideology." Jones, "A Representative of the Alternative Society of Restoration England?" in *The World of William Penn* , 59. On the relationship between travel and cosmopolitanism in the early modern period, see Alison Games, *The Web of Empire: English Cosmopolitans in an Age of Expansion, 1560–1660* (New York: Oxford University Press, 2008), 17–46.

12. Paul Warde, "The Idea of Improvement, c.1520-1700" in *Custom, Improvement and the Landscape in Early Modern Britain*, ed. Richard W. Hoyle (Furnham; Burlington: Ashgate Publishing, 2011), 128–148; Paul Slack, *The Invention of Improvement: Information and Material Progress in Seventeenth-century England* (Oxford: Oxford University Press, 2015).

13. Toby Barnard, "Gardening, Diet, and Improvement in later Seventeenth-century Ireland" in *Irish Protestant Ascents and Descents, 1641–1770* (Dublin: Four Courts Press, 2004), 208; David Dickson, *Old World Colony: Cork and South Munster, 1630–1830* (Madison: the University of Wisconsin Press, 2005), 170–171. See also, Toby Barnard, *Improving Ireland?: Projectors, Prophets, and Profiteers, 1641–1786* (Dublin: Four Courts Press, 2008); John Patrick Montaño, *The Roots of English Colonialism in Ireland* (Cambridge: Cambridge University Press, 2011).

14. "My Irish Journal," *PWP*, 1:110.

15. Barnard, *Improving Ireland?*, 32–33. See also, T. C. Barnard, "The Political, Material and Mental Culture of the Cork Settlers, c. 1650–1700" in *Cork History and Society: Interdisciplinary Essays on the History of an Irish County*, ed. Patrick O'Flanagan and Cornelius Buttimer (Cork: Geography Publication, 1993), 309–365.

16. Thomas E. Jordan, ed., *Sir William Petty, 1674: Letters to John Aubrey* (Lewiston, New York: the Edwin Mellen Press, 2010), 69–70.

17. Dickson, *Old World Colony*, 46–52, 203–205; Barnard, "Gardening," 226.

18. "My Irish Journal," *PWP*, 1:126. See also, *PWP*, 1:46–47, 51–54.

19. Barnard, *Improving Ireland?*, 41–72; "My Irish Journal," *PWP*, 1:106, 107. For the use of Petty's maps in Penn's land management in Ireland, see *PWP*, 1:163–164.

20. British Library Add MS 72867 ff. 47–89; The Marquis of Landsdowne, ed., *The Petty Papers* (London, 1927), 2:95–121. On Petty's use of the method of political arithmetic for various political and economic projects and of the form of "scribal publication," see Ted McCormick, *William Petty: And the Ambition of Political Arithmetic* (New York: Oxford University Press, 2010).

21. Letter from Sir William Petty to William Penn, August 14, 1682, *PWP*, 2:279, 280.

22. Hope Francis Kane, "Notes on Early Pennsylvania Promotion Literature," *PMHB* 63 (1939), 144–168; Edwin B. Bronner and David Fraser, eds., *William Penn's Published Writings, 1660–1726: An Interpretive Bibliography: PWP*, 5:265.

23. On the Free Society of Traders, see Gary B. Nash, "The Free Society of Traders and the Early Politics of Pennsylvania," *PMHB*, 89 (1965), 147–173; Mary K. Geiter, "London Merchants and the Launching of Pennsylvania," *PMHB*, 122 (1997), 101–122.

24. On the development of commercial and colonial policies in the seventeenth and eighteenth centuries, see Charles M. Andrews, *The Colonial Period of American History, vol. 4: England's Commercial and Colonial Policy* (New Haven: Yale University Press, 1938); John J. McCusker, "British Mercantilist Policies and the American Colonies" in *The Cambridge Economic History of the United States*, ed. Stanley L. Engerman and Robert E. Gallman (Cambridge, UK.: Cambridge University Press, 1996), 337–362.

25. On Benjamin Worsley, see Charles Webster, "Benjamin Worsley: Engineering for Universal Reform from the Invisible College to the Navigation Act" in *Samuel Hartlib and Universal Reformation: Studies in Intellectual Communication*, ed. Mark Greengrass et al.

(London: Cambridge University Press, 1994), 213–235; Thomas Leng, *Benjamin Worsley (1618–1677): Trade, Interest and the Spirit in Revolutionary England* (Woodbridge: Boydell Press, 2008). On the increasing importance of expertise and knowledge in commerce, see Thomas Leng, "Epistemology: Expertise and Knowledge in the World of Commerce" in *Mercantilism Reimagined*, 97–116.

26. William Temple, *Observations upon the United Provinces of the Netherlands* (London, 1673); Josiah Child, *A New Discourse of Trade* (1668; London, 1690). Armitage, *The Ideological Origins of the British Empire*, 146–169; Steve Pincus, "Rethinking Mercantilism: Political Economy, the British Empire, and the Atlantic World in the Seventeenth and Eighteenth Centuries," *William and Mary Quarterly*, 3rd ser., 69 (2012): 3–34.

27. William Petty, *Political Arithmetick* (London, 1690), [x–xi].

28. Charles Davenant, *Discourse on the Publick Revenues and on the Trade of England* (London, 1698), 15. On the balance of trade theory, see Joyce Oldham Appleby, *Economic Thought and Ideology in Seventeenth-century England* (Princeton: Princeton University Press, 1978), 38–44; Jonathan Barth, "Reconstructing Mercantilism: Consensus and Conflict in British Imperial Economy in the Seventeenth and Eighteenth Centuries," *William and Mary Quarterly*, 73 (2016): 269–271.

29. Barth, "Reconstructing Mercantilism," 269–271.

30. [Thomas], *An Historical Account of the Rise and Growth of the West-India Collonies* (London, 1690), 2, quoted from Appleby, *Economic Thought and Ideology*, 133.

31. Daniel Statt, *Foreigners and Englishmen: The Controversy over Immigration and Population, 1660–1760* (Newark: University of Delaware Press, 1995), 45–47, 74–79; Ted McCormick, "Population: Modes of Seventeenth-century Demographic Thought" in *Mercantilism Reimagined*, 25–45; Bertrand Van Ruymbeke, *From New Babylon to Eden: The Huguenots and Their Migration to Colonial South Carolina* (Columbia: University of South Carolina Press, 2006), 29.

32. Mildred Campbell, "'Of People Either Too Few or Too Many': The Conflict of Opinion on Population and Its Relation to Emigration" in *Conflict in Stuart England*, ed. William Appleton Aiken and Basil Duke Henning (New York: New York University Press, 1960), 192.

33. Statt, *Foreigners and Englishmen*, 77–78.

34. Roger Coke, *A Treatise wherein is Demonstrated, that the Church and State of England, are in Equal Danger with the Trade of It* (London, 1671), 16.

35. [William Petyt,] *Britannia Languens, or a Discourse of Trade: Shewing the Grounds and Reasons of the Increase and Decay of Land-Rents, National Wealth and Strength* (London, 1680), 154.

36. Carew Reynell, *The True English Interest: or an Account of the Chief National Improvement* (London, 1674); Samuel Fortrey, *Englands Interest and Improvement* (Cambridge, 1663), 35.

37. Penn, *Some Account*, 2.

38. On the influence of Harrington on Penn's political thought, see Dunn, "William Penn: Classical Republican," 139–143.

39. On neo-Machiavellian political economy, see J.G.A. Pocock, *The Machiavellian Moment: Florentine Political Thought and the Atlantic Republican Tradition* (1975; Princeton: Princeton University Press, 2003), 423; Istovan Hont, "Free Trade and the Economic Limits to National Politics: Neo-Machiavellian Political Economy Reconsidered" in *Jealousy of Trade: International Competition and the Nation-State in Historical Perspective* (Cambridge, MA: Belknap Press, 2005), 185–266; Steve Pincus, "Neither Machiavellian Moment nor Possessive Individualism: Commercial Society and the Defenders of the English Commonwealth," *American Historical Review* 103 (1998): 705–736; Pincus, "A Revolution in Political Economy?" in *The Age of Projects*, ed. Maximillian E. Novak (Toronto: the University of Toronto Press, 2008), 115–140.

40. Penn, *Some Account*, 3–4.

41. Penn, *Some Account*, 2.

42. Penn, *Some Account*, 4.

43. William Penn to Earl of Rochester, June 14, 1683, *PWP*, 2:398.

44. James Claypoole to Francis and George Rogers, January 21, 1681/1682, Marion Balderston, ed., *James Claypoole's Letter Book: London and Philadelphia, 1681–1684* (San Marino, CA: the Huntington Library, 1967), 101.

45. Thomas Budd, *Good Order Established in Pennsylvania and New Jersey* (Cleveland: the Burrows Brothers Company, 1902), 35–36.

46. "Charter for the Free Society of Traders," March 24, 1682, *PWP*, 2:246.

47. Gary Nash, "The Free Society of Traders," 148–158.

48. *The Articles, Settlement and Offices of the Free Society of Traders in Pennsylvania* (London, 1682), [ii].

49. Pincus, "A Revolution in Political Economy?," 252–255; Barth, "Reconstructing Mercantilism," 273.

50. William Penn to John Aubrey, 13 April, 1683, *PWP*, 2:395.

51. Barbara Shapiro, "Natural Philosophy and Political Periodization: Interregnum, Restoration, and Revolution" in *A Nation Transformed: England after the Restoration*, ed. Alan Houston and Steve Pincus (Cambridge: Cambridge University Press, 2001), 304–308.

52. Marion Balderston, "The Mystery of William Penn, the Royal Society, and the First Map of Pennsylvania," *Quaker History*, 55 (1966): 82. Cf. Henry J. Cadbury, "Penn, Collinson and the Royal Society," *Bulletin of Friends Historical Association*, 36 (1947): 20–22.

53. According to Michael Hunter, Penn is one of "the three wholly inactive Fellows proposed by [John] Houghton," the writer and promoter who was elected just one year before. *The Royal Society and its Fellows 1660–1700: the Morphology of an Early Scientific Institution*, 2nd ed. (London: British Society for History of Science, 1994), 253. On the nature of scientific community in this period, see, for example, Michael Hunter, *Science and Society in Restoration England* (Cambridge, UK: Cambridge University Press, 1981), 59–86.

54. Woodward, *Prospero's America*, 253–269.

55. Balderston, "The Mystery of William Penn," 84; Geoffrey Cantor, *Quakers, Jews, and Science: Religious Responses to Modernity and the Sciences in Britain, 1650–1900* (Oxford: Oxford University Press, 2005), 114.

56. William Penn to Robert Boyle, August 5, 1683, *PMHB*, 6 (1882), 472–473.

57. Nehemiah Grew, *Musæum Regalis Societatis, or, A Catalogue & Description of the Natural and Artificial Rarities belonging to the Royal Society and preserved at Gresham Colledge* (London, 1681). See Michael Hunter, "Robert Boyle and the Early Royal Society: A Reciprocal Exchange in the Making of Baconian Science," *British Journal for the History of Science*, 40 (2007): 1–23; Daniel Carey, "Compiling Nature's History: Travellers and Travel Narratives in the Early Royal Society," *Annals of Science*, 54 (1997): 269–292.

58. *The Petty Papers*, 2:115–118.

59. Steven Shapin, *A Social History of Truth: Civility and Science in Seventeenth-century England* (Chicago: the University of Chicago Press, 1994).

60. Philip Ford, *A Vindication of William Penn, Proprietary of Pennsylvania* (London, 1683); William Penn, *A Letter from William Penn, Poprietary and Governour of Pennsylvania in America, to the Committee of the Free Society of Traders of that Province residing in London* (London, 1683), 3.

61. Robert Boyle, "General Heads for a Natural History of a Country, Great or small," *Philosophical Transactions*, 1 (1666): 186–189. See Hunter, "Robert Boyle and the Early Royal Society"; Daniel Carey, "Inquiries, Heads, and Directions: Orienting Early Modern Travel" in *Travel Narratives, the New Science, and Literary Discourse, 1569–1750*, ed. Judy A. Hayden (Farnham; Burlington: Ashgate Publishing, 2012), 25–51.

62. Penn, *A Letter*, 3–9.

63. Joan Thirsk, *Economic Policy and Projects: The Development of a Consumer Society in Early Modern England* (Oxford: Clarendon Press, 1978), especially 75–77 (on the colonies).

64. Penn, *A Brief Account of Pennsilvania* (London, 1681), 10.

65. Francis Bacon, *The Essays of Francis Bacon* (New York, 1908), 106–109.

66. [William Loddington,] *Plantation Work, the Work of this Generation* (London, 1682), 14–16.

67. Drayton, *Nature's Government*, 55–59, William Cronon, *Changes in the Land: Indians, Colonists, and the Ecology of New England* (New York: Hill and Wang, 1983), 55–56.

68. Penn, *A Letter*, 8.

69. Francis Jennings, "Brother Miquon: Good Lord!" in *The World of William Penn*, 197–198.

70. *Pennsylvania Archives*, 4th ser. (Harrisburg: the State of Pennsylvania, 1900), 1:21.

71. *Pennsylvania Archives*, 4th ser., 1:22.

72. Drayton, *Nature's Government*, 50–54.

73. Joan Thirsk, *Alternative Agriculture: A History from the Black Death to the Present Day* (Oxford: Oxford University Press, 1997), 23–146; Thirsk, "Agricultural Conditions in England, circa 1680," in *the World of William Penn*, 87–98.

74. Samuel Hartlib, *Samuel Hartlib, his Legacie, or an Enlargement of the Discourse of Husbandry used in Brabant and Flanders* (London, 1652).

75. Thirsk, "Agricultural Innovations and their Diffusion" in *The Agrarian History of England and Wales: vol. 2:1640–1750*, ed. Joan Thirsk (New York: Cambridge University Press, 1985), 533–570.

76. Hartlib, *Samuel Hartlib, his Legacie*, Rare Book and Manuscript Library, University of Pennsylvania [Call number: EC65 H2554 651s 1652]. Hubertis M. Cummings, "An Account of Goods at Pennsbury Manor, 1687," *PMHB*, 86 (1962), 407.

77. Penn, *A Further Account of the Province of Pennsylvania and its Improvements, for the Satisfaction of those that are Adventurers, and enclined to be so* (London, 1685), 6–8, 11–12.

78. Penn, *A Letter*, 4; Penn, *A Further Account*, 7, 8.

79. As it is known today as Kentucky bluegrass, or *Poa pratensis*, this plant played a pivotal role in what Alfred Crosby calls "ecological imperialism," the process through which the European species of plants and animals conquered the new world's environments, sometimes even beyond the areas settlers could reach as feral species came in advance. Despite Crosby's emphasis on non-human agency in the process, Penn's introduction of this plant into the Delaware Valley suggests us to reconsider settlers' initiative in the transformation of the natural world in the early stage of colonization in North America. On "English grass," On this plant, see Alfred Crosby, *Ecological Imperialism: The Biological Expansion of Europe, 900–1900* (New York: Cambridge University Press, 2004), 157–158; Robert W. Schery, "Migration of a Plant," *Natural History*, 74 (1965): 41–49; Lyman Carrier and Katharine S. Bort, "The History of Kentucky Bluegrass and White Clover in the United States," *Journal of the American Society of Agronomy*, 8 (1916): 256–266. On the reconsideration of ecological imperialism, see Fredrik Albritton Jonsson, "Natural History and Improvement: The Case of Tobacco," in *Mercantilism Reimagined*, 117–133.

80. Cronon, *Changes in the Land*, 130.

81. Penn, *A Further Account*, 7.

82. Thomas Budd, *Good Order Established in Pennsylvania and New Jersey*, 33.

83. Thirsk, *Alternative Agriculture*, 135–139; Thomas Pinney, *A History of Wine in America: From the Beginnings to Prohibition* (Berkeley: University of California Press, 1989), 12–39; David Armitage, "John Locke, Carolina, and the Two Treatises of Government" in *Foundations of Modern International Thought* (New York: Cambridge University Press, 2013), 101–103.

84. Penn, *Some Account*, 4.

85. About Andrew Doz, see Albert Cook Myers, ed., *Narratives of Early Pennsylvania, West New Jersey, and Delaware* (New York: Scribner, 1912), 227–228.

86. Penn, *A Letter*, 8.

87. Penn, *A Letter*, 3–4.

88. Fredrick Albritton Jonsson, "Climate Change and the Retreat of the Atlantic: The Cameralist Context of Pehr Kalm's Voyage to North America, 1748–51," *William and Mary Quarterly*, 72 (2015): 121. See also, Anya Zilberstein, *A Temperate Empire: Making Climate Change in Early America* (New York: Oxford University Press, 2016).

89. Penn, *A Letter*, 3.

90. Penn, *A Further Account*, 7.

91. James Claypoole to William Popple and Robert Steward, January 9, 1681/82, *Letter Book*, 99. See also, November 15, 1682/1683, *Letter Book*, 182.

92. Penn, *A Letter*, 9.

93. Francis Daniel Pastorius, "Circumstantial Geographical Description of Pennsylvania" in *Narratives of Early Pennsylvania*, 376.

94. Jon Butler, *The Huguenots in America: A Refugee People in New World Society* (Cambridge, MA: Harvard University Press, 1983), 48–53; Van Ruymbeke, *From New Babylon to Eden*, 44–46. See also, Owen Stanwood, "Between Eden and Empire: Huguenot Refugees and the Promise of the New World," *American Historical Review*, 118 (2013): 1319–1344, especially 1333.

95. "Les personnes que la Providence semble avoir rendu propres pour cette Plantation sont, des Laboureurs, des Vignerons, & des Artisans industrieux, comme . . ." [William Penn,] *Recueil de Diverses Pieces, Concernant la Pensylvanie* (La Haye, 1684), 27.

96. Undated letter, in James Boyd, *A History of the Pennsylvania Horticultural Society, 1827–1927* (Philadelphia: Pennsylvania Horticultural Society, 1929), 4.

97. James Claypoole to William Penn, April 1, 1683, *WPW*, 2:370–371.

98. Nash, "The Free Society of Traders," 158–161.

99. William Penn to Thomas Lloyd, November 17, 1686, *PWP* 3:12. For the possible reasons why Huguenots did not choose Pennsylvania, see Jon Butler, *The Huguenots in America*, 52–53.

Acknowledgments

No volume, and certainly no volume incorporating the work of nineteen authors, comes to fruition without the hard work of many hands. We are (quite literally) indebted to the Rutgers British Studies Center, which provided the lion's share of the funding for "The Worlds of William Penn," a conference held at Rutgers, New Brunswick, in November 2015. For more than a decade, the Center, then directed by Seth Koven and Carla Yanni, has sponsored wide-ranging programming at Rutgers around the notion of British Studies broadly conceived. The Center's administrative staff (Curtis Dunn and, later, Miranda McLeod) provided outstanding support on the ground and dealt superbly with all the many details such events inevitably involve.

In addition to members of the Rutgers British Studies Center's Executive Board—Alistair Bellany, Ann Coiro, Seth Koven, and Carla Yanni—scholars from several other local institutions also contributed in various ways to the success of the conference. We are grateful for the assistance and participation of Mary Craudereuff (Quaker Collection, Haverford College), Christopher Densmore (Friends Historical Library, Swarthmore College), Stephen Hague (Rowan University), Maxine Lurie (Rowan University), Douglas Miller (Pennsbury Manor), Dennis Pickeral (Stenton House), Laura Keenan Spero (American Philosophical Society), and Stefano Villani (University of Maryland).

Additional funding for the conference was provided by the Rutgers Department of Political Science and the McNeil Center for Early American Studies at the University of Pennsylvania. Thanks go to Rick Lau, chair of the former, and Dan Richter, director of the latter; as well as to Fernanda Perrone in the Department of Special Collections at Rutgers University's Alexander Library, who took the lead in creating an exhibit of Penn's works held in the library's collections. And finally, we thank Micah Kleit, Elisabeth Maselli, and Daryl Brower at Rutgers University Press, as well as Angela Piliouras and the staff at Westchester

Publishing Services, for bringing this volume to print. Everyone at Rutgers University Press embraced the volume from our first conversations, and we are immensely gratified to see it appear in print.

Finally, we would like to thank the authors whose work appears in this volume. They submitted excellent and original essays, consistently met deadlines, and bore the inevitable delays in such a collaborative project with patience and aplomb.

Notes on Contributors

Patrick Cecil is a lecturer at Chapman University as well as a financial advisor with Merrill Lynch in Orange County, California. His research examines the security culture of colonial Pennsylvania from the 1630s through the 1780s. Previous publications include "Shifting Allies, Enemies, and Interests: The Fluidity of Coalition Warfare," in *Coalition Warfare* (2013).

Patrick M. Erben is a professor of English at the University of West Georgia, where he teaches courses on early American literature. His monograph *A Harmony of the Spirits: Translation and the Language of Community in Early Pennsylvania* (2012) and his forthcoming *Francis Daniel Pastorius Reader* focus on German Pietist immigrants.

Marcus Gallo is an assistant professor of history at John Carroll University near Cleveland, Ohio. He has published articles on early Pennsylvania's land distribution in *The Journal of Early American History* and *The Pennsylvania Magazine of History and Biography.*

Catie Gill is a lecturer in early modern writing at Loughborough University with research interests in gender and religion. Her publications include *Women in the Seventeenth-Century Quaker Community* (2005) and two edited collections: *Theatre and Culture* (2010) and (co-edited) *New Critical Studies on Early Quaker Women, 1650–1800* (2018).

Michael Goode is an assistant professor in the Department of History and Political Science at Utah Valley University. He is the co-editor (with John Smolenski) of *The Specter of Peace: Rethinking Violence and Power in the Colonial Atlantic* (2018) and is currently completing *A Colonizing Peace: Violence and the Quaker Struggle for Gospel Order in Early America.*

EVAN HAEFELI is an associate professor of history at Texas A&M University. He is the author of, among other studies of colonial America, *New Netherland and the Dutch Origins of American Religious Liberty* (2012) and *Pluralism by Accident: English Expansion and the Failure of American Religious Unity, 1497–1662* (forthcoming).

AUDREY HORNING is the Arts and Sciences Distinguished Professor of Anthropology, College of William and Mary, a professor of archaeology, and the former head of the School of Geography, Archaeology and Palaeoecology, Queen's University Belfast. She is the author of *Ireland in the Virginian Sea: Colonialism in the British Atlantic.*

EMILY MANN lectures in early modern art and architecture at the Courtauld Institute of Art, University of London. She was previously a research associate with the Centre for the Political Economies of International Commerce (PEIC) at the University of Kent. Her research focuses on visual and material culture in the context of emerging European empires, ca. 1600–1800, and she is writing a book on mapping the Caribbean.

ALEXANDER MAZZAFERRO is a postdoctoral fellow at the American Philosophical Society. He earned his PhD from the English Department at Rutgers University in 2017. He is currently at work on a book, *"No Newe Enterprize": Empirical Political Science and the Problem of Innovation in the Colonial English Americas,* and his essays have appeared or are forthcoming in *Early American Literature* and *Early American Studies.*

ELIZABETH MILROY is a professor of art and art history in the Westphal College of Media Arts & Design, Drexel University. She is author of *The Grid and the River: Philadelphia's Green Spaces, 1682–1876* (2016), which won the 2017 John Brinckerhoff Jackson Book Prize from the Foundation for Landscape Studies.

RACHEL LOVE MONROY is an assistant editor for the Papers of the Revolutionary Era Pinckney Statesmen and a research associate for the Institute for Southern Studies at the University of South Carolina.

ANDREW R. MURPHY is a professor of political science at Rutgers University. He is the author of *Conscience and Community: Revisiting Toleration and Religious Dissent in Early Modern England and America* (2001); *Liberty, Conscience, and Toleration: The Political Thought of William Penn* (2016); and *William Penn: A Life* (2018).

CATHARINE DANN ROEBER is the Brock W. Jobe Assistant Professor of Decorative Arts and Material Culture at Winterthur Museum. She is the executive editor of *Winterthur Portfolio: A Journal of American Material Culture* and is currently co-editing the *Handbook of Material Culture Studies* (forthcoming).

Elizabeth Sauer is a fellow of the Royal Society of Canada and a professor of English at Brock University. She is completing a term as president of the Milton Society of America. Recent publications include, as co-editor, *Women's Bookscapes* (2018) and *Milton in the Americas* (2017), as well as *Milton, Toleration, and Nationhood* (2014).

Sarah A. Morgan Smith is an Ashbrook Center fellow, the general editor of Ashbrook's Core Documents Collections, and a co-director of the Center's Religion in American History and Politics project. Her teaching and research focus on the intersection of religion and politics in American history, with an emphasis on questions of civic formation in sustaining political commitments.

John Smolenski is an associate professor of history at the University of California, Davis. He is the author of *Friends and Strangers: The Making of a Creole Culture in Colonial Pennsylvania* (2010) and the co-editor, with Michael Goode, of *The Specter of Peace: Rethinking Violence and Power in the Colonial Atlantic* (2018).

Scott Sowerby, an associate professor of history at Northwestern University, is the author of *Making Toleration: The Repealers and the Glorious Revolution* (2013). He is currently working on a book entitled *Battles of Belief: The Military Origins of Religious Toleration in Early Modern Europe.*

Shuichi Wanibuchi is an assistant professor of American history at Kyoritsu Women's University, Tokyo. His research focuses on the impact of European colonization on the environment and landscape of the Delaware Valley region in the seventeenth and eighteenth centuries.

Adrian Chastain Weimer is an associate professor of history at Providence College. Her research focuses on transatlantic Quaker, Puritan, and Baptist communities, and her publications include "Elizabeth Hooton and the Lived Politics of Toleration in Massachusetts Bay" (*William and Mary Quarterly*, 2017) and *Martyrs' Mirror: Persecution and Holiness in Early New England* (2011).

Index